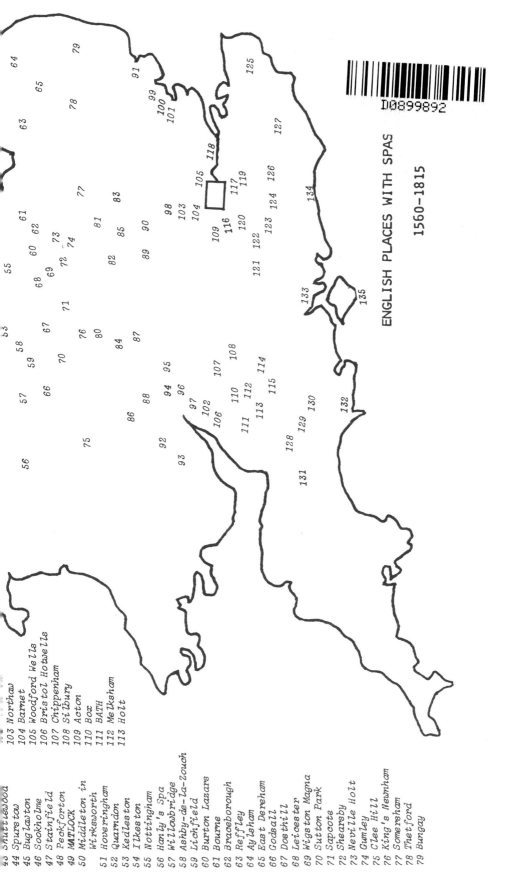

ENGLISH PLACES WITH SPAS

1560-1815

43 Shuttlewood
44 Spurstow
45 Buglawton
46 Sookholme
47 Stainfield
48 Peckforton
49 MATLOCK
50 Middleton in Wirksworth
51 Hoveringham
52 Quarndon
53 Kedleston
54 Ilkeston
55 Nottingham
56 Hanly's Spa
57 Willoughbridge
58 Ashby-de-la-Zouch
59 Lichfield
60 Burton Lazars
61 Bourne
62 Braceborough
63 Reffley
64 Aylsham
65 East Dereham
66 Godsall
67 Dosthill
68 Leicester
69 Wigston Magna
70 Sutton Park
71 Sapcote
72 Shearsby
73 Neville Holt
74 Gumley
75 Clee Hill
76 King's Newnham
77 Somersham
78 Thetford
79 Bungay

103 Northaw
104 Barnet
105 Woodford Wells
106 Bristol Hotbells
107 Chippenham
108 St Ibury
109 Acton
110 Box
111 BATH
112 Melksham
113 Holt

The English Spa
1560–1815

The English Spa

1560–1815

A Social History

Phyllis Hembry

The Athlone Press
London
•
Fairleigh Dickinson University Press
Rutherford • Madison • Teaneck

First published 1990 by The Athlone Press
1 Park Drive, London NW11 7SG

British Library Cataloguing in Publication Data
Hembry, Phyllis
The English spa 1560–1815 : a social history.
1. England. Spas. Social aspects, history
I. Title
306'.48

ISBN 0-485-11374-0

Associated University Presses
440 Forsgate Drive
Cranbury, NJ 08512

The paper used in this publication meets the requirements of the American National Standard for Permanence of Paper for Printed Library Materials Z39.48-1984.

Library of Congress Cataloging-in-Publication Data

Hembry, Phyllis M. (Phyllis May)
    The English spa, 1560–1815 : a social history / Phyllis Hembry.
        p.   cm.
    Includes bibliographical references.
    ISBN 0-8386-3391-9 (alk. paper)
    1. Health resorts, watering-places, etc.—England—History.
    2. England—Social life and customs. I. Title.
    DA665.H38   1990
    613'.122'09420903—dc20   89-45403
                                                          CIP

Printed in the United States of America

TO

Joyce Hayward

who helped me in so many ways

Contents

List of Illustrations

Acknowledgements

The author and publishers wish to thank the sources listed below for their kind permission to reproduce the illustrations which appear numbered as follows:

Bath Reference Library   VI, IX
The British Library   III, IV, XI
Cheltenham Art Gallery and Museums (by courtesy)   XIV, XV
Cheltenham Reference Library   XVI
Derbyshire Museum Service   II, XIX
Harrogate Corporation   XVIII
Kent County Library and Museum Service   XX, XXI
Mrs C. Sudbury   XIII
Victoria Art Gallery, Bath City Council   V, VII, VIII, X, XXII
Warwickshire County Library   XXIII, XXIV
North Yorkshire County Library   XVII, XVIII

Preface

No substantial book about the English spas has been produced since Dr A. B. Granville's *Spas of England and Principal Sea-Bathing Places* (1841) appeared in three volumes almost a century and a half ago. This was reproduced in 1971 with a new introduction by Dr Geoffrey Martin.

Granville's book, although a welcome quarry for all with an interest in English spas, is devoted mainly to descriptive topographical detail, gives little of the historical context of the subject, and is incomplete as a record of the not inconsiderable number of minor spas. It fails, for example, to include the charming Spa House at Box in Wiltshire or the equally delightful Horwood Well House at Wincanton in Somerset. As Martin says, it is 'a leisurely book, abounding in discursive detail'. My purpose has been to produce a study in more depth, relating the development of the English spas to their political, religious, economic and social context. The present volume traces the evolution of the spas to 1815, and I hope to cover the subject to 1914 in a sequel.

My debts for the material in this book are widespread. Mr J. C. Boswell drew my attention to Robert Lesse's little-known treatise and the Folger Shakespeare Library, Washington most generously gave me a microfilm of it. I am indebted to the British Museum (Print Room), the Bath Reference Library, the public libraries at Buxton, Cheltenham, Leamington Spa, Malvern and Tunbridge Wells, the Cardiff Central Library, the Wiltshire Public Library Service (especially the Warminster Library), Bristol University History Library, and to the Bath Record Office, the County Record Offices of Gloucestershire, Herefordshire, Northamptonshire, Somerset and Warwickshire, the Public Record Office, the Library of the Wellcome Institute for the History of Medicine, M. Georges Spailier the librarian at Spa, Belgium, the National Trust Administrator at Stourhead House, H. G. the Duke of Norfolk, H. G. the Duke of Northumberland and the Marquess of Bath. My thanks go also to those who helped me with references or suggestions, especially Mr C. Arnison, Dr S. T. Blake, Mr I. E. Burton, Professor A. Everitt, Mr J. P. Ferris, Professor A. Fletcher, Miss N. M. Fuidge, Miss E. Holland, Professor R. J. Knecht, Judge G. F. Leslie, Professor R. B. Manning, Professor H. S. Reinmuth and Mr B. S. Smith. Mr D. A. Bush, Mr V. J. Kite, Mr T. Marchington, Dr Sylvia McIntyre, Professor J. A. Patmore and Mr A. Varley kindly allowed me to quote from their theses. I am most grateful to Professor H. J. Perkin for advice at the final stage and to Mr C. R. Elrington and Professor Joyce Youings for their support. Considerable typing assistance was given by Mrs N. Buzzell and Mrs A. Nairn.

I owe a great deal to both the Institute of Historical Research and the British Library. I gratefully acknowledge that publication was facilitated by the help of grants from the British Academy, the late Miss Isobel Thornley's Bequest to the University of London and the Twenty-Seven Foundation who also helped with initial research expenses.

Finally I should like to emphasise that most of the surviving minor spa houses, like those at Glastonbury and Horwood, Wincanton in Somerset, Lower Swell in Gloucestershire, Sapcote in Leicestershire and Box and Melksham in Wiltshire, are in private occupation and are not open to the public.

P. M. H.

Introduction

One of the activities of the English nobility and gentry which has received too little attention from historians was their practice, in Elizabeth I's time and later, of taking relaxation in an inland watering-place. Most people of rank at some time faced the journey 'to the baths', originally at Bath or Buxton, often to stay for a week or more, and many of their kind congregated at these alfresco gatherings, which presented new and unique opportunities for informal social intercourse, the exchange of political and religious information, intrigue and gossip.

When the Elizabethans took up the practice of public bathing in England they were but readopting a well-established European custom dating from Roman times when extensive use was made of mineral waters and most of the thermal springs of France, Germany, Spain, Portugal, Belgium, Eastern Europe and even Africa were discovered, as well as those of Bath (Aquae Sulis) and Buxton (Aquae Arnemetiae) in England. Both Bath and Buxton became the location of settlements where baths were constructed.

As the Roman Empire declined the use of mineral springs diminished; the buildings were neglected, or destroyed by invaders, and in general only the poor of the neighbourhood continued to frequent them. Even such limited use was unpopular with authority; the doctors of Salerno were annoyed that the people of Naples used the local vapour baths, and the Christian Church denounced the warm bath as sinful. St Augustine's 'Rule' permitted bathing but once a month, and the Benedictines allowed it only for the sick, the young, the aged and guests. The Germans were, in any case, addicted to cold baths.

But the use of mineral-water springs as 'holy wells' was tolerated in the Middle Ages, and wells dedicated to saints proliferated in England as the poor carried their sick to them to be cured of a variety of ailments. At Buxton, now part of a royal forest, although the local spring was known as St Anne's Well and a chapel of St Anne, the patron of cripples, was erected, the Roman baths there apparently fell into decay and the king's deer roamed the neighbourhood. Saxon Bath, by contrast, became a borough and acquired a monastery, and in about 1088 both came into the hands of the Norman bishop of Wells. From the early twelfth century, under the guidance of physician John of Tours, now bishop of Bath and Wells, Bath became renowned as a centre of healing. The bishop had three baths, the King's, Cross and Hot Baths, under his jurisdiction but administered by the prior, and he is thought to have built two baths in the monastery: one public (the abbot's) and one private (the prior's). They were still being used in the mid-fifteenth century when the bishop issued warnings about stealing bathers' clothes.

Bishop John of Tours doubtless knew of the hot sulphureous springs at Aachen (Aix-la-Chapelle) where from about 800 Charlemagne had encouraged bathing. In Spain too thermal baths flourished under the Moorish Empire, their use encouraged by Arabian physicians. At the time of the Crusades, when Western people became acquainted with Eastern customs, the use of warm baths became more general. Surviving Roman buildings were taken into use again, but new establishments were erected under the patronage of rulers, such as at Warmbrunn in Silesia by Duke Boleslaus Crispus (1115), Carlsbad in Bohemia by the Emperor Charles IV (c. 1347), Wildbad by Count Eberhard of Württemberg (1367), Wiesbaden by Adolphus of Nassau and Gastein by Frederick of Austria. Pyrmont in the principality of Waldeck was a resort in the fourteenth century, as was Spa in the bishopric of Liège.[1]

The English interest in the merits of hot mineral-water baths developed much later, in the sixteenth century under Elizabeth I. At the English Reformation, under the orders of Henry VIII and Thomas Cromwell, the holy wells were suppressed, but when the English Catholic recusants began to leave the country for Spa in the Spanish Netherlands under pretext of drinking the waters at the Pouhon spring there, the government's attitude to the use of mineral waters was revised. The danger of allowing Catholic dissidents to emigrate to territory controlled by Spain under cover of real or pretended need to take the waters was obvious. As English intelligence agents reported, a potential fifth column of English recusants was being formed in the Netherlands, and they might assist the invasion of England. Faced both with this threat, and the reluctance of English people to abandon their practice of using 'holy' waters for the cure of illness, the policy of prohibition was abandoned. The government lifted its ban on the public bathing in and drinking of domestic waters and encouraged and promoted the use of a limited number, with a more secular and scientific approach shorn of its religious context.

With the patronage of the Privy Council and the nobility implicit official sanction was now given to bathing, mainly at Bath, the 'western Bath', Buxton to serve the North and a new and rather abortive watering-place in the Midlands, King's Newnham in Warwickshire. Learned men were recruited as propagandists, and they appealed to English patriotism in urging the use of waters at home. At the same time the Privy Council attempted to control the exodus to Spa by a system of passport licensing. Taking the waters became respectable and fashionable among the nobility and gentry, who toiled on long journeys following this new vogue. Queen Elizabeth herself, in the tradition of continental rulers promoting watering-places, went to Bath, and although she did not visit Buxton she sent for a consignment of its water and allowed Mary Queen of Scots, when her prisoner, to go there. Yet the traffic to Spa went on, although a new English 'spaw' was discovered at Harrogate where the water was drunk.

So the aristocrat on horseback attended by his retinue and accompanied by luggage wagons and carts going 'to the baths' became a familiar sight, but some came by coach, like Bishop Thomas Godwin (d. 1590), who possessed his own vehicle and went to Bath. This invasion of the shires by the elite and a host of hangers-on raised acute problems of accommodation. Inns became overcrowded and private householders took in lodgers, especially the physicians and apothecaries at Bath, who made a good living by letting rooms near the baths to their patients. The Earl of Shrewsbury invested in building a mansion especially to house visitors at Buxton, but later on at Tunbridge Wells and Wellingborough they had to be content with tents. Many forms of leisure activity were devised to help them pass the time in intervals between taking the waters.

By Stuart times taking the waters at a provincial 'spa' had become an accepted social fashion adopted by monarch and court. This vogue for gathering at baths and wells under their patronage, often in a rural setting, with the alleged intention of a quest for health, was free of the restraints of ceremony. The generally relaxed holiday mood allowed the court nobility to fraternize informally with backwoods local aristocrats and gentry, to their mutual enlightenment. The political and social implications of this easy and frequent means of contact between the capital and the local community has not previously been explored.

1

The Elizabethan Transformation

Among the dramatic actions of Henry VIII's government at the Reformation was the closure of the many holy wells, as when Sir William Bassett and his brother Francis, instructed by Thomas Cromwell, the vicar-general, destroyed the wells at Buxton in Derbyshire and Burton-on-Trent in Staffordshire in 1536. Ownership of the famed and profitable St Anne's Well at Buxton in the parish of Bakewell was claimed by local innkeepers, the Cottrell family, although successive vicars of Bakewell had contested their right to the offerings there. But the Bassetts now removed the images of St Anne from Buxton and St Mudwen from Burton, defaced the chapels to prevent their use and confiscated the pilgrims' relics, the crutches, shirts, sheets and wax. The keepers at both places were forbidden to take more alms and Sir William locked and sealed the baths and wells at Buxton.[1] Similar action was taken at other holy wells.

To Henrician and later reformers well-worship was a special problem, a Romish and superstitious practice, and pilgrimages to wells in search of healing cures offered cover for dissidents who rejected the new Erastian and Protestant regime. But gatherings at wells were a deeply entrenched custom traceable to ancient times, and certain wells, especially sulphureous or warm springs, were held to have mystic and curative properties. Many wells had been adopted into the Christian ethic by the early Church and dedicated to Our Lady or the saints. Chapels were erected over them and an attendant priest appointed, and some were closely associated with monastic houses. Holy wells were a familiar part of the medieval scene; a survey made in 1893 found that there had been about 450,[2] and although their use was proscribed, after the Reformation the credulous laity were loath to abandon them. Many laymen retained their faith in the miraculous, curative properties of certain wells, and social gatherings around a well in the summer months satisfied a communal need.

By the reign of Elizabeth I this popular addiction to springs and wells was a problem not to be ignored if the religious settlement of 1559 were to be secured against dissidents. Meetings at wells were, from the Establishment point of view, associated with the Catholic past and now masked recusant plots and intrigues. Complete prohibition was impossible to enforce, but an alternative was now permitted. A new and more secular approach allowed the bathing in and drinking of waters, under a measure of control and as demand arose, in a few widely dispersed places. This revised attitude was encouraged by the spread of secular learning, the growth of medical professionalism, and the government's awareness of the danger that if denied the opportunity to take the waters at home the wealthier people, especially Catholics, would migrate to the Continent to do so.

Secular knowledge, promoted by the development of printing and the growth of grammar schools, had by late Tudor times produced writers on a range of subjects and an enlarged reading public. Moreover, Protestant theology's sharp division between natural and supernatural knowledge helped to promote the independence of the former, and Protestant writers, sceptical of the notion of divine intervention, proclaimed the rule of law in the universe and no longer regarded disease as the product of sin. In England especially there was a demand for vernacular scientific literature suited to the popular market, and about 10 per cent of the books published between 1457 and 1640 dealt with the natural sciences, including medicine, physics and surgery.[3]

Before the sixteenth century the priest-physician had been the embodiment of medical learning, but his near-monopoly was attacked by the advance of the New Learning and the Reformation. Medical knowledge and herbal remedies were brought into secular life by the ex-religious from the monastic houses and reinforced the expertise of lay physicians, who now became organized. In 1518 the physicians were incorporated as a college privileged to license practitioners and so became the dictators of the profession, while surgeons, however skilled, had the status of humble craftsmen and worked to the physicians' direction. But in 1540 the surgeons too became incorporated with their 'brothers of the knife', the barbers, and acquired some autonomy in external treatments.[4]

The apothecaries who, directed by the physicians, supplied drugs also now achieved recognition. Previously allied with the company of Grocers who imported and sold their raw materials, they became a specialized mystery by an Act of 1540 and a new profession, pharmacy, began to emerge, although the charter of the Grocers' Company was not amended to recognize it until 1607. The pharmacists' own charter was finally achieved in 1617,[5] and they became influential in promoting spas.

Within a century from 1518 the physicians, surgeons and apothecaries had all become incorporated. The medical meritocrat now expected to have social status and the future direction of medicine, but his problem was how to secure his economic position. Dr John Jones was one such physician who typified the new scientific learning; in his *A Dial for all*

Agues (1566) he attacked ignorance and emphasized the need for self-knowledge to be obtained from physicians, not only from professors of divinity, lawyers and magistrates. Medical knowledge had been neglected recently and the art of healing had been 'marvellously abused'.[6] So the Elizabethan writers of medical treatises looked to a new market of a more secular and scientific mind, and to new subjects, including healing waters.

Popular allegiance to water cures and more informed enquiry about the nature and practice of medicine propelled Elizabeth I's government into adopting a new attitude about taking waters, allowing their use, but only if they were proven mineral waters where no miraculous element was claimed. A significant influence in this change was the international situation. Englishmen who could afford foreign travel often escaped to take curative waters on the Continent, where they mingled with rebel English exiles, both orthodox Catholics who had refused the oath of supremacy and later the radical Protestants impatient for change. The former were a political threat to the English government, a potential fifth column anxious to advance the Counter-Reformation in England; the latter fostered the exchange of notions of religious reform and scientific advance between England and Europe. At the accession of Elizabeth I some hundreds of English men and women returned home with a further influx of new ideas from the Continent.

Prominent among these travellers was Dr William Turner, the first propagandist to expound the official revised view of taking mineral waters. A prominent English reformer well equipped for his task, having read medicine and theology at Cambridge, he had from 1540 onwards, after a spell of imprisonment, studied medicine in Italy and Germany. In the more liberal, Protestant regime of Edward VI Turner returned to England and became physician to the king's uncle, the Protector Somerset. This connection brought him into the West Country near the baths at Bath in Somerset, for the Protector had acquired much of the episcopal estates of Bath and Wells, and he contrived to get Dean Goodman of Wells removed from his post in favour of Turner. But with the accession of Catholic Mary in 1553 Turner again became an exile, until under Elizabeth I in 1559 he returned to England and reinstatement in the Wells deanery.[7]

A scholar of the new religion and the new science, Turner had already introduced the serious study of botany and ornithology in England, and he was an obvious publicist of the new attitude to the most renowned English water cure, the hot springs and baths at Bath. Secure in the queen's patronage, he dedicated the final part of his great herbal to her in 1568, the year he died. He also that year republished a work of several years' reflection, the first version of which was dated at London in 1561, dedicated to Lord Edward Seymour, son of his old patron the Protector Somerset, and published in 1562. This was the first treatise on the baths at

Bath, comparing them with those he knew so well in Germany and Italy: *A Book of the Natures and Properties as well of the Baths in England as of other baths in Germany and Italy,* printed at Cologne by Arnold Birckman. The preface, which belongs to his second exile at Basle in 1557, reveals his lack of personal experience of the Somerset baths, but he subsequently went into them with 'a certain man diseased of the gout'.[8]

Turner, who rightly claimed to be the pioneer English writer in this field, addressed his treatise about the baths at Bath to his 'well-beloved neighbours' in the West Country, and he explained his purpose by reference to a homely metaphor. Just as birds call repeatedly to others if they find good food, so he wished to share his knowledge of wholesome baths in Italy and Germany and to enlighten both the ill, who need the help of the natural baths which Almighty God has given Bath, and others in England who will be spared the expense of going abroad. He cited twenty-five learned Germans and Italians who recommended the use of such baths to cure disease and named continental baths in use, as at Ems in the bishopric of Trier, Wiesbaden in Nassau, Baden in the Black Forest, Wildbad in Württemberg and Abano in Italy. He described eighty-nine illnesses which might be cured by taking the baths at Bath, which were a particularly good antidote to gout, as one of the players of his patron, Somerset, could testify.

Turner's object was both to popularize knowledge of Bath's healing waters and to stir the consciences of the wealthy men and physicians who had all neglected them and should be concerned to spread their use. Although, he argued, the baths had been known for a thousand years, because of the envy and ignorance of physicians they were seldom used by the public, but contemporary and more enlightened medical men recommended them. These noble baths could be made profitable for the whole realm, but no rich man had spent a groat on them for twenty years, although there was money for cockfighting, tennis-playing, parks, banquets, pageants and plays. Travellers who knew the costly and handsomely appointed baths in Italy and Germany – like Ems, where bedchambers adjoin the baths – must be ashamed of the English baths. The rich, although endowed by Almighty God, were so mean that they begrudged even one half-penny for the improvement of the baths to speed the cure of the sick poor.

Turner had specific suggestions for improvements, like a hole in the bottom of each bath for daily emptying and cleaning. Bathers should be excluded from the bath where the spring rises, to keep it wholesome, and it should be the feeder tank for other baths and cisterns. Baths should be roofed or easily covered in bad weather, and openings should allow vapours to escape. A vapour bath should be provided for sufferers from dropsy or gout, and there should be lofts from which water could be drawn up in buckets to fill wooden bathing vessels for the use of modest women and those wishing to bathe in privacy. The bestial mixed bathing should end and there should be separate baths for women and those with infectious diseases. Turner emphasized the need for a physician's personal advice about the nature of one's disease and the bath appropriate for its cure. May and September were the best months for bathing, and a consistent course of treatment should last at least three weeks or a month. He also made the·humane suggestion that horses with diseased legs and joints should be dosed with 'convenient drinks' by a horse-leech and allowed to stand in the waters almost to the belly.

In his plea for upgrading the baths at Bath to continental standards and encouraging the visitors' trade there Turner pledged the help of his professional knowledge – having, as he said, 'no store of other riches' – if a generous noble or gentleman would subsidize improvement costs. This appeal to the nobility to sponsor refurbishment of the baths and promote their use for the welfare of the common man was not ignored, although some of Turner's advice for the management of the baths was neglected; for example, they long remained uncovered and mixed bathing continued. But Turner, concerned for the underprivileged, spoke with the voice of the Commonwealth party, the group of reformers attached to the Protector Somerset, and during Somerset's rule Humphrey Cotton, a physician who had 'found how to cure diseases' by the Bath waters, was appointed keeper of the baths with a salary of 4*d*. a day from the central government on condition that one bath was reserved for the poor. Turner's views lived on; crucial sections of his *Baths* were reissued in 1586 by surgeons at St Bartholomew's with *The Englishman's Treasure* earlier compiled by Thomas Vicary.[9]

Turner's treatise reflects the clear shift of official policy about the use of healing waters, coinciding with renewed patronage of the baths at Bath and Buxton and the use of certain other springs. The nobility and gentry who responded to his appeal soon found that a sojourn of a week or two at baths or wells was not only a possible cure for disease but a pleasant relaxation from the responsibility of office or the management of estates, and a convenient means of enjoying the society of people of similar rank. Sir William Cecil, a patron of Turner, had plans to go to Bath as early as 1552,[10] and later he was a devoted visitor. As his son Sir Thomas Cecil said in 1594, if one went to Bath one was bound to meet courtiers, and he, when Earl of Exeter, returned at least three times.[11] So the new habit of going to the baths and wells became an accepted part of the social routine of the elite, drawing humble people there in their wake, and it was the origin of the secular English holiday. The use of prescribed waters for medicinal, as distinct from religious, reasons now acquired an aura of respectability, even of high fashion. Traditional habits of taking the waters could not be eradicated, but they were brought under control and given a new guise with emphasis on their medicinal qualities, as confirmed by scientific analysis.

The increasing patronage of the waters of Spa in the Spanish Netherlands by English visitors and the changing international situation made this adjustment all the more necessary. The English were probably introduced to Spa by the Venetian Dr Augustine Augustini, a physician of Henry VIII, but he left England about mid-1546 and then divided his time between the Netherlands and Italy, where he died.[12] Whether Augustini brought back news of the waters of Spa, a large village in the wooded Ardennes in the bishopric of Liège, or not, they were becoming better known in England.[13] In 1559, when the painter Aegidius Pierriers produced his view of Spa, Gilbert Lymborh, one of several author-physicians trying to popularize the Spa waters, published *De acidis Fontibus Sylvae Arduennae*, translated into French in 1577 under the title *Des Fontaines de la Forest d'Ardenne, et principalement de celle qui se trouve à Spa*.[14] So some English visitors travelled to the Spanish Netherlands in a genuine quest for health, but so also, using this excuse, did Catholic recusants who refused to conform after 1559. It was this aspect of the question – the English Catholic refugees' search for asylum at Spa near the Catholic university of Louvain in the dominions of Philip of Spain, where they could plot, intrigue and pass intelligence – that concerned Elizabeth I and her ministers.

The situation worsened in 1567, the year before Turner's book on Bath, when the Duke of Alba arrived in Brussels with the main field army of Spain, 'one of the turning points of western European history', for to Elizabeth and her ministers Philip II's intentions seemed aggressive. Alba's army was only about a hundred miles from London, and Spain was now the prime national enemy. So the Spanish-controlled Netherlands became a natural refuge for English malcontents, especially Catholics seeking haven abroad. Exodus to Spa to take the waters was their excuse, but the English government was kept informed by its agents there; in 1565 Sir Edward Warner wrote to Sir William Cecil, Principal Secretary, of the 'great repair' to Spa for the benefit of the water.[15]

The English Privy Council became yet more concerned as relations between England and Spain worsened after 1568, and the failure of the northern rising in 1569 brought a further dispersal of English Catholic refugees – like Sir Francis Englefield, who in May 1570 was at Antwerp, where twenty or thirty people had come in recent months on pretence of taking the Spa waters, and more were daily expected. The rebels at Spa included a leader of the rising, the Earl of Westmorland, and Lady Northumberland, the wife of another – as Cecil, now Lord Burghley, was informed in August 1571 – and a large gathering of them was at Antwerp in

July. Some of the more humble exiles, presumably illiterate, sent special tokens, 'Spaw rings', to their English friends as a sign that they were still alive. The queen made repeated attempts to flush these renegade English from the Low Countries, but to no avail.[16] Not all the English visitors to Spa, however, were fugitives. Under an Act of 1571 the crown tried to control foreign travel by the issue of passes if the recipients had taken the oath of allegiance. Christopher Hatton, then a gentleman pensioner of the household, planned to go to Spa with the Privy Council's consent because of his 'great sickness', accompanied by Dr Julio, court physician. He was back in England by August 1574.[17]

Another courtier legitimately at Spa was Henry Herbert, from 1570 the 2nd Earl of Pembroke, who, at his seat in Wiltshire, was naturally interested in the waters of Bath. The city of Bath paid the waits of Bristol 5*s.* to welcome 'my lord of Pembroke' – possibly his father – in 1569.[18] Pembroke's second wife Catherine, daughter of George Talbot, 6th Earl of Shrewsbury, had a fatal illness and may have tried the waters of Bath, or of Buxton in her father's territory. But as a measure of desperation in 1575 Pembroke took her off to try those of Spa, then, known as Spaw, from where he wrote to the queen and Lord Burghley; but the countess died that year.[19]

So the two earls, Pembroke and Shrewsbury, had lost, respectively, a wife and a daughter. In their common sorrow they had a mutual interest in the use of mineral waters as a cure for disease, and while Pembroke patronized Bath, Shrewsbury had begun to develop Buxton. Promoting English baths as an alternative to the Spa waters was not merely a personal interest but public policy, and they found a joint publicist for the waters they sponsored, the Welshman Dr John Jones. Educated at both universities, he had experience as a physician at Bath and in Derbyshire, and in 1572 he published two momentous treatises, *The Bathes of Bathes Ayde,* dedicated to the Earl of Pembroke, and *The Benefit of the ancient Baths of Buckstones,* inscribed to the Earl of Shrewsbury. The year 1572 is significant, coming after the northern rebellion and the Ridolfi Plot, when there was even more reason to publicize English waters and undermine the excuse for going to Spa. John Jones was a special protégé of Shrewsbury, to whom in 1574 he dedicated two more medical treatises, hailing him as 'a right Maecenas to all them that use their talent to the profit of the "Commonwealth"'. Shrewsbury, the creator of Elizabethan Buxton, was a wealthy patron; from his main seat at Sheffield he controlled vast estates and lived in great style. Dr John Jones was a small part of his empire.[20]

The mineral-water spring in a valley at Buxton had been owned by the house of Talbot since 1461, although Roger Cottrell claimed the well in 1568. Despite the earlier attempt to suppress its use, the 1st Earl of Pembroke had sent for Buxton water in 1559, at the cost of 4*s.* 4*d.* for carriage.[21] George Talbot, 6th Earl of Shrewsbury, succeeded to his estates in 1560 and in 1568, when William Turner was urging the nobility to improve existing natural baths, Shrewsbury married his second wife, Bess of Hardwick, who had a mania for building. Perhaps under her influence, as well as by government policy, by 1572, when Jones wrote his *Benefit of Buckstones,* Shrewsbury was engaged on Buxton's revival and had built a mansion hall there to accommodate noble visitors. The square Hall, between the spring and three ancient baths, was four storeys high with a battlemented roof and contained a great chamber and lodging-rooms for thirty; it appears, enclosed by a wall, in Speed's 1611 map of Derbyshire. Thomas Greves was in charge and kept Shrewsbury informed about the number of guests and the provisions there, the hogsheads of beer and ale, the bottles of wine and the casks of bread sent over from the Talbot home at Chatsworth. Lady Mildmay had the use of Shrewsbury's own furnished chamber. Meals for all visitors were prepared individually in the house, except that Mr Secretary, Sir Thomas Smith, had his 'at Heathcocks House', the New Hall or Talbot Inn which Anthony Heathcote, a Buxton yeoman, bought from Robert Newton on 7 September 1576. The earl was not the only one investing in Buxton's potential.[22]

To make public bathing there an accepted social habit Jones, in his *Buckstones,* followed Turner's lead in laying down guidelines for the management of the baths and the conduct and recreation of the bathers. The baths had seats around and places for fires to offset the cold winds, for Buxton was, Jones admitted, somewhat stormy in winter. Pastimes were necessary, for the protracted treatment involved long spells of idleness, so the ladies walked in the galleries or played Troule in Madame with little lead balls in eleven holes made in the end of a bench, while the men practised bowls or archery in the garden. The baths were not intended as the monopoly of the wealthy, and paternal provision for the poor included lodgings nearby. Also the Buxton Bath Charity was funded by a local poll tax on visitors and divided between the use of the poor and the support of a resident physician. The warden of the bath kept a register of visitors' status, dates of arrival and departure, and illness or other motive for coming, and a registration fee of 4*d*. carried an additional levy graduated by rank: 1*s*. for a yeoman, 3*s*. for a gentleman, 3*s*. 4*d*. for an esquire, 6*s*. 8*d*. for a knight, 10*s*. for a lord or baron, 13*s*. 4*d*. for a viscount, £1 for an earl, £1 10 *s*. for a marquess and £3 10*s*. for a duke. A duchess paid £2, but a gentlewoman only 2*s*. An archbishop was taxed £5, with an appropriate scale for other ecclesiastics and lawyers. This was the first of the charitable organizations which became a feature of several English watering-places.

After the rigours of the journey to Buxton, Jones advised, his patients should rest for several days before entering the baths, and he prescribed a visit of a fortnight, even forty days, which was good for the lodging business. Visitors should bathe for two or more hours morning and evening, after exercise but before eating. Then, with his clothes well aired by the fires and his body thoroughly dried, the patient could if necessary retire to bed, warmed by two bladders of hot water to sweat. Immersion followed by sweating in bed was also the normal treatment at Bath.

Strangers now came from all parts of the kingdom, and Jones suggested further exploitation of the Buxton waters: to the profit of the prince, meaning Elizabeth I, and of posterity, including right of sanctuary for the sick, except for major criminals (a proposal which might have sheltered Catholics) and a permit for them to eat flesh at all times. Two annual fairs and a Friday market should be established to draw in provisions for visitors; but Buxton's development was retarded by the lack of a market until 1813, despite this blueprint for an embryonic leisure industry. Although some visitors brought their own physicians (the Earl of Essex brought Dr Beech), Dr Jones's proposal of a permanent resident one was hardly devoid of self-interest. Full-time and permanent medical posts were few, and most physicians depended on clerical livings for economic support. Jones had the rectory of Treeton in the West Riding as his reward from Shrewsbury in 1581.[23]

After the Buxton treatise Jones did similar service for Bath, producing, also in 1572, *The Bathes of Bathes Ayde*. The North Baths, as he called Buxton, were under the supervision of Shrewsbury; now the hallmark of official approval must be given to Bath, 'the South Baths of England', under the patronage of Pembroke. The 2nd Earl of Pembroke, a partisan of the Earl of Leicester, was the lord lieutenant of Somerset and Wiltshire after 1570, and his seat at Wilton was only thirty-six miles from Bath. His players were at Bath in 1593, 1597 and 1599, and its burgesses looked to him for protection of their interests; in 1586 three of them met him at Bristol about the city's business, and in 1595 they presented him with an ox.[24] Bath was a city, a corporate borough with parliamentary representation, not a manorial village like Buxton, so Pembroke never had the influence there that his former father-in-law, Shrewsbury, had at Buxton. Here lay a reason for Bath's continued pre-eminence: it never rested on one man's patronage.

Shrewsbury may have introduced Dr John Jones to Pembroke as a propagandist for Bath, which in 1582–3 rewarded him with gifts of wine and sugar.[25] Government interest in Bath had been alerted by Thomas Churchyard, writer and adventurer, reporting to Sir William Cecil in May 1569, the year of crisis in the north. Bath, said Churchyard, attracted papists from all over England, some of them prominent and notorious, usually coming under licence on pretext of taking the waters, but, he implied, with rebellious intent. These camouflaged meetings were a matter for Lord Lieutenant Pembroke; 'undoubtedly under the cover of coming to the Bath many mad meetings there are'. Sir John Southworth, leader of the Lancashire Catholics, was at Bath in 1569, and seventeen years later he was released from Chester Castle and licensed 'to repair to the Baths for the recovery of his health', but he abused his freedom by meeting papists and was soon hustled back to Chester.[26]

The introduction of Dr Jones's *Bathes Ayde* was written by none other than Churchyard, the government informer, in significant verses:

> For Bathes did breed a heape of doubts and few disclosed the same
> Till he that wrote this skilfull book, a form thereof did frame,
> And tells us how, and when we ought, to use the Bathes a right . . .

'To use the Bathes a right . . .' is the key phrase and denotes Privy Council pursuance of a policy which, as Jones explains, looked to a partnership between the Church and the world of medicine in propagating the new interpretation of the use of mineral waters. His book included prayers to be said before bathing, and he urged consultation with experienced physicians. As at Buxton, he wanted resident physicians and suggested their endowment by the Church, with an impropriated benefice or a prebend at a cathedral not more than a day's journey away. All, rich and poor, should have medical services, and every cathedral church should promote a graduate in physic to give advice and medicine for the glorification of God and the monarch.

The *Bathes Ayde* also suggested precautions which helped to guarantee the reputation of the baths; some – the anxious, the feverish, the weak, children and pregnant women – should abstain from bathing, and, as at Buxton, visitors should rest for a day or two after their journey. The waters should not be taken on cold, windy or rainy days, nor when plague was about, and only during the five temperate months: April, May, June, September and October. A small amount of water should be drunk an hour after sunrise, followed by a gentle, short walk, then, having evacuated the bowels, one should enter the baths fasting. An hour's rest in bed, followed by light exercise, rounds off the treatment. Diet should consist of wheaten and leavened bread and the flesh of sheep, kids, rabbits, birds and certain fishes, but it must be boiled, not roasted or fried. Poached eggs and fruit such as almonds, raisins, damask prunes and quinces are permitted. Clean ale is the best drink.[27] Now that taking the waters was permitted, but in a new, secular and disciplined context, it lay with Protestant physicians like Dr William Turner, Dr John Jones and others to promote this new approach by such propaganda.

As well as Shrewsbury and Pembroke Jones had another noble patron, the Earl of Leicester, to whom in 1566 he dedicated his *Dial for All Agues*.

Leicester, the queen's favourite, was the archetype of the Elizabethan patronage system, a powerful and munificent benefactor of scholars in all fields. Contemporary men of letters, clerical and secular, were clients of magnates of wealth and authority who identified themselves with the existing regime, and whose approval was a shield against censorship and criticism. Such patronage was the means to payment, pension and place, but it often rested on dedication to a cause, almost a conspiracy to promote a certain point of view among the literate. Elizabeth delegated responsibility for this propagandist exercise to her nobles, and we should see the efforts of Shrewsbury, Pembroke and Leicester to encourage an interest in the English baths in this context. Leicester was the reputed champion of the sciences who, with other nobles, tried to make medical knowledge available in the vernacular.[28]

Among Leicester's followers was Dr Walter Baily (or Bayley), Oxford's Regius Professor of Physic from 1561 to 1582, who, with seventeen others – including Lady Essex, Lady Gresham and some gentlewomen – was at Buxton in August 1574 and whose name was inscribed on a glass window there, probably in Shrewsbury's great guest hall. Many visitors' names were scrawled on the windows between 1573 and 1582, including that of Pembroke. In the same column with Leicester's was, modestly expressed, the motto of Regius Professor Dr Baily: 'Hoc tantum scio quod nihil scio, Doctor Bayley'. (All that I know is that I know nothing). So Baily's inscription may be dated 1574.[29]

It was hardly coincidence that only five years later, in August 1579, there was news of a 'new bath near Coventry' in the Warwickshire village of King's Newnham (or Newnham Regis) only ten miles from Leicester's main seat at Kenilworth.[30] Two extant sheets of case histories list the cures at this 'new' bath in 1579, perhaps part of a register of visitors, like that kept by the warden of the bath at Buxton. Eighteen people recovered from a wide range of complaints between 18 July and early August, and about forty arrived each month and stayed on average seven days, but one man for twenty-one. Five visitors were Warwickshire folk but others came from six Midland counties, including Robert Storye of the old Hospital at Leicester suffering from migraine, black jaundice, the wind and colic, and John Flower all the way from Norfolk.

Clearly the King's Newnham baths had a more than local reputation and there was apparently a deliberate attempt to promote them as a Midland spa, an alternative to Bath in the South and Buxton in the North. In June 1580 Lord and Lady Warwick were at 'the wells in Warwickshire', which were known to another in court circles: William Harrison, canon of Windsor and household chaplain to William Brooke, Lord Cobham. Harrison, in his *Description of England,* corroborated the discovery of the King's Newnham spring in 1579, when it cured a wounded man's injury; in

1587 he claimed personal use of this bath, and that it drew as many customers as Bath and Buxton. Water from the best of the three wells was distributed throughout the country, a second well was reserved for healthy people, and the third was left for the 'common rag tag'. Both were cleansed daily, which implies a degree of supervision, but the owner of the wells is unknown, although the lords of the manor were the Leigh family. By the late 1570s there was a mania for well-finding and Harrison cites two other springs discovered in 1579, and now supplying a bath or medicinal well, in the hamlet of Newton, near St Neots in Huntingdonshire. Many flocked there, as to King's Newnham, for the cure of diseases as fast as from church to market and fair. St Vincent's Well at Clifton near Bristol and one at Ratcliff in the Mile End area of London were also in vogue. There were 'rumours' and 'vain tales' about almost every well at this time.[31]

The government could not ignore this new craze. In July 1579, when these wells were 'found', an invading papal force led by James Fitzmaurice reached Ireland, an apparent act of war. Since this was preceded by the Douai mission of Catholic priests to England in 1574, the Privy Council's concern lest gatherings at wells should be a cover for Catholic plots was understandable and was patent in their instructions on 13 June to the Council in the Marches of Wales about the daily disorders around St Winifred's Well in Flintshire, opposite the Irish coast. Many went there on a superstitious pilgrimage, pretending that the waters were medicinal, but the Privy Council was credibly informed to the contrary. On account of 'the present state of religion' and 'the great confused multitude' there the local council was to have the waters tested by experienced physicians, and take their advice. If the curative properties of the well were proved, diseased persons alone could be admitted, but if its waters were not medicinal its buildings and walls were to be demolished and the local justices were to prevent assemblies there.[32] So the superstitious use of holy wells was still forbidden; only those of accredited medical worth were recognized.

In this atmosphere of uncertainty the use of the King's Newnham waters had to be controlled, but since they, unlike those of Bath and Buxton, were *cold* waters a forceful medico-publicist was needed to promote them. The choice, possibly Leicester's, fell on his protégé Dr Walter Baily of Oxford University, where Leicester was Chancellor. Baily, according to the author of *Leicester's Commonwealth* a source of the earl's intelligence about the university, was a safe man at the peak of his profession. In October 1578 he had advised the queen about her toothache and rheum, and Leicester was one of two signatories of the order for a crown lease of lands belonging to Oxford colleges to him the next April.[33] In 1581 Baily became physician to the queen and at about that time also a Fellow of the College of Physicians, so he moved to London and acquired property and influential friends, including Sir John Popham, the Attorney-General. The next year, 1582, he became a publicist for the use of medicinal waters in England, the most prestigious scholar so far employed. His treatise, *A Brief Discours of certaine Bathes or Mineral Waters in . . . Newenam Regis* (1582), reappeared five years later with an adjusted title, the waters now described as 'medicinall', not merely 'mineral'. Although Baily had examined the waters at their first discovery he had delayed publication, waiting for the intended findings of another old and learned man now dead.[34] One senses Baily's reluctance to publish his work, which had no dedication or reference to a patron; perhaps he was unsure whether Leicester still retained the queen's favour.

The particular interest of the *Discours* lies in the argument of the introduction, linking the new role of medicinal waters with Anglican theology, and it places Baily foremost among those employed to promote the English baths. He began on a high note: '. . . the benefits no doubt are great and manifold which Almighty God . . . of late years hath plentifully bestowed upon this little soil of England, since the prosperous reign of our most gracious Sovereign, wherein the Gospel hath sincerely and freely been preached.' He stressed the long maintenance of peace, the abundance of all things, and the overthrow of evil plots to subvert the realm, all the outcome of 'God's well pleased mind with the government of our most gracious Queen'. Not least among contemporary benefits were the unknown baths and medicinal waters recently discovered with which God had blessed this country.

So, basing his propaganda on the appeal of Protestantism and patriotism, Baily descended to particulars. He had visited the well-established baths of Bath and Buxton, but among the many recently discovered medicinal waters those of King's Newnham had most credit, although, being abused, they had lost their first popularity. He had found many there using the waters indiscriminately, like their superstitious forefathers. Echoing William Turner, Baily reiterated the need to educate people in the use of the waters and for men of substance to subsidize the improvement of the baths, for those in England, even in Bath and Buxton, compared badly with continental ones. But such was the reputation of the Newnham wells that, he said with exaggeration, multitudes came for remedy from all over the kingdom, and experts in natural philosophy were examining reports of cures there. Baily spoke as the new man of science; it was impiety to detract from the omnipotent power of God, who was still able to perform miracles, but modern philosophers held that God used natural or inferior causes as his instruments. In these second causes, the laws of nature, man would find understanding of the hidden qualities of medicinal waters. So by appeal to second causes and the laws of nature Baily justified a new interpretation of the water cure. Establishment man though he was, he aligned himself with the Moderns against the Ancients.[35]

Baily admitted that exact diagnosis of the Newnham waters was in dispute, but he listed ailments which they might cure and, like Dr John Jones, he emphasized the importance of a disciplined approach. The Warwickshire waters, although cold, were suitable for both drinking and bathing, but only in the hottest part of the summer and in dry seasons. He suggested a routine like that favoured by Dr John Jones, and this became common form at watering-places, with emphasis on the need for expert advice and drinking small doses of water on a daily increasing scale. Treatment should be spread over ten or twelve days, which suggests that King's Newnham had accommodation for visitors.

Despite Baily's propaganda *cold* bathing was not yet an accepted habit, but although this embryonic Midland spa never became another Bath or Buxton, it had continuing custom. In June 1581 John Gifford of Stillington in Staffordshire, an imprisoned recusant, was licensed to go to the 'new wells' at King's Newnham for a fortnight to recover his health, as long as he employed no recusant as a servant. In March 1585 he was allowed to return there or to go to Bath, and in 1590 he again had 'special occasion to go to the wells in Warwickshire' as a favour because his son had helped to uncover the Babington Plot.[36] By then the King's Newnham experiment had lost its impetus, perhaps with the Earl of Leicester's death. After the Armada defeat in August 1588 he left on a long-promised holiday, by way of Kenilworth, to take the waters at Buxton again or near Leamington. He reached Cornbury near Oxford, where he died on 4 September; in his famous last letter to Elizabeth from Rycott he wrote hoping to find the perfect cure 'at the bath'.[37] He was not on the route for Bath; his objective, given time, was Buxton, but the alternative waters 'nearby Leamington' to which Leicester was journeying when he died were those at King's Newnham.

Although Bath was accessible from his home at Sudeley in Gloucestershire, Grey, 5th Lord Chandos, 'the king of the Cotswolds', also took the waters at Newnham in 1618, preferring them to those of Spa, where he had been six years earlier, but he returned to Spa and died there in 1621.[38] Had the Newnham waters cured nobles of the standing of Leicester or Chandos their history might have been different, but they probably attracted only local custom. Later editions of Baily's work, in 1654 and 1736, were produced in Yorkshire, prompted perhaps more by interest in the northern spas than by Warwickshire activity. With Leicester's death in 1588 and that of Baily in 1592 the Newnham project declined, although the water was still being taken in 1820. Only the Bath

Cottage at King's Newnham, a few documents, and a memorial brass with a full-length portrait of Walter Baily in the ante-chapel of New College, Oxford, remain as testimonies of the spa that never was.[39]

Bath, Buxton and King's Newnham were not, however, the only Tudor precursors of the English spas: another watering-place emerged in the North. Among the Englishmen who knew Spa in the Netherlands was William Slingsby, fourth son of Thomas Slingsby of Scriven, Yorkshire and uncle of the better-known William Slingsby, Member of Parliament for Knaresborough from 1597. In his youth Slingsby the uncle had drunk the waters of the Sauvenière and Pouhon fountains at Spa, and back in England he now took more notice of the many mineral springs at Harrogate, a small hamlet near Knaresborough. Slingsby's early home was a grange house in Harrogate near the Tewit Well, so called because of the lapwings there, and possibly the well in an intake held by Richard Benson in 1561. In 1571 Slingsby was elated to 'discover' that the waters of the Tewit Well resembled those of Spa. He and one Ingleby, another Yorkshire gentleman, had the well walled round, paved with two good stone flags and provided with an outlet hole. This was purely a drinking well; there was no bath.[40]

Although this spring was on his estate, Slingsby, who died in 1608, left its promotion to the medical men of Yorkshire, notably Dr Anthony Hunton (d. 1642). More important was the attention of a physician patronized by Lord Burghley and the Elizabethan court circle, Dr Timothy Bright (d. 1617), a Cambridge graduate, author of five medical books and a physician at St Bartholomew's, where some of his colleagues with an interest in mineral waters reissued parts of William Turner's *Baths* in 1586. In 1591 the queen presented Bright with the living of Methley, about thirty miles south of Harrogate, and he left for Yorkshire, where he was further bolstered by the rectory of Barwick-in-Elmet nearer to Harrogate. Bright too compared the Harrogate Tewit Well favourably with that of Spa, where he also had spent some time. He sent others to it and took the waters himself in the summer, and about 1596 he named the Tewit Well the 'English Spaw'. But he died in 1617 before producing his expected writing on the Harrogate waters, and the well – or the Northern Spa, as it was soon called – fell into neglect until some local physicians revived its use in 1625.[41]

William Harrison, whose *Description of England* had two editions, in 1577 and 1587, also promoted the new approach to the use of natural springs. He dismissed the many 'miraculous' wells of the past as baits for profiteers or those who suffered from excessive sexual indulgence, and he named the accepted baths and wells with which Almighty God had 'not a little enriched' the isle of Britain, emphasizing, like other propagandists, religious sanction allied to medical benefit. Apart from the baths of Bath,

Buxton and King's Newnham, Harrison explicitly mentioned those at St Vincent's Rock at Clifton near Bristol, at the Holy Well (either at Shoreditch or in Flintshire) and at Newton, near St Neots in Huntingdonshire.[42] So there were, including Harrogate but not the Holy Well, possibly in Wales, six recognized places for taking the waters, and a seventh not mentioned by Harrison, in Cheshire. Was it entirely fortuitous that these baths were geographically dispersed? Harrogate and Buxton served the North, King's Newnham the Midlands, Bath and the Bristol Hotwell the West, Newton the East and the Holy Well in Flintshire the North-West. It seems that a traditional bath or well was allowed to flourish or a new one to develop in each region.

But the Holy Well in Flintshire retained Catholic undertones, and so another well was belatedly promoted in that region, in Cheshire. Formerly St Stephen's Well, it was 'discovered' at Hollins in the township of Utkinton by John Greenway of Utkinton, whose physician advised him to drink and bathe there. News of his cure and that of his three sons attracted many to the well, but the promoter of this enterprise was the important John Donne of Utkinton Hall (also called 'The Chamber'), the chief forester. Donne was on the commission of peace for Cheshire in about 1593, the county sheriff in 1595–6 and a member for Cheshire in the Parliament of 1593, so he was in touch with London opinion.[43]

The Donne, or Done, family were clients of another Elizabethan grandee, Lord Keeper Sir Thomas Egerton, a local landowner, member for Cheshire in the Parliaments of 1584 and 1586 and chamberlain of Cheshire, whose younger son John Egerton owned land at little Budworth near the well in Delamere Forest, which was crown land. The well was in use by 1600 when an anonymous 'G.W.' described it in a pamphlet published in London, *Newes out of Cheshire of the new found Well,* which contains an illustration of the scene around the well, the naked bathers and people coming and going. The unknown author was conversant with the views of Dr William Turner and Dr John Jones on mineral-water baths, and he knew of the contemporary baths and wells at Bath, Buxton and St Vincent's, Bristol. He could have been John Greenway's unknown physician, or perhaps Dr John Donne (d. 1631), the poet and divine, who was possibly related to the Cheshire Donnes but was, in any case, from 1596 to 1599 the Lord Keeper Egerton's secretary. The Egertons knew of the new well in Warwickshire, for the lord keeper's daughter Mary married Sir Francis Leigh of King's Newnham. So John Donne the forester may have promoted the Cheshire well under the patronage of Sir Thomas Egerton.

The 'new found Well' at Utkinton, bordered by three or four flagstones, overflowed into two small pools where poor people came to bathe and wash, and allegedly 2,000 arrived daily from all parts, disturbing the neighbourhood and the queen's deer. So Donne the landowner appointed one of his keepers, John Frodsham, to preserve order and allowed him to provide entertainment for those who could afford it. Donne insisted on free access to the waters and posted servants to ensure that the keepers made no charge.[44] The fame of these waters spread among the now spa-conscious political and social elite. In March 1601 the gout-ridden Sir Henry Lee, the queen's champion, wrote to Sir Robert Cecil from Wood-stock that he intended to go to Bath or, as a desperate remedy, to the 'wells' in Cheshire, but he had doubts about the latter and by late May he still delayed his journey. John Donne, the governor of the wells, who with some friends 'had sought life but found death in that place' had died in Bath that month. 'That place' was ambiguous, either Cheshire or Bath, but the significant fact is that Donne lacked faith in his own waters and went to Bath. Yet his Cheshire bath was used for over a century, especially for the cure of lameness.[45]

None of these minor watering-places ever functioned on the scale of Bath and Buxton, but their existence helped to spread the new social habit of taking mineral waters. A philosophy and a regime for the water cure had been established under noble patronage and with guidance from leading physicians, and at least at Bath, Buxton and Utkinton the poor had free access to the healing waters.

2

Bath and Buxton: The New Vogue for Going to the Baths

After the setback of the Reformation both Bath and Buxton enjoyed an Elizabethan renaissance. With their custom stimulated by the publicity of Dr William Turner and Dr John Jones, they became renowned as watering-places where, during the summer months, the court element gathered for health and recreation in unprecedented fashion. Few courtiers of note did not at some time face the discomforts of travel to them, often several times, to stay for a week or more, and 'going to the baths' became an accepted social habit. Neither place was equipped to receive large numbers of visitors, although Bath had more accommodation than Buxton, but both had a long tradition of bathing and the advantage of natural thermal waters. Bath had three springs at temperatures varying from 117° to 120°F, and the abundant Buxton waters from nine springs were cooler but warm at 82°F.

Buxton

Upper Buxton, the old town, was little more than a village in the barren Peak district of Derbyshire and lacked even a church until 1625, when a modest, single-storey building dedicated to St Anne was erected behind the High Street to serve the growing settlement and the increasing number of visitors. St Anne's Well in the marshy valley of the River Wye, a hundred feet below, was fed by the mineral springs on the shale beds, one of which the Earl of Shrewsbury tapped when in about 1572 he built his hall with a bath. Few settled in this dale and the only buildings were lodgings near the baths.[1] According to John Jones in his *Benefit of Buck-stones,* in 1572 there were three chief baths. Remains of an ancient one, perhaps Roman, uncovered in 1697 showed a cistern of lead sheets over great pieces of timber, about four feet square, with surrounding ledges. A later excavation near St Anne's Well revealed another well of roughly worked limestone walls thirty feet by fifteen feet with a spring at the west end and an outlet opposite, but like the baths at Bath they were exposed to the open air, although Shrewsbury's bath attached to the Hall had fire-places.[2]

Uninviting though the baths might be, the legend of the miraculous power of St Anne still brought people there. Thomas Wentworth of Went-worth Woodhouse was directed to St Anne's Well by a vision; he re-covered from illness and had a son in 1562. The Earl of Shrewsbury's bad attack of gout in 1569 led him, urged by his physicians, to try the 'baynes of Buckstones', and he then built the Hall, the largest house in the village, to provide badly needed lodgings for visitors.[3] Roger Manners, later Earl of Rutland, intended to visit Buxton in 1571, and the erection of the great Hall in about 1572 encouraged more of the nobility and others to come to Buxton Well, which became a recreational centre with some organized social activity. In August 1574 nineteen people of some importance stayed in the Hall, including Lady Essex, Lady Mildmay and Lady Norris. A great assembly of ladies and gentlemen was there two years later, and in 1580 many Yorkshire and Lincolnshire gentry arrived and outshone the local folk in a series of contests with their cocks, dice, cards, balls and music which they brought with them. When Sir Robert Constable, trea-surer at the Berwick-on-Tweed fortress, came in 1567 seeking remedy for his ill-health, the Lord Regent of Scotland offered to send him the best surgeons and physicians but was confident that the Buxton waters were his best hope.[4]

Buxton's most famous visitor was Mary Queen of Scots, then in Shrewsbury's custody at Wingfield Manor, Derbyshire. Her repeated re-quests to visit the Buxton baths to alleviate her tertian fever and a pain in her side embarrassed the English government, who feared she would intrigue with visitors, especially the nobles. But apart from Shrewsbury's special interest in the place, a gentleman of her household, Robert Tunsted, was a native of Buxton and she was allowed to go there in late August 1573 since Shrewsbury guaranteed her security. After a stay of five weeks she longed to return and went altogether nine times to Buxton, the second time in June and July 1575 when she met Lord Burghley there, and then in early June 1576 when she wrote to Elizabeth on 30 June of the improvement to her health. The French ambassador pressed for a longer stay for her, but Elizabeth I wanted to prevent her meeting the Earl of Leicester and ordered her back to Sheffield, although they did meet there in mid-1577. Shrewsbury again reassured Burghley about security for another visit in August 1580; the beggars now wanted her gone so that they could be allowed to return to the town, and none of her household had ventured far from the well and then only if guarded by his soldiers, as when Mary came out to take the air one evening in the close around the house. Shrewsbury escorted Mary to Buxton again in July 1581 and June

1582 and was reprimanded when he allowed her a second, unauthorized visit that year.[5]

Finally, in May 1584, Mary requested her ninth visit to Buxton – her last. There was now such a shortage of lodgings that when Shrewsbury went there in June to meet Leicester he and his brother-in-law, John Manners, had to share a bedchamber and Manners sent a bed in advance. On 24 June Shrewsbury, back in Sheffield, planned a fortnight's visit with Mary, who wished to come after Leicester's departure but while Shrewsbury's staff were there. On 7 July she assured the French ambassador that the waters had benefited her nerves. The patronage of Mary and Shrewsbury made Buxton a social magnet for the nobility and it was a profitable investment for Shrewsbury, who supplied both lodgings and provisions. The queen thought he was making between £3,000 and £4,000 out of the place, but Leicester assured her this was not so.[6]

When Elizabeth's chief minister, Lord Burghley the Lord Treasurer, planned to visit Buxton in August 1574 Thomas Greves, Shrewsbury's agent, could find no free room for him unless his son Sir Thomas Cecil left the next week. Shrewsbury was anxious for him to come, to arrange a marriage between their families, so in 1575 Burghley faced the 159 miles from London to Buxton and stayed at least a week from 6 August. The Lord Chamberlain, Thomas Earl of Sussex, previously President of the Council of the North, was at the same time by order of the Privy Council provided with four carts to convey his possessions to Buxton, but Burghley required only one cart and post-horses on the route.[7]

Advised by his physician, the Earl of Leicester went to Buxton in July 1576 and again in June 1577 with his brother the Earl of Warwick and the Earl of Pembroke, patron of Bath, and enjoyed Shrewsbury's generous hospitality. Robert Knollys used three post-horses to go to him at Buxton and back, for statesmen had to attend to government business even while taking this new kind of holiday. Leicester, writing to Burghley, recalled that in 1575 the latter had overtaxed his strength when at Buxton by long journeys of ten or twelve miles a day and overeating at dinner and supper. The three earls, by contrast, lived moderately, dined together with one dish or two at most and had short walks or rides on horseback. The house where they stayed (presumably Shrewsbury's new mansion) was rather small, easily filled and hard to keep fresh, so Burghley was advised to reduce his retinue if he came the next year. Although his health had improved at Buxton, Leicester had taken cold coming from the bath, out walking, or sitting in the cold to hear a sermon on Midsummer Day, an experience well understood by those exposed to the brisk air of Buxton in summer. By 26 June Leicester, fearing that he had contracted tertian ague, was returning to Kenilworth with Warwick and Pembroke. Meanwhile the queen personally thanked Shrewsbury for his hospitality to Leicester, her forty-five-year-old favourite, but as he was becoming red of face and round of girth she urged Shrewsbury to restrict his diet, except to allow him his fill of St Anne's sacred water.[8]

Both Shrewsbury and Leicester hoped for Burghley's return to Buxton in the summer of 1577. Since Buxton was overcrowded Burghley asked for assurance of a lodging in Shrewsbury's house, the Hall, but only if his social inferiors, and not others, were displaced for him; and, resolved to keep a frugal diet, he set out with his son Thomas on 22 July. Elizabeth I herself never went to Buxton, although she visited Bath, but on Leicester's return she repeatedly commanded him to persuade Burghley to send her a tun of the Buxton water in well-seasoned hogsheads, which she received on 8 August. But now, angered by rumours that she needed the water for her sore legs, she pettishly spurned it as having lost some virtue in transit. Leicester still had faith in the waters and would have given 500 marks to be able to spend twenty days at Buxton to cure his rheum, and his June 1578 visit to the bath did indeed reduce the swelling in his leg.[9] In late June 1580 he again thanked Shrewsbury for his 'good entertainment' at Buxton, and his fifth and last visit was in May 1584.[10] So Buxton was a place of resort of some importance in the Elizabethan political scene, an alfresco setting for the exchange of gossip and information, where two leading statesmen, Burghley and Leicester, met Mary Queen of Scots.

Yet members of the government were sometimes alarmed about gatherings at Buxton Well, for its Catholic tradition endured and much intrigue went on under cover of taking the waters. The Privy Council were concerned about the visits of Derham, a priest from the diocese of Norwich, in 1578 and of William Davenport's wife of Bramhall in Cheshire in 1581, and in 1586 about the activity at Buxton during the Babington Plot, for Anthony Babington of Derbyshire had a house at Dethwick near Matlock. Sir Thomas Gerrard and others there planned to free Mary Queen of Scots, and a general meeting of priests was arranged at Buxton, where some arrived with £150 collected in London. In 1593 a rebel priest, Francis Ridcall, fled to Buxton to meet Sir Robert Dormer and other papists, but he dared not stay long and sheltered in a wood.[11]

By now the appeal of Buxton was declining: in 1582 Burghley questioned its future and the value of its waters, good only for wounds and encouraging exercise in journeying there. Lady Willoughby failed to find a cure in 1589, and although Roger Manners, now Earl of Rutland, wanted to return in 1591, on his visit in July 1594 he found nothing to commend the place apart from its waters. Mary Queen of Scots' execution in 1587 and Shrewsbury's death in 1590 shifted political attention from the North, and Buxton lapsed in importance. Some northerners were as ready to patronize Bath as Buxton; the Catholic William Hussey of North Duffield in Derbyshire left custody to go to Buxton in 1567 but in 1569 for Bath, and George Earl of Cumberland, from Yorkshire, sought health in 1595 at Bath, not Buxton. In the next century Yorkshire gentry frequently travelled to Bath for a cure, but few people of standing went to Buxton.[12] Yet Elizabethan Buxton had been of some social significance; although the queen and her court had never ventured there her rival Mary Queen of Scots paid nine visits, and at least eight English nobles and several of their wives went to Buxton, Leicester five times and others more than once, attracting a crowd of beggars whose invasion had to be deterred by Act of Parliament in 1572.[13]

Bath

By contrast, in 1590, when Buxton's decline had begun, Bath was recognized as an important city by a new charter of incorporation. Although Taunton was technically the county town, Bath was the premier city of Somerset and had had an independent magistracy since 1447. Elizabethan Derbyshire was dominated by the Earl of Shrewsbury, but Elizabethan Somerset had no noble family and looked to Wiltshire for its lord lieutenant, the Earl of Pembroke. Somerset was a county of gentry some of whom, with the prospering Gloucestershire gentry and clothiers from the Cotswolds and those from West Wiltshire, became consumers in Bath's leisure market.[14]

Bath, in a hollow of the limestone hills between the Cotswold escarpment and the Mendips, is about 107 miles from the metropolis, then a three-day journey for a fast rider and only two-thirds of the distance from London to Buxton; and as the fame of its waters grew, it attracted an increasing number of social and political magnates from afar, as well as local patrons. Elizabethan Bath had a contemporary social importance as great as that which the city enjoyed two centuries later.

The traveller to Bath in about 1560 entered a little city enclosed by walls of less than a mile, with four main and two smaller gates, the Ham Gate and St Peter's Gate, and partly encircled by the river Avon flowing under the bridge by the South Gate. Some of the fields within and without the walls, the Abbey Orchard, the Ham and others, had belonged to Bath Priory. Speed's map showed little expansion beyond the walls, even in 1610, and space remained for gardens, orchards and avenues of trees. Dominating it all was the shell of the Abbey or Priory Church of St Peter built, from 1499 onwards, on an earlier site but still incomplete. The adjoining monastic ruins were a quarry for house-builders; eleven loads of stone were taken away in 1573 alone. The Abbey gatehouse, the prior's or Abbey House by the main bath and some of the ruined bishop's palace remained, but in the twenty-five acres of the city there was little infilling of buildings. The parochial church was St Mary of Stalls in the centre of the city; the corporation had refused to buy the ruinous Abbey Church for 500 marks, for there were three other churches inside the walls – St Michael's Within, St Mary's Within and St James's – and just outside the North Gate a second St Michael's.[15]

After the dissolution of the Priory in 1539 Bath was reduced to being merely a cloth-making and market town, still with its medieval layout of narrow streets and alleys. With the departure of the monks the focus of activity was now the market place or market house of 1551–2 and the Guildhall in the High Street, and both were repaired in 1578. The Guildhall was, apart from the churches, the most important building in Bath; its door was painted in 1575, repairs in 1595 included new windows and a seat for the mayor, three yards of green cloth were provided in 1597, and the floor was remade in 1601.[16]

This hall was the meeting-place of the common council who now controlled Bath's destiny, for the Reformation had profoundly altered the balance of power in the city and opened the way for its transformation into a resort town. It had been subject to the mandate of the bishop of Bath and Wells, the lord of the manor and owner of the neglected palace and a little property there. The prior of the Benedictine monastery had also had some jurisdiction, but much ecclesiastical power was gradually transferred to the corporation. The prior surrendered his monastery to the crown in 1539 and the bishop his possessions in 1548, but in 1552 the crown granted all the monastic lands to the city, and the corporation's acquisition of a lease of the courts leet in 1568 became an outright grant in the charter of 1590. But the crown grant of 1552 conflicted with an earlier one in March 1543 of the Priory site and lands to the lawyer Humphrey Colles, who immediately sold them to Matthew Colthurst, the auditor of Edward Seymour, later the Protector Somerset. Colthurst also acquired the episcopal manors of Claverton and Monkton Combe and the monastic property of Hinton Charterhouse south of Bath, and he represented Bath in the Parliament of 1545.

Colthurst's possession of the Abbey property had enormous future significance; his purchase included the Abbey Orchard and a large close called the Ham, and created a private estate of about a quarter of the city in the south-east area. Matthew Colthurst died in 1560, and on 27 July 1569 his son and heir Edmund sold the Abbey House and its lands to Fulk Morley, who leased out the house as a lodging-house, but Colthurst retained private access to the baths. Edmund Colthurst also, by licence from the crown of 21 November 1572, passed the fabric of the Abbey Church to the corporation, who now made it their parish church to accommodate the extra visitors. In 1611 the Abbey House and lands passed from Fulk Morley to John Hall, a wealthy clothier of Bradford-on-Avon. In 1596 the corporation queried the original Colthurst rights to the Abbey Orchard, and in 1620 they challenged Hall's monopoly, but his tenant John Biggs asserted that the orchard, as part of the Abbey House estate, was privileged property where the maces were lowered and not carried before the mayor.[17] Relations between the corporation and the Abbey Estate long remained a source of conflict, especially when both later catered for the visitors' trade.

During the thirty years after 1552 most of the rest of the city area became civic property, including the baths. The tradition of the sick coming to bathe in the healing waters had survived from the Middle Ages, and from the mid-1570s onwards this town of about 300 houses and 1,000 to 1,500 people received a steady flow of visitors, high and low, who created an accommodation problem. There were a number of fine houses for the wealthier and eleven inns, such as the White Hart, the Cross Bow and the Three Tuns close by the King's Bath in Stall Street and the Bell and the George near the Hot and Cross Baths. But inns were intended for short-stay travellers in transit, and more lodging-houses for residential visitors were needed. Members of the corporation controlled several inns and lodging-houses and had a vested interest in promoting the use of the waters, as had the local physicians, some of whom took in private lodgers, and each extolled the virtues of the bath nearest to his own house. Dr Reuben Sherwood was well rewarded for his hospitality to Sir Robert Cecil's son William in 1599 in what he called 'my poor house', the Abbey House. Lady Rutland paid his son Dr John Sherwood £30 for a visit in 1605, and Sir John Harington lent his Stall Street house almost opposite the Queen's Bath to his friends and let it to Dr Ralph Bayley for his patients.[18]

The town council was swift to invest in its new leisure industry; in 1569, the year after the publication of Turner's treatise on Bath, it spent the then enormous sum of £4,095 11*s*. 6½*d*. on lime, stone, timber and labour for building houses. In 1583 the four city churches were amalgamated into one rectory under its control, and George Meredith was given this living in 1584 in return for a lease of all the church property for fifty years at an annual rent of £62. So the corporation acquired some very convenient building land as a result of the Reformation changes, and by the last decade of the century some fine lodging-houses had been erected.[19]

The impetus to Bath's renaissance was particularly marked in the 1570s. The city fathers' hold over both local government and much property meant that the promotion of Bath as a watering-place depended on the enterprise of the common council, helped by the interest aroused by Turner's treatise of 1568 and from 1570 by the patronage of the 2nd Earl of Pembroke. In 1572 came legal aid to control the influx of paupers, John Jones's *Bathes of Bathes Ayde* dedicated to Pembroke, the gift of the

Abbey Church from Edmund Colthurst, who was rewarded with the freedom of the city, and the initiative in restoring the church. Peter Chapman, soldier son of a Bath clothier, paid for repairs to the east end of the north aisle, but more were needed. So in April 1573, by royal proclamation, the city authorities were empowered to receive alms nationwide for seven years to rebuild the Abbey Church and improve the old Hospital of St John the Baptist for the sick poor. Bath certainly had friends at court that such demands were allowed, but according to Sir John Harington the money came in slowly. Six years later a forcible reminder went to the bishop of Durham that the contribution of his laggardly diocese was incomplete. The letter was signed by eight privy councillors of whom at least five had been to Bath.[20]

The contemporary bishop of Bath and Wells, Gilbert Berkeley, also helped to promote the Bath waters. About 1580 he commissioned Dr Robert Lesse, who had a house in Bath, to write a guide to the healthy use of the Bath waters. Lesse's resulting treatise, *A brief view of all baths. . . ,* was based on the arguments of the *De medicatis aquis* of Gabriel Fallopius (d. 1562), and is further evidence of the Church's sanction of the use of medicinal waters in Elizabethan times. Lesse held it important that the 'unlearned laity' and others of common rank should also be instructed about the Bath waters and dedicated his study to the Master of Trinity College, Cambridge, Dr John Still, who was also later bishop of Bath and Wells, arguing that his good name would give the people confidence in the benefits of the waters. Lesse's rather verbose manuscript pamphlet emphasized that Bath waters had been used for drinking, as well as bathing, in the past and that prolonged water treatment – sometimes up to forty days, under medical advice – was necessary.[21]

Bishop Berkeley and the new Earl of Pembroke may have initiated the queen's visit to Bath in 1574 which gave the accolade to the new cult of public bathing. Pembroke, had, apart from Bath, a general interest in mineral waters; he went to Spa in 1575 and to Buxton in 1577. The bishop, previously a royal chaplain, was in Bath in 1573 and subsequently two of its citizens went to Wells for his letter 'to London' on the city's behalf and paid for a copy. Berkeley's wife accompanied him to Bath in 1574 and received gifts of capons and chickens. He may also have prompted the Privy Council's request to the city in June 1573 to maintain and manage the baths better for the reception of important patrons. In 1573–4 there were bustling preparations for the queen's visit; the chamberlain paid for paving and painting and for 'one that kept the walls of the city at the Queen's Majesty being here', presumably a guard. A window in the church of St Mary of Stalls was glazed for the occasion, and a ring for the oration to the queen was laid out by the West Gate. The choristers were brought from Wells for her reception, which again suggests episcopal involvement in her visit.[22]

In July 1574 the queen and her household progressed to Sudeley in Gloucestershire, the home of Lord Chandos, to Bristol and on 21 August to Bath, where two days later she held a privy council attended by all the foremost courtiers: Burghley, the Lord Treasurer; Leicester and his brother Warwick; her two secretaries, Sir Thomas Smith and Sir Francis Walsingham; Lincoln, the Lord Admiral; and Sussex, the Lord Chamberlain. So for five days of glory the court was at Bath, and one must assume that some of them, if not the queen, took the waters. On 26 August they left by way of Longleat for Wilton and a grand reception by Pembroke. Elizabeth never went to Bath again.[23] Her progress planned for July 1602 to include Bath, where her cousin George, Lord Hunsdon, now the Lord Chamberlain, was taking the waters, was abandoned through bad weather and her increasing weakness, so she did not see the fine house which her godson Sir John Harington had built at nearby Kelston in about 1587 to the plan of Barazzi of Vignola. All the frantic activity at Bath to get the streets in order for her arrival by pitching loads of stones and recruiting paviours from Tetbury, Bristol and Warminster was in vain. Hunsdon had endured the treatment in May 1600 to please his physicians, despite the excessive heat and the draughts of the baths, but now in October 1602 he returned from Bath 'neither much better nor worse' than when he went, and had 'little hope or help' from that source.[24] The queen expressed surprise that he had not been drowned by the many pails of water poured over him, a reference to 'bucketing' at Bath. 'Those extreme water-pourers' angered her, and had she been there she would have restrained them; she urged Hunsdon to leave Bath.[25]

Despite her later reservations about methods of treatment, the queen's visit in 1574 had set the stamp of fashion on Bath and led to its economic revival, now as a watering-place, and many contemporaries spoke of going 'to the Baths'. They may have had doubts about the value of the water cure, but Bath provided recreation and the society of those of similar rank and interests in a relaxed atmosphere, and it became the custom, more than at Buxton, for many of the aristocracy to spend a part of the summer there. In 1604 the Earl of Cumberland professed to value Bath for its company as well as its waters, and between 1570 and 1600 at least ten earls and thirteen other nobles went there, some three or more times. The new habit of indulging in a holiday under pretext of a health cure was especially favoured by the Cecil family. Sir William Cecil went possibly in 1552, but certainly when Lord Burghley in 1574; he returned in June 1592, excusing himself from state business to recover from gout, and again in 1598. The Cecil patronage of Bath was maintained by his sons Robert and Thomas; Thomas went six times.[26]

The Earls of Leicester and Warwick were patrons of Bath, as of Buxton; they accompanied the queen there in 1574, Leicester went again in 1577, and in April 1587 both returned. The city presented Leicester with an ox worth £8 and two sheep and Warwick with a lamb and a calf, and engaged the waits of Bristol to play for them. Bath continued to court the powerful and sophisticated with gifts of a practical nature and little attentions to retain their patronage. Leicester's company of players added to the entertainment and were remunerated by the city in 1578, 1587 and 1588; so too was Warwick's bearward in 1576. But Leicester later disparaged the Bath waters, finding nothing to commend them; he was always worse the day after going into the bath. Warwick got some benefit there and returned in 1588 with his tumblers, but Leicester did not survive to see Bath again. His poor opinion of its waters supports the theory that 'the Bath' he was seeking in August 1588 was at King's Newnham or Buxton.[27]

Other nobles who went to Bath were Thomas, Earl of Sussex – four times in the 1570s – and Roger, Earl of Rutland – three times, to cure a swelling in his heart. Both had been to Buxton. Edward Nevill, Lord Bergavenny, later associated with Tunbridge Wells, came in 1595; as in 1589, 1594 and 1600 did Roger, Lord North, whose grandson Dudley 'discovered' the Tunbridge spring. Other nobles frequently sent their troops of players to enliven the social scene; those of the Earls of Sussex and Worcester came five times each.

All three of the contemporary bishops of Bath and Wells visited Bath: Bishop Berkeley in the 1570s; Bishop Godwin, doubtless in hope of curing his gout, in 1585; and Bishop Still, interested in the restoration of the Abbey Church, in the 1590s. Two of the bishops of Gloucester, Bullingham and Goldborough, were there in 1563 and 1600 respectively. Most people of note in Elizabethan society and politics now visited Bath – like William Davison, who was appointed Secretary of State when there in August 1586 to recover his health, but he delayed his return to court for some days.[28] In the wake of the peers spiritual and temporal flocked a host of others: gentry, clerics, attendants and servants. Shakespeare's lines

> I, sick withal, the help of Bath desired,
> And thither hied, a sad distempered guest,
> But found no cure. (Sonnet 153)

suggest that he too sampled Bath. For those seeking a courtier's patronage, a visit to Bath was a good alternative to going to the capital.

The visits of the nobility, with their great households, were not lightly undertaken. In 1600 the Privy Council ordered public officers to assist Lord Chamberlain Hunsdon with twenty horses for his retinue and five cart-horses to carry his clothes and household provisions. His predecessor Sussex had in 1578 been allowed four carts to carry his luggage from Norwich to Bath, and Lady Winchester was provided with a team of horses and oxen to take her possessions there in 1600.[29] Although Buxton was so much nearer his home at Alnwick, Henry, Earl of Northumberland was at Bath twice in 1590, for three weeks in June and over a month in October, for a further month with a retinue of twenty-five in April 1591, and in 1593. Dr Reuben Sherwood, the Bath physician, was temporarily attached to his household. Northumberland's friend Sir Walter Raleigh also haunted Bath, despite his moans that he was the worse for his April 1593 visit; in 1596 he eagerly awaited Northumberland's arrival there and urged Lord Cobham to join them. In 1597 Raleigh again wrote to Cobham to hasten his return that they might see Bath together, and he and his wife went there that winter. In 1601 Cobham and he were arranging another visit and Raleigh returned in 1602.[30]

Bath's attractions inclined men to neglect their duty. The Earl of Bath, from his Devon home, begged to be excused attendance on James I in March 1603 as he had a troublesome leg and had been ordered to Bath; he would arrange for a proxy in the Lords. Lords Russell and Audley also obtained leave of absence from the Lords to go there for their health, and the member for Ludlow, Robert Berry, from the Commons.[31] But some criticized Bath; Sir John Stanhope disliked it in 1593 and would not soon return, but he did so in 1597, and two years later Dr James and 'My Pady', possibly Sir William Paddy, advised him that a journey to Bath should be his 'last refuge'. Yet that year, 1599, Sir Robert Sidney was encouraged by Rowland White, Sir Robert Cecil's agent, to go to Bath or Spa as equal alternatives.[32]

The nobles were only some of the wide social range of people now making for Bath, which included many humble folk hoping to find a living in servicing the booming visitors' trade and paupers coming to beg. Some parochial authorities added to the social problems at the baths by subsidizing visits of the deserving poor, for justices could license the sick poor to travel beyond their homes to seek help. A lame boy in the Oxford alms-house was given 6s. 8d. or 10s. to go to the new well (possibly King's Newnham), and authorities at Nottingham in 1579 paid 1s. to four lame men from Kendal going 'to the baths'. The city of York in 1609 allowed 5s. to Anthony Cuthbert, a poor lame boy, to go to St Anne's Well at Buxton for recovery of his health.[33]

Bath was already such a magnet to paupers that 'the beggars of Bath' became a notorious nuisance, many coming daily from Bristol.[34] Eventually legislation was necessary for Bath, as for Buxton, to limit their numbers, and the contemporary mind saw no incongruity in bracketing these towns together, since one served the North and the other, also called 'the western bath', the South. This dual status was reflected in the 1572 Act covering the punishment of vagabonds and the relief of the poor, for 'great numbers' of poor and diseased persons were being drawn to Bath and Buxton, to which they were an intolerable burden. So a special provision offered some control; no diseased or needy person was to go to either place unless licensed by two justices of his own county and maintained by his own parish, and he must return home by a fixed date or be treated as a vagabond, for the people of Bath and Buxton could not be held liable for his relief. These restrictions were repeated in an Act of 1597/8, with the additional proviso that paupers at Bath and Buxton should not beg. The two members for Bath doubtless supported these bills in the Commons, but the first bill in 1572 coincided with Shrewsbury's initial development at Buxton, and either he, or his son the 7th Earl, or his son-in-law the 2nd Earl of Pembroke was present at all stages when the Acts of 1572 and 1597/8 passed through the Lords. The committee which considered the latter act included Roger, Lord North, who had had experience of Bath and, like many other peers remembering holidays there and at Buxton, would be prepared to support the interests of both places.[35]

But at Bath, like Buxton, more positive help was needed to cope with the sick poor. The Hospital of St John the Baptist took in eight almsfolk, St Catherine's Hospital housed ten poor inhabitants and the Hospital of St Mary Magdalen existed for the leprous poor. Now two outside philanthropists provided more assistance. Dr John Feckenham, last abbot of Westminster, like other recusants sought asylum in Bath when released from prison from July until Michaelmas in 1575. On his return in 1576 the corporation allowed him to purchase three tons of timber and 400 laths to build a poorhouse by the Hot Baths, the Lepers' Hospital attached to the Magdalen Hospital. He also compiled some medical advice on the use of the baths.[36] Thomas Bellot, formerly steward of Lord Burghley's household, in 1609 founded and endowed another hospital for poor persons resorting to Bath to take the waters: in Bell Tree Lane, the modern Beau Street. Bellot was also a generous benefactor to the Abbey, and Sir John Harington paid tribute to his munificence:

> Hospitals, Baths, Streets and Highways,
> Sound out the Noble Bellot's Praise.[37]

The practice of taking the waters was now such an accepted medical remedy that the government was prepared to release some imprisoned recusants, like Feckenham, under licence and with safeguards to take the cure at Bath. The first known case, in August 1574, coincided with the queen's visit: the Privy Council wrote from Bristol for the release of John and Nicholas Harpesfilde from the Fleet Prison to go to Bath to recover their health until late October on sureties of £100 each. Others released under order to go to Bath were Dr Yonge from the Marshalsea for six months in 1575, Edmund Beddingfield, who was very ill, freed by the bishop of Norwich in 1579, and Evans Fludde in 1580, let out by the sheriff of Cambridge despite his 'obstinacy in Popery'. Lady Stonor was allowed two months there from April 1582, but only if attended by her son Francis and a Protestant physician and not meeting anyone 'evilly affected in religion'. John Whitmore was freed to visit Bath after twelve years in Chester Castle, because his life was in danger. Despite the authorities' vigilance some active proselytizing went on at Bath where in 1581 Henry Clark was apprehended for popery and massing.[38]

Buxton, as we have seen, was also the resort of Catholics. Sir Thomas Throckmorton of Weston Underwood, Oxfordshire, was permitted to go to the Buxton baths in 1594 until 1 September, but a wet June and July made the journey impossible, so he begged an extended licence until Michaelmas to go to Bath. Michaelmas, 29 September, was the normal terminal date of travel permits when all the recusant birds had to be back in their cages for the winter. Francis Tregian, suffering from sciatica after twenty-four years in the Fleet, also begged liberty to go to either Buxton or Bath in 1601.[39] So Bath had become a Catholic centre; Sir William Catesby was allowed there for a fortnight in 1593 and Edward Winter after almost four years' 'barbarous imprisonment'. At Easter 1605 there were, as Thomas Winter confessed, many meetings at Bath about the 'hellish design', the Gunpowder Plot: Lord Monteagle, Robert Catesby, Thomas Percy and he all met 'at the Bath' and tried to recruit others.[40]

Although social fashion and religious dissent were motives for coming to Bath, the search for health predominated. Five baths were available in Elizabethan times: two new; three, the King's, Cross and Hot Baths, previously under the jurisdiction of the bishop and administered by the prior. The large King's Bath at the west end of the Abbey was for gentlemen only; it was surrounded by a high stone wall and the brim of the bath had a little wall around it. Less than half its size and separated from it by a wall was the New Bath built in 1567; it was moderately warm, square in shape, surrounded by a higher wall and provided with a public and a private dressing-place. This New Bath was known as the Queen's Bath after Queen Anne's visits in 1613 and 1615. The Cross Bath, with a cross in the centre, in the south-west of the town was surrounded by an almost triangular wall; it was reserved by 'the better sort' of people and had three dressing-rooms. The less popular Hot Bath of higher temperature, about 200 feet away, fed the Lepers' Bath only twelve feet square, possibly 'the poor folks' bath' mentioned in 1584. The Hot Bath had various private baths attached, including two which had served the abbot and the prior. Speed's map of Bath in 1610 shows the Horse Bath outside the South Gate, which suggests that William Turner's advice about the care of horses had been heeded.[41]

From 1552, when the baths were under civic control, they were constantly repaired and improved, often by private benefaction. The only income from them came from annual rents from a few favoured persons who had private doors into the King's Bath and the keeper's payment for farming the baths; for example, in 1569 Harry Mace, a town sergeant or mayor's officer, paid £3 1s. 10d. for the privilege, and in 1588 and 1590 John Strangwadge, ex-town sergeant, found £1 a year to be keeper of the Lower Baths. The town sergeant often held office as keeper, his function being to organize the lesser officials and ensure the orderly conduct of the baths. The post was no sinecure, for the keeper had to attend the baths morning and evening and at 10 p.m. during the bathing season to ring a bell to signal their closure and shut the doors. He also had to supervise the cleansing of the baths, the smaller Cross and Hot Baths daily and the larger King's Bath either twice a week or on alternate days. The baths gave employment to eight men guides and six women for the King's Bath and four men and four women for the Cross and Hot Baths; they had to supply linen, attend the bathers and work the pumps, and although paid wages they, like the keeper, depended mostly upon gratuities.[42]

The other source of civic income from the baths, a rent of normally 5s. a year from each person with a private door into the King's Bath, was probably an underpayment. The increase in the number of these doors and the competition to lease them indicates a growing revenue from customers using the doors for direct entrance from their lodgings to the bath; in 1569 there were six doors, in 1573 seven, by 1581 eight, nine in 1592 and ten in 1594. The city fathers tended to monopolize the doors, especially George Pearman, four times mayor and Member of Parliament for Bath in 1571–2. He paid the usual 5s. annual rent from 1573 to 1596, but for the last six years 'for Henry Blackleche'. Blackleach and Pearman angered some citizens, who made it a Star Chamber case when in 1573 they tried to monopolize the common footway to the King's Bath and made doorways in the wall round the bath to obtain access from Blackleach's house. But they retained their advantage, although Pearman stopped payment in 1597 and in 1601 owed the city chamberlain £4. Other monopolists included the Whibbens family, Thomas Turner, mayor and alderman, and from 1579 to 1601 Peter Chapman, sometime mayor. 'Mr Colthurst', probably Edmund Colthurst, in 1581 paid only a token rent of 4d., as did Dr John Sherwood from 1594 at least until 1602.[43]

The tenacity with which these monopolistic arrangements were maintained indicates their lucrative nature. In the 1590s Reuben Sherwood held the Abbey House, but the townsfolk resented his aristocratic clients having the privilege of a private bath and in 1598 a mob interfered with its water supply. The Privy Council were concerned about this and wanted to maintain the bath for the continued use of 'lords and ladies of great calling', so they intervened. In March they ordered the mayor and corporation to restore the damage and asked the Lord Chief Justice, Sir John

Popham of Wellington in Somerset, to see that the baths were repaired. The need was urgent, for the Swedish Lady Marquess of Northampton, a gentlewoman of the privy chamber from Longford in Wiltshire, planned to visit Bath in May. She came seven more times and in 1601 gave £100 to the city as a loan to poor clothiers.[44] Other doctors who made a lucrative living by supplying their patients with medical advice and also sometimes accommodation included Ralph Bayley (d. 1645), Edward Jorden (d. 1632) and Thomas Elton (d. 1618). They prescribed not only bathing but drinking the water; a fountain in the King's Bath was established for that purpose in 1578.[45]

The interest of the queen and the court in the city, and its growing importance, were recognized by the grant of a new and significant charter on 4 September 1590, replacing the original of 1189. The corporation now acquired control of a much-enlarged town and had the constitutional apparatus to supervise further advance. The corporation, never more than thirty, consisted of the mayor, recorder, aldermen and councillors, and its first mayor under this charter was William Sherston, six times Member of Parliament for Bath, who held much of the Walcot land newly included in the city boundary. Other civic officers were two justices, the chamberlain, two bailiffs or sheriffs and two chief constables, as well as minor officials like those at the baths.[46]

Both the Earl of Pembroke and Sir John Harington may have had a hand in obtaining this civic privilege. Sherston went to London to see Pembroke about the city's business. Harington was sworn sheriff of Somerset in 1591, and in May 1593 Burghley and others of the Privy Council suggested the stewardship of Bath for him, but the corporation refused him this post, fearing his power. Harington kept Burghley informed about Bath; in 1595 he met Bellot, Burghley's steward, there. The next year he described Bath as now 'wonderfully beautified' with 'fine houses for victualling and lodging' since the queen's visit – that is, after 1574. (Hetling House was, among other houses, erected in about 1570 for Sir Walter Hungerford.) But he deplored the lack of a common sewer, a disgrace '. . . for a town so plentifully served of water, in a country so well provided of stone, in a place resorted unto so greatly . . .'. In May or June 1598 Harington visited Burghley, now very ill and paralysed on one side, at Bath, but with the death of Burghley, his patron, that August and of the queen, his godmother, in 1603, Harington withdrew from court to the less exacting provincial life of Bath: '. . . I will keep company with none but my *oves* [sheep] and *boves* [oxen] and go to Bath and drink sack, and wash away remembrance of past times in the streams of Lethe.' Still a local patriot, he tried to persuade the capitalist Thomas Sutton to make a donation to the rebuilding of the Abbey Church, urging him to come to Bath, where he could use his warm and clean lodgings, with dry wood for his fire and plentiful supplies of good beef and beer. His company would be lawyers, divines and physicians and 'saint Bellot', by whose generosity the tower, the choir and the two aisles of the church were already finished.[47]

The death of the 2nd Earl of Pembroke in 1601 was the end of an era for Bath. From 1586 to 1601, as President of the Council in the Marches of Wales, he had wielded immense power in the West, but his youthful heir, in trouble, went abroad. Another Wiltshire magnate Edward Seymour, Earl of Hertford and son of the Protector Somerset, now became, from 1601 to 1621, lord lieutenant of Somerset, Wiltshire and Bristol, an assignment specifically covering the city of Bath.[48] So Seymour influence replaced Herbert influence at Bath, which in 1611 gave a gift to Hertford, whose friends included Sir Thomas Gorges, the second husband of Bath's patron, the Lady Marquess of Northampton of the queen's privy chamber. The abortive plans for the queen's visit to Bath in 1602 had included going to one of Seymour's Wiltshire homes, and in 1605 his brother, Sir Thomas Seymour, was living in Bath to avoid the plague. Yet when in 1612 the Earl of Salisbury, 'the last of the Elizabethans', went to Bath in a final desperate search for a cure, his constant companion was not Seymour but the 'Welsh earl', William Herbert, 3rd Earl of Pembroke.[49]

Salisbury retained the Cecil faith in the Bath waters, although they had failed his father Lord Burghley. When still Sir Robert Cecil he planned a summer visit to Bath in 1604 and Hertford hoped to entertain him *en route,* but rumours of plague there made him hesitate. Dr John Sherwood reported fewer than twenty-six cases, but they were dispersed throughout the city, so Cecil postponed his visit. Sherwood admitted that he had an interest in the King's Bath, but he assured Cecil that it would suit him best and was conveniently near the lodgings prepared for his party. He would provide stables and beer, but they must bring bed-hangings and plate. There was an infected house near the Cross Bath, the temperate bath which Cecil's brother the Earl of Exeter had advised him to use 'at the next fall of the leaf'; it had cured Exeter's swollen leg.[50]

As Cecil dallied figures of plague deaths came in: from mid-May to late August seventy-two people had died and twenty-four houses had been infected. As late as 26 August John Sachfield, the mayor, laid in stores in anticipation of Cecil's coming: three hampers of ale, a ton of beer, and wood and coal. At last on 16 September Captain John Winter reported that the plague was declining; all the houses near the baths were now safe. But Dr John Sherwood, overcome with the responsibility of bringing the great man to such danger, warned Cecil against coming, and although his coach was ready for the journey, between 20 and 22 September he turned back while Sir Edward Stafford waited for him in vain at the bridge in Bath. Captain Winter was depressed about the waste of provisions, but Sherwood had to face the angry citizens. 'The better sort' had hoped for Cecil's patronage for a renewal of the city charter with more immunities, and the less well off were frustrated of profit, but Sherwood told Cecil that the situation had been 'full of terror to those that truly love you'.[51]

Plague did not, however, deter the elite from coming to Bath in Stuart times. In 1607 the archbishop of Cashel was determined to get there, although he was delayed at Bristol by lack of money. The sick and lame bishop of Durham journeyed in 1612 from Bishop Auckland. Lionel Cranfield, later Lord Treasurer and Earl of Middlesex, stayed at the Bear for two or three nights in April 1608, when his nine-day expedition cost £15 2s. 4d. By contrast, in 1623 the forty-day journey of Lord William Howard to Spa, also in quest of health, cost £212 9s. 11d.[52]

Despite the fiasco of 1604, in 1612 Lord Salisbury, his life at risk from scurvy and dropsy, renewed his efforts to reach Bath. He left Kensington on 26 April accompanied by Dr Atkins and his chaplain Mr Bowls, but he was a broken man, saddened by the failure of his attempted financial reforms in 1611, and was fully prepared to be buried in Bath Abbey. His agent Michael Hicks, concerned about his low spirits, encouraged Sir Hugh Beeston to visit him at Bath with the prospect of winning £4 or £5 from him at the tables, or at least one small suit, a velvet cloak or a saddle; so gambling was already a diversion at Bath. Cormacke, James I's musician, was given £10 to accompany him.[53]

Salisbury reached Bath on Sunday 3 May and tried the bath on 5 May at 3 p.m., sitting in the water up to his navel, but on Wednesday, when the wind rose, the baths were deserted. He bathed for a whole week as the weather permitted, but on 12 May he began to decline. Sir John Harington, himself now sick of the palsy, visited him the next Monday and, as Salisbury remarked, 'Sir John, now doth one cripple come to see and visit another'. That day Salisbury inspected the Abbey Church and, impressed by its appearance, granted his servant 'old Mr Bellot' a life pension of £20 to repay his munificence to Bath. Salisbury also gave £4 a week to the poor of Bath, £3 to the hospitals, £10 to the guides at the bath, and £3 to the sergeant of the bath. By the next day, 19 May, his life was in danger, but he was now resolved not to die there. John Chamberlain reported that Salisbury had found so little value in the bath that he had hastened to leave 'that suffocating, sulphurous air'. He began the return journey two days later but died on the way at the parsonage at Marlborough on the 24th.[54]

For Elizabethan society taking the waters at Bath, Buxton and a few lesser places had become an accepted summer custom endorsed by the medical profession, the Protestant Church and the queen and her ministers, and Salisbury's visit to Bath in 1612 helped to continue the tradition in the Stuart age. Here were the origins of the resort trade, but in a political and religious context. The alfresco assemblies at the spas were a means of contact between members of the central government and the local community, where the Presidents of the Councils of Wales and the North, the lords lieutenant, bishops, Members of Parliament and justices of the peace rubbed shoulders and even shared the baths with London statesmen. Interspersed with the gossip serious information was exchanged and privy councillors became aware of local problems. Like the news gathered on court progresses or by assize judges on circuit or brought up to London by the Lords and Commons assembling for Parliament, the feedback from the informal gatherings around baths and wells was a significant means of communication between central and local government.

3
Stuart Patronage and the Drinking Spas

The government of James I – reluctant, like that of Elizabeth I, to allow an exodus to Spa – continued to endorse the custom of taking domestic mineral waters, and Sir Theodore Mayerne, the senior court physician, diplomatically advised the Queen, Anne of Denmark, to seek relief for her gout at Bath in 1613; the only royal visit since 1574. She and her retinue reached the city on 30 April and she immediately used the King's Bath and later the new bath, by 1615 known as the Queen's Bath. She was the first English royal to adopt the new practice of public bathing. There is record of a charge for preparing the King's and Queen's Baths that year and of the queen's bathing chamber and slip – that is, steps entering the bath – which implies that if there were only one bath a part of it was divided off as the Queen's Bath.[1]

The queen's treatment lasted for five weeks and on 4 June, much revived in health and spirits, she set out for Bristol, and so returned to Windsor. In early July her gentleman usher was settling accounts for her visit, but three weeks later he received advance payments for her next. By 21 August she was leaving Salisbury again on her way to Bath, where her household ushers prepared the houses of Dr Steward and Mr Hadnett for her party for twenty days in August and September. They also made ready the baths on ten occasions and her bathing chamber and her place at church five times. At the king's command Sir Theodore Mayerne sent him a detailed account of the improvement in her health, helped by her faith in the waters. By 22 September she had returned to court after a progress costing about £30,000. Bath had to pay for her footmen and the king's trumpeters 'at the Queen's being here in September'. There is ample evidence, then, that Queen Anne paid *two* visits to Bath in 1613.[2]

The queen intended to return in 1614, but the local people were less than enthusiastic about another visit. The city council resolved in March that the cost of her entertainment should fall on subsidy-payers and all able persons, and on 16 August to 'show themselves joyful by all the means they could' at her coming.[3] But these plans were abortive, and her 1615 visit was delayed by lack of funds. The Somerset folk feared having to meet the cost through the royal right of purveyance – that is, the requisitioning of goods and services with delayed payment. Beer casks for her household at Bath alone cost £10, and twenty carts were required to convey the royal provisions. The hundreds of both Bruton and Keynsham afterwards resisted the levying of rates for this purpose. Eventually the queen set out for her third and last visit about 20 July 1615 and stayed five weeks, although Bathonians were slow to pay for her presentation cup and other expenses. A fit of gout delayed her departure until mid-September and she was subsequently no better, but worse. She died in 1619.[4]

Despite the queen's death the stamp of Stuart approval was set on Bath and on taking domestic mineral waters in general, all the more so because the peril of dissidents going abroad remained. The Elizabethan government may have underrated the resilience of English Catholicism, but the danger of political disaffection was real enough to provoke increasingly stringent penal laws against recusants after 1581. Consequently their leaders were either imprisoned or they fled into exile, frequently with the avowed intention of taking the waters at the Pouhon spring at Spa, where by 1565 the English had a centre, a house named *Aux Armes d'Angleterre* in the rue Xhrouet.[5] Henry, Lord Morley and his family were among those who fled without a travel licence and lived in penury at Spa, watched by one of Burghley's agents.[6] Others equally dubious to the English government were Charles Paget, in exile after the Throckmorton Plot, who wrote to Mary Queen of Scots in 1586 of his intention to go to Spa 'for remedy of the stone'. Another declared Catholic, Robert Robinson, informed a London ally in 1592 of others intending to remain at Spa for two or three months, ostensibly to drink the waters, and naively suggested that their ruse would not be suspected. A more intellectual Catholic at Spa in the 1590s, again allegedly to take the waters, was Thomas Lister of Lancashire, an English Jesuit later charged with treason.[7] Spa was a centre of intrigue and the English government kept it under surveillance. By James I's reign the Privy Council were more reluctant to grant licences for overseas travel, as Hugh Speke, a known recusant, found. He had been allowed to go to Spa in Elizabeth I's time but his licence was countermanded in March 1605, and Sir Thomas Lake hesitated to intercede with the king on his behalf unless reassured by Secretary Cranborne.[8]

After the failure of the Gunpowder Plot in 1605, pressures on the Catholics increased. Early in 1612 leading papists were summoned to take the oath of allegiance, but a prominent Yorkshire recusant, Sir Ralph Babthorpe, was found to be 'at the Spawe'. Catholics were treated more severely from 1615 when the Pope authorized the English papists at Spa to choose a Catholic Archbishop of Canterbury. The English government procured a list of recusants there in July and August 1616, with their residences, and the crown tried, under the Act of 1571 which controlled foreign travel by licence, to ensure stricter control of the issue of passes.[9]

But despite this curb and the almost endemic state of war in Western Europe from 1585 to 1659, Englishmen continued to indulge in taking a Grand Tour on the Continent, which became commonplace for young noblemen and gentlemen. Spa, if they could afford it, was increasingly an accepted part of their itinerary, but even the Earl of Bedford's wife had to forgo a visit to Spa in August 1613 through lack of means.[10]

A survey of the licences issued specifically for Spa for a limited period, 1613–24, reveals at least 337 English men and women with the cover of passes. Peers were normally free, under the 1571 Act, to travel without a permit until required to return (when the 7th Earl of Argyll renounced the Protestant religion he was ordered home from Spa in 1618), but of these 337 other persons 124 were direct licensees and the other 213 were their gentlewomen, physicians, waiting-men and servants. These figures were probably incomplete, for some exiles would have escaped illegally.[11] The common form of licence was that issued on 21 May 1615 in the name of James I to all his officials and agents in favour of Lady Harris of Great Baddow in Essex allowing her to go to 'the Spawe in Germany' to recover her health after illness, as certified by Dr John Argent. She could stay for six months and take one manservant, two women servants and necessary trunks of clothes and provisions, and she had to go direct to Spa. Most licences were issued in the summer, in May, June and July; in the sample quoted there was none for December, January or February, but five for March and only one each for October and November. Licences were normally valid for six months but many for only three or four, and recipients had to take the oath of allegiance.[12]

Under James I the flow of licensees going to Spa between 1613 and 1624 averaged about twenty-eight a year, reaching sixty in the peak year, 1624, although only four or five in 1620 and 1621 during the marriage negotiations between Charles, Prince of Wales, and the Spanish Infanta. The English government then apparently tried to deter troublesome Englishmen from going to the Spanish Netherlands. Not all visitors to Spa were suspect, however, and an accepted English colony grew up there; in July 1611 Thomas Nevitt wrote of the nobility, gentry and others in this cosmopolitan centre, and in 1612 the Earl of Arundel, Lord Chandos, the Countess of Worcester and various Englishmen of standing hoped for cures there.[13] Viscount Lisle met the Earl of Southampton at Spa in July 1613 and they went off together to sample the warm baths at Aachen. Southampton returned to Spa the next August.[14] Sir Dudley Carleton, the British ambassador at The Hague, applied to Secretary Winwood for permission to go in 1616 and became a regular visitor to Spa, where he met the Earl and the Dowager Countess of Pembroke and Dr Matthew Lister, physician to Anne of Denmark. Lister was the countess's companion there in 1615–17. Lord Chandos returned in 1621 but died in his coach going home, his death allegedly hastened by his drinking the waters of Spa. About 1626 an Anglican chapel, equal in status to the English parishes and deemed to be a part of the bishopric of London, was erected there.[15] Spa was no longer the refuge only of recusants and the sick but had become a fashionable resort attractive to the wealthier English Protestants and Catholics alike. A forty-day jaunt to Spa in 1623 cost Lord William Howard of Naworth £212 9s. 11d.[16]

The medical profession now gave increasing approval to the consumption of Spa water, either at the place of origin or imported. By about 1600 there was a growing trade in Spa water with England. Dr Henri de Heer, whose *Spadacrene* was published in 1616, had already in 1603 sent 200 bottles of waters from the original Pouhon spring at Spa to 'Kensington near London'. When the waters arrived in good condition after over ten days' journey, more despatches followed accompanied by certificates of origin from the town authority, *la Cour de Justice de Spa*. Sir William Selbie brought 800 bottles of the water back from Spa in 1611, for, it was reported, 'he cannot live without it'. By 1632 England was receiving a large share of the about 100,000 bottles exported from Spa.[17]

English physicians who sponsored the other side of the trade, the local consumption of the waters, often enjoyed a good holiday out of it. A physician's opinion on one's medical condition was necessary to procure a Spa travel permit, and some patients took an English doctor with them, but Lord Cobham made an unfortunate choice. In June 1603 he engaged a Dr Foster to accompany him to Spa for a down payment of £100 and his travel expenses both ways, including horses for him and his servant. The day after Foster had received the £100 Cobham was committed to the Tower, suspected of complicity in the Main Plot, but Foster kept the money.[18]

Normally two physicians were required to sponsor each licence application, and the recurring names of some doctors on the certificates suggest the existence of a small group with a specialist interest in the water cure. Among the licences issued between 1613 and 1624 Dr John Gifford and Dr Henry Atkins sent four applicants each, Dr John Davis two and Dr John More five. Dr Richard Andrews, an eminent physician, accompanied Lady Gresley to Spa in 1617 and his co-signatory was Sir William Paddy, President of the College of Physicians from 1609 to 1611 and in 1618, and physician to James I. Paddy himself was at Spa about 1613 and he sent Lady Phillpot in 1619. Andrews arrived there soon after the publication of de Heer's *Spadacrene* in 1616, and both he and Paddy collaborated with de Heer in a study of the local mineral waters. On their return they introduced the study of ferruginous waters in England and helped to popularize those English springs which were of similar chemical composition to the Spa waters. In the early seventeenth century Andrews and

Paddy played a large part in promoting the use of the word *Spa,* or *Spaw* as it was then known, already in use at Harrogate in Yorkshire. It became a generic term in England, applied to all resorts where people went both to drink the waters and to bathe in them.[19]

So a generation of English physicians became familiar with Spa and its Pouhon waters and now tried to promote domestic spas, or drinking wells, at springs which they claimed to be like those at Spa. They stood to gain from establishing practices around the wells, and their treatises on mineral waters stressed the need for guidance from a local physician. In self-interest they argued that because of the volatile nature of the mineral content, the water spoiled in transit and should be drunk on the spot, not distributed in bottles.

The demand for mineral waters was now clearly established, but the Privy Council still viewed the exodus to Spa with disfavour, and courtiers with large retinues found the journey to Bath, or perhaps Buxton, both troublesome and expensive. So alternatives within easy reach of the capital were the obvious solution. But England had few thermal waters to use: only at Bath, Buxton and the Bristol Hotwell. Development at Bakewell and Matlock came later. So this shortage of places for bathing in comfort led to a movement for *drinking* cold mineral water, as at Spa and Harrogate, and the burgeoning of local spas, especially in the home counties. Landowners and their courtier friends were quick to designate a local spring a spa, and owners would then sink a well and enclose it with a fence, enlist the aid of a physician or apothecary to publicize it and employ a native woman to be a water-dipper. But owners as yet provided few amenities, such as a hut shelter or paved paths, for the water-drinkers who gathered there. These early rural spas were very primitive, yet in good summer weather they were a welcome alternative to hot, overcrowded, insanitary Bath.

James I had not accompanied Queen Anne to Bath, but his patronage was sought for some of the embryonic spas close to his palace at Theobalds, his favourite base for hunting in Epping Forest. Lord Mountjoy Blount entertained him at his nearby manor of Wanstead in Essex in 1611 and 1612, and the Wanstead waters were drunk perhaps as early as this. The Earl of Northampton advised James to be cautious in going since many had died there, but the king returned many times and Wanstead was popular with the courtiers. In 1618 young Mountjoy Blount was made to pass the manor to the favourite, George Villiers, then Marquess of Buckingham, but it soon went to Sir Henry Mildmay, who entertained the king there in June, July and September 1619 when the Wanstead Spa was established. A fountain was erected to mark the spot close to Blake Hall. John Chamberlain spoke on 23 August 1619 of '. . . a great noise of a new spa' so much resorted to by lords and ladies and other great company that it was almost drawn dry already, but if it continued it would rival the Tunbridge waters. However, the original well proved inadequate and never supplied water to the fountain.[20] Not far off, on the Middlesex–Hertfordshire border, another ephemeral spa near Theobalds attracted attention when the king stayed there: that at Cuffley in the parish of Northaw. Wells Farm in Cuffley hamlet takes its name from the King's Well, which lost custom after James's death in 1625 but regained popularity under Charles II.[21]

The most popular of these early courtiers' spas was 'the Tunbridge Wells', where the spring was 'discovered' by Dudley, 3rd Lord North (1581–1666), the grandson and heir of Roger, Lord North (d. 1600). Although the grandfather lived in Cambridgeshire, he had journeyed to Buxton in 1578 and, advised by his doctors, to Bath in 1589, 1594 and 1600, both to drink the waters and to bathe in them.[22] So his grandson Dudley, Lord North knew of the use of mineral waters before he drank those of Spa during the summer campaign in the Low Countries in 1602, as did other English nobles who went to fight and stayed to drink. But North returned in bad health and in spring 1606 he went off to stay in rural quiet with his friend Edward Nevill, 8th Lord Bergavenny (or Abergavenny) at his hunting seat at Eridge in Kent.

Bergavenny had been to Bath in 1595 and the talk may have turned to the efficacy of mineral waters as a cure, for on his homeward journey in 1606 North paid particular attention to some local springs on the edge of Bergavenny's estate in the parish of Speldhurst on the Kent–Sussex border. London physicians confirmed the healing virtues of the waters, and on their advice North returned to Speldhurst in 1607 to take them for about three months.[23] North's later claim in his *Forest of Varieties,* written in 1637, was not to have discovered but to have first popularized both the Tunbridge and Epsom waters in London and at court, as alternatives to those of Spa. His arguments against travel to Spa followed those of the Elizabethan establishment: it was costly and inconvenient to sick people, undesirable from a religious point of view, and carried bullion from the realm. He lived for eighty-five years, a living memorial of the efficacy of the Tunbridge waters.[24]

Meanwhile Lord Bergavenny, alive to the potential of the waters, with the consent of Mr Weller of Tunbridge, lord of the neighbouring manor of Rusthall, had wells dug over two of the springs and the site cleared of wood and bushes, paved round with stone and enclosed with wooden rails in triangular form. These wells were known as the Tunbridge Wells, for Tunbridge was the nearest town, and the company, or visitors, originally took lodgings there. Numbers of sick and diseased people found the wells beneficial, and as their fame grew it drew in many of the nobility and gentry. The traditional dating of the 'discovery', 1606, is that given by a local man, Thomas Benge Burr, the first historian of Tunbridge Wells, in 1766. Another version, derived from Richard Weller, the steward of Lord Bergavenny's estate, places the date as 1615 or 1616, but that would mean very rapid fame for the Tunbridge Wells, because in 1619 John Chamberlain wrote of many important people using them, especially that summer. A Cambridge tutor, John Preston, who may have heard of the Tunbridge waters from Lord North in Cambridgeshire, left for Kent in August 1621 with the intention of drinking them.[25]

Although Tunbridge was only a drinking spa it had a clear advantage over Bath: it was only thirty-six miles from the metropolis, compared with the more than a hundred miles to Bath. But apart from improving the road to the wells and clearing the site Edward, Lord Bergavenny (d. 1622) did nothing to promote them. The state of the roads in this Wealden clay area was very bad, and there were no houses by the wells on the common surrounded by woodland, except Mrs Humphreys' hovel. She monopolized the office of 'dipper' – that is, of serving well water to the visitors – until her death in 1678. Visitors lodged in Tunbridge town, six miles away, or in the neighbouring hamlets of Southborough or Rusthall.[26] It was not the Tunbridge Wells but another new spa which attracted the attention of Princess Henrietta Maria when she arrived in England to marry Charles I in June 1625.

The House of Bourbon, to which this princess belonged, had patronized the fashionable thermal springs at Bourbon l'Archambault, also known as Borminis, and she looked for an English substitute.[27] English courtiers were currently flocking to a well 'found' the previous summer (1624) on the manor of Wellingborough in Northamptonshire then held by Fulk Greville, Lord Brooke. It had acquired some fame, especially from the visit that August of the king's favourite, the Duke of Buckingham, accompanied by his wife and his mother, the Countess of Buckingham. The queen's Lord Chamberlain, Edward Sackville, 4th Earl of Dorset, liked the waters so well that he talked of building a house there, but he was a patron of Tunbridge Wells. A Dr Merry produced a pamphlet about the Wellingborough chalybeate before 1625, and according to John Chamberlain, the centre of all gossip, Wellingborough now vied with Tunbridge Wells. Although the Countess of Buckingham found little help there and departed to Harrogate, in the disastrous summer of 1625, when plague drove many from London, Sir Francis Nethersole, secretary to the king's sister Elizabeth of Bohemia, sought protection in the waters of Wellingborough.[28] For the new queen from France, Wellingborough was an obvious choice.

The spring most in vogue at Wellingborough was the Red Well about half a mile north-west of the town, and the queen spent nine weeks there in 1626, her first full summer in England. To protect her from annoyance and health hazards, the Privy Council sent the surveyor of the king's highways ahead with instructions to the justices of four counties to assist him in mapping a route for her retinue through the fields. Despite the excessive heat and the dustiness of the highways which her cavalcade followed in five stages, in late July she set off, accompanied by the Earl of Carlisle. Charles I and the court joined her at Wellingborough most of the time, but they had to lodge in tents on the hill above the spring and perhaps sometimes in the nearby Swan Inn, where two rooms were later called the King's and Queen's Rooms.[29]

The next summer, 1627, the queen was again advised to take the Wellingborough waters and returned, leaving the king to hunt, but Bishop William Laud found both the king and the queen at Wellingborough on 26 July.[30] On 3 August the queen was still held there by lack of money to pay her servants' wages; she had expected to receive £2,000 on leaving London but had only £1,000. In July 1628 she was thinking of Wellingborough again, but apart from the usual money troubles soldiers billeted there were causing disturbance and she lingered in London until 25 July. Her Lord Chamberlain, Dorset, intervened and she reached the spa, but by 18 August Lord Treasurer Weston had the problem of finding sufficient money to get her away again. A week later she still dallied there, enjoying rural life and entertained by the peasants' dances but with little physical benefit, for the waters were flooded by rain, and she left before 5 September.[31] Earlier the relatively unknown Huntingdonshire gentleman Oliver Cromwell came to take the waters at this, his nearest, spa, and he perhaps met the queen around the well. After Wellingborough's brief fame during Henrietta Maria's three visits, the dilution of the waters may have been its doom, but the distance from London, sixty-seven miles, was a deterrent to courtly patronage and the spa declined.[32]

The waters may have had some effect on the queen. Her first child was born on 3 May 1629 but soon died, and her medical adviser – perhaps Sir Theodore Mayerne, her physician since 1628 – urged her to go not to Wellingborough but to Tunbridge Wells, which was only half the distance from the capital, to recuperate. Several Kentish courtiers may also have influenced her decision to try Tunbridge Wells, like her chamberlain Dorset, a Sackville of Knole whose wife Mary became governess to the Prince of Wales. Henry, 9th Lord Bergavenny of Eridge, whose father erected the Wells, married a Sackville and was a groom of the bedchamber, and another loyalist nobleman, Ulick de Burgh, Earl of Clanrickarde, lived only six miles from the Wells at Somerhill. John Packer, Clerk of the Privy Seal, of Groombridge in Speldhurst, had built a chapel of ease in his parish to commemorate the safe return of the king (then Prince of Wales) from Spain in 1623. The king is reported to have repaired and ornamented parts of Speldhurst parish church, later dedicated to him as Charles the Martyr.[33]

So Tunbridge Wells was now the courtiers' spa, and the queen went there in 1629. In the last week of July Sir Robert Aiton forwarded her instructions from Tunbridge Wells to Secretary Dorchester, but she was bored apart from the king and 'not liking well her Tunbridge waters' she suddenly decided to return and was back in Somerset House by 6 August. As at Wellingborough, the queen had had to live in tents, but there was an atmosphere of gaiety among her impromptu court on Bishop's Common Down.[34]

Henrietta Maria's visit to Tunbridge Wells in 1629 was her last to any spa before the Civil War, for on 29 May 1630 she produced the necessary heir, Prince Charles. Her stay had put the mark of fashionable approval on Tunbridge Wells and, within easy reach of London, it offered a pleasant public diversion in July and August as an alternative to the heat and dullness of the capital out of season or the social isolation of country estates. Anthony Mingay from Norwich stayed there for six weeks in July and August 1635 and found six earls or lords at the Wells in the morning, besides many ladies, knights and gentlemen.[35] A publicist soon came forward, Lodowick (Lewis) Rowzee (1568–?), a doctor of medicine of the University of Leyden, who had considerable knowledge of the continental hot springs, including two, the Pouhon and Geronstère wells, at Spa. He may have gone to Spa in 1610 after being at the siege of Jülich with Sir Horace Vere; he certainly went in 1619 with Sir Henry Palmer of Bekesbourne, a justice of Kent, comptroller of the navy and 'a loyal subject', who on 27 June was licensed to go to Spa for the summer with him, two other Kent justices and two servants. Three years after the queen's visit Rowzee produced a pamphlet, *The Queen's Wells . . . a Treatise of the Nature and Virtues of Tunbridge-Water* (1632) about mineral waters in general but the Tunbridge waters in particular, which were very like the Spa waters, especially in creating a good appetite.[36]

Despite the queen's visit and the large numbers now coming to the Wells, as they were called, little was done to exploit them or to improve the primitive conditions there until around 1680. In 1636, however, shelter was provided for the water-drinkers when two small houses were erected, one each for ladies and gentlemen, and in 1638 the first of the promenades which became a feature of spa settlements was constructed at the Wells. A green bank, later paved and called the Upper Walk, was raised, levelled and planted with a double row of trees, and here the company found shelter and the opportunity for exercise and conversation, and tradesmen came to display their wares once a day. The visitors still lodged too far away to make permanent booths or shops practicable.[37]

During the queen's visit, statesmen had been able to keep in touch with public affairs in the metropolis while enjoying a holiday at the Wells, which now became a magnet to them. In July 1634 three ministers, the

Lord Treasurer Weston, the Attorney-General, and the Master of the Wards, were there, although some visitors, such as Viscount Chaworth, would have preferred to be at Spa and found the benefit of the waters debatable: '. . . with some they work not at all, with some by siege'. Sir John Butler died there, and Mr Noy returned worse than he went. The court faction tended to congregate at the hamlets of Southborough and Rusthall, where in 1639 a few small houses for lodgings were put up, but this modest investment in the spa trade was '. . . rather suited to the circumstances and apprehensions of the builders, than to the company they were intended for' – that is, hardly appropriate for people of rank.

During the season the shortage of accommodation was acute, but such was now the repute of the waters that visitors endured any inconvenience, and when the new houses were full they paid extravagant prices for cottages, huts, or any place of shelter. Anthony Mingay feared being homeless on reaching Tunbridge and in 1635 wrote to London friends for advice in getting lodgings, for which he and his daughter were each charged £1 for a room and £1 for food, and each servant 10s. for food and 5s. for a room. Tunbridge Wells was already becoming geared to the tourist trade, but between taking the prescribed doses of water the company had to make their own diversions in that rural setting. They walked beneath the canopies of trees and on the commons; as Mingay said, '. . . in the afternoons we have a young Hyde Park for the lords and ladies to frolic in', but tedium inevitably led to the introduction of excitements like gambling. The game then played, even by important people who hazarded 'great sums of money', was country scalebones, also called kettlepins or nine-pins. Lord Dunluce lost almost £2,000 at ninepins in 1635, the year he married the Dowager Duchess of Buckingham.[38]

Of all the embryonic spas of the early Stuart period Tunbridge Wells was the most successful, but two others struggled into existence south of the Thames: Epsom and Sydenham. In the dry summer of 1618 the waters of a pond on the common at Epsom, or Ebbsham, in Surrey attracted attention when farmer Henry Wicker's cattle refused to drink at an enlarged water-hole. Physicians tested the waters and proclaimed their healing virtues, so, doubtless encouraged by the example of the Tunbridge Wells, the owners of the estate, probably one of the Mynn family, enclosed the well with a wall and erected a shed for the convenience of invalids. Dudley, Lord North, later claimed to have had a hand in publicizing these waters as well as those of Tunbridge.

By Charles I's time the famous Epsom Salts were on sale at 5s. an ounce, and in 1629 Epsom Well was known to the traveller Abram Booth, who found many there drinking the water and carrying it away in bottles and jugs, while an attendant served the drinkers with glasses. Some customers were invalids, but more often the poor came there. Although the well-house was but a cottage and visitors had to lodge in huts on the common, by about 1640 the fame of Epsom had attracted distinguished persons from France, Germany and other parts of Europe, and it maintained a steady reputation during the troubled times of the Commonwealth.[39] At Sydenham in Lewisham parish in Kent, nearer the capital, a saline chalybeate spring similar to that of Epsom was discovered in 1640 among a few scattered dwellings, but it was not much used until after 1660.[40]

The use of mineral waters was now being stimulated by the growth of a body of serious scientific writing on the subject. Despite the lead given by Turner, Jones and Baily in the sixteenth century, the volume of such publications was slight before 1660, but it showed an awakening interest in mineral waters within medical circles and an increasing, popular demand for information. Most writing centred on the Bath and Harrogate waters. Two early anonymous pamphlets, the G.W. (?) *Newes out of Cheshire of the new found Well* (1600) and *A True Report of certain Wonderful Over-flowings in Somerset* (1607), were followed by the work of Tobias Venner and Edward Jorden at Bath, of Edmund Deane, Michael Stanhope and John French at Harrogate, and of Lodowick Rowzee at Tunbridge Wells. Two general writers were Dr Tobias Whitaker (d. 1666), who in 1634 produced *A Discourse of Waters, their Qualities and Effects. . .* , and Thomas Johnson (d. 1644), an apothecary who travelled extensively in England and in 1634 produced his *Mercurius Botanicus* with a section on baths, which was reprinted alone as *Thermae Bathonicae* in 1674.[41]

Many more doctors now recommended mineral waters for a variety of ailments, the most influential of them being Sir Theodore Mayerne, the distinguished French doctor and senior physician to James I who often attended Queen Anne and Queen Henrietta Maria. He came to England early in James I's reign, was knighted in 1624, and had a considerable and important clientele for twenty years. When the king died in 1625 Sir Theodore was already fifty-five, a bluff and benevolent man of ruddy cheek and white hair and beard, but he soon ingratiated himself with Henrietta Maria, whose father, Henry IV of France, he had advised.[42] Mayerne survived the vicissitudes of the Civil War, perhaps because Oliver Cromwell had been his patient in 1628, and he died in 1655 esteemed and enriched. He was catholic in his patronage of the English spas: Bath, Epsom, Tunbridge Wells and Wellingborough were favoured, and also Harrogate for his northern and Scottish clients. In June 1638 he recommended James, Lord Livingston of Almond (Count d'Amart) to take 'Spa waters', especially those of Knaresborough (Harrogate), which were sharp, vitriolic and ferruginous, in increasing quantities. But Livingston wrote from Harrogate 'near the spa' in August that excessive rain had spoiled the waters and he was returning to Scotland.[43]

By then the Harrogate, or Knaresborough, waters were becoming better known. Dr Timothy Bright (d. 1617) had failed to popularize them, but the highly qualified Dr Edmund Deane (d. 1640) of York became 'the father of Harrogate'. He and other York physicians had often been urged by Dr Bright, Dr Anthony Hunton, Sir Francis Trappes a recusant of Harrogate, and some Yorkshire gentlemen to publicize these waters. So there was a clear demand for a Yorkshire spa to serve the North, but the Tewit Well found by Slingsby in 1571, the only one much used, was now neglected and so it fell to Deane, in his own words, to 'set a new edge on this business'. Late in the summer of 1625, led by a Knaresborough guide, he, Dr Michael Stanhope, two other physicians and a 'worthy knight', possibly Trappes, set out to rediscover the well two miles from the town on a rough, barren moor. They found it decayed and filthy, but they cleaned it up and stopped other waters seeping into it. The water had 'a perfect Spa relish', and back at the inn the excited talk was all of 'our new spa', although Deane knew of its original discovery in around 1571. After chemical experiment on the water back home at York, in 1626 he produced his *Spadacrene Anglica, or, The English Spaw Fountaine,* to herald the Northern Spa.

By then the Thirty Years War had broken out in Europe, and Deane argued that Englishmen would find it more beneficial and less dangerous to visit the English Spaw fountain than the waters of Germany. The West Riding, he wrote, was stored with fountains and springs, including two holy wells, St Mungo's Well at Copgrove and St Robert's Well below Knaresborough, where the common people came in daily crowds. As to the Harrogate waters, apart from the chalybeate spring in the forest known as the Tewit Well to commoners and the English Spaw to those of rank, there were four others, the Dropping Well near the castle and three sulphur waters or Stinking Wells, one in Bilton Park, the Starbeck Old Spa near the town, and the Old Sulphur Well at 'Haregate-head'. Sulphur waters were especially beneficial for skin diseases and chalybeate waters for purging the blood of humours, preventing ulcers and tumours, and relieving catarrh, cramp, migraine, epilepsy and jaundice.

Deane admitted that the Pouhon waters at Spa had a wide distribution in Europe, but those of the Yorkshire Spaw lost potency in transit, even when carried into Knaresborough town in a stoppered vessel, and they were worthless twenty or thirty miles from their source. Yet the waters of the English Spaw had a speedier effect than those from the Pouhon spring, and Deane urged people to make the effort to travel to them, on foot if possible, but those with feeble legs might ride on horseback or in coaches or chairs. The bedridden and those confined to lodgings could drink the water at home if it were rushed to them in a well-stopped vessel or glass. The local gentry who showed such interest in the Yorkshire Spaw stood to gain from a developing social life there and perhaps some economic profit, although the Harrogate Wells in the Royal Forest of Knaresborough were common property.[44]

Dr Michael Stanhope of York, who had accompanied Deane in 1625, also wrote of the Harrogate waters in his *Newes out of Yorkshire* in 1626, with a second edition in 1627 dedicated to a member of the powerful Hastings family, Lady Katharine Stanhope, wife of his relative Lord Philip Stanhope, Baron Shelford. Stanhope's next work, *Cures without Care Or a summons . . . to the Northerne Spaw,* in 1632, was a further appeal to try the Northern Spa and it was more ambitiously inscribed to Sir Thomas Wentworth, from 1628 to 1641 President of the Council of the North at York. Stanhope claimed that preceding presidents had found the waters beneficial: Wentworth's immediate predecessors were Edmond, Lord Sheffield (1603–19) and Emmanuel, Lord Scrope (1619–28). Sheffield may have used the Harrogate waters, but in 1606 he was allowed to leave his post in York to go to Bath to cure his lameness. Wentworth was the nephew of Sir Francis Trappes, who had encouraged Deane's investigations.[45]

Dr Stanhope was the first writer to mention the 'Old Spaw', later known as the Sweet Spa, or St John's Well, a spring which he found in 1631 about a quarter of a mile from the Tewit Well. These two springs outside the main settlement of Harrogate were on the exposed open common at 'Haregate-head', where visitors faced much discomfort. There was no shelter from the cold winter blasts, no place for swift retirement after taking purging draughts of water, and no inn. The inhabitants, lowly husbandmen and cottagers on the north side of the present High Harrogate Stray, could not supply accommodation for people of rank. The 'better sort' of people were also deterred from coming to Harrogate, especially to the Sulphur Well, by the behaviour of the sick poor who left their putrid rags around and cleansed their sores where others dipped their cups to drink. Stanhope had no wish to exclude the poor, but he offered, if the Old Sulphur Well were carefully guarded, to find them an alternative spring nearby.[46] Dr George Neale of Leeds also tried to mitigate the disadvantages of the Northern Spa. He found a seasonal visit worthwhile for seventy years, and, far ahead of his time, in 1626 first introduced artificial warm bathing in heated sulphur water. As he explained in 1656, he copied a vessel of the kind used for baths on the Continent in constructing his bath.[47] The general movement to supply warm baths did not come until late the next century, but Harrogate was then the most northerly English spa.

Despite Harrogate's limitations, it filled a social void in the North and publicity about the spa brought in large numbers of people. The town of Knaresborough three miles away gained economically, for according to Deane it could provide 'good and commodious habitation', but visitors had to ride over to the wells daily. Sir Arthur Ingram stayed at Scriven with Sir Henry Slingsby in 1627 with the express purpose of drinking the waters, and in 1632 Stanhope reported scores of visitors assembling in the morning for the same reason. When vacant in 1642 the living of Knaresborough was said to need an able man because of 'the great resort to it in summer time by reason of the wells'.[48] Noble patrons were certainly coming. Stanhope's *Cure without Care* catalogued those who found benefit or cure in the waters, and out of twenty-four case histories thirteen seem to have been of the nobility and gentry, including the Countess of Buckingham. Some patients came from as far away as Scotland and Suffolk.[49]

Civil war broke out in 1642, but the new vogue for going to baths and wells was by no means diminished. Although the rural spas were difficult of access, had crude facilities, and almost totally lacked lodging accommodation, they offered a new kind of relaxed, informal social life to the leisured classes, as an alternative to the more restricted company of the country houses. Significantly, six of the new minor spas – Epsom, Northaw, Sydenham, Tunbridge Wells, Wanstead and less so Wellingborough – were within easy distance of the capital, and their discovery and use were prompted by the court nobility as well as by the local gentry and physicians. Harrogate became the northern place of resort, ousting the baths of Buxton, which were now in decline, but Bath held primacy over all, and it was there and not to Harrogate that the Archbishop of York went in 1630.[50]

4

Bath and the Civil War

Despite the enthusiasm for Tunbridge Wells in the early Stuart period Bath still remained popular with courtiers and in terms of social importance was the second city of the realm, although the squalid and dangerous effects of congestion within the walls were becoming apparent and the baths were not well managed. Queen Anne's patronage had given the city the royal accolade, earning it the soubriquet 'the loyal city' which it retained until the end of the Stuart dynasty, but in the confused politics of the seventeenth century its allegiance sometimes wavered.

Possibly while the queen was at Wellingborough in July 1628, Charles I was at Bath with Bishop Hall of Exeter and others.[1] Lord Zouche, President of the Council of Wales, came at least six times between 1603 and 1620, his visit in late August 1606 coinciding with that of Lord Sheffield, President at York.[2] Two other visitors of importance were the Earl of Northampton in 1621 and the Earl of Suffolk in 1625; the latter's heir subsequently came three times. One can only guess at the range of government affairs which were gossiped over while people were taking the waters.

The Earl of Huntingdon, the lord lieutenant of Leicestershire, to his deputy's concern, made an infirmity an excuse to go to Bath in September 1627. Henry, Earl of Northumberland, released from the Tower in 1621, wended his way there 'like a baron bold and opulent' with eight steeds attached to his carriage, but the weather was unsettled when he returned in May 1629, he used the bath only seven times and caught cold. The Earl of Totnes came to Bath in October 1626 to recover from the palsy which afflicted him at the funeral of James I, but returned weaker than he went.[3] Contemporary bishops of Bath and Wells frequented Bath, but also those from afar, Chichester and St Andrews in 1618, and the archbishop of York in 1630. The city encouraged the patronage of such important visitors by gifts: sometimes a sheep or lamb but often chickens, partridges, pheasants, capons, sugar-loaves, white wine or sack; in 1628 £8 2s. 7d. was spent on presents and entertainment.[4] Other watering-places could not compete with this hospitality, which with other advantages gave Bath pre-eminence.

The substantial group of doctors now practising in Bath had a vested interest in maintaining its social status. The local Dr Thomas Guidott catalogued the physicians there from 1598 onwards in his *Discourse of Bathe . . .* (1676), and in the early Stuart period to 1640 there were at least eleven of some note – say sixteen in all, but perhaps more. One of the earliest of them to write about the Bath waters was Edward Jorden (d. 1632), a distinguished physician practising in London who moved in court circles and came under the protection of Francis, Lord Cottington, later Chancellor of the Exchequer. Jorden settled permanently in Bath and his *Discourse of Natural Bathes and Mineral Waters . . . especially of our Bathes at Bathe . . .* (1631) was dedicated to Cottington and ran to four editions before the Civil War and two afterwards.

In this detailed account of the chemistry of waters Jorden deplored the general neglect of the baths at Bath, which were less known than others in Christendom and deserved better, and he made a special plea for the Bath habit of pumping, or bucketing. Recently there had been a drive to promote 'dry pumping' with pumps erected in the baths for this purpose. Under this treatment the patient sat fully clothed while the water was directed, like a douche, only on to the afflicted part of the body, without heating the rest of it. Some slow improvements were being made in the baths, but by private donation rather than civic expenditure. At Jorden's persuasion a wealthy London merchant, Humphrey Brown, had provided two pumps in the King's and Queen's Baths, and he undertook their repair in 1631. Archbishop Harsnett of York and Hugh May had been responsible for providing dry pumps at the Cross Bath and the Hot Bath, and Jorden hoped for similar endowment of the King's Bath. Guidott's tribute to Jorden was that he had gained the applause of the learned, the respect of the rich, the prayers of the poor and the love of all.[5]

Another effective advocate of the Bath waters was the popular Dr Tobias Venner (d. 1660), who practised in his native Somerset. This 'plain, charitable physician', very different from the sophisticated and learned Jorden, was not very articulate but ready enough with his pen in producing an analysis of the Bath waters: *Via Recta ad Vitam Longam . . . Also the true use of our famous baths at Bath* (1620). Seven editions of this work, the last in 1660, bear witness to the vastly increased popular and scientific interest in mineral waters. Venner wrote critically of the Bath physicians, and his professional sense was especially affronted by their involvement in the lodging-house racket. The lack of changing accommodation at the baths compelled visitors to seek lodgings adjacent to them, but some local physicians who also ran lodging-houses employed agents to waylay visitors in the streets and advertise their lodgings and the virtues of particular baths. Venner argued that only physic graduates should be allowed to practise in the city.

Venner also wrote of the water of St Vincent's Rock (the Hotwell) at Clifton near Bristol, a warm water increasingly used as a cure for stone, and, as at Bath, he deplored the fact that so few users took proper medical advice and that excessive use of the well would bring it into disrepute. No Bath physician could ignore the growing custom at St Vincent's Well about ten miles away in the rocky Avon gorge. Although John, Lord Paulet, of Hinton St George in Somerset, was among Bath's visitors in 1628, in July 1629 his wife drank the water at the Hotwell. In 1630 one John Bruckshaw made extravagant claims about it and was licensed to exploit the well for forty years, to make a wall between the spring and the sea (really the River Avon), enclose the fountain and the surrounding ground, and construct a bath. Venner's publicity may have prompted this initiative. When he died in 1660 his memory was honoured with a monument in Bath Abbey.[6]

Another outstanding Bath physician was Dr Samuel Bave (d. 1668), much favoured by Sir Theodore Mayerne and, like him, a foreign immigrant. Bave, born in Cologne but trained at Oxford, specialized in the use of chalybeate waters and no doubt knew of the continental ones, for he was proficient in several languages. His career began in Gloucester and, having made a fortune, around 1640 he settled in Bath, where he practised successfully and at his death left the largest estate of any physician who died in Bath.[7]

Despite the impressive number of well-qualified physicians operating and prospering in Bath, they did not always cure their patients. The burial registers for three Bath parishes from 1569 to 1625 show that out of 2,869 deaths 425 were those of strangers,[8] but many visitors were ill on arrival – like Lord Cobham, for whom Bath was a favourite haunt. Although he had been involved in the Main Plot he was released from prison in May 1617 to go to Bath with a keeper for the recovery of his health. On the journey back to the Tower he had a stroke and in July 1618 was licensed to return to Bath – or to any other place, since Bath had not noticeably improved his health – but he died in January 1619.[9]

The Privy Council were still prepared to release recusants from prison to seek health by taking the waters, either permanently or temporarily, even after members of the Gunpowder Plot had conspired at Bath. Catholic influences on the council, like Cottington, Dr Jorden's patron, may have sponsored this leniency. Buxton was not entirely out of commission, for in 1618 a recusant widow, Dianese Bulmer of Elmedon in the diocese of Durham, was licensed to go either there or to Bath for eight months for health reasons. The licensing of other known recusants – Jane Andrews of Longdon in Worcestershire in 1615, Edward Morgan of Lanternham in Monmouthshire in 1616, Eve Yaxley, a widow of Suffolk, in 1617, and in 1626 Thomas Theerle and Thomas Cornwallis, gentlemen of London – to go to Bath was a remarkable act of toleration.[10]

Outside the capital there was no place other than Bath where so many people of importance gathered, as in 1620 when it was very full for the season. The common council had to control a 'very poor' and congested city still largely confined within its walls, and the task of managing the inhabitants and the visitors and of making Bath more acceptable as a place of resort was not easy, but there was some attempt at improvements.[11] Accommodation was a particular problem, and a certain amount of building by infilling was going on. The city council minutes show four new houses on corporation property between 1613 and 1617, and in 1634 one George Parker was even allowed to encroach on the town timber yard, the Saw Close, and the next year to take another six feet for his new house. References to stables in 1632 and 1636 remind us that not only people came to Bath but also the horses that carried them or drew their coaches, wagons and carts.

There was little building outside the city walls and overcrowding accentuated the danger from fire so in 1621 the corporation acquired eighteen buckets, and in 1633 they ruled that slate and tiles should replace thatch in roof repairs. In an attempt to keep the streets clean a scavenger with a cart and collectors in every tithing were appointed in 1614 and paid by rate. Richard Ryall, the scavenger for 1632–3, received 20*s.* for collecting the soil in the city and suburbs and spreading it on the commons. From 1633 householders could be fined 1*s.* for sweeping rubbish from their doorways into the water channel in the streets. To meet the increased demand for domestic water, in 1616 water rates were levied for waterworks and conduits to bring water into the city. Although the market house may not have been entirely rebuilt, as a new Guildhall, allegedly to the designs of Inigo Jones, in 1625, a considerable amount of repair work went on for a year: 4,800 lathes were used, much glazing was done and a sack of lime was brought in to paint the hall.[12]

With the decline of the cloth industry Bath's economy depended largely on the visitors' trade, and the proper conduct of the baths, corporation property, was very much the council's concern. One of the oft-mentioned disadvantages of the baths was their exposure to the weather. William Turner had advocated covers in 1568 and a shelter was erected at the Hot Bath in 1569, but some disliked it and it was taken down in 1588. When the council hoped to lure Lord Zouche there again in 1621 they assured him that the covering of the Cross Bath had been undertaken by Dr Jorden, his brother-in-law Sir Ignatius Jorden and others without any cost to the city. But ten years later Jorden wrote of the need to cover the Cross Bath and the Queen's Bath and to make their slips close and warm; if they were made usable all year round the season could be prolonged into the winter, early spring and late autumn, which was economically desirable. The Earl of Marlborough then undertook to meet the cost of covering the Cross Bath but apparently did not keep his promise.[13]

Another criticism was that the officials employed by the corporation for the day-to-day management of the baths neglected their duty, and the misconduct of users and guides attracted attention. Both William Turner and John Jones had condemned mixed bathing, but it remained the current practice, except in the Queen's or Women's Bath. Dr Jorden and others drew up regulations for the Cross Bath which the city council in 1621 forwarded to Lord Zouche for approval and they wrote that the separation of the sexes was intended, but no immediate action was taken. About 1625 the Privy Council complained to the corporation about the 'great disorders' at the baths and of the 'very unseemly and immodest' behaviour resulting from their joint use by men and women. In 1629 the corporation drew up new bylaws, but no copy survives to show if they applied to the baths, and mixed bathing continued. An observer in 1634 wrote that people of all kinds '. . . appear so nakedly, and fearfully, in their uncouth naked postures . . . and put one in mind of the Resurrection'.[14] Since the guides still failed to keep decorum in the baths in 1633 it was ruled that none should enter the baths after 6 p.m. in winter and 8 p.m. in summer on pain of a fine of 2*s.* 6*d.,* and following the temporary dismissal of guide Richard Stevens, whose wife had made trouble, wives of guides were barred from the baths. Widow Broad, a guide, was dismissed the next year for drunkenness. The not infrequent drownings in the King's Bath, including two casualties in 1617 but none recorded after 1639 until 1698, also suggest a degree of disorder in early Stuart times.[15]

The many inns in the city caused trouble too, and when Sir Giles Mompesson lost his monopoly to license them many were suppressed. Philip Sherwood, keeper of a common inn and hostelry for fourteen years, refused to withdraw his sign in 1622, so the corporation forcibly removed it. The next year they assured the Privy Council that they had closed superfluous alehouses and regulated the strength of beer.[16] The interest of innkeepers and local traders was to exploit their brief season in June, July and August as best they could, but there were two great hazards to the locals: the influx of poverty-stricken people and the outbreak of epidemics, especially in 1625 when outsiders were likely to bring the plague with them. The pest-house was rethatched in 1626, and in 1636 the city council agreed to build houses for the isolation of plague victims on the common and to appoint attendants.[17]

Despite its several disadvantages Bath offered attractions not found in rural drinking spas, including a range of entertainment to enjoy between spells of drinking or bathing. Companies of players there included the king's in 1603, the queen's, the 'prince's players' (Prince Henry's?) and those of his sister the Lady Elizabeth; they acted in inn-yards or the town hall, which the queen's players rented for 3*s.* 4*d.* in 1618. Other performers drawn there included bagpipe-players, waits, bear-baiters, tumblers, acrobats and trumpeters. There were now two tennis courts, one east of the King's Bath and the other by St James's Church near the South Gate, and two bowling greens. The Old Bowling Green close to the Abbey was reserved for men of rank and in 1637 was leased from the corporation for £1, and the Outer Bowling Green was also leased out by 1658.[18] These investments in rented property show that commercialized entertainment was being introduced.

Out of season Bath was a comparatively quiet and empty place, but the elite came in high summer despite fear of plague and other discomforts. Significantly, in the autumn of 1639 a court masque, *Salmacida Spolia,* in which the king and queen took part, reflected the contemporary political scene and the fashionable preoccupation with taking mineral waters. Its theme was the taming of barbarians by their drinking at the fountain at Salmacis in the province of Caria in Asia Minor. The implication was that the king too had 'barbarians' to deal with, the rebel Scots. But in the current crisis that led to civil war he had matters of more concern than taking the waters, although many of his subjects continued to patronize Bath and other spas through all the upheavals of the war and interregnum. In June 1639 Sir Edmund Verney was in the king's camp near Berwick-on-Tweed, but he hoped to slip away to Bath to relieve his sciatica. He recalled visits in 1631 and 1635 when the town was empty on his arrival, but by August it was full of very good company which passed the time merrily; his son Ralph used the bath every day, but he, Sir Edmund, was sceptical of the value of the waters. Despite this doubt he left camp in autumn 1639 for a break in Bath.[19]

While the king wrestled with Anglo-Scottish relations on the border, his courtiers were not so willing to relinquish their pleasures. His Lord High Admiral, the Earl of Northumberland, was in Bath in July 1639, leaving Secretary Nicholas to worry about ship money delays and to hope for his return to the capital, but Northumberland laconically told Secretary Windebank that Bath suited him so well that he proposed to spend the whole week there. Other courtiers at Bath during the 1639 season were the Lord Treasurer Bishop Juxon, Lord Finch and Lord Essex, and when Lord Cottington, Dr Jorden's protector, came the bells were rung.[20]

As from 1641 the king's prerogatives were stripped away by Parliament, whose leaders tried to assert control over his family, even over the queen's person. In July 1641 she announced her wish to go to Spa for the recovery of her health, which had been undermined by the anxieties of the times. She proposed to travel to Utrecht in Holland, accompanied by her ten-year-old daughter, the betrothed of the Prince of Orange, and to have the

Spa water brought to her there. Some of the Commons, alarmed by the implications of her staying near the Spanish Netherlands, opposed the scheme, arguing that nothing was wrong with her and that her plans were a ruse to transport treasure overseas to raise troops for the king in Holland and France and to intrigue with papists. They appointed a committee to confer with the Lords, saying that if it were known that their queen went to Spa in quest not only of physical health but peace of mind it would reflect on the nation, and they were concerned about the cost of the expedition. They feared a dangerous design behind the queen's journey, for the Earl of Sussex and other papists had recently sold much land and exchanged gold and were leaving the kingdom. They argued that the season for taking the Spa waters had already passed, and the water could be brought to England as easily as to Utrecht. Finally they sent for Sir Theodore Mayerne and solicited his opinion.

Mayerne, the court physician, was equal to the occasion. It was not a question, he asserted, of whether the Spa water could be brought to London, for the queen was dangerously ill and not fit to take it at present; she would not live unless remedies were found. She had twice been helped by taking waters (at Tunbridge Wells and Wellingborough) and Spa water was the best, but it must be taken between the present date, 14 July, and mid-August. Then Mayerne hedged: he would swear that the queen would not survive in her present condition, but he was not convinced that the Spa water would cure her. Since the question of health was doubtful, the committee argued about the cost and impropriety of the princess's visit to her future husband's family. The king allowed a joint committee of lords and commoners to intervene with the queen, who reluctantly gave in to them.[21]

Henrietta Maria's faith in mineral waters never left her. In April 1644 she was with the king at Oxford, but she was pregnant and when the military situation worsened she had to leave. Flight to France was her obvious move, but she was convinced that she needed the curative waters of Bath so, escorted by Lord Jermyn, she reached the city on 21 April. Her brief visit shows in the chamberlain's accounts: 'paid for candles for the Queen's coming to town 6s. 8d.'. She dared stay only a few days and pressed on to Exeter where, attended by the faithful old Mayerne, her child Minette was born. In weak condition she thought longingly of the waters of Bath beyond the enemy lines, but the Marquis de Sabran, the French agent, was unwilling to procure a safe-conduct for her to go to Bath, so she fled instead to France, where she headed straight for Bourbon l'Archambault to take its waters again, as she did in subsequent seasons. At the Restoration she returned to England in October 1660 and in November went once more with her daughter Minette to Tunbridge Wells where she was joined by her son Charles II during her brief stay. In

January 1661 this royal addict of the spas returned to France and spent her summers at Bourbon, her favourite watering-place.[22]

With royal and noble patronage so firmly stamped on the embryonic English spas, not even the outbreak of the Civil War could undermine their usage. Those who sought to alleviate the cares and rigours of war, like soldiers on leave, slunk away to take the waters whenever possible. Sir Kenelm Digby, Henrietta Maria's chancellor, was at Tunbridge Wells in August 1640, using his visit as a cover to raise troops, and the next year he was at Spa. Later, when considering tincture of strawberries as a cure for stone, he thought that only the Spa or Tunbridge waters had done him more good. Another Tunbridge visitor was Ralph Cudworth, who left Emmanuel College, Cambridge in 1641 to take the waters. The Lord Admiral, Northumberland, had lurked both at Bath and at Tunbridge in 1639 and returned to the latter in July 1641, but its waters did not suit him, so in mid-August he went again to Bath, while Thomas Smith dealt with his state correspondence in London. He was still lingering 'at the Bathe' on 8 September when John Allen, a mariner, awaited his attention.[23]

So although the spas were not immune from the disturbance of war, they still drew custom. By the outbreak of fighting in 1642 two small hamlets of timber cottages had sprung up to serve the Tunbridge Wells, and they became increasingly inhabited during the season: Southborough, halfway between Tunbridge and the Wells, exclusively by Royalists; Rusthall, one mile from the Wells, by Roundheads. Local foundries supplied weapons of war, so rival troops haunted the district. Colonel Brown encountered Royalists at Tunbridge in 1643 and took 200 prisoners while releasing his parliamentary supporters from custody.[24]

When the Duke of Hamilton invaded England with the Scottish army in 1647 Ludovic Bray was drinking the waters of Epsom, but although he was ill he took horse to persuade the 15,000 Kentish men near Greenwich to unite to meet the advancing Lord Fairfax. After that ill-fated venture Lieutenant-General David Leslie was imprisoned in the Tower, and in 1653 he begged leave to retire to Tunbridge Wells. In 1648, after the collapse of the Kentish rising, Cavaliers met in the wild heathland south of Tunbridge and the Council of State repeatedly instructed the justices to dissolve 'dangerous meetings' at the popular wells near Tunbridge. During the interregnum they were well aware that drinking the waters could be a cover for royalist plots at Tunbridge Wells and Epsom, both within a day's journey of the capital; secret meetings were held at Tunbridge to plan the capture of Sandwich and Dover Castle.[25] Colonel Fitzjames from Dorset found 'a multitude' at Tunbridge in 1651, but many visitors were innocuous, such as John Evelyn escaping from smallpox in London in mid-June 1652 to take his wife and her mother to the Wells to drink the waters. They stayed in a nearby cottage for about a month.[26]

In August 1649 the Council of State were concerned about many dissidents, led by Lord Goring and Sir Thomas Bludder, who met privately in east Surrey under guise of drinking the now very popular waters of Epsom; although they stayed there quietly, they had good horses and arms. The council urged Cromwell, the Lord General, to quarter two troops of horse nearby as a safety precaution, and again during Booth's Rising in 1659, expecting trouble in Kent and Surrey, they posted Life Guards at Epsom and ordered Colonel Gibbon to the Tunbridge Wells with all the troops he could muster.[27]

Despite the suspicions of spas as a security risk, the Council of State, like the earlier Privy Council, allowed the release of prisoners to take the waters, a practice now generally recognized as a legitimate need. John Offley of Madeley Manor, Staffordshire, was temporarily released from the Tower in June 1650 on bond of £10,000 to go to Tunbridge or Epsom for two months for the benefit of his health. The Earl of Carnworth was given liberty in June 1652 to go to Epsom for six weeks, and Lord Beauchamp, urged by his father, the Marquess of Hertford, obtained a certificate from two doctors that the Epsom waters were necessary for his health and in late July 1651 was released for one month on a bond of £10,000.[28] Lord Saville hoped for liberty in 1645 to take the spa waters at Knaresborough (Harrogate), which were now sufficiently popular for Stanhope's *Cures without Care* (1632) to be reissued in 1649 and 1654.[29]

The war did, however, undermine the spa trade at Bath, which became a garrison town and suffered from proximity to military operations at Bristol. The immediate outbreak of hostilities was disastrous for Bath when from 1642 to 1643 it was held for Parliament; civic funds were no longer spent on gifts for illustrious visitors but for Colonel Popham and other military leaders, and on war supplies like barrels of match and bullets, setting up barricades, bringing in 'great guns' and raising the city walls. In July 1642 the inhabitants bemoaned the lack of company that summer; their chief benefactors had gone north to Knaresborough, although its climate and waters, both cold, deterred them from bathing. They complained that the unoccupied Bath guides were reduced to leading one another from the alehouse to keep in practice, and the ladies had become lethargic for lack of stirring cavaliers to keep them awake. There were few of these nymphs, now the only attraction for courtiers, and the poor unemployed fiddlers were ready to hang themselves in their strings. But hope of a resuscitation of trade came in July 1643 when royalist troops occupied Bath, the king passed through with his army early in 1644 and again in July and October, and the queen stayed briefly in April. The corporation offered them both gifts of plate that year. Charles, Prince of Wales, came in March and May 1645 seeking asylum from the plague in Bristol, but now the city had to pay for more essential goods: wood, coal, and candles for his guards and those commanded by Captains Chapman and Sherwood. Another change came when the Parliamentarians triumphed at Naseby in June and Lord Fairfax was free to deal with the western parts. Bath fell to him on 30 July.[30]

Although suspected of royalist sympathies and under military occupation, Bath now resumed some normal life. In October the corporation ordered that the baths should be shut at 4 p.m. every day and drained and refilled and again at 7 p.m. for the next day's bathing. In January 1646 Major-General Skippon took over the city and Bath began to assess the consequences of war: the taxes, contributions and billeting of soldiers. Lord Fairfax now found leisure there in June to have his portrait painted by one of the workshop of Sir Anthony Van Dyck, and the city's gifts of wine and sugar were now offered to him and Sir Thomas Fairfax. New bylaws were passed that year, and the respite was used to survey the damage of 'these unhappy wars' and the ruinous effect of armies and carriages passing on the three great roads converging on Bath from Bristol, Wells and Salisbury.[31]

After the king's execution the Commonwealth authorities still allowed royalist prisoners, and also some wounded soldiers, to seek relief in the Bath waters: Colonel Hungerford in 1649 with £100 arrears of his pay, in 1652 Captain Grimes with £40 arrears and Mrs Jane Roe, a war widow, with an allowance of £20. Among the Royalists under duress who were permitted to go in 1650 were William Hanmer of Flintshire with his apothecary for three months on a surety of £1,000 and Lord Kerry for two months; but some, like Sir John Wintour in 1652, were refused relief. The seriously wounded Captain Joseph Smith spent £250 on six visits to Bath to get cured. The more humble sufferers were a problem; the city of Bath, impoverished by the great burden of contributions, refused in June 1651 to spend money on some lame soldiers sent by order of Parliament. So a democratic and embryonic health service for war casualties was introduced. In April 1652 the Council of State sanctioned expenditure of £1,000 to conduct 186 wounded soldiers from Ely House in London to Bath to complete their cure; by contrast only £374 1s. 10d. was allowed for medical equipment for the army in Ireland.

By May 1653 a hospitals committee of a physician, surgeon and apothecary and four others were selecting those to be sent to Bath out of 220 claimants for this treatment; but there were financial problems and, to hasten its plans, the committee was allowed to rifle £1,000 from the Custom House money. Mr Malbone and three officers were given charge of taking the wounded to Bath and were made responsible for their care and proper behaviour there: Malbone was issued with £400 for travel expenses and a further £400 later. A fortnight later the treasurer at Ely House allowed him to take up £300 on credit 'in the country', presumably in the environs of Bath, but by July the cost of keeping sick and wounded soldiers at Bath so exercised the Council of State that the Irish and Scottish Committees had to find some of it, and £700 was taken from the excise.[32]

Aided by this philanthropic scheme, precursor of the welfare state, Bath's reputation as a health resort was maintained in Commonwealth times. Sir Thomas Pelham, a Sussex gentleman, lived near Tunbridge Wells but chose to spend £56 on a visit to Bath in 1652 to cure his gout. A Danish knight, Hannibal Sehstedt, Lord of Norargerard, had a pass to go there in August 1654 with his train and baggage. The Lord Protector Cromwell himself, having been indisposed, was advised to go there in 1656.[33] By the summer of 1659, when Lord Fairfax returned to Bath, the Protector was dead and army factions and politicians were jockeying for power. President Whitelocke ordered a strong military party to Bath to seize suspected persons and their arms and to search Colonel Alexander Popham's house near Bath while he was taking the waters at Epsom. In these uncertain times the new Lord Protector, Richard Cromwell, was feasted as lavishly as any monarch at Bath and his trumpeter and servants were given money, while he sent the city council a gift of venison in 1658.[34]

Obviously, however, despite some continued tourist trade – including a visitor from Jamaica in 1656 – Bath's embryonic leisure industry had suffered from the war and political instability, and the effect of the re-establishment of the Rump Parliament on Bath was that '. . . it makes us like men that dream'. There were great demonstrations of joy by ringing of bells, bonfires and other means. Bath was the first city to proclaim Charles II, on 12 May 1660, and on 4 June the first to offer a loyal address,[35] and the Restoration brought hope of a resumption of court patronage and a renewed social life.

Restoration Bath was to find, however, that not only the nobility and gentry, but also the middle ranks of English society were becoming spa-conscious, and an increasing number of small spas attracted their custom. At least three more – Barnet, Castleton and Witherslack, 'discovered' during the 1650s – were used with varying success. The mineral-water well in Arkley on Barnet Common in Hertfordshire was found in 1652 and was popular in Restoration times.[36] The medicinal virtues of a chalybeate spring called Holy Well at Witherslack in Westmorland were from 1656 exploited by one in court circles, Dr John Barwick, a native of Witherslack but now Dean of St Paul's while his brother Dr Peter Barwick was physician to Charles II. John Barwick built and endowed a chapel there about ten years later, and the spa remained noted for the cure of scorbutic diseases.[37]

The craze for well-finding sometimes caused local problems, as it did in 1656 when Dr Theophilus Haworth investigated a well or spa adjoining the house of Abraham Stott, a woollen-webster and smallholder on the edge of Castleton Moor between Rochdale and Manchester. When Haworth and others approved the water as medicinal many Lancashire gentry and multitudes of others descended there to drink, wash and carry away loads of water. Stott complained of damage to his hedges and grass, of having to graze his cattle on a neighbour's land, and of his family weaving business having suffered. In January 1657 he petitioned the justices for a licence to sell ale and beer the next season as compensation, probably in an attempt to cash in on a profitable trade, but the licence was refused. The fame of the Castleton Spa was short-lived.[38]

Nothing better illustrates the new habit of taking mineral waters with both serious and social intent than the travels of Colonel John Fitzjames of Leweston in Dorset. In 1650 he postponed a visit to Bath from March until August because of the cold weather, and his need was not urgent. But by 17 August, when he left Bath, he was 'weary and sick'. Two more visits, in September and in spring 1651, failed to cure him, so on physicians' advice he tried Tunbridge Wells. He set out in early July by way of the capital, where Sir Theodore Mayerne advised a course of drinking bottled Epsom water, then on sale in Westminster. After imbibing four bottles a day for six days Fitzjames moaned: 'I trade in nothing but waters', but he made no improvement and in late July Mayerne sent him to Tunbridge Wells for a month.

Fitzjames now resolved to abandon physic and 'any further seeking after secondary causes' and to leave his future welfare only to God. By 1 August he was lodged in Mr Kingsmill's house at Rusthall, a mile from the Wells. Getting up at 5 a.m. was, with the social obligation to play kettlepins, the greatest hardship, but he progressed from six flasks of water to eleven and then to thirteen of fourteen ounces each, obviously his limit. After ten days' drinking he reported to Mayerne 'of the effects of my waterworks'; his pains had subsided and he would remain at Tunbridge to the end of the month if Mayerne thought fit. In mid-September he returned home to Dorset, where he lived at least until 1668. But the drinking habits of an English gentleman were not easily transformed by mineral waters; during his first week of the Tunbridge Wells regime he had instructed his London agent to buy and fill three dozen glass bottles, two dozen with white wine and one dozen with Rhenish.[39]

In the early Stuart period court patronage had led to an increased number of secular spas and to the fashion of drinking, rather than bathing in, mineral waters. So agreeable were these rural summer gatherings, and so convenient for informal contacts, that not even government suspicion of Catholic plotting, military supervision, or the disruption of war could undermine the new social habit. Commonwealth leaders accepted the practice of taking the waters, but more for health than pleasure. When the first Stuart king came to the throne in 1603 only Bath and Buxton, and to a much lesser degree King's Newnham, had any importance as water-cure centres. At his grandson's succession in 1660 Bath, although much shaken by war, was still the supreme health resort, but now new drinking spas, especially Tunbridge Wells and Epsom, gave some challenge, as did Harrogate in the North, and there were twelve other minor watering-places, making sixteen in all.

5

Restoration Development: The Provincial Spas

During the half-century after the Restoration there was a marked proliferation of English spas, with Bath, although impoverished by civil war,
holding primacy of place, but sometimes eclipsed by Tunbridge Wells as a
fashionable venue. Epsom, too, attracted increasing custom, but Buxton
and Harrogate were slow to develop. Northaw revived, but the demise of
the ephemeral Wellingborough spa did not deter attempts to establish
other minor spas, although few visitors came to them from outside the
immediate region. A more commercial attitude to founding and maintaining spas now prevailed and, as in other spheres of activity, the government
saw no reason to interfere in entrepreneurial initiative. Religious and
political considerations were much less evident and economic paternalism
gave opportunities for minor capitalistic enterprise. The central government now generally displayed little interest in the spas, except as a form of
relaxation and entertainment for monarch and court, but the patronage of
the courtiers and the nobility was still important, and the immediate effect
of the return of the king and royalist exiles with experience of continental
watering-places was to stimulate the foundation of more English spas.

Charles II had inherited some of the enthusiasm of his mother,
Henrietta Maria, for healing waters. He had been in Bath in 1645, and
while exiled in June 1654 had stayed at Spa with his sister the Dowager
Princess of Orange and the court in exile. On 16 June his arrival at Spa,
where he stayed at the Hôtel du Cornet, was the signal for many festivities.
Although Charles had taken the Covenant in Scotland, he was regarded as
the head of English Catholicism and attended services at the church of S.
Remacle in Spa, so the connection between taking the waters and Catholicism was underlined again.[1] On his return to England in 1660 he went to
Tunbridge Wells in November with his mother, and in 1663 he returned
there with his wife, and they then proceeded to Bath with his brother the
Duke of York and the duchess. Charles II and his court subsequently went
to Epsom in 1662 and 1664 and to Tunbridge in 1668 and, it is said, at other
times. The queen and her ladies enlivened Tunbridge in June 1666.[2] So the

Stuart patronage of the spas was maintained, and the courtiers favoured both Tunbridge Wells and Epsom because of their proximity to the capital.

Sir Thomas Baines, describing in 1676 the flourishing new fashion of drinking mineral waters, held the physicians largely responsible for their exploitation. They made, he said, a profitable practice of treating their patients in the spring and sending them to a spa in the summer. As to the beneficial effects of the waters, a change of air, regular diet, the stimulation of conversation and the prescribed exercise were the reasons for improvement in health, but a patient's confidence in his physician was the true cause of his recovery. Far more cures were effected after the initial discovery of a mineral spring than later, for familiarity and custom diminished its reputation.

Despite scepticism about their curative effects, the spas supplied a popular form of relaxation for the patient's family and filled a social need for the elite as centres of public life in the summer. London still held a monopoly of fashionable amusements, as Dr Peirce of Bath wrote in 1697 '. . . after the return of Charles II all the world went to London to live'. But summer was a time of languor and discontent, when the healthy endured wearisome solitude in their country seats among peasant company whose uncouth manners were incompatible with their own, while the sick took the waters at small spas, content with purely rural pleasures. Then came a growing awareness that spas might provide not only medical cures but agreeable retreats where people of fashion could assemble and pursue the polite amusements available in the metropolis in the winter; spa mania had begun. Water-drinking, said Dr Peirce, had by the 1690s become universal, and medical practices adapted to the change of fashion. Scarcely a county in England now lacked 'a medicine water' frequented in season, but some of former fame became neglected, like the once famous water of Wellingborough.[3]

Here was a potential new leisure market, and spa foundation and development became a new industry – a holiday industry, especially after the 1688 revolution had made property rights more secure. Landowners saw opportunities to increase their revenues, and enterprising entrepreneurs to make money from a relatively modest investment in spa sites and amenities. They provided structures over wells to shelter the drinkers, baths and bath-houses, purpose-built lodging-houses and recreation facilities, such as long-rooms for assemblies, music galleries, coffee-houses – often with libraries attached – and raised walks between a double row of trees for promenading. By the early eighteenth century spas offered 'diversions' such as music and concerts and the performance of plays in a local barn to help to fill the long intervals between taking the waters.

These new spas brought valuable trade and employment to many rural areas, but there is little information about the recruitment and pay of their labour force. In some places old women made a useful living as water-dippers serving customers at wells, and tenants and retainers, like park-keepers and their families, became keepers or lessees of wells and lodg-ing-houses during the season and were rewarded with fees and gratuities. Apart from the inns many local inhabitants let lodgings on their own initiative to visitors from a distance. Some physicians and shopkeepers were attracted from the towns for the season, but all services were with-drawn in the autumn when the spa closed for the winter.

So the emphasis of spa life became more a search for pleasure and entertainment, although still under pretence of taking the waters for health reasons. But the company which gathered at the wells had little cohesion; there was no focus for community life and 'no general society' except in the few places where, later, a long-room was built. Social contacts were casual and a matter of chance, depending on personal relationships, and there was little attempt at civilized accommodation of manners. The great ones retained the haughtiness of nobility and had no notion of how to unbend to lesser people. 'In short, delicacy, politeness, and elegant plea-sures were then only just budding forth . . .'.[4] There was little attempt at social control or organization until the eighteenth century.

Such a primitive rural spa was one promoted by a royalist family and known to Dr Edmund Borlase (d. 1682), who practised at Bath and in Cheshire. In 1670 he wrote a tract to publicize Latham Spa in Lancashire, which belonged to Charles Stanley, 8th Earl of Derby, to whom he dedi-cated his work, and he had twenty years' experience of it, so it was probably used in the 1650s. During the Civil War Derby had gone into exile and married a Dutch wife, Dorothea Helena, maid of honour to the Stuart Elizabeth of Bohemia; she had had first-hand experience of the Ardennes spas and those of Wilong in Hesse. The Derbys tried to revive the Latham Spa site, now in the tenancy of Thomas Hulmes of Slade, and the spring at West-head was walled in and protected with a wooden cover. Rich and poor alike had access to it and the Stanley tenants living nearby supplied lodgings for the better-off. A perpetual problem at these small spas was provision for the needs of nature, especially acute after imbibing potent mineral waters, so Derby allowed both sexes to retire modestly behind the shrubs and undergrowth in an adjacent field. His countess ran a small business supplying salts of vitriol or steel, seeds of herbs such as coriander, lemon or orange pills and angelica roots to render the water more palatable and cakes of cream of tartar, which her neighbours dis-pensed to the water-drinkers. Some drank the water warm, or retired to bed with their potations.

A veneer of scientific respectability attached to this spa by the pa-tronage of at least three other doctors, including Dr Howorth (or Haworth) from Manchester, possibly the founder of the Castleton Spa, but few patients cured at Latham were of social importance. They mostly came from the Stanley's circle, their friends, servants, retainers and clients, such as Major Henry Nowell, the deputy governor of the Isle of Man, where the earl was overlord. The Frenchman Monsieur Pelate, a gentleman of the horse to the countess, had taken the waters of Bourbon and other renowned spas, including Holy Well in Flintshire, but he diplomatically, like others, found the Latham waters superior to all.[5] Nicholas Blundell was at Latham Spa with his wife in August 1703 when they met Cousin Scarisbrick and other acquaintances and danced there, but by the late eighteenth century visitors were deterred by the lack of proper accommodation.[6]

Many other rural spas of brief life and limited size proliferated after the Restoration. The definition of a spa, or spaw, in this study excludes the hundreds of 'healing' springs throughout the country which, although called spas, were nothing more than wells, or watercourses channelled into a basin, where only the locals came to dip and sip. A real spa was of greater importance; it served more than immediately local clientele, and there was some development around the site. Another criterion of a spa was that it received the imprimatur of mention or approval by a medical practitioner; it is rare to find one of any consequence which was not the subject of a treatise by a physician or mentioned in a general publication. The landowning nobility and gentry, quick to grasp that the vogue for taking the waters had become general and could provide a profitable form of speculation, searched their properties for a suitable spring to convert into a spa. Physicians and apothecaries were equally alert to opportunities to work up a practice by advising water-drinkers there, and spa proprietors enlisted their services in writing publicity pamphlets.

Although there was an accelerating movement in spa foundation provincial spas had tended to attract a mainly local custom, because of the difficulties of travel, but after 1660 a renewed effort was made to deal with the bad state of the roads. The parish repair system was in 1663 supplemented with a new concept of road improvement: the turnpike authority, under which travellers contributed towards road repairs by a system of tolls. The first one was on a section of the New Great North Road, but thirty-two years elapsed before the second Turnpike Act was passed in 1695. A new turnpike was then erected somewhere nearly every year by local justices. These justice trusts were by 1714 replaced by a new type of turnpike trust, but investment in them was slow and before 1720 there was little turnpike activity in areas remote from the capital.[7]

By 1660 the geographical distribution of the spas was wide, although some, like Castleton, King's Newnham and Witherslack, maintained a precarious existence and the nascent ventures at Northaw, Wanstead and

Wellingborough had almost collapsed. Dr Benjamin Allen listed Northaw and Wellingborough in his *Natural History of the Chalybeate and Purging Waters of England* of 1699, but not in the 1711 edition.[8] Their loss was immaterial; there was a steady rash of new spas. By the late seventeenth century, although travelling for pleasure was rather rare, people began to move around the spas as their increasing number offered a choice, and more horses, coaches and wagons, as well as some improvement of the roads, made travel easier.[9] In the plague-ridden year 1665 an element of panic crept in; Lady Elmes fled to Scarborough and also sampled Knaresborough, Buxton and a new spa, Astrop Wells in North-amptonshire. In 1686 Sir Ralph Verney, her ageing brother, was recom-mended by his physicians to try the waters of Islington, Epsom and Tunbridge, but those of Astrop he might drink at home; they were as good as the London ones. That year one Thomas Brown was reputed to go annually to the wells at Tunbridge, Astrop, Epsom and Knaresborough. The hot, dry weather in July 1684 made all the wells very crowded.[10]

The new well at Astrop in Northamptonshire was very popular among courtiers and Dr Peirce of Bath blamed it, being nearer to Oxford, for Wellingborough's eclipse. The well was associated with the shrine of St Rumbold at nearby King's Sutton, but an anonymous, crude pamphlet of 1688 about it, perhaps by Dr Richard Lower (1631–90), does not reveal the promoter of the spa, although Lower 'discovered' it in 1664. It quickly became fashionable with the local gentry, but suitable lodgings were lacking.[11] In 1665 Lady Elmes complained of having to endure 'the stink of sour whey and cheese' in her chamber, of having no coal fire to burn perfume to smother the unpleasant aroma, no food at night and no candle, so she had to borrow one. The Ishams of Lamport in Northamptonshire accompanied her on her tour of the spas, and Thomas Isham was at Astrop in July 1672, by which time a booth had been built and walks were laid out. A royalist friend, Sir Nicholas Steward of Hartley Maudit in Hampshire, Chamberlain of the Exchequer, was there taking the waters and intended to stay three weeks. Another courtier, the Earl of Sunderland of Althorp, James II's Secretary of State, was there from exile in Holland in August 1690.[12]

By 1740, as Dr Thomas Short of Sheffield found, some capital had been injected to improve the surroundings of the well. In 1694, Celia Fiennes, a connoisseur of spas, had seen the mineral water flowing into a dirty, mossy well, and two rooms, one for company and one for music. But now a basin caught the water in a small, stone-flagged enclosure presided over by a statue of St Rumbold. A well-house had a palisade in front and from here visitors could go under shelter into a large, wainscoted room to mingle and talk and take tea and coffee. Behind the well-house the fine, dry gravel walk ran 140 yards long and six yards broad between a close-set, clipped hedge twelve feet high with benches on each side, and beyond were 'conveniences' for the drinkers to retire to. Over the brook from the well was a fine tea-room, the second or dancing-room, a large kitchen and a shop, one of the earliest in a village spa. Astrop had in fact become 'a paradise of pleasure', and in 1749 another well was opened at Sutton, half a mile from the old spa.

Astrop remained a fashionable resort. Among its devoted patrons were the North family of Wroxton and their circle; Elizabeth, Lady North, told in 1739 of Lady Thanet ordering everyone there about, the great consumption of burgundy and champagne, and of the visit of Frederick, Prince of Wales and his wife, who had both been at Bath the previous year. Well-known Northamptonshire families who came included Mr and Mrs Brudenell in 1739, and Thomas Thornton III of Brockhall on an extended holiday from 21 July to 16 October 1740 with his wife and four children at a cost of £116 6s. 0d. He returned faithfully each year, joined by other local gentry, such as Justinian Isham in 1757 and throughout the 1750s by John Devall of Floors and his wife. Thomas Thornton described the delights of Astrop in verses addressed to Mrs Sarah Devall, beginning with a Monday public breakfast of buttered rolls and tea costing 9d. each from 9 a.m. to 10 a.m., then a walk with friends, a concert of instruments and voices, and yet another walk before a plentiful dinner at 1s. 6d. each and 6d. for wine. The ladies then retired for friendly talk, but the men sat quaffing wine until teatime. Except for the regular weekly ball on Monday, a card-playing session then began and continued until midnight, so there was no time for supper. Clearly Astrop, although still a minor rural spa, had acquired some organized social routine and its large kitchen did some busy catering.

Thomas Thornton remained a devotee of Astrop until 1782, and after his death in March 1783 his son, Thomas Lee, paid a subscription in August 'to the rooms & wells at Astrop', but it had already become less fashionable and was losing custom. Despite a disastrous fire in July 1785 the Great Room was opened each June or July until about 1800, but it was then deserted and the buildings decayed. J. C. Nattes's sketchbooks (c. 1810) show the well and a thatched cottage adjoining, but also the interior of a large shed with a tank, pump, shute and sunken bath; so the Astrop Spa may later have catered for bathers as well as drinkers. Although one of the more substantial of the minor spas of the Midlands, it lacked an entrepreneurial developer of the kind to be found in Cheltenham and Leamington.[13]

Roughly twelve miles east of Astrop Celia Fiennes visited a spa at Horwood in Buckinghamshire, which must have had a reputation, if ephemeral, for she stayed to drink for a fortnight. Almost equidistant from Astrop to the west was another Midland spa, a chalybeate spring 'discovered' at Ilmington in Warwickshire in 1684. Supported by Dr William

Cole and a pamphlet by Dr Samuel Derham in 1685, on the initiative of the Capell family, lords of the manor to 1700, it had a considerable vogue for some years.[14]

Royalist promoters were behind another Midland spa, at Willowbridge in Staffordshire. In 1660 Charles, 4th Lord Gerard of Gerard Bromley Hall, gentleman of the bedchamber to Charles II in exile, married the heiress Jane Digby, a cousin of Sir Kenelm Digby who was the Chancellor of Queen Henrietta Maria. Gerard's infant son Digby succeeded in 1668 and when, in about 1676, a spring was discovered near his residence, Willowbridge Lodge on Ashley Heath, the young earl's mother sponsored a spa, the Willowbridge Wells, for both drinking and bathing. She enclosed several springs in a stone bath-house with two large baths, one for men and the other not for women but for *horses,* which indicates the importance of horse transport in the economy of the spas. She also built a four-square stone conduit for drinking, and, between 1676 and 1686, some rooms for lodging the poor and changing-rooms for bathers of higher rank. Her chaplain Samuel Gilbert, rector of Quatt Malvern, was the propagandist; he claimed to be a physician, surgeon and oculist but also a farrier, hence the bath for horses. (In Tudor Bath William Turner had advocated this equine treatment.)

The spa already had a regional reputation when Gilbert's pamphlet appeared in 1676. He cited seventy cures, mostly of local people, about thirty-one from Staffordshire and twenty from Shropshire, with a sprinkling from Cheshire and Derbyshire. One aged man came all the way from Kendal in Westmorland to obtain ease of a dog-bite, and the water-takers included workers from a distance, such as a collier of Stoke-on-Trent and a tanner from Nantwich. Benefit of the Willowbridge waters was no longer confined to consumption on the spot for, as at some other spas, the bottling and distribution of them was now being organized, but to avoid adulteration and because the waters were volatile, the bottles were corked and sealed with Lord Gerard's arms. No charge was made for water taken at the well, but the wealthy Lady Gerard could afford to be philanthropic. By 1697 two more Midland baths were in use, a sulphur one at Godsall in Staffordshire and the Routhen Well in Sutton Park, Warwickshire where small cottages were built.[15]

Judd, an apothecary, was behind a brief spa venture at a bathing-pool near Leicester which had by tradition cured wounded soldiers after the Battle of Bosworth in 1485. Realizing its potential, Judd built a cold bath and apartments for customers at great expense, with partitioned rooms to accommodate patients of differing ranks and various diseases. After his death, but before 1724, the building was demolished.[16]

The new habit of cold-bathing was now developing, as at Willowbridge and also at Matlock, which emerged as a rival to Buxton in Derbyshire.

About 1698 a spring on the Woolley estate at Matlock was tapped to supply a bath, and the Reverend Mr Fern of Matlock and one Heywood (or Hayward) of Cromford built a wooden bath lined with lead for public use, surrounded it with a stone wall and paved it round. George Wragg confidently leased the site from the lords of the manor for ninety-nine years for a fine of £150 and an annual rent of 6*d*. each and built a few small rooms adjoining the bath. Despite the poor accommodation for visitors, from these slight beginnings one of the larger spas later developed.[17] Also in Derbyshire an old well on Sir Nathaniel Curzon's estate at Kedleston, now used as a bath, was publicized by Sir John Floyer in 1702, and in the West Midlands springs in the Malvern Hills, one 'new found' in 1622, were becoming famous for cures by 1688, but the development of Malvern Spa came later.[18]

The success of one spa often led to the foundation of others within its periphery to catch some overflow trade. The fame of Tunbridge Wells encouraged the attempt to mount one at Sissinghurst in Kent, but the immediate cause was a domestic financial crisis after Lady Baker's death in 1693. In 1695 the Bakers tried to retrieve their fortunes by exploiting the iron-bearing waters of the well in Sissinghust Park in Cranbrook parish. They had earlier attracted so many 'people of quality' that Lady Baker, objecting to the crowds, had closed the well and locked the park gates, but her heirs had the well repaired and the walks there restored. Sissinghurst lay on a good road only two miles from Cranbrook, a post town, and a coach service brought passengers from London forty miles away to the wells for 10*s*. each in one day. A cheaper but tedious route was from Billingsgate to Gravesend for 1*s*., by coach to Rochester for 1*s*. or sometimes 1*s*. 6*d*., by water to Maidstone for 6*d*. and the last ten miles by coach or horses.

This Sissinghurst Spa had its environmental attractions: a park about seven miles round with views for over twenty miles in the midst of birch woods and fruit-growing country. Abundant cheap provisions included cherries, strawberries, birch wine, cider at 6*d*. a bottle, and fresh fish from the ponds. Accommodation was no problem, for the impoverished Baker family rented out parts of their great Elizabethan house, furnished or unfurnished, with the use of their chapel, to persons of quality. The cloth trade had decayed, so many former clothiers' houses, large and timberboarded, could be leased cheaply. Mr Basden, a London merchant, had a vested interest in the spa's prosperity; he had a house near the well and provided pasture for visitors' horses. Despite the advantages of good transport services and lodgings the experiment at Sissinghurst did not succeed; as so often the proximity of an established spa – in this case Tunbridge Wells – to a new spa venture was a disadvantage.[19]

Another victim of Tunbridge Wells was Canterbury, where there were chalybeate springs and a sulphur one near the West Gate and a spring with a bath called St Rhadgund's Bath outside the North Gate. Celia Fiennes drank the waters at one of these sites in 1698 and compared them, not unfavourably, with those of Tunbridge. The walled-in well had a surrounding rail and steps down to the paved area where the company drank the waters, and fine walks, seats and places for music made it attractive. Some time after 1705 *A Short Account of the Mineral Waters of Canterbury*, published anonymously, referred to recent attempts to divert people from these waters. Tunbridge interests could have intervened.[20]

On the eastern side of England Benjamin Allen, a Braintree doctor, wrote about mineral-water springs in two pamphlets dedicated to Charles Montagu, 4th Earl of Manchester, not only to enlist aristocratic influence but because, although Manchester's main seat was at Kimbolton in Huntingdonshire, he had inherited estates in Essex with several springs. But only one temporarily flowered into a spa: that at Witham near the home of Sir Edward Southcote. An attempt about 1697 to enclose the spring in a well was mismanaged, and the spa lost its reputation. But Witham was well sited as a potential watering-place, near the centre of the county and midway between London and Harwich on a good sixty-mile road, and it was a focus of the social life of the nobility and gentry of East Anglia. Later George II brought it some fame by resting at Lord Abercorn's mansion there when journeying between England and Hanover, so Dr James Taverner of Witham, helped by Dr Legge of Braintree, attempted to revive the spa in 1736.

Greater care was taken in pumping the spring into a small receptacle, and the great hall of the mansion New Hall near Chelmsford was moved to Witham and adapted as an assembly-room. Local innkeepers and lodging-keepers invested in a network of entertainments and other facilities for the fairly numerous visitors who came, some by the daily stagecoaches. Taverner may have hoped for royal patronage; his *Essay upon the Witham Spa* (1737) was dedicated to the important Dr John Hollings, physician-in-ordinary to the king. But Hollings died two years later and the high hopes of the spa were not realized, although George III's queen stayed there on her arrival in England, and the local gentry came to take the waters and maintained their monthly assemblies in the summer months until about 1790.[21] Another East Anglian spring, listed by Allen in 1699, which had a brief life as a spa was at Aylsham in Norfolk.[22]

In the North of England the example of Harrogate inspired the establishment of periphery spas in Yorkshire in the post-Reformation period, the most popular one being at Scarborough, a coastal port. Local tradition was that a merchant's wife first noticed the medicinal qualities of a spring coming from a cliff to the south of the town in 1620 and the inhabitants soon adopted the water as a physic. Yorkshire gentry besieged in Scarborough Castle during the Civil War used the water as a cure for scurvy, so the fame of Scarborough spread in elite circles and after the Restoration it acquired a reputation among people of fashion, especially since it could provide the facilities of an established town. In 1662 Sir John Reresby saw many persons of quality there for both health and pleasure, but it also attracted attention as the focus of controversy between Dr Robert Wittie and Dr William Simpson.

Wittie practised at York from 1665 and was the author of *Scarborough Spa* (1660, 1667), in which he described the chemical nature and medicinal value of the Scarborough waters, discoursed on balneology at large and defended Galenical medicine, but his ideas were challenged both in the Royal Society and in public forum, especially by Simpson, who produced *Hydrologia Chymica: or the Chymical Anatomy of the Scarborough, and other Spaws in Yorkshire* . . . (1669), *The History of Scarborough Spaw* . . . (1679) and another pamphlet on Scarborough. Aristocratic patronage still mattered and Simpson dedicated his *History* of 1679 to a member of the Privy Council, Charles Paulet, 6th Marquess of Winchester, who had already acknowledged the benefits of the waters and about 1683 was at Scarborough again. Winchester's father had been to Epsom for five weeks in 1647 and he himself was an expert on mineral waters: there were few in England or France which he had not sampled.[23]

Others lending aristocratic flavour to Scarborough were James, 15th Earl of Suffolk, who after seeking a cure in England and France had found it there attended by Dr Wittie, and Lady Carey, Lady Rhodes and Lord Roos came on annual visits. Nearly all the visitors were from Yorkshire, with a scattering from Scotland and Newcastle, Grimsby, London and Cambridge, all before 1679. A physician, G. Smith, came from Berwick-on-Tweed on annual visits of 120 miles, and a Mrs Robinson preferred the Scarborough waters to those of her home town Buxton. Celia Fiennes gave Scarborough only qualified approval in 1697 on account of its dearth of amusements, and the spa well was vulnerable to tidal flooding, but the spa prospered and temporarily rivalled Bath, which, envious of Scarborough's fame, spread rumours of several distinguished persons dying there during the season. As at Bath, the spa site was owned by the corporation, which in 1698 built the first water cistern and secured the wells in front by a staith or wharf, a large body of stone bound by timber as protection against the sea. In 1700 they erected an adjoining house and rented it to a superintendent, the governor of the spa. In 1733 this was Dicky Dickinson, who was deformed and uncouth of speech but, with the wit to promote his rented property, built two houses, one each for gentlemen and ladies. John Cossin's map of 1725 shows Dicky's house, the Spaw Well and the coach road leading to it.[24]

Sir Walter Calverley of Esholt visited various northern spas. As a boy he had been to Buxton for a week in 1695, in 1699 he spent several days at the Harrogate spa, where he returned in 1702, but he then favoured Scarborough for three visits: in 1705, 1713 and 1715.[25] Had he wished he could have visited four other Yorkshire spas recently 'discovered'. At Malton a spring in Longster's garden was promoted as a spa by a Mr King and Dr Lister and Dr Simpson (possibly Dr William Simpson of Scarborough), who wrote the *Treatise on Malton Spa* in 1669.[26] A 'spa water' at White Wells near Ilkley was used by the Middleton family of Middleton Lodge to supply a small bath-house with a deep, circular plunge bath which they built in 1699. Nicholas Blundell bathed at 'brother Middleton's baths' in 1714. From this humble beginning there later grew a major spa.[27]

Also in Yorkshire at Aldfield, a sulphur spring in Spa Gill Wood found in 1698 attracted 'immense' numbers of people in the summer months but failed to become a fashionable watering-place through lack of accommodation,[28] and at Gilthwaite near Sheffield a local inhabitant, George Westby, in 1664 made a large bath, using a mineral spring, and built a house over it. Dr Yarburgh of Newark sent patients there and Westby's spa acquired an ephemeral reputation; many from Sheffield suffering from mineral fumes came annually and were relieved by bathing.[29] South of Sheffield at Bakewell in Derbyshire John, 10th Earl of Rutland, caught the fever for establishing spas and with the advantage of a warm natural spring of 60°F on his property, in 1697 erected the Bath House in Bath Street off Buxton Road.[30]

The most northerly spa was in a rocky dell at Butterby near Durham, where in 1684 Hugh Todd claimed a deep medicinal spring 'lately discovered' by workmen digging for coal. Also at Durham, in the Framwelgate district, a well of chalybeate water which flowed into a stone basin with an arch over it and a sulphureous one were on Celia Fiennes' itinerary in 1698. Another Durham spa was a vitrioline one in a field with a 'useful' wood adjacent, and a pamphlet, *Spadacrene Dunelmensis,* was published about it in 1675. The author, E.W., was probably Edward Wilson, trained at Padua and Oxford, who died that year. Dr R. Clanny of Durham Infirmary, in an account of these spas in 1807, claimed that they had a long reputation, although they were never developed.[31]

At the other end of England, in the south-west, a rash of periphery spas appeared within the ambience of Bath. The Alford Well west of Castle Cary in Somerset – a saline-chalybeate spring first 'discovered' by Thomas Earl, the local minister, in 1670 – was of sufficient reputation to draw Celia Fiennes among the company who resorted there. Dr Robert Peirce of Bath and Dr Highmore of Sherborne in Dorset both sent patients and Highmore went himself during the drinking season, presumably in search of custom. A trade in the waters had been developed by 1676, probably by Peirce, for they were, curiously enough, sent to Bath, and thirty years later Alford had, he claimed, become 'very famous', its waters being distributed as far as Exeter and Plymouth and even to Land's End. Peirce rated them with those of Barnet, Northaw or Epsom, but Alford failed to become an established spa, again because of the lack of lodgings suitable for people of fashion. The Somerset country folk were 'a clownish rude people', obviously incapable of appreciating the niceties of polite behaviour.[32]

Nearer to Bath a clutch of minor spas burgeoned in north-west Wiltshire. Of the many mineral-water wells in that area four qualify for inclusion in the list of commercialized medicinal wells the fame and usage of which spread beyond the local inhabitants in the Restoration period; Seend (1667), Box (1670), Holt (1688) and Chippenham (1694). John Aubrey, who wrote *The Natural History of Wiltshire* between 1656 and 1691, had a personal involvement in the Seend project. In 1665 he found a mineral well in the courtyard of John Sumner's house, and in 1667, encouraged by the results of analysis, he tried to interest the Bath doctors who, understandably, showed no enthusiasm for the Seend waters so near Bath. Aubrey and Sumner persisted in their enterprise, and by 1684 more company arrived than the village could accommodate, so they prepared to invest more heavily in building houses for the summer season. Sumner hoped to make £200 a year out of his well, and Aubrey intended to provide a handsome 'house of entertainment' and a fine bowling green. The origins of another spa, at Box, go back at least to 1670 when, according to both Dr Thomas Guidott of Bath and Aubrey, medicinal waters were being taken from a well in the street, but the spa that developed in the next century was at Ditteridge, three-quarters of a mile north-west of Box. The most important of the Wiltshire spas was Holt, where the medicinal virtues of its waters were known about 1688, following the 'accidental' discovery of its virtues by a local inhabitant while sinking a well near his home. Sir William Lisle of Moyles Court in Hampshire, then lord of the manor of Holt, lived for a time in a house opposite the well which was his property. His widow later took an active interest in it, with the support of Mr Hickes, a clergyman, who recommended the waters to Dr Guidott of Bath, but the fuller development of Holt came after 1713.[33]

Easier travel and increased publicity were producing more consumers for the embryonic spa leisure industry, which became less exclusive. Drinking the waters was no longer a vogue confined mostly to the nobility and gentry who could afford long journeys to notable watering-places such as Bath, Harrogate or Tunbridge Wells, although aristocratic patronage was still an advantage. Where lodgings were available customers were tending to remain longer for a holiday of several weeks, as at Astrop; the visitors there stayed at King's Sutton, four miles away. The lodgings question was the crucial one, as Aubrey and Sumner realized at Seend,

and many a village spa failed for lack of suitable rooms to let in season.
But some relatively humble people were now gingerly opening up spas and
in general their capital investment was limited to the provision of a well or
bath site; there was little physical expansion beyond, and so the spa
market was restricted, not so much by demand as by lack of accommodation.

The new spas of the early Stuart period had been drinking spas, but a
curious development after 1660 was that more provision was made for
cold-water bathing. Bakewell was fortunate in having a warm spring to
serve its bath-house, but cold baths were erected at Gilthwaite, Godsall,
Ilkley, Leicester, Matlock, Sutton Park and Willowbridge – seven in all.

6

Tunbridge Wells Rivals Bath: Late Stuart Changes

Tunbridge Wells

Post-Restoration Tunbridge Wells, once more the 'courtiers' spa', was the most fashionable drinking spa near London, drawing as much custom or more than Bath, and the quality of its waters was the touchstone by which others were assessed. To meet the needs of the growing number of visitors, the few local inhabitants at the Wells decided in 1676 to erect a chapel of ease at Tonbridge (then Tunbridge) five miles away, lest distance from a church and social distractions should lead to neglect of religion. The Purbeck family perhaps initiated the scheme, for that year Robert Villiers, Viscount Purbeck married the daughter and heiress of the loyalist Marquess of Clanricarde of Somerhill, Margaret, Dowager Viscountess Muskerry, who had shared exile with Queen Henrietta Maria.[1] Although she was a known papist, the Purbecks gave the site for a new church and 2,526 subscribers, including members of the court, Princess Anne, her stepmother Mary, Duchess of York, her uncles the Earls of Clarendon and Rochester, and Sidney Godolphin, raised £2,177. By 1678 the 'courtiers' chapel' stood in a key position near the chalybeate spring, but it had to be enlarged twice, in 1682 and 1688–90, to accommodate the increasing number of visitors. The square chapel with two octagonal domes of 1682 and 1690 was landscaped with a paved yard costing £60 5s. and fifty-two lime trees at £4, and in recognition of the Stuart patronage of the Wells it was dedicated to Charles the Martyr. In 1703 Lady Purbeck's son, the Earl of Buckingham, conveyed the chapel and its site to trustees, including George, 12th Lord Bergavenny, whose ancestor had originally enclosed the well.[2]

Sometime before 1660 the spring in Waterdown Forest discovered by Lord North had had a marble cistern set over it but no other improvement. The original site, enclosed by a rough wooden fence, remained in a primitive state in the highway at the end of the common. But the wells were valued as a means of livelihood by the common people, and when at the Restoration John Wybarne, a saddler, tried to monopolize them the locals saw their future prosperity in jeopardy and in May 1660 petitioned the House of Lords about his depredations, claiming that 'for fifty years and upwards' poor women had been free to dip and serve the water to the nobility, gentry and others. Wybarne had removed the cistern and paving stones and felled some birches in the Walk, and he threatened more destruction unless given charge of the spring. The Lords referred the case to the justices and ordered the restoration of the wells for the public good.[3]

Prompted by this decision, or the king's visit in 1663, in 1664 Charles, Lord Muskerry, first husband of the Somerhill heiress who held the manor of Rusthall, restored and improved the wells. A stone wall with a gateway adorned by his armorial bearings, his initials CM and the date 1664 replaced the triangle of railings, the area was repaved and a handsome basin was placed over the main spring. A sketch of the elaborate entrance porch topped with minarets, and one of the triangular ground plan, survive in the notebooks of Dr Edward Browne, and the 'triangle where the wells are' and the surrounding wall were mentioned in about 1720.[4] Muskerry also replanted the avenue of birch trees and built a hall to shelter the water-drinkers. About 1660–4 the pedestrian precinct of the well was developed, the first fixed booths or shops were laid out on the west of the Upper Walk (built in 1638) and the Lower Walk was marked out on the east.[5] There was also some illicit building of dwellings, shops and taverns on waste land on Bishop's Down near the wells in the 1670s.[6] Previously Rusthall and Southborough had provided lodgings and bowling greens for visitors, but after the royal visit of 1663 Mount Ephraim, or Culverden, was favoured for lodging-houses and had an assembly-room, brought from Rusthall, a bowling green by 1670, and a pleasure garden, the Fishponds.[7]

The post-Restoration settlement around the Tunbridge Wells was made possible because most of the huge forest area of Southfrith had by 1664 been disparked and divided into fifty holdings, including the Somerhill estate. A more commercial outlook now stimulated the enterprise of local people and, as at Epsom, of London speculators and shopkeepers, and a village of about a hundred largely timber-framed houses arose from about 1680 to cater for summer visitors. Development on the Walks began in about 1676, the year of the Purbeck marriage and the new chapel, but on the initiative of a courtier, Thomas Neale, groom-porter to Charles II and a manager of lotteries. Alive to the opportunities for commercial expansion, he bought the manor of Rusthall from the Purbecks and in about 1676 leased the grazing rights on the common from the freehold tenants at 10s. a year. Then in 1682 another London speculator, Thomas (later Sir Thomas) Janson, leased the Walks and the adjoining kettlepins place from Neale and the tenants for fifty years. But local interests were protected by the agreement that the Walks and bowling green remained open to all and that the freeholders' rights to grazing, to appoint the water-dippers, and to appeal to a tribunal against excessive rents were protected. Shops, booths, or rooms for coffee, drinking or games could be erected on the Walks, but not lodging-houses, nor premises for dressing meat, a process offensive to visitors. (At Epsom the less squeamish John Livingston allowed both a butcher and a fishmonger at his New Wells.) Wisely, part of the Lower Walk was reserved for coaches.[8]

Opportunities for commerce and employment were stimulated by continued royal patronage; accessibility from the capital still gave Tunbridge Wells the edge over Bath, and, like her mother-in-law Henrietta Maria in 1629, Queen Catherine's hope of an heir led her in 1663 to take its waters. The king and she went in July, he on a second visit, and they may have stayed in Mount Ephraim House, but their retinues, like that of Henrietta Maria, had to live in tents temporarily erected on Bishop's Down, and the removal of the queen's court cost £5,000. But the queen disliked the waters and on 11 August the royal couple left to seek instead the remedies of Bath,[9] although the Countess Dowager of Devonshire thought her livelier than ever. The queen gave Tunbridge a second chance in 1666, so providing some diversion in what Francis, Lord Hawley called that 'dull place'; but he was the recorder of Bath. The lords of the Treasury were left to find the costs of what the French ambassador, De Gramont, reported as an expensive and profitless visit.[10]

James, Duke of York also patronized Tunbridge Wells; in July 1661 his wife Anne forsook drinking the Barnet waters for those of Tunbridge, and in the summer of 1670, when she was unlikely to survive her pregnancy, they and their daughters Mary and Anne also took to tents on Bishop's Down, but she died in 1671. In 1674 the duke returned with his second wife, the Catholic Mary of Modena. Many Catholics still came there, and the new Duchess of York, with young Princess Anne and her husband George, stayed from 6 July to 11 August 1684 while the duchess drank the waters at the wells, and at night they watched the company dance on the green. The princess attended the new chapel and contributed £10 15s. for its erection and £53 15s. for its management.[11]

By 1684 Tunbridge had reputedly 'grown a place of gaiety' attracting all the good company from London, including 'an abundance of court soldiery', but physicians emphasized the health value of the Wells. Rowzee's treatise was republished in 1658, 1670 and 1671, and a weightier account, Dr Patrick Madan's *A Philosophical and Medicinal Essay of the Waters of Tunbridge* (1687) recommended the waters for a range of illnesses and advised a preparatory dose of Epsom waters for three or four days, then leisurely drinking at Tunbridge while banishing cares and listening to charming music.[12]

As at other spas, the search for health was gradually subordinated to social activities, and the company, some 'wholly employed in the amusements of the place', became increasingly mixed, as depicted in a comedy, *Tunbridge Wells, or, the Courtship of a Day* (1663) and another in Queen Anne's reign, *Tunbridge Wells or the Yeoman of Kent*. Both plays revealed the assorted humours, customs, diversions, dresses and manners of the contemporary company. John Verney, a Buckinghamshire squire, in 1684 found all sorts of gaming, dice and cards played daily and dancing every night, and Lady Essex Finch went intending to take the waters for the customary month, but her father-in-law wished her 'good company and much diversion' as well as physical relief.[13]

In August 1685, when Tunbridge Wells was so crowded that lodgings and all provisions were scarce and expensive, the visitors included the Duke of Norfolk, the Duke of Lauderdale (who died there), Lady Rochester, the politician Robert Harley, who was directed by his doctor to drink the waters for six weeks, Thomas Vivian with his family for five weeks, and many London citizens. Lord Chief Justice Jeffreys lived there at his house, Chancellor House, in September 1686 for a few weeks.[14]

The large gatherings of mixed ranks at watering-places presented a novel social phenomenon with no precedent for forms and routines of behaviour and, with the pressure on accommodation and services, led to informality in local society. Tunbridge Wells, like Hampstead and Islington, acquired a disordered and licentious reputation, but even so many officials were drawn there, as a matter of duty in the wake of the court or to take the waters in fashionable company. In 1667 Thomas Harper asked Samuel Pepys for a fortnight's leave from Admiralty business to drink the waters, and Christopher Pett requested three weeks' leave. Two admirals were there in 1697, and in 1685 Colonel Whitley begged absence from his post office accounts to go there.[15] A flow of official papers passed between the capital and the resort and authority was concerned about their transfer; in 1666 there was negligence with the king's packet containing special intelligence for Principal Secretary Sir William Morice, which was opened in transit. Obviously during the water-drinking season, from May onwards, better arrangements were necessary.[16] In 1667 William Loquer brought sixty or seventy letters a week in his wagon from Tunbridge and elsewhere. Henry Guy issued Treasury warrants there in 1686 and busily corresponded with the Attorney-General and the auditor of receipt while, presumably, taking the waters, and some of the diplomacy of the Triple Alliance (1668) was conducted from Tunbridge by Lord Keeper Bridgeman and Sir William Temple. In 1696 a necessary visit to Sir John Herne at the Wells was paid for from secret service money.[17]

The volume of traffic between the metropolis and the growing resort so increased that one August, possibly in 1685, seven full Tunbridge coaches passed Fleetwood Shepherd, leaving him stranded, but he was promised a place for the following day. Yet local roads were bad, although in 1709 the

one from Sevenoaks to Tunbridge was improved. Highwaymen were another hazard: Sir Orlando Bridgeman's children were robbed by six troop-
ers when going to Tunbridge in 1667, but generally the public and their
letters got through, for by 1678 a nightly post and a daily coach service ran
from the Three Tuns in Gracechurch Street.[18]

The rising pressure for accommodation and services led to more development after Lord Purbeck's death in 1684, when his widow allowed
the exploitation of the Mount Sion area of the old manor of Southfrith.
This became the fashionable lodging-place at the expense of Southborough, Rusthall and Mount Ephraim, and whole timber-framed houses
were moved on sledges from these hamlets to the wells area, one accompanied by the band playing music. During this boom period about half a
dozen speculators leased sites on Mount Sion or Mount Ephraim and built
much-needed lodging-houses or sublet unwanted ground; they included
Thomas Weller, steward of both the Somerhill and Rusthall manors, substantial local tradesmen like the mercer Richard Constable, and London
men. Abraham Spooner, a city vintner, spent £1,200 in his first year as
lessee, and Thomas Ashenhurst of Lambeth, gentleman, erected the Royal
Oak Lottery and the hazard or play-room and seventeen shops on the
Walks. Property at the Wells was held to be a fine investment, but houses
and shops on the west of the Walks had to be rebuilt after a fire in 1687.
The age of planned estates came later; most investors put up only one or
two individual houses, like Richard Dorsett, a local builder, on Mount
Ephraim, and Samuel Rose, a milliner from the Strand, London, who
favoured the Walks. Lodging-houses, the most profitable investment, were
built on or near the main road with several acres in the rear to pasture a
few livestock. As at Bath, the building lease with a small ground rent was
almost universal.[19]

The agreement between Neale and others in 1682 had provided for
'rooms for coffee', and there were two large coffee-houses at the Wells by
1697. After water-drinking the gentlemen could retire to the Pipe Office (or
House) to hire a pipe and smoke and talk over a dish of coffee, or to read
the newspapers for a subscription of 2*s*. 6*d*. This was an early example of
the subscription-based activity of the next century. After the 1687 rebuilding the Upper Walk was dignified by a continuous colonnade with shops
under cover, as they appear in Kip's engraving of 1718. By 1697 they
supplied a great variety of goods: toys, silver, china and millinery and also
Tunbridge Ware, wooden souvenirs like those sold at Spa, manufactured
locally on a small scale by George Wise in the 1680s.[20]

By 1700 there were twenty to twenty-five shops along the Upper Walk
and public assembly-rooms, a Great Room of eighty-two feet frontage and
a Long Room of fifty-four feet. On the Lower Walk, below the tree-lined
bank where the musicians played, were about twenty more shops, a
tavern, a coffee-house and a 'pissing house'. A new community had

formed to service the visitors, resident tradespeople who augmented their income by following a craft, leasing a shop, or farming. One such enterprising inhabitant, Nicholas Wood a fellmonger, in 1724 spent considerable sums on extending and furnishing his home as a lodging-house, had land adjoining, and ran a glove shop. Much of this commercial activity was only seasonal, from May until October, when a few Londoners with shops on the Walks came down and the local lodging-house keepers opened up.[21]

Visitors normally, as at Bath and later Cheltenham, booked lodgings without board and purchased their own food, and in summer many gentry visited the Friday market which existed at Tunbridge Wells by 1673 for corn and provisions. During the boom of the 1680s Lord Bergavenny was allowed, in 1686, to convert the weekly market into a daily one for general provisions, with a monthly cattle market and a fair on St James's Day (25 July). Epsom also gained a market – but only weekly – and two annual fairs, in 1684. The Tunbridge Wells market on the Lower Walk, where the country folk displayed their produce, provided plenty of meat, poultry and, since it lay on the road from Rye and Deal to London, very cheap fish. Several good taverns supplied wine, including by 1706 the Gloucester Tavern, named after Queen Anne's son the Duke of Gloucester, and there were brewhouses and bakers' shops. So Tunbridge Wells had become a small resort and commercial centre, but some traders from London spoilt the market by raising prices.[22]

The problem of filling leisure time at resorts such as Tunbridge became more urgent as they grew, and strolling and gossiping on the Walks was the usual occupation. (The Wells Walk beyond the two wells was paved with brick and stone and extended into a path of clay, but there was talk of a gravel covering.) The common opinion was that the water, which easily evaporated, should be drunk on the spot, but some drank it in bed in their lodgings, and there was a trade in bottled water sent to London. After water-drinking visitors took tea and chocolate in the coffee-houses and gambled at the lottery or hazard board in two rooms. The gentlemen still favoured playing bowls, as at Epsom and Bath, and by the late seventeenth century there were several bowling greens in surrounding hamlets, all with houses where the ladies danced on wet days; on fine days they performed outside. Tunbridge was among the earliest spas where the 'company' maintained musicians, certainly by 1697, although John Verney mentioned dancing in 1684. These players entertained the visitors at the water-drinking and provided music for nightly dancing at one of three greens. A different 'diversion' was listening to sermons in the chapel or in the Mount Ephraim ballroom, where from 1689 the local Presbyterians met on Sundays.[23]

For a time 'the Wells' enjoyed the patronage of Princess Anne, who reputedly came for many seasons and presented a Portland stone basin for one of the springs. She was there in 1670, 1684 and in August 1686, possibly with her father, James II; both came in 1687 and she returned in August 1688.[24] After 1688 her sister Queen Mary and King William avoided Tunbridge Wells, although Mary had been there as a child, but Princess Anne and her husband Prince George continued to patronize the spa; in 1691 three weeks' subsistence for two companies of Foot Guards to attend them cost £125 11s.[25] In 1697 Anne and George went again on 22 June and the Lord Chamberlain and other courtiers joined them later. When her boy son the Duke of Gloucester, who had water on the brain and tended to overbalance, fell down Anne entrusted £100 to a cottager to pave and level the Walks, but on her last visit, irate that the work was incomplete, she appointed a more reliable person for it and, justly angry, drove away. In 1700 the Walks were paved with pantiles, and to propitiate Anne the Queen's Grove of birch trees was planted later, but her favour had now switched to Bath.[26]

Better management of the wells area was needed, and from 1703 the chapel trustees became responsible for 'the comfort of the walks', with a subscription fund. By 1713 this fund was controlled by a majority of 'the company resorting to the Wells', so that, as later in other spas, the visitors claimed a share in organizing local social life. A regular monthly meeting of subscribers held in the summer season chose a treasurer and three or four trustees who paid for benches, laying the dust, attending to trees, fencing, paving and lamps, and in 1729 for making a cage to lock up miscreants. In winter the local gentry took over as trustees of the deserted walks and the closed chapel, but their duties were minimal.[27]

Although by the 1690s a more settled workforce of shopkeepers and labourers lived around the wells, the season still began in May and ended effectively in late August. Tunbridge was empty at Robert Harley's arrival on 27 August 1685 and when he was suddenly taken ill in early October he could find no physician and it was, as he said, then a wilderness. Normally some of the physicians and apothecaries who swarmed around in the summer lingered on; in 1702 there was little company on 1 September, but so many doctors that they had hardly a patient each, yet lodgings were still scarce.[28]

Tunbridge Wells was from 1660 to about 1720 the expanding courtiers' spa and now the rival of Bath. A gentleman and his wife who failed to find the fare after booking a place on the Bath coach in 1711 took that for Tunbridge Wells as second best, but those waters suited him so well that had he been able to afford it he would have stayed at Tunbridge all the winter.[29]

Bath

Bath had endured a traumatic time of fighting, changing military occupation and shifting political allegiance. Political settlement was essential for

its survival as a health resort and a trading community, and it acknowledged the restoration of the monarchy enthusiastically, celebrating the
coronation with cakes and wine for the citizens and tobacco, wine and
cheese for the soldiers. The king was sent £100 in gold in 1662. But after
the disruption of war the city chamber was in debt: it sold some municipal
property in April 1665 and in March some old armour by the hundredweight, and found the mayor's salary, which had been £55 in 1641, with
difficulty; in 1662 it was a part payment of £25 and from 1665 only £20
annually. Battles over the election of the two Members of Parliament and
the mayor also hindered civic revival, for Bath, despite its monarchist
reputation, was divided between loyalists and supporters of the Rump
Parliament.[30]

Apart from these impediments to expansion as a resort, Bath could not
absorb large crowds of visitors. In 1660 it was still a small town of about
thirty-two acres and fifteen streets, as a contemporary Bathonian, Captain
Henry Chapman, described: 'walled all around, with time-defying stone'.
Apart from ribbon development in Walcot outside the walls to the north-
east, the general position was one of stagnation. But Bath, in 1673 described as '. . . a fair and neat city, replenished with well-built houses . . .'
with good markets on Wednesdays and Saturdays and still some cloth
trade, did not compare too badly with other towns. Abundant supplies of
stone came from the local quarries and, as reported in 1699, the houses
there were 'very well built' and the city was better paved than Bristol. To a
visitor in 1724 the buildings were handsome and the streets well paved but
many courts and alleys were inaccessible to coaches, and traffic congested
the dirty, narrow streets.[31]

Although the resort trade was important to Bath's economy, its expansion was hindered also by the poor state of the approach roads. Pack-
horses, on which the town's commerce largely depended, could reach the
city by the old Roman roads, the Fosse Way from Exeter and the Via Julia
from South Wales. These merged at Walcot and left Bath to the north-east
as the London road, from which the Fosse Way diverted to the Midlands.
So Bath stood at the junction of four great routeways and the Bath to
Bristol road through Kelston, but they were at times almost impassable.
The River Avon circling the city walls on two sides, and the steeply rising
slopes on the north and south, constituted another impediment to expansion. Building to the west was blocked by the ninety-two acres of the
common lands, in 1661 farmed out by the corporation for £112 a year and
by 1677 for £123. The corporation listed other increased rents in the 1680s,
which indicated rising property values.[32] So physical difficulties and the
failure to attract outside capital, like that being invested in Epsom and
Tunbridge Wells, delayed Bath's physical growth. Just as the Cavendish
family were slow to promote Buxton, at Bath the stranglehold of the

corporation, who owned four-fifths of city property and were cautious of change, was a disincentive to investment.

Epidemics remained a deterrent to visitors. Henry Chapman's description of Bath, within its walls, as a 'coffin filled with earth' was not inappropriate. In July 1665 many fled from the plague-stricken capital 'to the great danger of our city', complained the city fathers, and inhabitants were forbidden to entertain anyone from London or other disease-ridden places. But despite precautions, in 1675 smallpox and fever were rife and in 1684 sickness was rampant, and the necessary drive for more sanitary conditions to fit the city for visitors did not come until 1755. Meanwhile for further safety, in 1662 an official bellman was appointed to preserve the city from fire and other dangers at night, with a stipend of £10 and a night coat.[33]

Inadequate accommodation for visitors and, as always in resort towns, the seasonal nature of their invasion, made the lodging question acute. Joseph Gilmore's map (1694) shows twenty-two inns, perhaps twice as many as in Elizabethan times, and twenty-eight lodging-houses. A military survey of 1686 assessing billeting reveals that inns and alehouses had 324 available beds and stabling for 451 horses; by contrast the city of Wells, also in Somerset, had 402 beds and stabling for 599 horses. But at Bath the local gentry, physicians and merchants also let out odd rooms as lodgings. The typical lodging-house was of three bays and three storeys with gabled roofs, bow windows and an imposing porch, but the interiors were unattractive: the floorboards were dyed brown with soot and beer to hide the dirt and deficiencies.[34]

So Bath lacked the economic resources to repair the roads and erect new buildings, although its commercial future lay in supplying the leisure needs of a growing consumer society. As a visitor wrote in about 1700: '. . . the inhabitants generally speaking have nothing to live on but what comes from those that frequent the baths . . .'. In gay summertime an inhabitant of Bath will be proud to say that he lives there, but in winter 'when he is cold in the mouth for want of summer's blessings', he will say '. . . I live at Bath, God help me'. Thomas Dingley corroborated the city's dependence on the baths and the manufacture of apothecaries' wares.[35]

Government of the city by a close corporation did not encourage initiative. By the 1590 charter authority was vested in the mayor, aldermen and councillors, and vacancies were filled by promotion from the freemen, also a limited body, and they alone could open shop in the city. Freedom of the city was gained by vote of the council, purchase or apprenticeship, but from 1697 by the latter only, although to retain the goodwill of the elite honorary freedom might still be conferred on noblemen and gentlemen. This inbred system of government gave traders little spur to activity.[36]

The political situation also had a stultifying effect on the city fathers.

Memories of the Civil War and anxiety to retain Bath's status as a corpo-rate town made them play for safety in the shifting relationship of king and Parliament. But royal patronage still mattered, and Bath's loyalty was displayed in 1663 when on 21 August, after a stay at Tunbridge Wells, the king and queen, with the Duke and Duchess of York, came for an informal visit with few attendants, although two carriages and three teams of horses were required for provisions for the escorting foot guards. They were greeted at Bath on 29 August by its recorder, Francis, Lord Hawley, and the king dined with the council, who, hard up though they were, presented the queen with a basin and ewer costing £31 10s. and paid £36 6s. for the king's officers' fees. The Duke and Duchess of York soon left, but the king and queen stayed on in Dr Robert Peirce's Abbey House, despite fears that she would find the air of Bath 'stifling'. The queen drank the waters and after 8 September bathed once or twice.[37]

The queen's visit had been encouraged by the Scotsman Alexander Fraizer, the king's physician and political agent, who showed great interest in the waters on this, his first, stay at Bath and afterwards corresponded with Dr Peirce. He likened the Bath waters to those of Bourbon, where he had attended Queen Henrietta Maria, and he subsequently sent clients to Peirce at Bath to avoid the expensive and hazardous journey to Bourbon and because Bath waters were more suitable, he said, for English people. The drinking of waters in Bath was encouraged by him, and in September 1664 Henry Chapman, the mayor, adopted his advice to erect a drinking-pump in the middle of the King's Bath, although a pump had existed since 1587 and both the King's Bath and the Queen's Bath had a pump-house for water-drinkers. Fraizer's pump was a part of the 'New Cross in the King's Bath' which cost £150 4s. 8d. in 1664. Fraizer himself returned to Bath with the Duke of Lauderdale in 1673.[38]

In 1663, while the queen took the waters the king went on local visits; they left on 22 September. But Bath did not immediately regain the courtiers' custom, partly because of the plague scare of 1665, and in July 1669 it was 'exceedingly empty' of persons of note, except Secretary of State Lord Arlington. Recognizing the importance of royal patronage for the restoration of Bath's reputation as a fashionable resort, Henry Chap-man in 1673 dedicated his *Thermae Redivivae: the City of Bath Described* to the king. The Cross Bath, now honoured as Queen Catherine's Bath, was given a new umbrella-shaped pump and cistern in the centre in 1665 and it had a gallery all around donated by Robert, Lord Brook, in 1675. The queen returned to Bath in 1677, and, as queen dowager, in 1686, possibly in June as well as on 7 September, and she intended to go in 1690 and 1691.[39]

But from the late 1660s the city fathers were anxious to establish Bath's status as an assize town not only as a resort. When the king's daughter-in-law, the Duchess of Monmouth, was at Bath from about 23 July to 2 September in 1668 and her husband came for ten days, the council petitioned Arlington through her for Bath to have one of the assizes or quarter sessions. They argued precedents for Bath, which paid £121 of the new hearth tax, about four times more than either Wells or Taunton, and was staunch for the Stuarts, the first garrison in the west for Charles I and the first to proclaim his son, and they sought the support of nearby grandees, the Duke of Somerset and the Marquess of Worcester.[40] In 1683 the high sheriff of Somerset pleaded for this 'very loyal city', but provisions there were one-third dearer than elsewhere in Somerset and it could provide only 'a very little hall', the Guildhall, in 1699 described as well built of stone, set upon pillars, open underneath, thirty yards long and ten yards broad. Lord Keeper North held the assizes there in 1682 but had little encouragement to return.[41]

The high cost of living at Bath was caused by the increased number of visitors, as from the 1670s onwards courtiers resumed their habit of going 'to the Bath'. The Duke of Hamilton arrived from Edinburgh in 1678 and the Duke of Lauderdale in 1662, 1673, probably in 1678 and certainly in 1680. In late summer 1674 and the next year Lord Treasurer Danby transacted government business from Bath and two of the Cabal ministers came: Lord Arlington again, and Lord Clifford for at least three weeks in 1672. Surrounded by much good company, they found drinking the waters more beneficial than bathing. A royal favourite, Louise de Kerouaille, Duchess of Portsmouth, dallied there in 1674, and when she was ill in 1676 she again chose Bath, as she also did in 1677.[42] The newly created Duke of Beaufort came from nearby Badminton in 1683. So with the Restoration the custom of the court was restored to Bath, and the greater traffic of wealthy visitors to the city shows in increasing references to stables: four in the council minutes of the 1630s, one in 1675, six in the 1680s, and six for the 1690s. In 1690 there was a newly built coach-house, and another in 1692. By 1699 congestion in the narrow streets was a major problem and part of the town common was set aside for the airing of gentlemen's coaches and horses.[43]

Despite the bylaws of 1646 and orders in 1663 for keeping rubbish off the streets, Bath was still a none-too-pleasant, overcrowded city, and it was so debt-encumbered that in 1685 the mayor's salary, now £40, could not be paid and a loan of £300 was taken up; so little was done to improve amenities. There was constant trouble over domestic water supplies, for private houses drew too much from the common conduit and their intake was temporarily stopped, but it was resumed in 1680. Members of the corporation paid only half the 10*s.* rent when in 1695 approval was given to bring water to every house. Until about 1690 there were only minor and sporadic improvements in the baths as elsewhere, such as the railing in of the walks around the borough walls by public subscription in 1674 and the building of a house of ease in the bowling green in 1681.[44] In general, however, there was a sense of lethargy in the city, the result of national uncertainties and fear of renewed civil war.

The city fathers behaved equivocally in politics, especially during the Exclusion Crisis in the dilemma of choosing between the two claimants to the throne, the Catholic Duke of York and the Protestant but illegitimate Duke of Monmouth, both patrons of Bath. The city council, seemingly pro-Yorkist, declared in May 1680 for the lawful succession, but Monmouth's arrival in Bath in August provoked demonstrations for him and, fearful of losing the charter, the council sought influential allies. In August 1682 they conferred the city's freedom on the Earl of Nottingham the Lord Chancellor, Viscount Newport the Treasurer of the King's Household, and two members of a locally powerful family, Sir Thomas Thynne and Henry Frederick Thynne. In 1683 two West Country peers, Charles, Earl of Worcester, heir of the Duke of Beaufort, and Thomas, Earl of Pembroke, were recruited to the noble patronage. By late 1684 the charter of 1590 had to be renewed; it cost £230 in 1685 but was not engrossed until 1688. On Charles II's death in March 1685 Bath promptly proclaimed York as king and refused support for Monmouth, celebrating the defeat of his rebellion in Somerset. The execution of two rebels at Bath and the burial of two soldiers in the Abbey churchyard in July and August showed how near to civil war the city had come. Lord Feversham and Colonel Kirke, who had suppressed the rebels, were made freemen of Bath.[45]

Yet the revolution of 1688 was perhaps precipitated by Bath. James II, when Duke of York, had been there with his first wife Anne in 1663, and its waters were obvious treatment for his barren second wife Mary. The queen arrived in Bath on 18 August 1687, but the king was at Tunbridge Wells, and five unfortunate owners had their coaches requisitioned to escort him to Bath, including the Earl of Pembroke, Lord Weymouth and the dean of Salisbury, but not Bath's high steward, Lord Fitzhardinge, who organized the muster. Once more Bath paid up, among other expenses, for the ringers when the royal couple arrived. While there they reputedly visited the mineral spring at Lyncombe Spa House, later called 'King James's Palace', to the south of the city.[46] The king left in mid-September but the queen lingered on to bathe in the Cross Bath, and the freedom of the city was bestowed on her general-of-horse, the Earl of Dunmore, Lord Waldegrave and five other courtiers, and two councillors escorted her home on 11 October. Back in Whitehall she 'found herself breeding', an event which the Earl of Melfort, Secretary of State, celebrated with a new cross in the Cross Bath.[47]

As Protestant opposition to James II grew after his son's birth on 10 June 1688 Bath continued to support him, with a loyal address on 25 June and on 3 August the appointment of the Catholic Lord Waldegrave of Chewton Mendip as its high steward to replace Viscount Fitzhardinge. They rang the bells when Waldegrave came. But Bath was on the losing side, and on 17 October received the order which removed all mayors, councils and servants of corporate towns, a last desperate effort by James at a Catholic takeover. The council minutes are silent on the events of November 1688, which brought the downfall of many of Bath's noble patrons when James II fled into exile. On the succession of his daughter Mary and her husband William the crown of thorns and the cross in the Cross Bath were taken down, as a conciliatory gesture, but a firm political settlement was to Bath's advantage and it celebrated the coronation of Mary II and William III with gusto.[48]

Once the uncertainty was over, the real period of expansion in Bath began tentatively in the 1690s. The 1688 revolution had given legal security to property-owners, which encouraged investment in building and amenities for visitors. The bowling-green walks were gravelled and re-planted with young trees in 1694, and as a hygiene measure the house of ease there was taken down in 1701 and built out over the river. As a further precaution against fire, from 1697 most tenants of city property were now required to provide six water-buckets each. But there was growing pressure of people on space, despite attempts to control building within the city. Seventeen people were renting 'encroachments' in 1687 and Robert Sheyler was allowed to build in Cheap Street in 1694, but four were fined for new building in 1697 and four more in 1701–2. By 1699 the process of burrowing under the streets for space had begun, so creating the cellars which are a feature of Bath. Joseph Gilmore's 1694 map refers to 'the most remarkable new building' and shows ribbon development also outside the walls to the north-east, 115 houses and the new bowling green, and eighteen houses along Southgate Street.[49]

Now commercial enterprises catering for the leisure industry were feasible and they included bookshops – those of Thomas Salmon by 1670, John Marthen (or Nalder) until his death in 1695, and Henry Hammond by 1697.[50] By 1690 Robert Sheyler ran a coffee-house, the Turk's Head; in 1718 its lease was renewed by Mrs Elizabeth Sheyler for ninety-nine years. The cockpit at the Saw Close, two bowling greens, the fives court outside the West Gate, and by 1708 a primitive playhouse in a stable by the Abbey Gate provided other recreations, but with too much leisure and too little purposeful activity, as reported in 1693, Bath produced nothing new, only intrigues.[51]

Serious publicity by doctors and others stimulated the now increasing custom. A second edition of Chapman's *Thermae Redivivae* (1673) came in 1675, and Dr Thomas Guidott of Bath edited the work of Dr John Maplet (d. 1670) on the Bath waters but is better known for *A Discourse of*

Bath and the Hot Waters there . . . (1676) containing biographies of the
Bath physicians from 1598.[52] His *Register of Bath* . . . (1694) lists his
patients from Cornwall to Scotland, a range of the nobility, middle ranks
and below, a Deptford shipwright, a London merchant and a Smithfield
butcher among them. Guidott's *Register* shows that his patients rapidly
increased in number as Bath's resort trade grew; sixteen in the 1670s,
sixty-nine in the 1680s, and in only four years – 1690–3 inclusive – seventy-
four.

The revival of Bath's fortunes was much helped by the arrival of Queen
Dr Robert Peirce, a grass-roots observer, published his *Bath Memoirs* in
1697 through Henry Hammond the bookseller. On his arrival in 1653 there
had been three resident physicians of repute besides several interlopers
from Oxford, London and elsewhere. While his seniors were busy in Bath
Peirce endured the 'very ill ways', building up a riding practice for thirty
miles around, but he later shared the Bath custom. He gives vignettes of
clients who stayed in his Abbey House, where he died in 1710: Major
Arnot from Fife, disabled by hawking in all weathers, and Sir John Gell of
near Buxton but 'a great friend of Bath' for twenty years. Colonel Hallet
and his brother came from Barbados and Richard, Earl of Tyrconnell,
from Ireland. Among West Country patrons the Duchess of Beaufort sent
her children 'to promote their growing', and Lord and Lady Digby of
Sherborne also lodged in Abbey House. Peirce favoured the practice of
dry-pumping, which had replaced the earlier bucketing and wet-pumping
and applied a greater force of water to the extremities of the body. The
Duke of Hamilton, who was among the Scottish nobles drawn to Bath by
Stuart patronage, had dry-pumping treatment in 1674 for a painful hip and
at the peak endured 800 to 1,000 strokes.

Another change was the altered timing of the season caused by the
competition of Epsom and Tunbridge Wells. Previously visitors had come
during the hottest time, from early July to mid-August or later, but now the
patients of London physicians preferred these new spas to facing the three
days' journey to Bath and the hot season there. Consequently two shorter
seasons developed at Bath: in the spring from April or May to late June or
early July, and in the autumn from mid-August to late September or early
October. The joint effect was to prolong the busy period, to the financial
benefit of Bath's entrepreneurs.

The revival of Bath's fortunes was much helped by the arrival of Queen
Anne in 1702, maintaining the Stuart interest in Bath. Although as Princess Anne she had favoured Tunbridge Wells, she had fled to Bath from
May 1688 until June, when the birth of James, Prince of Wales, put her in
an equivocal position.[53] In August 1692 she returned with her husband to
convalesce after illness, but she was in disfavour with Queen Mary and the
city records do not mention that visit, except the bell-ringing. Even so the
Earl of Nottingham, Secretary of State, expressed the queen's displeasure

to the mayor and requested less ceremony for her sister. Anne subsequently had bottled Bath water delivered at Windsor three times a week. Her visit had drawn in crowds and sent up prices (especially for lodgings, so that an inn now charged 9*s.* a week), and it focused attention on the difficult roads into Bath, for her cumbrous coach ran backwards while going up Lansdown.[54]

In 1702 Anne's household officials issued £100 for another journey to Bath. But she was now queen, and to atone for past slights the corporation voted to present her with a piece of plate which cost £46, to pay her servants' fees, and to illuminate the scene with ten convex lights; and to ease the passage of the queen's coach they had the old bridleway from the down into the Via Julia widened and levelled. Queen Anne was properly received by the sheriff of Somerset outside the city on 28 August and at the West Gate by the two Members of Parliament, the mayor and corporation and two hundred ladies richly attired; bells were rung and Morris dancers performed. She stayed at Abbey House and from 5 September drank the waters, which had alleviated her husband's asthma. For six weeks, until 8 October, the court was at Bath and, as when it was at Tunbridge, her ministers kept administration going: Lord Treasurer Sidney, Lord Godolphin and Secretary of State Sir Charles Hedges dealt with various matters, including negotiations for the Act of Union. Inevitably, however, this visit again made lodgings scarce and provisions expensive.[55]

The queen so favoured Bath that she returned in 1703, accompanied by Secretary Hedges and Attorney-General Sir Edward Northey. Twenty chairmen waited on Lansdown on 19 August with sedan chairs to carry her and her husband down to the city, but she remained in her coach to the North Gate and a civic reception. She again stayed with the aged Dr Peirce in Abbey House until 7 October, amidst much public rejoicing. But there was trouble with a deputy clerk of the market to the queen's household, when twenty-four citizens were summoned to the Bear Inn, and two councillors subsequently went to London with the charter and other city documents 'on trial between Her Majesty and Mr Chapman'. A bond of £100 was given for the charter's safe return. The ghost of the royal right of purveyance seems to rise here.[56]

So Anne went to Bath four times. Although her 1703 visit was the last by a reigning sovereign until 1917, it had underlined Bath's social significance as a resort. Tunbridge Wells, not Buxton, was now its rival; as reported in August 1696, the capital was 'very empty and no sign of money anywhere, but at Bath and Tunbridge where ladies shake the elbow' – that is, throw dice.[57] Four Stuart monarchs and six of their consorts had been to Bath, and Epsom and Tunbridge Wells also received royal patronage, but other early watering-places lacked it and remained in a more static position.

Buxton

Buxton had not entirely lost its custom; in 1665 Lady Elmes included it in her tour with friends but found its accommodation indifferent. As Richard Blome wrote in 1673, the waters attracted many people, especially the northern nobility and gentry; but it remained a backward place, deficient in lodgings and means of entertainment. In 1686 the inns and ale-houses had beds for only thirty-nine people and stabling for seventy-two horses; nearby Bakewell and Ashbourne both had far more space for visitors. The lord of the manor of Buxton, William Cavendish, 4th Earl of Devonshire (d. 1684) did little to promote it as a resort, except that in around 1670 he rebuilt and enlarged Shrewsbury's Old Hall. The 5th earl, elevated to a dukedom in 1694, was more concerned with rebuilding Chatsworth House, but he put a new tenant in the Buxton Bath-House, Cornelius White, attorney of the King's Bench, who in 1695–6 made some improvements. The ancient bath was repaired, paved with freestone and now protected with a roof, and a new bath was made for the poor. New lodging apartments were provided and more stables, and gardens, a bowling green and walks were laid out. But even more accommodation was needed, and opinions about Buxton were mixed.[58] In 1697 Celia Fiennes found the Hall overcrowded: guests shared four beds to a room, sometimes with strangers, and were disturbed by noisy people using the warm bath there. Meals, ale, wine and servants' attendance were a separate charge, and the mealtime beer was almost undrinkable. Buxton was disappointing; few stayed more than two or three nights but Lord Chesterfield, with Lord Stanhope lingered for ten days in 1707. By contrast, in 1699 J. Verdon thought Buxton the best and cheapest place on his journeys. The men and women constantly bathing at the Old Hall went at different times, so the sexes never mixed, as confirmed by Sir John Floyer, whose *Enquiry into the Right Use and Abuses of the Hot, Cold and Temperate Baths in England* (1697) was dedicated to the Duke of Devonshire and extolled the Buxton waters. Robert Downs the bath-keeper received not only Derbyshire patients but some from Nottinghamshire, Buckinghamshire and Yorkshire. They bathed in the morning when fasting and at night after supper and swam or walked about so they never caught cold, although the second bath was extremely cold. But Floyer disapproved of their bathing naked; men should wear drawers and women shifts.[59]

In 1719 John Scattergood too complained of lax behaviour at Buxton, a disreputable place and the resort of loose, revelling youths who came for pleasure more than need and whose music and dancing almost all night long kept him and his companions awake. So Buxton remained a primitive place, with few amenities or even shelter for the water-drinkers, until 1709 when Sir Thomas Delves erected an ornamental, arched building twelve feet square, with stone seats, over the drinking-fountain as a thank-offering for the Buxton water. Daniel Defoe was outspoken about Buxton's wasted opportunities, despite its many springs. Apart from the Bath-House, Old Hall, lodgers were dependent on the goodwill of house-holders, and the baths were unfit for winter use. If, Defoe said, a city were built for the entertainment of the nobility and gentry, instead of a few houses, more would come to Buxton, for its advantages were valuable medicinal waters, open country with a variety of trees, and a fine moor where ladies could ride out in their coaches. Bath, a close city, was by contrast more like a prison than a place of diversion and gave off a stink like a common-shore.[60]

Harrogate

Buxton in the north had to meet the competition of the wells of Knaresborough and Harrogate, but 'the Yorkshire Spaw' developed, not around Knaresborough town but on the open common at High Harrogate, outside the settlement of Harrogate to the north. These wells were by no means neglected; John French's *The Yorkshire Spaw or a Treatise of four famous Medicinall Wells* (1652) had another edition in 1654, and Michael Stanhope's *Newes out of Yorkshire* (1626) was reissued under another title in 1649 and 1654. But there was little to attract outsiders; Lady Elmes and her party of sixteen in 1665 paid 10*s.* a week each for lodgings and 7*s.* for their servants in an unpleasant, crowded house which sickened them more than 'the nasty water'.[61]

There was increased interest in Yorkshire waters, as in other mineral waters, after the Restoration, but the danger of plotting at spas remained. The 1663 Derwentdale Plot was a Presbyterian and Anabaptist intrigue by Dr Richardson and others at the Yorkshire Spa in June.[62] Most visitors, however, came to take the waters or to enjoy the social life, although this was limited, and the doctors at York, eighteen miles away, supported both Harrogate and its rival spa, Scarborough. Dr Robert Wittie's essay of praise *Scarborough Spaw* (1660) was countered by Dr William Simpson's *Hydrologia Chymica* (1669) and, at a lower level, by Dr George Tunstall's *A New Year's Gift for Doctor Witty* (1672). Tunstall, originally a devotee of Scarborough, switched his loyalties to Harrogate, as he explained in his *Scarborough Spaw spagirically anatomised* (1670). His first visit to Knaresborough Spa in 1667 had been during a wet spell when its mineral content was diluted, but now he argued its superior virtues. Good livings were to be made around all wells and doctors debated with acrimony the merits of those in which they were interested.

Dr George Neale of Leeds, who had introduced warm-water bathing at Harrogate in 1626, assiduously supervised further improvements there, so that in late Stuart times it ranked as a spa after Bath, Epsom and Tunbridge Wells and became less dependent on Knaresborough for visitors' accommodation. In 1656 the chalybeate Sweet Spa or John's Well, discovered in 1631, was provided with a stone basin, walled about and roofed in, and Neale called in workmen to restore the spring when it dried up. In 1670 Jane Eltoff was in charge of the Sulphur Well in Low Harrogate and received £1 15s. from the parish of Pannal, and in 1675 Neale had it dug out to increase the volume of water and installed a large basin covered with stone. By 1734 the other two springs had stone basins enclosed in small stone buildings. Neale's attempt at publicity, the unfinished *Spadacrene Eboracensis* (between 1690 and 1695), was later incorporated in Short's *History of the Mineral Waters* (1743).

At Bath visitors went to public baths, but at Harrogate they stayed in their bathing or lodging-houses and used the few bathtubs filled with sulphur water brought in casks from the well; after bathing, as at Bath, they sweated in a bed of blankets to cure rheumatism and other muscular pains. George Neale's son, Dr John Neale of Doncaster, also introduced a *cold* bath with visitors' accommodation in the later Cold Bath Road. By the 1690s bathing had become a minor local industry, with twenty bathing-houses all fully occupied in season. Francis Hardisty, for example, in 1692 had a bathing-room with a bedstead and bedding and a bathing-tub in his house of five rooms, two hogsheads and other vessels in his cellar, and a horse and cart to transport the water. His widow received 3s. for two baths in 1694. Others apart from lodgers used the bathing-tubs, and late bathers stayed overnight to avoid catching cold and drank the waters early in the morning before returning home. But this was a competitive trade; while Thomas Baskerville's party were still in bed in 1682 local women burst into their chambers with pots of water clamouring to serve them, either by filling their pots at the wells or bringing the water to their lodgings.[63]

Like Celia Fiennes in 1697 and 1698, most visitors had to find lodgings in Knaresborough and go daily to the Harrogate Wells. In 1686 Harrogate inns had only ten beds for visitors and stabling for ten horses, but Knaresborough provided thirty spare beds and stables for sixty horses. As the two distinct spa settlements emerged at the Old Sulphur Well at Low Harrogate and at High Harrogate more inns, lodging-houses and cottages were erected on the common, despite the manorial court's penalties for encroachment. High Harrogate was transformed by the building of inns: the Queen's Head in 1687, the Dragon and perhaps the Granby before 1700; and the company there, including fashionable society, became as much an attraction as the mineral waters. James Brome was captivated by it in 1700: 'We happened here at the season, when there was a great confluence of the gentry . . . whereupon we diverted ourselves for a few days in this place.'[64]

Despite its exposed position on a barren moor, Harrogate (122 miles from the capital), like Scarborough, increasingly supplied the northern nobility and gentry with an alternative to York's social life in summer. Yet Harrogate had no social amenities outside the inns – no coffee-house, no bowling green or even a shelter for the water-drinkers, the minimal facilities for most contemporary spas. Daniel Defoe was surprised, in about 1724, to discover more people there than at Scarborough, both drinking the waters and, in the new fashion, taking a cold bath, for it seemed the most desolate, out-of-the-world place. Both Buxton and Harrogate, although early spas, were handicapped by distance from the capital and lack of capital investment.[65]

Bristol Hotwell

By contrast the mineral water at St Vincent's Rock at Clifton near Bristol, used for over a century, was more fully exploited in late Stuart times because it had a *hot* spring, commercial capital was available, and a royal visit gave it some publicity. As its fame grew, local traders tried to control the Hotwell; in 1676 the Bristol Society of Merchant Venturers bought the moiety of the manor of Clifton, including the well 200 steps down the cliff-side by St Vincent's Rock. The next year Queen Catherine came from Bath, although the Bristol civic authorities delayed the invitation, failed to escort her to the well, and provided neither a gift to mark the occasion nor proper furniture for her reception. She went from her coach to the well in Lady Cann's chair, but there was no mat for her to walk on and no seats for her and her company, who had to sit on deal-wood forms supported by joint stools until a private citizen supplied a Turkey carpet and chairs.[66]

As at Epsom, people were now ready to rent spa property. In 1687 the society leased the Hotwell to two tenants for a mere £2 a year, but in 1691 the building of a high stone enclosure around the brick reservoir to prevent contamination by the tide nearly stopped the spring. So in 1695 a group of prominent Bristol citizens negotiated the rescue of their local spa with the Merchant Venturers, and in April the well was leased for ninety years to Charles Jones, a Bristol soapboiler, and Thomas Callowhill, a draper, who were committed to an annual rent of £5 and capital investment in a pump-room and lodging-houses and walks laid out to give better access to the well. In 1696 the gaunt Hotwell House was built on a rocky ledge of the Avon gorge to enclose the spring; it cost £500, the earliest figure we have for a pump-room. Now the Hotwell was an established spa; Dr Benjamin Allen in Essex received consignments of its water in 1706 and listed it in his *Natural History of the Mineral Waters of Great Britain* of 1711.[67]

No account of Stuart mineral-water resorts would be complete without mention of Holywell (or Holy Well or St Winifred's Well) in Flintshire, the only important well in Wales. After the setback of the Reformation the pilgrim traffic there was revived under Mary Tudor. James II and his wife Mary, as well as sampling the waters of Bath and Tunbridge Wells, went there on 29 August 1686, so contributing to his alienation from his Protestant subjects.[68] Holywell, now a flourishing Catholic venue, was an anachronism among the secular-based and more commercial spas serving the slowly developing leisure market. The survival of earlier watering-places into the post-Restoration period depended on various factors: court patronage played its part at the southern spas, but at Epsom and Tunbridge Wells it was also fashion and proximity to the capital; at Bath the control of the corporation, albeit lethargic; at Harrogate the initiative of local physicians; and at the Clifton Hotwell the support of Bristol's commercial wealth, that ensured continuity. Only Buxton, for lack of local enterprise, remained backward.

7
Metropolitan Spas

The pacemakers in providing more facilities at spa sites, especially commercialized leisure diversions, were the metropolitan spas. Astute businessmen found new opportunities for profit in providing small pleasure grounds within easy access of the city, and these promoters were often small traders, strongly supported by local physicians. In the post-Restoration period the improvement of the highways within a forty-mile radius of London helped this development of watering-places in the home counties, to which some of the elite – but mostly the middle ranks of society: professional men, merchants and shopkeepers – flocked in the summer months. Of these metropolitan based spas Tunbridge Wells and Epsom, the courtiers' spas, were still predominant, but now some of the legacy of the holy wells in the environs of the city, mostly suppressed at the Reformation and since forgotten, were resuscitated and popularized. In no other region of England was the transformation of the holy wells of the Middle Ages into the secular spas of Stuart and Georgian England so obvious.[1]

One of the most interesting resorts, dubbed The New Tunbridge Wells, was in the former grounds of Clerkenwell Priory. In 1683 Thomas Sadler, surveyor of the highways, rediscovered its holy well in his garden, where he had a music-house, a single-storey wooden building. An eminent physician advised him to mix the well-water with beer and distribute it in bottles, with so encouraging a result that in summer 1684 a Dr Morton sent patients there, as did many London physicians later. Dr Thomas Guidott of Bath produced a publicity pamphlet, *A True and Exact Account of Sadler's Well. . .* , in 1684, and Tunbridge Wells lost many patrons to Sadler's Wells, which had similar ferruginous waters. As many as 500 to 600 came early in the morning to drink the waters, then Rhenish or white wine, and to stroll in the garden with a pipe of tobacco while waiting for their waters to work. Sadler introduced the new device of a seasonal subscription, in this case 1*s.*, but he charged non-subscribers 6*d.* a glass for the water, enhanced by an orange-flavoured syrup. So Sadler's Wells became a thriving business, but its popularity brought criticisms from its older rivals, Tunbridge Wells and Epsom. From about 1687 it declined, but in around 1699 Francis Forcer, a song-writer, and his partner James Miles leased the playhouse, which flourished as Miles' Musick-house, while the spa was practically forgotten.[2]

The 'New Tunbridge Wells" were in fact two spas, Sadler's Wells and the Islington Spa on the opposite side of the New River, which had a more spacious and inviting site with lime trees, arbours and shady retreats and lasted longer. A poetical 'puff', *Islington Wells,* drew attention to it in 1684 when a Mr Jones, preparing to build there, discovered a well with a cover. John Langley, a London merchant, was quick to buy the site by September 1685, physicians approved the well water as a 'very good chalybeate', and the wells became known as the New Tunbridge Wells, or Islington Spa. Islington attracted some very mixed company and was the subject of numerous poems, plays, songs and satires, such as *Islington Wells or the Threepenny Academy* (1691), but it was a paying proposition. Around 1696 two hundred coaches were seen there, and a coffee-house forty feet long had been erected by 1716, when Dudley Ryder found 'multitudes' coming every morning to drink the waters at 3*d.* each.[3] The dancing-room, raffling-shop and card-room probably came later. In 1733 Islington Spa was news when the Princesses Amelia and Caroline, daughters of George II, came to drink the waters and a royal twenty-one gun salute was fired, about 1,600 people attended, and the proprietor took £30 that morning. A poem called *The Humours of New Tunbridge Wells at Islington* (1734) alluded to this visit and reinforced Islington's popularity. The garden was open two or three days a week from April or May until August, and for 1*s.* 6*d.* one could enjoy a public breakfast and dancing from 11 a.m. to 3 p.m.[4] Lodging-houses sprang up round about, but rumours of counterfeit mineral waters being distributed in the area threatened the spa's prosperity. In June 1748 these stories were investigated by the mineral-water expert Dr D. W. Linden, who advised the attendance of a physician to give advice at the spa.[5] In 1776, in *The Spleen or Islington Spa,* George Colman wrote: ' . . . the spa grows as genteel as Tunbridge, Brighthelmstone, Southampton or Margate . . .'; but already the growth of London was engulfing a large part of the gardens.

Also in Clerkenwell the proprietor of the Fountain Inn, John Halhed, claimed discovery of an excellent tonic water on his premises, and on 14 July 1685 he made a ceremony of changing its name to the 'London Spaw', but without effect.[6] Another London spa promoted more successfully by an innkeeper, Edward Martin, was the Pancras Wells adjoining a tavern, The Horns. The most notable feature of Martin's ambitious and expanding project in about 1697 was extensive gardens with long, straight walks shaded by trees, the Old Walk and the New Plantation. By 1700 the Horns development also had a long-room sixty-six feet by eighteen feet (much longer than Cheltenham's Old Room of 1738), two pump-rooms, the house of entertainment (135 feet long) and the Ladies' Hall.[7] Contemporary with Pancras Wells was the use of a medicinal spring in the Hoxton Wells, described in *A Short. . . Account of the late found Balsamic Wells at Hoxdon . . .* (1687) by Dr T. Byfield and dedicated to the proprietors of the wells at the Golden Heart in Hoxton Square. But Dr Windebank advised Lady Harley against these waters.[8]

Capital was not always available for development. Shooter's Hill – where John Guy, the tenant, found a mineral spring and had dug three wells, the Purging Wells, by 1673 – remained a modest medicinal spa, although the diarist John Evelyn sampled the waters in August 1699, Celia Fiennes knew of it, and it was said to have been used by Queen Anne. Celia Fiennes also knew of waters in the hamlet of Sydenham in the parish of Lewisham, often called Dulwich Wells. A physician discovered the Sydenham spring in 1640, or in 1648 according to Dr John Peter in *A Treatise of Lewisham, but vulgarly called Dullwich Wells, in Kent . . .* (1680). Nicholas Culpeper referred in 1653 to the juniper bushes by the new-found wells at Dulwich, and Evelyn went there too, in 1675 – 'I came back by certain medicinal spa waters at a place called Sydname Wells in Lewisham parish; much frequented in summer time' – and in 1677 he visited Lord Brounker, who was taking the waters 'at Dulwich'. Later George II went to the cottage in Wells Road where the waters were dispensed.[9]

By contrast, Richmond in Surrey was a sophisticated pleasure resort, a social centre for courtiers where Charles II went – to hunt in the park – and also his brother the Duke of York and his duchess in 1670 and 1682.[10] So a mineral well was 'discovered' about 1680 in the grounds of the later Cardigan House, assembly-, card- and raffling-rooms were provided, and in April 1696 the *London Gazette* announced the opening of 'The New Wells on Richmond Hill' in May. A 'Consort of Musick, both Vocal and Instrumental' was held on 13 June 1696 and the pleasure side predominated, with the emphasis on music and dancing. One Penketham, a humble trader, invested in a theatre there in 1719 and played in a comedy, *Richmond Wells: or, Good Luck at last* (1723), written for it by John Williams. The scenes were set in Richmond at the Wells and the dancing-room, and a character, Mr Gaylove, described the local scene:

> . . . the admir'd Richmond, the frequented Richmond, the seat of pleasures. . . . here's music, balls, walks, dancing, raffling, and to crown all, a play-house . . . In short, 'tis urbs in rure. . . .

By 1724 there were balls on Monday and Thursday evenings in the season and card-playing, and the new habit of public breakfasts, dinners and teas, with tea and coffee served at the meal, was adopted. Particulars of the tides in advertisements for Richmond suggest that some patrons came by boat, which may have been safer than taking the road over Hounslow Heath, for the Duke of Northumberland and Lord Ossulton were beset by robbers while returning from Richmond Wells. But Richmond gradually attracted a more settled population and after 1750 the popularity of the Wells declined.[11]

Another spa west of London, known to Dr Benjamin Allen in 1699, was the Acton Wells in East Acton, which were reputedly supported by the nobility, gentry and physicians and belonged to the Devonshire estate. They were most popular from about 1730 to 1790 when pleasure-seekers of all ranks crowded in, some staying for the season, so a New Room was provided by 1771.

Other spas to the south of the city were at Lambeth and Streatham. There was an attempt to exploit a mineral spring in the grounds of the Dog and Duck Inn at St George's Fields near Lambeth, which was known about in 1695, and Dr John Fothergill, a famed physician, approved it. Mrs Hedger, a barmaid, took the inn and in about 1731 promoted it as 'St George's Spa'; her son J. Hedger retailed the water at 4*d.* a gallon on the spot or a dozen bottles for 1*s.* Sarah Duchess of Marlborough had it sent to her at Windsor in 1734. From 1754 to 1770 the spa flourished and Hedger erected new buildings, including an elegant long-room lighted by large chandeliers. When he retired his nephew Miles was able to allow him £1,000 out of the profits, but the inn acquired a bad reputation in the 1790s, the magistrates suppressed it, and the house was pulled down in 1811.[12]

The other Lambeth spa, the Lambeth Wells in the Well House, surmounted with a gold ball in Three Coney Walk, was formally opened in April 1696 with daily 'consorts of very good music' until 4 p.m. on Tuesday, Wednesday and Friday and on other days until 7 p.m., and also French and country dancing. Dudley Ryder paid the usual 3*d.* for admission, which included the music, in July 1715, but was depressed to find that the many people there were mostly rakes, whores and drunkards, idlers such as Guards officers, or young pleasure-seekers like attorneys' clerks, mingling with loose women of the meanest sort.[13] The Lambeth Wells also became a public nuisance, so a dancing licence was refused in 1755 and the Great Room was used for Methodist meetings. Concerts were also held every Monday and Thursday and assemblies during the summer at the Wells House at Streatham in Surrey, 'the Hampstead of the South', which enjoyed a long reputation as a minor spa after the discovery of a mineral spring in 1660, although the landowner opposed its use and the water was not 'commonly drunk' until 1671.

Hampstead was the most important of the post-Restoration watering-places north of London and witnessed a scramble for profits in the new spa industry. There was some small-scale commercial activity at a well on

Hampstead Heath in Charles II's time when Dorothy Rippin was using half-penny tokens there, but the origins of Hampstead were earlier, in residential settlement. It was an urban village, with 146 dwellings by 1646 and a population of 600 to 650, many houses belonging to the gentry and the comfortable classes, who were ready customers as the spa developed. Edward Noel, 1st Earl of Gainsborough, a local landowner, had a warrant in 1684 for a licence to supply water to the City of London, but he died in 1689, followed two years later by his heir. Celia Fiennes saw a fine stone basin holding the Hampstead waters in about 1697, and in 1698 the decisive step was taken to exploit them commercially. The widowed Susannah, Countess of Gainsborough, on behalf of her son Baptist, the minor 3rd earl, vested six acres of the Heath with springs and wells in a syndicate of fourteen, the Wells Trustees, for the sole use of the poor of Hampstead for ever.[14]

This was the first legalization of public ownership of a watering-place, although the Tunbridge Wells arrangement in 1740 shared the same concept. But the poor of Hampstead did not benefit; the trustees became copyhold tenants of the Wells Charity Estate at a nominal rental, so in 1700 the manor court ordered the parish to pay for a second spring to be brought into the 'town' of Hampstead, but to use profits from it to reduce the poor rate. The syndicate had a valuable asset; customers soon came for health or pleasure and trade boomed, to the advantage of lodging-house keepers, speculative builders and property developers. By 1700 the trustees had organized a trade in bottled water from the Flask Tavern in Flask Walk; its London distribution at 3*d*. a flask was arranged by Mr Philips, an apothecary, from the Eagle and Child in Fleet Street. In April they advertised in the *Postman* that these chalybeate waters were taken by eminent physicians and many gentry who had previously drunk the Tunbridge waters.

In 1701 John Duffield, a speculator, leased the Wells Estate from the trustees and began an ambitious development; a walk, Well Walk, was laid out with a rapidly built ballroom to accommodate 500. It was possibly then the largest and most splendid long-room anywhere, thirty-six by ninety feet with thirty feet partitioned off to serve as a pump-room, and was adorned with figures of the nine Muses on spaces between the windows. The surrounding district, New End, was laid out with the Green Man Tavern, the Sion Chapel, various shops (some with souvenirs), gambling dens, gardens and a bowling green. Duffield's assembly-room was in use by mid-August, when he and his associates advertised a 'consort' of vocal and instrumental music, with admission at 1*s*. each or 6*d*. for afternoon dancing. These activities continued for some years, but Hampstead's exclusiveness was brief; its proximity to London soon drew in day-trippers, working people and disreputable elements. The comedy *Hampstead*

Heath (1707) reflected the social decline, and by 1715 there was 'much company but little genteel' in the dancing-room.[15]

Hampstead was no longer a fashionable spa. In 1719 Duffield astutely sublet his interest in the Wells site for £450 a year to William Luffingham, who relet the long-room to William Hoare, but he converted it into a chapel. Local doctors naturally attempted to revive the spa side of Hampstead life and praised the waters, and in 1734 Dr John Soame produced his *Hampstead Wells; or, directions for the drinking of those waters.* A Queen Anne house in Well Walk, Burgh House, was converted into a new assembly-room and in 1735 was enlarged with a new ballroom, much used for entertainments and lavish private parties, but the number of water-drinkers declined.

Barnet, to the north of Hampstead, was a much less important spa, well-known by 1652 and more renowned after 1660, but its economy depended more on its being a posting-stage and cattle market and horse fair than on its mineral waters. Samuel Pepys drank at the well in July 1664, and in August 1667 he cautiously took only three glasses of the water,[16] but a visitor in 1673 took the notoriously strong Barnet waters in preparation for a visit to Tunbridge. Sir Edward Harley's sister had four bottles of Barnet water sent to her in 1680, and Dr Benjamin Allen listed them in both the 1699 and 1711 editions of his *Natural History of Chalybeate and Purging Waters.* In 1693 Celia Fiennes found the well on the common to the west of the town walled in with lattices of wood and roofed over, but its water was muddied and full of leaves and it compared badly with the stone containers of the springs at Tunbridge, the Spaw (probably Knaresborough) and Hampstead, and she disliked it. Mr Owen, a London alderman, had in 1677 given £1 a year in trust to keep the well in repair, and there were purpose-built lodgings for visitors, but forty years later the once famous Barnet waters, much approved by physicians, were almost forgotten.[17]

Epsom

The waters of Epsom, also despised by Celia Fiennes, were most popular from about 1690 to 1710, when that spa was reputed to be as favoured as Bath and Tunbridge Wells. Although the Old Well, Whicker's Well, had been used since 1620, Richard Evelyn, lord of the manor from 1663, did not attempt to develop the site on the common between Epsom and Ashtead, and in 1667 the Surrey justices ordered the inhabitants to repair the protective paling. Yet an active social life developed at Epsom which, only fifteen miles from London and with 137 houses liable to the 1664 hearth tax, was outstanding among Surrey townships. The local nobles, gentry and merchants included Sir Robert Howard, who in 1681 was licensed to enclose the old highway from Epsom to Ashtead and to lay out another. Epsom retained its reputation as a courtiers' spa; when George Berkeley entertained Charles II there in 1662 John Evelyn met the king and queen, the Duke and Duchess of York, Prince Rupert and various noblemen. Charles dined there again in 1664, and Prince George of Denmark was another visitor. In July 1663 Samuel Pepys had to lodge at Ashtead and in July 1667 had to accept an indifferent room at the King's Head, because the town was so full. In 1667 Nell Gwyn and Sir Charles Sedley kept 'a merry house' next door.[18]

Authority was sometimes concerned about these crowds and consequent disturbances at Epsom. There were two convictions for running disorderly houses in 1667 and another for keeping an unlicensed common tippling-house. In the Great Plague year, 1665, the exodus of crowds from London worried the local justices, as at Bath, and fearful that the infection would be brought to Epsom, they asked Richard Evelyn to close the wells for the summer and to keep strangers out.[19] By 1668 a second well was in use, but Evelyn only built a wall around the original one, which he leased to some women for £12 a year. The failure to exploit such a profitable site is partly explained by an entry in the diary of his famous brother John. Richard's death from calculus in 1670 was attributed to excessive drinking of the Epsom waters, which would account for his family's reluctance to improve the Old Well area, but finally in 1675 his widow Dame Elizabeth built a house over the well and a paved brick walk for the visitors.[20]

So began the expansion of Epsom, although its reputation as a centre of intrigue died hard. In 1683 the Privy Council had a report of a conspiracy of fanatics there under guise of water-drinking and led by men of substance, mostly armed with pistols and with 300 to 400 horses. Even so in 1684 Dame Elizabeth Evelyn gained the right to hold a Friday market and two annual fairs on Michaelmas Day and St James's Day, each for three days – a concession which helped Epsom to compete with Tunbridge Wells, which had a Friday market by 1673 and in 1686 a daily one. Visitors who took furnished lodgings could shop there for their own provisions. Commercial growth was also aided by the commencement, on 19 June each year, of a daily post to Epsom and Tunbridge Wells from London for the water-drinking season.[21] But as Samuel Pepys found in 1663, Epsom lacked diversions except, by 1671, a bowling green in Phillips Close and from about 1680 a second one run by George Rickbell. In 1688 a monopoly of the pastime was established when Randolph Ashenhurst and Michael Cope, London gentry, acquired the first green and Ashenhurst and one W. Fox also paid £68 for the second and closed it.

Meanwhile an enterprise then unique among the spas was promoted by Nehemia Grew, secretary of the Royal Society, who read two papers about the manufacture of salts from mineral waters in 1679 and in 1695 published his *Tractatus de Salis Cathartici amari in aquis Ebeshamensibus.* . . .

contenti natura et usu, describing the preparation of Epsom Salt. Others competed with him in the manufacture of salts, in particular Francis Moult, a chemist and apothecary, and a dispute arose between Grew and Moult.

London capital was now being invested in the growing market for servicing visitors at Epsom, which by 1700 – as well as many brick-built lodging-houses with fine gardens, courts, gates and railings[22] – had four inns, including the older 'New Inn' (in existence by 1662). In 1687 W. Richardson, gentleman, of Bell Yard, London, sold the New Inn to William Steward, a barber-surgeon prominent in the city, knighted in 1717, and a director of the New East India Company. Two other entrepreneurs prepared to risk investment there were John Livingston and John Parkhurst of Nether Catesbury in Northamptonshire. Livingston, an apothecary, came to Epsom about 1690 and so flourished in his practice that in 1701 he was able to acquire land in Shoulder of Mutton Close, perhaps knowing of John Symonds's private well nearby. Dr Benjamin Allen, the mineral-water expert, saw Symonds's well of purging water when it was newly dug. It was 'in the town', as opposed to the 'Westerly One' – that is, the Epsom Well at the top of the hill – and Livingston may have used it when in 1707 he began to develop his New Wells in the town centre, competing with the Old Wells less conveniently placed on the common. When Dame Elizabeth Evelyn died in 1692 the trustees managed the manorial estate until in 1707 it devolved on John Parkhurst, who met the challenge from Livingston by more vigorous promotion of the Old Wells, perhaps with Astrop Spa in his home county in mind.[23]

Meanwhile Livingston acquired more land adjacent to Shoulder of Mutton Close in 1701 and planted it all as the Grove; in 1706 he also acquired some of the Old Manor House grounds, where he already had a bowling green and had erected some buildings. Here, next to his Grove, he laid out his New Wells development, a large house with an assembly-room for dancing, music and gaming and a pump-room at one end, and shops let to a bookseller, a picture-dealer, a haberdasher, a milliner, a shoemaker, a fishmonger, a butcher and other tradesmen. He advertised his unfinished venture in April 1707, the year when Parkhurst took over the manor, and after its completion in 1709 it attracted the company there from the more exposed Old Wells. Livingston left the New Wells land to one daughter and the Grove to another.[24]

Social life at Epsom centred around the two greens, especially on Mondays, and Celia Fiennes observed the dichotomy of interest between the Old Wells and the New Well. The Upper Green of the Old Wells, where the gentlemen played bowls and the ladies walked, was 'many steps up', and there were benches around, little shops, and a gaming- or dancing – room kept by the man who managed the well and sold coffee. 'Not far off', in the centre of the town, was the more sheltered Lower Green, one whole side occupied by Livingston's large assembly-room, with big sash windows and seats all around. It had two hazard-boards and a millinery and china shop.[25]

Parkhust, presumably unable to compete with the capital investment at the New Wells, soon let the Old Wells for seven years to a syndicate – John Grant, a joiner, John Maynard, and Daniel Ellicar, a bricklayer – but they still lost custom. Between November 1710 and May 1711 the opportunist Livingston purchased the remainder of their lease, due to expire in 1715, on condition that the syndicate renewed it with Parkhurst for twenty-one years. So Livingston established a monopoly of the Epsom wells, and in about 1720 he became the proprietor of the weekly market and two annual fairs, thus holding a large stake in Epsom's economic life.

The legend that John Livingston acquired the Old Wells to close them down has been discounted. Celia Fiennes saw both wells in operation in 1717 and John Macky found the Old Wells in use, albeit neglected, in 1724. Capital investment and the facts of geography shifted the spa centre from the common to the town, and Livingston was not the 'wicked apothecary' but a resourceful man who, after some eighty years of local lethargy, embarked on new enterprises and became a minor tycoon. Epsom did not decline from 1704 to 1714, as previously believed, but flourished under Queen Anne, when Prince George of Denmark came to drink the waters while she kept court at Windsor, and under George I. In 1716 (not around 1690) Sir William Stewart invested in rebuilding the New Inn with an extended frontage. Reputedly the largest inn in England, it was one of the earliest to have an assembly-room and was run by Mrs Wright. Epsom had four inns or taverns in the 1680s and nine by the 1730s.[26]

Epsom became noted as a leisure centre with a variety of commercialized entertainment. By 1708 Mrs Mynn's company was performing at the New Cockpit, presumably the playhouse in Hudson's Lane run by Powell, a well-known actor at Drury Lane. Public breakfasts were held at the wells with music and dancing every Monday morning, and in 1715 Dudley Ryder saw a great many gentlemen playing at dice or on the bowling green, where musicians performed each afternoon. As many as sixty coaches could be seen in the riding-ring on Sunday evening, the tradition of horse-racing went back at least to 1648, and other country sports survived: cudgel-playing, foot-races, cock-fighting and catching the pig by the tail. For the more sophisticated J. Lancaster had a coffee-house by 1716 on Coffee-House Walk and Coffee-House Buildings were erected for visitors' accommodation.[27]

The traditional view that Epsom society, which had earlier attracted more London citizens than Tunbridge Wells, was licentious was modified by John Toland's *Description of Epsom, with the Humours and Politicks of the Place: in a letter to Eudoxia* (1711). Thomas Shadwell's comedy *Epsom Wells* (1673) had satirized the mixed society and the ill-bred city wives staying at the well with their tame husbands, but Toland portrayed a more civilized and urbane society. Ladies of the court or city sat around on benches before their doors displaying their finery and bargaining with country girls for provisions, but some, especially those who sat up late at cards, had them brought to their bedside. It was a heterogeneous society where, from conversations overheard,

> . . . you would fancy yourself to be this minute on the Exchange, and the next at St James's; one while in an East-India factory, or a West-India plantation, and another while with the army in Flanders or on board the fleet in the ocean. . . .[28]

The company at Epsom, as in the other larger spas, reflected the multi-farious interests of a growing commercial empire.

The greater social mobility of the age produced a rich mixture of society and prompted the evolution of standards of polite conduct to achieve group cohesion. As in other spas, a sense of community was gradually created with the acceptance of a rational routine of taking the waters, exercise, amusement and cultural diversion. This new society demanded self-discipline, especially in the coffee-houses, which became schools of tolerance and good manners. In Epsom coffee-houses Tories did not stare and leer at Whigs, and Whigs did not look sour and whisper when a Tory came in. Social, religious and political distinctions were laid by, 'like the winter suit in London', and foreigners were well received. Abstract princi-ples were subordinated to the peace of society, and the sexes mixed more easily. Unlike Tunbridge, where they were not permitted, in Epsom ladies received visits in their lodgings, and despite opportunity for intrigue Epsom, it was claimed, was remarkably free from censure and observa-tion.[29]

Toland urged English society in general to adopt these admirable stan-dards of civilized behaviour, which were maintained and propagated by 'a gentleman of our society' called 'the governor'. He was the arbiter of all differences; he found virtue to be its own reward in promoting the town's interests, and was esteemed for his humour, breeding and good living. Toland does not name the governor, but he was a contemporary of Beau Nash, from 1705 the master of ceremonies at Bath. Licentious behaviour was also curbed by adopting religious observance as part of the estab-lished routine, as at Bath and Tunbridge Wells. There were prayers on Wednesday and Friday and two sermons every Sunday in the parish church of St Martin, while dissenters had a meeting-house.

From 1711 for six years John Toland divided his time between Epsom

and London, happier in his rural retreat, where permanent country pleasures were allied to the joys of civilized intercourse. But the Epsom which
he enjoyed was already changing; its decline as a spa while it grew as a
residential place was caused by the problem of all spa investors: only
intermittent use of the facilities and amenities provided. As these grew
more elaborate the underutilization of capital investment became more
serious. Epsom was a long-weekend resort where the city gentlemen came
down on Saturdays and escorted the ladies on the walks in the evening –
for unlike Tunbridge, where the ladies were seen daily, at Epsom they did
not appear during the week. On Sunday they went to church, on Monday
they attended the ball in the long-room, and on Tuesday the gentlemen
returned to the capital. Again Epsom, like most spas, was a summer
resort; out of season the lodging-houses were shut up and the walks were
neglected. As it became an increasingly residential place for rich merchants, wealthy Londoners met too many of their own kind there and
wanted a change of society when on holiday, and the nobility and gentry
thought Epsom too near London and, aided by the improved roads, were
able to travel to Bath or other more distant spas to seek variety in their
pleasures.

The late seventeenth century was a growth period in the history of the
English spas. Not only was it a time of physical expansion at Epsom,
Hampstead and Tunbridge Wells, and later at Bath, but between 1660 and
1710 about forty-four new spas of some significance emerged and five
undated ones, making a total of about sixty-five, including the earlier
group. Although dating is in many cases tentative, the momentum of spa
foundation apparently increased decade by decade (six new spas in 1660–
9, seven in 1670–9, eleven in 1680–9 and fifteen in 1690–9) but then fell to
five between 1700 and 1709, with five improved spas. Most remarkable was
the ring of seventeen 'drinking spas' serving the metropolis, which mostly
provided a day's recreation for London citizens, but some visitors stayed
on and lodging-houses were erected at least at Barnet, Epsom, Hampstead
and Islington. These metropolitan spas declined as 'other ranks' and
undisciplined customers increasingly frequented them. There were also
ten new spas in Yorkshire, perhaps inspired by Harrogate, five within the
ambience of Bath, two potential rivals of Tunbridge Wells in Kent, and two
aping Buxton in Derbyshire. Of the other scattered ventures Astrop was
the most notable.[30]

The provision of local amenities, such as pump-rooms and assembly-
rooms, sometimes with specialized card-, dancing-, raffling- and music-
rooms, and also coffee-houses, libraries and reading-rooms, often enhanced by landscaped surroundings, now became commercially viable.
There were coffee-houses at Bath, Epsom, Scarborough and Tunbridge
Wells by 1725, bowling greens at Bath and also at Hampstead, Epsom and

Tunbridge Wells, which all had also several shops, some for luxury goods and souvenirs. Sadler's combination of a mineral well with his 'musick-house' in 1683 was so popular that other London spas put on concerts for their patrons: Lambeth and Richmond from 1696, Streatham and Hampstead by 1701, and Epsom by 1707. Tunbridge Wells had a company of musicians by 1697, as had Bath at least by 1704. Astrop had a music-room in 1694, Epsom in 1708 and Richmond by 1719 had theatres; the only other spa with so early a theatre was Bath, where a company played in a stable in 1694 but a theatre was built in 1705. As commercial competition increased more capital was needed to initiate new projects, and syndicates took over the well sites at Epsom and Hampstead. The provision of lodgings for visitors gave other opportunities to entrepreneurs and, es-pecially in a small rural spa, to humble local residents. The erection of lodging-houses and inns often preceded other amenities, and at Epsom and Tunbridge Wells attracted the investment of London capital.

Public and communal meals, especially breakfast, became a new feature of English social life at the larger London-based spas – Epsom, Hampstead, Islington, Richmond and Tunbridge Wells – where people gathered picnic fashion as at Astrop. Many such social facilities were provided in return for a fixed seasonal payment, a subscription, distinct from a charge for the use of baths and wells, although that too was often covered by advance funding; and so the notion of a subscription society was born. This type of forward pricing offered a more secure return on capital and was more universally applied as the nascent spas developed, and bolstered by this committed economic support they made a marked contribution to a more sophisticated and cultured English society in the eighteenth century.

Another aspect of the post-Restoration commercialization of spa life was the embryonic domestic trade in mineral waters operated largely from the metropolitan market. Of the sixty-five spas already mentioned the waters of nine were by 1713 being bottled and distributed, often by carrier and cart, to those unable to holiday at a spa. Sir John Newton of Bitton near Bristol had regular consignments of the local Hotwells water, usually two or three dozen bottles at a time, sent to him by carrier when he was staying in London from 1720 onwards.[31] All this spa activity in general created a great deal of new employment in the leisure industry.

8

Bath: The New Towns

When the Hanoverian George I came to the English throne in 1714 he was accustomed to drinking mineral waters, those of Pyrmont in the principality of Waldeck, and he found the more affluent of his new subjects journeying around England to take the domestic waters as an established habit. Some also drank imported Spa waters. By about 1710, of approximately sixty-five places where local mineral waters were used, the most substantial spas were Bath and Tunbridge Wells, followed by Astrop, Barnet, Buxton, the Clifton Hotwells, Epsom, Harrogate and Scarborough, and the small resorts encircling the capital accommodated the overflow of metropolitan social life.[1]

Spa creation was now stimulated by improvements in travel, especially the introduction of turnpike roads which made remote areas accessible. Before 1720 there was little turnpike activity far from the metropolis, but trust investment boomed in the mid-twenties and there was a spurt of spa promotion between 1740 and 1770. During the two most active decades, 1751–72, 389 Turnpike Acts were passed. Not all new spas were on a turnpike road, but the better highways helped to create a travel mentality and increasing numbers of people became adjusted to the notion of mobility. Personal travel in vehicles or on horseback by well-off families within their own county or region, or even beyond, grew as the use of horses spread and very many more became available. The more careful breeding of them for work led to a 'horse revolution' between 1680 and 1750 and the number of horses multiplied many times, as did stagecoaches, post-chaises and private coaches.[2]

The middle ranks of society became more mobile and thousands of people now moved about the country on holiday to view outstanding houses, historic monuments and remarkable features of the landscape, or to watering-places. As personal diaries show, many families or groups of friends travelled around from spa to spa: Nicholas Blundell's wife went to Wigan Spa and in 1714 was accompanied by her husband and another companion to Middleton's Bath at Stockhill and to Harrogate. In 1739 Richard Kay journeyed from Stockport to Buxton and Matlock in a party of six.[3] These spa-seeking travellers were often helped by the new roads at some stage of their journey, by the increasing number of bridges and signposts, and from 1740 by milestones along the main roads. After John Ogilby pioneered road maps in 1675 a series appeared to assist the traveller: including in 1719 John Senex's pocket-sized road-book *An Actual Survey of all the Principal Roads of England and Wales. . .* , and Thomas Gardner's hundred strip maps, *A Pocket Guide for the English Traveller.*[4]

The success of the Tudor and Stuart spas, several attracting a steady local trade and some outsiders, also led to an upsurge of resort activity; the few of ephemeral existence, like Wellingborough, being exceptions. A vogue for spa-going encouraged speculators to invest in converting a local spring of mineral water into a spa. Social fashion and the search for pleasant society amidst the stimulus of a fresh environment had much to do with the foundation of new spas. To quote Dr W. R. Clanny, writing in 1807:

> Some mineral waters have arrived at high celebrity very justly . . . but habit and fashion, assisted by an agreeable neighbourhood, have done much for their celebrity, and many wander a considerable distance from their homes to watering-places, who have mineral waters in their neighbourhood, which are equally, if not better, adapted to their complaints.[5]

But although they abounded in numbers, some rural spas had a limited life. Long-term success lay with the evolution of the urban spas, which often acquired the appendage of a residential new town. Under the challenge of the accelerating holiday market, improvements were made in old towns: existing inns were rebuilt or enlarged to include public rooms and more bedrooms, walls were wainscoted and windows sashed; imposing porches were added, and larger stables and coach-houses were built in the rear. But even when adapted these inns were not the most convenient abode for long-stay visitors to spas, who needed more space and privacy than the itinerant traveller. So as the spa industry boomed a new town was built adjoining the historic settlement of an urban spa to meet the unprecedented and specialized accommodation and convenience needs of the health-resort industry.

The main feature of these new towns was that they were often built in planned units with a layout for leisure and space for all kinds of social activities. Wide streets eased the flow of traffic, while broad pavements, 'walks' and private squares provided promenades for visitors to enjoy an 'airing' and the delights of leisured conversation, divorced from the bustle and noise of commerce in the old town. Pavements were sometimes raised above street level to protect pedestrians from the filth of passing traffic – examples may be found at Bath and at Clifton near the Hotwells. New inns, and later hotels, were built with ample dining-rooms, parlours, assembly-rooms, many more bedrooms, and broader passages and staircases, and in the rear large inn-yards with spacious coach-houses and stables. Detached mews – rows of stables and coach-houses with accommodation for grooms and ostlers above – were also discreetly erected behind the grander buildings. Places of public assembly and entertainment, with spacious approaches where coaches and chairmen could manoeuvre, had to be incorporated in these purpose-built new towns, and usually at least one church or chapel. Most of all, terraces of lodging-houses, often arranged in squares or crescents, were built, usually uniform in exterior design and interior layout; in these almost totally residential areas a few individual, free-standing houses were no longer sufficient in the rapidly growing urban spas. The commercial district – with that necessary adjunct of a new town, a well-stocked provisions market and shops – usually remained in the old settlement. The workers who served the visitors also lived in the alleys in the old town or on the less desirable fringes of the new town.

Such an old town later transformed was Bath, still the premier spa although its development had been handicapped by difficulties of travel, political troubles and lack of capital investment. The city was at such low financial ebb in 1700 that it lacked a goldsmith and the council suggested luring one there under offer of the freedom of the city.[6] Unlike some metropolitan spas Bath as yet provided few social amenities, but in the eighteenth century – as Hampstead and Islington, for example, acquired a licentious reputation and declined – fashionable society preferred to travel further afield to the provincial spas, especially to Bath. The more settled political scene after 1688 made a new Bath possible by giving greater security of property, now an acceptable basis of credit, and led to an infusion of outside capital – much of it, as at Epsom and Tunbridge Wells, from London, but also now from Bristol. Some of the enterprising immigrants who were attracted there formed an elite of entrepreneurs who contributed not a little to Bath's development.[7]

At the Hanoverian succession in 1714 Bath was suspect as a Tory and pro-Stuart city, but it was careful to return both a Whig and a Tory to Parliament until 1741. Although a loyal address was sent to George I in 1714, when Jacobites were active in the west the next year the city was occupied by troops and arrests were made. To acquire a better image, in 1716 Bath gave its freedom to the Whig William Pulteney, Secretary of War, and to the suppressor of the northern rebels, General Wade, who represented the city in Parliament from 1722 to 1748.[8] At the ball celebrating the king's birthday in 1715 many nobles wore purple and orange favours, the colours of Hanover and the Prince of Orange. Yet although a succession of princes and princesses came to Bath, no reigning Hanoverian monarch visited the city, which certainly courted the dynasty; the church bells were rung at every conceivable royal event, especially birth-days and marriages and the king's return to England from Hanover.[9] The court, then, no longer came to Bath, but minor royalty and the presence of the elite gave the city a unique social flavour second only to the metropolis, although it was now more sparing with honours for noble visitors. From 1697 a new class of honorary freemen was created for them, distinct from freemen in trade, and the recognition was bestowed less often.

More important than high-ranking patronage in encouraging investment in Bath's tourist industry was the development of its winter season, made possible by Bath's sheltered position, mild climate and proximity to the Mendip coal-fields, and providing a more consistent return of profits. Previously a summer place for visitors, although a few came in the winter and bathed sparingly, Bath changed its routine as it became also a drinking spa. Dr Peirce claimed that his patient Lord Stafford was among the earliest to drink the waters during the cold months, in 1668. Consequently in 1726, even in November, Bath was full of invalids, but Tunbridge Wells was 'dull and empty'. Samuel Derrick wrote in 1767 that now the two extended seasons totalled six months, in spring from late February to early June and in autumn from late September to mid-December. The first attracted the invalids, and the quest for pleasure lured two-thirds of the company to the second. In some seasons there were allegedly 8,000 visitors.[10]

Improved access to Bath, as to other spas, came with the spread of better roads, making the city less dependent on sledges and pack-horses for transport. The 1707 Act allowing the turnpiking of those immediately leading into Bath was one of the earliest, but Tunbridge Wells also had a Road Act in 1709. By 1743 all the 107 miles between the capital and Bath through Reading and Chippenham had been turnpiked.[11] To promote the tourist industry the local roads had to be improved and their use properly regulated, so in 1706 between £1,700 and £1,800 was subscribed to repair the road to Lansdown, and in November 1707 Jacob Smith, the town clerk, was sent to London at the cost of £42 to obtain the necessary Act. The need for the Bath Act for enlarging the highways, cleaning, paving and lighting the streets and regulating the chairmen was stated unequivocally: the city had become 'a place of very great resort' of people from all parts of the kingdom and foreign countries to bathe in and drink the waters.[12] Under the Act trustees responsible for short sections of all main roads into Bath could levy tolls for improvements, including 1*s.* for a stage or hackney coach, 6*d.* for a two-wheeled carriage and 1*d.* for horse-riders. Those leaving the city to take the air, a favourite recreation, paid a deposit, refundable if they returned the same day. By 1820 the annual income of the Bath Trust was £11,870, and it administered fifty-one miles of road and fifty-one gates.[13]

Under the 1707 Act surveyors were appointed to ensure that house-holders pitched and paved the streets before their houses and swept them three days a week. To augment public lighting some ratepayers had to provide candles or lanterns outside their houses from sunset to midnight; a visitor in 1766 admired the lamps' 'daylight' effect. Scavengers were to cart away rubbish, and hay and straw had to be removed from public places to a stable or yard within an hour of unloading. As Celia Fiennes remarked in 1698, Bath's narrow streets were 'no place for coaches', so sedan chairs were used to carry the 'better sort' on social visits and Bath chairs to take invalids to the baths. But the Bath chairmen exploited the visitors, so the Act limited their number from 1 May 1708 to sixty, subject to annual licensing and a fixed tariff of charges. Unauthorized chairmen could be fined 13*s.* 4*d.,* and those who used abusive language lost their licence.[14]

The impetus to improvement, making Bath more attractive to visitors, which began in the 1690s continued, especially from 1704 to 1707, which R. E. Neale sees as the first high point of corporate economic activity. A fence of palisades was erected on the town wall next to the Abbey Orchard to prevent people falling into the river below, a row of houses was com-pleted in the gravel walks, and a ladies' 'piss-house' was made near the Abbey Church. There are thirteen references to new building on corpora-tion property between 1704 and 1708.[15]

Yet the social facilities of Bath, with about 2,000 people in 335 house-holds and the seasonal influx of visitors, compared badly with those of the metropolitan spas, although by 1710 it had two small theatres and two coffee-houses, Benjoy's and Sheyler's. No special room existed for water-drinking, the baths were still uncovered, and the company had no large place of assembly.[16] The focus of social life was the Grove north-east of the Abbey and the adjoining gravel walks, where musicians performed each morning and afternoon. In 1730 the palisades between the Upper and Lower Walks were removed and the ground was sloped and made fit to walk on, and in 1732 young trees were planted to replace old ones.[17]

Another amusement was dancing in the town hall, which in 1718 was 'sashed and wainscoted'. The 2nd Duke of Beaufort (d. 1714) was said to have introduced Captain Webster (d. 1705) as the conductor of the amuse-ments in 1703, although at most ten couples came to a ball, for which gentlemen subscribed 10*s.* 6*d.* So began the evolution of a regulated social life, paid for by the participants, and of the office of master of ceremonies, from 1705 held by Webster's assistant, Richard Nash (Beau Nash). Nash arrived in 1704, drawn to Bath, like other immigrants, by the opportunities of its expanding leisure market. Much of the improvement of Bath society has been credited to him, although some dispute his reputation. A Welsh adventurer from London with a social flair, he may have experienced the social life of the metropolitan spas. The office of 'master of ceremonies' or 'master of the ceremonies' was never a civic appointment and at first carried no emoluments. Both Webster and Nash were probably chosen by consensus of the company who continued to elect the MC.[18]

In the year of Nash's arrival Dr William Oliver of Bath reiterated the advantages of drinking the waters at all seasons, and the corporation encouraged also by Dr Richard Bettenson, planned to build the first Pump Room. In 1705 Bettenson gave £100 towards a simple, one-storeyed building north of the King's Bath, reputedly designed by John Harvey and opened in 1706. It cost £400 in labour alone. Dr Bettenson was rewarded with the freedom of the city.[19] The physicians also pressed Nash to move the music-players from the Grove to the Cross Bath Pump Room. He imported seven more from London to raise the musical standard, and they were now remunerated from the ball subscriptions, but also from 29 May 1711 by the corporation, which paid them 10s. 9d. then, various sums for later services at special events, and by 1734–5 an annual salary of £4 4s., raised in April 1759 to £5 5s. From 1754 they were known as 'Thomas Baker's company', or the 'city music' or 'city waits'.[20]

An early investor in Bath's expanding leisure industry was George Trim, a wealthy shopkeeper in the Grove and a member of the corporation, who in 1705 erected a playhouse in the borough walls for £1,300 and, to improve access to his theatre, in 1707 leased a passage between Gascoign's Tower and the North Gate and built Trim Street. The other theatre, ignored by many historians, was in a stable by the Abbey Gate and part of the Abbey Estate of John Hall, who on 21 January 1709 granted a ninety-nine-year lease 'of the theatre or playhouse with all housing and building' for a rent of 10s. to John Woodman, a carpenter, Richard Griffeth, a musician, and James Atwood, a glazier. Woodman assigned his share to Dr Richard Bettenson.[21] So there were two theatres in Bath then.

Another immigrant entrepreneur was Thomas Harrison, a young London tradesman who, passing through Bath to Bristol fair, saw the opportunities for speculation, especially on the unbuilt Abbey Estate held by John Hall, grandson of the original owner. On Hall's death in April 1711 the estate was divided into forty-seven leaseholds with an annual income of £1,864 10s.; reversions brought in an additional £13,737. Thomas Harrison had acquired part of the Abbey Orchard and other important tenants were Richard Marchant, a tailor, who from 1709 held part of the Ham for ninety-nine years, Peirce (Pearse) à Court with the Abbey House and garden, Charles Swallow with the Prince's Lodgings or the 'Star Chamber' near the Abbey, and Mr Masters with more of the Abbey Orchard.[22]

The heiress of all this increasingly valuable land in 1711 was John Hall's 'natural' daughter Rachel, whose mother was the wife of Thomas Baynton of Little Chalfield, Wiltshire. On 20 May Rachel married William Pierrepont, Lord Kingston, son and heir of the Earl of Kingston, from 1715 1st Duke of Kingston (d. 1726), and she brought him this Bath property as her dowry. Her husband died young in 1713, and when Rachel, Countess of Kingston came of age on 24 March 1716 Thomas Baynton, her trustee and she signed more leases. Benjoy's Coffee-house by the bowling green was acquired for a fine of £500 for ninety-nine years by another speculator, Humphrey Thayer, a London druggist and commissioner of excise, who invested heavily in Bath property. Leases were renewed by William Benjoy (alias Jellicot) of two tenements near the bowling green and in 1717 by William Seager, an apothecary who held the Garden House near Abbey Green and was backed by Charles Axford, the Bath banker. In 1718 Dr Richard Bettenson leased Widow Player's former ruinous house in Abbey Green, which he relet to Ralph Allen, and he sublet a garden to John Wiltshire, a carpenter, and his brother William.[23]

After Baynton's death in 1719, the Countess Rachel signed other reversionary leases. In 1720 Thomas Harrison provided his daughters Mary Webb and Sarah Harrington, both married to clergymen, with property there, and by 1722 Humphrey Thayer had a further grip on the Kingston Estate with a ninety-nine-year lease of the Abbey Orchard for the lives of his daughter Elizabeth Knollys, her husband and another daughter, Jane. When the young Countess Rachel died in 1722 much of the estate was held by entrepreneurs, Harrison, Thayer and the Wiltshires, who played a formative part in the social life around the Grove. Her son and heir Evelyn, as the 2nd Duke of Kingston, inherited the Pierrepont Estates in 1726. He died at Bath in 1773.[24]

Thomas Harrison used part of his Abbey Orchard site to build the first assembly-rooms in Bath: the Lower Rooms, opened in 1708 – a modest building on the east side of Terrace Walk overlooking his gardens, where he laid out walks, although the corporation challenged his right to build a wall there. In 1716 Harrison's Walks were 'very pleasant' and, despite a subscription of 10s. 6d., 'full of company'. In 1720 Harrison employed William Killigrew, a mason, to add a large ballroom on the north of his premises. This ballroom, enlarged in 1749, was then ninety feet long, thirty-six broad and thirty-four high: 'the finest and most elegant room I ever saw', said Mr Penrose in 1766.[25]

In February 1720 John Scattergood found Bath 'much frequented by the polite part of the world', but as Harrison had a monopoly of assemblies, the company urged Nash to promote a second public room, which gave Humphrey Thayer an opportunity to invest in Bath's growing leisure industry. In 1728 he employed John Wood to design a range of superior buildings with an assembly-room opposite Harrison's Rooms. His ballroom, opened on 6 April 1730, was smaller than Harrison's, only eighty-six feet long, thirty broad and thirty high, and was leased by Dame Lindsey, a retired singer and gaming-house keeper. Bath now had two assembly-rooms, both on the Kingston Estate, and balls with a joint subscription were held at each alternately on Tuesday and Friday from 6 p.m. to 11 p.m., and there were other 'well-regulated' amusements. On Harrison's death in 1735 Dame Lindsey's sister, Mrs Elizabeth Hayes, took his rooms, but when the two women kept up prices the company appealed to Nash, who insisted on a reduction and that after Dame Lindsey's death in 1736 the rival rooms did not maintain an antisocial monopoly. Humphrey Thayer (d. 1737) passed the Lindsey tenancy to Mrs Ann Wiltshire (d. 1747) and her son Walter. A much less known 'concert-room near the Parade' was also open in the mid-eighteenth century.[26]

The enterprising Mrs Hayes, who married Francis, 2nd Lord Hawley, purchased the rights of Trim's ailing playhouse, demolished in 1738, and started up a theatre in cramped conditions under her ballroom. Tickets cost 2*s*. 6*d*., but expenses left only £13 10*s*. to divide among twelve players. On Lady Hawley's death in 1745 her tenancy of Harrison's Rooms passed to William Simpson, who built another theatre under the great ballroom which was added to his premises in 1749. In January 1754 Simpson's theatre was producing Shakespeare's *Othello,* while Wiltshire's Rooms specialized in concerts. A third theatre, the New Theatre (1723) in Kingsmead Street, was only about fifty feet long by twenty-five feet wide with a gallery. Simpson died in 1755 and Mrs Mary Webb (d. 1773), daughter of Thomas Harrison, 'the first improver of this city', had his rooms. In 1772 Cam Gyde, the tenant, paid the Kingston Estate £140 a year for 'the long-room and walk by the river' which Harrison had erected. Gyde sold off Simpson's furniture, including bedsteads, card- and dining-room tables, silver coffee-pots and a full-length painting of Richard Nash.[27]

The Pump Room and Harrison's Rooms had been built before the start of the new town in 1727, when Bath was already a potential gold mine for landowner and speculator. But the massive provision of lodging accommodation was delayed by the difficulties of bringing in building materials, and also food and coal, by wagon and pack-horse. Sledges were used to transport goods in the city, but the steep north and south roads, repaired at great expense, would soon deteriorate under heavy loads. Passage by the River Avon, the obvious solution, was possible only at the spring tide, so in December 1711 the city council renewed an old project to make the Avon navigable, prepared to fund it by mortgaging or selling the common fields. A Tory administration had come to power in 1710, so help was enlisted from the Tory Henry, 2nd Duke of Beaufort, who had entertained Queen Anne in 1702, and from other West Country aristocrats. The preamble to the necessary Act of 1712 spoke of the convenience of the new navigation 'to persons of quality and strangers (whose resort thither is the principal support of the said city of Bath)' and the advantages to trade and the poor, presumably by way of employment. Thirty proprietors, headed after 1714 nominally by the thirteen-year-old 3rd Duke of Beaufort who succeeded that year, were given authority to levy tolls to pay for the undertaking. They included the quarry-owners Ralph Allen and Milo Smith, the Bristol timber merchant John Hobbs, seventeen residents of Bath and three of Bristol. Dr Charles Bave represented the local physicians, who were never backward in promoting Bath's resort industry.[28]

By June 1726 the Duke of Chandos, who planned to build in Bath, had hopes of bringing goods from Cannons in Middlesex by water; Bath carriers could not handle such bulk and charged exorbitantly. Making the river navigable between Bath and Bristol cost about £12,000, but from the inaugural voyage of a barge on 15 December 1727 Bath was closely linked with the second largest town and port in England by barges carrying 40 to 120 tons of heavy goods, and a passenger-boat service. The fruits of the new navigation were the subsequent great expansion of building in Bath and the substantial revenues from the Avon tolls, sometimes over £1,200.[29]

So when John Wood the architect, another immigrant, was drawn to Bath in 1727 he found a city of increasing prosperity, as reflected in the mayor's salary; in 1685 £40, then nothing until 1712; by 1712–13 £12 18s., followed by dramatic rises: £21 10s. annually for 1713–32 to £76 10s. for each of the two years 1732–4. Then for 1735–9 it fell to £60, but from October 1742 rocketed to £100 until 1766, when it became £160 and two years later £210.[30] At Wood's arrival the prime need was for more lodging accommodation and shops, investment in which was encouraged by the lengthening of the season and the tendency for families to stay all the winter. When in 1725 he heard of the navigation scheme he tried to interest two Bath landowners, Dr Robert Gay, a London surgeon, and the Earl of Essex, who held the manor of Bathwick, in his building schemes. Gay had acquired some of the Walcot Estate by his marriage to Mary Saunders in 1699 and was the Tory member for Bath from 1720 to 1722, but the corporation disliked Wood's scheme of November 1726, and it was shelved. The Duke of Chandos also rejected Wood's plan, but in February 1727 he contracted with Wood for his own investment in superior lodging-houses. Other contemporary ventures were Thayer's buildings designed by Wood and the Kingsmead development abutting the New Quay on the Avon by Bristol men, John Hobbs and the architect John Strachan.[31]

Much more significantly, Wood was engaged in his Queen Square project, the first stage in the creation of a new town in the Palladian style of architecture outside the city walls, where leisured visitors and inhabitants could live and meet apart from the city commerce and the labouring poor. The neoclassical Palladian style was then becoming fashionable – other architects in Bath were adopting it and Palladian country villas like those of the Italian Veneto were becoming a feature of the English countryside; Clandon was started in 1715, Stourhead in 1720 and Holkham in 1734. Wood also knew of the layout of the great estates of West London and he had a vision of a revolution in urban architecture, a new town made up of neighbourhood units of terraced houses in neoclassical idiom. The argument of his book *The Origin of Building, or the Plagiarism of the Heathens Detected* (1741) was that although the Palladian style of harmony and proportion was derived from pagan art forms, it had divine origins. He hoped to create a replica of a Roman city in Bath, complete with forum, circus and gymnasium.[32] Although this ideal was not fully achieved, Bath became the dignified prototype for a spa town, its classical style of architecture later adopted at urban spas like Cheltenham, Harrogate and Leamington, at Regency Malvern, the Clifton Hotwells, the Tunbridge Wells Calverley Estate and the Droitwich original brine baths, and at such minor spas as Ashby-de-la-Zouch in Leicestershire, Dorton in Buckinghamshire and the two in Brighton.

The next boom periods in Bath, 1726–32 and 1753–8, owed much also to the acumen and energy of Ralph Allen, who arrived from Cornwall in 1710 and acquired a fortune from management of the crossroad and byway posts. The Avon navigation made his future; he became treasurer to the proprietors in 1724 and in 1725 a freeman and a member of the corporation. In 1726 he acquired land on Combe Down and later Hampton Down, where he invested in stone quarries for the extensive new building in Bath. Operational costs were reduced by bringing the stone down the slopes by tramways of wagons in timber tracks. Bath freestone of a light honey colour, durable and beautiful, was highly suitable for ornamental masonry and also provided paving-stones. Allen reduced its price by lowering the wage rates of his hundred workmen yet providing them with steadier work and houses on the worksite. But Bath was built at the expense of mining casualties; in 1755 alone collapses in stone quarries caused three deaths.[33]

Ralph Allen amassed a tycoon's fortune from the expansion of Bath. In 1741 he left his town house in Lilliput Avenue for a palatial home built as a commercial showpiece to advertise Bath building stone at Prior Park on the slopes of Widcombe, where he could survey the growing city below and entertain distinguished visitors: the Prince of Wales in 1750, William Pitt the Elder, David Garrick and Henry Fielding and others. Princess Amelia borrowed his house in 1752 while he obligingly stayed at Weymouth, and again in 1754 when the corporation paid for sentry boxes to be taken up there for her guards' use. Allen outlived his contemporaries Beau Nash and John Wood, who also served Bath's development. He died in 1764.[34]

The building of Bath proceeded in periods of activity interspersed with years of depression. In 1727 John Wood's arrival and the opening of the Avon navigation initiated another boom time, despite the harvest failure that year. The Duke of Chandos had found Bath lodgings inadequate for people of fashion in 1725, so in 1726 he invested in property by the Cross Bath and in 1727–30 he erected five superior lodging-houses around Chandos Court and equipped them with good furniture, partly from his homes, Chandos House and Cannons.[35]

John Wood was also the sole contractor in building the great residential Queen Square, on the north side of the walled city. Robert Gay's family now only too willingly leased Wood and his son, between 1728 and 1766, some forty acres on ninety-nine-year terms for an annual rent of £560, an eightfold increase in the value of their land. This square, then a novelty in a provincial town, involved much expense in planting, turfing and levelling, but it let in far more light and air than the contemporary Chandos Court or Beauford Square. Wood began his work in late 1729 and completed it in seven years with twenty-five houses. Gay Street, where Robert Gay had a house, led out to the north by 1734; the inhabitants of its thirty houses advertised for a smith to make their railings in 1755. So began the new or upper town of Bath, divorced from the commercial and social centre of the old town, and its splendid and uniform buildings standing starkly amidst the fields were admired by visitors and citizens. Expansion north-west-ward outside the walls proceeded: St Michael's Church, Walcot, was rebuilt in 1734 and Walcot Street was lengthened. But the city fathers wanted to prevent the drift of custom from the old town to the new, and by the 1739 Paving Act the chairmen's fares from the assembly-rooms to the new town were fixed at double the rate to any part of the old town.[36]

So economic sanctions partly determined that the next development should be on the Kingston Estate, near the assembly-rooms, the pump-room and the baths, where Wood planned a forum extending southwards into the Ham, and here he was treating with a private landowner, not an obstructive corporation. In May 1739 Thomas Cromp, the Duke of King-ston's agent, leased him the Lower Abbey Orchard to erect two lots of buildings with 'ways' thirty-five feet between them and houses on one side of a square. Tenants were to convey rainwater from their houses, pave a footway six feet wide in front and pitch the streets and open spaces. A grass plot in the middle of Abbey Green was left open for ever, and in the general tidying-up Benjoy's Coffee-house was demolished. Wood, again the contractor for an ambitious project, drained this swampy ground, and in 1740–9 the houses of the Grand Parade (later the North Parade) and the South Parade were raised on vaults and fronted on to broad terraces connected by Duke Street and Pierrepont Street, which were named after the landowner. Eight builders with a total capital investment of £72,300 were involved. Wood, Allen and Nash were not only concerned with the leisure market and private profit; they also supported the building on the site of the old playhouse of a general hospital (1738–42) for the nation's sick poor.[37]

The boom of the thirties was over. The terrible winter of 1740–1, depression in the building industry, and the Jacobite scare of 1745 all contributed to the lull when even the mayor was not paid in 1741 and the Avon tolls reached their lowest level in 1745–6. But revival came. The new parades on the Kingston Estate were completed in 1749 and William Galloway's Buildings there were erected between 1749 and 1750, a new theatre was built nearby in 1750 and the Pump Room was enlarged in 1750–1. There was a new peak of activity in 1755–9 and the crown of Wood's work in Bath, the King's Circus, was started in February 1754 on nine acres acquired from Thomas Garrard, who had married a Miss Gay. The Circus, based on the Colosseum in Rome inverted, north of Queen Square, was linked to it by Gay Street and consisted of thirty-three terrace houses with three streets of entry in a paved centre which gave ample room for coaches and sedan-chairs to manoeuvre. Wood, a highly articulate and intellectual architect, died in May, esteemed at Bath for his 'great genius' and indefatigable efforts. His *Description of Bath* – published in 1742, revised in 1749 and reissued in 1765 – is a main source (if used with discretion) for the contemporary history of Bath, where in 1742 he estimated that there were 1,362 houses and 12,000 people could be absorbed. His son John Wood the Younger extended the concept of the new town by completing the Circus (1754–8) with £61,650 capital and five main builders. Two terraces north of Broad Street, Prince's Buildings by Wood and Bladud's Buildings by Thomas Jelly, were also begun outside the city walls in 1754–5.[38]

Faced with the competition of the new town, the corporation embarked in about 1750–65 on cautious improvements. A committee including Richard Jones, city surveyor and clerk of the works to Ralph Allen, met at the Three Tuns and directed the enlargement of the Pump Room in 1751; one Priggs was paid £2 2s. for his plans and Allen received at least £116 12s., including £9 for balustrades. The new building had five bays fronted by Corinthian columns and topped with urns. A pavement was made across the walks in 1753 and thirty-six barge-loads of gravel were laid in the Grove. In 1754 the North and South Gates were pulled down to ease the flow of traffic and the 1362 bridge over the Avon was rebuilt, the masons there encouraged with free beer that hot August.[39] A new reservoir on Beechen Cliff in 1765 met increasing demands for domestic water, but 5s. compensation was paid to a workman hurt during its construction. Among other improvements from 1755 the corporation allowed the demolition of parts of the borough walls for building; their lessee Charles

Milsom erected Edgar's Buildings on the Town Acre in 1761 and with Daniel Milsom, started Bath's premier street, Milsom Street, in 1763.[40]

The Duke of Kingston was still building. From May 1754 he sold off the remaining tapestry hangings and furniture of the Abbey House and in March 1755 demolished it; in April 1762, with the carpenter Thomas Jelly and the mason Henry Fisher, he laid out three new streets, Abbey Street, Church Street and Kingston Street, to erect houses with vaults. But in view of the discovery of Roman foundations in 1755 all hot-water springs, stones, timber, building, mineral and treasure were excepted from his lease in 1765 of the Abbey House site to Fisher and Jelly for ninety-nine years. The annual rent of £75 remained, like others on the Kingston Estate, unchanged at least from 1774 to 1784. Also from 1762 the Duke of Kingston's Baths were built for the wealthy, who paid 5*s.* a time, and the house – with five private baths, elegant dressing-rooms and a waiting-room for servants – was opened in 1766.[41]

From about 1758 activity lessened; war may have reduced the availability of capital and Baltic timber. But already the new building amazed visitors; in 1750 Dr Richard Pococke described the 'great pile of buildings' in Abbey Orchard and the 'great additions' of 'very fine buildings' outside the walls, and he thought Bath a very good place of retreat from the capital, attracting more people every year. Another visitor in 1763 admired the regularity, neatness and magnificence of the new building.[42]

The influx of company led to a demand for more shops, and Bath became an outstanding consumer centre serving both normal and specialized luxury needs: for example, its floral tradition had begun by 1755 when the Association of Gentlemen Florists was formed. Thomas Loggon's 'Little Fanmaker' in Abbey Churchyard by 1754 supplied newspapers for 2*s.* 6*d.* a season, perfumery, snuff, writing materials and fans. From October 1755 Mrs Clementine Foord and Elizabeth Taylor provided newspapers, breakfasts and tea in a large room by the Pump Room, and John Graham in Green Street sold lawns, cambrics, velvets and lace. There were shops in the new buildings on the Kingston Estate by 1754; James and Peter Ferry, London silk-weavers, and Paulin, a mercer and milliner, were in the North Parade, and Pettingal's Warehouse for silks and laces was in Pierrepont Street. The post office was in Duke Street, and as well as Charles Morgan's Coffee-house in Wade's Passage, Richard Stephens, a wine merchant, ran the Parade Coffee-house (replacing Benjoy's) and supplied jellies at 4*d.* a glass, whipped syllabubs and an assortment of mineral waters.[43]

Under the pressure of an expanding economy the corporation tried to protect the freemen's monopoly, but in vain. By 1765 restrictions had lapsed into an economic free-for-all. Trading opportunities expanded as the national population increased and the rising incomes of the upper and middling ranks produced more people able to make a seasonal visit to Bath. Some became the new social phenomenon noted by Dr Pococke in 1750, leisured residents. In 1761 it was remarked that ' . . . a great number of gentlemen have taken houses and reside here all the year . . .'. The initiators of most building schemes were enterprising attorneys, traders and especially building craftsmen, some Bathonians, some immigrants, who, as at Cheltenham on the Pittville Estate later, held a building lease either as a group or singly, sublet to others, and pooled their skills and labour on a communal basis. They included the surgeon John Symons and the coach-builder Charles Spackman, involved in Camden Place and Lansdown Crescent respectively.[44]

The purchasers of Bath houses found that the facts of topography and a unique market rendered them more expensive than those in most provincial towns. The commons and the river blocked expansion, so building spread along the lower Bristol to London road and to the North, where the heights of Lansdown involved much levelling, terracing and underpinning by vaulting and retaining walls. Since a good standard was expected, quality materials and much ornamentation went into house-building and amenity value was important. The typical housing unit was the purpose-built, narrow-fronted terrace lodging-house with three floors, an attic and a cellar backed by a garden or a yard. Sites were often chosen for their view, and the majority of houses cost £500 to £1,500, considerably more than in an industrial town, with a few larger occasionally free-standing houses at £1,350 to £2,400 to meet individual requirements. This high-quality terrace-building became the prototype for domestic premises at spa towns such as Buxton, Cheltenham, Harrogate, Leamington, and the Clifton Hotwells. Between the 1720s and 1800 about 5,000 houses were erected at Bath, about seventy a year, generating a vast amount of employment, a demand for capital and specialists in financing developers and working builders, like Richard Marchant, the Duke of Chandos's financial agent, who died in 1773 worth about £30,000; and John Jeffreys, attorney-at-law and town clerk from 1776 to 1800, who lent out some £11,000. Money could be made by those with sums to invest in Bath's leisure industry. The King's Circus cost £61,650 and the Parades £72,300, and the building of Bath was achieved by using the capital savings of people of diverse standing.[45]

The corporation did not initiate building schemes but now more readily approved those of speculators on corporation property, for Bath still had rival spas; even the Duke of Chandos, with interests there, went to Tunbridge Wells in 1728. Nearer home Cheltenham attracted patrons: Mrs Jane Edwards of Redlands near Bristol went to Bath for the winters of 1736 and 1741, to Cheltenhan in 1742, to Bath in 1743, and to Cheltenham in August 1745 and on to Bath, where she returned the two following years.[46]

By the mid-1760s another local and national boom led to the building in 1765–9 of the huge York House Hotel – to the Younger Wood's designs and strategically placed on the outskirts of the city to catch the coaching trade from London, Bristol and the Midlands. Coaches using its ample stables no longer had to penetrate the cramped streets of the old town; it became the premier hotel and the hub of Bath's transport services, and was the first purpose-built hotel in a spa town.[47] The Circus, said Lady Mary Coke in 1766, was 'the noblest building in the country', but the Younger Wood now extended the new town by building the Royal Crescent of thirty houses in 1767–74. This novel idea in town planning, then the supreme achievement in the field of English urban architecture, is a large half-ellipse terrace fronted by double-storeyed Ionic columns. Sir Harbottle Grimston thought in 1769 that for beauty and elegance the finished Crescent would compete with any other building in Bath or elsewhere. This new building form subsequently became a characteristic of an urban spa; Buxton and Cheltenham and later Leamington Spa each acquired a crescent and six were erected at Clifton by about 1820. In c. 1767 Wood linked the Crescent and the Circus at Bath by Brock Street and it stood up sheer and massive amid the Crescent Fields, the former Barton Fields, which, under the terms of Sir Benet Garrard's lease, were 'never to be built on'. While the Crescent was echoing to the clangour of builders, the curving terrace of the Paragon went up where the London Road came in.[48]

The axis of Bath's social life was shifting from the old city to the upper town with its superior lodging-houses, capacious coaching-inn and fine outdoor promenades, but it still lacked a social centre, so earlier suggestions of a new assembly-room were revived. Captain William Wade, master of ceremonies from 1769 and well aware of the overcrowding in the lower town rooms, directed the building of the New Assembly Rooms behind the Circus. Seventy-two shareholders subscribed £23,000 and the licensee, Robert Hayward, opened the Upper Rooms with a Grand Ridotto on 30 September 1771. This substantial building by the Younger Wood contained an elegant ballroom 105 feet eight inches long, forty-two feet eight inches wide and forty-two feet six inches high – supported by forty Corinthian columns, lit by five magnificent chandeliers, and warmed by seven marble fireplaces – and it became the focus of Bath's social life. The assembly-room at York (1730–6) was the largest in England, but no other English spa had a long-room to compare; the New Assembly Room at Cheltenham (1816) was only eighty-seven feet long, lower and narrower.[49]

The Upper Rooms also had the attraction of a large tea-room with a musicians' gallery, and an octagonal card-room. Access roads were wide and chairs were directed to the main door, carriages to the front corridor, and waiting chairmen to the north colonnade. Faced by the competition of these Upper Rooms, Walter Wiltshire now abandoned the smaller of the two rooms in the city and Cam Gyde was allowed to make a new road from the New Market to his rooms, originally Harrison's, in 1782. But he had died by 1784, when the new tenant, James Heavens, had his rent reduced from £140 to £40. So the old town was challenged by the new, but it was not moribund. In 1765 the Ambury development of sixty houses was begun outside the South Gate by Thomas Jelly and others, and two were on the market by 1772.[50]

The city council now worked energetically to maintain Bath's reputation against the increasing competition of other spas, and to control these boom conditions through subcommittees: that for general repairs of corporation property from 1784 and the waterworks committee from 1787. Temporary committees covered particular problems: there was one for improving the baths and the Pump Room in 1785 and one for considering the enclosure of the Upper Commons in 1789. The corporation's debt rose from £3,110 to £26,400 between 1765 and 1783 as they borrowed heavily for improvement schemes. An Act of 1766 empowered them to clear property and widen streets, to open a way from the lower to the upper town, remove markets, improve the Pump Room and baths and erect another reservoir. Only Bath workmen – except those opposed to the Act – were to be employed in these building improvements. To achieve more unified control the responsibility for supervising the streets, the chairmen and the night watch was transferred from the parishes to twenty commissioners.[51]

Both a larger provisions market and a new town hall were prime needs. Samuel Derrick, the MC, had said that the old town hall built by Inigo Jones about a century before might well fall down and in 1767 it was clamped with iron to prevent spreading. By January 1769 the market was on a new site nearby, but conflicting local politics delayed the building of the adjacent new Guildhall, although the foundation stone had been laid with a peal of bells in 1768. Thomas Baldwin, city surveyor from 1776, masterminded the building of the handsome Guildhall, completed in 1779. Its banqueting-hall was adorned with Corinthian columns and splendid glass chandeliers; the lustres alone cost £266 10s. and settees and other furniture £106 9s. 6d.[52] The citizens of Bath held their balls there but refused its use to visitors, and in 1794 the corporation ruled that to maintain their dignity, future civic entertainments would be there and not in inns and taverns. It was a fitting scene for the reception of the Duke and Duchess of York in 1795 and the Prince of Wales in 1796.[53]

But the upper town was now the fashionable area, and three new chapels – Lady Huntingdon's Chapel, the Octagon Chapel and the Margaret Chapel – were built there, with rapidly growing congregations. In 1780 Lord Herbert wrote: 'I cannot bear to go into the Lower Town', and his mother, Lady Pembroke, wanted lodgings in the upper town, not lower than Bond Street. On arrival at York House her party might have to remain in the street for two hours, but she *hoped* to find mutton chops and a room with a fire awaiting her. Lodgings were preferred to 'the Hotel' (York House) because they were cheaper. In 1773 153 of the 235 lodging-houses were still in the old town against eighty-two in the new; the Orange Grove had twelve and the Kingston Estate fifty-two.[54] Edmund Rack saw the winter of 1779–80 busier than for three years, with no lodging free in the upper town. On 8 January 1780 a dress ball at Gyde's Rooms coincided with a ball and supper at York House for 400 and a ball at the new Guildhall with 300. Gay Street blazed with flambeaux behind the carriages going to the balls, and the many chairs impeded foot passengers. After the disruption of the American War (1778–83) and the Gordon Riots (1780), which affected Bath, a building revival set in about 1785, coinciding with a period of credit expansion in the provinces, and Bath had at least six banks: the Bath Bank, opened in 1768 by Hobhouse, Clutterbuck, Phillott and Lowder; Clement's bank, founded in 1783; the Bladud Bank (1790), the Bath City Bank (1789) and two others.[55]

During the 1788–93 boom period roughly 1,000 houses were built, including some high-density working-class housing. Expansion to the north was bounded by two notable crescents, Lansdown Crescent (1789–93) and Somerset Place (1790), and included the attractive St James's Square complex. Another crescent, Camden Place (1788–), was never finished, but prolonged expansion took place along the London Road. The ambitious Grosvenor Place project was begun to provide informal pleasure gardens, like those at some metropolitan spas, and to replace two at Bathwick now threatened by building operations. The Spring Gardens – approximately three acres – had opened in about 1735; subscribers in 1766 paid 2*s*. 6*d*., and by 1791 3*s*., to enjoy public breakfasts on Monday and Thursday and teas to the accompaniment of clarinets and horns, and a Thursday ball with illuminations, fireworks and entertainments. The Villa Gardens (from 1782) catered mainly for the lower ranks, and although Marrett, the proprietor, mounted a grand fête for the Duke of Clarence on 21 August 1789, his gardens closed in 1790 and the Spring Gardens also shut down, in 1796.[56]

John Eveleigh, the architect, and other speculators saw the opportunity to provide a grander place of recreation for Bath's visitors and they planned an immense building scheme: the Grosvenor Gardens with 143 houses and a large hotel on fourteen acres on the London Road. The scheme included a 'saloon with organ, mechanism and orchestra, hot and cold greenhouses, conservatories, . . . a labyrinth with merlin swings and caves, grotto, alcoves . . .' and other devices. The hotel was started in 1791, and by September 1792 there were garden tea parties on the site, but it was too low-lying and when the Bath City Bank failed in 1793, work halted. Despite an attempted revival the hotel and many houses remained unfinished even by 1819; finally the hotel became Grosvenor College and the gardens closed.[57]

Two more main undertakings, before war halted expansion everywhere in 1793, were Bath's other new town on the Bathwick or Pulteney Estate, its largest development by a single landowner, and the corporation's improvements under the Bath Improvement Act of 1789. William Pulteney, created 1st Earl of Bath in 1742 and owner of the manor of Bathwick from 1726, had no particular interest in the Bath waters, although he frequented Tunbridge Wells and went to Spa in 1763. But his second cousin and heiress Frances married Sir William Johnstone, who took the name Pulteney and in 1767 set about the exploitation of her lowland estate east of the River Avon.

The first essential in the creation of the Bathwick New Town was a bridge (built 1770–4) to link it to the city. Robert Adam's elegant Pulteney Bridge, the second bridge in Bath, had a superstructure of shops and cost almost £11,000. Pulteney's attempt to divert traffic from London through his property from Melksham was defeated by the corporation and turnpike interests. He had miscalculated the market and costs so, except for the new gaol, no new building began until 1788 after he had obtained three Acts of Parliament and capital of about £83,535. Thomas Baldwin, the city surveyor, was heavily involved and planned the layout for 5,000 houses. Laura Place, an octagon of 'superb mansions', was named after Sir William's daughter, Henrietta Laura, who inherited the estate in 1782, and the majestic Great Pulteney Street, Henrietta Street and other streets were completed. The Bathwick New Town was a superior residential development, its superbly furnished houses inhabited by the opulent and distinguished and its shopping precincts limited to Argyle Street and Pulteney Bridge.[58]

Baldwin's original plan of 1791, approved by Miss Pulteney, had included a social centre with extensive pleasure gardens, but the financial collapse of 1793 ruined him. So in 1794 the commission for 'the Vauxhall of Bath', the Sydney Gardens, went to architect Charles Harcourt Masters from backers who included Marrett of the late Villa Gardens. The tenant of these incomparable gardens was James Gale, a haberdasher, who opened them in May 1795. The visitors' delights included groves, pleasant vistas, serpentine walks, waterfalls, pavilions, two elegant cast-iron bridges and a sham castle; and the Kennet and Avon Canal cut through in 1810. In these gardens in the summer subscribers could enjoy public breakfasts, promenades, illuminations and music for 7s. 6d. a head or 5s. each member of the family. On the four or five gala nights which drew in massive custom – 3,000 to 4,000 people – 5,000 lamps were lit. The gardens were a powerful conterattraction to the assembly-rooms.[59]

Bath was a magnet second only to the metropolis for those seeking pleasure, fortune and fashion. 'Bath', said Lord Herbert in 1784, 'I think a very proper preparation for the London world . . .' So the city council were spurred to further action to improve the old town: still mainly confined by walls, with few entrances and congested streets and lanes. Under the 1766 Clearance Act the Pump Room had already been enlarged and the King's and Queen's Baths improved, but now Dr John Symons campaigned for better bathing facilities at the Hot Bath. A house purchased in 1772 became the pump-house for its springs, in 1773 a committee was appointed to supervise the new Hot Baths, and in 1776–8 the Younger Wood built a single-storeyed house with dressing-rooms and small, private plunge-baths around the octagonal central bath, with a free mineral-water pump for non-subscribers. New baths were being planned by a committee for the Cross Bath in 1777. Dr Symons, who managed these baths, was in 1781 remunerated with 100 guineas, but he feared that private developers would ruin the springs and he urged Thomas Baldwin to promote an ambitious scheme for the improvement of the centre of Bath under the aegis of the committee for improving the baths and the Pump Room. From 1783 Baldwin was deputy chamberlain; in 1784 he built an annexe of water-closets to the Pump Room and also rebuilt, in neoclassical style, the Cross Bath, which John Palmer enlarged in 1797–8.[60] Next, in 1786, he built the colonnade on the north of the Pump Room as a barrier to coaches and to give chair-carriers and pedestrians more room to manoeuvre. In 1788–9 he erected a pavilion over the King's Bath spring and a new, compact, elitist arrangement of baths and dressing-rooms round a top-lit rotunda, with access to the King's and Queen's Baths.[61]

But more drastic action was needed to restore the dilapidated town centre and to retain Bath's health-resort trade, and despite a corporate debt of £26,400 by 1783 the city council embarked, from 1785, on a massive improvement plan. In 1788 Baldwin produced his scheme for the baths and Pump Room, the most grandiose project to date, and the committee scrutinizing it met every evening in the Guildhall. The total estimated cost of the improvements was £547,163 (Baldwin's plans alone ran to £47,163), but in March they decided to proceed. With help from Prime Minister William Pitt – a freeman of Bath from 1784 – and the city recorder, Lord Camden, a long overdue reform, the Bath Improvement Act of 1789, went through. Responsibility for its implementation rested with an oligarchic commission of the corporation, the two Members of Parliament, and twenty nominated property-owners with a stake in Bath's continued prosperity, including Sir William Pulteney, John Wiltshire and Jacob Mogg, the owner of several Mendip coalfields.[62]

The commissioners cleared decaying buildings and built five new streets: Union Street to link the upper and lower towns and Nash Street, Hot Bath Street and Beau Street to give better access to the Hot and Cross

Baths. Twenty years before Samuel Derrick had thought the Pump Room too small, too hot in summer and too cold in winter, and its steps inconvenient for invalids. From 1789 it was rebuilt as the impressive Great Pump Room, but during this disruption custom, not surprisingly, declined and its revenue was insufficient to pay the sergeants of the baths. The commissioners initially borrowed £25,000 and resold improved property, but the burden of the improvements fell on the visitors by substantial tolls on carriages and horses on the turnpike roads of the Bath Trust – except loaded wagons, carts and horses coming to market. Work was delayed by Baldwin's dismissal in July 1792 and the depression of 1793, and the commissioners had to find another £12,500 to finish it in 1799, with fresh plans from John Palmer.[63] At the completion of this massive improvement programme Bath had facilities for taking the waters unrivalled by any other English spa, as well as outstanding means of commercialized pleasure and recreation.

Another preoccupation of the Bath corporation was to retain the remaining common lands, the 106-acre West Field of the old Barton Farm, held by them on trust for the freemen, who accused them of taking more than £700 a year from the profits. With the pressure for building space this land was now of great potential value, so enclosure was suggested in 1787 and in 1789 the 117 freemen, encouraged by builders, challenged the corporation's refusal of building leases there, claiming that between £7,000 and £8,000 could be made, for it contained a limestone quarry and a vein of gravel. Turnpike officials and others had taken away loads of stone.[64] The corporation, led by mayor Leonard Coward, stood firm that the commons must never be built on and eventually, in 1804, they were relet to William Vowles for seven years at £400. But in 1806 demands for building leases or garden ground were raised again, and in 1812 the trustees allowed the Walcot surveyor of the highways to open a stone quarry for 200 guineas an acre. When Benjamin Vowles took the lease in 1818 the rent was £500.[65]

In 1791 the cry went up that Bath was overbuilt; but over 2,000 more houses were planned for and the city was a 'rapidly-improving place' with a 'rage for building'. When war brought financial collapse in 1793, building was dramatically halted; in 1801 Warner described 'the huge piles of unfinished houses' covering part of King's Mead fields and along the London road. By 1795 property values had fallen, and builders had little encouragement to start again.[66] In the eighteenth century, capital investment of over three million pounds had gone into the building of Bath – now, with nearly 33,000 people and about 3,652 rateable houses, one of the largest towns in the country. The population increase was most acute in the parish of Walcot; from 160–180 before 1700 to over 17,500 by 1801. A complete list of Bath's lodging-houses would, it was claimed, fill a directory, and every house not tenanted by the nobility and gentry was one, but there were cheaper ranges of high-density housing for the mass of labouring people, especially in the Snow Hill area of Walcot from the 1790s, and in Holloway, where in 1772 two tenements to let at £8 each annually, about one-eighth of the average rent of the best houses, had plenty of water, so were 'convenient for a woman who takes in washing'.[67]

Bath's two new towns, like those of other urban spas, were residential and originally had few shops. Even Milsom Street, later a renowned shopping centre, was originally built as lodging-houses. Unlike other expanding urban resorts, Bath as yet had no subsidiary spa centres with drinking-pumps or baths, except at Lyncombe. The only place for taking mineral waters in Bath was in the traditional centre of the city, and the new Bath was not universally admired. The stark barrenness of the buildings was 'disgusting' and 'inhospitable' in 1799 to one who preferred the old city; they were too detached and exposed to appear 'commodious and comfortable' and the proprietors should soften the effect with trees and bushes. But bookseller William Meyler, a loyal Bathonian, surveyed it all in 1813 with pride. The green fields and hills where he had played in his youth had been occupied by 'stately and well-established edifices', and what had been suburbs was now the heart of the city. He admired the spirit of the builders and the immense wealth employed in such magnificent works. Despite claims that Bath was overbuilt and builders would be ruined, houses in anything like eligible situations were purchased as soon as they were erected.[68] By then the building revival had begun.

9

Bath: The Regulated Society and the Leisure Industry

The evolution of a new kind of society at Bath in this incomparable architectural setting should be seen in the context of the contemporary commercialization of leisure, particularly from 1690, which, as J. H. Plumb has written, tapped the increasing affluence of the British people. The social signs of this wealth – the increased consumption of food, expenditure on houses, the preoccupation with fashion and the boom in books, music, entertainment and holidays – were all especially reflected in the rapid growth of leisure places, the spas, which borrowed ideas from the capital. London had over 500 coffee-houses by the early eighteenth century, but they were to be found also at Bath, Epsom, Scarborough and Tunbridge Wells.[1] The theatre, music, horse-racing and dancing all underwent dramatic developments from 1670 to 1770, stimulated by a more sophisticated exploitation of leisure which concentrated many activities in country towns.

There had been no provincial theatres, but within this century every town of any pretension acquired a purpose-built theatre and a regular company, often supplemented by London actors. Public concert-halls became established in the early eighteenth century, as in the metropolitan spas, and by 1722 112 cities and towns held race meetings. Private houses were generally too small for even the private theatres, orchestras and concerts of the prosperous gentry and the new leisured middle ranks, so subscription assembly-rooms were established in market towns where the local social elite could meet for balls, music, improving lectures and dramatic performances. Both Shepton Mallet and Frome in Somerset had assemblies by 1758 and they had emerged in at least ten Norfolk towns by 1776.[2] Assembly-rooms marked a transitional stage between private and fully public entertainment; the subscription was kept high to exclude traders and minor shopkeepers.

Important agencies of this social change were the increasing numbers of newspapers spreading publicity about new communal facilities, and newsrooms and libraries which fed the desire for self-improvement and spurred cultural advance. In the 1690s the first two London non-official newspapers appeared – the *Post Boy* and the *Post Man* – and the first London daily newspaper, the *Daily Courant,* in 1702. By 1712 twenty weekly single-leaf newspapers were being published in London. There were no country newspapers in 1700, but by the end of 1760 130 had appeared and the local ones helped to publicize the neighbouring spas. Coffee-houses and taverns kept racks of London and local newspapers and pamphlets. Circulating libraries were established in London and the provinces by 1720 and by 1750 were to be found in 119 towns; there were also some private-subscription book clubs.[3] Stimulated by this social activity, people became more competitive, even in their pleasures, and social emulation led to increasing consumption and expenditure and encouraged the entrepreneur to exploit and extend his market. Nowhere were these tendencies more marked than in the spas.

Princess Amelia's visit to Bath in April 1728 was of particular significance in encouraging investment there and the maintenance of Bath's social status. This event, the first occasion when Hanoverian royalty patronized the city, was celebrated with gusto. The princess sailed on the new Avon navigation and was awarded a mayoral reception, a firework display and the other usual gestures to royalty. When she returned in 1734 with her brother-in-law the Prince of Orange, the Grove, where Beau Nash erected an obelisk in his honour, was renamed the Orange Grove or Square. Special homage was paid to Frederick, Prince of Wales, and his wife in 1738: he merited another obelisk, in Queen Square, and the freedom of the city, and music for his dinner party in the town hall cost £9 9s. Royal visitors and some of their households normally received the freedom of the city, as did Edward, 10th Duke of York in 1761; Frederick, 11th Duke of York, in 1795; and the Prince of Wales, later George IV, in 1796.[4]

But no Hanoverian sovereign came to Bath, perhaps because of its tradition of Stuart loyalty. Despite extravagant celebrations of George III's coronation in 1761, in 1788, to the city's chagrin, he ignored it and went to Cheltenham to drink the waters. Bath reacted promptly: by unanimous vote of the city council on 1 August a deputation of the mayor and others was sent to Cheltenham, where on 5 August they invited the king to Bath. He replied civilly that he hoped to come soon but failed to do so, although in 1789 he visited Lord Weymouth, a lord of the bedchamber, at Longleat only twenty miles away. Lady Weymouth had accompanied the royal party to Cheltenham and her husband, a personal friend of the king, was now created the 1st Marquess of Bath. Aristocratic patronage still mattered, and Bath swiftly sought his support; in 1790 it made his heir Thomas, now

Viscount Weymouth, one of its Members of Parliament, and after his promotion to the Lords in 1796 replaced him with his brother Lord John Thynne in 1802.[5]

Although the court failed to come, the aristocracy still favoured Bath. The 'local' dukes, Beaufort, Kingston and Somerset, often came with their wives, but some peers died there – the 3rd Duke of Beaufort in 1739 and the 2nd Duke of Kingston—and the corpses of four successive Earls of Suffolk were carried away for burial. In 1766 Lord and Lady Abergavenny left their local spa, Tunbridge Wells, and gathered at Bath with the Earls of Northumberland and Chesterfield and their countesses and the 5th Duke of Beaufort and his wife. The Duke and Duchess of Devonshire came in 1782 and subsequently, comparing Bath with their local spa, Buxton. To many people of standing the possession of a Bath house was a social necessity. Pitt the Elder, a Member of Parliament for Bath from 1757 to 1766, built one for himself in the Circus, and many gentry lived at Bath permanently.[6] Famed throughout Europe as the leading English spa, Bath remained the haunt of minor royalty, the aristocracy and a number of foreign visitors. One evening in December 1779 nearly twenty dukes and lords and Count Manteufel from Saxony were in the Pump Room. A brilliant assembly of nearly sixty nobles, several distinguished foreigners and 800 ladies and gentlemen attended a concert at the New Rooms that month, the elegant scene enhanced by 480 wax candles and a blaze of jewels.[7]

Bath society was wide-ranging: the gentry came in their hundreds, as did the clergy. Bishop Sherlock of Salisbury was there in 1746, the primate of Ireland in 1784, but the bishop of Durham, past all hope of recovery, died there in 1752, as did the bishops of Worcester, Lincoln and Cork between 1774 and 1785. The deans of Gloucester and York sported in the King's Bath for three weeks in 1766, but those of Norwich and Durham died at Bath, in 1765 and 1766 respectively. A coterie of Wiltshire clergy left their rural solitude for Bath in 1783, including the rector of Bishopstrow, who escaped the dampness of local water-meadows in winter to cure his gout, and the vicar of Longbridge Deverill, who had a winter residence there.[8]

Serving officers on leave or half pay joined most gatherings at Bath, several used the King's Bath in 1775, and an increasing proportion of professional men, especially physicians, surgeons and attorneys, made a profitable living there. Members of Parliament were drawn in in the orbit of the rich and powerful. Pitt, now Lord Chatham, had a political 'congress' there in 1766 with the Duke of Bedford. Charles Edwin of Clearwell, Gloucestershire, the member for Glamorgan, and his family stayed for three weeks from mid-April 1783, in December 1784 and from mid-January 1793 for one month. Equally at home in Bath was a Gloucestershire farmer on a second visit in 1784, for all the company mixed freely, observing little pomp and ceremony, and a projected royal visit was something to talk about back in the Forest of Dean for the rest of his life. His family had 'a most excellent house, a good cook, and a hostess who keeps us like fighting cocks', and if he forsook farming he would live in Bath.[9]

Other visitors were more discriminating, or more sour. Sir William Jones, orientalist, eschewed 'the follies of the place' in 1777 '. . .knowing that one bath or assembly is as like another, as a fig is like a fig', and he preferred riding in the countryside to walking backwards and forwards on the parades. Bath also lured colonials from the West Indies who sometimes made block bookings for 100–150 people, with servants, horses and black slave attendants. The Pulteneys with their extensive West Indian estates, may have developed Bathwick for this market.[10] In the wake of all this company came a multitude of gamesters, tricksters, prostitutes and other hangers-on, and also servants and labouring people, creating social tensions.

The elite visitors imported London standards of courteous and elegant behaviour, but Bath society was perhaps less stratified than some provincial groups and observed little formality beyond the essential rules of politeness. The company mixed on equal terms in the rooms – except the local tradespeople who, however respectable, were excluded – and social life was very public; few conventions barred the making of new acquaintances or the exchange of invitations and visits, unlike Epsom and Tunbridge Wells, where the company met only on the walks. The mixed society was not congenial to all, and overcrowding exacerbated the incompatibilities. Lady Irwin wrote petulantly about 1729 that '. . .the company increases daily, but . . . they are people that nobody wants', and the Earl of Orrery said sourly in November 1731 that the company consisted of '. . .those who neither know or are known' in 'this censorious place' riddled by gossip. Harrison's Rooms were always too full to be agreeable, with not a card-table to spare.[11]

Such an explosive growth of mixed company could have been unmanageable had Bath not been a corporate city with the authority to enact bylaws. The maintenance of decorum was also assisted by the evolution of the office of master of ceremonies, which originated at Bath or at Epsom, where there was a 'governor', for as a new type of communal life emerged around baths and wells the need for a social ritual and an acknowledged leader was felt at the larger spas. The notion of an MC, an officer who determined and supervised acceptable forms of social behaviour on public occasions, was not new: in royal courts he was an official of high rank. As we have seen, the masses invading Bath during Queen Anne's visits had made some social discipline necessary under Captain Webster, and the concept of the office rested on both the persuasive qualities of the holder and on public assent. Richard Nash – who held the post for almost fifty years, 1705–61 – had invested it with importance by 1716, when a visitor observed that Nash was the man who mattered, and the life and soul of their diversions. By then the city council, in recognition of his services to Bath, had made him a freeman. Another visitor in 1723 acknowledged his great contribution to Bath society; although of low birth he had a good manner, dressed well and directed all their pleasure parties. Without 'that monarch Nash' there was no play, assembly or ball, and no one seemed to know what to do in his absence.[12]

His knowledge of metropolitan life made Bath society's lack of decorum more obvious to Nash. The prime need was to ensure that polite company from London was not affronted by the local gentry's uncouth manners in public assemblies, and to end the rule of the well-dressed roughs and adventurers in the streets. Under the aegis of Nash, backed by the city council, the company at Bath became a regulated society to a degree that may seem elementary today but was unparalleled in contemporary secular life except at court, in collegiate societies, trading companies and the declining guilds. The interests of the visitors were paramount, so all activities susceptible to organization were regulated for their protection. Rules were drawn up for the Pump Room, the assembly-rooms (at least by 1742), the baths and the conduct of the chairmen, and the daily routine became so institutionalized that little time remained for individual activity.

A ritualized leisure industry developed, its financial risks underwritten by advance payments – that is, subscriptions for assemblies, balls, concerts, public breakfasts, libraries, the use of newspapers in coffee-houses, the town band and other activities. Bath society became a subscription society, and the ritual and regulation began on arrival. Nobles were greeted by a peal of the Abbey bells, and lesser people by waits serenading them in their lodgings, both under a fixed tariff. Newcomers were expected to sign a book in the Assembly Rooms, and this was a useful guide for Nash, who paid them a formal call, and for tradesmen. Duelling became controlled and Bath was soon dubbed 'the swordless city'. Nash, no moralist, did not attempt to suppress the endemic gambling, nor the prostitutes and their managers drawn in from London and Bristol brothels, but in 1723 Bath was reputed to have fewer common women than Tunbridge Wells or Epsom, and to be a place of universal sobriety where drunkenness was scandalous.[13]

Gambling was a minor industry too entrenched to be killed in 'this place of hazard', and Bath city council were half-hearted in abolishing such a popular amusement, despite laws of 1699, 1711–12 and 1728 against gaming. Walter Wiltshire, who ran one of the rooms, became a freeman in 1742 and a member of the council in 1746.[14] Nash and the gamesters evaded the law with three new games, especially E and O, or Evens and Odds, a form of roulette invented by one Cook and played at Tunbridge Wells. Nash introduced it at Bath and took a cut of the profits in the rooms, but the proprietors in both resorts cheated him, and he foolishly sued two of them, Joye or Joyce at Tunbridge Wells, and at Bath Wiltshire was fined £500. Sir Edmund Isham, at Bath in January 1749, found that 'Lord Chief Justice Hills plays at EO continually as most everybody does and excessive high', but a new law that year banned all the games of chance popular at Bath, such as hazard, basset, ace of hearts and faro (Pharoah). Operators were to be fined £200, and even watchers could be prosecuted. In 1750 – when all games with numbers, including lotteries, were made illegal – gaming-houses in Bath were closed and the justices destroyed a number of gaming-tables: the city chamberlain paid 1s. 'for faggots to burn Little Dicks OE table'. In 1755 all play except cards was declared illegal, but in general whist came in for public play and noblemen gambled in privacy.[15]

Beau Nash's influence extended far beyond Bath; his pattern of social organization became a blueprint for other resorts, and by 1735 Tunbridge Wells had also enlisted his services. The two Bath seasons of March to June and September to December freed him in July and August for the Tunbridge high season, but the dual obligation was a strain. He was taken ill at the Wells in 1752 and his return to Bath was anxiously awaited. On 30 September 1754 the *Bath Journal,* to allay another crisis, forecast his imminent return from Tunbridge Wells, and he headed the next list of arrivals.[16] Nash's reputation and lifestyle were, however, undermined by the attacks on gaming, and to assist the old man a subscription was opened for his book, *The History of Bath and Tunbridge Wells for these last Forty Years,* although few believed that it existed. In acknowledgement of his contribution to Bath life the corporation in January 1755 paid £52 10s. for twenty-five copies and gave him an annual pension of £10 from February 1760, disguised as payment for five books. When he died, aged sixty-seven, in 1761 the council, urged by the Earl of Chesterfield, voted him a 'state' funeral in the Abbey, costing at most fifty guineas. Prominent in the long procession of mourners were Wiltshire, forgetting past scores, and Simpson II, the proprietors of the rooms. Nash's portrait by William Hoare was also hung in the town hall; the council's payment of £107 5s. to Hoare in 1767 presumably covered more than this picture.[17]

Nash's achievements in improving the quality of Bath society were widely recognized. An anonymous writer in *Characters at the Hot Well* hailed him as King at Bath, Prince at the Hot Wells, Duke of Tunbridge, Earl of Scarborough, and Lord of Buxton and St Winifred's Well. The commercial and social value of having an MC was obvious, the office became increasingly professionalized, and Bath became a nursery of potential MCs, experience there being a recommendation for similar posts in other resorts. Scarborough imported Charles Jones, Nash's assistant, in 1740, as the MC appointed by 'several persons of distinction'. After Nash's death the office at Bath was regularized to make the MC financially independent of gaming. He was elected by ladies and gentlemen who subscribed one guinea to the balls and he received the proceeds of two benefit balls, in spring and winter, and subscriptions from a book opened for him in the rooms, a method of remuneration copied at other spa towns. The post was not only profitable (the Bath MC in 1777 made about £1,500 a year), it was prestigious and was competed for with intensity, but its holder now had less independence and authority than Nash.

His immediate, brief successor at both Bath and Tunbridge Wells was his assistant Collett, then from 1763–9 Samuel Derrick, 'an insignificant puppy' of literary pretensions who was better received at Bath than at Tunbridge Wells, which took umbrage when he attempted to become MC at Brighton. In 1766 Derrick visited Liverpool, where a small spa was called Mount Sion in imitation of Tunbridge Wells. His *Letters from Liverpool . . .* (1767) contain a useful account of contemporary Bath. Although dangerously ill at Tunbridge in 1766, he arrived home in Bradley's Buildings, Bath, in mid-September and cleared about £150 of his benefits in May 1767. He died in 1769 and was buried at Bath.

Derrick's deputy Major William Brereton, tall, manly and elegant, was promptly elected by many Bathonians, including some Irishmen. But an unseemly squabble arose. The Bristol Hotwells now had an MC, Mr. Plomer, whose friends there attempted to bring him to Bath, and a protracted schism ensued during which Charles Jones, a gambler, (possibly the Charles Jones of Scarborough), intervened. The mayor and his officers were called in, the Riot Act was read three times, and eventually Captain William Wade, the illegitimate son of General Wade, Bath's benefactor and Member of Parliament from 1722 to 1748, was appointed. Brereton and Plomer withdrew, each compensated with half the surplus subscriptions and a benefit ball, and Mrs Brereton had an annual ball on guarantee of £200 from Wade. Tunbridge Wells now made a separate arrangement.[19]

Captain Wade's reign opened on 18 April 1769 with a splendid ball when he wore a badge of office, a medallion like that of the court master of ceremonies, presented by the company, and although he doubled as MC at Brighton from around 1770 he restored harmony at Bath. During his rule the Upper Rooms were opened in 1771 and Gyde's Lower Rooms were smartened up. He presided at both, but they were competing interests, so in 1774 the company set up a committee of users – nobility and gentry – to divide the market between the two sets of rooms. The proprietors of the New Rooms rejected this arrangement to safeguard their £23,000 investment, and opened their rooms every evening except Friday and alternate

Sundays. Although Wade tried to manage both rooms his resignation was forced in July 1777, but until his death in 1809 he held the post at Brighton, where his widow died in 1812.

The election at Bath in 1777 attracted seven candidates including Simon Moreau, a Bath socialite, who pledged a third of his remuneration to the general hospital if chosen; but he was rejected and became the first MC at Cheltenham. Finally the office was divided between the ever-optimistic William Brereton and William Dawson, the Southampton MC, so settling controversy over the relative use of the rooms; from October Brereton officiated at the Lower Rooms while Dawson had the senior position at the Upper Rooms.[20] But the post was a vulnerable one: Dawson had a dispute with the bishop of Worcester's lady about her wearing a hat at a dress ball, and the able Brereton retired after criticism in 1780 and died at Holt in Wiltshire, aged ninety, in 1813.[21] Richard Tyson of Tunbridge Wells replaced him in the Lower Rooms and so renewed the link between the two spas.

Tyson held the two masterships, at Tunbridge Wells alternating with Bath, from 1780 to 1801. He was at the Lower Rooms, Bath, from 1780–1785, then on Dawson's retirement in 1785 he was promoted to the Upper Rooms, where he remained until he too retired when the winter season began in 1805. The 'polite, worthy and well-conducted' Tyson had guided social events during the major expansion at Bath, four years longer than at Tunbridge, where he returned briefly in 1817. James King, who replaced Tyson at the Bath Lower Rooms in 1785, was promoted to the Upper Rooms on his withdrawal in 1805. King had witnessed Tyson's taxing assignment between Bath and Tunbridge – they headed the Bath list of arrivals on 20 October 1800 – but this link finished when in 1801 King succeeded Simon Moreau at the much nearer Cheltenham, now the second spa. Again the double post was possible because Cheltenham, unlike Bath, had a summer season. When King died in 1816 this dual appointment also ended; Bath and Cheltenham went their separate ways. Bath contestants included H. Madden, an ex-Royal Marine officer, eventually the MC at Tunbridge in 1825; and James Heaviside, the MC at Leamington Spa. Heaviside had taken charge of the Lower Rooms in 1815 but in 1817 – when transferred to the Upper Rooms at Bath, the ultimate promotion – was made to drop the Leamington connection.[22]

Apart from the MCs, other means of social control lay with the city council, who were responsible for the supervision of the inhabitants as well as meeting the new specialized demands of the visitors, which multiplied as Bath's tourist industry expanded. It was to the commercial interest of the city to improve the condition of the streets, and from 1755 men inspected them daily and scavengers' carts went round three times a week.

Lighting had to be sufficient to encourage people to patronize evening entertainments, and in March the *Bath Journal* urged inhabitants to pay up for street lighting:

> . . . the corporation of this city have set so great a pattern . . . in rendering avenues and other places more agreeable, in order to accommodate the nobility and gentry who resort here . . .

So an Act of 1757 allowed rates for lamps and scavenging to be levied within the city. Surveyors were to supervise the erection of lamps to burn from nightfall to daybreak from 1 September to 31 May. By 1801 960 lamps glowed in the city.[23] The Act also required all city property-owners to provide drainpipes to prevent rainwater from rooftops from soaking pedestrians. Domestic water supplies were still a civic problem, so in 1790 another reservoir of far greater capacity was built to supplement that of 1765 at Beechen Cliff, and in 1791 £749 was spent in repairing the waterworks on Beacon Hill. By 1792 a separate committee managed the corporation waterworks and fixed the water rate, a subject of controversy. In 1799 yet another reservoir was made on the High Common.[24]

Traffic congestion was tackled under the 1766 Improvement Act which prohibited narrow-wheel wagons with more than four horses, or carts with more than three, in the streets, where carriages full of stone and building materials were allowed to stop only briefly. Other improvements included removing obstructive signs to fix them to houses, setting back housefronts to widen streets, and breaching the city walls for new ways; in 1766 the West Gate was taken down. Fire remained a particular hazard; there was a civic fire engine by 1747 and several by 1755, and from 1777 city leases contained a covenant obliging tenants to insure against fire. The provision of night watchmen was ratified in the 1739 Improvement Act and there were payments to them in the 1740s; by 1752 they numbered ten.[25]

To protect visitors from the abuse of overcharging, price control of lodgings was imposed early in the eighteenth century: at a weekly maximum of 10s. for a furnished room and 5s. for a servant's garret, reduced by half out of season. In 1754 Mrs Galloway of Chapel Row, Queen Square, had furnished rooms to let at half price, 5s. each not including servants and linen, in August, and garrets at 2s. 6d. By 1800 prices had advanced only sixpence to 10s. 6d. a week (5s. 6d. for servants), and in June, July and August to 7s. 6d. and 5s. 3d. respectively. This tariff was uniform irrespective of the quality of the houses, but control relaxed after 1800 and by 1813 prices varied according to location, the size and number of the rooms and the quality of the furniture.[26]

Lodging-houses where only the furnished rooms were hired, often for a term of weeks, were distinct from boarding-houses providing all meals and services. Both could prove a valuable investment; some owners let entire lodging-houses for the season and their tenants sublet to visitors who took the whole house or a suite of rooms, but landlords were generally reluctant to split suites. The proprietor might supply plate and linen for an additional charge, and now that the Duke of Chandos and others had set higher standards, houses were better furnished. The Penrose family from Cornwall hired three rooms in a clergyman's house in Abbey Green in April 1766 for £1 5s. a week and luxuriated in a parlour with a handsome ceiling and a fine chimneypiece, equipped with a buffet (sideboard), six mahogany chairs with hair bottoms, an easy-chair, two mahogany tables and two looking-glasses. The better of two bedrooms had a blue and white flowered linen bed, matching window curtains, walnut chairs with blue seats, a chest of drawers, a dressing-table, a looking-glass and a closet.

The Penroses came provided with many household goods, and the carrier brought a box with more from their home. Mrs Penrose liked shopping in the 'very fine' market, although food prices were higher than at home. Miss Elizabeth Collett and her relatives had a similar experience in 1792: they found only linen in their South Parade lodgings and spent the next day purchasing provisions. When William Winstone from Gloucestershire removed his belongings from such a house after a visit from December 1814 to June 1815 he had to secure his fixtures against an invasion of whitewashers, painters, carpenters and stonemasons. But he was undeterred, and although '. . . never decidedly a Bath character, in the constant pursuit of frivolity and dissipation . . .', he made a return visit in 1817.[27]

In general Bath lodgings were noted for their comfort and elegance, with separate parlours, dining-rooms and dressing-rooms. Furniture provided by Mrs Phillips at Chandos Buildings included rectangular and oval tables, strong Dutch chairs, screens, looking-glasses, sconces, candlesticks, embroidered beds and best feather mattresses. Water-closets with seats, marble basins and leaden pipes replaced the old close stools and outdoor 'necessary houses'. The new imported Chinese wallpapers gradually replaced wainscoting: rooms lately hung 'with the most beautiful wallpapers' were advertised in 1772.[28]

On arrival at a coaching inn like the Christopher or the White Hart all that was necessary to find lodgings was to walk around the city (as William Meyler claimed) for only five or ten minutes, even in high season, so continual were the arrivals and departures. The Bath Universal Register Office – run by B. Wyatt, a linen-draper and hosier, near Queen Square – had a list of houses or lodgings for hire in 1758, and libraries often kept one. Visitors preferred the independence of lodging-houses to boarding-houses; in 1773 there were at least 235 lodging-houses, of which Milsom Street had twenty-three; by 1791 the total was 362, including twenty-two boarding-houses; and by 1799 457, but nineteen boarding-houses. The next decade showed another increase to 533, but even fewer boarding-houses – ten.[29] The growing consumer demand for room hire alone and the shrinking interest in rooms with meals and services was encouraged by improved market and shopping facilities. Bath was well endowed with inns, and after the York House Hotel no more hotels were built for about a century.

Although the erection or purchase and furnishing of a lodging-house was a sound investment, many lodging-house keepers had a dual occupation; in 1773 eleven in the marketplace all had other trades, including a grocer, a linen-draper and a brewer. Some ran more than one lodging-house: Mrs Gibson had two in the Circus, Mrs Welling two in Alfred Street and Mrs Shaw three in Duke Street. Lord Weymouth leased three houses from the Duke of Kingston and sublet them, and his large lodging-house in Bull's Yard was let to Mrs Robertson, 'a poor complaining widow', on an eleven-year lease (1749–60) for £66 a year. Some visitors stayed in neighbouring villages – like Weston, one mile from Bath, where houses were offered to let or sell in 1754 and 1755, one furnished. Dr Lowther advised patients from the North Country to take country lodgings two or three miles out and ride into the city daily.[30]

Lodgers who found provisions and coal themselves also brought or hired a cook and other servants. In 1766 the Penroses employed a fifteen-year-old maid for 2*s.* a week and her food, because their lodging-house servants cleaned rooms, made the beds, lit fires and prepared food but would not run errands, wait at table or do minor jobs, as in the boarding-houses. Bath claimed to be a nursery for cookmaids and many hired for the season went home with their employers. Servants could be hired through the Bath Universal Register Office by 1758, and later several libraries acted as servants' agencies. Lodging-house keepers normally gave no wages to servants, who depended on gratuities from lodgers and their leftovers for food. Some servants were coloured, the products of the Bristol slave trade; in 1755 the funeral in Walcot Church of a black girl employed by a gentleman living in Queen Square brought out six black men as pall-bearers and others as mourners.[31]

Local newspapers show a lively market in fully furnished lodgings, sometimes with servants. In 1772 Mrs Hetling had three substantial, well-furnished houses for sale with furniture available at valuation, a 'genteely furnished' house opposite her near the Cross Bath was free with or without servants, and another to let in Charles Street had linen, china and a servant. Furnished houses were also let by the quarter to seasonal visitors, or for a term of years to speculators who sublet.[32]

The two lengthening Bath seasons made capital investment in lodging-houses, shops and entertainment more profitable than in spas limited to a summer trade, but they left the city at its lowest ebb in July, August and early September when the leisured classes favoured more rural resorts. Bath's hill-surrounded position makes it hot in summer, but warm lodgings were available in winter because of the local coal trade. Mendip coal production increased markedly from 1750, promoted by Jacob Mogg and other landowning proprietors to meet the Bath domestic coal market and aided by improved local roads. Ten colliery owners joined the protesters when turnpike tolls were increased to pay for city improvements in 1789, arguing that higher rates would inflate prices and encourage the import of inferior water-borne coal.[33]

Coal was transported to the Saw Close inside the West Gate where quantities were checked by coal merchants – at least four found a living in Bath in 1784, and ten by 1799. Noisy coal wagons were a nuisance, and from 1757 they were barred from passing through the city at night. Under-vaults of houses served as coal cellars in the constricted town, and coal was so plentiful that it was freely burnt; '. . . cold winds, but we are happy in being so near the coalmines . . .', wrote Edmund Rack in January 1780. Coal money for the poor at Christmas appeared on corporation accounts from 1704.[34]

When Somerset coal-masters, faced with wage demands, combined in 1792 to raise the price of coal, the corporation reacted and in February 1793 appointed a committee to enquire into ways of lowering it. The coal proprietors had to compete with Welsh coal brought up the Avon, and in 1794 they planned a Somerset Coal Canal to reduce costs, but only one branch, from Hallatrow, was completed to join the Kennet and Avon Canal opened in 1810, at Limpley Stoke. The carriage of corn and timber to Bath became cheaper, but coal prices were not much reduced, although visitors often remarked on the cheapness of coal at Bath: by 1799 10*d.* a bushel, but in London 5*s.* Cheap coal lured both the winter visitor and the permanent resident to Bath. The corporation also purchased coal for public buildings: the old town hall and the new Guildhall had fireplaces, as did the slips in the baths where bathers undressed, and men were paid for sweeping the chimneys. By 1752 the city was dealing with Robert Wood-ruff for coal; but a woman, Mary Harries, supplied it in 1760–1.[35]

Bath increasingly offered comforts and amenities in a superb architec-tural setting, so that in 1772 it was said that most families of distinction 'in the three kingdoms' resided there for several months at some time. We may wonder why so many proud and spirited people of rank submitted to the ritual of an institutionalized social routine with detailed rules for specific occasions, which set a precedent for other urban spas. 'Rules' after the Bath pattern were adopted at least at Cheltenham, Southampton and Tunbridge Wells and influenced the social procedures of other spas. The explanation may be that social ceremony was a substitute for the lost glamour of the Stuart court; the first two kings of the new dynasty were often absent in Hanover, although some social life focused around the Prince of Wales at Leicester House. By contrast, the social ritual at Bath under the 'King of Bath', Beau Nash, offered stability, continuity and high fashion.[36]

Nash was concerned to exercise social control by uniting all degrees of society within the limitations he laid down, and to maintain decorum by enforcing standards of conduct by common consent, although the aristocracy at least demonstrated that an acquaintanceship made at the spa ceased with the visit. Nash's social rule, imposed by a mixture of audacity, urbanity and wit, was soon formulated in an elementary code of behaviour, copies of which were publicly displayed in 1707; it consisted mostly of hints to uncouth provincials of the expectations of polite circles, like avoiding malicious gossip and unseemly squabbles about precedence. Nash also insisted on several unwritten laws, mainly about irregularities of dress: for example, ladies should not wear aprons, nor gentlemen boots, at the balls. The code was apparently approved by the chief citizens and the company in spring of 1742.[37]

When the sumptuous New Rooms opened in 1771 the dichotomy between them and Gyde's Lower Rooms made the work of the MC, Captain William Wade, more onerous. He had to officiate at two establishments about half a mile apart and avoid a conflict of interests by integrating the social round, with two public balls a week in season: on Monday at the New Rooms and on Friday at Gyde's Rooms. The more private cotillon balls, public card-playing and concerts were arranged at each set of rooms once a week, never coinciding. Both rooms were open for walking in or playing cards, except for public tea-drinking on Sunday and on Friday when the New Rooms were shut.

Later MCs adapted Nash's regulations as, on 1 October 1772, did Wade, who formalized the conduct of balls with extra rules. Peeresses had reserved places in front, balls finished at 11 p.m. precisely, even in mid-dance, and no illegal games were played. The appropriate costume, that of the court of St. James, again implies that the company at Bath was aping the courtly life. Ladies and gentlemen dancing the minuets which opened the ball at 6 p.m. had to wear specified fashionable clothes and service officers were expected to have their hair or wig *en queue*. Front seats had to be left for minuet-dancers by those preferring the romp of country dances at 8 p.m., and ladies were barred from wearing clumsy hoops for sprightly dances. Later cotillons and country dances completely displaced the stately minuets.[38] By 1787 there was some relaxation of ladies' dress rules, except for minuets in the Upper Rooms; apart from ball or concert nights, hats were now allowed in the Lower Rooms, a concession to the current vogue for fantastic headgear. The elaborate dress in public places amazed observers – like Mrs Montagu, who thought young ladies must be wearing the scalps of Indian warriors brought from America; she had never seen such terrible dresses. A Gloucestershire farmer found the 'fancy dresses' very various; the ladies walked out with greatcoats like a coachman's, and heads were dressed wide and high in ten thousand different forms.[39]

After 1777 there were two MCs, Tyson and King, and in 1787 they formulated separate rules, both designed to protect a privileged society. The formal ones for the Upper Rooms (twenty-two points) were more ample and specific than those for the Lower Rooms. The proprietors of the rooms were now committed to twenty-six dress balls on the guinea sub-scription to each room (which carried two tickets) and thirty fancy-dress balls on the half-guinea subscription. Balls in the Lower Rooms still began at 6 p.m., but those in the Upper Rooms an hour later, perhaps to avoid traffic congestion, and both ended sharply at 11 p.m. The annual subscrip-tion for promenading in the Upper Rooms was retained at 10s. 6d. (pre-viously 10s.) for gentlemen and 5s. for ladies – except for Sunday-evening tea-drinking when gentlemen paid 6d. and ladies 1s. Non-subscribers were barred.[40]

The proprietors arranged for the musicians performing in the rooms, but the corporation paid those in the Pump Room, and in 1771 they still received only five guineas a season. When the Upper Rooms opened that year the New Assembly Orchestra was formed in the summer, a band of ten to fourteen players for the balls twice a week and a Wednesday concert in the rooms for 200 guineas during the autumn season. In 1784 the corporation tried to increase visitors' donations to the musicians' fund by placing a subscription book in the Pump Room, and further help came with Tyson's and King's new regulations in 1787. Some ball funds were now to be used to support a band of twelve performers, including players of a harp, a tabor and a pipe, the usual number of musicians in the Pump Room. Music was important to Bath's social life, and in 1795 the corporation agreed the request of the committee of the Upper Rooms to pay the Pump Room band three guineas a week for sixteen weeks – that is, £50 8s. a season, a much increased charge. Two years later they appointed a committee to supervise the music at the new Great Pump Room. Although the masters of the Upper and Lower Rooms contributed £50 and £30 respectively to the musicians' fund, by 1801 the total of £130 8s. was insufficient and musical performances were reduced.[41]

Regulations for the public baths were imposed on visitors and staff alike, even on 'people of the first quality' who favoured the moderately warm Cross Bath and left the others – the King's, Queen's and Hot Baths – to those of common rank. In 1735 an attempt to end mixed bathing by introducing separate fixed days for men and women was abandoned, but in

1737 it was ruled that men, except boys under ten, must wear drawers or a waistcoat, women a decent shift, and a male guide a distinguishing cap with a tassel. Offenders' fines of 3*s*. 4*d*. were used for poor relief, and servants and poor people could use the baths for only 6*d*. Staff were forbidden to levy 'footing-money' when a bather entered the baths or they began pumping, and they had to keep fires in the slips from 5 a.m. in summer and 6 a.m. in winter. Bathing was allowed daily (except on Christmas Day and Good Friday), a bathing-dress could be hired for 6*d*. a time, and small foot-tubs of water were provided or, for 8*d*., were brought filled with hot water to lodgings.

The committee of 1773 for improving the Hot Bath imposed a new tariff in 1778 to recoup some of the costs: 1*s*. 6*d*. for a private bath, 3*s*. for a vapour bath, or 4*s*. for both; dry-pumping cost 6*d*. for a hundred strokes and wet-pumping 3*d*. In 1779 a cold bath was added. But the better-off now spurned the public baths for private ones, and only about 20–30 gentlemen a week used the King's Bath. The corporation tried also to make the Pump Room a commercial success, and when some visitors refused to pay for drinking the water a fixed tariff was displayed in 1804. After a week's trial at 7*s*. the principal of a family paid a guinea a month for drinking and attendance, but all other members only 10*s*. The pumper could not exceed the set charge, but 'ladies and gentlemen of rank and opulence' might volunteer extra remuneration.[42] By 1800 the concept of inclusive terms for families was being introduced for various facilities as spa life in general became more sedate.

Although the sergeants of the mace supervised the baths, the corporation farmed out their custom on increasingly profitable terms as trade mounted. Thomas Sinnet paid £35 a year as pumper of the King's Bath in 1700; by 1706 this levy had risen to £200 for two pumps at the King's Bath and the use of a vault, and the Hot Bath was let for £20. In 1710 George Allen rented both concessions for £230, a constant figure until at least 1745. A visitor in 1772 thought the pumper's payment of £500 'a smart rent', but that the business was worth it. By 1778 the 'farmer' monopolized the profits of the Pump Room and of the baths, except the private ones, and in 1778–9 £630 was extracted from the tenant, widow Mary Harrington. Then declining profits prompted enquiries about the administration of the baths, which were supervised by Dr John Symons, but the pumper's rent remained at £630 until in 1786 it rose to £640, with the right to bottle and sell Bath waters in a bottling-house under the Pump Room.

The bottled-water trade dated at least from 1673, and in 1751 W. Lawrence, the accredited pumper, sold the water in containers bearing the city arms. The pumper in 1784–6 – William Tagg, a pastry-cook – was reminded not to exceed the price of 6*s*. a dozen bottles.[43] From 1783, under the drive for more efficient management, the sergeants were put on a salaried basis of fifty-two guineas a year with some 'military' duties. In 1786 Symons also acquired control of the Cross Bath, but in 1787 he lost the management of the Hot Bath to a committee which dismissed the staff and brought in new employees at appropriate salaries. The pumper's rent remained high – £830 in 1789 and £840 from 1790 – but the economic administration of the baths remained difficult, and by 1816 the fall in trade was so obvious that the rent was sharply reduced: to £630.[44]

Apart from regulations for the rooms and the baths there was an accepted daily social ritual at Bath: a visit to the baths between 6 a.m. and 9 a.m., a general assembly at the Pump Room for drinking the water while listening to music, and then diversions. Ladies withdrew to a neighbouring toy shop to read the news and to their lodgings for breakfast, which gentlemen took in a coffee-house. They had the choice of Morgan's, which existed by 1736, or Stephen's, on the Grand Parade by 1755 (in the 1770s kept by Ferry), where newspapers and domestic and foreign spa waters were available. The Exchange Coffee-house was open in 1766 and the Argyle Coffee-house in Argyle Street by 1804.[45]

Fashionable people often made this late breakfast a public party at the rooms and concert-breakfasts, where performers of rank joined the common band, were popular. Nash insisted that attendance at the Abbey service was the next social obligation, then from about noon two hours were allowed for promenading or taking an 'airing' on the surrounding heights. In 1725 the corporation were leasing Claverton Down for this purpose at an annual rent of £25, in 1743 during the depression only £10 10s., but in 1810 £30. Guidebooks to spas in general normally described local beauty spots in extravagant language, for local doctors encouraged visitors to take exercise by walking or riding as part of the cure. Less strenuous riders used a small ring on the common, 600 feet in circumference, called Hyde Park. Exercise over, the main meal of the day, dinner, was followed by 'evening' prayers, a second visit to the Pump Room to drink the waters, a short promenade on the walks, tea-drinking at the assembly-rooms, and the night's entertainment of balls, concerts, the theatre or visits. MCs tried to maintain Nash's custom of a ceremonial call on new arrivals, but as Richard Tyson said in about 1787, 'the late great extension of the city' made such contacts difficult. Private visits might be prolonged but public occasions finished by 11 p.m., when the night watch took over the streets. In the course of a century Bath society had become more complex and was organized in an unprecedented manner.[46]

As the health and leisure industry expanded, opportunities arose for entrepreneurs to invest in commercialized entertainment and visitors and residents to combine in select voluntary associations for cultural advancement. In 1793 it was claimed that Bath afforded universal satisfaction for the man of pleasure, the philosopher, the antiquarian, the man of letters, the poet and the painter. After the capital no other town in England then offered such quality and diversity of recreation and society.[47] Apart from the public rooms, the theatre, libraries and concerts were the main attractions, supplemented by travelling shows such as the New Circus with horse-riders, tumble-ladder-dancers and tightrope-walkers performing in Frog Lane in 1800. The considerable contribution of Bath society to the contemporary English cultural tradition is well known and cannot be more than touched on here.

When players from Trim's theatre retreated to Simpson's cellar in 1738 they also sometimes performed in an inn: in 1747 at the Globe and in 1748 at the George. As the resort of company grew the London actor John Hippesley, already connected with the Jacob's Well theatre at Bristol, appealed to the nobility, magistracy and gentry for support in building a better playhouse at Bath. He died in 1748, but John Palmer, a wealthy brewer and chandler, and nine others built a theatre by subscription in Orchard Street on the Kingston Estate, possibly near the primitive building leased by John Woodman in 1709.[48] The New Theatre in Orchard Street, started in 1747 and opened in 1750, was 'genteely and elegantly' equipped, with pits and boxes in semicircular form and proper dressing-rooms, and its challenge made Simpson enlarge the theatre below his great ballroom. In January 1754 the Orchard Street Theatre ran a tragedy, *The Gangster*. After Simpson's death in May 1755 the shares of the new playhouse came on the market, but there was insufficient custom for both theatres and their rivalry upset the visitors. In November 1757 Nash declared in favour of Brown, the actor-manager of the New Theatre, and persuaded Simpson's son to sell out to him, with £200 compensation from the Orchard Street proprietors, although Samuel Derrick, the next MC, had regarded Simpson's theatre as the better of the two. The Bath company of comedians performed on Monday, Wednesday and Saturday, even in January, and out of season went on circuit; in May 1758 the wagon conveying all their properties was accidentally destroyed by fire on Salisbury Plain.[49]

In 1768 John Palmer I (d. 1788), backed by the corporation, procured a royal patent for the theatre under the first Act in England to secure theatrical property, 'an Act to enable His Majesty to licence [sic] a Playhouse in the City of Bath', where it was 'much wanted'. This was the first Theatre Royal in the provinces, a status also acquired by the Cheltenham theatre in 1788, despite a law of 1773 which forbade performances except in a limited number of privileged theatres. In 1774 Palmer still paid a rent of £1 11s. 6d. to the Kingston Estate 'for part of the theatre in Orchard Street' and £15 for ground added to the theatre, which was rebuilt and enlarged in 1775. John Palmer II (d. 1818) found his recruiting drive hindered by slow postal communications, so, having successfully used fast coaches to take his players from Bath to the Bristol theatre opened in 1766, in 1784 he went into the transport business with new and faster mail-coaches. The Bath Theatre Royal flourished in the 1790s, managed by William Keasberry and principal performer William Wyatt Dimond; it was an elaborate theatre appropriate to the city's sophisticated society, a far cry from the playhouse barns of several resort towns.[50]

Extensive plans in 1767 to build another 'magnificent' theatre by the West Gate, from where a new road, 'the grandest in Europe', would link the old city with the new, were shelved, but the Orchard Street Theatre was too small and in a cramped position, so around 1800 the project was resuscitated. The old theatre closed in July 1805 and a new Theatre Royal, between the upper and lower towns with its grand front on the south side of Beauford Square, opened on 12 October. Designed mainly by George Dance, it cost £20,000 and was exceptionally well equipped with twenty-six private boxes and a suite of retiring-rooms. Bronze pillars of cast iron supported the tiers of boxes, the deep red and gold interior was lit by elegant chandeliers by Le Font of the Strand, and exquisite paintings by Casali, moved from Fonthill, adorned the ceiling. John Palmer II and William Wyatt Dimond were the joint proprietors, and Charlton was the manager.[51]

Investment in circulating libraries funded by subscriptions for the leisured society became a practice in spa towns, as in other provincial towns, in the eighteenth century. Bath already had bookshops and was possibly the first English town with a community library. Edinburgh had one in 1725, but in 1723 John Leake, son of a London bookseller and printer, succeeded to the Bath bookshop and printing business of his father-in-law Henry Hammond and his brother. Leake, Bath's foremost bookseller, printer and publisher, was lending books in 1728 when Thomas Goulding, in his *Essay against too much reading,* complained that Leake's customers' excessive reading undid the good of the mineral waters. Leake soon had rivals: William Frederick, also a publisher, opened his library at 18, The Grove in about 1740 and by 1770 had amassed 9,000 books and 1,000 modern novels and romances. Benjamin Matthews had a bookshop by 1725 and later a circulating library. After Leake's death in 1764 his sons sold out to Lewis Bull, a jeweller, goldsmith and lodging-house keeper, in 1770 and Bull's library flourished, from 1792 under his son John. When Frederick died in 1776 Joseph Sheldon and William Meyler bought his stock and announced a new catalogue in 1780. William Meyler (d. 1821), a magistrate and member of the common council, was famed for his circulating library in the Grove. By 1770 there were at least six libraries in Bath, seven in the 1780s and nine by the 1790s. When Miss Elizabeth Collett arrived in Bath in February 1792 she immediately sought out a library.[52]

Any book could be borrowed for a subscription of 5*s.* a season, or a guinea from people of more demanding tastes. After 1780 the price of books doubled, so borrowing rates crept up, and in 1789 six libraries combined to fix subscriptions at 15s. a year and 5s. a quarter. The most fashionable library before 1800 was James Marshall's in Milsom Street, where from 1793 to 1799 the mostly aristocratic and upper-class subscribers included two princes (the Prince of Wales and Frederick, Prince of Orange), five dukes, four duchesses, seven earls, fourteen countesses, many other nobles and forty-three knights. Professional customers were three admirals, four generals and many service officers down to twenty-six majors and seventy-one captains, and also ecclesiastics: one archbishop, six bishops and 114 other clerics. Of the total 1,753 subscribers, 639 were women. But with the depression of trade the number of Marshall's subscribers fell from 515 in 1793 to 258 in 1799, when the 25 per cent increase in subscription could not save him from bankruptcy. Smaller libraries provided middle-class ladies and servants with novels. Circulating libraries were also social centres and supplied various services and goods, such as patent medicines and tickets for concerts and balls, and the visitors' books with names and addresses there were a source of the local newspapers' rather inadequate lists of arrivals.

Visitors also paid subscriptions for reading newspapers at the coffee-houses – by 1754 at Thomas Loggon's Little Fanmaker, which supplied national newspapers and the *Bath Journal* for 2s. 6d. a season – or in the reading-rooms of bookshops and libraries. In 1784 one Hazard opened a large carpet-covered upstairs reading-room fronting the churchyard, with the comfort of a good fire. There were about six such reading-rooms in Bath before the mid-eighteenth century.

Apart from London and provincial newspapers, local ones often emerged early in the history of spa towns, providing an essential source of intelligence in advertisements of houses and lodgings to let, vacancies for servants, local shops, coming events and entertainments, as well as news. Bath was well served at an early date: its first newspaper was the *Bath Journal* (later *Keene's Bath Journal*) published by Thomas Bodley in 1744, then the *Bath Advertiser* of 1755 (later the *Bath Weekly Chronicle* or the *Bath Chronicle* established by Cornelius Pope in 1760), the *Bath Courant* of 1773, the *Bath Gazette* of 1778 and the *Bath Herald,* founded in 1792 by the bookseller William Meyler. In 1793 the *Herald* absorbed the *Bath Register and Western Advertiser,* also established the previous year, and the *Bath and Cheltenham Gazette,* founded by George Wood in 1812, was an attempt to serve both resorts. Not all survived, but their publication indicated the tremendous demand for information about Bath.[53]

Bath also pioneered in 1742 the production of local guides for visitors to spa towns. Tunbridge Wells provided one in 1766, Harrogate in 1775, Cheltenham in 1781 but Buxton not until 1792, and the later eighteenth century saw a rapid growth in general spa literature. These guides were more practical accounts than the earlier medical 'puffs' – usually a history of the town and a description of its mineral waters, places of amusement and worship, transport services and charges, posts and other information calculated to help the visitor to find his bearings. The *Bath and Bristol Guide* (1742) by Thomas Bodley, the newspaper publisher, was followed in 1762 by Cornelius Pope's long series *The New Bath Guide,* continued from 1770 to 1801 by Richard Crutwell, who in 1773 also initiated the *Stranger's Assistant and Guide to Bath,* a directory of tradespeople, the professions and lodging-house keepers.[54]

The flow of medical literature also continued. Prominent among these essayists was Dr William Falconer of Cheshire, from 1784 to 1819 physician to the Bath General Hospital, who produced *An Essay on Bath Waters* (1772), and Charles Lucas, whose essay *The City and Thermal Waters of Bath* (1765) was addressed to the Earl of Chesterfield, a patron of Bath. Mullet lists fifty-three publications on Bath in his bibliography of watering-places to the late eighteenth century, and Richard Warner's exhaustive and scholarly *History of Bath* (1801) met an enormous market for information.[55]

The above-average literate and leisured consumer society at Bath both patronized commercialized leisure activities and spawned voluntary cultural institutions. The contemporary urge to self-improvement influenced Bath's social and intellectual life, as in many provincial cities where lectures, discussions, lessons, concerts, catch clubs and glee meetings were seriously pursued. The 'City Musick' could be hired for private functions, and by 1799 at least fifteen male musicians and four music mistresses lived at Bath, augmented by itinerant virtuosi during the season. In 1772, for example, Mr Noel played the new pantaleon, an elaborate dulcimer, in the Great Room of the York House Hotel. At least two shops stocked musical instruments and printed music and arranged the short-term hire of instruments to visitors. Mr Underwood sold music to the corporation in July 1762, and by 1770 Henry Dixon Tylee, music teacher and Abbey organist, had a store of instruments and from 1800 a music library at 12, Bennett Street. Three men in turn controlled the concerts in the rooms and dominated Bath's musical life: Thomas Linley, composer and singing master; the Hanoverian William Herschel, composer, teacher and organist at the Octagon Chapel, who replaced Linley as the director of the New Assembly Room Band in 1776; and his successor from 1782, the Italian Venanzio Rauzzini, male soprano, keyboard player and composer. Rauzzini's funeral in 1810 was the best-attended since that of Beau Nash,[56] indicating the importance of the public performance of music which helped to stimulate the outpouring of private and informal music.

The institutionalizing of cultural and social life was a general tendency in England, but the new voluntary and elitist leisure groups of those with common interests seeking improving activities met in private and cost some disintegration of the old mixed public assemblies. Serious-minded societies of fifty to a hundred members had a formal committee, a fixed subscription and a regular meeting-place and helped to raise the cultural and educational level. The Bath Catch Club was established in 1784; by 1803 its 130 members met weekly in York House with a routine of catches, glees, songs and duets, and a cold supper. A more ambitious programme from 1804, with a five-guinea initial subscription and then three guineas annually, included a concert in the Upper Rooms, baited with refreshments of ices, jellies, negus, lemonade and cakes. The Harmonic Society also functioned in the Lower Rooms by 1800 and by 1812 claimed a Friday-evening place in the rota of public amusements. The third subscription musical festival was held in June 1810 with concerts in the Abbey and the New Rooms.[57]

Another serious organization was the Bath Society, founded in 1777 – from 1790 the Bath and West Society – for promoting rural improvement. Edmund Rack of Norfolk, who came to Bath in 1775, Dr Falconer the physician, and Richard Crutwell the printer and publisher were among the twenty-two founding members. Originally the society was interested in arts, manufactures and commerce, but because of the expanding food market in the Bath region its emphasis shifted to improved farming. Another cultural project involving both Edmund Rack and William Herschel was the ephemeral Bath Philosophical Society, active between 1779 and 1787 and concerned with rational learning in general.[58]

Bath was a magnet to artists in search of wealthy patronage, including Thomas Worlidge, a London portraitist who arrived in September 1754, and Thomas Gainsborough, who came in 1759 and from 1760, until he left for London in 1774, leased a house in Abbey Street from the Duke of Kingston at £75 a year, let it as lodgings and moved to better houses in Lansdown Road in 1763 and in the Circus in 1766. Confidently successful, in 1771 he insisted that the Countess of Dartmouth should come to Bath if her finished portrait were to be altered.[59] After his departure Joseph Wright arrived in Bath in 1775 and mistakenly hoped to replace him. Visitors liked crayon drawings, which could be done quickly, and young Thomas Lawrence drew heads in charcoal for a guinea each at Bath; in 1787 he too moved to London. But William Hoare (d. 1792) came from Suffolk in 1739 and stayed. His portraits of Bath notabilities included those of Lord Camden, the recorder, which cost the city £84 in 1765, Ralph Allen, and the famed physician William Oliver, portrayed with the surgeon Jerry Pierce. Hoare had at least eight other competitors in the 1770s, including Thomas Beach and Thomas Hickey: the latter produced portraits of two masters of ceremonies, William Dawson and William

Brereton. Charles Davis had joined these competitors by 1784.[60] Artists whose topographical sketches and paintings re-create Georgian Bath include John Claude Nattes, Bernard Lens III (d. 1740, in the city from 1718 to 1719), and Thomas Robins from Cheltenham, whom Bath acclaimed (1740–70) as 'the limner of this city'. Thomas Malton (d. 1804) left a similar record: a watercolour of the Crescent nearing completion in 1769, and other works. By 1779 sixteen artists and nine miniature-painters were trying to make a living in Bath.[61]

Eminent literary men were also drawn to spa centres for company and patronage and in search of copy, and they enriched English literature by their descriptions of the scene at Bath, Epsom, Harrogate, Tunbridge Wells and other resorts. At Bath they often enjoyed Ralph Allen's hospitality at Prior Park, and notable among his guests were Alexander Pope and Henry Fielding. Dr Thomas Smollett was a particularly acute observer of Bath society. His *Essay on the External Use of Waters, with particular Remarks on the Mineral Waters of Bath* (1752) undermined Bath's reputation; he argued that plain water was superior to mineral water for bathing, alleged mismanagement of the Bath hospital and baths, and supported Archibald Cleland, a surgeon, whose improvement plans had been rejected. But Smollett is better known as a satirical novelist whose work, like that of the dramatist, Richard Brinsley Sheridan (d. 1816), depicted the follies, vagaries and underside of Bath life. Here is evidence of the population explosion and the boom which attracted fashionable company when many genteel people were lost in a mob of impudent plebeians lacking judgement, propriety and decorum.[62]

But the leisured minority of the social elite and the rapidly growing middle classes provided a vast amount of employment; they all had to be transported, fed, and serviced in many ways by professional, manufacturing, retail and labouring people. Prominent among the workers were the chairmen, an essential means of transport in the narrow and many hilly streets. After 1739 the sixty or more licensed chairmen had to carry a distinguishing mark, keep their sedan chairs at allotted stands, and adhere to the tariff of charges – now fixed at 6*d.* within the city or 500 yards within the liberties and 1*s.* for other journeys up to one mile. They could be kept waiting up to ten minutes on a 6*d.* fare and twenty on a 1*s.* fare. The number of licensed couples rose from sixty in 1738 to seventy-eight in 1749, eighty-four in 1756, 120 in 1773 and 340 in 1801, perhaps not all on the streets at once.[63]

Even so demand exceeded supply, and many visitors complained of the independent and turbulent chairmen and of being stranded in public places of amusement. So in January 1791 Mayor John Horton called a meeting of chairmen and ordered a better distribution of the chairs, fifty to every public ball and thirty to each theatre and public concert performance, all to be in position by 9 p.m. The porters at the rooms and playhouse had to enforce the regulations and permitted fares, but dissatisfaction continued – especially at the Orchard Street Theatre, where coaches lacked room to manoeuvre and chairs were much in request, and licensees Keasberry and Dimond appealed for twenty extra sober and able-bodied chairmen. In 1793 the corporation tightened the control of the hackney coaches, chairs, basket-men and women and porters, and extended it to cover more of Walcot. The spread of houses up the northern slopes made the chairmen's job more arduous, so from 1794 the normal 6*d.* fare for 500 yards was applied to 300 yards on hilly ground in seven specified areas.[64]

The ebb and flow of visitors gave increasing employment to the transport services. In the 1730s Marchioness Grey thought that during her slow journey from Oxford she would read all the books intended for her recreation at Bath, but by 1766 the local roads were better and the slopes of Claverton and Lansdown were safer and easier, so an increasing volume of horse-drawn traffic congested the narrow streets of the lower town, and many stables were advertised to sell or let. Some visitors came intending to trade a horse; Lord Cardigan bought two in 1725 and Charles Edwin of Gloucestershire sold two horses in 1793 and hoped to get a butcher's hack for his servants. Five horse-dealers were in business in 1800.[65]

The transport industry and its ancillary trades rapidly expanded. In 1784 Walter Wiltshire was the sole carrier, but by 1799 there were five, and the one currier and one corn merchant in 1784 had in 1799 become three of each. Out of 1,267 traders listed in 1799 thirty-eight were engaged in transport, including ten coach-masters, four coach-makers, nine saddlers, six farriers, and the five carriers. Travel facilities between Bath and London grew especially rapidly; services of all vehicles covering journeys one way per week rose steadily from one in 1684 to seventeen in summer and fifteen in winter in 1740, twenty-four in 1760, ninety in 1781, 147 in 1800 and 265 in 1812. An improvement in 1754 was the introduction by six proprietors of Bath and Reading of the Bath flying-machines, swift coaches with steel springs reaching London in two days three times a week, instead of the lumbering stagecoach, the Old Bath Machine, now taking a changed route through Chippenham instead of the usual Lacock, Avebury and Marlborough. A daily summer coach service to Bristol from Bath also appeared in 1754. By 1772–3 a flying-machine from the Christopher Inn to London on alternate days was supplemented by an even swifter daily one in summer linking London, Bath and Bristol. Five coaches a day raced to Bristol, with an extra fare of 2*s.* 6*d.* to proceed to the Hotwells, and flying-machine services had now spread twice weekly to Exeter, Oxford and Salisbury. The alternative post-coaches three days a week to London from the White Hart and the White Lion took two days, the twice-weekly flying wagon took two and a half days, and a slow wagon ambled along for four.[66]

The picture twenty years later, by 1791, was remarkably different, for services had proliferated. York House was now the focus of some important coaching trade; the other ten dispersal points and ten stages for wagon and cart traffic were in the city. John Palmer's speedy mail-coaches took pride of place from 1784 and by 1791 seven left Bath daily: three to London and others to Exeter, Bristol and Birmingham. Sixteen other daily coaches raced to the metropolis and a slower post-coach on alternate days, compared with one swift and one slow in 1773. Services to Bristol, Exeter, Oxford and Salisbury were all better, and new coaches included one three days a week to the up-and-coming resort of Weymouth. Despite later links with Cheltenham the only transport service to it in 1791 was a once-weekly caravan of carts trundling along from the New Inn in Kingsmead Square, Bath, through Cirencester, and John Wildey's Bath–Cheltenham carrier service from his premises in Stall Street. But by 1809 a coach from Bath ran, through Gloucester, to the Plough Hotel in Cheltenham three days a week, in 1810 another started, and from 1812 a third ran on alternate days through Tetbury and Cirencester. There was an approximately equal amount of incoming traffic. Walter Wiltshire II (d. 1799), who traded as a carrier from 1752, was three times mayor of Bath, but in 1800 his son John sold the family business in Broad Street – the Bath, Bristol and London carrying trade – to George Lye, who operated the Bristol–Warminster–Salisbury route.[67]

Bath's economy now depended not only on servicing the visitors but also on providing a regional retail trade; by 1766 about 10,000 visitors came annually and at least £10,000 was estimated to be spent there weekly. Mrs Jane Edwards of Bristol purchased a cambric hood, a pair of doeskin shoes, a hat, some lace, and a sugar-loaf on several visits from 1736, and she frequently sent for some of Dr Oliver's famed biscuits. Sir William Codrington of Dodington in Gloucestershire purchased a box of candles and a woman's hat on two visits to the baths in 1779; in 1783 his harpsichord was tuned by one Ashman and in 1784 he purchased more wax candles (6 lb.) and a quantity of china. Much shopping was done in the lower town, still Bath's commercial centre, especially St James's parish. In 1784 the many clothing retailers near the Lower Rooms included seven drapers, a glover, a hosier, a milliner and a mercer. The overpopulated north-east Walcot area was also a commercial centre: in 1801 14,000 people were crammed in there compared with 9,150 in the other three parishes, and in 1799 it had over a third of the provision trades – seventeen bakers, fifteen butchers, eight fruiterers and thirty grocers – and fifty-one of seventy-six in the building industry, with six of ten coal merchants and five of six chimney sweeps. But Walcot also had a professional enclave of fifteen out of twenty-eight attorneys and eleven out of twenty-two apothecaries. The trades most evenly distributed in Bath by 1800 were those in demand by the fashionable clientele, clothing and personal services: twenty-two milliners and dressmakers, eight shoemakers, fifty-three tailors and habit-makers and forty-four hairdressers and perfumers. Another specialized group supplying sartorial expertise, twelve out of nineteen mantua-makers, was in St James's parish. Milsom Street, intended to be a residential area, already had fifteen retail businesses, including by 1784 that of Josiah Wedgwood, transferred from Westgate Buildings and described as 'potters'.[68]

The biggest group of Bath's retailers (about 31 per cent) were employed in the victualling trades: in 1799 the astonishing total of eighty-five grocers and tea-dealers, thirty-seven bakers, thirty-three butchers and sixteen fruiterers. Although visitors came ostensibly to drink the waters, much alcoholic liquor was consumed and some of the many inns took in lodgers, but the number of inns fell from 176 in 1781 to eighty-three in 1799, because of the brewers 'tying' public houses and rising costs. There were ten brewers in 1799, four of whom produced the new beer, porter, and ten wine merchants and three brandy merchants. The vendors of asses' milk may have been there for cosmetic purposes. Curiously, in mid-century two purveyors sold the mineral waters of other spas, foreign and domestic: including that of Nevill Holt in Leicestershire and Bourne in Lincolnshire.[69]

The second largest group of retailers (about 21 per cent) was in the clothing trade; the third (approximately 18 per cent) was the industrial element, many in building trades, and transport. Fourthly, in the expanding group of professionals the fourteen attorneys doubled in number and the apothecaries, surgeons and physicians, assured of a living in this haven of invalids, almost tripled between 1784 and 1799. But the *Medical Register* for 1779 and 1783 gives forty-eight surgeons and apothecaries, compared with twenty-two, including physicians, from the trade directory of 1784 and sixty-three from that of 1799. Trade directories may understate the number of medical men. There was also a steady middle-class market for teachers of music, languages, dancing and drawing, and schools where visitors' daughters were supervised and taught polite accomplishments while their parents took the waters. Such schools, sometimes for boys too, were an early feature of spa towns. A woman called Leslie opened a school for young ladies in 1755 on the corner of Abbey Green, and by 1766 the Bath Boarding School existed in Trim Street.

Fifth in the occupation groups were the assorted purveyors of luxury and leisure services, fifty-four in all, such as book- and musicsellers, gold- and silversmiths, pawnbrokers and fancy-dress makers, the majority being the forty-five hairdressers who cared for the ladies' wigs and the gentlemen's perukes. Finally, about 30 per cent of traders supplied Bath's household needs: cabinet-makers, dealers in earthenware, china and glass, ironmongers and others. The general conclusion is that Bath depended on a consumer economy largely oriented to the specialized retail needs of the region and the visitors; there was little independent industry.[70]

The Bath shops were supplemented by the expanding markets on Wednesday and Saturday behind the Guildhall, the basis of the fresh food provision in the city. Supplies for the butchers' market in the adjacent Shambles, enlarged in 1744, had been augmented from 1736 by a new beast market every Wednesday in the Saw Close. As the Bath general food market grew to provide for the growing population it splintered into specialist sections: a separate fish market operated by 1754 with two surveyors paid an annual £2 2*s.* whose duties were extended in 1755 to supervising the meat trade. A gradual change from arable to dairy farming on the town common to produce fresh milk, butter and cheese had been achieved from 1708 when the town oxen, plough and harness were sold off, and in 1742 the land was leased for fourteen years. To safeguard milk supplies, the corporation in 1747 sanctioned up to £80 to build a dairy-house there; it in fact cost £74 7*s.* Increased supplies of fresh vegetables were assured when a garden or green market was established in 1761, and was covered by the watchmen from 1765. By 1768 there was also a poultry market and by 1777 one for butter.[71]

The 1766 Improvement Act allowed the corporation to move the market, regulate it and change the market days, and by April there were plans for the new one. Regulations for the markets in meat, fish, skins and garden stuff were drawn up, and the busy Leonard Coward was appointed commissioner to superintend them. In 1767 £140 13*s.* was paid for work in guttering and lead done at the Shambles and the green market, and a long advertisement for the latter was to be placed in the *Bath Journal.* In 1776 the rent of the two bailiffs who farmed the profits of the markets and fairs was raised to £360 because of the expansion of business, and there was a premature attempt in 1776 to make the butchers' market a daily one. The Bath food market in the eighteenth century drew on a wide region and would repay detailed study. Lansdown mutton was renowned as the sweetest in Europe, local butter was brought in fresh every morning, and cheaper Welsh butter from Carmarthenshire came by barge in bulk lots in the winter. Large quantities of Severn fish – plaice, flounders, eels and others – were imported from the fisheries at Frethern, garden produce came from the Vale of Evesham, and from the North Wiltshire farms meat, milk, butter and cheese. Grain was bought in the markets at Warminster and Devizes.[72]

Contemporaries spoke of the variety and cheapness of food in Bath – for example, the poulterers supplied a fine range of game, snipe, woodcock,

wild geese, mallard, teal, fieldfares, starlings and larks. The food consumed at civic feasts also reflects the wealth of the Bath provision markets: turbot, soles, hams, turkeys, chickens, veal, creamed apple pie,
asparagus, lemons, nutmegs and sauces. Port wine at £1 for a dozen
bottles was frequently drunk, and the humble but no less potent Somerset
cider. Bath was renowned too for its pastrycooks.[73]

Fare of this richness was for the civic elite and had no relation to that of
the vast numbers of labouring poor in the city. Nor do the figures for trades
and occupations already cited include the working people: the coachmen,
ostlers, carriers, sedan-chairmen, waiters, male and female servants,
cooks, shop assistants, porters, scavengers, seamstresses, laundresses,
building workers and others. But those who enjoyed the comforts and
pleasures of Bath were not altogether unmindful of the workers, and the
city's long tradition of philanthropy fed its social conscience in the next
century.

10

Cold-Bathing at the Minor Spas

The urban spas which emerged as Bath's rivals in the eighteenth century were one aspect of the contemporary spa mania; there was also a further plethora of new minor spas as accumulations of capital from agricultural, commercial and, later, industrial profits gave surpluses not only for more travel but for investment in spa projects. The landowning classes not only founded the spas but with the middle and professional classes, especially the clergy and medical men, were the consumers of their health and entertainment services. But although the pacemakers in both the promotion and patronage of spas were the leisured people, the taking of mineral waters for *health* reasons was not their monopoly, for the poor were frequently provided for.

The growth of the medical profession as a whole, and its increased status, assisted the proliferation of the spas. The eighteenth century has been called 'the great age of the apothecaries'; in 1703 their standing was enhanced when the House of Lords ruled that their function was not only to compound and dispense but also to direct and order the remedy for disease. Now the local apothecary could join the physician in giving credibility to the virtues of neighbouring mineral waters, and they could make a living by treating patients and sometimes providing lodgings. They emphasized the advantages of consumption at the well of origin, arguing, as Dr James Taverner did about the Witham Spa in Essex, that mineral water was 'volatile' and lost quality in transit; it would 'make its escape upon carriage, tho' the bottles are ever so carefully cork'd and cemented'.[1] Landlords could charge for consumption on the spot and invest in leased-out lodging-houses often constructed near the well, but they also sometimes sponsored a trade in bottled water authenticated with their personal seals.

There was now considerably more solidity behind the medical profession, and its support for the spas – based on the analysis of mineral waters and the observation of case histories, and expressed in numerous publications – was a powerful aid to spa promotion. The physician, the surgeon and the apothecary were all progressing in skills and standing. In 1745 there were forty-five Fellows of the College of Physicians, and the surgeons broke away from the barber-surgeons that year and received their royal charter as the College of Surgeons in 1800. County hospitals and specialist hospitals were founded and dispensaries for outpatients, all contributing to the serious study of disease and its cure.[2]

Publicity was important to the creation of the Georgian minor spas, and even if motives for going to them were mixed, people pretended to accept the medical claims made for mineral waters. Consequently the landlord-promoter still enlisted a medical partner to write the necessary treatise, sometimes in Latin, until from mid-century the provincial press became organized and newspaper advertisements increasingly replaced the individual 'puff'. When John Kellaway discovered a mineral-water spring on his manor of West Tilbury in Essex in 1727 and sank a well in 1734, Dr John Andree of the London Hospital obliged with *An Account of the Tilbury Water* (1737), tactfully dedicated to Sir Hans Sloane, president of the Royal Society. The Nevill family of Leicestershire attempted to promote a newly found spring in their grounds at Nevill Holt in 1728, and the mineral-water authority Dr Thomas Short of Sheffield gave it a boost – *The Contents, Virtues and Uses of Nevill-Holt Spaw-Water* (1749) – dedicated to Cosmos Nevill, the proprietor, and – again – to the president of the society, now Martin Folkes. Disputes about the relative values of different mineral waters were pursued with acrimony and each treatise-writer tried to recruit informed opinion.

Fulwar, 4th Baron Craven, encouraged by Cheltenham's fame, tried to establish the nearby Hyde Spa on his Prestbury estate, perhaps interested in healing waters because of his lingering illness. A German expert, Dr Diederick Wessel Linden, supplied the publicity, *An Experimental Dissertation on the Hyde Saline Purging Water . . . near Cheltenham* (1751), dedicated to his lordship, and a tenant, John Timbrell, managed the spa and arranged the distribution of the Hyde waters in bottles sealed with Lord Craven's crest, and of mineral-water salts, at two London warehouses, the Duke of Cumberland's Arms in Covent Garden and James Coward's in Bridge-yard, Southwark. Craven invested in 'commodious' hot and cold baths and lodgings on the spot, but forty years later the spa was only 'a cot-house called Hyde'. The Gloucestershire historian Rudder blamed Linden's 'ill-written' treatise for the failure, but the more likely causes were Craven's death in 1764 and the growing reputation of Cheltenham.[3]

Publicity was essential. 'The want of a medical friend to analyse the water and recommend it by publishing its effects' explained the failure of Burton Lazars in Leicestershire to develop as a spa, although it had a drinking-room and an adjoining bathroom in 1760. The same argument was used about Shearsby, also in Leicestershire, in 1807:

> . . . this spring, if properly taken care of, and secured by a building over it, and the recommendation of a few M.D.s might be as beneficial

as several in the kingdom, which owe their celebrity more to the fashion, than the convalescence, of their visitants.[4]

Drinking spas received less attention in the eighteenth century in the face of new arguments in favour of cold-, as distinct from warm-, bathing. The few thermal springs in England already supported bathing-places, but despite the unsuitable English climate a new vogue for cold-bathing made many a landlord reconsider the possibility of exploiting springs of water on his estate. The protagonist of cold-bathing was a Staffordshire physician, Sir John Floyer (1649–1734), who practised at Lichfield and had a special interest in mineral waters.[5] He strongly recommended the temperate waters of Buxton (thirty miles from Lichfield), where he bathed and drank in 1696, about three years after visiting Bath. He also favoured three cold baths: at Willowbridge and the Godsall sulphur water, both in Staffordshire, and the Routhen Well at Sutton Park in Warwickshire.

Floyer's views about the virtues of cold-bathing were explained in his pamphlet, *An Enquiry into the Right Use and Abuses of the Hot, Cold, and Temperate Baths in England,* published in 1697, with five more editions.[6] It was dedicated to the Duke of Devonshire, owner of 'this jewel of nature', the baths of Buxton, which were in 'magnificent, pleasant and convenient buildings'. The duke had encouraged their use by his example, but despite recent improvements by Cornelius White, the tenant, the duke could do more – '. . . what is wanting for pleasure and convenience is by all expected from your generous hand' – as in the past when natural baths were lacking and great princes, or emperors, supplied artificial ones. Here Floyer echoes William Turner's appeal to the aristocracy in the sixteenth century.

Floyer argued that the Roman custom of cold-bathing was appropriate to the English climate and ought to be revived. Priests who had earlier dedicated medicinal wells to particular saints had deceived the common people, who attributed their cure to the merit of the saint rather than the physical virtue of the cold spring. After the Reformation the practice of bathing in and drinking the waters had revived, but the Civil War had led to the disuse of many famous waters. The general debauchery of manners in public places now deterred people from coming to the wells, and the Church was neglecting this problem. A proper form of service for use when bathing and drinking would be beneficial for both devotion and health, and baptism by total immersion should be revived – a suggestion no doubt popular with the cathedral society of Lichfield, Floyer's home town. There is no evidence of specific religious sanction for the readoption of general bathing, but church-going was a regular part of the social routine in the urban spas, which many clergy patronized.

Floyer explained cold-bathing as a means of concentrating strength during the summer. He despised all body-warming processes such as taking brandy, spirits, strong wine or ale, smoking tobacco, indulging in hot baths, wearing flannel and many clothes, warming beds, or continuous drinking of tea and coffee. He recommended the more spartan practice of taking temperate and cold baths, as at Buxton, where diseases ranging from leprosy to rheumatism were cured. He also favoured Holywell in Flintshire and St Mungo's Well near Harrogate. Floyer's appeal for more improvements at Buxton elicited no response from the 1st Duke of Devonshire, so his next pamphlet, *The Ancient Psychrolousia Revived: or, an Essay to prove Cold Bathing both Safe and Useful* (1702), was dedicated to the Royal College of Physicians in an attempt to enlist their interest; it ran to three more editions in 1706, 1709 and 1715. He now blamed the disuse of cold-bathing on the 'chemical doctors' of the last century, who had tried to promote cures by the use of salts, essences and strong tinctures of mineral sulphurs, and on the increase of foreign trade in the products of hot climates: tobacco, tea, coffee, wine, brandy-spirits and spices. These were unnatural to English bodies. He commended the novel manner of cold-bathing at Willowbridge; people entered the water in their shirts and on coming out dressed themselves in wet linen to close their pores.

Between 1697 and 1702 Floyer constructed his own bathing-place, St Chad's Bath at Unite's Well about a mile from Lichfield, encouraged by the landowner, Sir James Simon. Subsidized by the local gentry, he built a prototype for small bathing spas: two baths, each sixteen feet long and about ten feet wide, divided by a wall. The lower one for men received water from the upper or ladies' bath; in both the water reached to the neck, and they could be emptied and filled overnight. Each sex had a room for undressing and seating. Floyer also wrote a *History of Hot and Cold Bathing* in Latin, published in Leyden in 1699 and in Amsterdam in 1718, as well as English editions in 1709, 1715, 1722 and 1844.[7]

Floyer's ally in the campaign for cold-bathing, Dr Joseph Browne, addressed his *Account of the Wonderful Cures performed by the Cold Baths* (1707) particularly to the water-drinkers of Tunbridge, Hampstead, Astrop and Knaresborough and other chalybeate spas, hoping to convert them to bathing. Browne claimed that cold baths had recently effected 'many remarkable cures' in southern England and attracted 'multitudes'; and superstitious belief in Holy Wells remained alive in the North, where the common people flocked to cold springs, like St Catherine's near Doncaster and Our Lady's Well near York in the summer. He too blamed the luxury and degeneracy of the present age and foreign trade for the disuse of cold baths. Effeminate men preferred a *bagnio*, a warm bed and a flannel shirt, and imports like coffee, tea, chocolate and high spices spoiled their taste for cool and refreshing 'simples': herbs used in medicines, and spring water, cider, mead, lemons and cucumbers. Browne admitted that some physicians and apothecaries opposed the practice of cold-bathing as effecting too swift a cure. Generally speaking, however, cold-bathing had come to stay.[8]

This publicity had some influence in making cold-bathing fashionable, and opened up a further source of revenue for the landowner. In addition to a drinking-well he could provide a cold bath, a stone-lined pit covered by a simple house, for relatively small capital expenditure. Cold baths were constructed at Cornhill in Northumberland and Quarndon in Derbyshire, and Ilkley in the West Riding of Yorkshire had a small bath-house, the White Wells, in 1699. Thomas Greenway erected a cold bath in Widcombe just south of Bath in 1704, but the nearby Lyncombe Spaw – resuscitated in 1737 by Charles Milsom, who erected a circular pavilion over it – was a drinking spa. Ipswich in Suffolk had a cold bath in about 1716–17, as did Westwood in Leeds and Whittington in Derbyshire (both in 1769), and many others cannot be dated. As late as 1790 spa visitors to Horley Green near Halifax and in 1797 to Dinsdale in County Durham endured the rigours of cold, not warm, baths, which accounts for the seasonal nature of the trade. George Neale had introduced the practice of taking hot sulphur baths in Harrogate lodging-houses in 1626, but the Hyde Spa, Prestbury, was exceptional in providing a hot bath as well as a cold one as early as 1751. Not only were hot baths, except the thermal-water ones, lacking in the eighteenth century, but many watering-places were only drinking spas with no baths, and the spa building was primarily a well-house or a pump-room. There is no mention of a bath at Gumley in Leicestershire or Walton Spa near Tewkesbury in Gloucestershire, both spas which emerged late in the century. But as supplies of coal for heating boilers became available at the end of the century hot baths were introduced, as at Leamington Spa from 1786.

The leisured elite, those with some wealth who were not tied by common tasks at local level, journeyed round these rural spas, many visiting several and staying away from home for weeks. By mid-century these holidays were made easier by better roads: only 182 of the 1,563 miles on thirteen routes out of London were not provided for, and the 'turnpike mania' of 1751–72 and the speculative boom of the 1790s carried the process further.[9] Yet although travellers were helped by growing stocks of horses and vehicles and more commercial transport, the wonder is that they undertook such arduous journeys, often over unmade byways, to stay in remote spas in some discomfort.

One of the most successful cold-bathing ventures was at Bungay on the Norfolk–Suffolk border, although the first Suffolk spa at Ipswich, a drinking spa with a cold bath and a trade in mineral waters, was established by 1717.[10] The spa at Bungay, a market town on the River Waveney, was the brainchild of John King, a local apothecary who knew Floyer's 1697 pamphlet and was perhaps encouraged by the Waveney being made navigable from Yarmouth to Bungay from 1670. When King, after diligent search, found a spring on his land at Earsham, east of Bungay, he built a bath-house there on the north bank of the river in 1728 and planted a unique setting, a vineyard containing plants from Burgundy, Champagne and Provence. This expensive undertaking was supported by 448 subscribers and was publicized in 1737 by his explanatory pamphlet, *An Essay on Hot and Cold Bathing,* dedicated to physicians in the diocese of Norwich. Thirty-one subscribers were from Bungay and neighbouring towns, and eight titled people and many professional men, thirty-three surgeons, twenty-two apothecaries, eighteen physicians and forty-nine rectors were involved. Thirty-one fellows of Cambridge colleges were subscribers; Caius College provided fifteen and St John's the second largest group. Watering-places, even minor ones, had become accepted, not only as fashionable but respectable and worthy of serious attention. King's pamphlet described forty local cases of cures. His most astounding story was of a lady from Jamaica who came to Bristol and was advised by a Dr Baynard to try the waters of Bath, but in vain. So Baynard sent her to Bungay where, after 150 immersions, she contracted smallpox. Undeterred, she continued her bathing and recovered.

The illustrated frontispiece of King's booklet shows the delightful sylvan setting of the Bungay bath-house, a single-storeyed building with a central door flanked by two windows and fronted by a semicircular courtyard with two paths to the river, woodland and vineyards on the right and gardens laid out in parterres on the left. A sailing-boat preceded by two swans glides on the river towards the rustic bridge, which was wide enough to take a sedan chair. Three small houses – presumably lodging-houses – adjoin, twelve horses graze in the pasture, and visitors arrive: four on horseback, two in a phaeton and pair, and others in a coach and four. A fisherman sits placidly on the bank. Apart from its vineyards Bungay was typical of the minor spas in scale and solitude, the appendage of a thriving small town where in 1773 a theatre and a gentlemen's club were built. It was the occasional resort of the neighbouring gentry, but had declined by 1846.[11]

Somersham in Huntingdonshire was another exceptional venture involving Cambridge scholars; its ancient episcopal palace was held by the Regius Professor of Divinity. John Verdon went there to drink the waters in 1699, but John Moore, Bishop of Ely from 1707 to 1714, first encouraged its use, supported by Charles, 1st Duke of Manchester, of Kimbolton, Edward, Viscount Hinchingbrook, Bishop William Wake of Lincoln and the leading county gentry. A house was erected by subscription near the spring and, directed by the indefatigable Dr Samuel Knight, rector of Bluntisham, a pump-house was fitted up and a bowling green laid out. Some kind of accommodation was arranged, although most summer visitors had to find lodgings in St Ives or the surrounding villages. Bottled water was sent to Cambridge, Ely and parts of Lincolnshire and Norfolk. Despite this promising beginning rumours that the water produced calculus led to neglect and the attendants' profits were minimal.

Although the house had fallen into ruin, local physicians were loath to abandon the Somersham Spa and tried to disprove the allegations that the waters produced stone, supported in this by Daniel Peter Layard, physician to the Dowager Princess of Wales. He practised in Huntingdon from about 1750 to 1762 and then among high society in London. When in 1758 an attempt was made to re-erect the pump-house, now with a cold bath, some very influential people subscribed, so perhaps Layard's metropolitan connections had been canvassed. No other minor English spa had such an elaborate organization nor such high-powered support, and it suggests an attempt to mount a regional spa in eastern England. As well as the Montagu family of Kimbolton and the bishop of Ely, eight court physicians and surgeons and twenty-seven lesser ones, the deans of Salisbury and York and thirty-five other clergy, were involved. Their management committee of thirteen selected a chairman and two stewards, and on 19 May 1758 drew up a set of rules, the first of its kind, to put the administration of the spa on a commercial basis. The stewards' duties were to take payments, inspect repairs and improvements, meet expenses and give an annual account of expenditure, and a paid clerk acted as secretary and sent notice of forthcoming committee meetings to the Cambridge papers. The committee met at St Ives whenever the unnamed proprietor or the stewards desired.

As at Bath and Buxton, provision was made for the local poor; all who had right of common on Somersham Heath were given access to the mineral water. A commoner was admitted early, from 5 a.m. to 7 a.m., on presentation of a signed certificate from his parish minister, or another reputable person, that he was a proper object of charity, and on giving his name and address to the servant in charge. After the needy the subscribers came from 7 a.m. to noon, paying 5*s*.; non-subscribers paid 7*s*. 6*d*. a season, or 2*d*. a quart for the water. The servant in charge was paid 4*s*. a week from 1 May to 1 October, unless gratuities from drinkers proved sufficient recompense, but nothing was taken from the poor commoners. The servant was allowed to sell beverages, wine, spirits, tea, coffee and chocolate, and medicinal tinctures, drops and salts, on condition that he kept the establishment in good order. In about 1762 Layard returned to London and lived in Lower Brook Street, but he found time to write *An Account of the Somersham Water* (1767). The spa's effective life was probably brief; it had little repute by 1840.[12]

Somersham's detailed arrangements were exceptional among the minor spas, its patrons aping the organized social life of the larger spas. The only feature it shared with contemporary minor spas was the primitive nature of its accommodation: most spas had merely a well and a bath-house with a cold bath, and lodgings normally had to be procured in neighbouring villages. Lack of capital expenditure on adequate buildings explains why many springs were not developed into accepted spas. At Shuttlewood near Bolsover in Derbyshire Charles Basseldine, a gentleman of Clown, decided in 1732 to exploit a sulphureous spring but provided only a neat, small basin with a bath below. Nevill Holt, already mentioned, never had more than a well-head, although its waters were widely distributed.[13] The poor found the two mineral springs at Dosthill in Warwickshire beneficial, but they were neglected through lack of accommodation for respectable company until about 1765, when new proprietors built a 'neat' house with suitable offices and dry-walled gardens with stone and brick steps down to the wells, which were now enclosed, tiled over and locked against intruders.[14]

Even if hundreds of country people used a local spring, as at the so-called Crickle Spaw in the West Riding of Yorkshire, the medical profession often withheld its recognition of a spa. In 1765 the sulphur water there surged into a circular basin but it had no protection, such as a canopy, and in Dr Granville's words, later lacked 'every auxiliary resource to a well-established watering-place', and so had 'not yet been made available as a spa'. Again the Saltmoor spring in Worcestershire, much used by invalids, had been analysed by Sir Humphrey Davy, but failed to become a spa through lack of lodgings there.[15] Clearly positive effort in building and publicity was needed to convert a medicinal spring into a viable spa, as Nathaniel Curzon, Lord Scarsdale found at Kedleston in Derbyshire, where he built his mansion between about 1758 and 1761. A sulphur well in his plantations existed in 1673 and Floyer referred to the cold bath there in 1702, but only a small rustic building covered the well and the village had no lodgings available. So Scarsdale invested in the Kedleston Inn, built in 1768 to accommodate the drinkers and bathers, and a walk through the woods led to the bath-house. In 1795 the inn was kept by Mr Stephens and visitors lived in a 'communicative society', as at Buxton, Harrogate and Matlock.[16]

The main initiative in promoting spas came, as one would expect, from the leaders of local communities, the small landowners, many of whom exploited the mineral springs on their estates. Figures of cost for a complete Georgian spa building are problematic. The Hotwell House at Clifton in 1696 cost £500, but the primitive small houses called pump-house, bath-house or well-house involved little capital outlay, so landowners easily tapped an additional but seasonal source of income from fees for bathing or drinking and lodging-house rents. A more ambitious complex could be established if advance payments, subscriptions, were taken as financial security, as at Bungay and Somersham. The spa also provided employment for estate workers as stewards, pumpers, well or bath attendants and lodging-house keepers, and for labourers in erecting the spa house and landscaping the site.

The gentry were not slow to ape each other in establishing spas: John Baber of Sunning-Hill in Berkshire by 1711, John Kellaway at Tilbury in Essex in 1734, Cosmos Nevill at Nevill Holt in Leicestershire in 1728, Sir Thomas Mostyn at Spurstow in Cheshire in about 1758, and in 1772 James Booth at Idle in Yorkshire. They often acted as philanthropists to the neighbouring poor by admitting them free, as at Somersham in Huntingdonshire, Skipton and Slaithwaite in Yorkshire, and Willowbridge in Staffordshire. Out of forty-eight provincial minor spas where the promoter and approximate date of origin between 1660 and 1815 are known, twenty-four were initiated by local landowners of the gentry class and seven by the nobility. The next largest group involved were twenty-one physicians or apothecaries, either as principals or supporters, and three sponsors were ministers. Twelve others of mixed occupation included an artist, a judge and a woman, Anne Galloway.[17]

The contemporary social importance of the spas is illustrated by two examples of municipal enterprise. Northampton had maintained the pre-Reformation St Thomas's Well, but in 1702 a chalybeate spring was discovered and named the Vigo Well to commemorate the battle that year. Local men vouched for its extraordinary cures, and the city assembly, with ambitions of making Northampton a watering-place of renown, voted expenditure of £30 for development of 'the New Wells' recently found in Cow Meadow near Clack Mills by planting trees, making walks and whatever else was ornamental and useful. In 1705–6 additional work cost £2 2s. 9d.; four more trees brought from Kingsthorpe were planted, protected by stakes and a thorn hedge and watered ten times by two men. In 1784 a new sheltered gravel walk 300 yards long with a fenced row of trees was laid to connect the two wells, St Thomas's and Vigo, at 'considerable expense'.[18] Thirsk in Yorkshire was another example of municipal spa enterprise where by 1725 the corporation was exploiting a chalybeate spring north of the town. A thatched house was erected over it for bathing and drinking and the poor woman in charge made what profits she could. The waters, claimed to resemble those of Cheltenham and Scarborough, attracted a visit from the Earl of Bristol and his companions.[19]

The promotion of minor spas continued to be stimulated by writing on the subject of balneology, and there was a rapid growth of spa literature in the eighteenth century – both general, such as Charles Lucas's *An Essay on Waters* (1756) and John Rutty's *A Methodical Synopsis of Mineral Waters* (1757), and particular, like James Taverner's *An Essay on Witham Spa* (1736) and John Andree's *An Account of the Tilbury Water* (1737), by

1781 in a fifth edition. Many of these spa guides ran to several editions, like *Observations on the Sulphur Water at Croft, near Darlington* (1782, 1786 and 1815) by Dr Robert Willan of Darlington. Tilbury and Witham were two spas in Essex, where doctors were particularly interested in furthering medical science and were organized in three local medical societies.[20] English periodicals appeared – the *Gentleman's Magazine* in 1731 and the *London Magazine* in 1735 – and national newspapers, like the *Daily Advertiser* in 1731, and they and the proliferating provincial press, like the *Leeds Intelligencer* (from 1754), often carried advertisements of mineral waters and spas. The more specialist *Philosophical Transactions* (from 1665) had a series of essays on mineral wells, including in 1744 C.H. Senckenberg on the Cheltenham mineral water. The mid-eighteenth century produced an increased volume of literature on spas and the use of mineral waters, following Dr Peter Shaw's translation of *New Experiments and Observations upon Mineral Waters* by Friedrich Hoffman, the German physician. No writer in England exceeded Dr Thomas Short (1690?–1772) of Sheffield in influence and importance over forty years; his first survey, *The Natural, Experimental and Medicinal History of the Mineral Waters of Derbyshire, Lincolnshire and Yorkshire* (1734–40, 1743) mentions 131 mineral waters, but many were uncovered springs. Better known was his comprehensive *General Treatise on the Various Cold Mineral Waters in England* (1765).[21]

The German doctor Diederick Wessel Linden, who wrote of the Hyde Spa at Prestbury, contributed to this literary flow. He came to England in 1742, in the train of the Hanoverian court, bringing considerable knowledge of the spas of Western Europe, like those in his home district of Hommerde in Westphalia, and at Kleve, Pyrmont and Spa. In 1747 he set up practice at Holywell in Flintshire and in 1748 produced *A Treatise on the Origin, Nature and Virtues of Chalybeate Waters . . .* (second edition 1755) dedicated to Frederick II (the Great) of Prussia, whose dominions included Kleve. Linden, now something of an expert on English spas, gave analyses of the chalybeate waters of Tunbridge, Islington and Shadwell, and mentioned those at Bath, the Bristol Hotwells, Acton, Cheltenham, Harrogate, Nevill Holt and Scarborough. Despite the cult of cold-bathing he particularly urged the use of hot baths of chalybeate water taken in a bathing-tub up to the neck, as at the Hyde Spa, but preferably the Tunbridge waters. Linden knew Fairly Jones, the mineral-water merchant near Covent Garden and proprietor of the Shadwell Spa in Middlesex, so he published *Directions for . . . Berry's Shadwell-Spaw, in Sun-Tavern Fields, Shadwell* in 1749, and his Hyde Spa treatise came in 1751, when he was reputedly determined to 'travel himself into the inspectorship of the British waters'.[22]

From late 1753 Linden was a mining adviser to the 3rd Duke of Ancaster and in 1754, at ducal expense, he spent a month at Llandrindod Wells and was cured of scurvy, so he helped to boost the wells with *A Treatise on the Three Medicinal Mineral Waters at Llandrindod . . .* (1765). Subscribers to this pamphlet included supporters of the Somersham Spa, the Princess Dowager of Wales's physicians, Dr Francis Philip Duval and Dr D. P. Layard, the Duke and Duchess of Ancaster, and Lord Brownlow Bertie (later the 5th Duke). R. C. B. Oliver suggests that Linden now went to Bath or the Bristol Hotwells; certainly his *Letter to Dr Sutherland at the Hot Wells, Bristol concerning a remarkable phaenomenon of the Bath Waters* appeared in 1762, but C. F. Mullet claims that Linden was a physician at Exeter.[23] Although he wrote: 'Don't think that I want to employ myself to multiply mineral waters . . . there are already too many palmed upon the public', in 1766 he was interested in the mineral waters at Llangbi near Pwllheli and then in those first discovered in 1741 by Francis Boothby, master collier, among coal-mines at Hanley's in Shropshire on land owned by Thomas Powys of Berwick, to whom Linden's puff, *A History and Analysis of the Hanlys Spa . . . Waters near Shrewsbury . . .* (1768) was dedicated.[24] Linden's last contribution to spa literature was *The Theory and Uses of Baths . . .* published in 1772.

Many spas inspired more literary efforts and their virtues were often celebrated in poetry by the so-called water-poets, patrons with leisure to spare between bouts of drinking and bathing. At Tunbridge Wells such verse offerings for public perusal were inscribed in a book kept at the bookseller's on the Walks. The occasional poem or doggerel verse often revealed the quality of local life, as at Sunning-Hill in Berkshire. Its mineral waters, known in 1711, were taken at home in the 1730s by Sarah, Duchess of Marlborough, because they were supposedly like those of Tunbridge Wells, and she sometimes went by coach to the well, where a literary coterie gathered.[25] In 1725 a patron, Dr John Merrick, recently cured of fever lauded the spring in verse, *Heliocrene. A Poem in Latin and English on the Chalybeate Well at Sunning-Hill in Windsor Forest,* dedicated to John Baber, who lived there:

> . . . that Hill of Fame
> Which borrows from the Sun its name . . .

After the fountainhead on Mount Helicon had dried up Apollo directed the Muses to his house in Britain, blessed by Pallas:

> And lo! a noble structure near
> Worthy yourselves, and worthy her,
> A generous patron there you'll see,
> Who will your friend and guardian be . . .

The Countess of Pembroke persuaded the author to translate this poem from its original Latin and make it public. Dr Richard Pococke found an assembly-room at Sunning-Hill in 1754 and the well retained its literary tradition; in 1769 the group there included Elizabeth Montagu, Elizabeth Carter and George, Lord Lyttleton.[26] The Bristol Hotwells also inspired a delightful lyric, *'An Hymn to the Nymph of Bristol Spring'*, by William Whitehead (1751).[27]

Few spas were so socially exclusive as Sunning-Hill. Glastonbury in Somerset, which attracted pilgrims to its ruined abbey, briefly became a notorious spa when it exploited the cure of Matthew Chancellor, a yeoman of nearby North Wootton. He was probably the Matthew Chancellor born on 22 January 1693 and married to one Christian, five of whose ten children died in infancy. He claimed that in October 1750 he had been directed to the waters of a Glastonbury spring in a dream and his asthma had been dispelled after thirty years' suffering. Anne Galloway, a businesswoman with experience of spa towns who had kept a shop in Cheltenham and then lived in Bath, promptly came to Glastonbury. She was possibly the Mrs Galloway who ran a lodging-house in Chapel Row, Bath, and may have been related to William Galloway, who erected 'buildings' on the Kingston Estate there in 1749–50. At Glastonbury she built a large house over the springhead, the Bloody Well, for both drinking and bathing, and a new lodging-house with five rooms to a floor, almost finished in June 1752. She advertised widely in the *Bath Journal,* the *Gloucester Journal* and other newspapers, ran an agency for servants, lodgings and property, and had an assembly-room.[28]

The inhabitants of Glastonbury prepared to reap the harvest. 'Thousands', it was boasted, soon arrived to drink and bathe, finding lodgings, mostly at 10*s*. 6*d*. a week, with the Reverend Pratt, Mr White the mayor, Mr Rock the apothecary and others. John Fisher was prepared to let the Crown Inn, furnished or unfurnished. But acccommodation was in short supply, and there were only thirty-four visitors on 26 June 1754. Anne Galloway's pump-room was open every morning for taking the waters, and in the afternoon for tea and 'innocent amusements', excepting Sunday, Friday and days of abstinence. She also promoted a trade in bottled Glastonbury water which was sold in the Universal Register Office in the Strand, but in bottles supplied by the customer. Publicity pamphlets appeared; *A Short Description of the Waters at Glastonbury* (1751) by the Reverend J. Davies of Plympton listed thirty-four cases of cures: twenty-two of them local but others from Bath, Bristol, Hampshire, Wiltshire, London, and one from Norwich.[29]

Success, as always, brought its enemies. Some journals, such as *The General Evening Post* and *The Gloucester Journal,* attacked the Glastonbury project and hinted at a popish plot. In August 1751 the *Gentleman's*

Magazine alleged that fashionable people were forsaking Bath for this new spa, and a song with the refrain 'Derry down' prophesied the collapse of Glastonbury's inflated prosperity. Here are verses:

> This town, very late, was a place of no note,
> Where scarce one in ten could afford a new coat;
> But now since the Popish invention is found,
> In trade, and in plenty, and wealth, they abound.
> > Derry down, etc.
>
> By this well manag'd scheme to get rich by our folly,
> Their maids are grown buxom, their men blith[e] and jolly,
> Though humble before, now they're puff'd up with pride,
> His ruffles each wears, and a sword by his side.
> > Derry down, etc.

Charges of popish influence may have had some substance, for, alone among the English spas, the pump-room was closed on Catholic fast-days and there was a well-justified prophecy of imminent failure. Mrs Galloway could not afford to improve the pump-room and make it weatherproof, accommodation and services were inadequate for 'the better sort of people', and Glastonbury was overwhelmed by the influx of the poor, who had no shelter from the weather and caused disorder. An injection of capital was necessary, and the remedy proposed in the *Bath Journal* was an annual subscription of one guinea for the use of the rooms, drinking, bathing and attendance. Paupers could be subsidized by a two-guinea subscription from the better-off, carrying the right to send one poor person to take the waters with lodgings and maintenance for seven weeks; more generous subscribers had extra, proportional rights. A register of the poor – their names, time of admission, place of abode, sponsor, illness and cure – would be kept in the pump-room, and the Society for the Propagation of Christian Knowledge suggested the supply of books and persons to teach them to be useful to society. But the scheme failed to save the spa and when Chancellor died in 1765, with the vision of a prosperous Glastonbury unrealized, the burial register entry of 24 August was 'Matthew Chancellor, the dreamer'.[30]

By 1781 the spring was 'entirely ruined', the pump-room had become a shop, and visitors were more interested in the abbey ruins than the waters. In 1791 the Glastonbury Spa was denounced as a ploy to bring trade to the depressed town, but in 1794 an anonymous attempt was made to revive it with further publicity, *The History and Antiquities of Glastonbury . . .* [with] *an account of the Mineral Waters . . .*, printed by Crutwell of Bath. There were ridiculous claims that Glastonbury outrivalled the two major West Country spas:

> Cease, lofty Bath, aloud to sing,
> The virtues of thy sulph'rous spring:
> Hold Bristol, hold! boast not thy well,
> For Glaston spring doth both excel.

The revival, when it came, was ephemeral; by 1839 the pump-room had become a private dwelling (which it is today, charmingly restored).[31]

Another example of spa doggerel was on a signpost at a road junction directing travellers to the Spurstow White Water on the Bunbury estate of Sir Thomas Mostyn in Cheshire, which had some vogue in about 1750:

> If you are troubled with sore or flaw,
> This is the way to Spurstow Spa
> If all your sores you've left in the lurch,
> This is the way to Bunbury Church.

The Reffley Spring, a fountain with a chalybeate water on the estate of Sir W. J. H. B. Folkes in Norfolk, also inspired a poem, 'Reffly Spring, an Epistle in Verse', by John Grisenthwaite (1804).[32]

Not all the new Georgian spas were rural; some served the sophisticated rakes of the metropolis, the most popular one being Bagnigge Wells on the site of Nell Gwyn's country house, where King's Cross Station now stands. In 1757 the tenant, Mr Hughes, claimed medicinal qualities for two old wells in the gardens, which he opened in 1759 with an announcement in the *Public Advertiser,* and in 1760 Dr John Bevis gave support. The wells were dominated by a 'temple', a circular colonnade supporting a dome, surrounded by a low balustrade, and its amenities included a long-room where tea and muffins were served and formal gardens with arbours, a rural cottage, three bridges spanning the stream, a castellated hexagonal grotto and a goldfish pond. Bagnigge Wells inspired much verse, including a poem, 'Bagnigge Wells',

> Where 'prentice youths enjoy the Sunday feast,
> And city matrons boast their Sabbath best,
> Where unfledged Templars first as fops parade,
> And new made ensigns sport their first cockade.

John Davis, the tenant between 1775 and 1793, charged 3*d.* each person for drinking, or 8*d.* a gallon. He carried out improvements and attracted a sprinkling of aristocratic customers, but the spa became overpopular and declined. Thomas Salter, the lessee in 1813, was immediately bankrupted and all the stock, including 200 drinking-tables, was auctioned. W. Stock attempted a revival on a reduced site in 1814.[33]

Another contemporary new drinking spa of around 1762, St Chad's, a former holy well in spacious gardens at the north end of Gray's Inn Road, had higher charges – £1 a year or 6*d.* a person and 1*s.* a gallon – but in 1809 it was a resort favoured by the lower class of tradesmen. By contrast, the drinking spa at St Agnes le Clear near Hoxton became a bathing spa in 1731; it had a large cold bath thirty feet long, twenty feet broad and four feet six inches deep for ladies and gentlemen, and it was rebuilt in 1778.[34]

In comparison with the period 1660–1700 the early eighteenth century was a slightly less active period of spa foundation, producing only about thirty-four new spas, some of which were not commercially viable.[35] Apart from the ambitious Somersham project – and Quarndon, where Lord Scarsdale, lord of the manor, may have provided the cold bath in use by about 1727[36] – all the promoters between 1700 and 1750 were relatively modest. William Mason enclosed his spring at Cheltenham in 1718 and Captain Skillicorne developed it in a small way, and the Reverend Joseph Greene, curate and grammar-school master, supported by an anonymous gentleman, established the 'Spaw of Stratford-upon-Avon' at Bishopton in Warwickshire. From about 1742 people from twenty miles around came to drink those waters, 700 in one morning, but in primitive buildings, as Greene's drawings of 1744 showed. That year Dr Charles Perry, an authority on the Spa and Aix-la-Chapelle (Aachen) waters, analysed the Bishopton waters and suggested municipal support. The corporation of Stratford could exploit them at small expense, for the town could accommodate many strangers and good roads led to it. But although the spa was still 'much visited' in 1800 there was no financial support for building there until 1837.[37] Among the other new spas between 1700 and 1750 Jessop's Well at Claremont in Surrey was enclosed in a building by James Fox, lord of the manor, by 1739, when it drew mention from Dr Stephen Hales in his *Account of several . . . Chalybeate or Steel-Waters.*[38]

In 1744 John Shires, a labourer, found a mineral spring at Thorp Arch (or Clifford) in the West Riding of Yorkshire where the Gascoignes, lords of the manor, claimed its ownership. The Thorp Arch burial register commemorates him as 'John Shires who found the Spaw'. Although the spring on the south bank of the River Wharfe could be reached only by ford or ferry from the village, Sir Edward Gascoigne ordered the erection of a wall around it and good local turnpike roads facilitated the arrival of visitors, among them Dr Richard Pococke in 1751. Early visitors had to stay in the village on the north bank, mostly in Mrs Wright's house, but in 1753 an enterprising local, Joseph Tate (or Taite), built a house near the spa. 'Tate's', or the 'Spaw-House known by the sign of the Black Bull', with a maltkiln, stables and ten acres of land, was the nucleus of a new settlement on the south bank, Boston Spa, with good stone houses forming a High Street. Sir Thomas Gascoigne allowed local people to fix a pump over the spring in 1767 and to collect the revenues from spa-water sales, and neighbouring landowners with rising property values co-operated to build a bridge over the Wharfe in 1770.[39] Access by the bridge brought in more visitors: Dr Thomas Garnett of Harrogate and Drs Munro and Walker became interested in it, and Dr Hunter of Leeds analysed the waters in 1784. The Duke of Rutland, on a visit in 1796, found two 'very good inns' – the 'old established' house of Tate's, and the 'hotel', a 'capital hotel' designed to take many visitors. By 1792 a little pump-room, with hot and cold baths in an adjoining bath-house, had been erected over the spring, and Boston Spa had, the duke thought, the potential to become one of the most fashionable watering-places in the kingdom. By 1822 it indeed had 600 inhabitants and in the next decade it became a village resort of some renown, celebrated by William Bownas in his poem 'Boston Spa' (1852).[40]

The second half of the century, when improved roads spread to many parts of the kingdom, was a considerably more active period of spa promotion, especially 1780–9 also a time of expansion at Bath, Cheltenham and Clifton. Apart from extra investment in other existing spas, such as Boston, there were at least thirty-nine new and dateable foundations compared with thirty-four in 1700–49. Two new ones on the Essex coast, Mistley and Wivenhoe, were sea-water spas; they had covered baths constructed and did not originate as *sea-bathing* resorts. Liverpool and Wigan, both in Lancashire, were spa appendages to growing commercial towns which had profited by the construction of the Leeds–Liverpool Canal in 1774. Liverpool was an expanding port and Wigan's economy was based on coal and cotton, but it hoped to become the 'New Harrogate'.

The spa quarter of such towns provided an elitist social centre – not, as at Scarborough, primarily for visitors, but for enriched upper- and middle-class residents. Bath interests may have encouraged the embryonic spa at Liverpool, probably the chalybeate spring in St James's Walk. The Woods, Bath architects, directed the building of the New Exchange in Water Street in 1754, and Samuel Derrick, the Bath MC, visited Liverpool in 1760. There was a strong local medical fraternity: four physicians, seventeen surgeons and seven druggists and apothecaries in 1766, two of whom produced spa pamphlets in 1773. Dr Thomas Houlston wrote *An Essay on the Liverpool Spa Water* and Dr James Worthington produced *Experiments on the Spa at Mount Sion, near Liverpool.*[41]

But rural spas remained an attraction, as at Pear-tree House, an ale-house at Godstone in Surrey with a pear tree in the garden where a spring was found in the 1750s. Its well-water had some temporary fame, and the manager – Prentice, a jockey – was rumoured to make at least £100 a week in season by selling it at 2s. a gallon.[42] Norfolk's active social life, with its many market-town assemblies, led to attempts to mount a simple spa at

East Dereham as well as at Reffley. There was movement also in the Midlands; the new Derbyshire spa Whittington had a cold bath in 1769, in Leicestershire spas were promoted at Burton Lazars in the 1760s and Gumley and Leicester in the 1780s, and in Warwickshire the expansion of Leamington Spa dates from the foundation of Abbotts' Well in 1784.[43]

The fame of Harrogate and Scarborough and the increasing affluence of the middle classes from growing industrialization touched off a marked increase in spa enterprise in the North. Men employed by William Lambton, later Earl of Durham, found a sulphureous spring while prospecting for coal at Dinsdale near Darlington in 1789, and a bathing-house was erected nearby in 1797.[44] Idle Spa in the West Riding emerged in the 1770s, and Askern Spa in 1786 was an attempt of Humphrey Osbaldeston of Gateforth, lord of the manor, to exploit a disused sulphur-water well, but he did not live to see the Askern of the 1820s, an elegant, fashionable watering-place with lists of arrivals in the *Leeds Intelligencer* and other newspapers. Gipton Spa and other small wells had a following within the environs of Leeds, and Gilsland Spa in Cumberland attracted custom in the 1790s.[45]

The waters of the Old Well at Croft Spa on the Yorkshire–Durham border were on sale in sealed bottles in London in 1713, but so far the Chaytor family, lords of the manor, had failed to develop the spa, and its lack of suitable lodgings led to neglect. But by 1782 Croft, on the Great North Road, had a regular daily post and coach service and the landowner, William Chaytor (d. 1819), spurred on by the current spa mania, had elaborate plans to build a new bath with dressing-rooms for both sexes, and an adjacent lodging-house. Then came war in 1793 and economic collapse, bankruptcies at Bath, Cheltenham and Clifton, and a temporary halt to most spa foundation. Although the old posting-inn at Croft was extended, improved and renamed the Spa Hotel in 1808, nothing further was done until August 1827, when the discovery of the New Well made the spa economically viable.[46]

Another wartime casualty, too much in the ambience of Bath, was the spa at Middle Hill, Box, in north-west Wiltshire, founded by a physician, almost certainly Dr William Falconer of Bath, who in 1786 wrote a pamphlet, *A Brief Account of the newly-discovered Water at Middle Hill, near Box in Wilts.* (2nd edn, 1789). The proprietor invested in a pump-room, a lodging-house, coach-houses, stables and a tap-house there and put the property in the charge of William West, the baker who discovered the spring in 1783, but in 1791 he had to sell it all, including the mostly new furniture. The Spa House, which became a private dwelling, still exists.[47]

A more famous Wiltshire spa, Holt, was associated with Henry Eyre, a dealer in the mineral-water trade, especially in Spa water. English visitors still frequented Spa; the Earl of Bath, three other English peers, and eleven members of the House of Commons among others in July 1763, and some used the nearby warm baths at Aachen. English visitors founded an English Club at Spa in 1766, and by 1785 it had 534 subscribers.[48] There was now much demand for imported Spa water – the bulk of it, as Sylvia McIntyre has shown, coming to London, but some directly to outports, such as Bristol, Ipswich, Newcastle, Yarmouth and Boston. William Sutton's import of 300 flasks of Spa water into Stockton in 1743 was not unusual for that port. At the retail end it was handled by tavern- and coffee-house keepers and tea and coffee merchants, such as the tea merchant Tom Twining, who from 1714 to 1723 sold a great quantity.[49]

The Spa water dealers received a setback on the accession in 1714 of the Hanoverian George I who, like the House of Saxony, preferred the steel waters of Pyrmont and returned to drink them when visiting Hanover. In 1717 the presidents of the Royal Society and the Royal College of Physicians, Sir Isaac Newton and Dr John Bateman respectively, diplomatically allied to commend the Pyrmont waters as superior to those of Spa in strength, taste and virtue and more accessible by land carriage to the coast. Soon Mr Burges, a druggist at the Blue Anchor in Fleet Street, was importing vast amounts of Pyrmont water in sealed bottles, but Dr Frederick Slare, in *An Account of the Pyrmont Waters* (1717), was careful not to offend the vested interests of the Spa trade by denigrating those waters. George Turner's *A Full Account of the Mineral Waters of Spa and Pyrmont* (1723) followed, and the Pyrmont waters became more popular; by 1730 large quantities – 64,375 three-pint bottles and 7,702 larger ones – were imported, compared with 123,786 bottles of Spa water.[50]

The increasing volume and complexity of the English trade in mineral waters, both foreign and domestic, led to closer organization. London was its centre – nine-tenths of the Pyrmont water and most of the Spa water came there and by 1733 it was dominated by three London specialist merchants, each with a warehouse: James Turner in St Alban's Street, Pall Mall, John Fiddes of Scarborough at the Golden Wheatsheaf in Tavistock Street, and Henry Eyre at the Golden Tea Canister at Temple Bar, who in 1730 claimed to be the first 'to make the sale of mineral waters his only business'. Eyre had a house at Holt in Wiltshire, where in about 1713 there was an attempt to promote the Old Wells as a drinking spa with widow Grace Harding as their keeper. In 1727 Eyre was selling Holt as well as Bath and Bristol waters and in 1729 he advertised them from his London premises. In 1731 he was 'the Master' of the Holt Wells, but the lord of the manor, Edward Lisle (d. 1752) of Moyles Court in Hampshire, was the proprietor, and Eyre's treatise *A Brief Account of the Holt Waters . . . near Bath in Wiltshire* (1731) was dedicated to him. From 1732 Eyre had a Bristol warehouse to supply the west of England and Wales with foreign waters, but he also sent Holt water to Bath, Bristol, Oxford, Cambridge,

Winchester, Southampton, Reading, Salisbury and Chichester. Four baskets of it went out by ship from Bristol in 1752.[51]

Eyre's efforts to exploit the trade in the waters of Holt conflicted with a parallel attempt to transform it into a small resort, a drinking spa. By 1731 three more wells (one of the original pumps is still preserved) were being used, buildings had gone up and six houses offered lodgings, including the Great House, whose visitors had preferential use of the water. A doctor lived in a cottage, and a list of visitors cured shows that most – forty-one – were from Wiltshire, but fifteen came from Bristol, ten from Somerset, seven from Gloucestershire, a scattering from adjacent counties, ten from London and two from Scotland. In 1733 Eyre acquired a brief monopoly of the import of Spa waters, which he supplied to Queen Caroline, so from about 1738 he went to Spa more often. In about 1740 Edward Lisle sold his Holt property to Dr Simon Burton of Savile Row, who died in 1744, and in 1746 the wells 'commonly called Holt Waters', and several nearby lodging-houses and tenements, were sold to meet his debts. In 1754 the wells, with some furnished lodging-houses, were again offered for sale or lease – Mr Robbins, a Melksham attorney handling the negotiations – and by March 1755 Mary Burcombe was the new keeper. In 1766 Holt Wells was a spa of sufficient importance for arrivals there to be reported in the *Bath Journal:* over thirty in late June and more than nineteen in early September. When Charles Nott was the proprietor in 1780 a cold bath with dressing-room, fireplace and an attendant, had been added.[52] Holt's life as a spa lasted until about 1815, when Melksham became its competitor.

Tourists could drink domestic mineral waters at the location, but an increasing volume and variety of them was distributed by carrier. By 1733 at least sixteen English waters were on the market including those of another Wiltshire spa-let, West Ashton, on sale in Bath, Bristol, Salisbury and London. More soon appeared. Domestic waters available in London included those from Cheltenham in 1738, West Tilbury, Essex in 1739 and Nevill Holt, Leicestershire, in 1748. Both the Bourne waters from Lincolnshire and the Nevill Holt waters were stocked at the Parade Coffee-house and the Phoenix in the marketplace at Bath in 1755.[53]

Competition in the retail trade was keen. Henry Eyre distributed some of the Iron Pear-tree water and salts from Holcomb's New Well at Godstone from 1752 to 1753. The water, in stone bottles, was sealed with his emblem, the wheatsheaf, but it was also handled at Holcomb's warehouse in Coventry Street and the White Horse Inn, Cripplegate.[54] Fairly Jones, who in 1747 married John Fiddes' widow and took over that business, in 1748 handled Acton waters and those of Shadwell, bearing the coat of arms of the proprietor Walter Berry, and of Harrogate and Bourne. In 1751 his stepson Richard Fiddes also dealt in the Hyde waters of Prestbury, Gloucestershire.[55] By 1762 Thomas Davis had Pyrmont and Seltzer waters and sixteen domestic ones on his list, and two, Kilburn and Jessop's Well at Claremont in Surrey, were new. By the time Davis died in 1778 a commerce in at least thirty-one bottled domestic waters had been attempted – thirty-six in 1816.[56]

Even Buxton water, slow to come on the market, was advertised in 1782 when the 5th Duke of Devonshire was undertaking the expansion of Buxton, but the trade in mineral waters was beginning to decline. The proliferation of minor spas and the improvements in travel by the late eighteenth century brought a visit to a spa within the reach of more people and reduced the demand for bottled water.

II   The Earl of Shrewsbury's Hall at Buxton c. 1573 (from John Speed's map of
Derbyshire 1611)

III The Utkinton Well, Cheshire (from BL C. 123 d. 20)

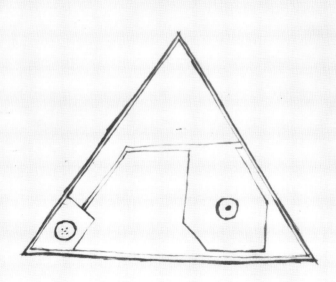

IV   The Tunbridge Wells, a) the triangular ground plan and b) Lord Muskerry's
entrance 1664 (Dr Edward Browne's Drawings, BL Add. MS 5233 fo. 72)

V   Bath, the first Pump Room 1705–6, copper engraving by John Fayram 1739

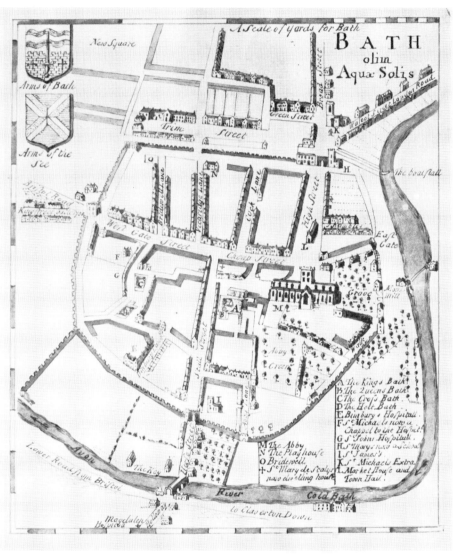

VI Bath Olim Aquae Sulis 1732–6 surveyed by Mr Strachey

VII Bath, Milsom Street 1769 by Thomas Malton

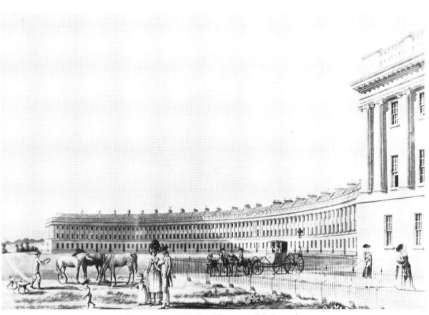

VIII Bath, The Royal Crescent 1788 by Thomas Malton jun

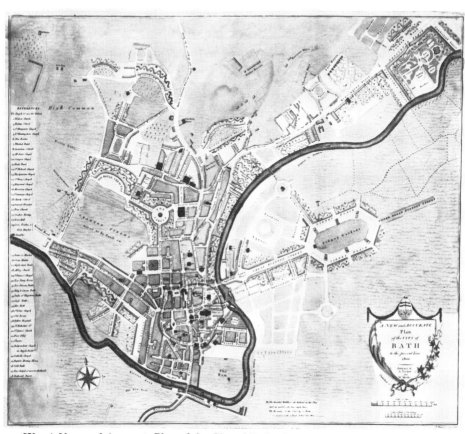

IX   A New and Accurate Plan of the City of Bath 1801 by A. Taylor and W. Meyler

X Captain William Wade master of ceremonies at Bath 1769–77, by Thomas Gainsborough

XI   The Bungay Spa from John King, *An Essay on Cold Bathing* **(1737)**

XII   The Pump House, Glastonbury (photo. Phyllis Hembry)

XIII   The Spa House, Box (photo. David Wiltshire)

XIV   The West Prospect of the Spaw and Town of Cheltenham c. 1748 by Thomas
Robins

XV   The Royal Party at the Old Well, Cheltenham in 1788. Etching by Peter La
Cave c. 1789.

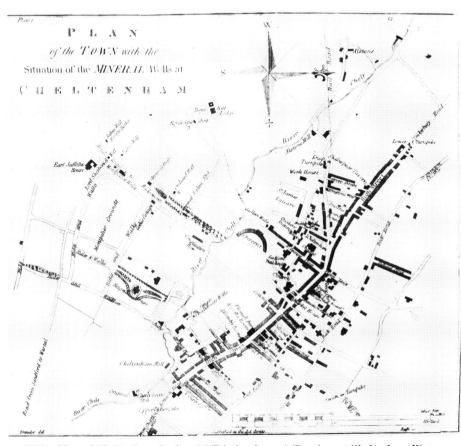

XVI Plan of Cheltenham by Daniel Trinder from *A Treatise on Cheltenham Waters and Bilious Diseases* by Thomas Jameson (1809)

XVII Low Harrogate by F. Nicholson (engraving by I. Walker 1796)

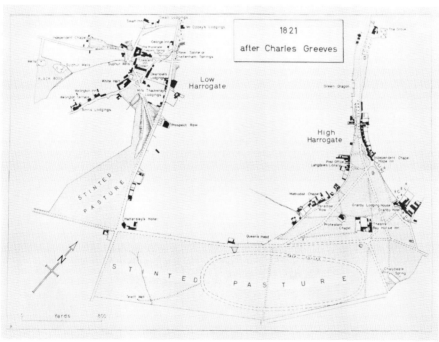

XVIII Harrogate 1821 after Charles Greeves

XIX   Buxton Old Hall and Crescent 1833 by D. Orme

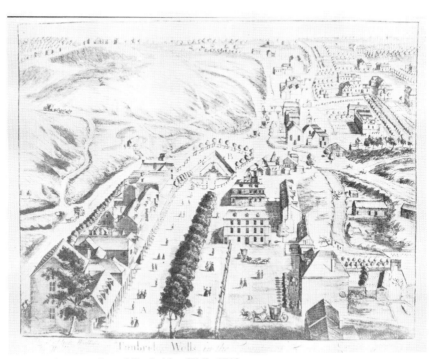

XX   Kip's engraving of Tunbridge Wells 1718

XXI   Tunbridge Wells, The Upper Walk 1772 by Samuel Green

XXII   Bath, the Sydney Hotel from the garden 1805 by John Claude Nattes

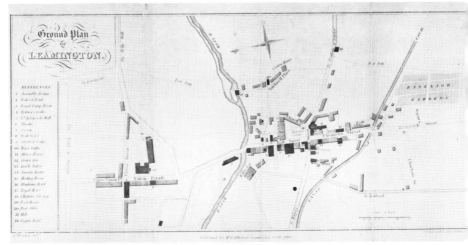

XXIII   Ground Plan of Leamington Spa 1818

XXIV   Leamington Royal Baths and Pump Room 1822

11

Cheltenham: The Village Spa

Another spa site which might have been a small, ephemeral watering-place was at Bay's Hill, about half a mile from the parish church of Cheltenham in Gloucestershire, where in 1718 William Mason put a rail around the spring on the slope, locked it and erected a little shed over it.[1] This, the Old Well, was for almost a century the focus of spa activity in Cheltenham and the origins of an urban watering-place which came to challenge Bath.

One version of the first use of the spring, inscribed on a painting by Thomas Robins, is that Gabriel Davis, a mason, found it in 1719. But it was generally accepted that Mason discovered it in his ground acquired in 1716 from Mr Higgs of Charlton Kings. Local inhabitants had earlier drunk the water for its purgative properties, and according to legend, pigeons had a marked partiality for the deposit of salts nearby. Mason would have known of the fame of the Hotwells springs at Bristol, where his son Joseph was a merchant, and he apparently thought of exploiting the spring, for Dr Baird of Gloucester and Dr Grevil of Worcester made experiments on the Cheltenham water and confirmed it as a mild chalybeate. Advertisements in the *Gloucester Journal* of 1720, and later in the London press, urged visitors to come to the pleasant town of Cheltenham to take the famous purging mineral waters, assuring them of 'convenient lodgings' with the diversion of a good bowling green and billiard tables. These were minimal amenities, but Mason made no further attempt to exploit the new spa. He leased it to a Mr Spencer, who paid an annual rent of £61 for this new business, and retired to Bristol.[2]

On Mason's death (by early 1725) his Bay's Hill (later Bayshill) property came to his daughter Elizabeth. In 1731 she married Captain Henry Skillicorne, a master mariner of Bristol who in 1738 retired to Cheltenham, where he set about the 'improvement' of his wife's inheritance. Much of the impetus for the development of Cheltenham was – as at Bath, Epsom and Tunbridge Wells – supplied by immigrants: Henry Skillicorne, born in the Isle of Man and a much-travelled man; then William Miller from London, Thomas Hughes from Monmouthshire, John Boles Watson, an Irishman, and Simon Moreau from Bath. Skillicorne promoted the first stage of Cheltenham's expansion as a spa, some of which he chronicled in his journal, no longer available but quoted by Goding.[3]

The Cheltenham which Skillicorne knew was a market town within the manor held by Sir John Dutton of Sherborne, twelve miles away. Although other landlords promoted minor spas, the Duttons did little to encourage Cheltenham's growth as a resort until the early nineteenth century. When the mineral spring at Bay's Hill was found the manor was being managed by a steward, John Prinn (d. 1735), the vestry managed parochial affairs, and the inhabitants, not anxious to attract visitors, accepted the status of a small town, in 1666 of 312 houses with 1,500 inhabitants. A traveller in 1682 dismissed Cheltenham as noteworthy only for its spired church; little could be said of the other buildings, except a very fine inn, formerly a gentleman's house. There was a fair on St James's Day (25 July). Cheltenham was a long, narrow town of farmers, maltsters, hosiers, mercers and shopkeepers, with one principal street running south-east to north-west for about a mile where water flowed down the centre. A grammar school could supply some sufficiently educated men to run its affairs, and its inns and ale-houses, presumably including the Plough Inn, could in 1686 provide forty-two beds and stabling for seventy-three horses.[4]

The way to the spa lay past the church, across the Church Meadow and over the River Chelt to the gentle rise of Bay's Hill beyond. In the summer of 1738 Skillicorne set about developing this site; he closed the well, which was five to six feet deep with doors to exclude the air, built an elaborate well-house, a square brick building on four arches with a dome over it, and erected a pump on the east side in the form of an obelisk. At the west end of the well he erected the 'Old Room', thirty-five feet by eighteen feet, with a billiard-room above (not to be confused with Mrs Jones's Old Room near the Plough), which protected the water-drinkers in bad weather and was used for dancing. Attempts were made to landscape the site, following the practice at other spas – such as the Tunbridge Wells Walk of 1636 and at Bungay, Hampstead and Islington – to provide a vista and a place to promenade.

Skillicorne's wealthy and travelled young friend Norbonne Berkeley, later Baron Botetourt and lord lieutenant of Gloucestershire, assisted him. In 1739 he proceeded to lay out the famous Old Well Walk, the first of Cheltenham's 'walks and rides'. Subscribers contributed £31 10s. 6d. towards the cost, and Sir John Dutton topped the list with five guineas. Skillicorne also, in 1739, laid out the Upper Walks, a double row of elms and limes, and made a new orchard adjoining. The next year the Lower Walk was planted with ninety-six elms at a cost of £56. The whole avenue was aligned with the church spire and led from the rustic Jemmy's Bridge over the Chelt, which formed the boundary between the parish of

Cheltenham and Alstone Tithing including Bay's Hill, to the well and some distance beyond. The original plan had been to extend the avenue through the Church Meadow by the church, but there were property objections and a winding six-foot-wide gravelled path was laid across it instead.[5]

The increasing number of annual subscribers to this project suggest strong local support at the outset: they mounted from 414 in 1740 to 667 in 1742, then fell slightly but recovered with 655 in 1748. So Skillicorne was able to improve the property by paving the yard round the well and building eighteen 'little houses' and in 1742 another 'room' two storeys high. But the droughts of 1740 and 1741 forced him to replant a considerable number of trees and quick-set hedges by the walk, assisted in 1743 by Mr Andrews, a surveyor of the town. This historic scene, on or near the site of the present Princess Hall of the Cheltenham Ladies' College, is shown in a watercolour painting on a fan (*c.* 1748) by the Gloucestershire artist Thomas Robins (1716–70) born at nearby Charlton Kings. The square four-arched pump-house had by then been enclosed by a square, stone-walled yard with ball-topped pillars at two entrances. The pump-room, built in three stages, was on one side of it.[6]

The Cheltenham Spa had the advantage of being linked to a market town which could supply lodgings and provisions, and the fame of 'Cheltenham Well' spread rapidly. In 1743 a London newspaper listed Cheltenham after Bath, Scarborough and Tunbridge as the most popular resorts and prophesied that its chalybeate water would attain great repute in Europe. There were 600 'persons of great fortune and gentility' at Cheltenham then, including the Duke and Duchess of Argyll, the Earl of Chesterfield, the 4th Earl of Westmorland and his wife, courtiers and several more nobles. Lady Stapleton, a granddaughter of Lord Westmorland and the wife of Sir William Stapleton, who died in January 1740, had already in about 1739, perhaps because of her husband's ill-health, built a new house, the Great House or the Grove House, for herself in Cheltenham. Close to the Old Well Walk, it was then unique among Cheltenham's buildings and Thomas Robins sketched it in 1748: a tall two-storeyed house with five bays and two recessed double bays on either side, a pedimented doorway reached by a flight of steps, and a west-wing extension.[7]

The vigour with which Captain Henry Skillicorne promoted the amenities of his well, and other entrepreneurs provided resort facilities at Cheltenham, should be seen in the context of Bath's example of a new kind of leisure society and its contemporary commercialization. Among other outsiders who descended on Cheltenham and took the opportunity to promote this embryonic watering-place was Thomas Hughes, the Monmouthshire attorney, reputedly there by 1749 when he was sixteen.[8] He rented the Old Well from Skillicorne and developed the mineral-water trade of the 'Cheltenham Spaw' or, as in the *General Advertiser* of 1751, the Cheltenham Wells. But in 1743 Henry Purefoy had purchased Cheltenham waters at 9*d*. a sealed bottle at Shalstone in Buckinghamshire – brought there, presumably by carrier, every Friday afternoon. His friend John Wentworth of Livingstone Lovell also bought them at 10½*d*. a bottle,[9] and Cheltenham water was on sale in Bath in 1748. The identity of this early trader operating before Hughes's arrival is unknown; Goding mentions a handbill referring to Hughes's trade in 1738, the year Skill-icorne began the development of the Walks, but Hughes was then only a boy of five. Thomas Hughes was certainly the keeper of the well later and traded in Cheltenham waters and mineral salts under the seal of his 'Spaw'. He packed his bottles in the Old Room and had London outlets through Thomas Davis's warehouse in St Alban's Street and the well-known Henry Eyre at Temple Bar, as well as agents in the West Mid-lands—Nantwich, Chester, Whitchurch in Worcester; and in Gloucester, Bristol, Bath and Oxford. The public were warned against other, spurious sources, and some false agents who were named. By 1752 Cheltenham water was being exported from Bristol.[10]

Hughes, a good businessman and a clever lawyer, began humbly at Cheltenham apprenticed to John de la Bere, whose partner he became in 1762. The next year he married into a powerful spa-conscious family; his wife was Elizabeth Bridges, the joint heiress of Henry Bridges of Key-nsham in north Somerset and a kinswoman of the Duke of Chandos, who was then building lodging-houses in Bath. Also that year, 1763, Henry Skillicorne died. He had, in the words of his memorial tablet in the parish church, 'brought this most salutary water to just estimation and extensive use'. His son and heir, Captain William Skillicorne, now acquired the Bay's Hill well and made a partnership with another newcomer, William Miller, who replaced Hughes, as the well's tenant. But Hughes, bolstered by his wife's wealth, was set to become their commercial rival; he became the under-sheriff of Gloucester in 1772 and in 1776 he set up as an independent solicitor. He also switched his interest to the High Street, where he bought the old Powers Court house and estate adjoining the Plough Inn. This included a ballroom and gardens run by a Mrs Jones, and he concentrated on developing his new property.[11]

Hughes later claimed that he had had to delay putting his plans into action. Certainly the mid-century economic slump was not a propitious time for capital risk, and in 1753 he was excused payment of poor rates on the well, which suggests that it was not very profitable. This is the first reference to a mineral-water spring being rated. In 1781 Moreau blamed the inhabitants, nervous of further investment, for neglecting the spa for thirty years, but outbreaks of smallpox may have been a deterrent to visitors. Before a visit in April 1742 Henry Purefoy of Shalstone wrote to the Cheltenham postmaster asking for assurance that the town was free of infection, and in 1757 journals of nearby towns reported that Cheltenham had been free of smallpox for the past six weeks. The next year the parish authorities warned that sufferers bringing it to the town would be prosecuted, but they claimed that the disease was on the decline—because a few had escaped it![12]

Transport problems also inhibited the growth of Cheltenham as a spa. The wealthy, like Lord Chesterfield, came in their own coaches, but those travelling from the metropolis by stagecoach had to go first to Gloucester and take another conveyance to Cheltenham, or leave the coach on the heights at Frog Mill Inn, Andoversford, and come on by post-chaise. The first recorded coach to cover the route between London and Gloucester, the 'Gloucester Flying Machine', took three days. By 1773 the journey had been reduced to twenty-six hours by the 'Old Hereford' stage, but there was still no direct coach from London to Cheltenham. Communication between Cheltenham and Gloucester was improved in 1756 when that stretch of road was turnpiked.[13]

Shortage of lodgings was another handicap. A survey of 1756 showed only sixty-seven beds available in inns, but stables for 150 horses. William Winterbotham found only one lodging-house – presumably the Great House – for visitors in 1773, and two inns which took lodgers. The Plough, at least from 1727 to 1763 was run by Thomas Pope and another inn, the George, was by 1745 in the care of Thomas Harvey, who in 1754 took over the new, large Swan, which had good stables and coach-houses and ran a coach 'from the hill' to this inn, presumable a shuttle service from the Frog Mill, where the London coach put down passengers. Two other inns were the Crown Inn, by 1745 run by Josias Cooke, and by 1763 a fifth, the Fleece; and Mrs Hyett had a coffee-house in Coffee-House Yard. But Moreau listed only four inns in 1783 – the Plough, the Swan, the George and the Fleece – and he thought that some good boarding-houses and a coffee-house, presumably a second one, were much needed and would be profitable.[14]

Another local spa, the Hyde Spa at Prestbury, provided some competition and was supported by lodgings. A more formidable rival was Bath, which had so much to offer forty-two miles away. But although Mrs Jane Edwards of Redlands in Bristol lived near the Hotwells waters and was a frequent visitor to Bath, she went to Cheltenham in 1742 and was there again from about 1 August to 6 September 1745, when she paid 2s. for a subscription to the walks and 10s. 6d. a week for the hire of a chair – so at least one sedan chair was available then – and went to the assembly, either at the long-room at the well or at Mrs Jones's room. She paid £7 10s. for the five weeks' hire of her rooms at Mr Ketheway's but bought her own provisions, including beer and 14 lb of honey, and a ton and a half of coal. She also gave 7s. 6d. to the bell-ringers, which suggests that Cheltenham had adopted the Bath habit of ringing in new visitors.[15]

But Cheltenham was not in an entirely static condition in the 1750s and 1760s. Not all came for health or pleasure, and although John Wesley was critical of spa life the Methodists drew large crowds, nearly 2,000 on the large bowling green of the Plough in 1739, 'thousands' in the churchyard in 1757, and a large audience in 1766. Some public social life was also being organized: assemblies by 1745 and by 1758 balls every Monday and Thursday and card assemblies on four other nights. A band of musicians performed at the well, as earlier at Bath, Tunbridge Wells and several metropolitan spas. They played from 8 a.m. to 10 a.m., and visitors subscribed 5s. a season towards their emoluments. The Great House was not only a lodging-house but a social centre; in August 1757, when run by Mr Pope, a concert there was followed by a ball, no isolated occasion. In 1744 the Warwick company of comedians introduced dramatic perform-ances, and in July 1758 Mr Williams's company performed in an old malt-house in Coffee House Lane converted into a primitive theatre by Mr Pope, who ran the coffee-house. If he was the same Thomas Pope the proprietor of the Plough Inn and the owner of the Great House, he dominated Cheltenham's social life.[16]

The small Cheltenham theatre, like that at Bath, was a nursery for the London stage and attracted the attention of the Irishman John Boles Watson, later an important theatrical manager and proprietor. About 1772 he bought Pope's malt-house and played on alternate nights at the Coffee House Yard Theatre and in Tewkesbury in company with John Kemble, whose sister Sarah married William Siddons. In 1774 both John Kemble and Sarah Siddons were in the company of Chamberlain and Crump engaged by Watson to play at his theatre. She and Kemble frequently returned.[17]

Cheltenham was mainly a drinking spa, and the cold bath in 1763 kept by Miss Stapleton in a building close to the Chelt, with conveniences for warm bathing, was disused by 1783. So Cheltenham might have remained a minor spa with the Bay's Hill well and the Long Walk beyond Church Meadow, the Great House near the church, and the busy commercial High Street with the inns. As Dr Pococke found in 1757, there was a 'tolerable' meeting-room, lodgings near it, and a physician, Dr Tomlinson, had set-tled in. But unlike the city of Bath, with its common council and tradition of self-government, Cheltenham was dominated by a vestry of limited agricultural and trade interests and lacked the constitutional framework for expansion. In 1780 the *Morning Post* accused Cheltonians of a 'narrow-minded mode of thinking'; they 'seem displeased that chance has brought them to public notice, by their constant opposition to every improvement for the convenience and accommodation of those who visit them'. But this local lethargy was challenged by William Miller, the Londoner of wealth and ability who went into partnership with William Skillicorne at the Bay's Hill Estate. In 1775–6 they built a new long-room, or assembly-room, measuring sixty-six feet by twenty-three feet, on the east side of the pump at the well, and converted the old room into private dwellings.[18]

As Cheltenham developed as a spa it adopted many of the fashions and customs of Bath, its prototype, and recruited its first master of ceremonies, Simon Moreau, there. Moreau, whose father was a lieutenant-colonel, claimed to be proficient in several languages and to have moved in polite society at home and abroad – including Bath, where in 1777 he had aspired to become the MC but had been rejected. Four years later Moreau became Cheltenham's first master, allegedly self-elected and at first not very popular, but he himself claimed that he had been appointed in 1780, the year before he came to Cheltenham.[19] Not only Bath and Cheltenham but the Bristol Hotwells, Scarborough and Tunbridge Wells all now had such a social arbiter.

However, there was already an active division of interests among the social centres: Miller's new long-room of 1775–6 at the Old Well, Mrs Field's Great House in the Grove, and the inadequate Old Room near the Plough now belonging to Thomas Hughes. Miller's long-room was open for water-drinkers every morning during the season, for public breakfasts on Monday from the first week in June as long as the weather permitted, and balls from the last Monday in June until the first in September, except in bad weather. Mrs Field's room competed with its main balls, also on Monday, cotillon balls every Thursday, and cards and public tea every other evening. Dancing at both rooms ended at 11 p.m., and when Moreau arrived in 1781 regulations for the balls were drawn up, inspired by his knowledge of the rules at Bath.

Following the example of other spas, a subscription society was being developed at Cheltenham, based on the notion of advance funding to secure capital investment. The general season subscription for the use of the well and of Miller's walks and avenues was 2*s*. 6*d*., and for the balls at his long-room the comparatively high charge was 10*s*. 6*d*. For Mrs Field's room it was less than half, 5*s*., but gentlemen were expected to find 1*s*. extra for the music for the cotillon ball on Thursday, and for Mrs Jones's Old Room in the High Street the rate was only 2*s*. 6*d*. Non-subscribers at the long-room at the Old Well and Mrs Field's paid 2*s*. for each ball. Subscribers at the long-room also paid 2*s*. 6*d*. for the newspapers and 5*s*. for the musicians at the well. Subscription books, as at most watering-places, served as registers for visitors and guides to local tradesmen in their dealing with customers, and all these payments represented a return on investment for the Skillicornes, William Miller and Mrs Field.[20]

The 1780s marked the first real boom in Cheltenham's development as a spa and provoked publicity. From a Birmingham press in 1786 came anonymously *A Treatise on Cheltenham Water,* and the next year John Barker's *Observations on a late publication on Cheltenham Water.* The number of visitors, including the neighbouring gentry, increased sharply: 374 in 1780, 500 in 1781, and 650 in 1782. In 1781 Monday public breakfasts alone attracted 200 or 300 and frequently included aristocrats like Georgiana, Duchess of Devonshire in 1780. Henry, 3rd Earl of Fauconberg, hoped to cure a scorbutic humour on his face there in 1776 and was so much attracted to Cheltenham that William Skillicorne was commissioned to build a house for him on Bay's Hill. In June 1781 the Honorable John Byng saw this building – Fauconberg House or Bayshill House, on the site of the present Sidney Lodge – being erected, while Lord Fauconberg and his family stayed at the Great House, as did Byng and his wife. Fauconberg House, the first residence of an aristocrat in Cheltenham, was a modest three-storeyed building, and bricks were burnt for it in nearby kilns. Byng walked out with Fauconberg to watch the foundations being dug and tried to persuade him that a basement was unnecessary in this rural site with ample space for expansion.[21]

Byng sampled the growing pleasures of Cheltenham: the summer breakfasts, riding during the day, dancing minuets in the pump-room, playing whist at Mrs Field's and a cotillon ball at Mrs Jones's which, 'from want of skill' in that semi-rural community, ended in country dances. He visited Watson's playhouse for a concert of both music and drama: *Much Ado About Nothing* and a farce, *High Life Below Stairs.* Most of all he liked the walks behind the town by the trout stream, and he found 'much company' about, many from Bristol and around and more expected, for the waters were the vogue and the last season had been the best. This was possibly because inland places were considered to be safer in wartime, when invasion threatened the coast, and Britain was then at war with France and Spain.

Like Mrs Edwards of Bristol at Cheltenham nearly forty years earlier, Byng and his wife had no meals at Mrs Field's; they had to purchase their own provisions with the family servants to market and cook for them. This self-catering at lodgings without board, and servants paid for separately, was customary at Cheltenham, which had a market, as it was then at Tunbridge Wells and Bath, but Byng found much to complain of in the exploitation of visitors. He and his wife had come for a quiet, cheap holiday, but all sorts of provisions were dear – even the Severn salmon was 7*d.* or 8*d.* a pound, owing to the competition of the London market. Current prices of everything were as high as in the most polished places of entertainment. Two sedan chairs were now available but at exorbitant fares, a minimum of 1*s.*; Simon Moreau dared not exert his authority against the profiteers, and the company also failed to take action. Byng was pleased to leave Cheltenham and hoped never to return; it was the dullest of places – sombre to look at, lacking inns or stabling fit for gentlemen or their horses – and the lodgings were pitiful and dear.[22]

Thomas Hughes and other enterprising entrepreneurs attempted to change this unpromising opinion. Hughes concentrated on improvement of the High Street area and built some of the best lodging-houses in the town on the first stretch of the east end where the visitor entered from the London Road. A larger assembly-room was urgently needed to accommodate the increasing company and Hughes had plans to improve his High Street Old Room, which had drawn only six dancing couples and one card-table at the opening of the 1781 season. Alarmed by the prospect of losing custom from Bay's Hill and the Grove to the historic centre of the town, Miller and Mrs Field opposed him and formed a powerful faction against the newcomer Moreau and Mrs Jones, supported by most of the company. Byng sympathized with Moreau:

> If Mr Moreau continues to behave with decency, I hope he may preside as such a character seems necessary at a public place; and his opponents seem so [to] be guided by ill humour and self interest.

Miller and Mrs Field refused to serve Moreau and his wife and their followers with the waters, or to give Moreau's subscription-book house-room. These were tough economic sanctions, and Byng – saying 'I hate oppression' – and some of the company sent a deputation to Miller who, rather unwillingly, accepted a compromise. Moreau's alignment with Mrs Jones indicates that his coming to Cheltenham in 1781 was engineered by Hughes, who in 1776 had leased and then purchased Mrs Jones's Old Room and might have thought that some regulation of social life was necessary.[23]

When Thomas Hughes set about the improvement of the Old Room Mrs Jones proved uncooperative, so a more amenable tenant, Henry Rooke, came in on Lady Day 1783. Hughes was now able to erect new rooms in the High Street, possibly designed by a well-known London architect, Henry Holland, and more worthy of fashionable customers. Opened on 24 June 1784, this was a single-storeyed building of a classical style entirely new to Cheltenham, with a rusticated front, an entrance portico, four sashed windows and a pedimented doorway topped by a fanlight. Four doors gave entrance and there was an anteroom or card-room and the grand ballroom, sixty feet by thirty, similar in size to Miller's long-room at the Old Well, which was sixty-six feet by twenty-three. But Hughes's new room had some distinction of style, with Corinthian pilasters, windows in a concave end-wall and a small music gallery.[24]

Simon Moreau presided in these splendid rooms, now the focus of Cheltenham's social life, from 1784 to 1801, and he contributed a great deal to the impetus for improvement in Cheltenham. The first *Guide Book to Cheltenham* by Ridley had appeared in 1781, but Moreau's useful and factual *A Tour to Cheltenham Spa* appeared in 1783 and ran to eight editions during his life, the last in 1797, with a reissue in 1805. Hughes's rooms were called the Lower Assembly Rooms, but by 1791 Miller had built and owned yet another competing set of assembly-rooms, also in the High Street and opposite the new playhouse, as shown on Mitchell's 1806 map of Cheltenham. The main room sixty-eight feet long and twenty-six feet wide, was adorned with lustres, chandeliers and ornaments, but they were unenthusiastically described as 'adequate to the respectability of the company who visit them'. In 1791 Harry (or Henry) Rooke was acting as master or manager of both the Upper and Lower Rooms. Thomas Hughes died in 1794 and the ownership of his rooms was eventually settled on his second son, Robert, in 1805. Rooke was still in theory the manager of both sets of rooms in 1811, but the Upper Rooms were superfluous when yet another long-room was opened at Montpellier in 1809, and by October they had become R. Crump's Universal Auction Room.[25]

The notion that social life should revolve around the two sets of rooms, controlled by a committee of amusements and supported by subscriptions, was also imported from Bath. The Cheltenham committee originated by vote of the company in 1784 when Hughes's rooms were opened. Moreau implies that regulations drawn up in 1784 to replace those of 1781, and revised in 1791, applied to both assembly-rooms in the High Street. More probably the 1784 rules related to Hughes's rooms and the room at the well, which by 1791 was superseded by Miller's new room in the High Street, so they were revised. Clearly from 1781 Moreau acted as master of ceremonies at both rooms, the Monday balls being held alternately at each. The more ambitious 1784 and 1791 programmes reveal a social life of increasing complexity; a cotillon ball was introduced, held alternately in each set of rooms on Thursday, and card-playing on Tuesday and Friday with two nights for play-going. The revised schedule of 1791 changed the second ball from Thursday to Friday and increased the theatre nights to three, with a card-playing alternative. On Wednesday there was card-playing only. The subscription for the Monday ball remained, as in 1781, 10*s*. 6*d*., but after 1784, by vote of the company, three members of a family could be admitted for one guinea. Some charges went up; non-subscribers now paid 2*s*. 6*d*. for a ball, as against 2*s*. in 1781. Separate subscriptions had been introduced for card nights: 2*s*. 6*d*. for ladies, 5*s*. for gentlemen and 1*s*. for non-subscribers. The subscriptions for the Well Walks were unchanged at 2*s*. 6*d*., like the 5*s*. for the musicians, although they now performed on Wednesday evenings in good weather as well as in the mornings. The company was reminded that the contributions entered in the book at the pump-room were the musicians' sole remuneration, except their payments from the proprietors of the rooms for playing at the balls, as the musicians themselves reiterated in 1810.[26]

As at Bath, a regulated but unprecedented choice of various social options was being offered to the upper ranks of society who were prepared to pay for it, with (from the 1780s) an expanding commercial provision of entertainments and more basic services. Thomas Price, the Gloucester publisher and bookseller, had premises from at least 1735 until 1769 at the 'New Inn', but in 1780 Samuel Harward opened the first circulating library.[27] John Boles Watson's old playhouse was inadequate for the increasing number of visitors, and in 1782 he built a new theatre north of the High Street and charged 5s. for a box seat, 2s. for the pit, and 1s. for the gallery. In 1787 better bathing facilities were introduced by Daniel Freeman at 61 High Street, with warm and tepid baths for 3s. 6d. and temporary baths supplied to invalids' apartments at short notice, but with no suggestion that the water used was mineral water. The occupant of Gallipot Farm near the Old Well cashed in on the boom and provided tea and syllabub for visitors, and to the north-east at Prestbury Mr Darke laid out a pleasure garden and built a summerhouse and grotto for breakfast, dinner and tea-drinking parties.[28]

Yet despite these attractions, Cheltenham's expansion as a resort town was hampered, especially by insufficient lodgings. There were at most thirty-three lodging-houses in 1780. Moreau's opinion in 1783 was that more were needed and the first hotel, with a long-room, was opened by Mrs Edwards opposite the Great House in 1785. Better paving, lighting and market facilities were also necessary. The manorial court, the vestry and the justices of the peace had no authority to make the changes required for the convenience of the growing number of visitors. Other expanding towns – for example Bath in 1766 – had already found the need for Improvement Acts, so the momentous Cheltenham Paving Act (1786) was obtained, petitioned for by some residents on the grounds that 'the town is a place to which great numbers of people of distinction and fortune resort, on account of its mineral waters', but the footways were inadequately paved, some old buildings obstructed traffic, and the town needed to be cleansed and lighted.[29] Under this Act fifty-eight commissioners with special powers – the paving or town commissioners – were appointed, including representatives of the old Cheltenham families, Thomas Higgs and Thomas Pope, and enterprising businessmen, Thomas Hughes, William Miller, William Skillicorne and Samuel Harward. Among the local social hierarchy on the commission were the attorney John de la Bere of Southam and the Honorable John Dutton, son of the lord of the manor. Although Lord Fauconberg was interested in Cheltenham he apparently took no hand in obtaining this bill: he was absent from the Lords on 31 May and 12 June 1786, when it came up.[30]

Initially the commissioners acted speedily and called a nascent municipality into being, appointing the first town clerk, a treasurer and town surveyor, and two scavengers to keep the streets clean. They raised the first loan of £600 for public works and demolished the old market-house and butter-cross and erected a new one on the site of the old prison. A new stone prison was built later in Henrietta Street. Having removed the 'coarse old buildings', the commissioners proceeded to light, pave and clean the town. The contract for paving the streets was signed in 1787, so presumably the water had been diverted by then. 'Till within these few years', runs an account of 1800, 'the water ran through the middle . . . now a good road through the town with a channel on each side.' Occupants of houses in the High Street were obliged to pave the footpath with flat Hannam stone, so a visitor in 1796 found the town 'neatly flagged and paved'. Houses were numbered – a rational idea to assist visitors in finding their way about – signs and spouts were removed from exteriors, and to encourage attendance at evening assemblies 120 street lamps were ordered. These improvements cost the inhabitants a new rate of 2s. 6d. in the pound above the usual parish rates, so early enthusiasm waned and protests forced a reduction to 1s. Deprived of money for wide-scale developments, the commissioners held only irregular and poorly attended meetings and future initiative remained with the private speculator.[31]

12

The Challenge of Cheltenham

It was Cheltenham's good fortune that George III suffered a series of severe abdominal spasms in June 1788 and Sir George Baker, president of the Royal College of Physicians, advised a royal course of drinking the medicinal waters of this small rural spa. The suggestion may have originated from the Earl of Fauconberg or the Cheltenham landowner the 4th Earl of Essex, both lords of the bedchamber. Fauconberg, a great favourite of the king, lent the royal party his new house at Bay's Hill, and the king and queen and their three eldest daughters, the Princesses Royal, Augusta and Elizabeth, arrived on 12 July 1788 and stayed five weeks, with a small ménage which included Lady Weymouth of Longleat near Bath. To the chagrin of Bath, the Cheltenham visit was the only occasion when a Hanoverian sovereign stayed at an English watering-place, although George II went to Sydenham one day and passed through Witham in Essex on his way to Hanover, and numerous princes and princesses went to the spas. Bath swiftly sent a civic deputation to Cheltenham on 5 August to invite the king and queen there, but the quieter style of Cheltenham life was more to the liking of 'Farmer George', despite the cramped accommodation at Bay's Hill. When his son the Duke of York wished to join him a portable wooden house was moved from the end of the town to join up with Fauconberg House, a laborious operation employing a Mr Ashton, 'an ingenious mechanic and surveyor', and twenty or thirty men for several days.[1] There was similar movement of wooden houses on sledges at Tunbridge Wells to meet the fluctuating demands of seasonal company.

The king's daily early morning visit to the Old Well soon revealed another Cheltenham handicap, the insufficient volume of mineral water. To increase the flow Lord Fauconberg had a pump placed over the well, but to no avail. For religious reasons, or to conserve the supplies, the king ordered the closure of the well on Sundays, and had another sunk nine feet deep to tap domestic supplies. This well on Lord Fauconberg's estate, twelve feet from the old one, proved to have the same mineral water and became known as the King's Well, with Mr Clerk, an apothecary, in charge.[2] The keeper of the Old Well, whom the king met, was Hannah

Forty, the wife of a local gardener. She had been the pumper since 1772 and had the monopoly of sales of Moreau's guidebook. On her death in 1816 a mural tablet in the church recorded her 'long and meritorious services', forty-three years as pumper. Spa wells seem to have produced a breed of redoubtable women organizers, pumpers and dippers.

George III's visit to Cheltenham was kept as informal as possible, unlike the progresses of Elizabeth I and Stuart monarchs, who went to spas accompanied by large retinues. He dispensed with guards, which pleased the local populace, and appeared to have enjoyed his visit. He thought the waters similar to those of Pyrmont, which he and other Hanoverians favoured, and, like so many visitors to spas, he filled in the long hours of leisure with journeys to local places of scenic or historic interest, and he went to nearby farms. On Sunday mornings the royal party attended the parish church, but mostly they spent the time quietly strolling on the walks or visiting friends staying in the town.[3]

The royal visit to Cheltenham made a great impression locally and nationally and left the title 'Royal' attached to two Cheltenham institutions, the theatre and the Old Well. The king twice patronized John Boles Watson's newly built theatre (1782) in York Passage, on the first occasion using a hastily improvised box to watch the vivacious Mrs Jordan. Before the second visit on 15 August Queen Charlotte held court with music in the long-room. At the theatre more boxes were laid in the pit and the first two rows of the gallery for the most splendid occasion Cheltenham had ever seen, when the king and queen came attended by four earls, six lords, several ladies, and local people of fashion. Watson's arrangements were excellent; the playbills were printed on satin, Mrs Watson served tea to the royals in the interval, and Mr Charlton gave a poetic address which began:

> When the Majestic spirit of the law
> Feels a Relief from Cheltenham's humble Spa;
> When George, our Constitution's sacred shield,
> Here, aids his Own, the Sceptre long to wield,
> All hearts must worship this dear, hallow'd ground,
> Health at whose Fount the King of Freemen found.

So pleased was the king that he constituted the playhouse a Theatre Royal, it is claimed by letters patent. The theatre in Bath had been similarly honoured in 1768. He left Cheltenham on 16 August.[4]

For Simon Moreau the royal visit was the zenith of his career as master of ceremonies. He was presented to the king and queen – an honour he would not have received had he been, as he had wished, the MC at Bath – and gave them copies of his *Tour*, the fourth edition of which in 1789 was newly entitled *A Tour of the Royal Spa at Cheltenham*. He also commissioned a commemorative medal; copies were handed to the king and queen and six of their children in April 1789 by Lord Courtown, the comptroller of the household, who had accompanied the king to Cheltenham. There were hopes of a repeat royal visit the next year; in June 1789 it was reported that 'the Cheltenham people much wished it, tho' only for a week or ten days', because the company was inexplicably thinner than for several seasons. Possibly the French Revolution in 1789 had an upsetting effect, for the number of visitors dropped by nearly half: from 1,550 in 1788 to 860 in 1789, although in 1790 it recovered and reached 1,100.[5] But in 1789 the king went to Weymouth for his relaxation, and he never returned to Cheltenham.

Even so, Cheltenham's future as a spa was assured. For five weeks the town had been in the national news and the king had transacted a certain amount of state business during his stay. Not only was the visit reported in the *Morning Post* and the *Gentleman's Magazine* but it was depicted in illustrations, including two by Peter La Cave. One shows the royal party traversing Well Walk through the open fields on either side with the Great House on their left; the other shows them at the Old Well with the Union Jack flying over all. A great number of people had been attracted to Cheltenham, putting pressure on existing accommodation and services, although Moreau had tried to control prices in an explosive seller's market.[6]

As a result of royal patronage the town became fashionable while Bath was suffering a recession following the financial crash in 1791. Cheltenham was then described as a handsome and well-built town, recently much improved, well-paved and lighted, and a place of great beauty with long gardens behind each house abounding with fruit and walnut trees and providing pleasant walks. After the setback in 1789 the number of visitors attracted there again increased: from 1,350 in 1791 to 1,560 in 1792, between 1,500 and 1,600 in 1795 and 1,600 to 1,700 in 1796. The company of the growing spa now had an even more pronounced aristocratic flavour, and the Gloucestershire squires, farmers and tradesmen found themselves rubbing shoulders with the elite of London society.

Cheltenham's economy was also changing and becoming more diversified to meet the demands of the spa business. The simple community of farmers, tradesmen and maltsters was being progressively supplemented by a lodging industry for temporary inhabitants. By 1791, a residential core of gentry – headed by Lord Fauconberg and including John Boles Watson – had also emerged, of whom twenty let lodgings, so the term 'gentry' was rather elastic. The occupation structure was now more complex: the ten professional men included three surgeon-apothecaries and four attorneys, and the retail trade had seventeen purveyors of food and drink. One of the two brewers was John Gardner, establishing his family's long connection with the town. The fourteen traders in the clothing business included three milliners and a peruke-maker; the five luxury or semi-luxury trades comprised a printer and bookseller (Samuel Harward), a musician, a cabinet-maker and a silver- and goldsmith. Travel services were almost non-existent and the town depended on Gloucester for them. There was only one horse-dealer and four others – a mealman, a saddler and two carriers – connected with transport in Cheltenham, which lacked even a coach proprietor. There were eight employers in the building trade, led by Edward Smith and William Marshall. Equally busy in 1791 were the four directly involved in the spa business: Simon Moreau, the MC; Harry Rooke, in charge of the rooms; Daniel Freeman of the warm baths; and Watson of the theatre.[7]

The most remarkable change in the last two decades was the increased number of lodging-houses; the only one in 1773 had been Mrs Field's Great House, but in 1780 there were about thirty-three and now in 1791 forty-two, of which the best and most elegant were the Great House, now run by Richard Hooper, and five others. Watson, Harward and Rooke ran lodgings in addition to their other businesses, and in March 1792 Watson advertised his house, 21 High Street, opposite the New Rooms and near the theatre, to be let completely furnished with a coach-house and stabling; it was one of the first lodging-houses taken the previous season. In all twenty-two traders combined letting lodgings with another occupation. In addition Mrs Edward's hotel (about 1785) stood opposite the Great House, and the five main inns were the Plough and the Swan, 'the two great inns opposite one another', and the George, the Fleece and the Lamb, all in the High Street. (The Crown is not mentioned in this 1791 list, which may be incomplete.) The number of lodgings proliferated to about 150 in 1800, but there were still too few to meet demand. The overflow was accommodated in houses fitted up for the purpose in neighbouring villages and hamlets: Charlton Kings, Sandford, Arle, Alstone and Prestbury. Two banking firms, Higgs & Cook and John Bedwell & Sons, supported this general activity, drawing on London money.[8]

The influx of seasonal visitors strained the town's resources severely, although the population had risen to 3,076 by 1801 with 710 occupied houses and fifteen being built, compared with 1,500 people and 321 houses in 1666. In season visitors formed about two-fifths of the inhabitants, expansion did not keep pace with demand, and prices were forced up. In 1796 an American visitor, Joshua Gilpin, thought it the most extravagant place, with the worst accommodation of any watering-place in England. Sir Richard Colt Hoare paid two guineas a week for lodgings for himself, a servant and a kitchen-maid in 1796 and in 1801 two-and-a-half guineas and 18s. for a cook and a housemaid.[9] These were high prices compared with the maximum of 10s. 6d. a room at Bath. Visitors were also preyed on by the crowds of ne'er-do-wells who were drawn to the growing resort in the guise of musicians, jugglers and other entertainers, and servants. Gilpin deplored the ubiquitous subscriptions and resolved not to pay them but to adhere to a minimum list. By 1801 some of them seem to have doubled even since 1797, or the local proprietors regarded the official tariff as a minimum, not a maximum. Admission to the balls had been 10s. 6d. but now it was £1 1s., and the use of newspapers, 2s. 6d. in 1781, was now 5s., but they were provided in a new coffee-room. The lack of coffee-rooms, which Moreau had deplored, had been made good at the Plough Inn, where for 5s. one could enjoy the *Sun,* the *Star* and the *Morning Post* newspapers. Another coffee-room, for ladies, was open at the bowling green for tea on Sunday and public breakfast on Thursday. The woman at the pump had to be given 5s., against 2s. 6d. in 1784, and an unnamed museum cost another 5s.[10]

Despite the pressure for more accommodation there was little significant expansion in the 1790s. An obvious development was to connect the old town, with its High Street, with the spa area at Bay's Hill. St George's Place, a street of unpretentious houses on the east side of Stills Lane, was begun in 1788–9 and was for many years the only avenue from the town to the Royal Well and Fauconberg House. The Colonnade, planned as a prime shopping area at the entrance to a narrow lane (the future Promenade) across a marshy field was also destined to link the old town and the new. The first stone was laid by Lord Fauconberg in 1791, and the three-storeyed building of twenty-six bays, fronted by Doric columns on the ground floor, was slightly crescent-shaped. Samuel Harward by 1800 owned Numbers 2 and 3 and also Number 4, where he later opened a second library. The Colonnade was the most impressive building in Cheltenham to date, and the beginning of its new town.[11]

The site of Cheltenham was well suited to urban spa development, but it had drawbacks. There was no lack of springs for domestic water, but supplies of proven mineral water were hard to come by and until 1801 were limited to the two wells on the Bay's Hill estate. Dr Thomas Jameson (d. 1824), one of the increasing number of doctors drawn to the town, took forty borings on the south side of the present Queen's Hotel in his search for mineral waters. The speculator, Henry Thompson, made eighty borings in a similar hunt. Another serious impediment was the difficulty of transport, for as late as 1826 many local roads were described as 'execrable', although various commercial interests had tried to make Cheltenham more accessible. The first stretch of a long-distance road to be turnpiked was that towards Andoversford in 1756 to join the Crickley Hill to Oxford road, improved five years earlier. The inconvenience to coach travellers of alighting at Frog Mill to make their way to Cheltenham, or going through to Gloucester and doubling back to Cheltenham, went on until 1785, when Thomas Hughes and Simon Moreau, as commissioners, supported the improvement of all roads from Cheltenham, including part of the Gloucester to London road, and a new main road to Winchcombe was constructed in 1792.

Although Moreau wrote rather over-enthusiastically of the consequent great amendment of local roads, by 1797 or earlier there was a direct coach link between Cheltenham and the capital. The London to Gloucester mail-coach now called at the George in Cheltenham High Street daily both ways. By 1800 it had been joined by other services: a daily heavy coach on the same route stopped at the Lamb Inn, John Byrch's weekly stagewagon ran from the Plough Inn and Rowland Hearne's twice-weekly wagon from the Lamb Inn. More local services appeared: twice a week Mr Hooper's wagons went to Gloucester and Mr Dobbins's to Tewkesbury. The first direct link with Bath was Wildey's Light Cart, which left his Cheltenham house on Tuesday and Friday mornings during the season to reach his warehouse in Bath fourteen hours later.[12]

Moreau and Hughes had backed road improvements. Their rival William Miller supported the 1792 Act for the construction of a canal to bring coal 'to the growing spa of Cheltenham' from the mouth of the Chelt on the Severn to a wharf at Coombe Hill to meet the Tewkesbury road into Cheltenham. So Miller now had interests in the Old Well, the Upper Assembly Room and the canal. Although he and the other proprietors, Sarah Mumford of Cheltenham and Thomas Burgess of London, failed to bring the canal into the town, by 1798 Staffordshire and Shropshire coal was coming in by it. But it had cost £5,000 and from 1802 a high toll of 2s. 6d. a ton on coal made it profitable by 1808.[13]

Besides the transport difficulties and the shortage of mineral water and coal, neither of which Bath lacked, another impediment to Cheltenham's physical expansion was that much land there was still open fields and rights of common pasturage prevented conversion to separate holdings for building plots, particularly on the common called the Marsh north of the High Street, although the common lands of Leckhampton to the south were enclosed in 1788. The de la Bere family of Southam had large holdings, as did the Earl of Essex in Cambray and around the church. Bath's physical growth was restricted by the surrounding hills but Cheltenham, on a gentle slope 205 feet above sea level and sheltered by the Cotswold escarpment, was geographically well placed for urban development, as the speculator Joseph Pitt, a successful Cirencester lawyer, was aware. The open plain of the Severn Valley offered prospects of easy urban spread, with room for the 'walks and rides' which became a marked feature of the town's layout. 'Cheltenham', ran an account of 1800, 'is much indebted to art for the agreeable walks and little promenades which surround it. Summer heat is much alleviated by the shade of trees, and the pathways are sound, firm and gravelled.'[14]

Another of the natural advantages of Cheltenham was that it had quantities of the raw materials for building to hand: sand came from the subsoil and also blue lias clay, which gave rise to works making the bricks of which, with a facing of stucco, most Cheltenham houses are built. The proprietors of the houses built in the Colonnade in 1791 supplied bricks for the whole building, made on the spot at 13s. a thousand. During the early building boom, around 1800, Mr Billings of Albion Cottage had brickworks to let with ground sufficient for three work companies, and there was a brickworks in Portland Street. When Charles Brandon Trye, a surveyor of high repute, took over the estates of the Norwoods of Leckhampton Court in 1797, the Leckhampton quarries of oolitic limestone were developed and provided lime and a cream-coloured freestone for building, the best of which compared well with that of Bath. Like Ralph Allen at Bath, Trye installed a tramway on an inclined plane to transport stone; in 1810 this was linked to the new Gloucester and Cheltenham Railway, a horse-drawn tramroad.[15]

North Gloucestershire was well wooded and could also easily meet the demands of the local carpenters. In 1800 Prestbury was covered with foliage 'so thick as almost to embower the houses and form a canopy of leaves over the inhabitants', and a vast number of timber trees was offered for sale in the neighbourhood, especially during the building boom of 1809–10, including 500 oak and ash trees at Standish alone. The building of Cheltenham undoubtedly led to some denudation of the surrounding landscape, but even after fifty years of construction it was said of the town itself that the 'rich luxuriance of foliage imparts a rural and verdant appearance not often to be met with in large towns'.[16] Cheltenham was indeed well placed to become a large and pleasant resort.

The turning point of Cheltenham's rapid expansion was the 1801 Enclosure Act, which released land from the open-field system and made development north of the High Street possible. The prime mover in this was Joseph Pitt, the owner after 1791 of large estates in Gloucestershire and Wiltshire and the holder of interests in John Gardner's brewery and in the County of Gloucester Bank. When Lord Essex died in 1799 Pitt purchased the impropriate rectory and other land, including about 85 acres of glebeland, Cambray Meadow and Church Meadow, from the disposal of the Essex estates, and by 1801 he was the chief landowner in the central part of Cheltenham. Essex Place on Mitchell's 1806 map reminds us of the earl's connection with the town.[17] The final enclosure award was not made until 1806 and Alstone and Arle, to the north-west, were not enclosed until 1830–4. Joseph Pitt emerged as the largest property-owner in Cheltenham with about 250 acres in twenty-five allotments, one of the largest being in the Marsh, where he planned to develop a distinct spa town called Pittville, but his scheme was delayed for a quarter of a century. Lord Sherborne, the lord of the manor, gained little, but he was still entitled to rights which were valuable in an expanding economy, heriots and fines on the exchange of manorial land and the market tolls.[18]

Joseph Pitt's first building project was the one which became the hallmark of a developing spa: a crescent of buildings like those at Bath (1767–74) and Buxton (1780–6). The Royal Crescent – erected between 1806 and 1810 on part of the Church Meadow to provide lodgings for visitors – was, with the Colonnade, the first of Cheltenham's Regency buildings and set the architectural style of the town for the future. Building arrangements were made in 1805, by 1807 the roofs were on, and in 1809 T. Fisher was offering Number 6 completely furnished for sale, obviously as a lodging-house investment; it contained a drawing-room, a breakfast parlour and nine bedrooms. Fisher's plot was probably on a building lease, for Pitt's practice, like that of many landlord-speculators at Bath, was to have an architect's plans approved before he sold to builders. The architect for the Crescent was Charles Harcourt Masters of Bath.[19] The attorney Walter Hylton Jessop had a large interest in the Crescent; he lived in Number 7 and owned three more houses there. By February 1810 the foundations of the eight remaining houses were being laid and a new 200-yard stone road, Crescent Terrace, was begun to link it with the Colonnade. The gardens behind the Crescent houses adjoined the carriage road leading to the wells where John Ballinger opened the Crescent Mews, the first mews in Cheltenham, with private stables and a lock-up coach-house.[20] The Crescent proprietors also owned the remains of the Church Meadow in front: this was to be planted, and surrounded with iron palisades, at a cost of £4,000.

E. Cossen's pictorial map of Cheltenham (1820) shows these Crescent Gardens, and one must deplore the fact that, central and convenient though it is, Cheltenham cannot find an alternative to this historic site for its bus terminus today. At its completion in 1810 the Crescent, with the earlier Colonnade, stood stark and bare among the fields, in sharp contrast with the older buildings of the High Street. Although in 1851 they were described as having been 'built in Cheltenham's more primitive days' the Crescent's terraced three-storeyed houses with basements, each of three bays with fanlit doorways, first-floor balconies and good interior plasterwork, made it the fashionable place of residence and set the pattern for Cheltenham's future development. One of the local celebrities, Dr H.C. Boisragon, lived at Number 11 and gave musical parties there.[21]

Meanwhile Mr Billings of Albion Cottage, a land surveyor, was promoting St James's Square, the first square to be built in Cheltenham, with access to the road leading from the spa to the High Street. At least one house, 24 St James's Street, was erected by 1809 and more were built between 1809 and 1810. St George's Square, Chapel Street and also Albion

Street to the north of the High Street were all in existence by 1809 and there was a certain amount of infilling or rebuilding in the High Street, such as the two unfinished houses, each with a shop, a cellar and lodging-rooms, offered by W. H. Jessop in 1809.[22] But the piecemeal construction of individual houses, or even of terraces, became less common.

A new approach to spa development was now putting the monopoly of the Old Well at risk. The water-drinking and bathing at Bath were concentrated in the Abbey area, except for some minor peripheral spas, but Cheltenham's development after 1801 was as a series of estates, each located around a spa. Neither the Woods' new town at Bath nor the Grosvenor or Pulteney Estates there had had a spa centre incorporated in their layout, but the concept of the planned estate of homogeneous neo-Grecian architectural style and a garden-city-type environment, with ample avenues for walks and rides, had been born there. Capital for such grandiose development could come only from the wealthy or from joint-stock companies, and meanwhile the hunt for new mineral wells was on.

The first challenge to the Old Wells came in 1801 when a chalybeate spring was found near the Cambray mill. William Humphris Barrett, the owner, built a large room for the company and laid out gravelled walks, so making the Cambray area a social centre. John Boles Watson was swift to buy much of the Cambray Meadow, where in 1803 he began the erection of yet another and larger theatre in Bath Street, also called the Cambray Colonnade. The new playhouse, the Theatre Royal or the Cambray Theatre completed in 1805, was 'superior to most theatres' and cost £8,000. The old theatre became the assembly-room of the York Hotel. Watson and his son controlled a circuit of theatres in the West Midlands, but Cheltenham was their headquarters. Many famous players appeared there, including the Kembles in 1809. In the words of the local press, Mr Watson had 'learnt the way to wealth' before he died on 17 March 1813.[23]

As the Cambray development went on, James King, now the master of ceremonies, built his home, Cambray Lodge, there in 1804, conveniently near the Assembly Rooms. That year the eccentric visitor Colonel John Riddell tasted the water of a well where Watson had placed a new pump, and so in addition to Barrett's spa the Cambray chalybeate spa was born in 1807. Riddell astutely bought Watson's land as a speculation, together with a half-built house subsequently enlarged, Cambray House or the later Wellington Mansion. News of the colonel's purchase leaked out within a day and the remaining property more than doubled in value. 'All were purchasers.' Riddell enclosed the land, laid out a carriage road to the spring, Cambray Street, in 1809, and planned to build 'twelve handsome houses' on the south-east side with £30,000 raised by a tontine of subscribers. For a time Riddell leased his Cambray property to Sir Edward May, who spent £3,000 on it, but he reclaimed it in 1813. In 1815 Cambray

House was to let for the season; it stood amid lawn and shrubbery with pleasure and kitchen gardens and a coach-house and contained a break-fast-room, a library, a large dining-room, two allegedly magnificent draw-ing-rooms and fourteen bedrooms, nine of them best bedrooms. Cheltenham was now acquiring domestic houses of a new scale in size and elegance. There was even talk of building a church in Cambray in 1817, but the real development of Cambray Spa came later.[24]

The next threat to the Old Wells' proprietors, a momentous one, came from Henry Thompson, a Liverpool and London banker and an entrepre-neur of extraordinary vision. Another Liverpool merchant, Bertie Great-heed, involved in similar speculation at Leamington Spa, described him as 'the new improver, a chattering box', but he injected a great deal of vigour into the development of Cheltenham.[25] A new spa, several wells, the manufacture of Cheltenham salts initiated by Thomas Hughes about fifty years earlier, the establishment of a suite of baths, a superb pump-room which became the new social centre of Cheltenham in summer, and the layout of a new estate were all Thompson's contribution to Cheltenham. He left an abiding and extensive impress on the new town which emerged.

In 1801 he bought about 400 acres of common land, now the Montpellier and Lansdown Estates, to the south-west of the town for a nominal price. In 1804 he built Hygeia House (Vittoria House from 1813) as his first spa, a rectangular house of great charm, which has fortunately been recently restored; it is in the present Vittoria Walk. In 1808 Thompson's 'walks and rides' were laid out marking the boundaries of his Montpellier Estate. Daniel Trinder's map of Cheltenham in 1809 shows these avenues com-memorated today as Montpellier Spa Road, Montpellier Parade, Montpellier Terrace, Montpellier Villas and Montpellier Grove, and here in this estate Thompson created another spa. In March 1808 he opened his Montpellier Well in a field east of the Badgeworth Road, and in 1809 he built a pump-room and a long-room, with a veranda supported by wooden pillars and surmounted by a wooden structure, and laid out tree-lined walks as an approach. Granville implies that Thompson did not settle in Cheltenham until 1809 and that he invested £10,000 there.[26]

Visitors now had a choice of drinking wells and the new ones, Barrett's and those at Cambray and Montpellier, were a considerable threat to Mrs Forty, the manager of the Old Wells. There is some evidence that in 1803 the owner of the property, Mr Nash, or the renters of the wells, Messrs Capstack and Matthews, had built a new pump-room, and 'Mrs Forty's New Well', where in 1809 a visitor was amazed to find servants with their hats on unceremoniously mixing with ladies and gentlemen in a small pump-room, may have been the Orchard Well close to the Old Wells, or the Essex Well at the end of Well Lane, now Montpellier Street, both in existence by 1809. When Thompson's spas opened Mrs Forty allowed visitors to use her walks as a cool and refreshing short cut to them by opening a gate in the Grove, but she later regretted this generosity as she lost custom. The *Bath and Cheltenham Gazette* in 1813 suggested that she should have 3*s*. 6*d*. compensation from each individual. Perhaps old Mrs Forty was then past caring; she died on 16 August 1816 aged seventy-one. The proprietor, Captain Matthews, had already taken over the Old Wells in April and carried out various improvements, 'unsparing of expense'. Three years later he was trading as Messrs Matthews & Company, and he invested more money in extending the wells to offer five types of water and salts. The war of the wells had truly begun.[27]

Cheltenham was the most rapidly expanding of the wartime spas and was, for the time being, more fashionable than Bath. An index of the prosperity of the town is that local tradesmen, who were excluded from visitors' gatherings, began, like those in Bath, to promote their own communal social activity. On 30 October 1809 they held their Jubilee Ball and Supper at Sheldon's Hotel and 180 people of 'great respectability' attended. In general a more sophisticated social life evolved, its success largely engineered by Moreau. A visitor in 1791 pronounced that Cheltenham could not have found a better conductor of the amusements who exerted himself to give visitors an agreeable stay, and nowhere else could a family spend the summer months more comfortably.[28] When Moreau died in 1801 he was buried in the parish church, and again Bath's social example was acknowledged when the experienced James King, now master of the Upper Rooms at Bath, was elected in his place.[29]

13

The Innkeepers' Rule: Harrogate and Scarborough

The social life of the northern spas in the eighteenth century was entirely different from that in the South. The trying northern climate restricted outdoor activities and visitors kept to the shelter of the inns, which were the centres of communal life at Buxton, Matlock and Harrogate. Scarborough had a more hybrid social life. Visitors to these northern spas relied on the inns' catering excellence and their 'social meal' and did not, as in the southern spas, take individual lodgings and find provisions independently. So the northern innkeepers were key people in promoting the popularity of their resorts, where a new type of social routine emerged and spread to some seaside resorts, as explained anonymously in *The New Brighton Guide; or, Companion. . . . to all the Watering-Places in Great Britain* (1796). The company at an inn or boarding-house assembled for a communal meal, with the head of the table acting as their president and smoothing all social blunders. Controversial subjects like politics or religion were banned, on penalty of supplying a pot of coffee to fellow-guests, but Irishmen were allowed a second chance. Accepted modes of address were adopted for those meeting casually in this new kind of mixed society: a duke greeted his inferiors as 'honest man' or 'honest woman'; a marquess, earl, viscount, baron or bishop used the blunt term 'man' or 'woman'; and the plain epithet 'friend' was appropriate for a baronet, knight, physician or one of the lesser gentry.

The role of president of the table was achieved by seniority of stay. The last newcomer ranked as the most junior visitor, sat at the bottom of the table and ate his way up by regular gradation. Such a regulation preserved order and prevented disputes but, as in all prearranged successions, there was the frequent disadvantage of an inadequate chairman whose clumsy carving and clownish manners were tolerated by the company until his departure.

Harrogate

Visitors to Harrogate were confined to their inns and boarding-houses in a very public life, dependent on their limited home-made amusements. At the Granby, the best inn, they dined together in a long-room, although breakfast was taken at separate tables, and they sat in another room morning and evening. Only those who could afford the luxury of a private parlour had an escape other than their bedrooms. In this informal but claustrophobic family atmosphere women mixed with men on more equal terms than in the southern spas, their presence at the common board curbing uncouth conversation. It was customary for men and women to treat each other mutually after dinner: the men paid for the wine and the women for tea. Women were even allowed in the billiard-room, but for amusement, not for play. Gambling of any kind was discouraged as detrimental to mixed parties. But the visitor, denied public balls or assemblies until 1800, paid the price for female society: sobriety.[1]

Not only the bleaker climate of the northern spas, which kept people in the inns with their internal bathtubs, but also lack of capital investment meant that these spas, except Scarborough, were slow to provide large, public, indoor and central places of assembly which could accommodate all the visitors. Until the industrialization of the North yielded more profits for investment and more customers in the nineteenth century there were few communal facilities and the company was never integrated under the aegis of a professional master of ceremonies, except again at Scarborough and briefly at Buxton. When Hargrove's room was opened at Harrogate in about 1800 a visitor chosen from among the company served as MC during his stay. Intrigue for the appointment was forbidden and he was elected for his suavity and good manners, but he lacked the status of a regular and received no fee.[2]

Harrogate, Scarborough, Buxton and Matlock all slowly expanded in the eighteenth century. Low and High Harrogate, settlements nearly a mile apart within the common land of the Forest of Knaresborough, belonged, as part of the duchy of Lancaster, to the crown. Harrogate had no clearly defined centre but was well placed for future development in the Vale of York, a natural corridor for north–south traffic, and it was a convenient stop for travellers between London and Edinburgh. As the Harrogate Spa became better known it attracted not only travellers and the Yorkshire gentry but the new industrial middle classes of the North. But climatically it is less congenial than the southern spas, with rather low temperatures, and it stands on moorlands rising from 350 to 600 feet, except the valley of Coppice Beck in the Low Harrogate area.[3]

Unlike Cheltenham, which was always short of mineral water, Harrogate had a never-failing supply, eighty-eight springs within a radius of two miles, although only sixteen were used medicinally. Recent development had been around the Old Sulphur Well at Low Harrogate, the focus of several roads, in the parish of Pannal, where John Hogg was allowed to make an enclosure in October 1739. The Crown Inn was built adjacent to this well and from 1740 was run by Joseph Thackwray, according to his self-epitaph in Pannal churchyard:

> In the year of our Lord 1740
> I came to the Crown;
> In 1791 they laid me down.[4]

By contrast the chalybeate Tewit and John Wells remained isolated on the open common of High Harrogate, apart from the mile-length settlement of lodging-houses. After the erection of the new inns there in the upper town – the Queen's Head, the Dragon, the Granby and also possibly by 1700 the Salutation – visitors were less dependent on lodgings in Knaresborough or with the local farmers and linen-weavers of the township of Bilton and the adjacent parish of Pannal. In 1756 Bishop Hare's widow stayed at an unnamed lodging-place with a long-room where there was dancing on three consecutive nights and people drank tea, played cards and supped, but acquaintances of hers lodged at the Queen's Head and the Salutation. From about 1662 a musician called Morrison played at the spa until he died in 1732, and he must have had successors for the dancing. But the visitors organized their own amusements; there was no commercial entertainment until about 1760.

The company at the various inns gave mutual invitations for social occasions, as when Mrs Hare's company and those at the Queen's Head, eighteen at least, hired a wagon, put in benches and six pairs of horses and went off on an expedition to Studley. Several of the local gentry came two or three times in a season for a few days, and Mrs Hare enjoyed seeing many people and living gaily at small expense, for at other public places one paid for both lodgings and diversions, but here only for board. Dr Pococke, there in mid-century, found board for 1s. 8d. a day, breakfast excepted.[5] Harrogate certainly lacked the contemporary pleasure facilities of Bath and Tunbridge Wells, but it increasingly drew more people of note and long-distance customers to use these wells although they were in an exposed position and lacked amenities. Earl FitzWalter of Moulsham Hall, Chelmsford, in Essex came in 1734 with twenty-two relatives, friends and servants, using eleven saddle-horses, seven coach-horses, his own carriages, and a hired coach and six for the journey. Mrs Hare noted Lord Warkworth, Lord Willoughby and Lord Northumberland's sons there in 1756, and Lord Bute went to take the waters of Harrogate on the fall of his ministry in 1763. Harrogate was still renowned for its moderate living in 1806.[6]

From the early eighteenth century the term 'Harrogate Spa' came into use instead of 'Knaresborough Spa', and Dr John Neale's bath-house was in 1750 known to Dr Pococke as 'the best cold bath in England'. By 1743 the growing number of visitors and residents at Harrogate needed a place of worship, and the Anglican chapel of St John was built at High Harrogate, 'convenient for the inhabitants of Bilton and those who resort there for the use of the mineral waters', backed by ninety-two subscribers headed by Lady Elizabeth Hastings. Its erection was interrupted by soldiers coming through during the '45 rebellion, but in 1749 the small, plain chapel surmounted by a bell-turret was completed and eighty-three acres of duchy land were let off to provide the curate's stipend of £30.[7]

Previously the poor roads around Harrogate had made access difficult; in 1710 even that between Knaresborough and Harrogate was but a 'forest lane' in a bad state, as in 1744 was the Leeds to Knaresborough road through Harrogate. Then in mid-century came considerable improvement in the local roads. The first Act for turnpiking that part of the Great North Road nearest to Harrogate, from Doncaster to Boroughbridge, in 1741 helped to open up the area, and three trusts covered highways between Harrogate and Boroughbridge, Hutton Moor and Leeds by 1752, while Knaresborough became another centre. Travellers soon noticed the better roads; Mrs Hare enjoyed her expedition to Studley in 1756 because the wagon had broad wheels and the road was turnpiked, and so her party 'trotted away very expeditiously'. By 1768 the roads from Harrogate to Leeds and Ripon were 'good', and the enclosure of the Forest of Knaresborough from 1770 helped the improvement of others.[8]

Soon there was a market for public stagecoaches, and by 1743 one ran daily both ways from Wakefield to the Queen's Head in High Harrogate. Wealthier visitors came in their own carriages but public services expanded, and by the 1750s regular Monday services operated from Leeds to Harrogate during the season. Two new services started in 1772: Joseph Myers at Leeds ran a post-coach twice daily to the Crown in Low Harrogate, again for the season only, and Gilbertson used his Queen's Head at Harrogate as a stage for a Leeds to Newcastle coach. Long-distance coaches, such as the London to Carlisle coach three times a week, were diverted through Harrogate to pick up the spa traffic, and by 1789 the 'Liberty' coach from Leeds to Harrogate ran daily, supplemented in 1791 by a new service three days a week from the Swan Inn, Low Harrogate, to Leeds.[9]

As the growing settlements at Harrogate became more accessible, more amenities were introduced. A Knaresborough grocer, John Ross, had a shop there in 1736, and by August 1760 a barn fitted with boxes, a pit and a gallery behind the Granby Hotel was rather grandly called the 'Theatre in High Harrogate'. It was repainted in 1772 and opened on 8 July, financed by subscriptions for a brief season of fourteen plays, comedies, tragedies and a pantomime, at £1 1s. for a box and 14s. for a pit seat.[10]

The growth of the spa was both a cause and an effect of continual intakes on the common of the forest. An enquiry by the duchy of Lancaster in 1766 revealed 494 encroachments in cottages and/or land between 1708 and 1766, including large and valuable ones near the Sulphur Wells. So an investigating commission in 1767 resulted in the Forest of Knaresborough Enclosure Act (1770, amended in 1774). The award issued in 1778 introduced a new class of large landowners in the Forest, including Daniel Lascelles, who acquired 600 acres, and Alexander Wedderburn, whose grant of 272 acres in 1775 was the largest single block in Harrogate and included Woodland Cottage, which he rebuilt in 1786 and enlarged as Wedderburn House. To soften the bleak aspect of the locality he laid out plantations and well-wooded walks, one of them a two-mile promenade. Wedderburn became Lord Loughborough and Chief Justice of the Common Pleas in 1780, and he was to Harrogate what Fauconberg was to Cheltenham. At some time he visited the Pouhon spring at Spa, which had a lofty dome, and in 1786 he paid for a similar one over the John Well near his home.[11] The crown kept 600 acres within the later borough of Harrogate from the enclosure, including 240 along the edge of the West Park Stray, where it granted long building leases, a connection recalled in the names of local roads – Duchy, York, Clarence and Cornwall – built during the later residential expansion.

Harrogate's essential interests as a growing spa were, as at Buxton the next year, safeguarded by clauses in the Enclosure Act protecting the mineral springs.

> . . . certain wells or springs of medicinal waters, commonly called Harrogate Spaws, to which during the summer season great numbers of people constantly resort . . . to the great advantage and emolument of tradesmen, farmers and other people in the neighbourhood.

Near the springs 200 acres were set aside as permanent unenclosed common where visitors could take an 'airing' and have free access to the springs at all times; in 1789 about fifteen more acres were added and the enclosure commissioners were authorized to carry out more landscaping by draining, levelling and improving land and planting trees for shelter and ornament. This spacious stretch of common land, the Stray, was, like the common at Tunbridge Wells, an important amenity helping to create a relaxed resort atmosphere. It is still one of Harrogate's most distinctive features. The Enclosure Act led to a release of activity and from the 1780s there was purposeful improvement. Labour was in much demand, wages rose sharply and hundreds of workers migrated to Harrogate from a distance, especially joiners, carpenters, smiths and masons. Several local quarries supplied millstone grit for building. Food production also increased as a result of enclosure and the pace of Harrogate's expansion quickened. By 1783 there were more inns: at least the Globe and the King's Arms.[12]

The innkeepers had a special interest in finding and promoting springs. The master of the Half Moon in Low Harrogate discovered one resembling the Sulphur Well behind his house in 1783 and a second one like the currently fashionable Leamington waters in his cellar. Dr Thomas Garnett, a physician, had settled in Harrogate by 1791, when he publicized the first spring in his *Experiments and Observations on the Crescent Water at Harrogate* and in his *Treatise on the Mineral Waters of Harrogate* (1792), dedicated to Lord Loughborough. By then Mr Jaques, a surgeon and apothecary, was also drawn to Harrogate during the season. The profitable springs were known as the Crescent Waters and the landlord upgraded his inn to Crescent Hotel and by 1814 could afford to reject customers unaccompanied by servants. Another chalybeate water, St George's Spa, was found near the George Hotel in about 1792. Other propagandists of the Harrogate waters were Dr William Alexander in a popular treatise, *Plain and easy directions for the use of Harrogate waters* (1773 ?), and Dr Walker of Leeds in an *Essay on the Harrogate Waters and those of Thorp Arch* (1784). About 1783 the famed Betty Lupton, 'the Queen of the Harrogate Wells', took up her duty as well-woman.[13]

The 1780s marked a period of prosperity for the spas in general, and the boom at Harrogate encouraged investment in recreations. A better theatre replaced the barn behind the Granby and attracted two touring companies: those of Tate Wilkinson, who introduced the system of advance booking for seats, and Tryphosa Wright, who married Samuel Butler. Butler erected a new theatre in High Harrogate on Church Square, financed by Mrs Wilks, owner of the Granby. It opened on 1 July 1788 with regular performances: three a week from July to September and the normal programme of two plays and an interval entertainment. The block subscription for the season was superseded by separate charges: 1*s.* for gallery seats, 2*s.* for the pit and 3*s.* for the boxes – as at Buxton and Cheltenham, except that Cheltenham boxes cost 5*s.* Butler's players included Mrs Dorothy Jordan, lured there by a subscription purse from the company in the Harrogate hotels to play four nights. Harriet Mellon, later the Duchess of St Albans, also performed there, as did Jane Wallis, granddaughter of Tryphosa Butler, who, sponsored by Lord and Lady Loughborough, made her way to Covent Garden. Many aristocratic patrons sponsored plays: the Countesses of Home, Ormond and Shaftesbury and Lady Castlereagh. Another diversion for the company was a racecourse, a mile and a half in circumference and sixteen yards wide, laid out in the Stray in 1793 by Colonel Clement Wolsley. When, in that same year, the French wars closed the Continent to the grandees, more of them patronized the domestic spas, where an increasingly sophisticated life developed. By 1800 Harrogate had a museum, as did several spa towns, displaying handmade wooden articles. It had also by 1800 belatedly acquired an assembly-room, rather inferior to the norm but with a good circulating library and billiard-rooms, in the Library House run by Ely Hargrove (d. 1818) in Regent Parade between High and Low Harrogate. The modest assembly-room was often well filled, and its temporary MC presided over the balls on Monday and Friday.[14]

Harrogate's short season began late, in July, and did not warrant an elaborate assembly-room like those of the southern spas; its social life still centred around the long-rooms of the 'five or six large inns'. The 'best' company favoured Upper Harrogate, the socially superior Granby or 'house of peers', the Green Dragon or 'house of commons' with more and better parlours, or the biggest and oldest inn, the Queen's Head. In 1800 Low Harrogate was still dominated by the recently improved Crown, now the town's largest inn. Apart from these early inns there were now lesser ones, like the White Hart and the Swan in Low Harrogate, and visitors could enjoy the moderate cost of living in all. There was abundant mutton, fish from Hartlepool and trout from the Nidd, but vegetables were scarce and backward. The society in this inn-orientated life was in 1800 said to be living in harmony and 'better cultivated than the soil'. A more integrated social life had evolved with a routine of balls at the Dragon, Granby and Queen's Head in rotation on Wednesday and Friday, where entrance cost 1*s.* and dancers paid more for music, and theatre performances on Tuesday, Thursday and Saturday. About 8 a.m. each day the water-drinkers went to the well, where Dr Adair, 'a very sensible and well-informed young man', had now joined Dr Jaques in attendance, or serving-women brought the water to their lodging-houses. Breakfast was at 10 a.m., dinner at 7 p.m. and, after a ball or the theatre, supper at ten and bed at 11 p.m. But many complained of Harrogate's deficiencies as a spa; in 1800 it lacked such elementary conveniences as a pump-room to shelter the drinkers or a simple well-house to protect the well-women. The springs' odour made the lower town objectionable in hot weather, and except for Lord Loughborough's two-mile path the few walks were poor and of dry, sandy soil, and the marshy heath on the borders of the upper town required draining.[15]

Despite these inconveniences an increasing number of visitors gravitated there, according to Ely Hargrove, printer and proprietor of the rooms, whose *History of the Castle, Town and Forest of Knaresborough with Harrogate* (1775) ran to six editions by 1809 and a seventh, posthumous one by 1832. In 1781 1,556 visitors came and 2,458 in 1795, exclusive of servants. The Reverend Robert Mitton, curate of St John's Chapel, High Harrogate enlarged his church in about 1791 and 1812, hoping to augment his stipend by accommodating more seasonal visitors, for Lord Loughborough and others had annexed some chapel land. Mitton also, in 1810, spoke of the greater influx of visitors; 5,858 had come that season. He allocated pews first to the local gentry, Mr Watson of Bilton Park and Mr Brown of Harrogate Hall, but then to the influential inn-keepers.[16]

Harrogate's slow physical expansion continued. By 1801 there were 234 houses and 1,195 inhabitants in Bilton with Harrogate, excluding part of Low Harrogate in Pannal parish, and improvements were belatedly put in hand. The Old Sulphur Well with three adjacent springs remained in a primitive state, with covered stone basins in a walled enclosure in 1773, and in 1804 an eleven-pillared dome was erected over one and the other three well-heads were taken down. Dr. G. Cayley suggested some shelter for those coming to drink the waters in the morning, so in 1804 an assembly-room, the Old Promenade Room, was built: seventy-five feet long and thirty feet broad, set in a large garden. By 1814 four doctors had settled in Harrogate and more shops had appeared, mostly in High Harro-gate. Roby's vast stock included jewellery and gold watches; Smith's of New Bond Street, London was one of two milliners' shops; Batchelor's dealt in gold and silver. Eight years later there was Hargrove's and another library and thirty-five shops, but only three in Low Harrogate.[17] East of his Crown Hotel Joseph Thackwray's land, purchased in 1765, became the Montpellier Gardens where in about 1810 his great-nephew, also Joseph Thackwray, discovered several springs, three of which were given fancy names – the Strong and Mild Montpellier Sulphurs and the Kissingen Saline Chalybeate – and were used to supply baths in the hotel. The Thackwrays ran the Crown so profitably that they were able to build up a large local estate, including Devonshire House. Part of their success lay in making bathing comfortable, with fires and beds in the bathrooms. A visitor in 1816 paid 3*s.* for a warm bath and the attendant expected to receive 6*d*. Other proprietors of hotels and inns also promoted new springs, but the control of bathing and social facilities was passing from them to commercial entrepreneurs.[18] The growing industrialization of the North produced both capital for investment in the leisure industry and more middle-class spa customers, and the greater commercial potential of Harrogate as a health resort became more apparent to enterprising busi-nessmen in the nineteenth century.

Scarborough

Harrogate's rival among the spas of Georgian Yorkshire, Scarborough, was a port with a spa quarter, while Harrogate was an embryonic urban spa. The distinctive features of Scarborough, still confined within its medieval moat, were its damaged castle, St Mary's Church on the hill, and the harbour. Its population of about 6,000 was chiefly engaged in fishing, shipping and shipbuilding, and catering for those who came to drink at the Spa Wells or for sea-bathing was only a minor part of its economy. But in 1686 Scarborough had more visitors' accommodation than Harrogate – seventy-four beds in inns alone, and stabling for 144 horses – and by 1801 its population was still about six times larger.[19]

Scarborough and Bath were the only spa boroughs – except Southampton, with an ephemeral spa – and spa facilities in both were controlled by the corporation. In Scarborough in 1691 they set about promoting the trade in bottled water, which was initiated and monopolized by the mineral-water merchant John Fiddes. He had a house in Scarborough and used the corporation seal on his bottles, but from 1733 he traded in London from the Golden Wheatsheaf warehouse in Tavistock Street, Covent Garden. In December 1733 Dr Peter Shaw, then an unlicensed practitioner at Scarborough, and apothecary Culmer Cockerill, the senior bailiff, attempting to eliminate fraud, gave Fiddes a so-called certificate of authenticity for the waters, and Shaw wrote the publicity puff, *An Enquiry into the Contents, Virtues, and Uses, of the Scarborough-Spaw Waters* . . . (1734). In 1735 he began the manufacture of Scarborough salts. A steady trade in Scarborough water developed in the 1730s: in 1733–4 alone 74,586 bottles, much of it exported to London and Hull. Municipal revenue also came from the 5s. subscriptions for the use of the spa house which Dicky Dickinson collected.[20]

Although a traveller of 1723 found that the Scarborough Wells and spa house down by the shore drew many customers during the hot summer months, Scarborough was not an attractive spa. In 1722 the corporation contracted to pay John Bland, a merchant, £85 to construct a coach road down the cliffs to the sands and a substantial staith or wall facing the sea, the 'coach road to the spa' of Cossins's map (1725). But in 1732 the Duchess of Marlborough found it extremely steep and disagreeable for coaches and chairs, and she complained that there were no walks, as at Bath and Tunbridge Wells, only sands for driving in coaches or riding on saddle-horses. But she thought the lodgings were good and preferable to the inns, although her own lodging-house was noisy and dirty.[21]

Social life at Scarborough had a different pattern from that of most northern spas; the inns were important but they seldom offered residential facilities, only travellers' accommodation, and there were some lodging-houses. So places for public assembly were necessary. Although the Duchess of Marlborough complained that there was no fit place for water-drinking or public assembly, there was a long-room in Low Westgate Street and in 1725 a second one, later the Royal Hotel, in St Nicholas Street, which in 1734 was kept by Vipont, master of the long-room at Hampstead. He provided a service for visitors who stayed in lodgings by putting on a dinner at 2 p.m., assisted by cooks and a poulterer from London. Balls were held *every* evening, the room illuminated like a court assembly, and sedan chairs from London plied the streets. In 1725 Cossins noted the surprising improvement in buildings to cater for visitors, or 'Spaws' as they were called: several more inns, the New Inn, the New Globe and others appeared. Between 1686 and 1756 accommodation at inns more than doubled; the number of beds available increased from seventy-four to 151 and places for horses in stables went up even more from 144 to 358, not counting some of both just outside the town. Leisure facilities by 1733 included a bowling green on the site of St Sepulchre's Church, a coffee-house at Newborough Bar, and a bookshop in Longroom Street. In May Mr Keregan was allowed to erect a booth as a primitive theatre in the Horse Fair near the Market Place, which was convenient for coaches. The author of the *Journey to Scarborough* (1733) claimed that the principal nobility and gentry had come from all over the kingdom in recent years, including the wealthy Richard Lumley, 1st Earl of Scarborough (d. 1721). A subscription list of 1733 showed 1,053 visitors, including two dukes, one marquess, seven earls, three lords, nineteen baronets and six knights; so Scarborough had a distinctly aristocratic flavour. There was commercial potential in providing diversions for visitors, who passed the afternoons gambling.[22]

Drinking spa water at Scarborough was now rivalled by outdoor bathing and swimming. Doctors had long recommended sea-bathing as a cure for melancholia and hydrophobia, and Dr Robert Wittie, the author of *Scarborough Spa* (1667), suggested it as a remedy for gout. Floyer's *Enquiry into . . . Hot, Cold and Temperate Baths* (1697) did much to popularize cold-bathing in general, and sea-bathing was first mentioned at Scarborough when the Duchess of Manchester and other ladies tried it out in August 1732. John Setterington's engraving of a view of Scarborough in 1735 shows people bathing in the sea and the earliest recorded bathing-machines. Scarborough became alarmed at rumours of a government intention to tax bathers, who before 1750 were to be found in the sea at Deal, Eastbourne, Portsmouth, Exmouth and Brighton.[23]

Sea-bathing increased Scarborough's attractions and many visitors both bathed and drank the waters, so the spa wells remained a source of prosperity until, to the consternation of the corporation, the sea damaged the spa buildings in 1735 and in December 1737 the cliff-face collapsed, destroying the well-house and cistern, forcing the weighty staith out to sea, and burying the springs. Dicky Dickinson, governor of the wells, lost all his household goods and died in February 1738. But the corporation acted promptly and the local people rejoiced when, after diligent search, the spa springs were recovered. In 1739 another building, the 'Old' Spa House, was erected over them, the staith was repaired, and attempts were made to restore the spa trade and to recover the cost of restoration under a new governor, William Temperton; he died in 1755. Subscriptions covering both the North and South Wells were raised from 5*s.* a season, as in 1733, to 7*s.* 6*d.*: one-third for the water-servers and the rest for the corporation.[24]

When John Fiddes died in 1743 Culmer Cockerill took over the trade in bottled water, which dropped rapidly to only 2,934 bottles and twelve bags by 1779–80 and a mere twenty-four bottles in 1800–1; by then the national trade in mineral waters had declined. But 'The Spaw' site remained in business: a long single-storeyed hut with a shed, perhaps the coffee-room erected by Mr Cooper, member of the corporation and tenant of the spa in 1796. William Allanson, the governor from 1755, believed that spa water was a sovereign remedy, and he was 103 when he died in 1775. Thomas Headley was governor in 1797.[25]

Neighbouring places had tried to profit from Scarborough's disaster of 1737, with rumours that the mineral water now had a brackish taste. Bridlington advertised a spa water, and Hartlepool subscribed to building a long-room but could barely afford lodging-houses. Scarborough held its own; although about 240 miles from London and away from major centres of population, it was one of Bath's rivals. In the summer of 1745 Cass, a Scarborough innkeeper, kept coaches to run sightseeing tours for the 'Spaws', as the visitors were called. Eight coachloads of the company departed in one morning that season.[26] Some visitors came by sea, a cheaper but less fashionable journey of four or five days from London, and after 1736 a road from Lincoln was linked by a ferry over the Humber at Winteringham, especially for travellers to Scarborough Spa. Better roads helped Scarborough, as they had helped Harrogate. The turnpiking of the Great North Road neared completion in 1750, and the case for improving the road between York and Scarborough in 1752 was that it had long been used ' . . . by persons resorting to Scarborough . . . from most parts of England, for the benefit of the mineral waters . . .', especially those in heavy coaches. By 1754 a regular coach from Leeds to Scarborough ran every Wednesday from 9 July for the season; by 1781 two coaches ran daily through York connecting with north Midland towns, and diligences went to Hull three times a week.[27]

Despite the expansion of accommodation in the first half of the eighteenth century, Scarborough was still complacent about its resort facilities; the season beginning in early July was short, and although stimulated by the mid-August races at York it did not encourage investment. Contemporary accounts were generally critical; in 1744 the drinking-room of the well and the paths around were 'miserably mean and dirty', and the lack of public walks was still deplored. Another visitor in 1768 thought Scarborough a 'dirty, ill-built, and very badly paved town'. But the more residential Newborough, built for visitors, was better, Longroom Street, covered with broad stones and set with posts from about 1733, was called its Pall Mall, and purpose-built lodging-houses, the 'handsome and stately' New Buildings, were erected by 1750.[28] There were lodgings to be had in the two best streets, the elegant Queen Street and Newborough, as well as in the inns, such as the George and New Inns and the Scarborough Arms. Charges for rooms matched those at Bath: 10s. a week but 10s. 6d. by 1806, including the use of towels, sheets and table linen, with servants' rooms at half price; but, as in Bath, landlords were reluctant to break their suites. A kitchen and utensils could be rented for £1 a week, and a servants' hall for 10s. There were two or three boarding-houses, but many visitors hired lodgings and foraged for provisions at the local market on Thursday and Saturday, and in full season an 'ordinary', a public meal at a fixed price and time, was available at most inns.[29] But visitors led rather isolated lives in their separate lodgings, except when the public rooms were open for entertainment.

The Old Long Room in Low Westgate Street and the New Long Room in St Nicholas Street were at least from 1784 run by Edward Donner and William Newstead respectively, but Arthur Young thought them 'paltry holes', and in 1789 they had 'a naked and scurvy appearance'. Dancing on three evenings was less popular than card-playing on other nights. The rooms' charges, agreed by the company in 1783, were in 1806 – and still in 1813 – the usual spa formula: one guinea for a season's subscription, 2s. for music from every male dancer, 1s. for tea, and 5s. for each event from non-subscribers. Scarborough alone among the northern spas had a master of ceremonies, whose services were needed to integrate social life since, although the inns were important, social life did not revolve around them. The first MC – Charles Jones, Nash's assistant at Bath – was imported in 1740, so the Old Long Room was presumably open then. Robin Farside held the office in 1783 when the charges were agreed, and, although over eighty, he was still there in 1797. When he died Newstead's long-room closed, apparently by 1800. Mr Dormer had acquired Donner's Old Long Room by 1789 and he opened a subscription room for newspapers and dinners.[30]

When the playhouses were suppressed in 1752 and 1755 the bailiffs were attacked for allowing a company of players to perform in the town, but a playhouse, later the Theatre Royal, was erected in Tanner Street in 1761, which in 1768, managed by James Cawdell, was functioning from June to October. Described as the 'equal of those elsewhere' in 1800 and 'generally well-attended' in 1813, its charges remained at the 1788 level, 3s. for a box, 2s. the pit, and 1s. the gallery. The Duchess of Rutland was the theatre's patron and entertained the corporation there in 1787, as did her son the 5th duke in 1796 after dining them in Donner's Room. Visitors could use two libraries by 1797 – one Mr Scholfield's – but Ann Park's coffee-house kept its monopoly. So Scarborough had some of the commercialized entertainments which Harrogate so conspicuously lacked.[31]

When Sir Harbottle Grimston wrote in 1768 that Scarborough was 'much resorted to by company for the benefit of bathing in the sea . . .' spa life there was already secondary to sea-bathing. By 1785 there were twenty-six bathing-machines, with two women guides for every lady bather and one each for gentlemen, and forty machines by 1813. Sea-bathing was indulged in by the Duchess of Beaufort, from Badminton near Bath, in 1787. Her husband, the 5th duke, was the recorder of Scarborough and had a house there, and she, her children and her sister-in-law Mary Isabella, wife of the 4th Duke of Rutland, arrived late in the summer, on 15 September, but there was still 'a fair amount of company', and Her Grace of Rutland bathed in the sea at least until 1 October. But already by 1768 Scarborough had become a pleasure resort rather than a health centre:

> They provide lodgings for themselves in the town and generally meet once a day at some kind of diversion either at the rooms or the playhouse . . . or at the billiard table. These amusements and the pleasure of seeing company induces many to come who are not really in want of the water.

Even so, there were still a great many water-drinkers in 1788.[32]

Scarborough's development as a watering-place accentuated the divorce between the old town, with its steep, narrow streets, and the 'polite parts': the Newborough with the assembly-rooms and the theatre to the west. Even the post office, near the harbour, was moved to Palace Hill for the convenience of visitors by 1806. But Scarborough lacked a large pump-room, and even public walks until gardens were opened to subscribers for 2s. 6d. in about 1806, so Harrogate, more conveniently sited, replaced it as the leading North Country spa. By 1774 the *York Courant* listed visitors to Harrogate but not to Scarborough, and the *York Herald* in 1813 reported 1,320 visitors there against 500 at Scarborough.[33]

Scarborough's population in 1801, excluding Falsgrave, was little more than in 1750 – 6,409 – and only 6,710 in 1811, but a new sense of enterprise was developing then. Under an Act of 1805 improvement commissioners were given the usual powers to pave, light and watch streets and alleys, to purchase land and levy a rate up to 2s. in the pound, but even so voluntary subscriptions were collected for street lamps in 1810.[34] Harrogate had no

Improvement Act until 1841, but from about 1800, with the wartime boom in English spas and the greater industrial prosperity of the North, came more investment and employment in the leisure industry to service the growing number of middle-class residents and more mobile visitors to both spas.

14

The Innkeepers' Spas of Derbyshire: Buxton and Matlock

Buxton

Daniel Defoe thought Buxton a watering-place ripe for commercial exploitation but it remained a backward spa, handicapped by its uninviting environment. The old 'town', Higher Buxton, stood on a limestone plateau at 940–1,050 feet amid the millstone-grit uplands of the southern Pennines where gorge-like valleys impeded communications to the north and west. Below the old town the spa settlement of Lower Buxton, in the marshy shale valley of the Wye, had some walks and plantations. Many contemporary travellers wrote of the bleakness of the landscape around Buxton in the eighteenth century, and of the hard local roads. William Gilpin said in 1772 that there was 'hardly a tree' and 'nothing but absolute want of health could make a man endure a scene so wholly disgusting'.[1]

Yet Buxton was endowed with naturally warm waters for bathing, and the chalybeate spring of St Anne's Well, covered by Delves's Well-house in 1709, for drinking. Compared with the thermal springs of Bath, held to be too hot at 116°F, and the too-tepid Bristol Hotwell (76°F) and Matlock (68°F) waters, Buxton waters were warm, 81°F in St Anne's Well and 82°F at the bath, and even in the very dry summer of 1780 their volume was undiminished.[2] Hawking on the moor was another attraction, so despite dreary surroundings and only elementary tourist facilities, a few aristocrats and some people of middle rank still patronized Buxton. Lady Pye – who, with her daughter, spent ten days there in July 1707 – preferred the Buxton bath to all other medicines. On her arrival there was only one coach besides her own, but later there were thirteen and more were expected. Buxton's Catholic tradition died hard; in 1713 it was still a haunt of many papists and Jacobites. Tomson, an apothecary from Ashbourne, mixed in 1731 with many visitors, possibly hoping for patients, and Dr

Richard Kay from Lancashire stayed three days in August 1739 among several clergymen. When he returned in 1744 and 1747 to bathe in 'Buxton Wells' he found many there bent on pleasure.[3]

Buxton was another spa where social life focused on the inns, especially the Old Hall in Lower Buxton, held from about 1730 to 1750 by landlord Alexander Taylor. Upstairs there was a beautiful dining-room seventeen yards long and nineteen feet wide, and there were seven other entertaining-rooms, eleven single bedrooms and twenty-nine others – altogether sixty beds, and some for servants. The Reverend John Nixon found the company of forty to fifty ladies and gentlemen lodging there in mid-September 1745 a stimulating experience. They ate at a common table, 'conversing promiscuously with the greatest freedom imaginable'. But amenities were limited to a billiard-table, a bowling green surrounded with sycamore trees, and a pack of hounds for the gentlemen's diversion. Some local inhabitants also took in lodgers; Dr Thomas Wilson, a prebendary of Westminster, stayed in a private lodging and took his warm baths, which gave great relief, at the Hall, but he soon left for Tunbridge Wells. In the mid-eighteenth century the Hall was improved and enlarged, and in 1781 Lady Newdigate found that some rooms had acquired names: the Lamb, the Lion and the Blue Parlour. But many visitors were critical of Buxton; one Carr in 1742 spoke of its 'melancholy situation, the accommodation bad and little company but invalids'. Another in 1766 thought it 'a shocking place', and the Earl of Mornington in 1787 could recommend only the bath; it was not a lively resort.[4] Buxton had been living on its long tradition as a water-cure place and substantial investment in tourist facilities was needed to meet the competition of developing spas like Bath and Cheltenham.

From mid-century, apart from enlargement of the Hall, there was some increase in accommodation, proof of a steady flow of visitors. By 1768 there were 'three large inns': the Hall, and also the Eagle and the White Hart, the 'good inn or two on the hill'. The oldest inn – the Eagle, or the Eagle and Child, in the marketplace in Higher Buxton – was rebuilt, probably before 1766. The White Hart opposite existed in 1752, and was 'a handsome inn'; by 1776 it had a dance-room with blue wallpaper and three chandeliers, but its company, although 'vastly civil', was less polished than that at the Hall. The more convenient Hall in Lower Buxton was the visitors' first choice and remained completely full, with many advance bookings.[5] The town could absorb 300 visitors, but in August 1776 the White Hart and the Eagle and Child were also full, and a lady visitor had to endure the inferior Angel where breakfast was 8*d.*, dinner 1*s.*, supper 1*s.*, and afternoon tea 8*d*. Later two of her party and an invalid got a room at the Hall, now managed by Brian Hodgson.[6]

Hodgson and his son were typical promoters of the inn-centred social life of the northern spas, and of Malvern, expecting visitors to reside fully under their roof and find their pleasures there. Brian Hodgson I, born around 1709, was an innkeeper at Stamford who took the Hall at Buxton about 1753, became the Duke of Devonshire's agent, retired in about 1780 and died 1784. Although Brian Hodgson II paid the duke an annual rent of £1,200 he ran the Hall during a new period of prosperity, so he graduated to become a country gentleman and claimed the standing of an esquire before his death in 1827. Under Brian Hodgson I the prices for food at the Hall were uniform with those for the Angel, and 3*s.* a week for a poor bedroom. The charge for a fire, a necessary comfort at Buxton, was 6*d.* a day in 1781 for poor-quality coal. As in other northern spas, the visitors dined communally at a long table in order of seniority as guests, but with five side-tables. Breakfast, with muffins toasted to perfection, was served in a small room downstairs. Musicians, who expected a gratuity from leaving visitors, played during meals, and the evening amusements included a harpist, dancing, card-playing and raffles. In 1784 about seventy 'noisy and disagreeable' people were there, and, nervous of the Hall's reputation, Mrs Hodgson broadcast that four lords and seven baronets were expected.[7]

From 1730 a number of 'excellent' lodging-houses were erected to supplement the Hall, and the nearby Grove Coffee-house (later the Grove Inn) was opened by 1778 and accommodated about twelve people, who dined together or took a private parlour for half a guinea a week. The George Inn, close to the Hall, existed in mid-century, and in Higher Buxton the Seven Stars and the Cheshire Cheese by 1788, or earlier. The medical profession, such as Dr Alexander Hunter of York, still encouraged people to take the Buxton waters; he published a treatise praising them in 1761. The upper town had an apothecary in 1743, but in 1769 there was still only one resident surgeon or apothecary, Samuel Buxton, 'a sensible and worthy apothecary near the wells', although outside physicians came for the season. By contrast Bath, Buxton's past rival but now acquiring a splendid new town, had forty-eight surgeons and apothecaries.[8] Some of Buxton's lethargy stemmed from undue dependence on ducal initiative.

The Duke of Devonshire held Buxton as part of the king's manor of the High Peak and lived in style nearby at Chatsworth with a household of 180. William, Lord Hartington, later the 4th duke, was enormously enriched by marrying Lady Charlotte Boyle, heiress of the 3rd Earl of Burlington and 4th of Cork, and so obtained the Irish and Yorkshire estates, Chiswick House in Middlesex and Burlington House in Piccadilly. He succeeded to the dukedom in 1755 but suffered a stroke in 1764 when he was only forty-four, and, sent by his doctors to drink the waters there, died at Spa. His heir William, the 5th duke, then only sixteen, inherited an immense fortune and an annual income of £35,000, including the profits of the lucrative copper- and lead-mines at Ecton in Staffordshire. He devoted some of his wealth to an attempt to transform Buxton into a major spa to attract the aristocratic and polite society in which he moved.[9]

The expansion of Buxton from the 1770s onwards was helped by the opening up and improvement of the surrounding countryside. Turnpiking of the local roads had been intermittent since 1725, when an Act covered the Manchester to Buxton road, and several road Improvement Acts were passed in the 1750s. Lord Kinnoul wrote in 1759 that this wild country, previously inaccessible to wheeled carriages, now had turnpike roads, which opened up communications with all the kingdom. Also to the duke's advantage, 977 acres in Fairfield were enclosed by an Act of 1771, completed in 1774, but, as at Tunbridge Wells in 1740 and Harrogate in 1770, the right of public access to 'the spring or well of water near Buxton Hall called St Anne's Well', the source of Buxton's prosperity, was safeguarded. All common roads or paths leading to it were to be left open and unenclosed, for the use and benefit of nearby inhabitants and 'all other persons resorting thereto, for their healths or otherwise'. A poor person, appointed by the vestry, was to care for the well and serve the water.[10]

The young duke also had, as it proved, the advantage of a long life, and with ambitions to make Buxton the rival of Bath and Cheltenham, he invested heavily in Buxton's holiday industry. He and his duchess, Georgiana, had much experience of spas. From 1763 and 1789 she went regularly to Spa in the Netherlands, and early in 1775 they both spent a few weeks there, although when the corpse of the 4th duke was returned to England it had been remarked that he might have lived long but for Spa. In 1776 the duchess spent three months at Tunbridge Wells, in 1780 she sampled Cheltenham, and with her husband visited Bath in 1782, 1783, for Christmas and New Year 1787–8, and in 1791. She thought Bath 'the dullest of places', but in November 1793 the couple took a house there for three months.[11]

The duke proposed to build in Lower Buxton around St Anne's Well and the Hall, on the recently enclosed higher common land, after first buying out several small owners. In 1780 he was free to pursue his project but his grandiose schemes needed an architect of calibre, like those employed at Bath. He chose a master-stonemason of his grandfather Lord Burlington, John Carr of York, the principal architect in the North and already the creator of assembly-rooms at Beverley, Newark and Nottingham. Devonshire had three considerations in mind: the bleakness of the northern climate (Buxton is the highest town in England), better facilities for visitors' health cure and pleasures, and more lodging capacity.[12] He may have gone to Bath before 1782, in which case he would have seen the outstanding feature of its new town, the Crescent of 1767–74; his plan was to provide a similar structure with social amenities at Buxton. His crescent would have been better framed on higher ground, but he chose the lower site to avoid taxing the sick and disabled. In 1780 the grove of trees near the Hall was felled, the river was arched over, and piles were sunk to secure the foundations. Stone for the main walls was extracted on-site and facing freestone from a quarry two miles away. In September 1781 Lady Newdigate found Buxton full of fog, noise and confusion; the walls of the Crescent were rapidly rising and men were moving about with barrows and carts, climbing ladders, shouting, hammering, filing, sawing and cutting stone.[13]

The magistrates had empowered the duke to divert the road near St Anne's Well, which, to the outrage of visitors, was demolished in about 1779. They demanded that Carr, who periodically rode over from York to supervise operations, should restore the well, but he said that was impossible. Some families then left Buxton, but a group of 'spirited' men, with some masons, actually poked a hole in a wall until they found the springs. Carr had it arched over and the women dippers put their glasses through the hole, but in 1782 he built a more appropriate well-house, a 'chaste little building of the Grecian order', to harmonize with the Crescent, opposite its south-western end. Lady Newdigate called it an octagon. Water from the original St Anne's Well was tapped to flow into a white marble basin, with two pumps, for cold and tepid water, and another pump outside the Hall. The water was free, and the four attendants, who were elected by the ratepayers, depended on gratuities. The most prominent of them was Martha Norton (d. 1820), who served at the spring for fifty years.[14]

By September 1783 the magnificent Crescent was, to the delight of the duchess, nearing completion, although she thought it would ruin her family. The Devonshire arms carved in stone by Thomas Waterworth of Doncaster surmounted the duke's lodging in the centre with 'fine effect'; they cost £65. Begun in 1780, partly occupied in 1784 and completed in 1786, the Crescent cost £38,601 18s. 4d., the last payment made in June 1790, and it is still the glory of Buxton. It is semicircular and smaller than that at Bath, which is semi-elliptical, and consists of three Roman Doric storeys, the lowest supported by a paved arcade forming a promenade seven feet wide and eleven feet high along the whole front and raised up a flight of steps. This building had – unlike the Bath Crescent, built solely for lodgings or residence – a multiple use to provide better standards of comfort and amenity for visitors. Each end contained a 'hotel', the first two of that name in Buxton, with four private lodging-houses between and shops in the lower rooms.

St Ann's Hotel at the west end, nearest to the well, opened first, probably under Charles Moore (d. 1811): it had thirty-seven rooms and the best bedrooms. The Royal Hotel (by 1813 the Great Hotel) at the east end, run by James Hall in 1790 and then by his widow until her death in 1815, had seventy-two best bedrooms. In keeping with Buxton's traditionally inn-oriented social life, the Royal had what Buxton had lacked, a splendid assembly-room. In the style of Robert Adam with giant Corinthian columns, it was 75½ feet long, thirty feet two inches wide and thirty feet high, less than three-quarters the length of the Upper Rooms at Bath, but larger than the contemporary Assembly Room at Cheltenham. The middle block of the Crescent had, around 1808, become the third and smallest hotel; its proprietor in 1812 was Robert Smith (d. 1820). The remainder of the Crescent was private lodgings.

The Crescent, a striking departure from the vernacular architecture, provided visitors with every convenience in close proximity; they could exercise on the handsome piazza while sheltered from the weather, shop there, drink at New St Anne's Well, and use the Assembly Room and the baths, which the duke enlarged.[15] By 1795 four extra baths were formed: two private ones for gentlemen, a private one for ladies, and another, now seven altogether, so the disreputable mixed bathing ended. All, except the charity bath, had dressing-rooms attached and servants in attendance. The accounts of the Buxton Bath Charity, originally the Treasury of the Bath, survive from 1785.[16]

By 1800 Buxton had recovered its reputation as a spa and could accommodate 400 more people, many coming in coaches or on horseback. Unlike the older free-standing inns, however, the new Crescent hotels had no yards and stables, so the duke's next venture, costing £40,000, was an octagon-shaped set of stables built from 1785 to 1796; it had stalls for 110 horses, a vast coach-house for sixty coaches, and a circular, covered gallery or ride 160 yards in circumference for exercise on horseback in bad weather. The upper storey, originally intended as visitors' rooms, was let off as family dwellings or artisans' workshops. Said to be the handsomest in Europe, aping those of Wentworth Woodhouse, these stables had their critics; one person thought them 'useless, ill-contrived grandeurs' where an hourly watch had to be kept, and he preferred small stables adjoining snug lodging-houses.[17]

The duke controlled the holiday industry in Buxton, with a monopoly of the baths and a near-monopoly of the hotels, inns and lodging-houses. Lower Buxton was now the fashionable quarter and he provided yet more lodging room there. By 1812 Carr's other 'New Buildings' included the so-called New Square, an oblong built on three sides, where the Crescent arcade continued as a covered walk about 200 yards long. The duke placed tenants in four lodging-houses there, and seven more in a new range of houses 'well adapted for shops and lodging-houses' on Hall Bank, the slope connecting the New Town of Lower Buxton with the old Higher Buxton. The duke also purchased and rebuilt the Eagle Inn in Higher Buxton and converted an adjacent large building into separate lodging-houses. His total holding in 1812 was eight hotels or inns and fourteen lodging-houses, against nine inns and seven lodging-houses which were 'free', excluding the meaner ones. The Grove Inn, for example, was kept by the Wood family for over sixty years. In this period of expansion innkeeping, often combined with farming, was a profitable business and gave rise to propertied dynasties. Some families ran more than one inn: the Bennetts had the Shoulder of Mutton and the Sun in 1812, and the Mycocks the Queen's Head and the Cheshire Cheese. In season every inhabitant prepared to take in lodgers.[18]

The overheads of innkeepers and their investments in stock were, the scanty evidence suggests, high: the annual rent of the Hall in 1784 and 1795 and that of the Great Hotel in 1816 was £1,200. The valuation of the furniture and stock, excluding liquors, at the Hall in 1808 was £1,918 8s. 4d. As at Bath and Malvern and Matlock later, uniform charges at the inns from June to October in 1801 suggest price-fixing agreements; a single bedroom cost 10s. 6d. a week, a double bedroom 14s., and a sitting-room 14s. to 16s., according to quality. Breakfast was 1s. 6d., an 'ordinary' dinner – a set meal – 2s. 6d., tea 1s., and supper 1s. 6d., but during the French wars Buxton prices increased. As well as rents the ducal revenues included profits from the baths, in 1795 £1,400. A public bath cost 1s. and a private bath 3s., but visitors in the duke's hotels and lodgings had a monopoly of them until 9 a.m., a privilege first mentioned in 1800.[19]

By 1789 the fifty or sixty houses of 1774 had become seventy-seven with 238 inhabitants, excluding Fairfield, which was also expanding. By 1801 Buxton alone had 180 houses and had more than trebled its residents – to 760 – and by 1811 934 inhabitants lived in 186 houses, chiefly of stone. Buxton was a very small township compared with Bath (population 38,408) or even Cheltenham (8,325) in 1811, but in 1813 it could absorb 800 to 900 visitors in private lodgings alone, not including the recipients of the Buxton Bath Charity, who had to walk to cheap lodgings in Burbage and Fairfield.[20]

Buxton, now transformed into a resort, drew an 'astonishing' influx of company which drove hundreds of invalids to neighbouring villages for lodgings. This expanding leisure market prompted the provision of more retail services, some previously unknown to this remote village. Reading was an obvious occupation of weather-bound visitors, and by 1790 William Bott, a haberdasher, had opened a circulating library. Now that there was something to write about, Bott also supplied Buxton's first non-medical guide, *A Description of Buxton and the Adjacent Country, or the New Guide for Ladies and Gentlemen* (1792, with possibly eight editions before his death in 1804). Bott's Circulating Library and stationer's shop at 6, Hall Bank had by 1812 passed to John Goodwin, and Mrs M. Goodwin brought out the tenth edition of Bott's *Guide* in 1813. Two other libraries had appeared by 1812, one run by Mr Abel in Bank Place and the other by William More, whose outstanding collection, more like a private library, included English and French works on philosophy, antiquities, biography and travel, and novels. This investor in commercialized leisure was also the proprietor of a newsroom with a 6s. subscription, a lodging-house in the Crescent, the post office and a stable of horses for hire.[21]

By 1790 Buxton's economy, based partly on the leisure industry, supported forty traders in twenty-two occupations, including four bakers, three blacksmiths and five grocers, but also three hairdressers and two jewellers. Four traders came for the season only. By 1795 an elementary transport service used Higher Buxton as a stage. The Manchester coach halted at the Eagle and Child three days a week each way and met the London coach at Leicester. Another coach to Manchester and Sheffield three days a week stopped at the White Hart. Pickford's wagon supplied a regular carrier service through Buxton on its Manchester to London route twice a week, and there were other carrier links with Manchester and Midland towns. The shift of focus from the old town to Carr's new lower town affected the transport services. The White Hart had lost the Manchester–Sheffield coach to the Grove Inn below by 1800, and was temporarily named the Scarsdale Arms after its owner, Lord Scarsdale. In 1796 it was bought out by the proprietor of the new St Ann's Hotel, George Goodwin, who closed it down in 1803. Even the London–Manchester post-coach now stopped at the Eagle and Child only one way, for breakfast, and on return its passengers dined at the Grove Inn in the new town.[22]

The new Buxton offered more employment, but agriculture was still its main support, with the visitors in season. The minority of about 200 who worked and lived in the limestone quarries were a race apart. By 1812 the innkeepers had lost their near-monopoly of the holiday trade; of the forty hotels, inns and lodging-houses twenty-three were lodging-houses. But the regular lodging-house keepers had only a seasonal trade and, as at Bath and Tunbridge Wells, they followed a secondary occupation; Charles Crowder was also a hosier and kept a fluorspar museum and mineral repository; Michael Clayton was a tailor and Thomas Clayton a shoemaker. Like Tunbridge Wells, Buxton had a trade in tourist mementoes; in 1812 there were ten 'petrifaction shops' selling vases, obelisks and candlesticks fashioned from natural or artificial fossils.[23]

Other Buxton people made a living from providing diversions for visitors. The small, dirty theatre in a thatched and boarded barn may have existed by 1776; it held only a few people but was comfortable inside and admission charges were normal: boxes 3s., the pit 2s. and the gallery 1s. Under the management of Mr Welsh (Welch) and his company it recruited a famous comedian, William Blanchard (then Bentley) in 1785, and in 1788 Welsh and one Ferrizer were licensed for theatrical performances in

Buxton and Bakewell. In 1790 Welsh's Buxton company had seven other members, including the comedian John Kane, who in 1799 died of eating hemlock instead of horseradish, as recorded on his gravestone in St Anne's churchyard. When the duke built his stables the barn-theatre was demolished, but he replaced it with a new but modest theatre in Spring Gardens or Theatre Street, built about 1792 and managed by Welsh's company. It opened around 1 July for three nights a week until the end of October and in 1812, when the company's lease was due to expire, Buxton hoped that the duke would build a more comfortable theatre appropriate to the 'improved state of the town'.[24]

To soften the framework of his new town, provide places for exercise and ease communications, the duke spent a great deal on improving the environment. Young trees had already been planted in the boggy Wye vale near the Hall, and its conversion into the enchanting Serpentine Walks was begun by 1810. The Duke's Drive through Ashwood Dale over the high ground to the old London road and back to Buxton was made about 1795, and another pleasure ride of over two miles was constructed to a high point on the Matlock Road. To link Matlock and Buxton more easily, in 1810 the duke obtained a Turnpike Act for the Ashford to Buxton road following the Wye, cut in 1811. The 5th duke's policy of extensive planta-tions was continued by his heir, who in January 1812 ordered 40,000 trees for his Buxton estates and in about 1818 laid out St Ann's Cliff in terraces and walks facing the Crescent.[25]

The outcome of the enormous ducal outlay was not only a changing landscape. The lower new town, with its elegant buildings and walks, became a fashionable spa centre, a miniature Bath, but there were critics. Byng complained that the duke had lavished his money upon a 'huge mausoleum' and 'a laboured quarry above ground' with 'great noisy hotels'. Local inhabitants, however, resolved to make 'a quick harvest', like Dr Norton, who erected some bath-buildings in an abortive attempt to challenge the ducal monopoly. The duke certainly had a return on his investment in the leisure industry; he left the 6th duke an enormously inflated annual income of £125,000 compared with his £35,000 in 1764, so large capital investment in Buxton appears to have been profitable. Yet some expected even more from the duke, especially in providing Buxton with a new church to replace the old and now inadequate chapel of St Anne in Upper Buxton, for during the season the minister read daily prayers in the Crescent Assembly Room. The 5th duke persuaded the patrons of Buxton in the parish of Bakewell, the dean and chapter of Lichfield, to allow the building of a chapel of ease, St John's in Lower Buxton, which cost him £30,000, but he died in 1811 before its con-secration on 9 August 1812. The church of St Anne was then closed; another example of the shift of emphasis from the old town to the new.[26]

No other English spa was so dependent on one man's initiative. The 1813 edition of Bott's *Guide* acknowledged Buxton's indebtedness for the patronage of the late duke and his successor

> . . . for all the embellishments and conveniences which render it so interesting to company, and which contributed to raise it so high in the rank of places of health and amusement . . .

But Buxton still lacked the convenience of a local market; there were difficulties in obtaining a charter for one, and complaints of high prices were frequent. The powerful innkeepers were losing their pre-eminence and had no wish to see more visitors depart to the independence of lodgings and the purchase of their own food. So although Buxton consumed a greater volume of foodstuffs than neighbouring market towns, it had to draw on them for supplies. Consequently butter prices were usually 2*d*. or 3*d*. a pound higher than elsewhere locally, and charges for bacon, cheese, eggs, meat and vegetables had to cover transport costs from Macclesfield, Stockport, Sheffield and Chesterfield. Itinerant higglers, who ransacked the country for forty miles around to find supplies for Buxton, forced up prices and frequently produced only market refuse. So in 1813 the 6th duke allowed a small Saturday market for corn and provisions in Higher Buxton during the visitors' season, and four annual fairs for sheep, cattle, horses and pedlary.[27]

Social life in Buxton had remained largely self-sufficient, confined to hotels and large inns, where the company dined communally. The elite avoided social promiscuity by the use of side-tables, as when Lord Thurlow dined with Lord Frederick Cavendish and Lord Hood and his ladies. As well as the 'president' each house appointed a steward to collect 1*s*. for the Buxton Bath Charity from each visitor who stayed more than one day. Entertainment had been minimal; in 1774 there was dancing after supper, but in 1782 Lord Thurlow went to bed at nine for lack of anything else to do, and the Misses Ellison in two consecutive years, 1781–2, found Buxton 'the most dismal of places'.[28]

Completion of the Crescent in 1786 with shopping facilities, the first purpose-built hotels, and the Assembly Room, now the town's social centre, brought new life to Buxton and, as Bott remarked in 1795, it had become 'a resort for pleasure as well as for health'. As in other spas, London retailers were drawn there to take shops for the season, and a London doctor always resided at the Great Hotel. Buxton lacked a long-room or even a pump-room by the well, but now that the Crescent ballroom had the capacity to hold most of the company some social life was organized there. A band was provided, balls had already begun in 1783, and a master of ceremonies was instituted to ritualize social events.

To avoid expense and disputed elections one of the company was proposed to take office; in 1788 it was G. Bluett. In 1791 a hotel president refused this unpopular, unpaid responsibility and no one would accept it, but eventually another visitor obliged. The existence of the powerful innkeepers, the presidents of the hotels, and the ducal agent to exercise social control in fact made a master of ceremonies almost superfluous. The ducal agent had no direct responsibility for social life, but he had considerable local influence. Mr Heaton, the agent when the Crescent was being built, was succeeded from 1801 to 1851 by the all-powerful Philip Heacock, who lived among the respectable Buxton families in the Square.[29]

Perhaps because of the absence of a professional MC, there were no restrictions, except at dress balls, about dress or the rank of people admitted to the Buxton assemblies, and only sufficient ceremony to preserve decorum. Yet at another assembly-room also furnished by the 5th Duke of Devonshire, at Derby, tradespeople and those incorrectly dressed were barred. The subscription for admission to the Buxton assemblies, as at Scarborough, was one guinea a season, or two and a half guineas for families, although at Cheltenham one guinea admitted three of a family. Non-subscribers paid 4s. each night at Buxton, compared with 5s. at Scarborough and only 2s. at Cheltenham in 1781 and 2s. 6d. in 1791 – so northern charges were high. During the Buxton season three balls a week, dress balls on Wednesday and undress balls on Monday and Friday, alternated with theatre nights, and gloves were sold at the door. There was card-playing every night in an adjoining room, and tea-drinking for 1s. on Wednesday, but from 1791 both were prohibited on the Sabbath. The ballroom remained open from about 4 June each year as long as there were twenty subscribers, and, as at other spas, balls began at 8 p.m. and ended at 11 p.m.[30]

Use of the Crescent ballroom introduced a new standard of behaviour. A visitor in 1789 found the Old Eagle Inn noisy, very different from Harrogate and Matlock, and only twelve couples for dancing, so the next night he and his wife sampled a dress ball at the Assembly Room. But Buxton's extra lodging capacity and the now considerable number of visitors made for a more divisive society; some retired to 'aristocratic loneliness and state' with meals sent in from the hotels, and the 'universal familiarity', when small parties cheerfully combined in communal activities to offset the inconvenience of crowded, gloomy and dirty rooms, was disappearing. The annual average number of subscribers to the ballroom for five years from 1783 was 400, and even more from the outbreak of war in 1793 until 1799. Miss Seward wrote in 1798 of an immense crowd, although the 'soldierized' young and middle-aged men had gone, and so a few prim parsons and dancing doctors were the forlorn hope of the Buxton belles. Originally strongly patronized by the nobility and gentry, the balls lost their social appeal as more mixed company was admitted, and in 1800 there were only 248 patrons.[31] The death of the 5th Duke of Devonshire in 1811 marked the end of an era in Buxton. His building enterprise had produced an elegant new town and shifted the axis of activity from Upper to Lower Buxton, but a period of relative decline of this fashionable watering-place then set in.

Matlock

Matlock, twenty-two miles from Buxton, was a much less important spa, different in nature and situation; it lies by the sheltered Derwent gorge at only 200–750 feet, between craggy hills rising to about 600 feet, with less rainfall than Buxton, so it is a warmer, sunnier and drier and more relaxing spa. Both were primarily agricultural settlements, but Matlock had no ducal patron; its leisure industry depended on the initiative of several modest people, and its economy was diversified by lead-mining and later cotton-mills.[32]

The original nucleated settlement at Matlock around the parish church of St Giles was even in 1782 a 'little town' of a few miserable houses. To the north cottages straggled up Matlock Bank, and a mile and a half down the dale, among miners' cottages, were the several warm springs of 68°F which gave Matlock an advantage as a spa. In 1723 a visitor to the bath-house constructed by Fern and Heywood found it 'indeed a rural one': a leaden basin could take eight or ten bathers and a few rooms were a 'poor convenience'. The rough mountainous road to the bath-house and the lack of good accommodation on the spot deterred visitors, although he found a satisfactory lodging, with stabling for horses. But now two Nottingham promoters with a fair amount of capital, Smith and Pennel, undertook some development, including the building of a lodging-house fit to entertain people of quality. They purchased George Wragg's lease and property around 1727 for about £1,000 and erected two large buildings – one the Villa, or Old Bath House, with stables, later enlarged and known as the Old Bath Hotel.

Pennel, who subsequently bought out Smith, left his property on his death in 1733 to his daughter and her husband, Stephen Egerton. The Egertons rebuilt the baths on a larger scale in 1734 and over them the Liverpool Gallery Rooms, chiefly the resort of visitors from Liverpool, and soon afterwards added a splendid drawing-room, other rooms and stables.[33] Smith and Pennel had also improved access to the bath-house, linking Matlock Bath with Matlock Town by a coach road to Matlock Bridge and a better bridleway from the north. Soon another road was made down the valley to Cromford communicating southwards, a section of the Derby to Sheffield 1756 turnpike road through Duffield and Wirksworth.

So Matlock Bath became more accessible to visitors and attracted many by the reputation of its waters and the natural beauty of its situation, and some for amusement. Dr Richard Kay of Lancashire had to find lodgings in Wirksworth in 1747, and Matlock Bath Inn, where Richard Yorke stayed in August 1763, was 'very noisy'.[34]

This steady custom at Matlock warranted the 'discovery' by 1762–7 of another spring, just south of the first, where the New Bath and a lodging-house were erected. Sir Harbottle Grimston spoke of the Matlock 'Wells' in 1768, which suggests that both baths were then operational. Most houses now became lodging-houses; the Old Bath was the largest and most popular, but the New Bath lodging-house was more handsome and more pleasantly situated. The company, as at Buxton and Harrogate, had their meals at 1s. each in common 'in a very sociable manner'; they dined at 2 p.m. and had supper at 8 p.m. and were free to drink as they pleased. The evening concluded with dancing or card-playing. Visitors inclined to exercise could take the ferry near the Old Bath, rowed by Walker the boatman, to the other river bank where he had made a Lovers' Walk.[35]

Matlock had to compete with Buxton, so attempts were made to separate yet another hot spring which mixed with a cold one on the hill beyond the Old Bath. In 1778 it was claimed that if this hot spring could be saved, the two spas would possess equal advantages for invalids. But Matlock had an incomparably more pleasant situation: all visitors extolled its natural and picturesque beauty; one in 1774 described the many cottages near the baths standing on mountain ledges, several nearly hidden by little gardens, and the foliage spread over every cliff. Another traveller wrote in 1782 of elegant houses for the bathing company, other lesser houses, and a mile-long 'prodigious' stone wall bordering the Derwent.[36]

The sheltered valley allowed a long season from April, against late June at Buxton, to late October, which drew in the neighbouring gentry as well as distant visitors. After the last had left in 1796 the Duke of Rutland and some companions arrived on 26 October and had the whole inn to themselves. Part of Matlock's appeal was that it avoided 'the infection of southern manners' – that is, the formality of social life at Bath, Cheltenham and Tunbridge Wells. But from 1771 this peaceful retreat was disturbed by industrialization when Richard Arkwright built his cotton-mill at Cromford, a mile to the south and the Masson Mills at Matlock in 1783, depriving the tourist of quiet retirement and wild scenery. According to Byng, in 1790, ' . . . these vales have lost all their beauties; the rural cot has given place to the lofty red mill and the grand houses of the overseers . . . Every rural sound is sunk in the clamours of cotton . . .'. Matlock's expansion was also stimulated by the opening in 1793 of the Cromford Canal, which was linked to the Erewash Canal. In 1789 there were about 1,469 people in 373 houses, but by 1801 2,354 people in 492 houses, more than double those of Buxton and Fairfield together, but they depended on a mixed economy of which the spa business was only a part.[37]

But some of the new industrial wealth could be spent in the leisure industry, and when, during the very dry summer of 1780, Matlock's warm springs flowed unabated, although the cold springs in Derbyshire failed, further investment in the spa trade seemed feasible. Another hot spring, drawn off near the Old Bath in 1786, fed a third hot bath in the Fountains Gardens known, with a cold bath, as the Fountain Baths. Mr Maynard, who held a large share in the Old Bath House, built a third hotel, the Temple Hotel, on terraces to give a magnificent view and used it as a private lodging-house for customers who wished to escape from the crowded, noisy inn. The Old Bath and the New Bath were the best inns until, in 1807, Maynard sold the Temple to Mrs Evans, who improved and enlarged it. Speculators who built the enormous Hotel or Great Hotel, claimed to be one of the largest in England, lower down the vale overestimated the market. Byng saw it in 1789, but after only four years' use it was sold in separate lots, and when Mawe's Old Museum was moved into the former fine dining-room it was known as the Museum Parade.[38]

The period from about 1790 to 1846 was Matlock Bath's zenith as a coaching spa, although by 1800 it was 'much deformed by manufacturies' and the 'depravity' of working people. But when the French wars made a continental tour impracticable from 1793 the nobility and gentry flocked to Matlock to stay for three weeks to three or four months, although generally parties perpetually came and went and few remained long. Like all the lodging-houses, the 'three spacious hotels' – the Old Bath, the New Bath and the Hotel – had by 1800 become the property of a syndicate of Derbyshire gentry, who placed their dependants there to service the company. About 1794 the proprietors added a large dining-room and a billiard-room to the Old Bath Hotel on the site of the old stables, and a coach-house and new stables were built lower down. The New Bath Hotel, from about 1813 managed by George Saxton, was also extended with a north wing and some spacious sitting-rooms. After 1780 the improvement of the roads and the daily coaches through Wirksworth to Manchester from London and Nottingham made Matlock more accessible, as did the turnpiking of the Cromford–Belper road down the Derwent valley in 1817.[39]

By 1800 Matlock could absorb a maximum of 200 visitors and the overflow had to seek beds in nearby villages, like Middleton, which that July was 'full of company from Matlock'. Prices of lodgings and food were reasonable, although Matlock's market no longer existed and provisions came from neighbouring ones. The narrow dale restricted space, so horses and carriages were usually left a mile away at the Boat-house Inn, which had an assembly-room and a good garden. From here for over eighty-three years Walker and his son ran a boat service at 6*d.* a trip with a band of instrumental music on summer evenings. Another who cashed in on the holiday trade as the expansion of Matlock continued was one Brown, who by 1810 had a small shop on the village green. By 1813 two more 'commodious' lodging-houses had brought accommodation up to 400 or 500 for visitors, who lived like one large family at moderate expense. Matlock was never a fashionable spa; its homely company was socially inferior to that of Buxton; but by 1815 it was a spa of moderate importance, with 'innocent and cheap' amusements.[40]

15

Georgian Spas of the South: Tunbridge Wells, Epsom and Southampton

Georgian Tunbridge Wells was a backward although popular southern spa compared with Bath, Cheltenham and the Bristol Hotwells, but it had an important share of the spa trade of the south-east, for despite the bad roads the return journey to the metropolis took only one day. From June to August the Wells settlement offered country pleasures in a picnic atmosphere and beautiful, sylvan surroundings as a retreat from the languorous heat of the capital. So in the reign of Anne (1702–14), earlier their patron, the Wells remained fashionable, although even by 1750 the emerging township had only a few hundred inhabitants.[1]

Speculators still found Tunbridge Wells visitors' trade worthy of investment. Tunbridge was a drinking spa, but with the new vogue for cold-bathing James Long of Marylebone in Middlesex in 1708 built the first bath there at great expense: a cold one at Rusthall equal, it was claimed, to any in the kingdom, in a garden with yew hedges, fountains and hewn stone steps. A visitor in 1720 described Rusthall as 'a mighty pretty place', very low, with steep hills on every side. A 'handsome and convenient house' covered the waterworks in a grotto adorned with a cascade of shells, with a bathing-pond in the middle, toads and birds carved on each side, and an orange tree on the further side, all spouting water for the amusement of visitors. When Long died in 1714 he was given a fine marble monument in Speldhurst Church.[2]

Slow expansion continued at Tunbridge Wells in the early eighteenth century, helped by the turnpiking of the Tunbridge to Sevenoaks road in 1709, on the grounds that Tunbridge Wells was 'a place of very great resort from all parts of the kingdom and from foreign parts for the use and benefit of the mineral waters'. Also, under pressure for land for building and to repair the Muskerry-Purbeck family fortunes, the heir John, the so-called Earl of Buckingham, between 1702 and 1710 sold off much of the manor of Southfrith, including building land on Mount Sion, mostly under lease. But four acres of open land were legally secured on 20 April 1703 to be planted and preserved as a grove with carriageways and footpaths for the use of inhabitants under the direction of trustees. So Tunbridge Wells acquired a pleasant amenity, its second Grove. The notion that walks and rides where the visitors could exercise were an essential feature of a spa influenced the layout of Bath's Pulteney Estate and that of other spas, notably Cheltenham and Harrogate.[3]

Although Queen Anne no longer came to Tunbridge Wells it was still the haunt of the aristocratic and fashionable; in late August 1704 the Duchess of Cleveland was there and three lords and six lords had just left, and in August 1708 the Duke and Duchess of Buckingham and the Duchess of Queensborough. But Tunbridge, like Bath, was never favoured by a reigning Hanoverian monarch, although other members of the royal family were visitors. The Prince of Wales, later George II, was there in September 1716 and in 1724 and gave lavishly to the parson, the poor, the coffee-houses, the water-dippers and the musicians. Frederick Prince of Wales and his wife in 1739, the Dukes of Gloucester and York in 1765, Princess Amelia in 1753, 1762 and 1763, and Princess Sophia in 1773 were some royal patrons.[4] Aristocratic visitors included Sarah, Duchess of Marlborough in 1729, and in August 1733 she stayed a month and took the waters in bed from a very hot cup; those with Kentish connections were Lord and Lady Lichfield and Lady Thanet in 1731.[5] Lord Bath, although a Bath land-owner, was at the Wells in 1752, 1760 and 1761 and found the waters much to his liking, although his chaplain Dr John Douglas, who accompanied him, thought it a 'foolish place'. They went to Spa in 1763.[6]

The middle classes also flocked to Tunbridge Wells, or the Speldhurst Wells, in increasing numbers. John Scattergood from Northampton found a great many gentry there in 1719–20, and whereas formerly the disabled took the waters, now many came for the pleasures of the company. As at Bath they were catered for with diversions subsidized by subscriptions – in 1724 10*s*. 6*d*. for the band, 10*s*. 6*d* the chapel, 5*s*. the assembly-rooms, 5*s*. the coffee-house and 2*s*. 6*d*. for Morley's library. In 1760 these revenues produced only about £200 a year, which suggests that few visitors took up all the services. Yet after the initial novelty some found the social routine tedious and behaviour lax. Unregulated gambling and the sharpers and shopkeepers who defrauded the consumers were no less a hazard than the lack of social ceremony. There was 'no better place to begin an intrigue'; ladies could be engaged in play at the tables or accosted on the Walks without introduction, but might not be visited in their lodgings.[7]

The lack of more positive action to exploit the Wells area may have stemmed from uncertainty about Sir Thomas Janson's lease, due to expire in 1726.[8] It was followed by a thirteen-year dispute between Maurice Conyers, the new lord of the manor of Rusthall, and the freeholders led by Lord Abergavenny, who held 226 acres, including the Lower Walk, where he had already erected houses. The freeholders wanted to prevent further building encroachment and to have compensation for the loss of pasturage, but a compromise, the Rusthall Manor Act, was given the royal assent on 29 April 1740. The Walks Estate was divided into three lots; two went to the lord of the manor, and one, lot B, now Nos. 18–44 The Pantiles, on trust to some fifty freeholders who received shares based on the value of their respective 391 holdings, of which Abergavenny had 100 and some only one or two. Again the future integrity of the commons, the wells and the Upper and Lower Walks was safeguarded; they remained open and free for the public use of the nobility, gentry and other persons coming to Tunbridge Wells. The medicinal wells, the source of local prosperity, were specified as part of the waste at Bishop's Down, the common of the manor, together with the ninepins or kettlepins place there. Buxton and Harrogate later secured their wells by similar protective measures.

No new building or improvement to buildings was to take place on the Walks except upon existing foundations; the pillars and colonnade were to remain; and the lord of the manor or his tenants were to maintain 'the Musick Gallery' over two shops and keep it open for free musical performances. He was also to select a water-dipper, with preference for the freeholders' womenfolk. No more enclosures were to be made on the common, except by his agreement and that of a majority of the larger freehold tenants. The freeholders retained grazing rights and a third of the manorial dues arising from the common, as from circuses and fairs. The significance of this 'charter of the town' was that the freeholders, including Lord Abergavenny, had some control over the future of Tunbridge Wells, it also conserved the distinctive character of the spa, its open common and the Walks, and was as momentous for Tunbridge Wells as the 1770 Enclosure Act which preserved the Stray at Harrogate. Seventy years later Tunbridge Wells's continued prosperity was said to rest on it; without it building would have spread and company from the deserted brothels of the metropolis would have occupied the houses.[9]

As the Wells settlement in the valley grew at the meeting-point of three parish boundaries, Tunbridge (or Tonbridge) and Speldhurst in Kent and Frant in Sussex, the increasingly licentious character of its company and the problems of social management underlined the lack of an overall authority, like the corporation at Bath or the vestry at Cheltenham, to take appropriate action. The Kent justices sitting at Maidstone tried in 1729 to suppress unlawful games—fairchance, faro and ace of hearts—at Tunbridge Wells, but they had no jurisdiction over the Sussex part of the Wells colony. Undesirable company was not the only problem. The Wells was a summer place, alive from May to October at the most, but despite the off-season exodus of visitors, shopkeepers and lodging-house keepers, a permanent settlement of working people with a subsidiary living in agriculture now formed a 'poor neighbourhood' in the vicinity. In default of an authority for social control and to preserve the local amenities, the duties of the trustees of the chapel of Charles the Martyr had been extended to include supervision of the Walks and of the charity school for about fifty or more children held in the ante-gallery of the chapel, or in winter in a coffee-house, to provide a future semi-trained labour force. The trustees' revenues came from collections on the Walks and two or three charity sermons a season.[10] This embryonic self-governing community, unique in the history of the English spas, had a wider scope than the later committees of public amusements at Bath and Cheltenham.

More social regulation of the ever-fluctuating and rather promiscuous company was called for to provide stability and direction to 'an extended system of pleasure'. Deference to persons of rank no longer sufficed as a steadying influence, and the continued prosperity of the Wells depended on the control of social life there. Since the high season – June, July and August – came between the two Bath seasons of spring and autumn, many visitors moved between the two spas, bringing news of Beau Nash's welcome influence at Bath. Nash himself came to Tunbridge in 1721, as he said, on the advice of Dr Thomas Pellett at Bath, not to drink the waters but for a rest cure, and he attended the first ball of the season at the Mount Sion assembly-room. He may have seen the need for a skilled social organizer at Tunbridge Wells, but meanwhile a remarkable woman – like those who so often dominated drinking wells – Bell Causey, had by 1725 established herself as 'absolute governess' at Tunbridge Wells and conducted the gaming-room for two guineas a day.

When she died in 1735 Nash, although over sixty, declared himself master of ceremonies, doubtless persuaded by local residents, and he retained the dual role of MC at Bath and Tunbridge until his death in 1761. Both places eagerly awaited his arrival for the season to maintain confidence; when gunfire signalled his coming to Tunbridge on 21 July 1754 all rejoiced, for now trade would flourish, but on 30 September Bathonians were assured that he would return the next day and his name, in large type, headed the list of arrivals at Bath published on 7 October. His two possible routes from Tunbridge to Bath were the Sevenoaks road to Farnborough, Hounslow, Salisbury and so to Bath, 141 miles in all, or the more southerly way through Brighton to Chichester, Winchester and Salisbury, a total of 154 miles. Nash is alleged to have covered one route for a wager in less than twenty-four hours and so danced at both Bath and Tunbridge Wells on the same day at the expense of fifteen horses. Normally he travelled more sedately in a post-chariot with six greys and outriders, footmen, French horns and elaborate trappings.[11]

At Tunbridge, in proximity to the metropolis, manners were more polite than at Bath, and Nash played his midsummer role of governor firmly but more quietly, and more as a relaxation, for in 1759 he kept a bathing-machine at Ramsgate in Kent. As at Bath he imposed a social code, mostly a matter of improvements, for a daily routine was already established. The Bath programme of dancing was introduced, two public balls a week in the rooms were opened with minuets followed by tea-drinking, then country dances, and all ended strictly at 11 p.m. Again as at Bath, Nash brought in London performers for better music, and while bells greeted new arrivals at Bath, the band of musicians welcomed them at Tunbridge. Nash compelled everyone to follow the social routine, including religious services twice a day, and his direction had immediate effect. The next season, 1736, was the best for six years: by 9 August there were 900 visitors, although few stayed the full term; a month to six weeks was normal and many had gone by 6 September, when seventeen coaches left. On 30 September departing visitors still filled nine coaches.[12]

Nash's success and the impending settlement of the commons dispute generated a new spirit of enterprise and some minor capital investment. Recent investigation has shown that another chalybeate spring, in which local apothecaries were interested, was enclosed with a stone wall by 1738 or earlier. The public room on the Upper Walk, where the Tuesday balls were held, belonged to the tenants' middle lot and was enlarged in 1739. The old assembly-room at Mount Sion fell into disuse; by 1736 only about six couples appeared for dancing, and it was then replaced by the Lower Rooms by the Sussex Tavern on the Lower Walk run by Mr Tod, and the Friday balls were held there. So social life was concentrated around the wells. In mid-century Tod tried, at considerable expense, to develop another spring behind his tavern and laid out new walks and plantations, but 'Tod's Folly' failed and by 1810 the site was a wilderness. In 1767 the Gloucester and the Sussex were still the only 'two taverns or inns' near the wells.[13]

Accommodation was now scarce. Dr Wilson had paid £1 5*s.* for lodgings in 1736. In 1743 Lord Fermanagh, who lodged on the Walks with Wood the ironmonger, tried to find rooms for a friend, but many houses were taken by 26 June and more people were expected; eventually he was able to engage 'commodious' rooms at a guinea a week. His friend had to pay 8*d.* a night for stabling for each horse, with hay and plenty of currycombs provided, but corn was extra. Most families brought a butler with them and kept a servant out of livery to go to the market, for ladies hardly ever went there. Fermanagh advised packing certain domestic articles with one's luggage: knives, spoons, salts, cruets, castors, tea-making apparatus and two or three china plates. As for provisions, beef, mutton, veal and lamb were to be had at 4*d.* a pound, but wine was very dear, 8*s.* a gallon, and many brought it with them.[14]

Various people invested in lodging-houses. Lord Egmont's 'very noble'

Mount Pleasant House was the best, with well-furnished rooms, five parlours and eight chambers, and stabling for thirty horses. His tenant sublet its rooms; Princess Amelia – and, for the 1736 season Lord and Lady Lichfield – stayed there, but Egmont sold it at considerable loss to Gratton of the Gloucester Tavern. For about twenty years Gratton rented it annually to the Duke of Leeds; he also held four lodging-houses at the foot of Mount Sion. Ladds, a wine-merchant, made £400 to £500 a year from lodgings, and the Wood brothers took in visitors in a handsome house on Mount Sion.[15]

In the 1750s the social appeal of Tunbridge Wells attracted a successful Portsmouth physician, Dr George Kelley (Kelly), who bought the manor of Rusthall, including houses on the Walks and Mount Ephraim and 250 acres of land in Speldhurst for £19,000. The first resident magistrate, he had by 1762 become Sir George Kelley of Bishop's Down, Speldhurst, and sheriff of Kent. Unfortunately, however, the continued success of the Wells as Nash saw it depended on the excitement of the public gaming-tables. After the 1749 Act banning some games of chance and its extension in 1750 and 1755 to cover others, a Tunbridge man, one Cook, invented EO, Evens and Odds, which Nash introduced at Bath. Nash rebuked a lodging-house keeper for privately using an OE table, for the prosperity of the Wells, traders and physicians, depended on the maintenance of the public life of the rooms; lodgings were temporary accommodation for eating and sleeping only and visitors were expected to live in public. But following Nash's disastrous lawsuit to reclaim a share of the profits and the Act banning all play except cards, gambling was driven into private houses. Nash's decline had set in, he was taken ill with apoplexy at the Wells in 1752, and his last recorded visit, after allegedly starting his *History of Bath and Tunbridge Wells,* was in 1755. This left Sarah Porter, the Queen of the Touters, as his substitute.[16]

Both Bath and Tunbridge Wells valued Nash's services and both commissioned portraits of him by William Hoare, and they continued to share an MC after his death in 1761. His two immediate successors were Caulet, or Collett (1761–3), a French dancer and fencer, and the diminutive and literary Samuel Derrick, whose *Letters* (1767) were a commentary on life at both spas, but who offended Tunbridge by angling for the post of MC at Brighton. When Derrick died in April 1769 Major William Brereton, lately his assistant, officiated briefly, but when Bath deposed him Tunbridge went its own way with one Blake (1769–79). In 1780 Richard Tyson took over and the link with Bath was restored with his appointment to its Lower Rooms, and in 1785 he was promoted to the Upper Rooms there. So once more, for twenty-one years from 1780 to 1801, the rival spas were linked. Tyson, one of the most competent MCs, issued his own code of social behaviour in both Bath and Tunbridge.[17]

In spirit the Tunbridge code was the current formula there and at Bath, but now the tea-break at the two weekly public balls was followed by a cotillon, chosen by the MC, and country dances. There was no restriction on dress, except for ladies dancing minuets, and Tyson insisted that a gentleman should keep his partner for only two consecutive dances. Tyson called on new arrivals, who were expected to pay subscriptions in advance for the two assembly-rooms, the circulating library, the two coffee-rooms and the post office. A list of charges, considerably increased in his time, was displayed in the Upper Rooms in 1785; they included donations for the minister at the chapel, the water-dippers at the well, who received no allowance from the lord of the manor, and 1s. for the sweeper of the Walks and the rooms. Doubtless worn out by his double assignment, Tyson retired from Tunbridge in 1801 but kept the senior Bath post for four more years. But James King of the Bath Lower Rooms elected to go to Cheltenham, a nearer and now more prestigious post, and so Bath and Tunbridge finally divided. One Fotheringham presided at Tunbridge from 1801 to 1805, possibly the Captain Alexander Fotheringham who was at Cheltenham from 1816 to 1820. He was succeeded by Paul Amsinck (1805–17), 'very like a gentleman, and not at all a coxcomb', as Miss Berry said. He, like Simon Moreau, MC at Cheltenham, produced a local guidebook, *Tunbridge Wells and its Neighbourhood* (1810). The highly regarded Richard Tyson – still living at Tunbridge, where his servant Thomas Parson died in 1816 – was briefly recalled from retirement in 1817.[18]

So a more formalized subscription society had emerged at Tunbridge Wells, which still offered some competition to Bath. Samuel Derrick, knowing both places, said: ' . . . few places are pleasanter for a couple of months than Tunbridge Wells. You are here with the most elegant company in Europe, on the easiest terms . . .'. Tunbridge's continued custom was helped by the vast improvement of the local roads. The turnpiking of the Sevenoaks to Tunbridge road from 1709 was followed by a lull until action on the Sevenoaks–Farnborough stretch in 1749. Much activity came in the 1760s when twenty Kentish roads were improved, opening up communications in all directions around Tunbridge Wells, as Derrick noted in 1767. So at least by 1780 Parman and Hargreaves ran a daily stagecoach to London, leaving Tunbridge at 6 a.m. and reaching Charing Cross at 2 p.m.[19]

The marked expansion of Tunbridge Wells started in the 1760s, the boom period of building in Bath and some other provincial towns, but the significant phase came later.[20] By 1780 there were at least seventy-three lodging-houses – eight people ran more than one – providing 226 parlours, 378 chambers, and stabling for 504 horses. In 1786 there were ten more. As in other spa towns, many lodging-house keepers had another occupation:

in 1776 one was the schoolmaster. By 1800 the total was about 100 boarding- and lodging-houses, well filled in season, and three inns: the well-established Sussex Tavern, the Angel, and the New Inn. Grattan's Gloucester Tavern had presumably by then become a shop.[21] By contrast Cheltenham, with only forty-two lodging-houses in 1791, had 150 by 1800 and was displacing Tunbridge as Bath's rival.

Samuel Derrick deplored Tunbridge Wells's lack of enterprise; despite its potential, in fact, except for Sir Thomas Janson, it had no immigrant speculators with the drive of those at Bath or Cheltenham. Yet it had plenty of good provisions: poultry, game, beef and pork; skilled cooks at the taverns, and fair accommodation at the inns. 'A little money well laid out would make them better', observed Derrick, but landlords were as reluctant to make improvements as were the tenants, whose rents were high and whose families had to live on two months' profits for the other ten. Consequently the visitors complained of exploitation, although from late September to mid-June – when, said Derrick, the face of a stranger was a curiosity, and there was time for contemplation until the mind burst with thinking – a man could live at Tunbridge as cheaply as anywhere. He especially deplored the 'touters', a name derived from the tradesmen of Tooting who formerly accosted those going to the Epsom Wells to solicit their patronage.[22]

The underuse of public facilities at Tunbridge Wells, because its short season offered a poor return, was a deterrent to further investment in the leisure industry. Alone among the major spas Tunbridge had no pump-room of any size until 1877, although a large public building of that kind was a desirable insurance against bad weather. The open aspect of the Wells made visitors more than usually weather-conscious, as Edward Young wrote in 1740: there was 'almost universal complaint' about the bad weather and 'the excessive rains have washed away all our company'. In 1736 Dr Wilson found that many houses, timber-framed and tile-hung, were so thin and badly fitted up as to be no protection against the weather, and in June 1777 Mrs Montagu complained 'I durst not name Tunbridge . . . we have indeed had a churlish season . . .'. Yet in a dry season there was 'a prodigious dust' from the underlying Hastings sands.[23] By contrast, the stone-built solidity of Bath gave it decided advantage.

Nevertheless, despite the short season, a few small initiatives were undertaken. During the vogue for cold-bathing in 1748 the mineral-water expert D.W. Linden urged the proprietors of wells to erect baths at once and eventually, about 1766, a second bath was constructed, more centrally placed on the common at Fonthill near the Walks. Pinchbeck, master of one of the rooms, also purchased the land around Adam's Well near the High Rocks in 1768 and erected a bath, the subject of an anonymous pamphlet in 1780.[24] The Rusthall bath, difficult of access for invalids, then declined, and in 1807 its ruins were inhabited by peasants.[25]

Another investment was the establishment in 1786 of a theatre at the Wells. Strolling players had come earlier and the company of 'Canterbury Smith' in the fifties, then Sarah Baker became to Tunbridge what John Boles Watson was to Cheltenham. After her acrobat husband's death in 1769 she toured Kent, probably with a puppet show, and set up her theatre, the Temple, on Mount Sion at Tunbridge Wells. She had ten other theatres, mostly in Kent. A rival theatre run by Glassington in a warehouse in Castle Street was ousted by 1789, when she demolished the Temple and rebuilt it on the Lower Walk; it was still very small but fairly well attended, and between about 1802 and 1804 she rebuilt it again. The Georgian façade of this 'neat little theatre', as it was described in 1813, is visible beneath the stucco of the Corn Exchange. In the 1790s Mrs Baker's company played at Tunbridge two or three times a week in August and September, with distinguished patrons: the Duchess of York; Richard Cumberland, who wrote plays for her; and Grimaldi, the famous clown. William Dowton, her actor son-in-law, took over in 1816, prolonged the season by beginning in June or July, and opened four days a week with standard contemporary charges: boxes 5s., upper boxes 3s., pit 2s. and gallery 1s.[26]

Racing was an early entertainment. By 1738 a two-day meeting in mid-August was held at a race-course on the common, supported by subscriptions. A later diversion, as at Malvern, was the use of asses, brought into fashion as a means of transport by Lady Seymour in 1801 when the Prince and Princess of Orange, the Duke and Duchess of Northumberland and many other noble visitors were there. Cock-fighting was organized on the common, and cricket from about 1750. Lectures added to the range of entertainment, and Dr William King gave a series on astronomy. Recitals were advertised and pianofortes, harpsichords and other musical instruments could be hired by the short-stay visitors, who could also browse in the two libraries on the Parade.[27]

Listening to the memorable sermons, both Anglican and Nonconformist, preached at Tunbridge Wells was, as at Bath and Epsom, a recognized group activity. Charity sermons for chapel finances brought in £50 a year, £80 in a good season. Nonconformist groups were already established, and inevitably Tunbridge Wells, like Bath and Cheltenham earlier, came under the attacks of the Methodists. John Wesley first went to the Wells in 1762–3 and preached in the parlour of Sir Thomas Janson at New (Little) Bounds in Southborough. Selina, Countess of Huntingdon, 'the Queen of Methodism', who had congregations at other spas – Bath, Cheltenham and Malvern – leased Culverden House to settle at Tunbridge in 1768 and erected a chapel, a timber building in the Gothic style, opened by George Whitefield in July 1769.[28]

A substantial permanent population had now been attracted by the more developed social life, including from 1783 the Prime Minister, Lord North, whose grandfather had discovered the mineral waters, Lord Chief

Justice Mansfield, and Martin Yorke, grown rich in the East India Company. Tunbridge became an increasingly stable and quiet resort favoured by the more serious-minded residents and visitors, and, like Bath, men of letters such as Dr Johnson, Oliver Goldsmith and Lord Chesterfield; and a stream of dilettante writing, some from the water-poets, emanated from there.[29] To cater for this informed community a local man, Thomas Benge Burr, in 1766 produced *The History of Tunbridge Wells*, the first attempted account of the spa's evolution.

Late in the eighteenth century some stagnation set in at the Wells; the profits of the fifty or more shops and the public rooms in the freeholders' block declined, and Tyson, the MC, complained of lack of support by the company. A contemporary described the Wells as made damp by the dense atmosphere and surrounding obstructions, and the pavements were covered with moss. But in 1793 Britain's involvement in war against France revivified Tunbridge Wells. While some sought asylum in the western spas away from possible attack, Tunbridge was invaded by refugees and the military; twenty-three French *emigré* priests were lodged in cottages on Mount Ephraim, and a military camp for 7,000–8,000 men was pitched in Waterdown Forest in July. That year the Upper Walk was repaved with Purbeck stone flags for £710 raised by subscription, replanted with limes, and renamed the Parade. The Lower Walk, used chiefly by servants and country people, remained unpaved. Noble visitors to whom the Continent was now closed also descended on the Wells. Lady Wellington stayed at Douro House on Mount Ephraim in 1809, 1810 and again in 1812. When news of her husband's victory at Salamanca arrived on 12 August Tunbridge Wells was illuminated that night, although smoke from the furze bonfires on the common obscured the lights, and the Pantiles were decorated with branches of oak. But in 1816 when the couple, by now Duke and Duchess of Wellington, were free to have a holiday they went to Cheltenham, not to Tunbridge Wells.[30]

The wartime inflation of its population prompted a building boom, but Tunbridge Wells was still a drinking spa, the three cold baths were in decay, and contemporary demand was for warm mineral-water baths. The lady of the manor, now the enterprising Mrs Elizabeth Shorey, ran three lodging-houses on Bishop's Down and was determined to maintain the wells, the source of local prosperity. About 1789 she replaced the corroded stone basin of the chalybeate spring with a handsome marble one, but she feared that bath construction might damage the spring. John Thomas Groves, from 1794 clerk of works at Whitehall, assured her that an inexpensive cold bath could easily be built on the same site as the well, and he became the architect of the new Bath House around 1804, a 'handsome structure' which catered for the new fashion of varied treatments – cold, warm, vapour and shower baths – with comfortable apartments above for invalids, but the premises were still incomplete in 1810.[31]

Tunbridge was slow, compared with the larger spa towns, to provide amenities for visitors, although it was well patronized and now attracted sufficient company for private balls and elegant suppers at the height of the season. In 1806 the four principal inns, with good rooms, were the Sussex, run by the proprietor of the Lower Rooms, the Kentish, the New Inn and the Angel Inn, and the well-off had excellent lodgings, but the middle and lower classes were less well served. To make investment more worthwhile efforts were now being made to extend the season from March to late November, especially for invalids, and there were two resident apothecaries, both mineral-water experts.[32]

Tunbridge Wells remained essentially a rural spa, as late as 1819 described as 'the hamlet of Tunbridge Wells consisting of four little villages named Mount Ephraim, Mount Pleasant, Mount Sion and the Wells, which together form a considerable town'.[33] Its urbanization came late and it sought no Improvement Act until 1835, compared with Bath in 1766 and 1789, Cheltenham in 1786 and even the new spa Leamington in 1825. Cheltenham had overtaken it and was now its rival to Bath.

Epsom

Epsom and Tunbridge Wells had originally been companion spas receiving the exodus of people from the metropolis in search of relaxation, but by the eighteenth century Epsom was relatively unimportant as a spa. Good communications with the capital, several daily stagecoaches each way, town and country wagons once a week or more, and the ordinary post converted it from an agricultural village into a residential place for the gentry and Londoners, like Tunbridge Wells later. A survey of resident gentry in every Surrey parish in 1725 showed Lords Yarmouth, Guildford and Baltimore, Sir John Ward, eight gentlemen and eight well-to-do widows in Epsom. No other Surrey parish could compete with this total.[34]

Yet the Epsom Wells were not entirely neglected. In 1717 John Livingston's New Wells property included a long-room occupied by widow Margaret Bowes, a coffee-house held by R. Williams, some houses and a bowling green, and before Livingston died in 1727 a cold bath had been erected at Epsom following that at Tunbridge Wells in 1708.[35] On Livingston's death another John Parkhurst, grandson of the original one, repaired the Old Wells building, but by 1738 its hall, galleries and other public rooms had decayed and only one house remained, inhabited by a countryman and his wife, who carried the bottled water around the neighbourhood. For some years Mrs Hawkins, supported by Mr Dale Ingram, a London surgeon who settled in Epsom, tried to revive the Monday breakfasts, and in the 1760s he advertised a magnesia preparation obtained from the mineral waters. Currently the anonymous article which blackened Livingston's reputation appeared in *Lloyd's Evening Post* in 1769, claiming that the waters of the Old Wells had never lost their potency. But the promotion failed, the Old Wells became deserted and the public rooms were demolished in 1804.[36]

Southampton

Like Epsom the Southampton Spa presented no real competition to Tunbridge Wells; in the second half of the eighteenth century, like the Bristol Hotwells and the Scarborough Spa, it flourished as the resort quarter of a port. Southampton otherwise showed signs of decay, but in the 1740s the reputed medicinal virtues of a Spa Well outside the town wall to the north-west drew in people of all ranks, and in about 1765 sea-bathing was established and appealed to great numbers of people.[37]

Southampton began to acquire a veneer of fashion when royal patrons of Tunbridge Wells also arrived – including Frederick, Prince of Wales, also popular at Bath, who came to Southampton to bathe in 1750. When he died the next year his three sons, the dukes of York, Gloucester and Cumberland, continued the connection. To cater for the gentry and other middle classes now attracted to the town, country houses were built on its fringes and villas and marine cottages nearer in. The townspeople, quick to profit from the boom, improved public buildings and provided more amenities.

About 1755 the town council had the mineral-water spring pumped into a fountain where it fell into a basin on a fluted pedestal; accommodation, including a reading-room, was provided, and fine gardens were laid out at the spa in the area now marked by Spa Road. Three separate sea-water baths were constructed: those of Seaward, Simcox, and John Martin, who built the largest bath-house near the West Quay and in 1761 added a long-room where interested spectators could promenade and watch the bathers. By 1775 Martin had a hot bath too, and in 1767 he developed his long-room into a spacious assembly-room with magnificent pier glasses, to replace the old assembly-rooms in the High Street. Other appurtenances of a resort society appeared; in 1766 a large playhouse was erected by sub-scription in French Street on the plan of Covent Garden, with three performances a week. Later Mr Collins, the manager, built an even greater but elegant theatre on the St John's Hospital site. By 1775 a circulating library adjoined Martin's Rooms with English, French, Italian and London newspapers, and there were coffee-houses, banks and a newspaper (the later *Hampshire Chronicle*).[38]

The town's approaches and promenades were improved and houses were fitted out 'in the neatest and genteelist manner' for visitors, but in 1764 lodgings were dear. Improved coach services to London, Bath, Bristol, Salisbury, Oxford and other towns brought visitors to the eight substantial inns, including the Dolphin, which was rebuilt with an assembly-room in 1775. In 1770 an Improvement Act allowed for better paving, lighting and watching, and the main parts of the town were lit to encourage visitors to go out at night.[39]

By 1775 the social life of Martin's assembly-room warranted the introduction of a master of ceremonies, William Dawson, to organize Tuesday dress balls and undress balls for cotillons on Thursday. Dawson's regime resembled that of Bath in other ways; for example, no lady was to dance in an apron or black gloves, and servants were not to crowd the stairs to the rooms but wait in the appointed place. But Martin's rooms were badly situated with insufficient carriage space among dark, dirty and dangerous lanes. So Jacob Leroux, an architect of Great Russell Street, London, backed by the wealthy General John Carnac of Cams Hall near Fareham, conceived the idea, in about 1768, of erecting a spacious amusement centre on a twenty-two-acre site north-east of the town. The planned layout was a twelve-sided polygon with an encircling carriage road and twelve large houses, the gardens of which tapered behind to a central block of a hotel, assembly-room and shops. This unique Polygon Estate, incorporating amusement and commercial facilities with residences, attracted sightseers from miles around. In August 1771 Mrs Harris from Salisbury thought the Polygon 'a most magnificent hotel'; it had a fine ballroom, card and tea-rooms, two billiard-rooms, several eating-rooms, fifty good bedchambers, elegant shops, and stabling for 500 horses. The incorporation of shops in the building was unprecedented, and the hotel was, with the York House Hotel at Bath (1765–9) and the Clarence Hotel, Exeter (1769), among the pioneer purpose-built English inns providing visitors' accommodation on an unusually large scale.[40]

Although the hotel was still incomplete in 1773 balls were being held there, the focus of two brilliant seasons under the aegis of the royal dukes. But Thomas Baker, a prominent bookseller and librarian, fought to retain the social life in the old town and argued the convenience of Martin's Rooms. Carnac, in financial difficulties, returned to the East; by 1806 only four houses were finished, and the original Polygon was eventually pulled down.[41] In the uncertainty about Martin's Rooms William Dawson had moved to Bath as MC of the Upper Rooms in 1777, but Martin's Rooms survived, later under another name. In 1792 their MC, W. Lynne, reissued social regulations, including fixed rates for the hire of chairs. Although the royal dukes ceased to patronize Southampton after 1778 people of rank and fashion still came, and from 1785 the MC supervised fortnightly winter assemblies at the Dolphin, with a set of rules like those for Martin's Rooms.[42]

The outbreak of war in 1793 accelerated Southampton's growth, for, as at Tunbridge Wells, armies camped in the neighbourhood, and by 1800 this invasion had sent up the price of lodgings, although during the boom more of the respectable inhabitants let rooms from early July to late October.[43] The advent of peace in 1815 brought some recession and the demand for the mineral waters dwindled, although doctors still praised their virtues and a spa revival came later.

The major spa activity in Georgian times was in the west of England: at Bath, Cheltenham, the Brisol Hotwells and increasingly at Leamington and Malvern. Those on holiday from the metropolis now favoured more distant places than Tunbridge Wells and Epsom, and even Southampton benefited from the westward drift.

16

The Severn Spas: The Bristol Hotwells and Malvern

The Severn valley, mild of climate, became a region of watering-places in the eighteenth century. Apart from the boom town Cheltenham and its minor periphery spas – like Stow, the Hyde Spa at Prestbury and the Walton Spa near Tewkesbury – two spas about fifty-five miles apart, the Bristol Hotwells and Malvern, acquired a more than local reputation. The original Hotwell in the Avon gorge, where the purpose-built Hotwell House of 1696 provided the shelter of a pump-room and convenient lodgings on the spot, became more popular and a widespread trade in bottled Hotwell water developed through the port of Bristol. By 1702 a 'New' Hotwell, about 200 yards along the river bank, was in use, and although difficult of access it gained a brief repute in 1754 when John Wesley thought it had cured his consumption. A small pump-room and lodging-house were built in this remote position but it could not compete with the first Hotwell, and by 1792 quarrymen occupied the buildings.[1]

Dudley Ryder, who knew Islington Spa and Tunbridge Wells, met Lord Percival and others at the Hotwells in 1716, and John Scattergood from Northamptonshire found almost as many of the beau-monde there as at Bath in 1720. Proximity to Bath added to the Hotwells' success, for its season – from May to September, between the two at Bath – gave an alternative to Tunbridge Wells in summer, particularly in July and August, the 'dead' time at Bath. A short stay or daily visits from Bath, thirteen miles away, were possible, so the Hotwells benefited from Bath's overflow trade. From 1754 a daily coach ran in summer between Bath and Bristol, and by 1772 a post-chaise journey from Bath to Bristol cost 10s. 6d., and an extra 1s. 6d. to the Hotwells. Clifton's expansion was also stimulated by the settlement of merchants grown rich on Bristol's foreign trade, who could afford to build and live there and to invest in its leisure industry.[2]

Like Matlock, Clifton's main attraction was the scenic beauty of its gorge, making it – as Rudder, the Gloucestershire historian, claimed – 'one of the most agreeable villages in the kingdom'. The rocky banks of the Avon rose about 200 feet, bare and craggy in places but covered with shrubs and hanging coppice wood, and the ships passing through provided a never-ending distraction. Most houses were on the hill around the church, where riding and driving on the downs were favourite recreations. Other diversions were sailing down the river for woodland picnics, often accompanied by musicians, or from 1729 attending the small Jacob's Well Theatre halfway between the city centre and the Hotwells. John Hippisley of the Bath theatre backed this venture, where in July 1755 the company from the Theatre Royal, London played.[3]

By 1723 the local gentry and merchants had begun to build 'handsome modern houses' in Clifton and to live there: in 1779 at least nine men of substance, like Sir William Draper, Isaac Elton and Henry Hobhouse. But there was also a demand for visitors' lodgings, and John Power sold part of his estate for building to Thomas Oldfield and George Tully, a prominent house-carpenter and surveyor. By March 1721 Tully had laid out Dowry Square and planned lodging-houses on three sides. Dowry Chapel, of moderate size and finished in 1746, was, like other chapels in resorts, built by subscription, to save visitors the two-mile journey to St Andrew's Church from the Old Hotwell. The chapel had no endowment for repairs or a minister, and, like that at Tunbridge Wells, was maintained by the visitors' annual contributions of about sixty guineas.[4]

By the 1750s the Clifton Hotwells was a crowded, fashionable resort attracting people of rank. When the Duke and Duchess of Beaufort drank the waters in July 1753 the place was full to capacity, not a bed was to be had near the wells and hardly any in the city suitable for the company who patronized the spa. Lords Boyle, Dillon and Jersey and their wives were also there, and 'we are as full as we can hold', wrote Sir Charles Howard. The Dillons planned to give a public breakfast in the long-room. Mrs Powys, too, saw 'a prodigious deal of company' in 1759, and the Duke of York, patron of the Southampton Spa, was there in 1766.[5] A more organized social life had now emerged, partly promoted by enterprising traders who came from Bath in its off-peak season.

Bath and Clifton were complementary rather than competing spas; Bristol newspapers of the 1770s reported arrivals at both, but none at Bath during the Hotwells season. The record of Hotwells' visitors likewise ceased abruptly in early autumn when Bath traders at Clifton went home for the winter season. Bath newspapers, such as the *Bath Journal* from 1754, publicized Hotwells events from April onwards. The social centre was the later 'Old Room', the assembly-room mentioned by the Duke of Beaufort in 1753, a 'very handsome' building, ninety feet long, thirty-five feet wide and the same height, with a reading-room supplying the Bristol, Bath and Dublin journals for 2s. 6d. from Lady Day to Michaelmas. In 1754 it was run by Clementine Foord, who out of season partnered Elizabeth Taylor at Bath in providing teas and breakfasts in a room adjoining the pump-room. By June 1755 there were Thursday balls in this Hotwell Long Room, later run by Mr Beresford, then from May 1758 by Mr Shirley of Wiltshire's Room, Bath, and in the 1770s by his widow.[6]

Another entrepreneur from Bath was Thomas Loggon, who ran the Little Fanmaker's in the Abbey churchyard. By 1754 he had opened the Hotwells ladies' tea-room, fifty feet long, which accommodated over a hundred, with free admission to the adjoining walks. Balls were held here on Tuesday and Friday by 1759, so Loggon had presumably built his assembly-room, Loggon's New Rooms, by then. Certainly by 1766 his premises had been extended to include an inn where rooms with well-aired beds could be hired weekly or nightly. Bathonians involved in the Hotwells trade also included Elizabeth Trinder from Lebeck's Head Tavern, who by 1754 had opened a Clifton tavern and eating-house with board and lodgings for single gentlemen and servants, and an ordinary, a set meal, for 2*s*. 6*d*. daily at 3 p.m.[7] So consumer services for tourists were a growth industry at Clifton.

With two assembly-rooms operating the Hotwells needed a master of ceremonies, but the Bath MC departed to Tunbridge Wells in summer, so a Mr Plomer was found for Bristol. When the Bath MC, Samuel Derrick, died in March 1769, Plomer's friends, backed by Bristol merchants and traders, met in Bath town hall and got him elected there instead of Major Brereton, Derrick's deputy. At Plomer's first official appearance at a Bath ball one of Brereton's supporters actually led him from the room by his nose, but by compromise both stood down in favour of Captain Wade. Plomer remained at the Hotwells until 1778, when he left to conduct the social life of Weymouth until 1783. The Bristol businessmen's attempt to impose Plomer on Bath may have been an effort to link Bath and Clifton more profitably. A later Hotwells MC, William Pennington, appointed in 1785, wore a gold medallion as an insignia of office, like Wade at Bath, and he copied the Bath regulations for balls. He lived in Dowry Square and was still in office in 1811.[8]

Some Bristol merchants' interest in the Hotwells was in its mineral-water trade. The widespread popularity of the Bath, Bristol Hotwells and Scarborough waters partly derived from the advantage that Bristol and Scarborough were both sea-ports, and their departing ships often carried cargoes of baskets of bottled mineral water, which was a cheaper – albeit slower – method of transport than wagon or cart. Bristol also, by the end of the century, had the asset of fifteen local glassworks which produced bottles for the Hotwells water as well as for exports of beer, cider and perry from Herefordshire and Somerset. A few baskets of Bristol water went to Gloucester and Chester in 1701, to St Ives in 1710, and in 1720 three shipments went to Dublin, 1,669 baskets, eight hogsheads, nineteen casks and eight barrels to London, and a lesser amount to the outports.

Nine years later Hotwells water was being widely distributed around British coastal ports from Glasgow to Plymouth, and by 1752 it was sent overseas – most of it, 2,388 gallons and one 'tun', to Jamaica but some to other West Indian islands, so nurturing the habit of taking the waters which brought so many planters to Bath and Cheltenham. Ireland now took 730 gallons, and cargoes went out to Rotterdam, Bremen and Hamburg, passing those of Spa, Pyrmont and Seltzer water coming in, and to Gibraltar and Africa.[9] One wonders how genuine was the vast volume of exported 'Hotwells' water.

So wealth flowed into the Hotwells leisure industry and the building of visitors' accommodation continued steadily. By the 1760s Clifton parish had about ninety houses and 450 inhabitants and could absorb the inflow of visitors who found its lodgings 'commodious and cheap'. In 1772 one of them paid 10*s*. a week for a room and 14*s*. for board. By then Thomas Nichols offered lodgings and stables at the New Inn Tavern (or the Hotwell Inn) in Dowry Square. Among the speculators was Thomas Boyce, a peruke-maker of King Street, who also owned property in Bath. He spent £3,000 on erecting and furnishing Boyce's Buildings, a handsome range of three lodging-houses designed by Thomas Paty, with gravel and grass walks, a pleasure garden, three summerhouses or tea-rooms, and five stables, as advertised in 1772, fit for the reception of the nobility and gentry. But he had miscalculated and was bankrupted in November. Other new buildings were Albemarle Row, erected in about 1762, and Brunswick Square, where Joseph Loscombe, a merchant, granted building leases in 1766. A new Clifton with handsome terraces of three-storeyed red-brick houses faced with stone appeared, and by 1770 there were about 1,367 inhabitants exclusive of lodgers, but the supply of houses now exceeded demand. The church, too, had been enlarged 'on account of the resort to the Hotwells', although some invalid visitors were beyond cure; about nineteen died every year.[10]

The patronage of persons of rank coming to take the waters was argued for the concession of the style 'Theatre Royal' to the new King Street theatre in Bristol in 1778, but in the next decade the boom period ended in local mismanagement and national financial disaster. The ninety-years lease of the Hotwell premises by the Society of Merchant Venturers expired in 1785, and they unrealistically expected the next tenant to invest at least £1,000 on building a quay wall before the pump-room, £500 to protect the spring from the tide, and a large sum to repair the pump-room, so no tenant came forward. The society then carried out the improvements and put in a salaried caretaker. A sheltered promenade near the pump-room was badly needed, and in May 1786 the society leased ground there to Samuel Powell, who erected the charming Tuscan-style Colonnade, a curved building with, like the contemporary Crescent at Buxton, shops on the ground floor, a single storey of living-rooms above, and a wide walk in front. Powell also, in May 1789, promoted St Vincent's Parade and Prince's Buildings, and by 1790 his speculative empire included the tenancy of the Hotwell, but he imposed higher charges to meet his increased rent.[11]

In Powell's time the building boom inspired by the example of Bath was at its height, with entrepreneurs buying up large sites and subletting plots on building leases to craftsmen-tradesmen. Ambitious projects included Berkeley Square and the minute Berkeley Crescent in December 1787 and the Mall in 1788. In about 1790 Windsor Terrace, a crescent of twenty houses on the edge of the gorge and one of Clifton's most impressive buildings, cost William Watts, a prosperous plumber, at least £20,000; it was probably designed by John Eveleigh, the Bath architect. Clifton was infected by crescent mania; the spectacular Royal York Crescent was promoted in about 1790 and the Cornwallis Crescent of Harry Elderton, a Bristol attorney, in 1791. Despite these great piles of buildings and houses 'nearly like palaces', Clifton was still in 1797 a 'delightful village'. However, the labourers who quarried the building stone were so poorly paid that their wives resorted to a souvenir trade in polished crystal stones from St Vincent's Rocks.[12]

Clifton's tourist boom encouraged a search for more mineral-water springs, with success about 1786 near the Mardyke ferry in Hotwells Road, where a small pump-room and hot and cold baths were built, but the 1793 recession killed the venture and by 1810 the site had become Poole's Mineral Spa Coal Wharf. The warm Sion Spring was found in 1793 by Mr Morgan, a local attorney of Sion Hil, who also built a small pump-room and bathing-places, but in 1798 the building was for sale and 'suitable for any genteel business'. Some revival followed, for by 1806 the proprietor had established a library and laid out gardens. In 1816 and 1820 J. Schweppe and Company advertised soda water manufactured from the Upper Hotwell or Sion Spring for sale in Bath.[13]

Dr Garrick, a local physician, surveyed a prospering Clifton in the 1780s. Scores (so he said) of the nobility and invalids of all ranks patronized it every season, so many innkeepers had made handsome fortunes in a few years. The pump-room was so crowded from noon to 2 p.m. that one reached the well to drink the waters with difficulty, and the keeper received hundreds a year in voluntary donations. The Downs and all paths to the Hotwell were filled with strings of carriages, parties on horseback and pedestrians. Independent corroboration of 'much company' there came from the Reverend William Hopton, staying with Mrs Robbins at Hotwell House in 1796 for a month or five weeks.[14]

Then in 1793 came war with France and, as at Bath, financial disaster, bankruptcies, and the cessation of building for a decade. An American, Joshua Gilpin, walking on Clifton Hill in February 1797, saw an immense number of incomplete and nearly ruinous buildings. Government plans in 1801 to convert the unfinished Royal York Crescent into barracks were supported by the Bristol brewers, but when local residents objected that such a change of use would ruin Bristol as a watering-place the scheme was abandoned. There was some building revival from 1807; in 1812 the Paragon, a crescent of twenty-one houses, was being built and the Royal York Crescent was finished in about 1820.[15]

Other signs of revival included increased hotel accommodation. The 'spacious and elegant' Clifton Hotel in the Mall was built between 1806 and 1809, but F. H. Greenway, the architect, was bankrupted. In 1812 the hotel incorporated a pastry and confectionery shop, some hot, cold and vapour baths, and the Lower or New Assembly Rooms, all run by William Mangeon (d. 1816). Apart from the old New Inn and Hotel in Dowry Square, three other hotels existed by 1812: Barton's Hotel or Gloucester House, the York House Hotel and Tavern in Gloucester Place, and the Bath Hotel. Two libraries served the visitors in 1806: Mrs Yearsley's and Philpot's.[16]

But Clifton had, like Bath, been overbuilt and overinvested. The now neglected spa had in 1816 'the silence of the grave': not a carriage appeared in an hour, nor a solitary invalid approaching the spring. One of the ballrooms and taverns had closed and the other had few customers. National recession and Cheltenham's competition accounted for this decline, but also the increase in Hotwell charges – from 10*s.* for a whole family for a season to £1 6*s.* for each person – which drove away many who formerly went more for pleasure than for health. A visitor in 1800 had complained of the high price of lodgings: 'Everything is dear at the wells. The visitors are rather driven by necessity than invited by fashion.' Hotwells patrons were now mostly incurable invalids, and the mortality rate was no advertisement for the spa. The 1816 Act to rebuild the parish church allowed for an additional cemetery. The dangerous and precipitous way down from Clifton to the well and the increased charge of hiring a carriage two or three times a day were other deterrents to visitors coming to a spa past its fashionable prime.[17]

Malvern

Malvern, a spa village in Worcestershire, had, like Clifton, attracted attention in the seventeenth century, but it could not command the same capital investment and it was slow to become a major spa despite its abundant springs. A map of 1633 shows wells on the western side of the Malvern Hills, including the Holy Well which, with the chalybeate St Ann's Well mentioned in 1744, became famous.[18]

The initiative for the expansion of Malvern came not from the local landowners, the Foleys, but from Worcester people who stood to gain by it. John Wall, a Worcester physician who knew the Pyrmont waters, and William Davis, an apothecary, analysed the Holy Well water in 1743. In 1747 Edward Popham of the Lodge, Tewkesbury, grateful for the cure of his gout, built a bath under the spout of the Holy Well to replace a ruined one. By 1756, when Dr Wall tried to develop this well as a spa, there was a little hut nearby for poor visitors. Wall published his *Experiments and Observations on the Malvern Waters,* with forty-seven case histories of cures, almost all of Warwickshire and Worcestershire people. A third edition in 1763 revealed yet more customers; a lady of quality had the water sent to her in London, and visitors of higher social standing, and more of them, were coming from a wider area – from Berkshire, Dorset, Gloucestershire and Leicestershire. Even the famous Dr Oliver of Bath had sent a boy with troublesome glands there. Wall intended to use profits from his pamphlet to improve the primitive and overcrowded Holy Well and he recommended drinking the waters on the spot over a long period, although he was aware of their deficient mineral content. Local self-interest again led some of the neighbouring gentry to meet in Worcester in October 1756 and form a committee to arrange better accommodation here in the hamlet of Malvern Wells, where a walk had been laid out, and by 1763 a growing settlement with several new buildings was emerging.[19]

In the main settlement, Great Malvern, John Lugard took the opportunity to turn the three-storeyed Jacobean Abbey House into a lodging-house for about fifteen visitors, who used the other well, St Ann's. Malvern had no market where lodgers could shop, so full board was the rule, and charges were low: 15*s.* a week for food and lodging, exclusive of tea, sugar, fire and candles, but hot rolls with tea and chocolate were available for 1*s.* 6*d.* extra. In 1757 Abbey House was so full that Benjamin Stillingfleet got a place with difficulty, for Lugard organized some social life in his assembly-room: a public breakfast at 10 a.m. every Wednesday during the season at 1*s.* 6*d.* per person, followed by a gambling game, The Shepherd's Lottery, music for dancing or a concert, and a public meal at a fixed price on a fixed day. Abbey House was described as 'a good hotel' in 1796, and apart from the balls on Wednesday there was card-playing on Monday. Also in Great Malvern William Mence built the Crown or New Inn just before 1760, and many ladies and gentlemen now came to enjoy the convenience of the walks and the variety of fine rides in Malvern Chase.[20]

An alternative to staying at the Abbey House was the large brick house at Malvern Wells, the 'new house at the wells' built in about 1741 and improved in 1761. When the Well House reopened Lord Walpole and others gave public breakfasts there, and a long-room was added in 1769. The house opened every 1 May and could take twenty-five people and their servants; in late June 1781 John Byng found it full. He, like other visitors, had come from Cheltenham, which he hoped never to revisit, but after enduring a very bad bed and room, and company which he was unlikely to meet again, he was equally keen to leave Malvern. Yet living there was 'very good and very cheap', and he returned in 1784 when the house was half empty. Sir Richard Colt Hoare was among the company there in 1796 living and boarding together on familiar terms, as at Buxton, Harrogate and Matlock; the charges were very reasonable and the food very good. The Well House tariff was 1*s*. less than at Abbey House: 14*s*. a week with dinner at 2 p.m. and a hot supper at 9 p.m. Red Rooms, presumably private parlours, were 5*s*. to 7*s*. 6*d*. extra. But Byng observed that visitors preferred to stay in Great Malvern and drive over to the Holy Well, and Sir Uvedale Price congratulated Miss Berry on being able to stay in the jasmine-covered parsonage house in the village in 1798 – he had a horror of 'that staring red house'. Colt Hoare also chose Great Malvern in 1801; the view was much richer and the accommodation more comfortable than at the Well House. Another option was the Crown Inn, now the 'unrivalled' Crown Hotel and posting-house in the centre of Great Malvern, run from 1796 by Mr Roberts, who abandoned teaching for the more profitable career of innkeeper.[21]

Colt Hoare also noticed the new cold bath, 'of purest water without any taste of mineral', near the spring in a house of several apartments built by subscription and opened in 1773. The next year Dr Wall had retired to Bath, where he died in 1776. His initiative had prompted the improvements, and although he was replaced by another doctor Malvern's popularity temporarily declined. His son Martin reprinted the *Experiments* with medical tracts in 1780 and 1781, and J. Barrett produced the first guidebook, *A Description of Malvern,* in 1796, but Malvern remained a quiet rural spa, its houses and cottages 'dispersed in the most picturesque manner' on the eastern flank of the Malvern Hills in orchard country. The focal point was the Gothic Priory Church, the Abbey House and the Crown Hotel in the centre of Great Malvern. Contemporaries estimated that there were about forty houses in 1796 and fifty in about 1805, almost all let for lodgings in season, not including the many more humble homes covered by the 1801 census, which gives 163 inhabited houses and 819 people, of whom 289 were engaged in agriculture and fifty-eight in various trades. So catering for visitors was important but not fundamental to Malvern. When the company came to this idyllic scene, ' . . . the creeping hop-plant, and myriads of apple and pear trees', in May the 'genteel visitors' were seldom more than could dine at one table in a large room at the Well House, in 1796 run by William Steers. He rarely had winter visitors. Unlike Cheltenham, only twenty-five miles away, with an active, sophisticated social life, there was

. . . nothing of high life about this place, except its hills: its company do not rise above the common level . . . it is a calm and reasonable resort, in which those who expect much of life and fashion will be disappointed.[22]

Malvern had scenic advantages, however, and was a retreat from the hectic pace of life at Cheltenham, and in about 1808, during the latter's boom and contemporary with the Hotwells' revival, some enterprising individuals began to see its potentialities. The Malvern Hills, the 'Alps of England', nine miles long and about 1,310 feet at their highest point, not only offered picturesque and romantic scenery like Clifton and Matlock, but also supplied the building stone, ancient and durable granite from the local quarries, for the expansion of Malvern.[23]

When the lord of the manor, Edward Thomas Foley of Stoke Edith in Herefordshire, succeeded to his father's estates in 1808, the first stage in Malvern's development began, stimulated by Cheltenham's success and attempting to catch its overflow of visitors. Many of them went from one spa to the other, helped by a regular coach service from 1815, and the centre of Great Malvern eventually became a small classical-style spa similar to contemporary building in Cheltenham. Malvern was dominated by its hoteliers, Joseph Downs, William Steers, J. Beard and Samuel Essington, and they took new initiatives. By 1802 Beard had taken over the Crown Hotel, which he enlarged, and in May 1809 he advertised lodging, board at a public table, meals served in private apartments, and neat post-chaises, open carriages and lock-up coach-houses for hire. He also organized a daily post (with the postmark 'Malvern Penny Post') to and from London, except Mondays, in the summer season; in 1809 it was extended to the whole year. Now stagecoaches ran to and from London three days a week, breaking the 120-mile journey at Oxford overnight and reaching Malvern at 3 p.m. the next day and Malvern Wells at 3.30 p.m. On coachless days a horseman linked the Worcester post, eight miles away, with Steers' Well House.[24]

The three original hotels, the Abbey House, the Crown and the Well House, were soon inadequate for the increasing invasion of visitors, and Edward T. Foley, owner of most of the village, saw his opportunity. An inn, the Foley Arms, in the centre of Great Malvern by 1807, was converted into a hotel for Joseph Downs, the proprietor, to the plans of Samuel Deykes, a Malvern saddler. The new building of three storeys and five bays, with a projecting veranda supported by five ironwork pillars at ground level, was opened in early August 1809, completely fitted up by the next May, and had wings added on either side by Downs in 1812–13. In September 1815 Downs had at least nineteen visitors and in 1818 over forty-one at one time. William Steers at Malvern Wells also branched out and by May 1810 had opened the Rock House, offering the privacy of separate rooms, and he enlarged his Well House so that he could contradict the rumour at Cheltenham, in 1818, that it was too full to take more visitors.[25]

Others cashing in on Malvern's first boom included Samuel Essington, who in May 1810 offered a 'genteel residence', Essington Lodge, consisting of two front parlours, a kitchen and cellar on the ground floor, five good lodging-rooms, a coach-house and a four-stall stable, as a lodging-house investment to be let furnished or unfurnished. This kind of business deal, new to Malvern, was handled by R. Gill, a Worcester auctioneer. By 1814 there were several more ready-furnished houses available, so Essington installed hot and cold baths and ran his house as a more profitable hotel. J. Beard of the Crown Hotel had also built up a little empire by 1815; he ran a coffee-room, a subscription newspaper-room, by May the adjoining Belle Vue Hotel, the Balcony House to let with or without board, and Trafalgar House, vacant from 1 June. Other early hotels were the Mount Pleasant in Belle Vue Terrace next to the Crown, and the Admiral Benbow in Wells Road.[26]

So there was a decided expansion of lodging accommodation, but because Malvern was another spa where social life tended to concentrate in the hotels and inns it was devoid of suitable spa amenities and other diversions, except for Beard's coffee-room and newsroom and the social events at Abbey House. Among the small improvements, both the Holy Well and St Ann's Well were now protected by buildings, the Holy Well and its cold bath from 1773. St Ann's Well acquired an approach path in 1807, its original house was built in 1808–9 and the small pump-room and hot and cold baths later. Samuel Deykes, humble but enterprising, as well as planning the Foley Arms Hotel and some hill walks, established a small library near the hotel. John Southall, the Worcester organist who came to Malvern in 1812, moved the library to his house, 1 Paradise Row, and made it a respectable collection, but the room where he kept it was too small and crude to shelter people of rank in bad weather. Malvern had no building of sufficient size to accommodate a crowd and no assembly-room until 1884; there was no long-room attached to either well and as yet no central promenade, as in other spas. It lacked even a small playhouse, although in 1794 William Meil, who held theatres in the West Midlands, obtained a licence to perform in Malvern and operated there in 1802.[27] No attempt was made to promote a communal life guided by a master of ceremonies, and outside the Abbey House balls and dances were unknown.

In 1815 Malvern was still a small, unambitious spa depending on Worcester for specialist services, and its company was, as in the northern spas, inn-orientated. Apart from encounters at the wells and on the hill walks visitors normally met only for the 'social meal' at a public table, but even then with the option of withdrawing to private apartments.

17

Wartime Cheltenham: Problems of Expansion

In 1793, when the continental spas were closed to Englishmen by war, Cheltenham, like Bath, offered a refuge in the west away from possible invasion, as members of the French royal family found. The town entered a period of the most remarkable expansion when the population rose from 3,076 in 1801 to 8,325 in 1811 and 13,388 in 1821, and the number of visitors doubled from about 2,000 in 1802 to 4,000 in 1809. But this rapid growth generated tensions between townsfolk and visitors, intense competition among traders, overspeculation, and the burden of immigrant poor.

The most marked commercial growth, apart from housing, was in transport, helped by further improvement of the local roads under three Acts of Parliament and transforming the town into a coaching centre. In 1810 a new road leaving Cheltenham from Albion Street opened up the way through Alcester to Birmingham. The New Bath Road (1813–20) was, by the co-operation of Colonel Riddell and Henry Thompson, linked with an improved 'ride' through pleasure grounds at Cambray to make a better entrance to the Montpellier and Sherborne Spa rides, and, extended through Leckhampton and Painswick, improved the route to Bath. Thirdly, the new turnpike road to Gloucester (1809) off the lower end of the High Street, further improved in 1825, remained the main road between Cheltenham and Gloucester until 1968–9.[1]

By 1809 the multiplication of transport services brought complaints of overladen stagecoaches coming in at the gallop and endangering passengers' lives. The George Inn was now an important coaching inn, and as traffic increased other inns took their share, but the old Plough Inn, by 1789 dignified as the Plough Hotel, held pride of place. Significantly, Cheltenham's coaching links were primarily with London. A daily post-coach from the Plough, Bickman's Original Day Coach, to the metropolis or back in the season took twelve hours, and in November 1809 was continued for the winter. Even the daily post-coach service from the Bell Inn to Oxford was a seven-hour stint, but in 1810 a new, competing service, the Bang Up coach from the Commercial Hotel, reached Oxford in only five hours. Before 1809 a seasonal light post-coach commenced service from early May to November transporting visitors between the York

House, Bath and the Plough in Cheltenham. The next season, 1810, this service, taking the Gloucester and Petty France route and entering Bath from the north, faced a competing daily service from the George in Cheltenham, which left Gloucester for Bristol and the Hotwells to pick up spa customers and approached Bath from the west. By 1812 the service between the Plough, Cheltenham and York House, Bath had been augmented by a new, elegant and light post-coach, the Maskelyne Coach, via Tetbury and Cirencester on alternate days when the older coach through Rodborough did not run.[2] So now there was a comprehensive service between Bath and Cheltenham.

Proprietors of inns were as competitive as coach-owners. In February 1813 Mr. E. Hughes took over the George Inn, now a 'Hotel', enlarged it, brought in new furniture, advertised his coffee-room, coach-houses and stables, and opened his regime in style with a grand dinner. But Bickman at the Plough was not to be outdone; to the service to London and two to Bath in early 1814 he added a Birmingham coach, through Worcester, and the Hibernia to Shrewsbury to catch the Irish trade, both three days a week, and a daily, slower post-coach to Shrewsbury. In June he introduced a light coach to the Royal Hotel at the growing resort of Weymouth, but it took two days and passengers slept overnight at the York House, Bath.[3]

For transport about the town there were sedan chairs for hire. From 1807 the town commissioners controlled the provision of chairs by annual licensing of the chairmen, who wore a compulsory uniform of a long, loose blue coat with a scarlet badge showing the licence number, and by 1810 there were ten couples of chairmen, compared with 340 in Bath in 1801, which reflects the far greater custom at Bath but also its taxing, hilly walks. In 1810 Jonathan Wildey, who already ran a light cart to Bath, introduced a fly-carriage to convey visitors to the ballroom and the theatre, but like other contemporary Cheltenham traders he had miscalculated the market and went bankrupt in 1811.[4]

The town was still in the stage of *rus in urbe,* its charms displayed in John Claude Nattes's drawings (1804) of the Well Walk, Fauconberg House and the back entrance to the Old Well.[5] But change came rapidly; 1809, when Henry Thompson's Montpellier Spa was fully operational, was the peak of Cheltenham's second boom period from 1801 to 1814. A town newspaper, the *Cheltenham Chronicle,* produced by Humphrey Ruff at his High Street library, appeared on 4 May 1809. Thompson may have had an interest in it, for it gave favourable accounts of his activities. Cheltenham's fame, now secure against the fickleness of fashion and the rivalry of less favoured towns, extended, said the *Chronicle,* to the remotest British colonies. Most people of affluence from the East or West Indies came there to restore their health. But it urged the creation of a new town planned by an experienced architect and it deplored false so-called improvements. Cheltenham's future beauty should not be sacrificed to self-interest and large property-owners should support the building of the new town – as at Leamington, where visitors had subscribed £50,000 for this purpose; information which doubtless came from Thompson's acquaintance Bertie Greatheed. The responsibility for improving Thompson's walks and rides, said the *Chronicle,* should not be his alone but that of all who let houses or lodgings. If these wells and their surroundings were neglected, who would come to Cheltenham? Whatever the financial funding of his newspaper, it spoke with the voice of Henry Thompson. In July 1809, when £15,000 was needed to purchase ground bounded on three sides by Thompson's walks and rides and to erect six villas costing £2,000 each, as at Cambray, the tontine method was used to raise the capital.[6]

As well as his Montpellier Pump-room Henry Thompson had mineral-water pumps in a small octagonal building by the Gothic Cottage in Montpellier Field, but the supply of mineral water was a problem, although physicians promoted its use. Dr Thomas Jameson's *Treatise on the Cheltenham Waters* appeared in 1803; in 1804 a reviewer mentioned the persistent rumours of the supply of mineral water failing to meet the increasing demand at the Old Well, and only a few drank the scanty and dirty water at the King's Well, except servants. Thompson now tried to promote bathing as an alternative to drinking and extended his empire to include baths and salts manufacture. His Montpellier Baths, with three Doric-style entrances, in the New Bath Road were more elaborate than Freeman's Baths in the High Street and received publicity in 1809 when Jameson, now a town commissioner, argued in the second edition of his treatise that hot- and tepid-bathing should supplement drinking saline waters. In August the *Chronicle* claimed that Cheltenham had become a bathing as well as a drinking spa, and that Thompson's Baths had over 100 customers every week, independently of Freeman's. Thompson should construct more baths – twenty would not be too many; but by 1825 there were only nine: two large cold ones; the others tepid and warm. In 1815 Thompson tried to maintain his trade by an extraordinary plan to transport quantities of Cheltenham water to Bath for sale at the Kingston Pump Room.[7] Now that the production of salts by Paytherus and Co. at the Old Well, to be marketed by Savory Moore and Co., had slumped, he also began their manufacture in his laboratory by the Montpellier Baths, as he showed Bertie Greatheed from Leamington in 1822.[8] Thompson's salts were retailed at Bath and through the sole agents, Messrs Butler, chemist, of Cheapside, London, with outlets in Dublin and Edinburgh.[9]

To meet the growing consumer demand, attempts were made to establish other spa centres in Cheltenham. A New Well which attracted much custom lay adjacent to Montpellier on land owned by the Earl of Suffolk of Charlton in Wiltshire, who had married a niece of Lord Sherborne. Like

Thompson, in 1801 he purchased land from John de la Bere, only thirty acres for £2,800, but it included Gallipot Farm, a thatched cottage where parties went to drink syllabub. Here he built Suffolk House, where in May 1809 he and the countess took up residence. He had become a town commissioner in 1806 and another house, Suffolk Lodge, existed in 1817, but development of the Suffolk Estate came after his death in 1820, and the New Well was never transformed into a spa.[10]

A more successful venture was the original Sherborne Spa, Lord Sherborne's Well at the top of Old Well Lane, founded about 1804 after Dr Jameson had discovered the spring while boring for waters. Trinder's 1809 map shows it, but it ran dry and was superseded in 1818 by the second Sherborne Well. The developers here were the Harward family, who acquired some marshland with brickworks between the High Street and the Sherborne Well of 1818 from Lord Sherborne. Samuel Harward, like the other commissioners in 1806, had a clear interest in the construction of a road to replace the footpaths and the plank bridge across the Chelt, which linked the High Street with the growing spa area. The commissioners continued the road begun in the Colonnade, perhaps persuaded by Harward, whose library was there; in 1806 he sold them the right of way for £450, and so the first stretch of the future Promenade was laid. In 1807 Harward netted a further 100 guineas for a second right of way to connect that road with another up and past the Sherborne Well.[11]

Another attempted spa development before 1815 was at Alstone Green. Mr Smith of Alstone Villa discovered a mineral spring in his grounds on 10 October 1809; he had the water analysed by Frederick Accum of London, author of a guide to the contemporary Thetford Spa, and later built an octagonal pump-room surrounded with pleasure grounds and promenades. Jung and Schneider's Alstone Spa Nursery Gardens were developed in front of it. But Smith's 'New Spa', advertised in the autumn of 1810, was the least successful.[12]

All this spa activity was both the result and the cause of an even greater influx of visitors, the most important being the Prince Regent, who in 1808 was entertained at Lindsay Cottage near the Vittoria Spa. Despite the war Cheltenham was a boom town; speculators in bricks flourished and in April 1810 new building was 'arising in all directions'. Newly built houses, fully and 'elegantly' furnished, were frequently sold or let, and at least fifty villas and lesser houses were erected during the year ending March 1813. The premature announcement of peace in 1814 was celebrated heartily in June with illuminations and decorations on the main buildings. Justice was depicted restoring Peace and Plenty with the national hero, Wellington, and a huge bonfire at the end of the Colonnade was fed with gifts from coal merchants and timber dealers. But recession set in from 1814 to 1815; in May 1814 rumours that Henry Thompson proposed to transport spa water to distant places caused much anxiety and in late June public places were nearly deserted, although a revival came later. Of at least fourteen bankruptcies in Cheltenham between 1809 and 1819, six occurred in 1814–15. The stoppage in May 1815 of the Gloucester bank of Evans and Jelf had repercussions in Cheltenham.[13]

Cheltenham seemed like a speculators' paradise, but this was an illusion. In 1791 only two builders were listed in a trade directory, William Marshall and Edward Smith, who on his death in 1813 had a memorial in the parish church. But other builders became involved in the hectic activity: the Billings brothers, one of whom, in 1809, planned to build fifty-two houses in St James's Square; Henry and Thomas Haines; and one Parker, who built St George's Place. At least nine helped to more than double the number of houses in Cheltenham between 1801 and 1811 – from 710 to 1,556 – and to maintain expansion between 1811 and 1821 to 2,411 houses. Other promoters of the building mania were the solicitors Walter H. Jessop, who owned houses in the Crescent; Richard Pruen and Theodore Gwinnett, clerk to the commissioners; and G. R. Wilmot, an architect and estate agent at 3 the Colonnade.[14] With the doctors they helped to form a professional core in the town, which now depended less on Gloucester for such services.

The inevitable outcome of this rapid expansion was a lack of social control. Builders under pressure left carts and wagons in public places overnight; rubbish and building materials clogged the High Street; and the scaffolding of the chapel in King Street collapsed, killing a bricklayer. House construction outstripped the provision of support services, roads and footways, water supplies and other sanitary measures, so a further Paving Act was needed in 1806 because '. . . the streets both old and new are still incommodious, unsafe for passengers and not sufficiently lighted'. The commissioners, now increased to seventy-two, had more powers to deal with paving, repairing, and cleaning streets, and to maintain a police force. Several of them – the Earl of Suffolk, John Boles Watson, William Humphris Barrett, Henry Thompson, Colonel John Riddell, Dr Jameson and Joseph Pitt – had commercial commitments in Cheltenham, but they were too many to be efficient, and the novelty of their corporate authority was not easily accepted. They were frequently accused of neglect, especially of the state of the roads which, because of increased building, were sometimes brought into use prematurely.[15]

Building was chiefly for lodging-houses, but also for stables and some shops. By 1815 servicing the visitors was, as at Bath, the town's principal occupation, and almost every householder supplemented the 'five good inns' by taking in lodgers. The well-established Plough, run by Mr Bickman, had ample space for families, their servants and carriages, and was the envy of the other innkeepers at the George, the Fleece, the Crown and the Lamb. Hotels were now built to meet the needs of long-stay visitors; Smith's Boarding-house, erected by Lord Sherborne in the grounds of the Great House, at 110 High Street and run by Edward Smith, auctioneer, shopkeeper and builder, was prominent. When Smith's widow became Mrs Fisher it was renamed Fisher's Hotel. By 1805 the York Hotel – or the Dublin and Bath Hotel – in the High Street was run by Charles Eldridge,[16] then by Mrs Weaver, and when Thomas Sheldon acquired it on her death in July 1809 it had the extraordinary capacity of forty-three bedrooms, a spacious dining-room, four parlours, five drawing-rooms and three kitchens. As Sheldon's Hotel it had an enviable reputation at least until 1816. When Thomas Hughes opened the new Wellington Hotel, with some publicity and the new fashion of a house-warming dinner at 3 p.m. on 12 December 1814, sixty people paid one guinea each to attend.[17]

But although the new building could absorb more visitors, more came, and in late August 1809 many had difficulty in finding lodgings. Lists of vacancies occasionally appeared in public places, but these 'solitary flags of distress' soon disappeared. During the 1810 season few lodgings were long vacant, and to avoid Cheltenham's 'bustle' some visitors escaped to the quiet of Malvern. The *Cheltenham Chronicle* dismissed this move as a 'temporary' secession and in July 1810 initiated a lodgings register, which at first showed vacancies in three large houses but subsequently at few addresses. It disappeared as the number of visitors grew to over 5,000 in 1814.[18]

Immense capital investment went into the local leisure industry, providing accommodation, entertainment and other services, but in 1810 the average profits of a newly built house, furnished in modern style were allegedly, after taxes, less than 6 per cent on the building and 10 per cent on the furniture, and where rents were high below 5 per cent and 7 per cent respectively. Far from exploiting visitors, the *Chronicle* averred, lodging-house keepers charged moderately. But public buildings and lodgings were under-utilized, in demand mainly from mid-April to late October, and the return on investment was inadequate. So from about 1809 onwards the fiction of a winter season was propagated, although lists of arrivals show only about twenty-three visitors in the third week of November and nineteen and sixteen in the subsequent two weeks. Fortnightly winter balls were introduced at the Assembly Rooms, and an inhabitant recalled that no visitors had arrived in past winters, but now they and the residents outnumbered the previous summer populations. It was claimed that 400 families arrived for the winter season in October 1812.[19]

One of the difficulties of transforming Cheltenham into a winter as well as a summer spa was in obtaining adequate supplies of domestic coal. Bath tapped the Mendip coal-fields, but most of Cheltenham's coal came from

Staffordshire and Shropshire by barge to Gloucester and then by inadequate roads, and sold at one guinea a ton or 1s. 3d. a hundredweight. When the Coombe Hill Canal project failed in 1808 the need for cheap coal from the Forest of Dean led to the construction of a railroad for horse-drawn trucks from Gloucester to Cheltenham under Act of Parliament in 1809. A branch line was also constructed from Charles Brandon Trye's Leckhampton stone quarries to the terminus of the Cheltenham and Gloucester Tramway in the Lower High Street where 'The Wharf' covered 1¼ acres of coal and stone yards.

The Earl of Suffolk laid the first stone of the railroad in November 1809 and the first stone carts came down in July 1810, accompanied by gentlemen on horseback and greeted by a band of music and a great crowd. A celebration dinner for fifty at the Plough was attended by Brandon Trye, and the Honourable John Dutton, son of Lord Sherborne, took the chair. The tramroads, it was confidently predicted, would materially aid Cheltenham's development; forest coal would sell at two-thirds the present price, and timber and high-quality stone for houses and hard stone and gravel for roads at about a quarter. Cheltenham had been too much a summer resort only, and the extension of road and water communications, especially to Bath and Birmingham, would make it more residential. So enlarged market wharves and warehouses were erected at the railroad terminus, and by April 1810 J. and B. Thompson had opened a yard at Gloucester to supply Cheltenham with cheaper coal and slack for brickfields. Thomas Weaver also opened a yard at the Wharf, and by 1815 the Cheltenham and Gloucester Coal Company in St George's Place offered lower-priced coals from Staffordshire, Shropshire, the Forest of Dean and Wales. In 1814, when strata 'like those preceding coal' were found, there was an abortive project to mine coal near Cheltenham, and the company formed to make trials hoped to have a profit and save the town £3,000 a year. But the plan was abandoned in September, only to be unsuccessfully revived in 1825.[20]

The attempted winter season and the growing residential population established a steadier consumer market and a complex social life developed, beyond the earlier simple routine of playhouse, billiards, bowling green, assemblies and 'airings'. As at other resorts, speculators now invested not only in houses but in a range of diversions for the leisured elite. Circulating libraries, pleasure gardens and musical performances were introduced, travelling shows arrived, and clubs and societies were formed. The *Cheltenham Chronicle* was founded, as explained in its first issue of 4 May 1809, to publicize such enterprises; a resort with such a changing population needed a newspaper with an extensive circulation to inform visitors about available lodgings and consumer services. From 7

October a second local newspaper significantly linked Bath and Cheltenham; the *Bath and Cheltenham Gazette* was published at Bath but also gave Cheltenham news.

The multiplying activities were both serious and entertaining; Cheltenham, like other leisure markets, attracted performers apart from theatre players, and John Boles Watson brought the famous Madame Catalini to perform in Handel's *Messiah* among a hundred vocalists in the parish church in 1811, but admission cost 10*s*. 6*d*. The so-called Sadler's Wells Theatre, a well-known marionette theatre of Fantoccini puppets in 1800 run by one Seward of Bristol, functioned at Cheltenham as well as at Bath and other watering-places, with box seats at 2*s*., the pit at 1*s*. and the gallery at 6*d*. To meet competing diversions, Watson refurbished his theatre in 1812 with new cushions, better lighting and fresh paint. Diversions in 1815 were demonstrations of glass-blowing in miniature by Mr Aubin and Mr Lloyd's astronomical lectures, both at Heyne's Regent Rooms.[21]

Nevertheless local entrepreneurs were concerned that, as at Bath, public assemblies under the aegis of the master of ceremonies were being undermined by private parties. In 1814 the *Cheltenham Chronicle* censured private and illegal balls at boarding-houses as damaging to both proprietors of established assemblies, who provided accommodation at enormous expense, and local traders. But the lack of a sufficiently large assembly-room until 1816 caused the dispersal of social life and the temporary use of Sheldon's Hotel and the Regent Ballroom for public balls and assemblies. The Regent Ballroom, set in a delightful ornamental garden, was opened in June 1809 by the Regent Library proprietor Humphrey Ruff, who added a music-room in 1810 and recruited a band of vocal and orchestral musicians who sometimes performed in the brilliantly lit gardens.[22] The vogue for pleasure gardens stimulated an interest in gardens in general and provided a new field for commercial investment. In 1809 C. Webb, a nurseryman and land surveyor of Painswick, advertised the laying out of lawns and pleasure gardens 'in the modern style', and land agents offered two acres of 'capital garden land', with a house to be erected, to let in 1810 – especially suitable for gardeners.[23]

A necessary leisure service for visitors was the provision of books and newspapers. Miss Penelope Newman from Bristol kept a bookshop at Cheltenham from mid-century, but left in 1783. A circulating library was more necessary; Bath had six in 1776 but Cheltenham had none until Samuel Harward, who had shops at Gloucester and Tewkesbury, opened one at 162 High Street in 1780 with fifty-two subscribers, and offering novels and books, 'as in other watering-places,' for 5*s*. a season. He also hired out musical instruments, including harpsichords and pianofortes, and fitted up the Old Pump Room as a reading-room. After 1791 he ran a secondary library of 30,000 volumes at 4 Colonnade Buildings, which his widow Kitty continued after his death in 1809 until it was sold in September 1814. In 1800 two other libraries in the High Street were kept by Mrs. J. Jones at Number 59 and Mr Buckle at Number 167, one '. . . more adapted for *looking* than *learning*'; in other words a social centre. Libraries here, as at Bath, were the focus of news and gossip both national and local, places where London daily newspapers were available in reading-rooms and subscription books were displayed for balls, concerts, card parties, music lessons, benefit occasions and a host of charities, especially relief funds.[24]

On 29 April 1805 Humphrey Ruff, who wrote the first *History of Cheltenham* (1803) as distinct from Moreau's *Guides* and was later the editor and publisher of the *Cheltenham Chronicle,* opened Ruff's New English and French Circulating Library at 329 High Street; this also combined a registry for servants and lodgings with an estate agency. As we have seen, Ruff's extended premises later became the Regency Gardens and Ballroom, but he faced the hazard of extreme competition and overinvestment in contemporary Cheltenham and went bankrupt in November 1813. Thomas Jordan acquired his business in January 1814, reopened it in April, and in a brief flush of prosperity provided a billiard-room and gave a public dinner of roast beef and plum pudding to the poor in June; then he also went bankrupt. By November E. Hughes of the George Hotel was operating the Regent Ballroom, but Stoke Heynes, a wine merchant, held all the premises by May 1815.[25]

The rapid turnover of ownership and the precarious town economy were apparent elsewhere. In 1810 T. Henney operated as a bookseller, stationer, medicine vendor and servants' registry at 343 High Street, with a circulating library of 15,000 volumes supported by a high annual subscription, 16*s.* He was patronized by the French royal family in 1814, survived the depression of 1814–15 and gave £10 to discharged soldiers and soldiers' widows, but in March 1816 he sold out to Samuel Bettinson Junior of Margate. W. Buckle's library at 167 High Street changed hands several times, and another ephemeral one was opened by C. Liddell in 1812.[26]

Despite commercial risks other diversions tended, as at Bath, to splinter the company into more selective groups with a wider choice of entertainment and cultural activity. Mr Spornberg opened the Cheltenham Museum of Natural and Artificial Curiosities in June 1810. Local clubs and societies emerged, some for members bent on self-improvement; in February 1810 the New Subscription Club had its own house and manager. As well as the musicians who, led by the clarinettist James Haldon, played daily at the Old Well and at the Assembly Rooms, a new band performed at Ruff's Gardens in the evenings and, at least from 1813, at Thompson's Well in the mornings. In June 1815 some fifty noblemen and gentry held a dinner at

Heynes' Regent Concert Room to inaugurate the Harmonic Society, and several businesses catered for the needs of musicians; by 1803 Charles Hale had a music warehouse to sell or hire instruments such as pianofortes, as did Samuel Harward and Mrs. Jones. In about 1810–12 Hale moved to larger premises by the churchyard and then to Promenade House, and in 1810 his new music included a dance, the Cheltenham Fling. Like other urban spas, Cheltenham promoted race meetings; in May 1814 a committee of twelve gentlemen, backed by a subscription of £350, made plans to establish annual local horse-races. Colonel W. F. Berkeley donated £1,000 a year, and the first race meeting was held in August 1818.[27]

Retail services were stretched to their limit to cater for the visitors' more material needs. In 1791 Cheltenham had about thirty-seven shops, but any new buildings were mostly houses. An analysis of seventy-six property 'units' on the north side of the High Street in 1802 shows forty available for commercial boarding and ten private dwellings, but only sixteen shops. The commercial community was overextended and undermanned: in 1813 out of about 3,176 inhabitants, not including any of the 5,000 visitors or inhabitants in outlying districts, 459 were engaged in trade. Shopkeepers were expected to crowd into the High Street, where a dwelling-house could be adapted for lodgings or trade. Owners of newly built estates tried to preserve their residential character and a few shops only gradually appeared outside the High Street. The Colonnade shops were probably the first to be purpose-built, but in 1812 Mrs A. Lovelock, a milliner from Bath, moved from 312 High Street to 1 Crescent Place.[28]

As at other urban spas, immigrant retailers captured some of the summer trade. By 1809 a few came from London and many from Bath, moving their stock to Cheltenham in April. The Bath Union Shoe Manufactory offered high-fashion footwear from Bath, 'the first place in the world for taste and elegance in the manufacture of boots and shoes' at 1 Cambray Street. Also from Bath, Mrs Langdon brought laces, millinery and dresses, and W. Cox laces and silks; he shared premises at 322 High Street with Henry Smith, agent of a Nottingham hosiery manufacturer. The reverse process was seen in October when Mrs Lovelock and other traders sold off stock at bargain prices to return to Bath. Two fashionable London shoemakers, J. Jones and T. Draper, shared premises in April 1810 at 336 High Street, and some newcomers opened permanent shops in Cheltenham: Charles Harrison, a cutler from Bath, and W. Rouse, a watchmaker and jeweller from Worcester. The proliferation of new businesses in the town would repay further study. So undeveloped were its resources that Gloucester had to supply a hearse until T. Kidman & Co., the coach proprietors, provided one in December 1809.[29]

Ample provisions for this expanding population came from the fertile Severn Valley where as a contemporary said, 'eight months are summer and four too warm for an English winter', and at first the only problem was distribution. Country carriers brought in corn, fish, butter and vegetables to the two old markets in the High Street, but even in the early nineteenth century transport difficulties frustrated the need to forage further afield. Preachers sometimes announced the arrival of eagerly awaited goods at the end of a sermon. By 1810 the effects of the Napoleonic blockade and the wheat crop failure affected even the Severn Valley, and the planting of potatoes on thirty acres of Battledown was urged. Carrots – said to be good for horses – and potatoes were grown around Westhall Green.[30]

Gloucestershire had been chiefly a food-exporting county, except for corn from Oxfordshire and Berkshire, but by 1811 the Vale of Gloucester was normally the granary of the region. This switch from importation to surplus production of the best corn in about a decade was a local farming revolution stimulated by the expanding Cheltenham food market, which also took in bacon, butter and tons of the famous Double Gloucester and Double Berkeley cheese. Cattle, game and poultry abounded, and the Severn was rich in fish such as salmon, lampreys and eels, but as meat prices climbed a market for more fish grew. In 1814 Lord Somerville of Newbold Comyn in Warwickshire promoted a novel enterprise to provide fresh fish for 'populous and wealthy' Cheltenham and perhaps for his neighbouring spa, Leamington. He built six smacks, equipped with wells to keep the fish alive, and employed them in the Bristol Channel. Relays of coaches, carts and caravans transported the fish from Bristol to local markets, and by October Cheltenham had regular consignments handled by a Mr Cossens, Somerville's agent. So unlike Buxton, where retailers had to forage in distant markets, the Cheltenham food market was well provisioned.[31]

Lord Sherborne, lord of the manor, claimed the tolls from the Thursday market now proving so profitable, and from the three or four annual cattle fairs. After the improvements in 1786 the rebuilt Butter Cross and market house stood in the Lower High Street, but twenty years later it was too small and in 1808 the commissioners erected yet another, the 'Town Hall' adjoining the Shambles, where they met monthly on the upper floor. In 1809 they had a special meeting about the state of the market and soon leased the market tolls for twenty-one years from Lord Sherborne and appointed a clerk of the market to collect them, but in 1810 they considered subletting the market house, with its several butchers' stalls and two large vaults, and in 1815 they farmed the tolls by annual auction for £490.[32]

Not only food supplies but a large labour force had to be mustered and housed to underpin the leisure life of the elite at the spa: workers in building and allied trades, coachmen, ostlers, carriers, porters, shop assistants, clerks and a horde of domestic servants. As well as the growing spa trade Cheltenham had malting and clothing industries, and its considerable job-generation potential led to a marked immigration of rural labouring people, attracted also by its reputedly fairly lenient Poor Law regime. The Michaelmas fairs were also local mop fairs where servants were hired on annual contract, but they coincided with the end of the season and other methods of recruiting labour were adopted.[33]

The libraries ran registries for servants and employers and the workhouse was another pool for domestic labour. But improved standards of service came to be expected in this fashionable resort, so methods of selecting and training servants were evolved, and in better-class domestic service hiring by the year superseded monthly wages and warning of dismissal. The Cheltenham School of Industry for Girls in Queen's Buildings was established in about 1808, supported by subscriptions and closely watched by the Association of Married Women, one of its aims being to produce under-servants. In 1818 a more commercial servants' registry, the Intelligence Office for Servants, was opened by C. Hayward, a greengrocer in Chester Walk.[34]

Inevitably the unfortunate members of society seeking easy pickings migrated to this venue of the better-off. There were constant complaints about beggars – in 1808 that every morning 'four of these miserable objects' roamed between the churchyard and Well Walk – and of the commissioners' failure to police the streets. During the war years, 1793 – 1815, food prices rose beyond the level of wages and, as at Bath, alarming disorder among the poor detracted from the image of the pleasant resort. By 1809 there was large-scale pilfering in gardens and fields around Cheltenham, and riotous groups damaged property. So like Bathonians, householders formed the Cheltenham Association for Prosecuting Felons and the Protection of Property in 1809 and invited evidence of wrongdoers. In 1810 a quantity of meat was stolen from the new market house, and in 1813 hooligans wrenched door knockers off in the Crescent and broke forty-two street oil-lamps and the next summer fifty-two. By 1814 a number of disorderly houses had been unearthed. But the maintenance of law and order was undermined by friction between the magistrates and the town commissioners, many of them newcomers or non-resident property-owners. In 1810 the vestry asked in vain for a better police force than the two high constables and the petty constable nominated by the court leet.[35]

Much of the social unrest was, as in Bath, caused by the over-rapid expansion of the town and lack of adequate support for the sick, disabled, old and unemployed, aggravated by poor harvests and wartime high food prices. In autumn 1809 it was proposed to celebrate the anniversary of the king's accession not with illuminations but by opening a poor-relief subscription list headed by Colonel Riddell, and as at Bath the better-off were urged to forgo pastry as part of their dinner. Individual relief funds were sometimes taken up; in 1808 £156 was raised for Widow Parsloe and her five children when her husband, a building worker, was killed.[36]

By 1811 the problem of rising food costs was so serious that the commissioners urged the justices to fix corn prices in Cheltenham by the market prices in Gloucester and Tewkesbury. The situation was aggravated by the unprecedented pressure on the poor rates as unemployed immigrant workers attempted to obtain a settlement in the town to qualify for poor relief. In 1809 a new workhouse was built off New Street, and in 1813 the vestry founded a dispensary for the sick poor. But these palliatives, aided by certain local charities, were inadequate to meet the crisis. Householders resisted the rising poor rate but in 1812 the overseers of the poor were in debt, despite the rapid increase in the amount of rateable local property, then 1,261 assessed houses. So the vestry decided to apply Gilbert's Act of 1782 by which the able-bodied poor were denied workhouse accommodation but were found work.[37] In theory jobs generated by Cheltenham's booming leisure industry should have absorbed many of the unemployed, but their fate in the hands of speculators, tradesmen and fashionable visitors awaits a detailed study.

Expenses mounted as the commissioners laboured to render Cheltenham a more agreeable place to the visiting company. In 1814 they improved public lighting, with 350 lamps for 264 nights in the year. Orders were given for paving, cleaning and lighting more of the streets and to control the stench and noise of blacksmiths' shops, brewhouses and slaughterhouses; to prevent chimneys from smoking and building materials and rubbish being left in the public highways. Street clearance alone was a financial burden, involving a surveyor and other salaried officials. The scavenger of the rubbish was paid £150 a year.[38]

Local-authority income failed to keep pace with urban growth, and both the vestry and the commissioners struggled with problems beyond their competence. The commissioners took up capital loans at 9½ per cent, and both bodies attempted to raise money on the expanding holiday industry by taxing the considerable new building. In 1810 the vestry ordered a survey of the parish for a fairer poor-rates assessment, including private and commercial buildings, public wells and gardens, and the commission also accepted that valuation, doubled it and charged 2s. 6d. in the pound with a resultant total rate of £2,334 13s. 0½d. for 1811–12. The inhabitants of Cheltenham reacted vigorously at protest meetings led by attorneys Robert Hughes and Henry Wilkinson and supported by local bankers and businessmen, like Henry Thompson and the library proprietors. Even the Assembly Rooms were rated at £88 and the Plough Hotel at £133. There were rumours of informers from the London tax office staying at the Plough, armed with a secret list of fifty or sixty local landlords and housekeepers who had made inadequate returns of their enormous profits, but the accusation of exorbitant charges was rejected by 'those who dabbled in bricks and mortar'.[39]

Profits from commercial investment in Cheltenham depended on both prolonging the season and on the competence of the MC. However, Simon Moreau's successor from 1801, James King, spent the winter at Bath as the master of the Lower Rooms from 1785 and from 1805 of the Upper Rooms. King held the Bath and Cheltenham posts simultaneously, as others had held Bath and Tunbridge Wells. He departed to Bath in late October and in mid-May reappeared in Cheltenham where he built his 'elegant villa', Cambray Lodge, which in March 1813 was robbed of plate, food and clothes.[40]

During King's tenure of office a larger assembly-room became necessary. Thomas Hughes's Lower Rooms (1784) were used until 1809 but were demolished by March 1810, when a new building was 'rapidly rising' on the site. Meanwhile the ill-attended winter coteries were held at Hooper's Lodging-House and the balls at the Dublin and Bath (or Sheldon's) Hotel. The east wing of the unfinished rooms was in use in May when James King announced a ball to honour the king's birthday at the 'New Assembly Rooms', and by the autumn there were plans to divide the superfluous Upper Rooms in the High Street into shops. One large assembly-room now sufficed instead of two in the town centre, for the new Montpellier Pump Room and Long-room was an alternative social venue from 1809 and was rebuilt in 1817–18. In March 1813 the new Assembly Rooms were still undergoing considerable additions and improvements, so Ruff's Regent Ballroom was used for public balls. When Thomas Jordan took over Ruff's business in 1814 he opened the ballroom for the summer with a superb gala and ball, jellies and refreshments provided by Mr Gunton, but a competitor to James King, Thomas Morhall, acted as MC.[41]

Some Cheltonians were restive about King's performance as MC, although by 1806 he was reputed to have established an elegant standard of amusements and contributed much to Cheltenham's prosperity. He had been indefatigable in helping to establish the Cambray Spa and had invested between £5,000 and £6,000 in lodging-houses let at a moderate rent by way of example. But his double assignment at Cheltenham and Bath made difficulties. The attendance when the Cheltenham rooms opened in mid-May 1814 was under par owing to the absence of 'so essential a character', and the next week he was 'still awaited' to organize the amusements; he headed the list of arrivals on 4 June. His benefit ball, a Bath institution imported to Cheltenham by 1809, was attended by 800 in August 1814. Nevertheless a winter MC was indispensable, and in the late autumn there were rumours of such an appointment. Morhall of the Regent Gardens, an obvious candidate, may have written the anonymous letter to the local press signed 'No Candidate for M.C.' alleging that King treated Cheltenham with contempt, as a place of no consequence in winter. He should be replaced by a master who could officiate all the year: 'We want no Summer Friends, who when they have bowed and scraped all the money they can out of our pockets, leave us in the winter to shift for ourselves.' Common sense prevailed; on 4 November the subscribers confirmed King in office, with thanks for his 'constant attention to the welfare and harmony of the society of this town'. Two stewards on a fortnightly rota were to cover the winter season, beginning with F. C. Burton and W. White. Under their aegis the first winter ball of 1814 was held at the Regent Gardens Ballroom, now run by E. Hughes of the George Hotel, and the card and dancing assembly met at Sheldon's Hotel and subsequently at Hughes's Regent Rooms.[42]

The next summer season, 1815, James King was careful to arrive from Bath on 11 May, much earlier than in 1814, and with his position now secure, he soon dissipated some of the boredom in fashionable circles. The last ball at Sheldon's was held in February 1816, when the new Assembly Rooms were almost complete. There are few references to James King after this; the aged grand old master of ceremonies lived to enjoy the first summer ball in the splendid new rooms on 26 May and a special dress ball on 29 July attended by the Duke and Duchess of Wellington and 1,400 people. The proprietors, J. D. Kelly and his associates, gave effusive thanks to the duke and his lady and also to King for their support. King's benefit ball was held on 19 August, but he did not return to Bath. He died at Cambray Lodge on 16 October, aged seventy, and his obituary praised him as a highly respected and urbane man with an enlightened mind, a polished understanding and a liberal heart. He left estate in Cheltenham, Cambray Lodge and its furniture, Cambray Villa, an elegant mansion with a pleasure garden and shrubbery, and two plots of building ground.[43]

Cheltenham's first two masters of ceremonies, Simon Moreau and James King, had served her well, both importing and establishing the new social ethic of Bath, an organized leisure society. King was buried near Moreau's remains in the parish church and honoured with a memorial plaque. They had both helped to establish Cheltenham as the second spa and the one favoured by the Duke of Wellington, the international hero of the hour.

18

Bath: The Price of Primacy

James King MC, dividing his time between Bath and Cheltenham from 1801 to 1816, would have been aware of their similar problems resulting from over-rapid growth, wartime depression and food shortages. Bath had the veneer of a well-organized, flourishing and fashionable society; in 1792 Hannah More exclaimed: 'Bath, happy Bath, is as gay as if there was no war, no sin, nor misery in the world',[1] but this impression concealed social tensions between visitors and residents, commercial competition and the increasing unrest of the poverty-stricken. The undercurrent of discontent in Bath occasionally erupted into riots which threatened the leisure industry on which so much employment and profit depended.

Religion might have been a palliative. Bath had the advantage of four old parochial churches, but its rapid expansion and the influx of visitors placed great demands on them and led, for example, to a shortage of burial space. Interment in the Abbey cost £10 by 1766 and most corpses were taken across the river to Bathwick and Widcombe for burial. The over-crowded churches could accommodate only a tenth of the visitors and residents by then and, especially during the winter, the sick found them cold and damp. The erection of places of worship in Georgian Bath was as much a part of the building mania as that of lodging-houses and mews.

Of the four churches, the Abbey Church of St Peter and St Paul was complete, but the other three, St James, St Michael and St Swithin, Walcot, were all enlarged or rebuilt. In addition new Anglican chapels, apart from dissenting and Catholic places of worship, were built by subscription in developing areas outside the old city, mostly on the proprietary principle, to provide reserved pews for the more affluent residents and visitors. The first privately owned chapel, designed by John Wood between 1732 and 1734, was St Mary's (1735) for the inhabitants of Queen Square: visitors paid 5*s*. a time or one guinea a season; another was the Margaret Chapel, Brock Street. These proprietary chapels were more comfortable than the churches and were equipped with fireplaces, like the Octagon Chapel in Milsom Street (1767), the Kensington Chapel in Walcot (1795) – whose three fireplaces made it 'very warm' – and the Laura Chapel (1796) of the Bathwick development. All Saints Chapel, Lansdown Place (1794), was another proprietary chapel.[2]

Despite the fashion for proprietary churches and chapels, the poor were not forgotten. Lord Rivers gave land on which Christ Church in Montpelier (1798), Bath's first free church since the Reformation, was built by voluntary subscription for their use; only gallery seats were leased to help defray expenses. Trinity Church, James Street (1812–13) also had 700 free sittings out of 1,000.[3] But the poorer people were inclined to attend the two Methodist and six other chapels which existed by 1811. The Methodists contributed to both chapel-building and the creation of a social conscience in Bath. They regarded Bath, with its prostitutes ('the nymphs of Avon Street'), its growing number of casinos and its pleasure-seekers, as 'Satan's Headquarters', and in June 1739 John Wesley had a confrontation with Richard Nash.[4]

Despite Wesley's criticism, however, Bath was not an entirely aristoc-racy-dominated, pleasure-loving city; a high proportion of responsible middle-class residents and visitors and the city fathers were, as their deeds show, aware of a growing social problem. To the agony of occasional disaster, such as flooding in the lower town and epidemics, was added the stress of over-rapid expansion and the continued invasion of thieves, rogues and other parasites. Earlier, expulsion had been the remedy; in 1709–10 two men, by the mayor's order, were paid 1*s.* to drive beggars from the city, but among the immigrant poor were many looking for honest employment. Workers' lives were dislocated by the fluctuating nature of seasonal work, wage rates were generally low, and there was persistent poverty. The many domestic servants were particularly vulnerable; in season they lived on the vails, gratuities, of rich households but in leaner times, when on humbler fare, they were tempted to steal. Even when working they were in jeopardy if they were ill, for temporary employers, the visitors, felt little obligation to them.[5]

Bath was paying the price of mushrooming prosperity and the city council were aware that social unrest could be a deterrent to visitors, but the early and undimmed tradition of philanthropy in Bath helped to prevent disruption. The council gave the ground and a liberal subscription to the Charity School founded in 1721 by Robert Nelson; it cost £1,000 and the boy and girl pupils, fifty of each, placed out as apprentices at the age of fourteen contributed to the pool of semi-skilled labour. When, during the terrible winter of 1739 and the depression in the nearby coal-fields and textile industry, starving people poured into Bath, Nash opened a subscription list for the unemployed with ten guineas, but he took a tougher line with professional beggars. He also encouraged the erection in 1738 of a general hospital, later the Royal Mineral Water Hospital, opened

in 1742, to make the mineral springs available to sick and poor strangers –
provided, as the *Bath Journal* reiterated in 1755, that they had proper
credentials. So general was the belief in the curative powers of the Bath
waters that some parish authorities gave assistance to their poor to come
to take them: the overseers of Box in Wiltshire lent young William Shill £1
'to try the benefit of the Bath,' and in 1791 those of Charlcombe, Somerset
sent William Miles there, in vain, to seek cure of his rheumatism, for he
died. The Pauper Charity was founded in 1747 in an attempt to assist the
poor of Bath with advice and medicine during illness; sometimes this help
was given in their homes.[6]

But charities were only cosmetic. By the late eighteenth century
the distress of the poorer citizens sometimes came to crisis point, especially in the overcrowded north Walcot area, the easily flooded Dole-
meads, and in steeply rising Holloway, where thieves and beggars lived
among dreary pot-houses and the stables of the carriers' carts. After the
bad harvest of 1766 the high corn prices brought out mobs at nearby
Beckington, many in the district lived on salt and turnips, and the Bath
magistrates issued a proclamation against engrossing corn supplies. In
1763 the first group of Bath workers, the journeymen tailors, had organized to protect themselves; in 1775 they went on strike and in 1784 used
force against their employers.[7]

During wartime shortages and high prices, in 1779 when mob agitation
became manifest, a Provisions Committee was formed and used subscription money to buy coal and food. Following the Catholic Relief Act (1778),
the Gordon Riots of June 1780 were a crisis for Bath as well as London.
This was ostensibly a Protestant protest: on 9 June a Bath mob of nearly
1,000 attacked the elegant new Roman Catholic chapel and new houses
near St James's Parade. The civic authorities read the Riot Act and
despatched the Bath Royal Volunteers to suppress the disturbance, but
during the night of 10–11 June they also in desperation summoned the
Queen's Dragoons from Devizes and the Herefordshire Militia from Wells,
and most of the corporation stayed up all night to keep watch. Seventeen
rioters were arrested and order was restored. Afterwards the city council
voted compensation for losses and the chairmen and others who had
patrolled the streets were rewarded with £100, the soldiers on duty with
100 guineas, and the Volunteers with official thanks. But two troops of
Dragoons and about 200 of the Herefordshire Militia were retained, and
the North British Greys kept order when the ringleader of the riot, John
Butler, was executed in Bath on 9 August. Troops remained in the city in
late April 1781.[8]

Bath had received a severe shock and could never be so complacent
again, for such disturbances marred its image as a resort. Some nibbling
measures of social relief now eased the consciences of the better-off and

prepared the way for more radical reforms in the next century. In 1785 Henry Southby, supported by the corporation, started Sunday schools 'for the improvement of poor boys'; by 1811 these took in 700 boys and girls, of whom one hundred proceeded to the School of Industry in St James's Street and the Weymouth House Schools, and contributed to both social stability and the supply of useful servants. Charitable collections were made for the victims of accidents to workers in the stone quarries on Combe Down and on the erection of lofty buildings. When, in September 1766, scaffolding around the Octagon Chapel being built in Milsom Street collapsed, and one workman was killed and others were injured, funds were collected for them at the booksellers and Morgan's Coffee-house. In 1791, when a builder's labourer received head injuries, subscriptions were opened for his family in five libraries. James Norman, a surgeon, helped in 1786 to found a small Casualty Hospital for such victims in King Street; it was operating fully from 1788, and in 1790–1 had seventy-six new patients with six from the previous year and 413 outpatients – the majority, 253, suffering from contusions, and 134 with wounds.[9]

Against the background of revolution in France and fear of social revolt at home, the pace of remedial measures in Bath quickened. The Strangers' Friend Society inaugurated in 1790 helped poor, sick strangers on proof of distress with food, clothes, coal and medical aid, and since sick-visiting under the Pauper Scheme was overstretched the Bath City Infirmary and Dispensary for the Sick Poor was established in 1792 and dealt with the more urgent cases and with the less serious as outpatients, but only those supported by a ticket from a subscriber. Between 1790 and 1811 Bath spawned a total of fourteen charitable societies.[10]

These were merely relief measures; stronger action was required to keep social order during the economic depression after 1793. Bath's contemporary historian, Warner, wrote of 'the melancholy effects of war' when several Bath banks and builders went bankrupt; widespread unemployment was added to previous squalor, and fear of unrest grew. In 1794 the corporation, by an additional charter, acquired the right to elect from four to nine extra justices. Night watchmen were introduced in the overcrowded parish of Walcot by the Walcot Police Act of 1793 and from 1801 in the parish of Bathwick, then being transformed into a new town, but no daytime patrols. The town commissioners provided the watch in the old city, but some inhabitants resisted the attempt to introduce a police force in 1807. At last the 1814 Police Act gave authority to establish a large force which though fairly effective had no powers as 'day police', nor jurisdiction in densely inhabited Lyncombe and Widcombe.[11]

As in some other provincial towns, by 1791 men of property were forming groups in self-defence against felons, forgers, receivers of stolen goods, swindlers and highwaymen, supported by voluntary subscriptions of 5s. each from people in the city but 7s. 6d. in the suburbs. The secretary, the ubiquitous William Meyler, reimbursed subscribers for their costs in bringing offenders, such as servants stealing coal from wagons and carts, to court. When the 'Loyal Association' movement swept the country in 1792–4 to combat revolutionary ideas the Bath Association for Preserving Liberty, Property and the Constitution against Republicans and Levellers was formed in December 1792; the corporation donated £50 to it, followed in 1798 by a further £21, and members were allowed to be armed. It was hoped that the free Charity School in Corn Street, opened in 1810, would improve the morals of the young and reduce the number of their crimes.[12]

On two occasions, 1800 and 1812, the city flared into riot again when bad trade and poor harvests worsened the situation. In the disastrous year preceding the spring of 1801 the price of wheat at nearby Warminster rose from 82s. a quarter in January 1800 to 160s. by late June, and bankruptcies in Bath extended beyond the building industry to include five in other trades: a tallow chandler, a silversmith and jeweller, a tailor and haberdasher, a coach proprietor and an ironmonger.[13] The city council had been concerned about the high price of coal in 1793 and of corn in July 1795 and had voted 200 guineas for poor relief. As at Cheltenham, inhabitants were urged to eat more vegetables, to keep to the assize of bread and in February 1800 to forgo pastry and rolls at home. Now, in early 1800, the Provisions Committee for the Relief of the Poor solicited subscriptions, and Lord John Thynne, one of Bath's MPs, headed the list with £205s.; coal and soup were distributed and rice was bought as a substitute foodstuff. By June 1800, 1,900 families, about one-third of the population, received weekly relief, and the following winter four tons of rice were distributed weekly to 3,000 families. Poor-relief expenditure went up by 50 per cent and at least £13,000 was spent publicly on relief and charity in one year. But disorder spread and among the crimes in 1800 a shop had forty dozen loaves of bread and other food stolen; forty-six poplar trees in a private garden were felled and taken, and one Michael Moloney went thieving in the inns, including York House.[14]

The culmination of the unrest came, after a 50 per cent rise in wheat prices in two weeks, in March 1800 when alarming leaflets were distributed and Messrs Williams's brewhouses and premises were burnt down. The government and the civic authorities offered rewards to informers and in late March, at a meeting in the Guildhall, the largest ever assembled in the city, the mayor explained the measures to restore order. An emergency committee was formed and the middle classes enrolled as night constables. In April the riotous servants and footmen were banned from public assembly places, so constables and civic officers had to help customers to their chairs.[15] The military stood by in July and attempts were made to secure the next harvest; neighbouring farmers, such as the Duke of Beaufort's tenants, promised the bulk for the Bath market. By 22 October the situation seemed stable, for the civic authorities invited representatives of the 6th Dragoons, the Bath Cavalry and the Bath Volunteers to a corporation dinner in May 1802 to thank them for their services 'during the late disturbances'.[16]

Yet the unrest among the working classes and the danger of mob rule continued, although R. S. Neale finds that after the disastrous years of 1800–1 there was stability and even improvement in real wages. Another study shows recovery between 1803 and 1804, a decline from 1806 to 1807, but a fairly consistent rise between 1809 and 1824, coinciding with the slow revival of building and improvement schemes. The population explosion added to the social pressures, especially in the poorer districts, like the parish of Walcot where between 1801 and 1821 the population, largely of traders and labourers, went up by 37 per cent – from 17,559 to 24,046. St. James's parish in the city moved out at least 139 persons and their families under settlement orders between 1800 and 1802 to relieve ratepayers. Other evidence of the undercurrent of poverty and misery was the bodies not infrequently taken from the River Avon. The fourth young woman's corpse in five weeks was retrieved in December 1813 when the local press asked whether the Bath Humane Society, earlier established by subscription, provided drags to assist people struggling in the water, a house to receive the body, and medical assistance.[17]

By 1805 there was great concern about the number of beggars and deserving poor in the streets. On the initiative of Lady Isabella King a society for 'the Relief of Occasional Distress, and the Encouragement of the Industrious Poor' was formed, backed by an annual subscription of five guineas from the corporation and followed in 1807 by the Society for the Suppression of Common Vagrants and Imposters. The public were asked to support it and avoid casual charity. Applicants for help had to take tickets of reference to an office in Monmouth Street, and there was a vigorous attempt to weed out frauds, but in the first year over 400 cases were handled and only twenty-five rejected. Many sufferers were helped during the unprecedented flooding of January 1809. The National Benevolent Institution founded at Bath in 1811 also assisted a few old people with pensions and coal.[18]

Domestic servants were particularly vulnerable in this resort, which employed so many, and a liability when incapacitated. The City Infirmary set aside two rooms for the servants of subscribers who paid two guineas, but 14s. a week extra was charged for inpatients and the cost of medicines for outpatients. The growing number of war widows and prostitutes was also no small problem; in 1810 a pimp used two 'genteel' houses in the best position as brothels. But the burden of relief work was not entirely placed on visitors and residents; self-help or benefit societies emerged at Bath from 1749: for example, the Servants' Fund started in 1808 had 101 servant-investors by 1811, and by 1814 there were twenty-nine benefit societies covering nearly 6 per cent of the population.[19]

Against the background of social distress and local political conflict, the amount of philanthropic help should not be forgotten. The subscription society which had evolved at Bath operated not only for pleasure or personal health but also for social welfare at lower levels. However, visitors in the better residential quarters may not have been fully aware of the erupting discontent. The city council, helped by the military and the watch, made vigorous efforts to contain the unrest and to preserve Bath's image as a fashionable resort. Astonishingly, the distress of the humble did not apparently undermine the social life of the elite, and the normal public assemblies and private visiting continued. In December 1797 Thomas Coutts, the banker, found such a crowd in Bath that only one house was free around Laura Place. In the crisis year 1800 at least 129 visitors arrived in the week beginning 22 September and the 160 a fortnight later included the Duchess of Grafton and Earl Howth.[20] Another visitor that year obtained lodgings with difficulty, and in 1805 she reported 16,000 strangers there. Bath's holiday industry survived the uncertainty of war, and the social unrest would have been more acute without the employment it generated. In mid-October 1800, the year of the riot, Richard Tyson arrived from Tunbridge Wells and, with James King, took up duty – at the Upper and Lower Rooms respectively. Bath was never officially 'Royal Bath', but it still attracted royalty and the aristocracy. The Duke of York, a frequent visitor, disposed of his house and furniture in the Crescent in January 1800 but returned in February 1801, with his duchess, to another home in Great Pulteney Street. The city council had abandoned civic entertainments from February 1798 for the duration of the war, but most normal social life continued. Jealous of the visitors' exclusivity, the citizens of Bath inaugurated their own assemblies in December 1800 'for the respectable members of the middle class' and by 1810 had their own MC, Dr James Merry.[21]

But the Lower Rooms on the Kingston Estate, which now faced the competition of the Sydney Gardens and the Upper Town, *were* losing custom. The second and last Duke of Kingston had a house, 5 South Parade, where he and his duchess had stayed in April 1772 before going on to the Bristol Hotwells, but he died at Bath in September 1773 when he was only thirty-six. On his widow's death in 1788 the estate in Bath, which in 1801 drew in about £2,400 in rents, went to his nephew Charles Medows; in 1796 he became Baron Pierrepont and Viscount Newark. During wartime Lord Newark tried to revive the social life of the old city. He enlarged and improved the Lower Assembly Rooms on Terrace Walk at 'enormous expense' and planned a new coach road, the later York Street, to link North Parade with Stall Street and make the Kingston Baths and Lower Rooms more accessible. His scheme of building a 'grand and spacious square' to be called Kingston Square, on the Ham opposite South Parade, was not realized, but he encouraged builders to renovate the old town. This improvement programme was initiated in 1796 when Newark's steward, Joseph Smith of Bradford-on-Avon, asked corporation permission to construct the new carriageway, but the city council, fearing damage to their baths and hot springs, appointed a committee to supervise the work. The council found negotiations with Newark expensive, so by February 1799 Charles Davies was acting as umpire to settle their differences, such as the length of an aqueduct leading into Lord Newark's baths.[22]

In 1806, when Newark was sixty-nine, he was created Earl Manvers, and his son and heir, styled Viscount Newark until his father's death in 1816, was involved with him in the management of the Kingston Estate, where the Lower Rooms were a particular problem. From 1801 onwards their able MC, James King, had spent half the year in Cheltenham, and when in 1805 he was promoted to the Upper Rooms his successor in 1806, Charles Le Bas, the MC at Margate and Ramsgate, also retained his previous post, so the rooms became neglected and were abandoned for a season.[23] An attempt in 1807 to raise money by tontine to reconstruct the Lower Rooms failed, and plans to erect a pump-room on part of the old Priory site in the autumn of 1809 were also unsuccessful. A Dr Wilkinson, now the tenant of the Kingston Baths in Abbey Street, made alterations which encroached on the pavement, so again there was trouble with the corporation. In January 1810 he made improvements at the baths which included a temporary room for daily water-drinking from 10 a.m. to 3 p.m. at one guinea a season and 5*s.* for the pumper. Bathing facilities now comprised a private bath for 2*s.* 6*d.,* a public bath for 1*s.* 6*d.,* and a shower bath, and new medical treatments, galvanism and electricity, were available. Wilkinson also ran morning and evening lectures on Experimental Philosophy at one guinea for twelve lectures, or 2*s.* 6*d.* for a single one, in Kingston House for at least six years. But despite the attraction of more specialized bathing and improving lectures his pump-room was not successful, for the one-guinea drinking fee was soon reduced to 2*s.* 6*d.;* he also sold bottled water at one guinea a dozen bottles.[24]

Although Le Bas nominally remained the MC the Lower Rooms were deserted by 1810, except by the Harmonic Society in January. But in August William Wilkins, Manvers' London agent of New Cavendish Street, and William Boord, a Bath solicitor acting for the Kingston Estate, made another attempt to revive the use of these 'very desirable' premises, offering a long lease to make their enlargement worthwhile. Thomas

Hobbes and J. T. Finegan undertook the risk of restoration at 'enormous expense', but the result was intensified competition for the visitors' trade. At the opening of the 1801–11 season the Lower Rooms were rented by G. Lanza, a musician, who advertised a series of twenty-four grand subscription balls, and later concerts, and to the outrage of Le Bas in Margate, ball-subscribers were invited to elect an MC on 1 November 1810. Le Bas publicly denounced this as a mean action, especially since the state of the rooms made his attendance entirely superfluous, and he undertook to return to Bath to act as MC immediately his Margate duties ended in early November, but Lanza retorted that Le Bas's previous efforts had not enabled Mr Gale to keep the rooms open. The subscribers unanimously elected Lanza's nominee Francis John Guynette, an officer in the Bath Volunteer Cavalry and a 'respectable and enterprising man', but on condition that he resided in Bath summer and winter and held no other post. New regulations were made for the rooms, a committee of twelve was elected to supervise them, and Guynette's first ball was held on 20 November.[25] Subscribers were opposed to an MC taking both a summer-season post at a spa or a seaside resort and one of the two Bath posts, which entailed a winter season.

This revival of the Lower Rooms brought their new tenants, Finegan and Hobbes, into conflict with James King, MC of the Upper Rooms. Guynette advertised an ambitious programme of twenty-six balls, exclusive of the MC's ball, for the winter of 1812–13 and promenade and card assemblies from the first Friday in March; but the weekly rota of public amusements was weighted in favour of the Upper Rooms and the new theatre:

Monday	– Ball at the Upper Rooms
Tuesday	– Ball at the Lower Rooms
	– Theatre
Wednesday	– Concert at the Upper Rooms
Thursday	– Fashionable Ball at the Upper Rooms
	– Theatre
Friday	– Harmonic Society at the Lower Rooms
	– Theatre occasionally
Saturday	– Fashionable Night at the Theatre

Hobbes and Finegan tried to introduce vocal concerts and promenades at the Lower Rooms on Monday nights as agreed by Andrew Ashe, the proprietor of the Upper Rooms, but King, to safeguard his Monday balls, objected. Hobbes retorted that with 10,000 visitors each season there was room for two simultaneous amusements, but he relinquished his concerts because King was said to have intimidated Finegan. Even so Thomas Hobbes was credited with having transformed that 'long-neglected pile', the Lower Rooms, into a 'temple of fashion and elegance'.[26]

Gynette guided the Lower Rooms until 1815 when 350 attended a ball in February and about 400 in March. The patrons were now significantly described as 'residents and visitors', the residents placed first, and the balls, previously ending at 11 p.m., now went on until 1 a.m., followed by an elegant banquet. But even with this attempt to enlarge the market, at the last ball on 9 May Finegan was in financial difficulties and the subscribers held a benefit ball for him on 29 May to offset his losses and in recognition of his 'general meritorious conduct'. Guynette was partly blamed for the economic plight, so James Heaviside of 14 Westgate Buildings acted as MC. He had already been the MC at Leamington Spa for a season and his dignified and polished manners made a good impression; after Finegan's ball he departed to Leamington, although another ball was held in the Lower Rooms for race week.[27]

But an MC had to be found for the 1815 winter season, and on 25 September Heaviside put forward his candidature from his Bath home, citing his Leamington experience; the election was deferred from 3 October until 15 November. Meanwhile James King arrived at the Upper Rooms from Cheltenham in late October; Finegan simultaneously announced his winter programme of twenty-four balls costing £1 6s. for three nights. Another would-be MC came forward – Thomas Jessee of Sydney House, an immigrant businessman from Reading – but the subscribers' meeting, chaired by the Reverend James Haviland, unanimously elected Heaviside, although the once 'indefatigable' Guynette was still in Bath; he helped to organize the Glee Club in 1825. Surprisingly, Heaviside was allowed to retain his Leamington post; a committee of eight, including Haviland, was set up to manage the balls; and the rooms, renamed the Kingston Assembly Rooms, were given a fresh start. Heaviside acted as MC for the first ball on 21 November, but persistent troubles led to a subscribers' meeting in December to place the rooms under 'express and determinate laws'.[28] Despite the efforts of subscribers, public social life was being undermined by falling custom and local rivalries.

The disruptive wrangles also continued between the corporation and the Kingston Estate. William Boord, Manvers' attorney, made a financial claim against the corporation in October 1810, but in January 1811 its water committee heard charges that Manvers' agents had laid a water-pipe to supply new houses in Philip Street; however, they decided to meet Lord Newark and Dr Wilkinson in hope of an amicable agreement about two clauses in the 1766 Improvement Act which gave the Kingston Estate rights to water supplies from corporation pipes at Abbey Gate for building activities. Again in November 1812 Manvers was ordered to remove stone posts erected on corporation ground south-east of the Orange Grove.[29]

The opening of Wilkinson's pump-room had increased the consumption of water on the Kingston Estate, but in January 1815 he claimed to have taken an extraordinary measure to remedy his shortage of mineral water. Henry Thompson, proprietor of the Montpellier 'New Spas' at Cheltenham, had agreed to construct a reservoir of over 1,000 gallons at Bath, replenished from his Cheltenham springs, so that Cheltenham water and salts could be sold at the Kingston Pump Room. The practical difficulties of transporting this water from Cheltenham to Bath, and Cheltenham's chronic shortage of mineral water, makes one suspect a hoax. Presumably to cover the extra expenditure, Wilkinson raised his water-drinking terms in February to 9s. 6d. a month, 18s. a quarter and £1 6s. a half-year, compared with only 2s. 6d. a season in 1810. In 1815 the corporation refused to allow Mr Mills, Manvers' engineer, to check the water supply and in May 1816 queried the possible diversion of water from the King's and Queen's Baths to the Kingston Pump Room.[30]

The long season at the 'Sydney Gardens Vauxhall', from April sometimes until Christmas, also lured custom from the Kingston Rooms. Subscribers paid 4s. a month or 10s. a season at this pleasure ground. (James Gale, the tenant, seems also to have had an interest in the Lower Rooms while Le Bas was MC.) The proprietors in 1803 were forty-three shareholders with a capital of £7,700, who paid a ground rent of £142 12s. to the Pulteney Estate. When the 'elegant and superior' Sydney Hotel and Tavern was offered to lease from Lady Day 1813 the rooms were let at one guinea a week each, although the rate fixed by the city in 1800 had been 10s. 6d. a week and 5s. 6d. for servants' rooms. By 1815 Thomas Jesse of Castle Hill House, Reading, who had aspired to become the MC of the Lower Rooms, had taken the lease.[31]

There is other evidence that despite wartime recession and fear of civil unrest, efforts were made to preserve the normal social life of Bath, which gained from being an inland spa away from possible French attack; in 1803 some Colchester families moved there. Indeed, Bath was now one of the twelve largest cities in the kingdom; and its population had multiplied to 10,127 by 1801 – 27,686, including Walcot, and with Bathwick, Lyncombe and Widcombe 33,196.[32] But its economy still almost exclusively depended on the leisure industry, and to safeguard this the corporation, the improvement commissioners and private entrepreneurs tried to maintain stability.

There was renewed activity from about 1805, when the new Theatre Royal was opened, the Guildhall was painted and repaired for the first time since 1784, and the waterworks committee built a reservoir on the High Common to serve St James's Square. John Palmer's Hetling Pump Room near the Cross Bath, with a four-column Tuscan portico, dates from 1804, and the work of completing the new Great Pump Room ended in 1806. Palmer, the city architect, planned a new street from Burton Street to Northgate Street, so in 1805–8 Thomas Emery, a wine merchant, transformed Frog Lane into New Bond Street with houses on the north side, and in 1809–10 Joseph Cave, a carpenter, built on the south side. By January 1810 Norman, a ladies' hairdresser from London, had opened shop at 22 New Bond Street.[33]

The corporation widened the bridge over the Avon in 1806 and the improvement commissioners steadily bought and abolished old and awkwardly placed properties, the legacy of the medieval city, to improve 'ways' and ease the flow of traffic. From 1809 property in Union Passage was demolished to construct Union Street, the essential link between the lower and the upper town, opened in July 1810, and the entrance from New Bond Street to the bottom of Milsom Street was enlarged to ease communication between the old town and the new. The building of West Green Park Buildings and East Green Park Buildings on the Kingsmead Estate was completed in 1808, and the improvement of the inconvenient and dangerous way from the Upper Bristol Road into Queen Square was from 1810 paid for by the landowner, Lady Charlotte Rivers. 'Improvements', reported the *Bath Journal* in July 1810, 'are increasing every year.'[34]

Another private landowner still investing in Bath was Henrietta Laura Pulteney, daughter and heiress of Sir William Pulteney, created baroness in 1792 and Countess of Bath in 1803, to whom the Bathwick Estate had devolved. Despite the financial setback of 1793 the development of the Bathwick New Town – which had great potential – proceeded, but in 1807 trouble like the Manvers dispute arose between Lady Bath and the corporation about her estate's private water supplies from three springs on Bathwick Down. She died in 1808 and the Bathwick Estate went to the Earl of Darlington, descendant of Anne Pulteney, and in September 1808 he tackled the water-supply question. The corporation filed an injunction against him to stop his workmen from digging, but by an agreement of June 1810 the Bathwick Estate obtained its water from one of twenty private companies. Darlington Street, Daniel Street and parts of Sydney Place were built in 1810, and Widcombe Hill, a road sixty feet wide from the end of Pulteney Street to Claverton Down, opened up Lord Darlington's estate for further development. Of more importance to visitors and residents of Bath who liked to take 'airings' on the down was the corporation's agreement with the tenant, Mr Faulkner, as approved by the estate trustees, to continue to pay the annual rent of £30.[35]

The original intention of the Pulteney Estate development had been to provide superior lodging-houses, pre-eminently the Pulteney Hotel in Great Pulteney Street, but the new Bathwick which emerged was a select residential suburb for the retired middle classes of means rather than accommodation for visitors, so reflecting the changing pattern of settlement and social activity in Bath. No attempt was made to 'discover' a spring or found a spa there, even though the nearby Lyncombe Spa, or St James's Palace, had been defunct since 1793. By 1811 residential penetration had so affected the original core of the Bathwick development – Argyle Buildings, Henrietta Street, Laura Place and Great Pulteney Street – that only seventy-seven out of 121 houses, or 64 per cent were registered lodging-houses, although some others may have provided furnished lettings.[36]

After a period of rapid expansion between 1789 and 1792, then recession, from 1805 the slow inching out of new house construction went on in all directions, providing employment in road-making, quarrying and building in the Bathwick Estate, in Widcombe Crescent and Terrace (*c*. 1805), Park Street (1808), Cavendish Place (1816), and some of Norfolk Crescent in 1810.[37] The seasonal fluctuations in employment declined as a more permanent population of the middle classes living on pensions and investment income infiltrated and gave stability to the local economy. So the Bath workforce did not in general suffer so much from the economic changes experienced in industrial towns. Although the 'lower orders' there, as elsewhere, were much feared and Bath was reputed to have one of the worst mobs in England, it was apparently no deterrent to increasing residential settlement, nor to wartime visitors. Visitors' lists, although deficient, were still of the usual length and retained a sprinkling of aristocrats, and compared with those for Cheltenham show more people favouring Bath than the newer spa. Social tensions between visitors and the residents, natives and immigrants, rival traders and different classes were now usually localized disturbances and did not erupt into general civil unrest and demonstrations. Among the porters of the coal market in the Saw Close, notorious for their insults and impositions, one in 1810 refused to load a coal wagon, but there the matter rested. Some groups of workers became organized and asserted themselves by strikes, notably the journeymen tailors from 1763, the staymakers and the shoemakers, all trades which catered for the fashionable visitors.[38] But the issue which once more crystallized some of the discontent was political.

Bath was a 'corporation borough', its two members even in 1831 elected by only thirty-three voters. From 1790 the Marquess of Bath's family supplied one member; after 1802 it was Lord John Thynne, who consistently opposed reform measures. The second member from 1808 was Lieutenant-Colonel (later General) Charles Palmer, who succeeded his father John Palmer, the mail-coach proprietor. Both were returned in the October 1812 election which provoked a self-appointed John Hampden, the Bathonian John Allen, to demand a vote for the freemen. A great mob assembled, the Riot Act was read, and the windows of the Guildhall were demolished. The situation became so alarming that all shops were shut, the Bath Cavalry and Volunteers were again called out and a party of dragoons was sent from Bristol and the militia from Oxford. Some of the rioters were imprisoned. The mayor had to explain 'the night of the riot' to the Secretary of State, and the abortive Bath Police Bill of 1807 became law in 1814. The peace of the city, it was held, had never been so interrupted, and the disorder was strongly condemned as a deterrent to visitors and likely to damage the early season.[39]

With the ending of the war in 1815 the civic authorities and local businessmen hoped for an era of prosperity, but receipts from the baths were falling and although Bath was now one of the largest cities in the realm the disorders of 1780, 1800–1 and 1812 had somewhat marred its image; newer spas were now in vogue, notably Cheltenham and Leamington Spa.

19

Leamington Priors and Wartime Minor Spas

During the recession of the 1790s, spa foundation halted. Philip Burton, lord of the manor of Burton Lazars in Leicestershire, optimistically erected a 'drinking-room' with an adjoining bath-room, but he died in 1792, and although in 1794 there were plans to demolish and rebuild the spa buildings on a more ambitious scale, war intervened and the lack of accommodation and medical publicity killed the spa.[1] Another casualty was Godstone Spa in Surrey; despite plans to refit it in about 1799 its custom had been lost by 1819.[2] Development of the Horley Green spring on the Drake Estate in the West Riding coal-mining area, discovered just before 1790, was also delayed. Dr Thomas Garnett gave approval in his *Experiments and Observations on the Horley-Green Spaw, near Halifax* (1790) and so many people came to drink the waters that Drake was induced to build a lodging-house, to be in use by spring 1791. Plans included a serpentine walk through the wooded spa site, a circular space round the house, planted with shrubs, a bath and more houses. Many water-drinkers lodged in Halifax, but the roads from there were a deterrent to travel and the enterprise collapsed. Dr Alexander, who sent patients in the 1790s, was astounded when he visited the site with Dr Granville in 1830 and found only vestiges of the spa-house. Alexander attributed the neglect to changes in ownership, but the two doctors thought the spring beneficial to the labourers from the factories, coal-pits and foundries of populous Halifax, and the revival of the Horley Green Spa was already in hand.[3] Another wartime casualty was Sutton in Shropshire where Lord Berwick, the landowner, intended to erect baths, but 'military avocations' in 1803 postponed his 'benevolent' plans until peace returned. He died in Naples in 1832, his project unrealized.[4]

By contrast the waters at Nottington in Dorest acquired some fame as Weymouth became a resort where Bath influences played a part. In 1763 Ralph Allen of Bath, advised to use sea-bathing for his health, came there and acquired his own bathing-machine. Others copied his example and Weymouth soon had hot and cold salt-water baths. Sproule of Bath invested £6,000 in the construction of a hotel and assembly-room in 1772 and Weymouth replaced Dorchester as the social centre for the local gentry.

Mr Plomer left the Bristol Hotwells to become its MC from 1778 to 1783, and by then local turnpike roads eased the way for visitors, some of whom came from Bath in the Bath and Weymouth diligence three times a week. Royal patrons arrived: the Duke of Gloucester for the winter of 1780 and George III, now spurning both Bath and Cheltenham, almost annually until 1805. Weymouth had everything to make it a fashionable resort except mineral waters, and that, wrote the Duke of Rutland in 1795, was a considerable drawback. But there was a mineral spring nearby at Nottington in the parish of Broadwey. Its water had been analysed in 1719, and Dr Archer had placed a strong protective cellar over it. Now its potential was such that it was deemed to deserve a cellar of gold. George III is said to have visited Nottington in 1789; he certainly went to nearby Upwey in 1794. So in 1791 Dr Robert Graves of Weymouth attempted to launch the Nottington Spa and published *An Experimental Inquiry into . . . the Sulphureous Water at Nottington near Weymouth* (1792). But again development was delayed until 1830.[5]

Not only wartime uncertainty but the success of a large spa could abort ventures within its periphery. Oldens Spa, or Spa Inn, at Stonehouse in Gloucestershire, a cottage north of Oldend Hall, had been in business for several years before an advertisement in the *Gloucester Journal* (16 April 1804) claimed that many and various people came there. However, like the wartime spa of Lower Swell, also within the orbit of Cheltenham, its appeal was limited.[6] In 1807 the spring at Lower Swell, west of Stow in Gloucestershire, was found to be a carbonated chalybeate water and attempts were made to promote it as the Stow Spa. The spa-house was an adjoining ashlar-faced cottage built in a style reminiscent of the architect of nearby Sezincote (*c.* 1805), Samuel Pepys Cockerell. A walk was laid out along the road from the spa to Stow, where turnpike roads met at the famous Unicorn Inn. In 1808 R. Farmer produced some publicity, an *Analysis of the Carbonated Chalybeate, lately discovered near Stow,* and once more the muse expressed the spirit of improvement; a poem on *The Stow Mineral* opened:

> What unto thee do not a myriad owe
> For the fam'd Fount discovered near to Stow,
> How many tongues, oh, Farmer will impart
> Th'indebted tribute of a feeling heart . . .
> New houses built in every part we meet
> And late improvements garnish every street . . .

There were well-furnished lodgings and other attractions for civilized living: Archer's lending library, an elegant room at the Unicorn fit for the nobility and used for the annual ball, the inn's well-stocked cellar of wines, and a pleasant bowling green with a neatly painted alcove where a good meal could be taken. Clifford's water-engine pumped water to each private house. Despite these advantages the Stow Spa failed because of its proximity to Cheltenham, and in 1814 the lease of the Swell Spa building, its pump-room and warm and cold baths, and two adjacent dwelling-houses with a garden, was up for auction. These buildings, one with an oval tablet over the door inscribed 'Carbonated Chalybeate, discovered 1807', still exist. Other small spas peripheral to Cheltenham which were doomed by its competition were the earlier Hyde Spa at Prestbury, the Newent Spa of the 1760s, the original Gloucester Spa, and the Walton Spa near Tewkesbury, where Cheltenham interests intervened to check its development.[7]

After the initial shock of being at war, the social life of the better-off went on as usual. The closure of the Continent to English visitors helped to boost domestic spa life, and between 1800 and 1809 spa promotion revived, with at least thirteen new spas. Horwood near the small town of Wincanton in Somerset was, like Nottington, well sited on the Bath to Weymouth road, and a new spa, Horwood Well House, was erected there by local businessmen. Wincanton had a good economic base for a spa venture with several inns, a direct coach service to London by Whitemarsh and Brown and a carrier service by Brown and Brice, and it was dominated by the Messiter family, attorneys and bankers. In 1770 Mr Messiter, the most eminent attorney in Somerset, had been to Bath. The Messiters had business premises in the High Street and drew on Bosanquet & Co. of London, but the head of the family lived at Bayford Lodge.[8]

When in 1805–7 Richard Messiter went into partnership with William Capper of Balsam House, owner of the mineral-water well at Horwood, south of the town, Messiter paid for most of this 'considerable expenditure' and used his London connections in its promotion. A two-storeyed limestone villa was built over the spring with a sunken bath and pump, a public room for visitors, six bedrooms, a kitchen, a cheeseroom and a larder. Other detached buildings were a milk-house, a double coach-house, stall stables and other conveniences. By 1807 a pamphlet about the Horwood Well water, printed in London, had run to ten editions and the bottled water was distributed from four London warehouses. London customers of this ideal rural spa included Clark Durnfold of the treasury of the Tower, who had six bottles of the mineral water sent by carrier and ordered a further three gallons. Despite the spa's ambitious beginnings, and the fact that in about 1810 Wincanton was a depot for French officers who were prisoners of war, and they were among the spa's customers, the Horwood Well Bank stopped payment in 1810 and Richard Messiter went bankrupt in 1819. The spa site was sold by Felix Faugoin, possibly the mortgagor, and by 1839 it was completely written off. It was still 'defunct' in 1869, but in 1970 Frank Mogg, aged eighty, could remember people coming in wagonettes to drink the water.[9]

The developing industrial areas of the Midlands had as yet no urban spa for middle-class recreation, but they were more promising ground for spa promotion. The most important of three new spas in Leicestershire was at Ashby-de-la-Zouch, where Enclosure Acts in 1768 and 1800 had given mineral rights within the commons to the Hastings family, lords of the manor. When in 1793 the Hastings Estates passed to the 2nd Earl of Moira, he prospected for coal and a mining village grew up around the Moira Colliery three miles west of Ashby. A saline spring was discovered during mining in 1805, and baths and a hotel were erected to serve the new Moira Spa, but real development came in the 1820s.[10] Sapcote was a hosiery-manufacturing centre where the lord of the manor, Thomas Frewin Taylor of Cold Overton Hall, in 1806 tapped the old Golden Well, which was reputed to cure scorbutic complaints, and erected a simple, rectangular bath-house of rough stone, now a private house.[11] Meanwhile Mr Reeve, a landowner at Shearsby, thought of enclosing a salt spring; the Bath Inn existed there at least by 1846, and a public well in Spa Lane in Wigston Magna, Leicestershire, suggests similar activity there.[12] Also in the Midlands, people drank the waters at Braceborough in Lincolnshire, where there was a shed beside a spring. Visitors lodged in neighbouring villages, and to encourage custom Dr Francis Willis the lord of the manor, who ran a private lunatic asylum, erected a cottage in 1803 to enclose a bath.[13]

These new Midland spas were insignificant; by far the most successful was Leamington Priors in Warwickshire, close to the county town, Warwick, and well sited for the exploitation of a spring there, Camden's Well, first noted by William Camden in 1586 and later by others, including medical men in the eighteenth century. By 1784, when a second spring was discovered, this village south of the River Leam consisted of the church, the vicarage, a mill, the manor-house where Matthew Wise lived, Thomas Abbotts' and two other farm-houses, the post office, the poorhouse, the smithy, the well-house and a few thatched cottages. William Abbotts owned one of the two inns, the Black Dog, where Warwick lawyers liked to come on summer evenings. The population was below 300.[14]

Leamington Priors had certain natural advantages for the commercial exploitation of its mineral-water springs which helped to transform it from a minor spa into a leading urban watering-place. The Leamington waters, rich in sodium chloride or common salt, are practically inexhaustible, whereas the Cheltenham Spa proprietors were often desperate to maintain supplies; Leamington publicists proclaimed the shortage of water at Cheltenham, and its fly-blown streets.[15] Leamington was endowed with three classes of mineral waters, and the gentle slopes of its promenades were comparatively clean because the dry subsoil quickly absorbed rain-water. The Forest of Arden provided the 'soft beauty of a woodland setting' and the shady walks so beloved by visitors, but also abundant timber. Other building materials were readily to hand; advertisements of building land in 1810 mention the wealth of brick earth and clay, but purchasers were not allowed to erect brick-kilns, except those needed for building on the spot.[16] Bertie Greatheed had a useful quarry at Guy's Cliffe, where in 1812 the Warwick builder John Morris was making bricks and erecting houses. In February 1811 alone Morris paid Greatheed £81 7s. for brick and stone. In 1812 Greatheed was told that his quarry would be needed for stone to enlarge the church, and to his delight, also that year, gravel was found for road repairs on his land north of the river.[17]

Leamington was also well placed to command the custom of the growing industrial West Midlands, ten miles from Coventry and twenty-two from Birmingham, and to attract travellers from other spa towns – Cheltenham, forty-four miles away; Malvern, thirty-eight; and Bath, eighty-eight. London is ninety miles away and the London to Birmingham road through Warwick, only three miles from Leamington, had been almost completely turnpiked by 1750, so metropolitan visitors reached the town with ease.[18]

Enclosure Acts had aided the development of Cheltenham and Harrogate by creating private estates, and the Leamington common lands, 990 acres to the south and west of the Leam, were enclosed by Act of 1767. The chief beneficiaries of the 1768 award were Matthew Wise, with 473 acres, and Mrs Ann Willes, and the yeomen John Lawrence and Richard Lyndon with seventy-six and sixty-eight acres respectively. In 1789 Lyndon sold out for £1,800 to the Earl of Warwick, who in 1791 passed the estate to Thomas Read, a wool-stapler of Kidderminster. Francis Robbins, a local gentleman, bought the Lawrence Estate in 1800 for £3,200.[19] So the Wise and Willes families, and Thomas Read and Francis Robbins, secured an investment in Leamington's future.

The lord of the manor, Heneage Finch, 3rd Earl of Aylesford, received only twenty-one acres. He lived about twelve miles away at Packington Hall and had some knowledge of the resort life of Bath. His mother died there in 1740, and he married Charlotte, daughter of the Duke of Somerset of Maiden Bradley near Bath. In 1781 the 4th Earl of Aylesford married Louisa daughter of Thomas Thynne, later the 1st Marquess of Bath, and her two brothers represented Bath in Parliament. From 1777 until his death in 1812 the earl held posts at court and was lord steward of the household from 1804 to 1812, so his influence in bringing the aristocracy and the fashionable people of the day to Leamington may have been underrated.[20]

A more practical aid to the rise of Leamington as a spa was the construction of the Warwickshire canals. By 1800 the Warwick to Napton branch of the Warwick–Birmingham Canal of 1792, to the south of Leamington, had been constructed and joined the Oxford Canal at Braunston. John Parkes, a Warwick banker and textile magnate, his brother William, and John Tomes, another Warwick banker, all had shares in the Warwick and Birmingham Canal Company in September 1810, and they became deeply involved in building operations in Leamington. Building materials and grain, and passengers in flies, came into Leamington by the waterways and the rivers Leam and Avon, which joined at Emscote. Bertie Greatheed often came in from Guy's Cliffe 'by land and water' and owned a boat in 1816.[21] Coal was also brought in by canal, chiefly from pits near Birmingham, and this 'Warwick and Napton Canal coal' was available at a reasonable price at the wharfs and the market in Leamington. In December 1811 Bertie Greatheed walked to the wharf to order sixteen tons of coal at £1 a ton, and he had his own wharf at Guy's Cliffe. Commercial concerns on the Leamington Wharf included Joseph Hirons, a dealer who sold out to Joseph Stanley in 1818.[22] The opening of the Warwick to Napton Canal was as important in speeding the development of Leamington as the new Avon navigation had been to Bath in 1727.

Despite its geographical advantages, the town which initially grew up between the Leam and the canal to the south might have remained a lesser spa, a mere appendage of Warwick, especially since the Finch family was slow to take an interest in it. At the height of the spa mania and the success of nearby Cheltenham the 3rd Earl of Aylesford (d. 1777) had refused an offer of £1,000 from Dr Holyoake of Warwick for a building lease or grant of the original well with a nearby cottage on his land – perhaps, like the next two earls, he was aware of Leamington's potential. The crude bathing arrangement at Aylesford's Well was a tub in the ditch near the spring, and the 'dipper' was the usual character at such wells, one Thomas Dilkes (or Dawkes). A register kept by him ran from June 1778, the year after the 4th earl's succession, to June 1786, and listed 114 cures of hydrophobia. William Abbotts, local farmer and owner of the Black Dog, determined to discover his own spring of mineral water and, helped by Benjamin Satchwell, the village shoemaker, found one on his own land on 14 January 1784. When Dr Kerr of Northampton and Dr Johnstone of Birmingham approved this saline water Abbotts erected two baths, one hot and one cold in a simple, single-storey bath-house, opened in June 1786. Visitors now 'flocked' in, including in 1788 the Honourable Mrs Leigh, a relative of Lord Leigh of Stoneleigh Abbey, a 'truly patroness visitor', as Satchwell described her, and Abbotts' Dog Inn was generally so full that in 1790 he began the erection of the New Inn, the first new house in the town.[23]

Encouraged by Abbotts' success, Matthew Wise of the manor-house found a third spring in 1790, the 'Road Well', on his land on a corner site opposite the bowling green and by the Warwick to Southam road, the later High Street. Here he built Wise's Baths, a single-storeyed but elaborate structure with a pedimented, arched doorway and a tall chimney; it contained two large cold baths and two hot baths with dressing-rooms. Cold baths were now less popular, but with canal coal for heating the water, Leamington could provide hot baths. In 1800 during the town's boom period, Wise built a new pump-room in front of the original building and improved the façade of his baths with attractive railings, and in about 1815, with ever-increasing custom, four more baths and a new pump-room were added. These baths, in an orchard, were sometimes known as Curtis's Baths under Mrs. Curtis's management. Wise prospered from the spa mania; in 1811 he sold off an acre of land in nineteen building lots in a new street, Wise Street, and another, Spa Street, was planned. But 'old Wise' had a fall in August 1812 and died at the age of seventy-six in May 1816.[24]

The enterprise of Abbotts and Wise and favourable publicity from Dr W. Lambe of Warwick, who in 1798 argued the waters' similarity to those of Cheltenham, added to Leamington's reputation and alerted Lord Aylesford to the commercial possibilities of his well. In 1803 Aylesford built a small stone well-house approached by a flight of steps, with a water-pipe outside for free public use. Those who came inside to take the waters were charged 7s.6d. for the season, 5s. a month and 2s. a week by Widow Webb, inhabitant of the well-keeper's house at the corner of Church Walk. As in many other contemporary spas, there were family-group terms: two members 10s., 7s. 6d. and 3s., and a whole family £1, 10s. 6d. and 4s. 6d. for corresponding lengths of time, prices which compared favourably with those of contemporary minor spas.[25]

Local people quickly cashed in on the boom. Richard Robbins conveniently discovered a fourth spring, the Bridge Well, on his land south of the Leam, where waters were drunk from 1804. He erected a bath-house and a small pump-room, the later Victoria Baths, opened on 7 July 1806. Standards were going up; his six baths were of marble with dressing-rooms, and there was a cold bath, a children's bath and reception rooms. He also let lodgings, but Mrs Cussans, Bertie Greatheed's friend, although paying four guineas a week, found her rooms so bad that she left to seek some in the newer part of the town. In June 1812 Greatheed thought the town fuller than ever at that season, but Robbins' Bath-house was untenanted. Robbins lost money and soon had to sell it. And yet another spring was exploited in 1806; the Reverend William Read, a Baptist minister from Warwick, built six baths over one in the High Street opposite Wise's Baths.[26] Leamington was now a flourishing spa with a choice of five places for visitors to drink the waters and four to take baths.

When Robbins' and Read's Baths were established in 1806 Leamington had grown very little – its population in 1801 was only 315 with sixty-seven houses – but local people were bent on exploiting the tourist trade. In about 1802 Thomas Sinker had taken over William Abbotts' Dog Inn in the High Street and converted it into Sinker's Hotel. When he retired in May 1812 it consisted of a dining-room, a spacious and elegant drawing-room, three good sitting-rooms, twenty-five bedrooms and other offices, with stables for twenty-two horses, and coach-houses. On Abbotts' death in March 1805 his other inn, the New Inn and Baths in Bath Street, came to his daughter, who still ran them in 1818. Her husband William Smith enlarged and rebuilt the baths and the premises were renamed Smith's Hotel and Baths.[27] The third of the early three inns was the old Bowling Green Inn, where in 1811 Mrs Shaw kept a good table with a bottle of port and 'a noble cask' always ready. This inn had a primitive assembly-room, only fifteen feet wide and thirty feet long, in use at least until August 1812. Apart from these inns accommodation was limited to a few humble cottages.[28]

Benjamin Satchwell, Abbotts' friend, played some part in Leamington's development. His cottage in Mill Lane doubled as a post office, and in 1807 he built a row of houses, Satchwell Place (later the Hopton Boarding-Houses), which led to Gordon House built by the Duchess of Gordon as a seasonal residence. When he died in 1810 his daughter Elizabeth managed the post office, as did her husband from 1816. Satchwell's main contribution to Leamington was his attempt to deal with the invasion of needy invalids drawn in by the renown of its waters. Assisted by the Reverend James Walhouse, in 1806 he founded the Leamington Spa Charity to help the sick poor, like the charity funds at Bath and Buxton. A set of rules was drawn up, collections were made through the hotels, and a subscribers' committee met at Sinker's, Smith's or the Bowling Green Inn. Beneficiaries had to produce a certificate of need from a respectable person or a parish officer and might receive a weekly lodging allowance of 5s., subject to medical supervision by Dr Watson of Warwick, or from June 1812 by Dr Wake.

Benjamin Satchwell was both secretary and treasurer of the fund, and annual receipts rose to over £39 in 1808 and £44 in 1809, falling slightly to £35 in 1810, the year he died. In August 1812 he was honoured with a raised tomb in the churchyard, fit for a nobleman or a gentleman and inscribed 'a patron and friend'. His successor as secretary and treasurer, T. Campion, was allowed 1s. in the pound as commission, and demand was so great in the 1812 season up to 8 September that 868 baths were provided for invalids – nearly half of them, 396, at Read's Baths, 210 at Smith's, 142 at Robbins' and 120 at Wise's. In 1816 750 free baths were given but, with the increase of visitors, donations totalled £119 a year. Leamington now had a resident physician, Dr Amos Middleton from Warwick, who produced *General Rules for Taking the Waters* (1806) and *A Chemical Analy-*

sis of the Leamington Waters with Instructions for Cold and Warm Bathing (1811) and advised poor patients. Mrs Greatheed was active in finding suitable lodgings for them and in procuring subscriptions.[29]

From 1808 the development of the adjacent Read and Robbins estates to the south began with piecemeal building, and a narrow lane leading due north from the High Street became Bath Street. Sites continually came up for auction: in August 1810 sixteen facing Smith's (the Bath) Hotel were sold and by late September nine. There was need of another hotel and other accommodation when, in September, two acres of land opposite Wise's garden and baths were for sale. They were suitable for a front building, large-scale improvements and the erection of superior baths, with the certainty, it was claimed, of finding springs of medicated water.[30] On this site the Balcony Boarding-house, Leamington's first purpose-built boarding-house, with a balcony fit for a hotel, was erected and completed in September 1811; it contained a dining-room, two parlours, a drawing-room and eleven bedrooms and had stabling for twenty-five horses and two open coach-houses for ten coaches. T. (or J.) Fisher took it, fitted it up in elegant style and opened in August 1812; in October it was advertised in both Bath and Cheltenham. A second lodging-house, the Oxford or Stoneleigh Hotel, built in 1812 before the street, Clemens Street, existed, was also owned by T. Fisher in 1814, but in 1815 this 'intended hotel' was still unoccupied and the Congregationalists met there.[31]

Builders remained busy; in the decade to 1811 the number of houses rose from sixty-seven to 138 and fifty more were being built. Leamington Priors was transformed into a small but fashionable resort which attracted some of the social elite: in 1810 the Duchess of Gordon, Lord Dormer, Frederick, Lord Montague, Earl Romney, and the Earl of Moira, who from 1805 was promoting his own Leicestershire spa. So some simple diversions were introduced for visitors; T. S. Palmer's 'well-stored shop' in Clemens Street, probably the first in Leamington, had a billiard-room which was opened with a ball in June 1810, and a temporary theatre behind Read's Baths was managed by John Simms.[32]

The development of Leamington had so far depended on the initiative of local worthies, mostly shrewd but simple rustics. It had no medical element until the advent, in around 1811, of Dr Amos Middleton, and by mid-1818 of the surgeons Dr Charles Chambers, Dr Birch and Dr Franklin, and no businessmen with adequate capital and experience to promote large enterprises. But by about 1810 'the spirit of speculation' infected Leamington, which became 'the magnet of speculators and builders'. Whole streets, it was said – with some exaggeration – were created in a day, and buildings sprang up as by magic. The opening of the two new baths in 1806 and the sale of an acre of land for 700 guineas in 1807 prompted some principal landowners to sell more land for building. Warwick supplied the necessary expertise, the solicitors, surveyors, auctioneers and bankers, and almost ran Leamington, where obvious opportunities also drew in immigrant entrepreneurs from the capital, Birmingham and Oxford, and some with experience of the resort trade at Bath and Cheltenham. Risks in this volatile boom market were great; in 1813 depression set in and several lost money. In 1809 William Olorenshaw provided Leamington's first reading-room and library with a shop for jewellery and fancy goods, and Stephen Probett, lately superintendent of Lord Middleton's stables, opened a large mews to take fifty horses and twenty-five carriages, both by 1814, but Olorenshaw, Probett and T. S. Palmer of the shop, all of Clemens Street, were soon bankrupt.[33]

Immigrants brought improved facilities and a more sophisticated life-style to Leamington. Fancy dressmakers and milliners came from London in 1814, the Birmingham builder John Webb opened a Leamington office by early 1811, and the wealthy and well-known James Bisset took his wife and daughter to try the Leamington waters that year. The potential market for the service and entertainment of visitors brought him back early in 1812 to stay in Fisher's new Balcony Boarding-house, and he opened a picture gallery and newsroom in the Apollo Rooms in Clemens Street and had had 400 customers by the first week in October. In March 1813 he settled permanently in Leamington with his museum of curiosities from Birmingham and charged a subscription of a guinea a season, 5*s*. a month or 3*s*. a week. He survived in business for twenty years and served the interests of the town. S. J. Pratt had already anonymously produced *A Brief Account of the Rise, Progress and Patronage of the Leamington Spa Charity* in 1812 with a second edition in 1813, and in 1814 Bisset's *Descriptive Guide of Leamington* followed. Another immigrant was W. King, mews manager at the York Hotel, Bath, who in 1810 opened a mews and livery stables with servants' lodging-rooms opposite Union Row in the new town now being built over the Leam, and by 1813 one Thomas Rackstraw from Oxford had a library of French and English books.[34]

The 4th Earl of Aylesford's death in 1812 had repercussions in Leamington. He had resigned from court in February, retired to Packington, and attended the opening of the new Leamington assembly-rooms in September, but he died on 21 October. The new 5th Earl of Aylesford now renounced his army commission and his parliamentary seat, presumably to manage his estates, but he was a serious-minded man, a bachelor until 1821, and the social leadership of Leamington went to the 6th Lord Middleton of Middleton Hall near Sutton Coldfield.[35] Yet Leamington eagerly awaited the new earl's arrival in 1812 in anticipation that he would soon make some improvements, such as filling up a noisome ditch in the town centre and demolishing some ruinous cottages. He refused several offers to purchase his well, being determined to maintain it for the free use of the poor, but his plan to provide a bath for them was abandoned. In 1813 he replaced the original well-house by a rectangular, single-storeyed pump-room with an arched entrance and an enclosing fence, but only for drinking, at 2*s*. 6*d*. a week, and the outside pump was still reserved for the poor.[36] Two of the earl's servants, William Squires and his wife, took charge and sold the Leamington or Squires' Salts prepared from the waters of both Aylesford's and Abbotts' Wells at 2*s*. 9*d*. and 4*s*. 6*d*. a bottle. Other capable servants trained in large households found opportunities in Leamington's expansion: Probert of the mews and a couple from Bertie Greatheed's employment who opened an hotel. Also in 1813 Lord Aylesford, as lord of the manor, allowed a Wednesday market near the Bowling Green Inn; as Bertie Greatheed noted on Wednesday 5 May, 'a market was held in Leamington today for the first time'.[37]

More hotel accommodation and better transport services were soon provided for visitors. By 1810 the Mercury Post Coach between London and Birmingham, operated by C. Hall & Co. of Warwick, came through three days a week each way, and the daily Leamington Post Coach came from Warwick. From May 1815 Bickman of the Plough at Cheltenham ran the 'Star' coach to Leamington three days a week, so visitors could easily go to both spas. High Street sites became even more valuable, and in 1814 Joseph Stanley purchased the vicarage house opposite Wise's Baths and converted it into the Crown Inn. Also in 1814 Michael Thomas Copps from Cheltenham bought Sinker's Hotel (the original Dog Inn) next door with its useful stables and coach-houses, and the Balcony Hotel on its other side, and converted them into the Royal Hotel, so that section of the street became the Royal Parade.[38]

The population of Leamington multiplied over sixfold, from 315 inhabitants in 1801 to 2,183 in 1811–12, as commercial opportunities increased. During the early boom, from about 1806 to 1813, businessmen and traders settled in and around the old town, and householders and cottagers alike hastened to improve their homes and let rooms at 10*s*. a week or more. Whole houses could be booked for five to ten guineas a week. By 1812 shopkeepers were coming for the season: Mrs Park with millinery and dresses from Dover Street, London, to 2 Clemens Street from mid-July until 1 October, and J. Smith with millinery. In May 1817 Mrs Allan brought her collection of hats from Oxford Street, London, to 2 Clemens Street.[39] As in other spa towns, a local education industry began to cater for visitors' children, especially their daughters. In 1812 the Misses Walker opened their 'select seminary for young ladies' in the new town being built across the Leam. Board with tuition cost thirty guineas a year, tea and coffee included. In January 1813 Mrs Clarke and Miss Brickman opened a competing school at 16 Union Place at twenty-five guineas. Such schools often took pupils just for the bathing season.[40]

Another investment in the leisure industry by some gentlemen in 1813 was a 'very neat though small' theatre, Simms' Theatre in Bath Street, replacing the temporary one; it opened on 26 October. John Simms, proprietor and manager of a company of comedians, was licensed in 1815 to perform there from 10 July for four months but not more than sixty days, normally three days a week. At the opening of each season between 1814 and 1817 Miss Simms, his daughter, read a prologue written by James Bisset; in 1814 a play, *The Earl of Warwick,* and a farce, *Fortune's Frolic,* were performed. There was not much profit in it; Simms sometimes wrote the plays and painted the scenery himself, and one Matthews, appearing there in 1815, had only 'one wretched country-dance fiddler' to accompany him. Yet the charges were normal: 4*s.* for the best boxes, 3*s.* for others, 2*s.* for the pit and 1*s.* for the gallery.[41] An alternative place of recreation was the new Ranelagh Pleasure Gardens and Exotic Nursery, ten acres of flower and fruit gardens east of Brunswick Street indifferently run from 1811 by Mr Mackie. John Cullis took over in 1814 and improved them by 1817 to match their fashionable name, with gravel walks and an orchestra where a military band played in the evenings.[42]

The search for mineral springs continued unabated. In 1812 Sinker's Hotel was advertised for sale with a spring of medicated water in an adjoining paddock where baths could be built as a valuable speculation. But the discovery late in 1806 of another spring, the North Well, over the old brick bridge, the only one north of the Leam, was momentous for Leamington's future. A 'group of spirited speculators' had decided by 1800 to lay out a 'new town' north of the river, contemporary with the old-town developments. To ease communications between the old and new towns a stone bridge (1807–9) replaced the old brick one, and by 1810 Greatheed had received £382 18*s.* for the stone.[43]

The diaries of Bertie Bertie Greatheed give some fascinating detail about the evolution of the new town. A Liverpool banker with a plantation on St Kitts in the West Indies, he lived in his Palladian-style house at Guy's Cliffe, and when he was bankrupted in 1809 he was saved by building promotion on his sixty-five-acre farm north of the bridge. He wrote exuberantly to Miss Berry in 1808 that he could help her to a fortune at Leamington Spa:

> I will let you land for garden ground, sell you stone, or sell you clay; you shall have salt water, or fresh water, or anything you please; for if we could but get you and Agnes into the undertaking, what a place should we make of it! Cheltenham should expire with envy, and Bath itself turn pale . . . .[44]

Other owners of land north of the Leam were Lord Aylesford and Edward Willes of Newbold Comyn. Some earlier building in the old town had been subsidized by profits from the Coventry silk industry, but the speculators of 1808 were a consortium of Warwick bankers and businessmen formed to promote the growth of Leamington as a spa, particularly north of the river. Warwick capital accumulated from the agricultural and textile industries was invested in Leamington, and Warwick labour was employed there. Through the Leamington Building Society, which terminated in 1811, the Union Society was formed by Warwick bankers John Tomes and John Russell, the treasurers, to subsidize the expansion. Other Warwick men involved were Richard Sanders, auctioneer, timber merchant, surveyor and self-styled architect; John Parkes, banker and textile magnate and his brother William, both with canal interests; the wealthy cloth manufacturer Joseph Brookhouse and some Warwick Dissenters. Dr. Amos Middleton, who had every reason to promote the expansion of Leamington, was also a shareholder.[45]

In 1809 Cheltenham envied the ease with which Leamington had raised a large capital sum, £50,000, as confirmed by Miss Berry. A recent suggestion is that George Russell's Birmingham merchant-banking firm helped, or that John Russell, 6th Duke of Bedford, invested profits from his London properties in Leamington,[46] which he visited at least three times, the first in 1808 accompanied by his Duchess Georgiana, whom he married after his first wife died at Bath in 1801. He persuaded his mother-in-law, the Duchess of Gordon, to stay at Leamington for two months in 1810, and he took a new house near Bridge Well in 1811. The first hotel in the new town was the Bedford, which stood on a plot purchased by a John Russell. Russell relationships are complicated – the 6th duke had twelve children – but this John Russell probably belonged to Russell and Tomes, the Warwick bankers. The link-man between the duke and the Leamington developers was possibly the Reverend Dr Samuel Parr, from 1783 to 1825 the incumbent of Hatton, north-west of Warwick, with whom the duke sometimes dined and who escorted the Duchess of Gordon to an assembly. He and Bertie Greatheed dined with Tomes in January 1810.[47]

There were Whig-Radical undertones in the Leamington situation, perhaps in reaction to Tory-Anglican control at Warwick; John Parkes, for example, was a Whig and a Dissenter, and William, Duke of Gloucester, a strong Whig, was 'much delighted' by a visit to Leamington with the Whig magnate Lord Craven of Combe Abbey in October 1812. Bertie Greatheed was no Whig, but the Union Society wanted his land, and between 1808 and 1826 he sold his entire estate for £37,827 0s. 10 d., less £2,013 13s. 3d. in costs and £1,000 for John Tomes's services. In the frantic speculation of 1810 some land sold at £1,200 and £3,500 an acre, but until 1814 the standard rate was about £400, compared with only £26 per acre on the Lyndon estate in 1789 and £42 on the Lawrence estate in 1800, both in the old town.[48]

By autumn 1808 the Union Society had raised £20,000 to build an elegant terrace of forty houses, Union Row. Pump-makers, brickmakers and labourers were advertised for and on the line of Lillington Lane, Union Street, or Lower Union Parade, was marked out. A Warwick mason laid the first brick in 'New Leamington' on 8 October 1808, for a house owned by Mr Frost of Warwick, and a new street parallel to the Parade was called Frost Street (later Bedford Street). Bertie Greatheed took his land out of agricultural tenancy, persuaded, T. H. Lloyd suggests, by the Union Society, who purchased the entire western side of Lower Union Parade for £4,090, but his diary shows that the stoppage of his West Indian rents forced his sale of further property in 1810. On 21 October, depressed by his 'very deranged' finances and advised by Tomes and Parkes, he decided on domestic cuts which his servants, especially John and Sarah Williams, his butler and housekeeper, took 'extremely well'.[49] On 9 October Greatheed conveyed eight houses to Tomes, on 2 November he sold frontage property for £441, and in May 1811 a further fourteen building lots for £1,805 10s. In September 1812 he ejected his Gunnery Farm tenant and sold the land for building. To his dismay, in October Richard, John Tomes's son, wanted to buy some of it at a price 'too low to be talked about', only £80 or £90 an acre. But by late November Tomes and Greatheed were expecting profits of £700 a year from Gunnery Farm land.[50]

In June 1810 Greatheed wrote of Leamington: 'the rapid growth of the place is really curious', and it 'assumes daily the appearance more and more of a confirmed bathing place', and in September: 'Leamington is extremely crowded and struggling to expand.' By March 1810 the new houses in the Union buildings were sold and the Union Society's profits rose. In July 1811 the society joined three houses to form the Bedford Hotel in the middle of the Parade, with the Bedford Mews behind run by Tomes's tenant, W. King. Obvious candidates to be the manager of the hotel were Greatheed's servants John and Sarah Williams, who, after much hesitation, took it in September 1811 and so embarked on a successful career. These 'excellent servants' left Guy's Cliffe on 25 October and by 11 November Greatheed rejoiced 'to see our business begun'. He frequently visited the Williams at the Bedford Hotel and once found them there with William Squires and his wife from Lord Aylesford's household, who had had a 'similar' domestic crisis earlier. The Squires now managed the Aylesford Well and some adjoining houses so profitably that in 1812 they were able to buy a building lot from Greatheed for £110 5s. 'How different from West Indian considerations', he thought.[51]

Lord Middleton was a patron and perhaps a proprietor of the Bedford Hotel, and he helped to negotiate the Williams's tenancy on 23 October 1811; they had free use of the premises until Michaelmas 1812, then a seven-year lease at £350 a year. The promoters of the new town, especially

Greatheed and Tomes, hoped that Middleton would use his influence to extend the season at Leamington into the winter by keeping his hounds there and making it a hunting centre. The underemployment of capital invested in public buildings was a problem in all spa towns. The Leamington solution of inducing wealthy men to take up winter residence for the pleasures of the field by day and the social round with their womenfolk by night was made possible by the proximity of the Warwick and Napton Canal, by which abundant coal for winter warmth was transported from the Birmingham coal-fields. The nearness of the Mendip coal-mines had already helped to establish a winter season at Bath.

By early September 1811 Middleton had decided to move his hounds from Wasperton, four miles south-west of Warwick, and although he lived nearby in Staffordshire he took the whole Bedford Hotel for six months and promised to fill it. He arrived there on 27 October and was out with his hounds the next morning. Lord Anson also came for a month with his relatives the Blackwells. On 4 December the worthy Williams held a house-warming dinner, a novel public-relations exercise copied at a Cheltenham hotel in 1813 and subsequently in others. Lord Middleton was among the 128 gentlemen guests paying one guinea each. Williams hired Anson's cook and paid £31 3s. for 109 bottles of port and forty-nine bottles of sherry, but he received so many gifts of game, venison, fish, pork and poultry that he hoped to clear £50. Despite this promising start Greatheed and Tomes were concerned in August 1812 that the Bedford was not living up to its fashionable pretensions and was too much like a lodging- and boarding-house, but by mid-October the fifty bedrooms were all taken at £17 each a week, and in late November Middleton returned for the winter. By September 1813 John Williams was discussing extension plans with Greatheed, Russell and Charles Smith, the architect.[52]

The shift of the bias of the town's social and commercial life from the south to the north was a gradual process. The first essential to propagate the social life of the elite in the new town was a new, large assembly-room to replace the two inadequate ones in the Bowling Green Inn and the Apollo Rooms in Clemens Street. Warwick businessmen, now including Thomas Heydon, again took the initiative, in February 1811 offering a premium of twenty guineas for plans for public rooms on a rectangular site where Lower Union Parade joined Cross Street. Richard Sanders, the Warwick timber-merchant turned architect, had supervised much new building, but in 1810 Mary Berry scorned his work: '. . . the houses now building are in rows, like any street in London, and are in the very worst possible taste'.[53] The rooms company appointed Charles S. Smith as architect, and Parkes and Tomes persuaded the reluctant Greatheed to invest some of his land profits, £1,200, towards the estimated total cost, including furnishing, of £6,000. The mason John Morris was almost certainly the builder of this classical-style, single-storeyed assembly-room, typical of the Regency spas. The main block, flanked by two wings, was faced with columns and had its principal entrance and seven windows fronting Regent Street (then Upper Cross Street). The ballroom, only eighty-two feet long by thirty-six feet broad, was smaller than that of Cheltenham of 1816 or either of the two Bath rooms. Two stove-grates four feet high, protected by brass-mounted wire fenders, warmed it, and when complete it was furnished with twenty-four mahogany seats with stuffed cushions, two large chimney glasses in gilt frames, three 'magnificent' chandeliers, and seven pairs of crimson drapery curtains. A card-room, a reading-room and two billiard-rooms adjoined.[54]

By May 1812 the Roman stucco was being applied to the exterior walls, but the premises were in use before they were fully furnished. A splendid ball to open these Upper Rooms on 24 September 1812 was attended by the old Earl of Aylesford and other local notables, about 300 people, and Bertie Greatheed thought it 'all very handsome and well conducted'. When between late October and April 1813 the proprietors discussed final furnishing details, including the chandeliers costing £1,000 each, the billiard-table, the advertising and the subscription, expenses had reached about £7,000. Subsequent legend was that £10,000 was involved. Thomas Rackstraw, the librarian in Union Row, and his wife were to manage the rooms. When these Upper Rooms opened, a Mr Owen followed the example of Bath and Cheltenham and in 1812 initiated a citizens' ball at the Old Bowling Green room for the middle-class residents, 'ladies and gentlemen, farmers and tradespeople of respectability' who were debarred from the social functions of the local and visiting elite.[55]

The proprietors hoped that the Upper Rooms would become the focus of a more sophisticated leisure life in Leamington, but the water-drinkers and bathers still depended on the old town's facilities, so while the rooms were being built plans were made for a new pump-room and baths using the North Well. Greatheed agreed alterations to the well on his land with Tomes in February 1810, hoping to make £700 from the deal, but the supply of mineral waters north of the river was uncertain, so on 31 May 1810 they fixed the spot for another well, and boring 'opposite Harry Williams's house' began on 2 July. The progress of this well became Greatheed's obsession; he went there seven times in the next month as the level dropped thirty-two feet into hard rock but produced only copious fresh water. In September labour was withdrawn for the harvest, then boring was resumed in October and reached forty-five feet, but only brackish water. At last in September 1811 the 'old salt well' produced a sufficient supply of water, and by late November Tomes, Parkes and Greatheed had approved plans for the baths 'on a handsome scale' sent from London by Charles Smith, the architect of the Upper Rooms. But the baths company needed more capital, and by January 1812 they had drawn in Harry Tancred, a lawyer, although Greatheed hoped that he would not repent of 'the baths speculation in which he is so comically engaged with us'.[56]

The building of the baths, conveniently sited between the old and new towns, went ahead from April 1812, supervised by Richard Sanders, but Smith, the architect, saw the foundations being marked out on 19 May. Greatheed received £1,947 15s. for 7,791 square yards of land. By mid-June the foundations for a stone building were being laid, but there was a crisis in July when the spring of the new well temporarily failed, and Greatheed was exasperated by the 'knavish and foolish cement-man' Scope.[57] This feverish search for a mineral spring on Greatheed's land illustrates the economic potential but also the capital risks of spa projects.

Smith's plan for the pump-room and baths, elaborate by contemporary standards, was a rectangular single-storeyed building with a garret floor above, a colonnade of Doric pillars on three sides, and an entrance at each end. The long pump-room was to be eighty feet by thirty-six feet, and the pump at the south end had an ornamental pedestal and basin of Derbyshire marble enclosed with a mahogany balustrade. There were hot and cold baths, fifteen in all, dressing-rooms, ladies' and gentlemen's privies, a waiting-room for each sex, a drying-yard, and a bedroom and linen-room. In September 1812 Greatheed had estimated for ninety hot baths a day requiring 7,000 gallons or more, besides the cold baths.[58] To maintain the essential flow of water a two-horsepower Boulton & Watt steam-engine was introduced. This was the first application of steam power to pumping mineral waters in England, but it was adopted at Lockwood Spa in Yorkshire in 1827 and the Hot Bath in Bath in 1831. It was one of the wonders of Leamington: '. . . the beautiful engine . . . could force up as many tons of the mineral fluid in a few hours as would fairly *float* a British Man of War . . .' boasted Bisset. One Binns 'the bathmaker' supplied the bath apparatus for £1,140, a sum settled in September 1812 after consultations with Fox of Derby – 'a clever man', said Greatheed. Warm baths were no problem with abundant coal supplies to hand, and beneath the terrace were an engine-house and two 'boiling-rooms', each containing a boiler erected by William Murdock, a well-known engineer employed by Boulton & Watt.[59] This was the new concept of mineral-water baths, far removed from the old cold bath in a cottage.

By mid-October 1812 the slaters were roofing the baths, but progress was slow in 1813 and the proprietors upbraided John Morris, the builder. In late August the plasterers and plumbers got to work, and fluted columns brought by water to Guy's Cliffe and thence by wagon were being erected. Although it was not finished until 1820 the building was opened in July 1814 from 7 a.m. to 3 p.m., except during divine service, and Charles

Elston's band played there daily. The building, by 1817 known as the 'Royal Baths and Pump Room', had cost about £30,000, and in 1813 the proprietors invested more in laying out adjacent gardens and spacious walks, bounded on the north-west by the Mall, later the Promenade, where in 1811 Greatheed planted extra limes. A military band played from a bandstand during summer evenings,[60] so two bands contributed music to this pleasant health-cure and leisure centre, which added considerably to the quality of a stay in Leamington.

The first phase of the urban expansion of Leamington, from about 1806, was halted in 1814 and followed by four years' depression, as at Bath and Cheltenham, and at Gloucester where the existence of the new Gloucester Spa was threatened. By 1814 the fashionable 'new town' at Leamington consisted of the Baths and Pump Room, the Upper Assembly Rooms, the Bedford Hotel and Mews, and about twenty-two houses on the west side of Lower Union Parade and two dozen in Cross Street, but much new building had been erected south of the river. Yet although Leamington Priors was still little more than an enlarged village spa with a population of around 1,000, in relation to its size it had much to offer visitors in search of health or pleasure, with the advantage of both a winter and a summer season. The proprietors of the rooms now looked for a master of ceremonies to organize the social life there, and they were able to lure one with knowledge of spa society, James Heaviside of Bath, to come to view the place. Heaviside was recommended by Brookhouse and had 'very agreeable manners', and with his appointment to the post on 4 April 1814 Leamington's future as a major spa seemed more assured.[61]

Conclusion

In spite of the Elizabethan government's efforts to deter it the exodus of English people to Spa continued, although a domestic substitute, the 'Spaw' at Harrogate, was discovered and the water was drunk there, and at the other English spas which soon emerged. The only thermal waters in England then in use were at Bath, Buxton and the Bristol Hotwell, and cold-bathing was not then considered practicable, so in the early Stuart period a more convenient series of *drinking* spas developed. These, notably Epsom and Tunbridge Wells, were generally within easy reach of the court or, like Wanstead, near James I's hunting grounds in Waltham Forest. The Stuarts, especially Queen Henrietta Maria, were ardent patrons of the spas, and since court and aristocratic favour was important for spa establishment and survival distant Buxton, now neglected by the elite, declined. Religious and political considerations still coloured governmental attitude to taking mineral waters, but the medical profession, especially the apothecaries, gave marked support to the practice of bathing and drinking. Physicians wrote pamphlets to extol their local spas and built up profitable livings giving advice to patients at the wells. So although journeys were impeded by bad or nonexistent roads, the mostly rural spa sites were primitive, and accommodation, except at Bath, was hard to find, the social elite soon became addicted to taking the waters as a health cure during the summer months. By 1640 there were thirteen 'spas' in England.

The Civil War by no means entirely disrupted the spa trade. At first Bath suffered as a garrison town, but it later became a hospital centre for the wounded and prisoners were often released to take its healing waters. The restoration of Charles II – who, like many returning royalist refugees, had a first-hand knowledge of Spa – gave a new impetus to the foundation of watering-places, and Stuart patronage of the English spas was resumed, with royal visits to Bath, the Bristol Hotwell, Epsom and Tunbridge Wells. Astrop near royalist Oxford was a new spa especially favoured by courtiers, displacing Wellingborough in the Midlands. The North was generally neglected, although by 1700 Harrogate, with three large inns, and Scarborough had a limited following. The government no longer tried to monitor the life of the watering-places; religious and political supervision was abandoned in favour of a purely secular approach and free enterprise by local landowners in minor capitalist ventures, as at Sissinghurst in

Kent. Serious scientific interest in the chemical composition of mineral waters also boosted spa endeavours and there was a growing body of informed literature on the subject. The Royal Society listened to a paper on the Wiltshire springs by John Aubrey in 1668.[1]

But the medical men did not dominate the spas. A new type of social life evolved around the wells in the late seventeenth century, as health resorts were largely transmuted into pleasure grounds for people of importance and fashion when they dispersed from the capital during the summer months. Spas provided a novel kind of rural public life with varied social intercourse, a welcome alternative to the boring limitations of the country house. Land speculators and builders, physicians and others took the new opportunities for capital investment, not only in spa buildings and the growing trade in mineral waters but in the leisure industry, to serve the transport and accommodation needs of the visitors and to provide commercialized diversions to fill their ample free time. This vast market attracted huge investment, creaming off the surplus profits of agriculture, overseas trade, and increasingly later, especially in the North, of industry. Investment in the spa industry was a part of the commercialization of leisure in the eighteenth century to which J.H. Plumb has drawn attention.[2] It was bolstered by the better security of property rights after the 1688 revolution, the increasing provision of horses for transport, and the better roads to ease the way of travellers. The average speed of coaches, between five and seven miles an hour in the 1780s was double that of 1750 and encouraged spa visiting.[3]

A primitive well-house with a woman dipper, or a cottage bath-house, was no longer adequate for the people of quality and fashion whom the spa owners, especially the metropolitan ones, hoped to attract. The provision of local amenities, pump-rooms and assembly-rooms in landscaped surroundings with sometimes specialized card-, dancing-, raffling- and music-rooms, and also coffee-houses, libraries, reading-rooms, pleasure gardens, and even shops, now became commercially viable. Originally primitive buildings like barns served as playhouses, but seven spa towns – Bath, Buxton, Cheltenham, Harrogate, Leamington, Scarborough and Tunbridge Wells – had purpose-built theatres before 1815. The shortage of lodgings for visitors, especially where spas developed in rural areas and tents were used at first, gave other opportunities to entrepreneurs. The erection of lodging-houses and larger inns, and later a few hotels, often preceded the provision of other amenities, and Epsom and Tunbridge Wells supplied an outlet for London capital. Bristol interests were involved at Bath and Clifton, and Liverpool merchants bought up land at Cheltenham and Leamington. Leamington also attracted capital from Warwick. Many lodging-houses and spa premises operated under lease; tenants came forward for even comparatively humble spa sites – like one

Spencer, who leased the Cheltenham Well in its original state from William Mason for £61 a year.

There were people with surpluses to spare for investment in lodging-houses, usually built in terraces, but the financing of bathing-places and drinking wells and of commercialized amenities and diversions was often achieved by the concept of a seasonal subscription, a device never before used on such a scale, by which the consumer paid for the use of premises and for services in advance for a fixed period, not at the point of consumption. Not only the proprietor but a number of employees depended on the financial stability of spa enterprises for their livelihood, and so the subscription society was born. Subscription could be used to anticipate revenue and to underwrite the cost of new ventures with comparatively little risk to the entrepreneur. Once captured by the initial payment the consumer's attendance at the relevant place or function was almost assured, and he might be lured into other incidental expenditure. Subscription, a sure way to commercialize leisure, was applied to all manner of projects – the provision of music and music-rooms, small theatres, coffee-houses with the use of newspapers, reading-rooms, libraries, pleasure gardens, balls and assemblies, as well as bath-houses and pump-rooms. John King the apothecary had recruited 448 subscribers to mount his Bungay Spa by 1728, and the environment of the Old Well at Cheltenham was landscaped with the Well Walk paid for by subscribers, 655 in 1748. The seasonal subscription to the walks there was 2*s.* in 1745, but had risen to 2*s.* 6*d.* by 1781.

The more modest spas with a primitive and utilitarian well-house or a cottage-type bath-house involved little capital expenditure and were mostly promoted by the landowning classes, who saw them as a profitable addition to their estate revenues. Out of forty-eight spas founded between 1660 and 1815 for which the relevant details are available, over half were established by landowners, twenty-four by the gentry and seven by the aristocracy, but twenty-one medical men were involved, some as supporters. For obvious reasons the local physicians and apothecaries generally favoured consumption on the spot rather than the retail distribution of waters, although both were practised. A considerable domestic trade in mineral waters had been organized by the eighteenth century. Largely concentrated in the hands of four specialist London merchants, it was part of the coastal trade, but mostly depended on carriers' carts and wagons. So there was a proliferation of minor spas after 1660; by 1699 there were sixty.[4]

A revised approach to spas then stimulated the formation of others. A new school of publicists, notably Sir John Floyer, decried the water-drinking prescribed by the seventeenth-century 'chemical doctors' and argued in favour of a revival of the bold practice of cold-bathing, in the manner of the Greeks and Romans. This opened more opportunities for landowners with convenient springs of water on their estates, and from 1700 to 1750 thirty-four new spas were established.[5] At the same time the expansion of Bath, Epsom and Tunbridge Wells accelerated but the rate of new promotions had slowed down, and apart from the venture at Somersham none of the aristocracy were involved, except as visitors. This was perhaps because monarchical patronage had been withdrawn in 1714. The Hanoverian kings drank the waters of Pyrmont in Germany which, with those of Spa, were now imported into England in large quantities; and, perhaps suspecting Stuart loyalties among the spa-goers, none of them or their queens went to an English spa, except George II briefly to Sydenham and George III with his family to Cheltenham in 1788.

But the Hanoverian princes and princesses were frequent visitors to spas and, like the nobility and lesser people, they travelled round to several, so general was the habit of taking a holiday at a watering-place. Frederick, Prince of Wales (d. 1751) was, for example, at Bath in 1738, Astrop and Tunbridge Wells in 1739 and Southampton in 1750. Princess Amelia, his sister and daughter of George II, was the first Hanoverian belatedly to honour Bath in 1728, and she returned in 1734, 1752, 1754 and in October 1767, when she said that she did not go to bed for nine nights.[6] She also went to Tunbridge Wells in 1753, 1762 and 1763. Edward, 10th Duke of York, brother of George III, patronized Southampton and was at Tunbridge Wells in 1765 and the Hotwells in 1766. Another indefatigable patron was Frederick, 11th Duke of York, his nephew, who was at Bath and Cheltenham in 1788 and revisited Bath in 1795, 1800 and 1801. Bath tried in vain to attract George III after the Cheltenham visit and attempted to gain the accolade of a visit in October 1800, following his two months at Weymouth, but nothing came of this.[7]

The second half of the eighteenth century, from 1750 until the outbreak of war in 1793, saw the most remarkable expansion of this holiday industry, helped especially by the improvements in transport, the provision of more horses, an expanding coach industry, and the turnpike mania of 1751 to 1773. Although the impetus to road improvement then declined it revived sharply in the 1790s. Many spa travellers on horseback or in their horse-drawn vehicles, the coaches, calashes and cabriolets, and the wagons and carts conveying their luggage or bringing in their provisions had the advantage of better roads for at least a part of their journey. Commercial transport, the public coach and wagon services, also proliferated, although some of this was only seasonal, expressly for the holiday trade. Improvements in water transport, as at Bath in 1727 and Leamington in 1790, also helped the movement of building materials, coal and food, and Enclosure Acts at Buxton, Cheltenham and Harrogate made possible the creation of private estates, all of which precipitated some development towards a few large, urban spas. Older settlements, notably Bath and Cheltenham, with existing houses adaptable for visitors, markets and shops, on which the spa industry could be grafted, had an initial advantage. But new towns, residential and purpose-built for the visitors, began to be constructed as appendages to older spa settlements, beginning with Bath in 1727; at the same time, between 1750 and 1790, thirty-nine new minor spas had been created as well as many which cannot be dated, and there were developments at thirteen existing spas.

The vast amount of capital invested in the spa holiday trade up to 1815 is impossible to assess, but it is obvious that this growth industry generated an enormous volume of employment in accommodating visitors and servicing their needs, especially among domestic servants. Large sums were spent on building lodging-houses and inns alone, and the social revolution brought about by the introduction of spa holidays bolstered the national economy, like developments in commerce, agriculture, transport and industry. It has been estimated that £3 million was spent on the building of Bath alone up to 1812, and 5,000 houses were erected there between 1720 and 1800. Building on the Kingston Estate in Bath between 1740 and 1749 cost £72,300 and improvements on municipal property there nearly £600,000 between 1786 and 1799. The New Assembly Room at Bath in 1771 took £23,000 from its investors, but the much more modest one at Leamington in 1812, with its furniture, absorbed at least £7,000. Standards and costs rose, and the Leamington Pump Room of 1812–14 cost £30,000, but the Manor Baths at Askern were erected in 1814 for only £1,000. The Duke of Devonshire invested at least £78,600 in Buxton's Crescent and stables for the holiday industry between 1781 and 1800, and the merchant Henry Thompson ploughed a reputed £10,000 into his Montpellier Spa at Cheltenham. The capital invested in diversions was also considerable; the Bath theatre erected in 1805 cost £20,000.

The increasing scale of finance tied up in buildings which were unused or under-used for about six months of the year led to attempts to prolong the season, which normally ran from mid-April to mid-September into October. In the North it began later, in June at Buxton and July at Harrogate, but in April at Matlock, which was in a sheltered position. At the more isolated rural spas it was shorter. Bath had a double season, in spring and autumn, to avoid the extreme heat there in July and August, and domestic coal from the adjacent Mendip coal-fields provided warmth for visitors in cooler months. Some retailers at the Bristol Hotwells and Cheltenham took advantage of this variation; they maximized their trade by packing up in mid-September and moving their stock to Bath to catch the winter season. Cheltenham also tried to establish a winter season by supporting the construction of a canal from Gloucester to bring in coal, and coal brought in on the Napton Canal made a winter and hunting season at Leamington possible.

Immigrants played an important part in the provision of capital, services and retail supplies in the urban spas, sometimes moving from one spa to another, so transferring skills and experience. London traders, such as milliners and shoemakers, invaded Bath and Tunbridge Wells from an early stage and later penetrated Cheltenham, Harrogate, Leamington and Scarborough, and to reduce the expense of setting up temporary shop often shared premises. Even remote Buxton had four seasonal traders in 1791. Harrogate drew in shopkeepers from Sheffield, Leamington from Birmingham, and Clifton, serving the Bristol Hotwells, from Bath. These roving shopkeepers were an important influence in promoting new ideas and fashions in the provinces, especially from London. Doctors and apothecaries also made seasonal moves to the spas, but Bath had a large resident medical group from Elizabethan times. As late as 1806 one or two London doctors welcomed a regular summer sojourn at Tunbridge Wells, where there were only two resident apothecaries, and Buxton had no resident physician until about 1769. Some of the wealthier spa visitors brought their personal physicians with them.

Initially spa visitors sought accommodation in existing inns, many of which were enlarged and improved, and new ones were erected from the post-Restoration period onwards. Hundreds of lodging-houses were also built, often in terraces, and a few even in remote, small spas. Cheltenham had one in 1733, more than thirty in 1780, but between 150 and 200 by 1800. Lodgings in the larger spas were usually let in suites of five or six rooms, and at Bath and Scarborough the proprietors were generally unwilling to break up apartments to let rooms individually. At Bath the city council, anxious to prevent excessive profiteering, maintained a strict price control of all lodgings, and there is some evidence of price-fixing arrangements at Buxton. Visitors staying in lodgings were expected to live on a self-catering basis, purchasing their own provisions and employing at least one servant if they failed to bring one with them, and they often had to procure some of the domestic equipment they needed. Although visitors bought their own provisions, the usual location of the kitchen in the basement was inconvenient for them, and cooking had to be left to the household servants. Visitors in lodging-houses depended on the facilities of the local market and shops, but some inns and taverns helped them by providing an ordinary, a fixed meal at a set price and time, usually in the early afternoon.

From about 1780, as expectations of what should be provided at the spas rose, the rambling and cramped old inns, unsuitable for the leisure hours of long-stay company, and the lodging-houses in some cases became neglected in favour of hotels and boarding-houses where families were entirely relieved of the chore of housekeeping and received more specialized domestic help. Full meals and basic services were provided in hotels and boarding-houses, although extras, like private parlours with fires, and candles and drinks were additional charges. The York Hotel of 1765–9 in Bath's new town, with its ample stable accommodation in the rear, was the first purpose-built hotel in a spa town. In 1785 Mrs Edwards's hotel was erected at Cheltenham, which by 1805 also had the York Hotel and Smith's Boarding-house, later known as Fisher's Hotel. The Crescent at Buxton (1786) originally had two hotels, and Matlock was aggrandized by the Great Hotel in 1789. William Abbotts' New Inn at Leamington (1790) was by 1810 transformed into Smith's Hotel, later the Bath Hotel, and his Black Dog Inn, enlarged and improved by Thomas Sinker, was in 1812 dubbed 'the long-established hotel of Sinker'. The growing number of boarding-houses were less grand and were favoured by those of middling and lower rank.

Lodging-house keepers endured a precarious livelihood and a brief season, so they often found a second employment as traders. As the consumption of retail goods and specialized services grew, and some achieved a high standard of quality, the occupation structure of the spas became more complex. This was especially true of Bath. Epsom and Tunbridge Wells also had shops by 1700, Hampstead by about 1701; Astrop had one by 1740, and Harrogate had one kept by J. Ross in 1736 and E. Hargreaves's mixed emporium by 1792.

Any figures of the number of visitors coming to the spas must be tentative and based on contemporary – possibly rather wild – estimates, which speak of people coming in their 'hundreds', even to the minor ones. Bath dominated the spa market, allegedly drawing in about 10,000 for the season 1812–13. Harrogate, beginning a belated but rapid expansion, boasted 5,858 visitors in 1810, apparently seducing custom from Scarborough. Cheltenham, with a rapidly increasing appeal after the royal visit of 1788, came third with perhaps 4,000 by 1804, and in 1806 about 2,000 were signing its Well Book alone. Tunbridge Wells, originally second to Bath, had its figure inflated by wartime followers of the military to 2,458 in 1795. Buxton came bottom of the first league with lodging capacity of about 700 in 1806 and between 800 and 900 in 1813. By 1750 leisured residents living on rents were settling in Bath to enjoy its rich social life and varied retail services, thus giving more stability to the consumer market there, as they did later in other urban spas.

But the unprecedented seasonal movement of population put great strains on the local community and provoked tension between residents old and new, visitors and traders, and there were also strains within the 'company', as the visitors were called. Social control had to be preserved among the largely mobile population to ensure the success and economic survival of this new leisure industry; the price paid by visitors and local gentry alike was the acceptance of a degree of regulation, and payment for private space and activity. Bath set the pattern for the elite by initiating a sophisticated ritual of social behaviour which was quickly adopted by Tunbridge Wells and eventually by some other spas and seaside resorts, its participants divorced from the 'barbaric' traditional and popular recreations like cock-fighting and street football.[8] All who wished to indulge in the benefits of spa society had to accept this ritualized, 'polite' and public social life following a recognized programme of daily events lasting from early morning to 11 p.m. and the mixing of all ranks who belonged to the exclusive community. Social ceremony was enforced by the institution of a committee of amusements elected from the leading visitors and residents who were subscribers to the balls. They took action to prevent social anarchy where the local authority was inadequate to the task of maintaining order and a pleasant environment. Even the minor spa of Somersham had a governing committee for a while.

Another device for maintaining social control initiated by Bath was the institution of the office of master of ceremonies, whose occupant was elected by the committee of amusements. By the 1770s the MCs at Bath and the Bristol Hotwells wore the insignia of office, a badge. The function of an MC was to educate the sometimes uncouth provincial assemblies in standards of polite behaviour acceptable to fashionable London society. The Bath MC proved to be of such value that he was soon persuaded to share his services with Tunbridge Wells, and the precedent of having an MC was also copied at the Bristol Hotwells, Cheltenham, Leamington, Scarborough and Southampton. At Buxton and Harrogate, where there was less organized public life, the MC was chosen from among the visitors for the duration of his stay only. Quiet Malvern and Matlock, both inn-orientated and with little public life, never elected an MC.

The office of MC became professionalized, some of its holders making a career of it. The plum post at Bath was the ultimate promotion, then Cheltenham, and experience at Bath was always a recommendation for recruitment elsewhere. Bath had two MCs from 1777, and even the small spa of Melksham attempted to ape it when it borrowed one in 1818. Seaside resorts also copied the example, and Brighton, Weymouth and Ramsgate with Margate all had MCs by 1806. The MC received no salary, only the proceeds of two benefit balls a year and donations from subscribers to the balls. His chief duties, as Richard Nash developed the post at Bath, were to preside over the functions in the rooms, to ritualize them by 'rules', and to integrate newcomers into local society. The balls and other social functions held in the assembly-rooms followed a fixed weekly pattern, and where two sets of rooms were in operation, as at Bath, Cheltenham, Harrogate and Tunbridge Wells, a joint programme operated.

The elite visitors tried to maintain their social exclusivity by their choice of residential district, the use of subscription and the power of the purse. In 1766 a customer at the private Kingston Baths in Bath could have fourteen baths at 5s. a time – for the sum which a servant girl took a whole year to earn.[9] Even the local tradespeople, however affluent, were debarred from the assemblies of the company, so they began to organize their own social life. When the new Guildhall at Bath was opened the city council reserved it for the use of citizens only, and from December 1800 the tradesmen, aping their betters, began to hold their own balls there. Cheltenham copied this example with a tradesmen's ball and supper in 1809, and Leamington followed suit in 1812.

Publicity about local functions and facilities was essential to their success. By the mid-eighteenth century the original kind of medical puff extolling the virtues of the local waters was being supplemented by historical and descriptive accounts of the spa towns and their local places of interest, part of a general movement towards the writing of town histories.[10] By 1800 more general surveys of several watering-places combined in one volume were appearing to aid the tourists who frequently visited several spas. Local sources of information from the mid-eighteenth century were the proliferating local and county newspapers which carried advertisements of spas from April to October. Bath had its own newspapers from 1744 and Cheltenham from 1809, and the commercial libraries also acted as news centres and registries for lodgings and servants.

Although the social life of the spas was geared to the elite, in their train came a multitude of labouring poor, the unemployed, tricksters and other doubtful characters, and the sick poor for whom specific charitable provision in taking the waters was frequently made. The social tensions resulting from this influx and over-rapid expansion were particularly acute in Bath and Cheltenham, where in each case two Improvement Acts were obtained before 1815, and vigilante groups were organized there when a national rash of rioting, the result of harvest failure and trade slumps, broke out between 1792 and 1801.[11]

The outbreak of war in 1793 caused a recession in spa promotion, halting much building at Bath and Clifton, and the number of new spas established between 1790 and 1799 sank to five, but the Regency Revival soon began. There were thirteen new foundations between 1800 and 1809, three at Cheltenham; Tunbridge Wells then acquired its first bath-house, and Lord Aylesford rebuilt his well-house at Leamington Priors. Five more spas were established by 1815, when peace brought hopes of a more active social life. Askern, a small Yorkshire spa with pretensions to becoming fashionable, acquired a hotel in about 1812 and the Manor Baths, using water from the Manor Well for hot and cold baths and a pump-room, were erected in 1814; the Capland Spa, the most westerly, at Ashill in Somerset, was 'discovered' in 1815, and the Gloucester New Spa was promoted between 1814 and 1815. Also in 1815 the Melksham Spa Company was formed at Melksham in Wiltshire to promote a spa after abortive attempts to find coal had uncovered two springs, and the spa mania reached Herefordshire with the discovery of a chalybeate spring at Ross-on-Wye, where a pump-room was erected. Apart from Askern, older spas where new development was attempted were Gilsland in Cumberland from about 1812 and Newent in Gloucestershire, which reopened in 1815.

But there is evidence that Bath, although by 1815 one of the twelve largest towns in the country, was losing some of its appeal, partly because its spa facilities were concentrated in the congested centre of the city, whereas the newer urban spas, Cheltenham and Leamington, had the advantage of several spa centres and more space. At Bath the number of subscribers to Marshall's library fell annually in the 1790s and he joined the several bankrupts in 1799; public musical performances were abridged because of insufficient support in 1801 and the revenues of the baths continued to fall until 1816. Cheltenham, by contrast, although experiencing social strains, was a booming and expanding spa town from 1801 to 1814 and was favoured by the Duke Wellington for a victor's relaxation in 1816. Leamington Priors was emerging as Leamington Spa and expanded between 1806 and 1813, and Malvern became known as a desirable and quiet retreat from the gaieties of Cheltenham.

Throughout the country some of the older rural spas declined and even ceased business, because of new rivals in the region, new coach routes which passed them by, or too little capital investment in lodging-houses, but in particular because their primitive, cold baths, so much extolled by Floyer, were now out of fashion. The day of the smaller landowner investing in a modest spa was passing. Contemporary visitors had higher standards and expected a spa complex of different kinds of baths, hot, tepid and cold, with better-quality fittings, instead of a simple, one-room structure. In particular they wanted the use of warm baths, now that the production of coal was rising and its easier distribution by canal was possible. In 1783 the architect James Playfair wrote a pamphlet explaining a method of constructing vapour baths to meet this demand but, like other contemporaries, referred to the 'enormous expense' now involved: several hundred pounds. Playfair suggested a London builder who could do the job for much less (This name and address could be obtained from J. Murray, 32 Fleet Street) and he published the plan and elevation of such a small, single-storeyed building, about twenty-five by fifteen feet, suitable for a rural situation and containing a cold, a warm and a vapour bath. It would cost about £100, or even less, but if, in the prevailing Palladian fashion, it were ornamented with a pedimented and pillared porch, £18 would be added to the bill. A boiler house, too, was an essential part of the equipment.[12]

Between 1560 and 1815 about 173 spas had operated in England, not all at the same time, and many cannot be dated precisely; by 1816 thirty-six of them had had some trade in mineral waters.[13] Some of these rural spas were a spin-off from some larger resort in the locality, periphery spas, like the many in Yorkshire around Harrogate and Scarborough and those near Bath and Cheltenham. The development of the English spas should be seen in the context of the growth of the English provincial towns in general in the eighteenth century.[14] Their original monopoly of the holiday trade was increasingly challenged by the seaside resorts, of which there were fifteen by 1806, not counting Scarborough, which was both spa and seaside. Marine resorts copied the physical features of the spas, their baths, assembly-rooms, theatres, libraries, reading-rooms, as well as their crescents, squares and terraces (some in the Palladian style) and their parades or promenades.

The social attractions of resort life had been observed by a contemporary in June 1792:

> . . . London is emptying very fast. The grandees are popping off to their country seats & the Cits to the watering places: washing off the smoke at Margate is I hear the favourite diversion.
>
> I suppose Cheltenham is very full this summer: tho' the weather has been rainy & unfavourable. I admire one effect that public places have namely that of bringing people together who would not otherwise meet: it sometimes also occasions people to meet together so that they cannot separate again for life . . .[15]

In 1815 the position of the English spas seemed secure, although they were under challenge from the seaside resorts, and the consequences of opening up the continental spas to the English visitor when peace came in June had yet to be experienced.

Abbreviations Used in Notes and Bibliography

The series of county histories, directories and gazetteers by S. Bagshaw and F. and J. and W. White are shortened to, for example, Bagshaw, *Derbyshire* (1846) and White, *W. R. Yorks* (1838).

County record societies are abbreviated as follows:

Beds Hist Soc — Bedfordshire Historical Record Society
Som Rec Soc — Somerset Record Society

Abbey Reg	*The Registers of the Abbey Church of S.S. Peter and Paul, Bath,* ed. A. J. Jewers, II (1901), Harl. Soc., XXVIII
APC	*Acts of the Privy Council of England*
BCA	Chamberlains' Accounts of the City of Bath 1601–, I and II (typescript, Bath Reference Library)
B & C Gaz	*Bath and Cheltenham Gazette*
BCM	Bath City Council Minutes (typescript, Bath Reference Library)
BJ	*Bath Journal*
BL	British Library
BM	British Museum
BRL	Bath Reference Library
BRO	Bath Record Office
Cam Soc S	Camden Society Series
Capper	B. P. Capper, *A Topographical Dictionary of the United Kingdom* (1813).
CC	*Cheltenham Chronicle*
CP	*Complete Peerage*
CPR	*Calendar of the Patent Rolls*

CSP Dom	*Calendar of State Papers Domestic*
CSP Scot	*Calendar of State Papers relating to Scotland*
DNB	*Dictionary of National Biography*
Gents Mag	*Gentleman's Magazine*
Granville	A. B. Granville, *Spas of England and Principal Sea-Bathing Places* (1841), (1971 edn)
GRO	Gloucestershire Records Office
HMC	Historical Manuscripts Commission
Lewis	S. Lewis, *Topographical Dictionary of England* (1840 and 1849 edns)
LP	*Letters and Papers of Henry VIII*
NRO	Northamptonshire Record Office
Pevsner Cherry Hubbard Nairn Verey Williams	*The Buildings of England* series by counties
PRO	Public Record Office
UBD	P. Barfoot and J. Wilkes, *The Universal British Directory* (1791)
VCH	*The Victoria History of the Counties of England*
WA	The *Warwick Advertiser*
WAM	*Wiltshire Archaeological & Natural History Magazine*
WAR	Warwickshire Record Office
WRO	Wiltshire Record Office

Notes

Introduction

1. J. Althaus, *The Spas of Europe* (1862), 267–8, 271–3; H. C. Tiebel, *Official Handbook of Spas, Watering Places and Health Resorts* (1896), 47; J. Haddon, *Bath* (1973), 43, 45, 46; R. Dunning, *Somerset and Avon* (1980), 36.

1 The Elizabethan Transformation

1. R. C. Hope, *The Legendary Lore of the Holy Wells of England* (1893), 51, 89; *Suppression of the Monasteries,* Cam Soc, 1st S, XXVI; Buxton Public Library, E. Axon, *Historical Notes on Buxton* (5th Paper, 1937), no pagination.

2. Hope, xiv–xxii, xxix–xxx.

3. C. Hill, *Intellectual Origins of the English Revolution* (1965), 16, 21, 25.

4. Antonia McLean, *Humanism and the Rise of Science in Tudor England* (1972), 199, 204–5; HMC *8th Report,* App. I, 226.

5. W. S. C. Copeman, *The Worshipful Society of Apothecaries of London: A History 1617–1967* (1967), 16–19.

6. Eleanor Rosenberg, *Leicester Patron of Letters* (1955), 32, 35.

7. F. D. and J. F. M. Hoeniger, *The Development of Natural History in Tudor England* (The Folger Shakespeare Library, 1969), 17–20; McLean, 212–14; P. M. Hembry, *Bishops of Bath and Wells 1540–1640* (1967), 121; Whitney R. D. Jones, *William Turner: Tudor Naturalist, Physician and Divine* (1988), 37.

8. BL W. Turner, *A Book of the Natures and Properties as well of the Baths in England as of other baths in Germany and Italy* (1568); Whitney R. D. Jones, 39.

9. *CPR 1549–51,* III, 309; Mr A. D. K. Hawkyard has evidence of an edition of the *Baths* and *The Englishman's Treasure* in 1596.

10. *CSP Dom 1547–80,* 43.

11. HMC *Salisbury,* IV, 587; BCA 1604 No. 45, 1607 No. 47, 1608 No. 49.

12. A. F. Pollard, *Wolsey* (1929), 295–6; *LP,* VIII, 408, X, 12, XXI (i), 568, 677, (ii), 291.

13. P. Lafagne, *Spa et les Anglais ou l'influence anglaise dans l'histoire de Spa* (1946), 3; E. A. Hammond, 'Doctor Augustine, Physician to Cardinal Wolsey and King Henry VIII', *Medical History,* 19, 240–1.

14. Both in the Musée des Eaux, Spa.

15. R. B. Wernham, *Before the Armada: The Growth of English Foreign Policy 1485–1588* (1966), 290–2; *CSP Dom Add. 1547–65,* 571.

16. *CSP Dom Add. 1566–79,* 295, 354, 365, 496; P. McGrath, *Papists and Puritans under Elizabeth I* (1967), 61, 66; Alkin Body, *Spa: Histoire et Bibliographie,* tome III (Liège, 1902), 216–18.

17. 13 Eliz. c.iii; E. St John Brooke, *Sir Christopher Hatton* (1946), 120; H. Nicholas, *Memoirs of the Life and Times of Sir Christopher Hatton* (1847), 24, 31. I thank Miss N. Fuidge for this reference; McGrath, 104.

18. *The Accounts of the Chamberlains of the City of Bath 1568–1602,* Som Rec Soc, XXXVIII, 4. 200.

19. *CSP Dom Add. 1566–79*, 486, 487; *DNB*.

20. R. W. Goulding, *Four Louth Men* (1913), 5–7; *A Calendar of the Shrewsbury Papers in the Lambeth Palace Library*, Derbyshire Arch Soc Record Series, I, ix–x.

21. HMC *Rutland*, IV, 387; Axon (5th Paper).

22. J. Hunter, *Hallamshire. The History and Topography of the Parish of Sheffield in the County of York* (1869 edn), 80; Axon (4th Paper, 1936); BL *The Benefit of the ancient Baths of Buckstones* (1572), 2 (in John Jones, Medical Tracts 1572–79); HMC *Bath*, V, 20–1.

23. Ibid., 21; Hunter, 81.

24. *DNB; Bath Chamberlains' Accounts*, 92, 124, 126, 141, 155, 167.

25. Ibid., 6, 63.

26. J. Anthony Williams, *Bath and Rome* (1963), 6–8.

27. BL John Jones, *The Bathes of Bathes Ayde* (1572), (Medical Tracts 1572–9).

28. Rosenberg, *Leicester*, xiv–xviii, 6–36.

29. HMC *Bath*, II, 20–2, V, 20–1.

30. PRO SP 12/131/2123; *CSP Dom 1547–80*, 631.

31. HMC *Bath*, V, 28; *Harrison's Description of England*, ed. F. J. Furnivall (1877), 347–9.

32. BL Cotton MSS, Vitellius C. I. fos 78–82. The original is PRO C.66/1181. I am indebted to Professor R. B. Manning for this reference.

33. HMC *Salisbury*, XIII (Add.), 171: L. G. H. Horton-Smith, *Dr. Walter Bailey (or Bayley) c. 1529–1592, Physician to Queen Elizabeth* (1952); D'Arcy Power, *Dr. Walter Bayley and His Works, 1529–1592* (1907).

34. Baily, *Brief Discours* (1587 edn).

35. Hill, *Intellectual Origins*, 96.

36. *APC 1581–82*, 111, *1586–87*, 19; HMC *4th Report*, App., 333.

37. *CSP Dom 1581–90*, 538; M. Waldman, *Elizabeth and Leicester* (1944), 198–9.

38. *CP; CSP Dom 1611–18*, 138, 531.

39. I. N. Brewer, *A Topographical and Historical Description of the County of Warwick* (1820), 88–9. I am grateful to Mrs J. Ward, the inhabitant of Bath Cottage in 1969, for information. In 1907 the baths were known as Rainbow's Cottage.

40. *A History of Harrogate and Knaresborough*, ed. B. Jennings (1970), 219–20; W. J. Kaye, *Records of Harrogate* (1922), xxix–xxx; BL Edmund Deane, *Spadacrene Anglica, or, The English Spaw-Fountaine* (1626), 7–9, and the J. Rutherford edition (1921), 9.

41. J. H. Raach, A *Directory of English Country Physicians* (1962), 119, 121; Deane, *Spadacrene*, dedication.

42. *Description of England*, 347–54.

43. Information by courtesy of the History of Parliament Trust.

44. D. and S. Lysons, *Magna Britannia*, II,ii (1810), 416–17, 791; Pevsner and Hubbard, *Cheshire* (1971), 366; BL G. W., *Newes out of Cheshire of a new found Well* (1600): *DNB*.

45. HMC *Salisbury*, XI, 110–11, XIV, 178; Lysons, 791.

2 Bath and Buxton: The New Vogue for Going to the Baths

1. T. Marchington, 'The Development of Buxton and Matlock since 1800' (London Univ. MA thesis, 1961), 33–4, 53; Pevsner and Williamson, *Derbyshire* (1978), 112; A. Jewitt, *The History of Buxton* (1816), 33–4.

2. Ibid., 28–9; *Benefit of Buckstones,* Preface, 2, in John Jones's Tracts.

3. HMC *6th Report,* App., 459; *Wentworth Papers 1597–1628,* Cam Soc 4th S, XII, 9, 28–9; *VCH Derbyshire,* II, 120.

4. *CSP Dom 1547–80,* 526; HMC *6th Report,* App., 456, *12th Report,* IV, App., 94, 109; HMC *Bath,* V, 21.

5. *Talbot Papers,* Derbys. Arch Soc Record Series, IV, 94, 120–1, 357, 366; HMC *Salisbury,* XV, 180; *CSP Scot 1547–1603,* V (1574–81), 204–5, 209, 214, 217, 219, 405, 408, 484; Arundel Castle MS, Autograph Letters 1513–85, No. 78. I thank Miss N. Fuidge for this reference; A. S. MacNalty, *Mary, Queen of Scots* (1960), 146, 224, 225, 238; HMC *Bath,* V, 4.

6. HMC *12th Report,* App., 167; *CSP Scot,* VII, 162, 191–2, 226–7; *Talbot Papers,* 106; HMC *Bath,* V, 5; MacNalty, 226.

7. *Talbot Papers,* 97; *APC 1575–77,* 7, 12; *CSP Dom Add. 1566–79,* 488, *1547–80,* 502.

8. *CSP Dom Add. 1566–79,* 488; *APC 1575–77,* 12; HMC *Salisbury,* II, 154; HMC *12th Report,* App., IV, 111; *CSP Scot 1547–1603,* V, (1547–81), 229; A. Kendall, *Robert Dudley, Earl of Leicester* (1980), 164.

9. *Talbot Papers,* 94, 98, 101, 102, 374; Arundel Autograph Letters 1513–85, No. 80; *APC 1575–77,* 361; HMC *Salisbury,* II, 154, 156, 157, 159, V, 69–70; HMC *12th Report,* IV, App., 112, 166, 167; *CSP Scot,* V, 234, VII, 162.

10. HMC *Bath,* V, 25; A. Fraser, *Mary, Queen of Scots* (1969), 438; Kendall, 174.

11. *APC 1577–78,* 325–6, *1581–82,* 123; *CSP Scot,* VIII, 650.

12. *CSP Dom 1581–90,* 63; Hunter, *Hallamshire,* 499; HMC *Salisbury,* V, 323; J. T. Cliffe, *The Yorkshire Gentry: From the Reformation to the Civil War* (1969), 21.

13. See p. 14.

14. T. G. Barnes, *Somerset 1625–46: A County's Government During the 'Personal Rule'* (1961), 3, 9, 11, 19–20.

15. J. Haddon, *Bath* (1973), 58–9, 68; *Bath Chamberlains' Accounts,* 19; P. Rowland James, *The Baths of Bath in the Sixteenth and Early Seventeenth Centuries* (1938), 12.

16. *Chamberlains' Accounts,* 26, 34, 57, 143–4, 159, 179; James, 16; E. Holland, The Earliest Bath Guildhall, *Bath History,* II (1988), 168.

17. R. Warner, *The History of Bath* (1801), 135; James, 15, 23–4, 31; Hembry, *Bishops,* 107; *LP 1543,* I, 197, 198, 551; *APC 1551–52,* 462; *Chamberlains' Accounts,* 149; *CPR 1550–53,* 439; S. T. Bindoff, *The House of Commons 1509–1558,* I (1982), 679–80.

18. James, 12–13, 113–17, 120; HMC *Salisbury,* IX, 179; Raach, *Country Physicians,* 113.

19. *Chamberlains' Accounts,* xii–xiii, 6–13; Warner, 241.

20. *CPR 1572–75,* 129; F. L. Hughes and J. F. Larkin, *Tudor Royal Proclamations,* II (1969), No. 593, p. 367; *The Injunctions . . . of Richard Barnes, Bishop of Durham, 1575 to 1587,* Surtees Soc, XXII, 120; Haddon, 68.

21. *Chamberlains' Accounts,* 44, 55, 71, 75, 85; Folger Shakespeare Library, MS v.a. 483, Robert Lesse, *A brief view of all baths . . . . c.* 1580.

22. *Chamberlains' Accounts,* 20–1, 25–8. Was the bishop's wife Anne Smarthewett? See Hembry, *Bishops,* 103–4; *APC 1571–5,* 112.

23. *APC 1571–5,* 28; E. Green, 'Did Queen Elizabeth Visit Bath in the Years 1574 and 1592?', *Proc Bath Field Club,* IV, No. 2, No. 19.

24. J. Nichols, *Progresses of Queen Elizabeth* (1823), III, 578; *The Letters and*

Epigrams of Sir John Harington, ed. N. E. McClure (1930), 393; *Chamberlains' Accounts,* 189–90, 208; *CSP Dom 1601–03,* 220; *The Chamberlain Letters,* ed. E. McClure Thomson (1966), 146–52.

25. J. H. Jeayes, *Descriptive Catalogue of the Charters and Muniments . . . at Berkeley Castle* (1892), 322–4; HMC *4th Report,* 365.

26. The main source for visitors to Bath is James, *Baths of Bath,* App. I, 153 ff.; HMC *Salisbury,* XVI, 269; *CSP Dom 1547–80,* 43, *1591–94,* 237.

27. HMC *De L'Isle and Dudley,* II, 439, 465, 466; *Chamberlains' Accounts,* 29, 38, 96.

28. Ibid., 69, 83, 135, 155, 170; *CSP Dom 1581–90,* 303.

29. *APC 1577–78,* 310; *1599–1600,* 286, 289–90.

30. *The Household Papers of the 9th Earl of Northumberland,* Cam Soc 3rd Series, XCIII, 8–15; HMC *Salisbury,* XIII, 481; *CSP Dom 1595–97,* 266–489; *1601–03,* 96, 238; R. Lacey, *Sir Walter Raleigh* (1973), 190, 258.

31. HMC *Bath,* II, 53, 54; HMC *Salisbury,* XVI, 52; *Lords Journal,* II, 274b, 284a; *Commons Journal,* I, 417b (I thank Lady Russell for this reference).

32. HMC *Salisbury,* IX, 128, XIII, 481; *CSP Dom 1595–97,* 266; HMC *De L'Isle and Dudley,* II, 446.

33. J. H. Thomas, *Town Government in the Sixteenth Century* (1933), 119–20; *VCH Yorks.,* III, 470. I thank Miss N. Fuidge for this reference.

34. James, *Baths of Bath,* 101; *CSP Dom 1547–80,* 43.

35. 15 Eliz. c.v; 39 Eliz. c.iv; *Chamberlains' Accounts,* 110, 135, 170; *Lords Journal,* I, 12, 15, 17, 19 May 1572, II, 6, 8, 14, 19, 20 1597.

36. James, *Baths of Bath,* 18, 69, 101, 103; *APC 1575–77,* 8, 147.

37. A. E. Bush and J. Hatton, *Thomas Bellot 1534–1611* (1966), 5, 10–12; James, *Bath,* 104–5.

38. *APC 1571–75,* 284; *1578–80,* 52, 117; *1581–82,* 236, 397–8; K. R. Wark, 'Elizabethan Recusancy in Cheshire', *Chetham Soc,* XIX, 120–1.

39. HMC *Salisbury,* I, 510, IV, 571, XI, 218.

40. HMC *Salisbury,* IV, 314, XIII, 473, 481; HMC *5th Report,* App., 311; James, 100.

41. Ibid., 55–7, 64–6, 68.

42. *Chamberlains' Accounts,* 105, 130; James, 74–7.

43. Payments abstracted from *Chamberlains' Accounts.*

44. *APC 1597–8,* 373–5; James, 71.

45. Ibid., 120, 138: Thomas Guidott, *A Discourse of Bathe and the Hot Waters there* (1676), 164–6, 174–5.

46. Sylvia McIntyre, 'Towns as Health and Pleasure Resorts, Bath – Scarborough – Weymouth' (Oxford Univ. D.Phil. Thesis 1973), 59–62; BCM 2 October 1616.

47. *APC 1592–93,* 266; *Letters of Sir John Harington,* 131, 135, 139; Haddon, 63; P. W. Hasler, *The House of Commons 1558–1603,* III (1981), 371.

48. *The Earl of Hertford's Lieutenancy Papers 1603–12,* Wilts Rec Soc, XXIII, 3, 5, 17, 150–1; James, *Bath,* 155.

49. BCA 1611 No. 51; *Chamberlain Letters,* 146–7; HMC *Salisbury,* XVII, 73; *CSP Dom 1611–18,* 140.

50. HMC *Salisbury,* XVI, 179, 310–12, XVII, 231.

51. Ibid., XVI, 276–7, 295, 308, 310–14.

52. Ibid., XIX, 132; *CSP Dom 1611–18,* 113; HMC *Sackville,* I, 213; HMC *Cranfield 1551–1612,* 158.

53. BL Lansdowne, xcii, no. 114, fo. 203. I thank Miss N. Fuidge for this reference; HMC *Salisbury,* XXIV, 203.

54. HMC *10th Report,* App., IV, 12–16; HMC *Salisbury,* XXI, 362–3; *Chamberlain Letters,* 90.

3 Stuart Patronage and the Drinking Spas

1. HMC *8th Report,* App., II, 29; James, *Baths of Bath,* 48–9, 117; E. Green, 'The Visits to Bath of two Queens: Anne Consort of James I and Anne Queen Regnant', *Bath Field Club,* VII, 222, 224.
2. E. Carleton Williams, *Anne of Denmark* (1970), 159–61, 163; *CSP Dom 1611–18,* 119–120, 185, 186, 189, 198; HMC *1st Report,* App., 107, *12th Report,* App. IV, 433; McLure Thomson, *Chamberlain Letters,* 154; BCA 1614, No. 54.
3. BCM 6 March 1613, 16 August 1614.
4. *CSP Dom 1611–18,* 274–5, 296, 308; HMC *De L'Isle and Dudley,* V, 307; James, 117; BCM 29 August 1615; *Quarter Sessions Records for Somerset, I, 1607–25,* Som Rec Soc XXIII, 67; *Chamberlain Letters,* 153–4; BCA 1616, No. 56.
5. Georges Spailier, *Histoire de Spa. La plus ancienne ville d'eaux du monde* (2nd edn, 1961), 55.
6. *CSP Dom 1547–80,* 503, *Add. 1566–79,* 491, 496.
7. HMC *Salisbury,* III, 141; *CSP Dom 1591–94,* 217, 234, 476–7; HMC *De L'Isle and Dudley,* II, 229.
8. HMC *Salisbury,* XV, 89.
9. Cliffe, *Yorkshire Gentry,* 177–8, 198; 13 Eliz. c.iii; *CSP Dom 1611–18,* 285, 300, 392; *APC 1619–21,* 395, *1613–14,* 41.
10. L. Stone, *The Crisis of the Aristocracy* (1965 ed), 15–16, 58, 618; *Chamberlain Letters,* 128.
11. *CSP Dom 1611–18,* 595, *1619–23,* 412, 586; *APC 1616–17,* 286, 336.
12. *APC 1601–4,* 53–4, *1613–14,* 41, *1615–16,* 164–5, *1619–21,* 206–7, 395.
13. HMC *De L'Isle and Dudley,* IV, 284; *APC 1613–14,* 447, 463; *1615–16,* 171, 432, *1618–19,* 185; Cliffe, 198–9; HMC *10th Report,* App., I, 599.
14. HMC *De L'Isle and Dudley,* V, 110, 112, 113, 221n.
15. HMC *13th Report,* II, App. 22–3; Lafagne, *Spa et les Anglais,* 4–6; *CSP Dom 1611–18,* 286, 384, 427, 458; W. Munk, *Roll of the Royal College of Physicians 1518–1700,* I (1878), 23.
16. *Household Books of the Lord William Howard,* Surtees Soc, LXVIII, 206. I am indebted to Professor H. S. Reinmuth for this reference. Lord William Howard (1563–?) was the third son of Thomas, 4th Duke of Norfolk by his second marriage. He had been tutored by a Catholic, Gregory Martin of Oxford. He lived at Naworth Castle from about 1604.
17. Gaston Dugardin, *Histoire du commerce des eaux de Spa* (1944), 15, 23–4; Lafagne, 4; HMC *De L'Isle and Dudley,* IV, 284.
18. HMC *Salisbury,* XV, 138, XX, 74.
19. Munk, *Roll of Physicians,* I, 100–2; *APC 1616–17,* 286, 1618–19, 442; HMC *De L'Isle and Dudley,* V, 110; Lafagne, 4.
20. W. Addison, *English Spas* (1951), 51–2; *CSP Dom 1611–18,* 135, 145, 381, 504, 568, *1619–23,* 54, 62, 72, 75; *VCH Essex,* VI, 324.
21. Addison, 47; *VCH Herts.,* II, 358–60; Capper.
22. HMC *De L'Isle and Dudley,* II, 466; *CSP Dom 1598–1601,* 415, 463; *DNB; Bath Chamberlains' Accounts,* 110, 135, 141, 170.
23. *DNB;* R. Onely, *A General Account of Tunbridge Wells, and its Environs . . .* (1771), 1–3.
24. *A Forest of Varieties* (Printed by Richard Cotes, 1654), 134.

25. A. Savidge, *Royal Tunbridge Wells* (1975), 25–8; *Camden Miscellany,* III, C. S. 61, iii–vi; J. Sprange, *Tunbridge Wells Guide* (1780), 12; *CSP Dom 1619–23,* 72; G. R. Smith, *Without Touch of Dishonour: the life and death of Sir Henry Slingsby 1602–58* (1968), 19.

26. C. W. Chalklin, *Seventeenth-Century Kent: a social and economic history* (1965), 157; Savidge, 26.

27. C. Oman, *Henrietta Maria* (1936), 162; *The Diary of John Evelyn,* ed. E. S. de Beer, II (1955), 155fn 6.

28. *VCH Northants.,* IV, 139; HMC *11th Report,* App., I, 168; *CSP Dom 1623–25,* 327, 329–30, *1625–26,* 61–2.

29. P. Whalley, *The History and Antiquities of Northamptonshire,* II (1791), 149; *CSP Dom 1627–28,* 276; HMC *11th Report,* App., I, 122; *APC January 1627–August 1627,* 407–8.

30. *Diary of William Laud,* in *The History of the Tryal of William Laud,* ed. H. Wharton (1694), 41.

31. *CSP Dom 1627–28,* 276, 283, *1628–29,* 218–19, 227, 258; *APC July 1628–April 1629,* 64; HMC *11th Report,* App., I, 158, 161–2, 316; Oman, *Henrietta Maria,* 61.

32. R. Blome, *Britannia: or a Geographical Description of . . . England* (1673), 177; A. Fraser, *Cromwell, Our Chief of Men* (1973), 36.

33. Oman, 61; Samuel Derrick, *Letters written from Liverpool . . . Tunbridge Wells . . .* (1767), 58, 74; Savidge, *Royal Tunbridge Wells,* 23; *CP; Laud's Diary,* 44, 45: Onely, *Tunbridge Wells,* 13, 14.

34. Savidge, 30; E. Hamilton, *Henrietta Maria* (1976), 97; Oman, 67; *CSP Dom 1629–31,* 20, 25; *Wentworth Papers 1597–1628,* Cam Soc, 4th S, XII, 318.

35. HMC *10th Report,* App., II, 152–3.

36. *APC 1618–19,* 485, *1619–21,* 1; Lodowick Rowzee, *The Queen's Wells . . . a Treatise of the Nature and Virtues of Tunbridge-Water,* Harleian Miscellany, VIII, ch.IV; H. F. Abell, *Kent and the Great Civil War* (1901), 252; Raach, *English Physicians,* 78.

37. Sprange, 20–2; Savidge, 31.

38. St John Colbran, *Guide and Visitor's Handbook to Tunbridge Wells and Neighbourhood* (1881), 59; HMC *10th Report,* App., II, 152–3, *12th Report,* App., II, 58, 59, 61; *CSP Dom 1635,* 256, 385.

39. H. I. Lehmann, 'The History of Epsom Spa', *Surrey Arch Coll,* LXIX, 89; E. W. Brayley, *A Topographical History of Surrey,* IV (1841), 353–6.

40. Lewis, IV, 270; Addison, *Spas,* 53.

41. C. F. Mullet, *Public Baths and Health in England, 16th–18th Century* (1946), 5–59; Raach, 120.

42. HMC *De L'Isle and Dudley,* V, 418fn; *CSP Dom 1611–18,* 57, 198; Oman, 60–1; *The Nicholas Papers,* II, *1653–55,* Cam Soc N S, L, 257; HMC *Salisbury,* XXIV, 62, 64.

43. Oman, 117; Fraser, *Cromwell,* 36; *CSP Dom 1637–38,* 526.

44. E. Deane, *Spadacrene Anglica* (1626), 3–7, 9–11, 27; ibid., Rutherford edn (1921), Introduction, 19–27; Jennings, *Harrogate and Knaresborough,* 220–1; Raach, 119, 120, 121, 124; Cliffe, *Yorkshire Gentry,* 193, 220.

45. HMC *Salisbury,* XVIII, 256; Cliffe, 220; Mullet, *Public Baths,* 49.

46. Jennings, 222; Thomas Garnett, *A Treatise on the Mineral Waters of Harrogate* (1792), 13.

47. Ibid., 11; T. Short, *A General Treatise on Various Cold Mineral Waters in England* (1765), 71.

48. Jennings, 223; Smith, *Without Touch of Dishonour*, 62.

49. Michael Stanhope, *A Relation of certain particular Cures done by the Mineral Waters near Knaresbrow* . . . (1649, 1654), 27 ff.

50. BCA 1630, No. 73.

4 Bath and the Civil War

1. HMC *9th Report*, App., II, 428.

2. HMC *Salisbury*, XV, 234, 245, XVII, 240, XVIII, 234, 256, 272, 292, 297; BCA 1607 No. 47, 1615 No. 55, 1620 No. 62.

3. *CSP Dom 1625–26*, 447, *1628–29*, 338, 559; Colbran *Tunbridge Wells* (1881), 47–8.

4. BCA 1618, no. 58, 1630 No. 73.

5. E. Jorden, *A Discourse of Natural Bathes and Mineral Waters* . . . *especially of our Bathes at Bathe* . . . (1632 edn), Preface, 135; Guidott, 166; Mullet, *Public Baths*, 59; Munk, *Physicians*, I, 100–2; Raach, 60; BCM 19 September 1631.

6. HMC *5th Report*, App., 479; James, *The Baths of Bath*, 97, 117; Mullet, 5–6; Guidott, 168; *CSP Dom 1629–31*, 18, 222, 276.

7. Guidott, 148–151, 176–7.

8. James, 109.

9. *APC 1616–17*, 244–5, 330, *1611–18*, 515, *1618–19*, 220; *CSP Dom 1601–03*, 27, 87, 96; HMC *De L'Isle and Dudley*, II, 454, 459, 460–1; *Chamberlains' Accounts*, 176; HMC *Salisbury*, XI, 382; *CP*.

10. *APC 1615–16*, 234, 438, *1616–17*, 245, *1618–19*, 143, *June–December 1626*, 43, 318.

11. *CSP Dom 1619–23*, 186, 391.

12. James, 17–18, 112–13; BCM 1613–34; BCA 1625 No. 68, 1626 No. 69; Holland, Bath Guildhall, *Bath History*, II, 168–9, 172.

13. James, 62–3; *CSP Dom 1619–23*, 250; BCA 1634 No. 77.

14. James, 81–2, 83, 85; *CSP Dom 1619–21*, 250, *1625–26*, 209.

15. BCM 22, 29 April 1633; *Registers of the Abbey Church, Bath*, II, ed. A.J. Jewers, Harleian Soc, XXVIII, 346, 350.

16. *CSP Dom 1619–23*, 374; *APC 1621–23*, 123, 195–6.

17. BCM 10 October 1636.

18. James, 98–9; BCM 4 September 1637; BCA 1603 No. 44, 1607 No. 47, 1608 no. 48, 1612 No. 52, 1658 No. 101.

19. *Letters and papers of the Verney Family*, Cam Soc, 1st S, LVI, 255–7, 275; *Memoirs of the Verney Family during the Seventeenth Century*, ed. F. P. and M. M. Verney, II (1907), 78, 120, 127.

20. *CSP Dom 1639*, 377–8, 393; BCA 1639 No. 82.

21. *Verney Papers. Notes of Proceedings in the Long Parliament*, Cam Soc, O.S., XXI, 105–9; HMC *12th Report*, App., II, 289; *CSP Dom 1641–43*, 69.

22. Hamilton, 208–9, 250; Oman, 157–66, 235, 259, 285, 321; BCA 1644 No. 87; HMC *6th Report*, App., 219; *CSP Dom 1660–61*, 326, 350, 354, 470.

23. E. W. Bligh, *Sir Kenelm Digby* (1932), 248; HMC *4th Report*, App., 101, 303, 420; *CSP Dom 1641–43*, 38, 42, 52, 93.

24. M. Barton, *Tunbridge Wells* (1937), 75–6, 106; HMC *7th Report*, App., 561.

25. *CSP Dom 1656–57*, 145; A. M. Everitt, *The Community of Kent and the Great Rebellion 1640–60* (1966), 268, 287, 304.

26. BL Northumberland MS 549/49/5 (Letterbook of Col. John Fitzjames,

1649–51) (microfilm). I am indebted to H. G. the Duke of Northumberland for permission to use this microfilm and to Mr J. P. Ferris for drawing my attention to it; *Diary of John Evelyn*, III, 68, 71.

27. *CSP Dom 1649–50*, 269, *1659–60*, 55, 61, 68, 87.

28. *CSP Dom 1650*, 216, 518, *1651–52*, 301; HMC *12th Report*, App., IX, 47–8, *15th Report*, App., VII, 158.

29. HMC *6th Report*, App., 53; Mullet, 59.

30. BCA 1643 No. 86, 1644 No. 87, 1645 No. 88; BL Thomason Tract, E. 108, 6. I thank Dr A. Fletcher for this reference.

31. BCM 13 October 1645; HMC *6th Report*, App., 266; BCA 1646 No. 89; *Somerset Assize Orders 1640–59*, Som Rec Soc, LXXI, 15.

32. *CSP Dom 1651–52*, 600; *1652–53*, 320, 322, 338, 341, 349, 350, *1653–54*, 40, 292, 430; BCM 9 June 1651.

33. *CSP Dom 1653–54*, 440; HMC *12th Report*, App., VII, 22; A. Fletcher, *A County Community in Peace and War: Sussex 1600–1660* (1975), 41–2. I thank Mr A. A. Dibben for this reference.

34. *The Nicholas Papers, 1657–60*, IV, Cam Soc, 3rd S, XXI, 179; *CSP Dom 1659–60*, 50, 68; BCA 1658 No. 101.

35. HMC *13th Report*, App., I, 690; J. Wroughton, *The Civil War in Bath and North Somerset* (1973), 133.

36. *VCH Herts*, II, 42.

37. Lewis, IV, 564; Pevsner, *Cumberland and Westmorland* (1967), 298; J. Nicholson and R. Burn, *The History and Antiquities of Westmorland and Cumberland*, I (1777), 234.

38. A. Fessler, 'A Spa in 17th Century Lancashire', *Man. Univ. Med. School Gazette*, XXXIII, 245–6.

39. Fitzjames Letterbook, 549/49/5, fo. 7r-117d.

5 Restoration Development: The Provincial Spas

1. Pierre Lafagne, *Spa ancien, figures de Bobelins et pages d'histoire* (1934), 78–80; *Nicholas Papers*, II, *1653–55*, Cam Soc, NS, L, 50, 78; HMC *Bath*, II, 110; HMC *5th Report*, App., 314.

2. HMC *Finch*, I, 275; M. Ashley, *Charles II* (1971), 153; Barton, *Tunbridge Wells*, 143.

3. HMC *Finch*, II, 32–3; Robert Peirce, *Bath Memoirs: or Observations in Three and Forty Years Practice at the Bath* (1697), 250, 387.

4. Sprange, *Tunbridge Wells* (1780), 14–15.

5. E. Borlase, *Latham Spaw in Lancashire* (1670); *VCH Lancs.*, III, 252; Lysons, *Magna Britannia*, II, Pt II, 623; *Camden's Britannia*, ed. R. Gough, III (1789), 137.

6. *The Great Diurnal of Nicholas Blundell of Little Crosby, Lancashire*, I, *1702–11*, Lancs and Cheshire Rec Soc, CX, 40.

7. W. Albert, *The Turnpike Road System in England 1663–1840* (1972), 14, 16, 20–2, 24, 31, 36, 44, 202.

8. See Schedule A; B. Allen, *The Natural History of the Chalybeate and Purging Waters of England* (1699); B. Allen, *The Natural History of the Mineral-Waters of Great Britain* (1711).

9. J. H. Plumb, 'England's Travelling Circus', *The Listener*, 5 October 1978.

10. *Verney Family during the Seventeenth Century*, II, 243–5, 452–3; *CSP Dom Jas. II*, 257; HMC *14th Report*, App., I, 308.

11. BL Anon., *A brief Account . . . of the Famous Well at Astrop*; C. Baker,

The History and Antiquities of the County of Northamptonshire (1822–30), I, 703; Peirce, *Bath Memoirs*, 250–1; J. Bridges, *The History and Antiquities of North-amptonshire,* I (1791), 180.

12. Verney, II, 244; *The Diary of Thomas Isham of Lamport 1671–73,* ed. N. Marlow (1971), 133; HMC *8th Report,* App., I, 557.

13. *The Journeys of Celia Fiennes,* ed. C. Morris (1949), 31–2; C. Tongue, 'Thomas Thornton at Astrop Spa', *Northants Rec Soc,* IV, No. 5, 281–5; K. Denbigh, *A Hundred British Spas* (1981), 28; *Thomas Isham,* 133; Stourhead MS, E.10, Illustrations by J. C. Nattes.

14. *Celia Fiennes,* 29; Samuel Derham, *Hydrologia Philosophica, or an Account of Ilmington Waters in Warwickshire* (1685); *VCH Warwicks.,* V, 98–9; Allen, *Chalybeate Waters* (1699); W. Dugdale, *The Antiquities of Warwickshire* (2nd edn, 1730), 631; Lewis, II, 501.

15. S. Gilbert, *Fons Sanitatis or the Healing Spring at Willowbridge . . . (1676);* 'Gentry of Staffordshire', *Staffs Hist Col* 4th S., II, 13; Pevsner, *Staffordshire* (1974), 207; R. Plot, *The Natural History of Staffordshire* (1686), 103; J. Floyer, *An Enquiry into the Right Use . . . of the Hot, Cold, and Temperate Baths in England* (1697), Preface.

16. J. Macky, *A Journey through England* (1732), II, 191.

17. Bagshaw, *Derbyshire* (1846), 377, 380; J. Dugdale, *The New British Traveller* (1819), 69.

18. *VCH Worcs.,* IV, 124–5; J. Floyer, *Essay to Prove Cold Bathing both Safe and Useful* (1702), 24.

19. N. Nicholson, *Sissinghurst Castle: an Illustrated History* (1964), 28–33; BL 778.K.15 (4) Pamphlet Collection.

20. Lewis I, 455; *Celia Fiennes,* 125; Bagshaw, *Kent,* II (1847), 51, 99; BL Anon. *A Short Account of the Mineral Waters . . . in Canterbury* has the date 1668 in ink [1171.h.18(2)].

21. J. Harvey Bloom and R. Rutson James, *Medical Practitioners in the Diocese of London 1529–1725* (1935), 54; Munk, *Roll of Physicians,* II, 94, 118; P. Morant, *The History of Essex,* II (1768), 102–3, 113, 419; Capper; Dugdale, *British Traveller* (1819), II, 412; Lewis, IV, 562; James Taverner, *An Essay upon the Witham Spa* (1737).

22. F. Blomefield and C. Parkin, *Topog. Hist. of County of Norfolk,* VI (1807), 284; *Camden's Britannia,* II, 110.

23. Munk. 413–14; *Scarborough 966–1966,* ed. M. Edwards, Scarborough Arch Soc (1966), 63; *CSP Dom October 1683–April 1684,* 11, 39; *CP.*

24. Fiennes, *Journeys,* 92; *Scarborough 966–   ,* 63; S. McIntyre, 'Towns as Health and Pleasure Resorts', 190–9.

25. *The Diary of Sir Walter Calverley of Esholt,* Surtees Soc, LXXVII, 65, 81–2, 97, 106, 135, 137.

26. Granville, I, 148–9; Denbigh, 211.

27. White, *W. R. Yorks* (1838), 510–11; *Nicholas Blundell, II, 1712–19,* 103.

28. T. Allen, *County of York* (1831), 378; Granville, I, 106; Denbigh, 209.

29. Hunter, *Hallamshire,* 499; White, *W. R. Yorks,* II (1838), 223; Thomas Short, *The Natural, Experimental and Medicinal History of the Mineral Waters of Derbyshire, Lincolnshire and Yorkshire* (1736), 269–70.

30. Pevsner, *Derbyshire* (1953), 53–4; White, *County of Derby* (1857), 476–7.

31. Lewis, II, 109; Munk, *Physicians,* I, 246; BL Anon., *Spadacrene Dunelmensis* (1675); W. R. Clanny, *A History and Analysis of the Mineral Waters . . . at Butterby, near Durham* (1807), 19–31, 52, 59; *Celia Fiennes,* 216.

32. Peirce, *Bath Memoirs,* 251–2.

33. J. H. P. Pafford, 'The Spas and Mineral Springs of Wiltshire', *WAM*, LV, 1–29, and *VCH Wilts*, IV, 386–8.

6 Tunbridge Wells Rivals Bath: Late Stuart Changes

1. *CP.*
2. A. Savidge, *The Story of the Church of King Charles the Martyr* (1969), 5–13.
3. HMC *7th Report*, App., 84; *Lords Journal*, XI, 29–30.
4. NRO H(K) 183 John Scattergood's Letters, 24 February 1720; Macky, *Journey*, I, 118; BL Add. MS 5233.1.3 Dr Edward Browne's Drawings.
5. *Walks around Tunbridge Wells*, No. I, Royal Tunbridge Wells Civic Society (1974), 1; Newman, *West Kent and the Weald* (1969), 559.
6. Chalklin, *Kent*, 12, 26, 157–8, from which much that follows is taken.
7. Savidge, *Tunbridge Wells*, 38.
8. Ibid., 43; Clifford, *Descriptive Guide of Tunbridge Wells* (1818), 7.
9. Barton, *Tunbridge Wells*, 137, 139; HMC *Finch*, I, 275; HMC *15th Report*, App., VII, 170–1; *The Diary of Samuel Pepys*, ed. R. Latham and W. Matthews (1971), IV, 240.
10. *CSP Dom 1665–66*, 541; *Cal. Treasury Books 1667–68*, 99.
11. J. Ross, *The Winter Queen: the Story of Elizabeth Stuart* (1979), 152; *CSP Dom 1670*, 151, 384, *1679–80*, 561; HMC *7th Report*, App., 482; Barton, 150–2, 159; HMC *Harley*, I, 375.
12. HMC *Egmont*, II, 152, 159; Mullet, *Public Baths*, 17–18.
13. HMC *Harley*, II, 118; HMC *Finch*, II, 82; HMC *7th Report*, App., 482; Onely, *Tunbridge Wells* (1771), 4.
14. *Verney Family Seventeenth Century*, II, 401; GRO D 1799/C2 Blaithwaite MS; HMC *Harley*, I, 386; HMC *12th Report*, App., V, 95; Colbran (1881), 168; *CSP Dom January 1686–May 1687*, 264.
15. HMC *10th Report*, App., IV, 130; *CSP Dom 1667*, 293, 305, 374; *Verney Letters of the Eighteenth Century, I, (1696–1717)*, ed. M. M. Verney (1930), I, 22; *Cal Treasury Books 1685–89*, I, 271.
16. *CSP Dom 1666–67, 102; ibid., 1667*, 323.
17. *CSP Dom 1667*, 407, *1667–68*, 503; *Cal. Treasury Books 1685–89*, VIII, ii, 853, 856, *1689-92*, IX, iii, 1224, *1702*, XVII, ii, 784.
18. HMC *Bath*, II, 172; HMC *10th Report*, App., IV, 130; *7th Report*, App., 482, 486.
19. Savidge, *Tunbridge*, 42; Chalklin, *Kent*, 26, 157.
20. Sprange, 20–3; *Fiennes*, 133; Savidge, 41–2, 44.
21. Clifford, *Guide* (1818), 12; Chalklin, *Kent*, 158.
22. R. Blome, *Britannia* (1673) 196–7; *CSP Dom January 1686–May 1687*, 280, 297; Savidge, *Tunbridge*, 44.
23. *Fiennes*, 134–5; HMC *Harley*, I, 400; Savidge, 48.
24. Barton, 155, 168; *CSP Dom January 1686–May 1687*, 235, 243; HMC *Harley*, I, 416; Savidge, 48.
25. *Cal. Treasury Books 1689–92*, IX, iii, 1224; *The Autobiographies and Letters of Thomas Comber*, II, Surtees Soc., CLVII, 199–200.
26. *CSP Dom 1697*, 207, 276, 381, 383; Barton, 168–9; H. W. Chapman, *Queen Anne's Son* (1954), 127.
27. Savidge, *Church of Charles the Martyr*, 11.
28. *Verney Family, Seventeenth Century*, II, 401; *Verney Letters of the Eighteenth Century*, I, 114.

29. HMC *Harley,* III, 98.

30. Wroughton, *Civil War in Bath,* 87, 133; BCM 2 October 1661, 1662 p. 77, 8 April 1664, 27 March, 7 April 1665; BCA 1641 No. 84, 1661 No. 103, 1662 No. 105, 1665 No. 108; *British Association Handbook to Bath,* ed. J. W. Morris (1888), 68–9.

31. H. Chapman, *Thermae Redivivae: the City of Bath Described* (1673), 2; R. S. Neale, *Bath* (1981), 49; Blome, *Britannia,* 196; Cardiff Central Library MS 4,370 J. Verdon, *Travel Journal,* 1699, VI, 110; James, *Bath,* 13; Macky, *Journey,* II, 144–5.

32. R. E. Peach, *Bath, Old and New* (1891), 133; Dunning, *Somerset,* 78, map; Neale, 96; BCM 22 April 1661, 11 February 1677; BCA 1685 No. 130.

33. *Thermae Redivivae,* 3; BCM 28 October 1662, 9 July 1665; HMC *12th Report,* App., IX, 66.

34. PRO WO 30/48, fos 161d, 166r (I thank Professor A. Everitt for this reference); John Wood, *A Description of Bath* (1765. 1969 reprint), Preface.

35. Verdon, *Journal,* 1699, VI, fo.111; Thomas Dingley, *History in Marble,* Cam Soc., O.S., XCIV, xliiii.

36. *Handbook to Bath* (1888), 75–6; BCM 27 September 1697.

37. BCA 1663, No. 106; HMC *14th Report,* App., IV, 71, *15th Report,* App., VII, 170–1; *CSP Dom 1663–64,* 247, 264–5; HMC *Finch,* I, 275; Peirce, *Bath Memoirs,* 257.

38. Ibid., 255, 258–9, 270; *DNB;* BCA 1664 No. 107; BCM 7 April 1665; Thomas Dingley, xxvii, xlvii, 1; James, *Bath,* 138; Wood, *Description,* 218.

39. BCM 7 April 1665; *CSP Dom 1663–64,* 268, 270, 275–6, *1677–78,* 244, *January 1686–May 1687,* 176, 260, *1690–91,* 383; HMC *7th Report,* App., 503, *11th Report,* App., VII, 197, *12th Report,* App., VII, 273; BCA 1686 No. 131; Thomas Dingley, xxxix.

40. *CSP Dom 1668–69,* 113–14, 432, 505; BCM 9 November 1668.

41. Peach, 132; *CSP Dom January–June 1683,* 40–1, 45, 305; Verdon, fo. 111.

42. HMC *7th Report,* App., 490, *9th Report,* App., II, 446, *12th Report,* App., V, 29; *Cal. Treasury Books 1672–75,* 570, 595, 807; *CSP Dom 1672,* 414, 457, 469, 479, *1673–75,* 308, *1676–77,* 166, *1677–78,* 184; *Selections . . . Correspondence of Arthur Capel, Earl of Essex 1675–77,* Cam 3rd Ser., XXIV, 50. *1678,* 312, 346, 610, *1680–81,* 34.

43. e.g. BCM 9 April and 23 May 1632, 27 June and 26 December 1636; *CSP Dom 1683,* 133.

44. BCM 30 June 1673, 22 September 1674, 4 October 1680, 13 February 1681, 23 September 1685, 30 February 1695; BCA 1685 No. 130, 1686 No. 131.

45. *CSP Dom 1679–80,* 429, 475, 597, *May 1684–February 1685,* 239, 249; BCM 25 February 1679, 28 August 1682, 4 April, 17 July, 1 October and 21 November 1683, ? January and 8 February 1685, 15 October 1686; BCA 1685 No. 130, 1688 No. 133; *Registers of the Abbey Church, Bath,* II, 387.

46. BCA 1687 No. 132; *The Limner of Bath . . . Thomas Robins 1716–1770* (Holburne Museum, Bath, 1978), 16.

47. HMC *11th Report,* App., V, 134, *13th Report,* App., II, 52; BCM 3 October 1687; *CSP Dom June 1687–February 1689,* 67, 77; Peach, *Bath,* 70; BCA, Bk II, list of honorary freemen.

48. BCM 25 June, 3 August and 17 October 1686, 13 December 1688; BCA 1688 No. 133; Haddon, 96.

49. BCM 11 December 1693, 1 January 1693/4, 28 March 1694, 29 March 1697, 27 March 1699, 30 March 1702/3; BCA 1687 No. 132; Neale, *Bath,* 103, 111.

50. Jorden, *Discourse* (1669 edn), 329; Peirce, *Bath Memoirs,* title; *Abbey Reg.,*

393; BCA, II, freemen, gives John Marteh as John Nalder; BCM 7 July 1718.

51. HMC *Harley*, I, 535; Wood, *Description of Bath*, 220; BCM 7 July 1718; BM Egerton MS 3647, fo. 93r.; Thomas Guidott, *Register of Bath* (1694).

52. Mullet, 14.

53. HMC *11th Report*, App., VII, 201, *9th Report*, App., II, 469.

54. *CSP Dom 1691–92*, 381; HMC *8th Report*, App., I, 58, *12th Report*, VII, 330; *Handbook of Bath* (1888), 77; Peach, 134 fn; D. Green, *Queen Anne* (1970), 102; BCA 1694 No. 137.

55. *Cal. Treasury Books 1702*, XVII, i, 76, 338, 352, 356, 358; *HMC 10th Report*, App., IV, 337; *CSP Dom 1702–3*, 217, 225, 235–7, 240, 250, 262; Peach, 135 fn; Green, 'Visits to Bath of Two Queens', 226–30; BCA 1701 and 1702, No. 145; BCM 22 August 1702; *Verney Letters, 18th Century*, II, 113–14.

56. Green, *Visits*, 230–2; *Cal. Treasury Papers 1703*, XVIII, 367, 406; *CSP Dom 1703–4*, 92, 98; BCA 1702/3 No. 146; BCM 28 August 1703, 15 May 1704.

57. HMC *12th Report*, App., II, 361.

58. *Verney Family, Seventeenth Century*, II, 243–5; Blome, *Britannia* (1673); PRO WO 30/48 fo. 39r; Macky, *Journey*, II, 206; Pevsner, *Derbyshire* (1978 edn), 127.

59. Verdon, *Journal*, 1699, fo. 60; *Fiennes Journeys*, 103; HMC *12th Report*, App., III, 168; Floyer, *An Enquiry into the . . . Baths in England* (1697), 136–7, 143–4.

60. NRO H(K) 183 John Scattergood's Letters, 27 October 1719, 17 January 1720; I. E. Burton, *Historic Buxton and its Spa Era* (1971), 8; Defoe, *Tour Through England*, II, 165–8.

61. Here and later I have drawn heavily on *A History of Harrogate and Knaresborough*, ed. B. Jennings (1970), 219–32; *Verney Memoirs, Seventeenth Century*, II, 243; Mullet, *Public Baths*, 59.

62. D. Ogg, *England in the Reign of Charles II* (1934), I, 209; *CSP Dom 1663–64*, 376, 540.

63. Kaye, *Records of Harrogate*, 108–9, 132; HMC *13th Report*, App., II, 314.

65. PRO WO 30/48, fos 210r, 214r; *Fiennes*, 79–80, 219; Jennings, 232.

65. Defoe, *Tour*, II, 212–13; Jackson, *Handbook for Tourists in Yorkshire* (1891), 333.

66. *CSP Dom 1677–78*, 426.

67. Vincent Waite, 'The Bristol Hotwells', *Bristol in the Eighteenth Century*, ed. P. McGrath (1972), 114–15; B. Little, 'The Gloucestershire Spas', *Essays in Bristol and Gloucestershire History*, ed. P. McGrath and J. Cannon, Bristol & Glos Arch Soc (1976), 171–2.

68. S. Lewis, *A Topographical Dictionary of Wales*, I (1840), I; Defoe, *Tour*, II, 4–5; *Camden's Britannia*, ed. Gough, II, 593.

7 Metropolitan Spas

1. Accounts of London spas are based on A. S. Foord, *Springs, Streams and Spas of London* (1910) and W. Addison, *English Spas* (1951).

2. BL T. G., *A True and Exact Account of Sadler's Well . . . lately found at Islington* (1684).

3. *The Diary of Dudley Ryder 1715–1716*, ed. W. Matthews (1939), 295–8.

4. HMC *5th Report*, App., 400.

5. D. W. Linden, *A Treatise on the Origin, Nature & Virtues of Chalybeate Waters . . .* (1748), 108–111, 121–2.

6. BL 778.k.15(7), Advertisement for the London Spaw.

7. BM Prints and Drawings, Grace Collection, XXI, No. 57, fo. 22.

8. HMC *10th Report,* App., II, 399.

9. *Celia Fiennes,* 132; *Diaries of John Evelyn,* IV, 74, 112, V, 351.

10. Lewis, III, 589; *CSP Dom 1660–61,* 71, 140–1, *1661–62,* 393, *1670,* 317, 323, 333, *Add. 1660–70,* 716, *1682,* 323; Allen, *Natural History* (1699).

11. Post Office, *Directory of Surrey* (1862), 1435; J. Williams, *Richmond Wells* . . . (1723); *Verney Letters Eighteenth Century,* I, 31; Macky, *Journey,* I, 79.

12. Foord, 192–9; G. Scott Thomson, *Letters of a Grandmother 1732–1735* (1943), 141–43.

13. *Dudley Ryder,* 57.

14. Foord, 139; *CSP Dom May 1684–February 1685,* 77, 111; *CP;* F.M.L. Thompson, *Hampstead: Building of a Borough 1650–1964* (1974), 18–20.

15. Ibid., 21–5; C. Wade, *The Streets of Hampstead* (The Camden History Society, 1972), 31–5; *Dudley Ryder,* 29–30.

16. *VCH Herts,* II, 329; Blome, *Britannia,* 114; Albert, *Turnpike System,* 202; *Diary of Samuel Pepys,* V, 200–1, VIII, 380–1.

17. *CSP Dom 1673,* 476; HMC *14th Report,* App., I & II, 368; Defoe, *Tour,* 3–4; Fiennes, 121.

18. BL Anon., *Some Particulars Relating to Epsom* . . . (1825), 63; *Surrey Quarter Sessions Records 1666–68,* IX (Surrey County Council, 1951), 144; Surrey Hearth Tax 1664, *Surrey Rec Soc,* XVII, ciii, cxxiii, cxxxvii; *Fiennes,* 341–2; *VCH Surrey,* III, 272, 276; *CSP Dom 1680–81,* 358; *Samuel Pepys,* VIII, 336, 338.

19. *Surrey Quarter Sessions Records 1663–66,* VIII (Surrey County Council, 1938), 70–1.

20. F. L. Clark, 'The History of Epsom Spa', *Surrey Arch Coll,* LVII, 21. Much of what follows about the history of Epsom is taken from this important revision of 1960; *Fiennes,* 350; *John Evelyn,* III, 544–5.

21. *CSP Dom 1683 July–September,* 172, 208, 210, 428, *May 1684–February 1685,* 83; Anon., *Some Particulars,* 64.

22. *Fiennes,* 349.

23. Lehmann, 'Epsom Spa', 89–95.

24. Ibid.

25. *Fiennes,* 350.

26. Macky, *Journey,* I, 152–3; Nairn and Pevsner, *Surrey* (1962), 185–6.

27. *Dudley Ryder,* 33; W. Lee, *Report to the General Board of Health. Epsom* (1849), 18.

28. Anon., *Some Particulars,* 76, 85; *Toland,* II, 100–1.

29. *Some Particulars,* 74; Macky, 139.

30. See Schedule A.

31. See Schedule D; GRO D. 1844 Newton Correspondence, C4, C17.

8 Bath: The New Towns

1. See Schedule A.

2. Plumb, 'England's Travelling Circus'; Albert, *The Turnpike Road System,* 44–5.

3. *Diurnal of Nicholas Blundell* . . . , *I,* Rec Soc, Lancs and Cheshire, CX, 178–9, *II,* CXII, 103; *The Diary of Richard Kay, 1716–51* . . . , Chetham Soc, 3rd S., XVI, 120–1.

4. A. G. Hodgkiss, *Discovering Antique Maps* (?), 32, 49, 51.

5. W. R. Clanny, *A History and Analysis of the Mineral Waters . . . at But-terby* (1807), 2.

6. BCA, II, List of honorary freemen.

7. Neale, *Bath*, 99.

8. R. Sedgwick, *The House of Commons 1715–54* (1970), I, 563; BCM 27 August and 1 October 1716; Neale, 306.

9. *Dudley Ryder*, 245–6; BRO Chamberlains' Accounts, 1736–7, 3 September 1745, 24 November 1748; BCM 1 April 1734.

10. *The Marchioness Grey of Wrest Park, 1726*, Beds Hist Rec, XLVII, 10; *Samuel Derrick, Letters . . . from Liverpool* (1767), 85; E. Clarke, *A Tour through the South of England in 1791* (1793), 141.

11. Albert, Map p. 35, 37, 42, 202, 204, 205.

12. Wood, *Description*, 224; BCM 20 November and 1 December 1707, 28 June 1708; 6 Anne c.xlii; Albert, 44.

13. *Bath in the Age of Reform*, ed. J. Wroughton (1972), 68.

14. 6 Anne c. xlii; *Letters from Bath, 1766–1767*, ed. B. Mitchell and H. Penrose (1983), 54.

15. Neale, 116–17; BCM 1 April, 1 July, 30 September 1706, 17 February 1707, 27 December 1708, 27 March, 27 June 1710, 16 May 1718.

16. Neale, 47; BL Egerton MS 3565, fos 26r, 30r, MS 2647, 93r; Wood, *Description*, 220.

17. BCM 28 December 1730, 20 November, 11 December 1732; BRO Chamberlains' Accounts, 1733–4.

18. McIntyre, 'Health and Pleasure Resorts', 38; J. Walters, *Splendour and Scandal, The Reign of Beau Nash* (1968), 34–7.

19. Wood, 222; BCM 27 November, 31 December 1705, 22 January, 1 April, 1 July, 24 October 1706; BCA 1706–7.

20. Meyler, *Original Bath Guide* (1813), 90; BRO Chamberlains' Accounts, 1710–11, 1733–4, 29 March 1753, 1 April 1754, 2 April 1759.

21. BCM 1 July 1706, 31 March 1707; W. Ison, *The Georgian Buildings of Bath* (1948), 101; BL Egerton MS 3647, fo. 93r; Wood, 220.

22. B. L. Egerton MS 3565, fo. 16r, MS 3647, fo. 107r.

23. *CP; VCH Wilts*, VII, 15; Egerton MS 3565, note inside cover, MS 3647, fos 26r, d, 28d, 30r; Neale, *Bath*, 166.

24. Egerton MS 3647, fos 67r, d; *CP; Abbey Reg*, II, 459.

25. BCM 7 May 1711; Wood, 225; *Dudley Ryder*, 239; Meyler, *Guide* (1813), 90; Ison, 49; *Letters from Bath*, 123.

26. NRO H(K) 183, John Scattergood's Diary; *Diary of Thomas Smith . . .*, WAM, XI, 92; Derrick, *Letters*, 84; Ison, 50; BJ 20 May; 11, 18 November 1754; Wood, 288, 319; Pope, *New Bath Guide* (1761), 28–9.

27. Ison, 89; Meyler, 107–8; BJ 14 January, 15 April, 14 October, 11 November 1734, 13 January 1772; *CP; Theatre Royal, Bath – A History* (Bath Theatre Notes, 1981), 2; BL Egerton MS 3648, fo. 7d.

28. K. R. Clew, *The Kennet and Avon Canal* (1968), 16, 17, 18; BCM 6, 29 January 1695, 10 December 1711, 25 January 1712, 20 June 1714, 1 April 1728, 27 October 1729; *CP;* 10 Anne c.ii.

29. C. H. Collins Baker, *The Life and Circumstances of James Brydges, First Duke of Chandos* (1949), 297–8, fn, 315 fn; Clew, 18; Wood, *Essay*, 331; McIntyre, 422, quoting J. R. Ward, 'Investment in Canals and Housebuilding in England' (Oxford D. Phil. thesis, 1970), 183.

30. BCA; BCM 30 June 1766.

31. Collins Baker, *Chandos*, 298, 300, 302; Sedgwick, *House of Commons*, II, 60–1; Neale, *Bath*, 103–4; H. Colvin, *A Biographical Dictionary of British Architects* (1978), 787.

32. J. Summerson, *Architecture in Britain 1530–1830* (1953), 222–4; Neale, *Bath*, 189–191, 204; R. S. Neale, 'Society, belief, and the building of Bath 1700–1793', *Rural Change and Urban Growth 1500–1800*, ed. C. W. Chalklin and M. A. Havinden (1974), 272.

33. B. Boyce, *The Benevolent Man: A Life of Ralph Allen of Bath* (1967), 1, 4, 5, 10, 18, 20–6, 31, 35.

34. Boyce, 56, 61, 98, 103, 113, 213; BCA 24 January 1754; K. Hudson, *The Fashionable Stone* (1971), 44–5: M. Williams, *Lady Luxborough Goes to Bath* (1945), 54.

35. Collins Baker, *Chandos*, 297–9, 300, 314–15.

36. Ibid., 334; Ison, 32; Wood, 246-8, 343–5; Neale, *Bath*, 151; BCM 9 February, 18 July 1739; BJ 1 September 1755; 22 Geo. II, xx.

37. BL Egerton MS 3647, fo. 91r, d; Ison, 32–3, 88–91; Neale, *Bath*, 155.

38. Ibid., 185, 261, 265; C.W. Chalklin, *The Provincial Towns of Georgian England* (1974), 74–6; BCA 1740–1; BJ 27 May 1754; Ison, 150–1, 154; *Shardesloe Papers of the 17th and 18th Centuries*, ed. G. Eland (1947), 123; Ison, 150–1, 154; Wood, 351.

39. BCM 31 December 1750, 10, 30 May 1751, 6, 8 August 1752, 10 March 1753, 17, 24 June 1754; Chamberlains' Accounts 14 May, 10 July, 30 August, 23 September ff. 1751, 21 April 1753, 15 July 1754 ff.

40. BCM 12 April 1756, 10 November 1757; Chamberlains' Accounts 10 May 1756, 24 January 1757; Neale, *Bath*, 183–4.

41. BJ 27 May 1754, 17 March 1775; BL Egerton MS 3647, fo. 113–14r, MS 3648, fo. 2d; Pope, *Bath Guide* (1761), 13; *UBD*, II, 87; *Letters from Bath*, 84.

42. *The Travels of Dr Richard Pococke*, I, Cam Soc., N. S., XLII, 154; ibid., II, XLIV, 32; *Marchioness Grey*, 70.

43. BJ 2 February, 1, 29 April, 3 September, 21 October 1754, 17 March, 12 May, 30 June, 6 October 1755; Williams, *Lady Luxborough*, 31.

44. McIntyre, 70–3, 143; Neale, *Bath*, 67–9; Chalklin, *Provincial Towns*, 77–8, 182–3; Pope, *Guide* (1761), 30.

45. Ison, 32, 105, 109; Chalklin, 80, 218, 220; BL Egerton MS 3565, fo. 16r.; Neale, 'Society, belief . . .', 257–8; Neale, *Bath*, 155.

46. McIntyre, 142; GRO Batsford Park MS D. 1447, Accounts of Mrs Jane Edwards.

47. Ison, 159; Pevsner, *North Somerset and Bristol* (1958), 127, 128.

48. *The Letters and Journals of Lady Mary Coke, 1756–67* (1970), I, 81–2; Neale, *Bath*, 207; HMC *Gorhambury*, 249; Pevsner, 130–1, 134; Neale, 'Society, belief . . .', 266; A Taylor and W. Meyler, Map of Bath (1796).

49. Meyler, *Guide* (1813), 100; Neale, *Bath*, 221; Ison, 51–3; Warner, *History of Bath* (1801), 356; Lewis, IV. 647; BL Add. MS 27951 Anon., Travel Journal August–September 1772, fo. 22.

50. Neale, *Bath*, 159, 210; Egerton MS 3648, fo. 52r; Ison, 50, 51; *UBD*, II, 90; BCM 7 January 1782, 26 January 1798; BJ 17 February 1772.

51. Neale, *Bath*, 251; 6 Geo. III, c.lxx; BCM 20 December 1765, 21 April 1766, 4 October 1784, 3 October 1785, 15 September 1787, 28 September 1789.

52. Warner, 227; Derrick, *Letters*, 105; BCM 5 January 1767; Ison, 35–6; BRO Chamberlains' Accounts, 2, 16, 23 December 1778; Neale, 249, 453.

53. BCM 29 September 1794, 8 January, 14 November 1795, 15 September, 26 November 1796.

54. *Pembroke Papers (1780–1794)*, ed. Lord Herbert (1950), 74, 77, 78, 79–80; (R. Crutwell), *The Strangers' Assistant and Guide to Bath* (1773), 63–72.

55. BRL R 69/12675, Edmund Rack, *A Disultory Journal of Events at Bath,*

1779, 1, 7, 10, 20: quoted by McIntyre, 48 (from Ward, Investment in Canals); Warner, 345 fn.

56. Ison, 37, 40, 92, map facing 212; Neale, 'Society, belief . . .', 268; *UBD*, II (1791), 95; BJ 7 April 1766; S. Sydenham, *Bath Pleasure Gardens of the Eighteenth Century* (1907), (1969 facsimile ed), 2–11, 16–20. I thank Mr J. Ede for this reference; Peach, 198–9.

57. Ison, 93–4.

58. Ibid., 38–40, 65–6; Meyler, *Guide* (1813), 121; Peach, 196; *CP;* Sydenham, 21–2; Warner, 235; Neale, *Bath*, 227–40.

59. J. Savage, *The Original New Bath Guide* (1804), 46; J. Browne, *The Historic and Local New Bath Guide* (1811), 116–17; Sydenham, 23–6.

60. *Pembroke Papers*, 262; BCM 28 December 1772, 2 March 1773, 29 June 1778, 23 June 1781, 31 March, 6 October 1783; McIntyre, 152–3, 155; Meyler (1813), 27; Ison, 57; Neale, *Bath*, 250; Chamberlains' Accounts 25 April 1777; J. Manco, The Cross Bath, *Bath History*, II (1988), 68–74.

61. BCM 24 September 1781, 3 October 1785; Ison, 42, 61–2.

62. BCM 18 February 1784, 3 October 1785, 5 February, 18 March 1788, 10 July 1789; Neale, *Bath*, 180, 251; 29 Geo. III c.xxiii.

63. Derrick, *Letters*, 83; BCM 18 March, 21 May 1788, 2 June 1789, 10 July 1792, 10 December 1793, 7 January, 12 February 1794; Ison, 42; Neale, *Bath*, 251–2.

64. Warner, 190–9; BCM 11 July, 24 August 1776, 6 April 1778, 27 March 1780, 31 January 1781, 10 December 1787, 10 July 1789, 9 January 1796.

65. BCM 9 January 1796, 4 January 1803, 22 March 1804, 22 September 1806, 3 June 1812, 20 December 1814, 17 April 1816, 6 March 1818.

66. *UBD*, II, 89; *Gents Mag* (1790), I, 23; Chalklin, 281; Warner, 226, 234, 235; BJ 3 January 1791.

67. Warner, 236, 266, 269, 271–2; McIntyre, 50–1; Meyler, *Guide* (1813), 138; BJ 20 January, 2 March 1772.

68. *Gents Mag* (1799), II, 1014; Meyler, *Guide* (1813), 121–2.

9   Bath: The Regulated Society and the Leisure Industry

1. J. H. Plumb, 'The Commercialisation of Leisure in Eighteenth-century England', *The Birth of a Consumer Society,* ed. N. McKendrick, J. Brewer, J. H. Plumb (1982), VI, 265ff.; P. Clark and P. Slack, *English Towns in Transition 1500–1700* (1976), 74.

2. BJ 1758; *Norfolk Chronicle and Norwich Gazette* 1776; Plumb, 281.

3. Ibid., 269–70; G. A. Cranfield, *The Development of the Provincial Newspaper* (1962), Preface.

4. Boyce, *Ralph Allen,* 36; BRO Chamberlains' Accounts 1738–9; BCM 25 October 1738, 14 December 1761, 14 November 1795, 26 November 1796, 21 September 1808, 24 October 1817, 1, 17 November 1817.

5. BCM 15 September 1761, 1, 11 August 1788, 21 June 1790; *CP;* J. Brooke, *King George III* (1972), 12; A. Aspinall, *The Later Correspondence of George III, I (Dec. 1783–Jan. 1793),* (1962), 12, 20–1, 443.

6. *Handbook of Bath,* ed. W. Morris (1888), 86; HMC *13th Report,* App., VIII, 141, *14th Report,* App., I, 315; HMC *Rutland,* III, 395; BJ 1, 29 September, 10 November 1766; *Abbey Reg,* 414, 419, 459, 465; *Letters from Bath,* 37, 42.

7. Rack, Journal, 2, 3.

8. *The Diary of Thomas Gyll,* Surtees Soc, CXVIII, 190–1; HMC *10th Report,* App., I, 294; HMC *Bath,* I, 355; *Wiltshire Returns to the Bishop's Visitation Queries, 1783,* Wilts Rec Soc, XXVI, 33, 37, 84, 145; *Abbey Reg,* 452, 460, 464,

473; BRO Weekly List of Gentlemen Bathing in the King's Bath, 1774–6.

9. Ibid.; HMC *9th Report,* App., III, 25; GRO Parsons Correspondence, D. 214/F1/45, 61, 69, 115, 137.

10. *The Letters of Sir William Jones,* ed. Garland Cannon, I (1790), 229–30; Derrick Knight, *Gentlemen of Fortune* (1978), 87–9.

11. Meyler, *Guide* (1813), 107; Macky, *Journey,* II, 137; HMC *Bath,* I, 334; HMC *11th Report,* App., V, 327, *15th Report,* App., VI, 61.

12. Macky, II, 138; *Diary of Dudley Ryder,* 240; BCM 1 October 1716, 6 August 1752; HMC *Bath,* I, 331.

13. Walters, *Splendour and Scandal,* 36–45, 66; J. Cannon, 'Bath Politics in the Eighteenth Century', *Som Arch & NH Soc,* LXXXVIII, 105; Anon., *A Guide to . . . Watering and Sea-Bathing Places* (1806) (pub. R. Phillips), 16–17; *Letters from Bath,* 40; Macky, II, 143–4.

14. NRO Isham Correspondence, 1C/2093, 11 January 1749; Savidge, *Tunbridge Wells,* 67; Walters, 171–9; BCM 7 July 1746; BCA, list of honorary freemen.

15. 22 Geo. II.c.xxviii, 28 Geo. II, c.xxxiv; BRO Chamberlains' Accounts, 2 January 1749; R. Baldwin, *A New Present State of England,* I (1750), 208–9; McIntyre, 100.

16. Savidge, 61–2, 68; Walters, 117; BJ 30 September, 7 October 1754.

17. BRO Chamberlains' Vouchers, 1760, nos 102, 114, 126; Walters, 192, 193, 195; BCM 14, 20 February 1761; E. Waterhouse, *Painting in Britain 1530–1790* (3rd edn 1969), 144; BCA 1766–7.

18. Walters, 118; McIntyre, 9, 10; BC 17 July 1777; E. W. Gilbert, *Brighton: Old Ocean's Bauble* (1954), 13; *Letters from Bath,* 174; BJ 12 May, 15 September 1766; Meyler, *Guide* (1813), 97.

19. Savidge, 74; Meyler, 97–8; McIntyre, 315.

20. Neale, *Bath,* 221–2; B & C Gaz 18 November 1812; Gilbert, 176; Meyler, 101; B. Little, 'The Gloucestershire Spas', 188, but Little is wrong about the date of Moreau's death; see pp. 201, 338 n. 29.

21. Rack, Journal, 20; B & C Gaz 20 January 1813.

22. Savidge, 74–5, App., III, 208; M. Villiers, 'Pump and Promenade', *Quarterly Review* (April 1941), vol. 276., no. 548, 190; BJ 20 October 1800.

23. Warner, *Bath,* 335, 340 fn.; BJ 17, 24 March 1755; BCM 24 January 1757; 30 Geo. II c.lxv.

24. BCM 10 November 1757, 30 June 1777, 15 September 1787, 5 July, 4 October 1790, 4 May, 6 September 1791, 7 December 1792, 20 March, 15 April 1797.

25. BJ 30 June 1755; BCM 29 June 1747, 20 December 1765, 27 January 1766; BCM 30 September 1765, 30 June 1777; BRO Chamberlains' Accounts, 11 June 1742, 5 November 1744, 2 November 1752; McIntyre, 150; Warner, 228.

26. Wood, *Description,* Preface, 4; BJ 12 August 1754; Meyler, *Guide* (1813), 139; (H. D. Symonds) *A Companion to the Watering and Bathing Places of Great Britain* (1800), 12; W. Mavor, *The British Tourists* (1800), VI, 272–3.

27. *Letters from Bath,* 26–9, 38, 89; BRL Diaries of Elizabeth Collett, 1792 (typescript), ed. H. Collett, 8; GRO D 123/F4 Winstone Correspondence, 21 January, 5 June 1815.

28. Collins Baker, *Chandos,* 307, 311, 314–15; BJ 11 May 1772.

29. Meyler, *Guide* (1813), 138; BJ 13 March 1758; (Symonds), *Watering and Bathing Places,* 12; (Crutwell), *Strangers' Assistant,* 63 ff.; *UBD,* II, 111–13; Warner, *Bath,* 216; Browne, *Historic Guide* (1811), 177–80.

30. E. Hughes, *North Country Life in the Eighteenth Century,* I (1952), 399; Longleat MS (uncatalogued), Lord Weymouth's Estate in Bath, 1752; Crutwell, 63–72.

31. Browne, *Guide* (1811), 99; Collins Baker, 317; BJ 10 February 1755, 13 March 1758; *Letters from Bath*, 24–5, 27, 72.

32. BJ 6, 27 January, 10 February, 16, 30 March 1772, 3, 17 January 1791.

33. Wood, *Description*, 58, 368; J. A. Bulley, ' "To Mendip for Coal" – a study of the Somerset Coalfield before 1830" ', *Proc Som Arch N.H. Soc*, XCVII, 46, 62, XCVIII, 24, 30.

34. Bulley, XCVII, 58; Bailey, *British Directory* (1784), 336 ff.; Warner, 214–16; BCM 1 October 1753, 24 January 1757; Rack, *Journal*, 23; BCA 1704.

35. Bulley, XCII, 51–2, 58, XCVIII, 44; BCM 15 February 1793; Mavor, *British Tourists*, VI, 273; (Symonds), *Watering Places*, 12; *Passages from the Diaries of Mrs. Philip Lykke Powys . . . 1756–1808*, ed. E. J. Climenson (1899), 328; BRO Chamberlains' Vouchers, 1706 nos 103, 104; BRO Chamberlains' Accounts, 11 October 1752, 12, 19, 27 January 1753, 28, 30 November 1754, 25 February 1761.

36. BL Add. MS 27951, Anon., Travel Diary 1772, fo. 25; Brooke, *George III*, 12; D. Jarrett, *Britain 1688–1815* (1965), 160, 200.

37. Lewis Melville, *Bath under Beau Nash And After* (1926), 55–6; Peach, 170.

38. *Strangers' Assistant* (1773), 32–6; *Dr. Campbell's Diary of a Visit to England in 1775*, ed. J. L. Clifford (1947), 89; Anon., *A Guide To . . . Watering and Sea-Bathing Places . . .* (1806), 36.

39. Warner, 356–60; HMC *Bath*, I, 334; GRO D 214/F1/61 Parsons Letters.

40. Warner, 356–60; Anon., *Guide to Watering Places* (1806), 30–1, 37.

41. BCA 1770–71; BCM 16 April 1784, 22 April, 19 September 1795, 9 November 1797; Anon., *Guide* (1806), 34.

42. Macky, *Journey*, 139, 140; BCM 26 September 1737, 8 January, 26 April 1753, 16 May 1778, 24 August 1804; Anon., *Guide* (1806), 26; BRO Weekly List of Gentlemen Bathing in the King's Bath.

43. BL Add. MS 27951, Travel Diary, 1772, fo. 25; BCM 2 October 1704, 7 October 1706, 29 June 1778, 11 June, 4 October 1779, 5 January, 23 June 1781, 28 June 1784, 3 July 1786; D. W. Linden, *The Hyde Saline Purging Water* (1751), 68.

44. BCM 21 January, 3 July 1786, 25 June 1787, 10 July 1789, 5 July 1790, 12 February 1794, 10 July 1811, 21 October 1812, 6 May 1814.

45. Browne, *Guide* (1811), 97–100; BJ 17 March 1755, 17 March 1766; Savage, *Guide* (1804), 37; *UBD*, II, 90, 93; BCA 1736; BL Egerton MS 3648, fo. 2d.

46. BCM 12 November 1743, 12 January 1810; BL Add. MS 27951, fo. 25; Warner, 358–9.

47. Clarke, *Tour through the South of England in 1791*, 145–6.

48. Macky, *Journey*, 137; BJ 20 January 1800; A. Barbeau, *Life & Letters at Bath in the Eighteenth Century* (1904), 65–6; *Theatre Royal* (Notes, 1981), 2.

49. BJ 14 January 1754, 1 May, 14 July, 17 November 1755, 11 February 1757, 22 May 1758, 13 January 1766; Derrick, *Letters*, 111; Browne, *Guide* (1811), 107–8.

50. BL Egerton MS 3648, fo. 2d; *The Statutes at Large, 1765–1770*, 452; Barbeau, 68–9; *UBD*, II, 94; Browne, *Guide* (1811), 108–9.

51. Derrick, *Letters*, fn 105–6; Browne (1811), 109–10; Ison, 102–4.

52. Diaries of Elizabeth Collett, 1792, 8–10; I have drawn heavily on V. J. Kite, 'Libraries in Bath, 1618–1964' (FLA thesis 1966, copy in Bath Reference Library) and V. J. Kite, 'Circulating Libraries in Eighteenth-century Bath', *A Second North Somerset Miscellany* (Bath & Camerton Arch Soc, 1971); *UBD*, II, 97 ff.

53. BJ 2 February 1754, 12 May 1755; *Bath Guides, Directories and Newspapers* (2nd edn, 1973, Bath Municipal Libraries); L. E. J. Brooke, *Somerset Newspapers 1725–1960* (1960), 13.

54. *Bath Guides*, Preface; A. J. Turner, *Science and Music in Eighteenth Century Bath* (University of Bath, 1977), 12.

55. Mullet, *Public Baths*, 69; Munk, *Roll of Physicians*, II, 278–9.

56. Kite, 'Libraries' (thesis), 63; BCA 1762–63; BJ 4 May 1772; CC 19 April 1810; Turner, 25, 37, 43.

57. Ibid., 47–8; Browne, *Guide* (1811), 113; BJ 20 January, 13, 17 February 1800, 26 January 1801; B & C Gaz 4, 25 November 1812; CC 11 June 1810; Anon., *Guide* (1806), 42.

58. K. Hudson, *The Bath and West Show* (1976), 3–9; Savage, *Guide* (1804), 47; *Science and Music,* catalogue, 82–3, 95, 115; Rack's Journal, 2–4.

59. BJ 16 September 1754; HMC *15th Report,* App., I, 193–4; BL Egerton MS 3648, fo. 4d; W. Orpen, *The Outline of Art* (n.d.), 312–13; E. Waterhouse, *Painting in Britain 1530–1790* (3rd edn 1969), 175; J. Hayes, *Thomas Gainsborough* (Tate Gallery, 1980), 23–4, 30.

60. Bailey, *British Directory* (1784), 336–8; BRO Chamberlains' Accounts, 3 October 1765; Orpen, 330; Waterhouse, 144; William Hoare's mural tablet, Bath Abbey; G. Breeze, 'Thomas Hickey's Stay in Bath', *Proc Som Arch N.H. Soc,* cxxviii, 83–93.

61. I. Williams, *Early English Watercolours* (1970), 49; *Limner of Bath: Thomas Robins,* 4, 6, 10; Warner, *Bath,* 214 ff.; Turner, *Science and Music,* 11, 12; BM, Prints & Drawings, Catalogue of Topographical Drawings.

62. R. A. L. Smith, *Bath* (1945), 66–7, 75–80, 83–7; L. M. Knapp, *Tobias Smollett* (1949), 146–8; T. Smollett, *Humphry Clinker* (Everyman edn, 1943), 35.

63. 6 Anne c. xlii, 12 Geo. II c.xx; Wood, 378–80; McIntyre, list of licensed chairs; *Strangers' Assistant* (1773), 79; (Symonds), *Watering Places,* 6.

64. BJ 24, 31 January 1791; BCM 12 March, 1 August, 10 September, 1 November 1793, 7 January 1794.

65. *Marchioness Grey,* Beds Hist Rec Soc, XLVII, 49; HMC *15th Report,* App., VI, 61; Albert, *Turnpike Road System,* 204, 205, 208; BJ 13 January 1772; GRO 214 F1/115 Parsons Letters; *UBD,* II, 97 ff.

66. Bailey, *Directory* (1784), 336–41; Warner, 214–16; McIntyre, 436; BJ 11, 18, 25 February 1754, 30 March 1772; *Strangers' Assistant,* 90–5.

67. *UBD,* II, 110, 113–15; BJ 7 April 1800; BCA, list of honorary freemen; *The Journals and Letters of Fanny Burney,* ed. Warren Derry (1982), IX, 217; Meyler (1813), 154; B & C Gaz 28 October 1812; BCM 30 March 1752.

68. *Letters from Bath,* 73, 92; GRO D. 1447 Household Accounts of Mrs Edwards; GRO Coddrington MS D. 1610/A75; Bailey, *Directory* (1784), 336 ff.; Warner, 236, 266, 269, 272.

69. Bailey, 336 ff.; *UBD,* II, 97 ff.; Warner, 214–16; R. Wilcox, 'Bath Breweries in the Latter Half of the Eighteenth Century', *A Second North Somerset Miscellany,* (Bath & Camerton Arch Soc, 1971), 27–30; BJ 17 March, 20 October 1755.

70. BJ 19 May 1755; *Letters from Bath,* 146; Bailey, *Directory* (1784), 336 ff.; *UBD,* II, 96; *The Medical Register, 1779, 1783;* J. Haddon, *Bath* (1973), 207.

71. *UBD,* II, 94; BCM 26 April 1708, 11 March 1742, 8 March 1744, 13 February 1756, 22 July, 11 October 1761, 23 October 1762; BRO Chamberlains' Accounts, 12 October 1754, 7 April 1777.

72. BCM 21 April 1766, 5 January 1767, 16 February, 23 September 1776, 5 June 1777, 7 March 1778; Pope, *Bath Guide* (1761), 33; Rack's Journal, 5, 21.

73. Williams, *Lady Luxborough,* 29, 31; BJ 30 March 1772; BRO Chamberlains' Vouchers, November 1767, No. 236, April–June 1767, No. 240.

10   Cold-Bathing at the Minor Spas

1. J. Taverner, *An Essay upon the Witham Spa* (1737), Preface.

2. Copeman, *Society of Apothecaries,* 47–8, 52–4; R. Porter, *English Society in the Eighteenth Century* (1982), 90–1, 302–3.

3. D. W. Linden, *An Experimental Dissertation on the Nature, Contents and Virtues of the Hyde Saline Purging Water* . . . (1751); *UBD*, II, 551; S. Rudder, *A New History of Gloucestershire* (1779), 235.

4. J. Nichols, *The History and Antiquities of the County of Leicester* (1795), IV, i, 234.

5. *DNB*.

6. Mullet, *Public Baths*, 19.

7. *DNB;* BL Catalogue.

8. J. Browne, *An Account of the Wonderful Cures perform'd by the Cold Baths. With advice to Water Drinkers at Tunbridge, Hampstead, Astrope, Nasborough, and other Chalibeate Spaws* . . . (1707, two edns).

9. Albert, *Turnpike Road System*, 35, 42, 49.

10. BL Anon., *Hydro-Sidereon: or a Treatise of Ferruginous-Waters, especially Ipswich-Spaw* . . . (1717).

11. J. King, *An Essay on Hot and Cold Bathing* (1737); *Gents Mag* (April 1734), 224; A Suckling, *The History and Antiquities of the County of Suffolk*, I (1846), 128–9.

12. Cardiff Central Library MS 4370; J. Verdon, Travel Journal (1699), fo. 125r; D. P. Layard, *An Account of the Somersham Water in the County of Huntingdon* (1767); *The Medical Register 1779 & 1780; VCH Hunts*, II, 224–5; Kelly, *Dir Hunts* (1924), 69; Lewis, II, 487; Munk, *Roll of Physicians, II, 1701–1800*, 181–2; *CP*.

13. Bagshaw, *Derbyshire* (1846), 596; T. Short, *Nevill-Holt Spaw-Water* (1749), Preface.

14. T. Short, *A General Treatise on Various Cold Mineral Waters in England* (1765), 114–17.

15. Ibid., 71; Granville, I, 368–9.

16. Blome, *Britannia* (1673), 75; BL Anon., *Sketch of a Tour into Derbyshire and Yorkshire* (1778), 66–71; *UBD*, II (1791), 889; HMC *Gorhambury*, 231; W. Bott, *A Description of Buxton* (1795), 31–2; J. Floyer, *An Essay to Prove Cold Bathing both Safe and Useful* (1702), 24.

17. See Schedule B.

18. J. C. Cox, *The Records of the Borough of Northampton*, II (1898), 262–3.

19. HMC *Portland*, App., VI, 98; *UBD*, IV, 598; E. Baines, *Hist Dir & Gaz County of York*, II (1823), 558.

20. A. F. J. Brown, *Essex at Work 1700–1815* (1969), 140.

21. Mullet, *Public Baths*, 24, 66, 78; BL Catalogue; T. Garnett, *The Mineral Waters of Harrogate* (1792), 21.

22. I have drawn heavily on R. C. B. Oliver, 'Diederick Wessel Linden, M.D.', *The National Library of Wales Journal*, XVIII, 241–66 for this section; D. W. Linden, *Directions for the use of that . . . mineral water, commonly called Berry's Shadwell-Spaw, in Sun-Tavern Fields, Shadwell* (1749).

23. Mullet, 30.

24. I thank Mr G. C. Baugh for this information.

25. Savidge, *Tunbridge Wells*, 36-7, 65; Scott Thomson, *Letters of a Grandmother*, 131.

26. BL Anon., *Heliocrene. A Poem in Latin and English on the Chalybeate Well at Sunning-Hill* (1744); *The Autobiography & Correspondence of Mary Granville, Mrs Delany*, ed. Lady Llanovery, 2nd Series, I (1862), 236; *UBD*, IV, 788; *Travels of Dr Richard Pococke*, II, 61.

27. *Gents Mag* (1751), 33.

28. SRO 2/1/2 and 2/1/3 North Wootton Parish Registers; Neale, *Bath*, 205; BL

Egerton MS 3648 fo. 2d; *Topographical History of Shropshire and Somerset,* ed. G. L. Gomme, *Gents Mag* Lib. (1898), 262–3.

29. J. Davies, *A Short Description of the Waters at Glastonbury* (1751); *Gents Mag* (1751), 411; BJ 1 July 1754, 24 February 1755; W. Gould, *An Enquiry into the Origin, Nature and Virtues of the Glastonbury Waters* (1752), unpublished MS, Stanley Crowe Catalogue 83 (1973), 33. I thank Miss P. Jacobs for this reference.

30. BJ 24 February 1755; *Gents Mag* (1751), 373; R. Warner, *An History of the Abbey of Glaston: and of the Town of Glastonbury* (1826), 276.

31. *Gents Mag* (1751), 294–5; S. Saunders. *A Description of the Curiosities of Glastonbury* (1781), 45–6; BL Anon., *The History of Glastonbury collected from Various Authors* (1794), 40, 45–6; *UBD,* III (1791), 152; J. Collinson, *The History . . . of Somerset,* II (1791), 266; W. Phelps, *History . . . of Somersetshire,* II (1839), 499. I am grateful to Mrs S. Jones for allowing me to see the renovated Pump House.

32. Bagshaw, *Chester* (1850); White, *Norfolk* (1836), 454; S. Woodward, revised W. C. Ewing, *The Norfolk Topographer's Manual* (1842), 54.

33. Addison, *English Spas,* 39–40; Foord, *Springs, Streams and Spas of London,* 68 ff.

34. Ibid., 74–7, 110–11.

35. See Schedule A.

36. Defoe, *Tour,* II, 158; Blome, *Britannia,* 76.

37. *Correspondence of the Reverend Joseph Greene,* Dugdale Soc, XXIII, 18; C. Perry, *An Account of . . . the Stratford Mineral Water* (1744).

38. S. Hales, *Philosophical Experiments . . . An Account of several Experiments . . . on Chalybeate or Steel-Waters* (1739), 113–14.

39. White, *W. R. Yorks.,* II (1838), 305; A. B. and M. D. Anderson, *Vanishing Spas* (1974), 26; *Extracts from the 'Leeds Intelligencer' & the 'Leeds Mercury' 1769–1776,* Thoresby Soc, XXXVIII, 22, 81–2; Short, *General Treatise on Cold Mineral Waters* (1765), 58–61; *Travels of Richard Pococke,* I, 175; B. M. Scott, *Boston Spa* (1985), 10, 12.

40. T. Langdale, *A Topographical Dictionary of Yorkshire* (1822), 238; *Gents Mag* (1804), i, 513; *UBD,* IV, 722; J. H. Manners, Duke of Rutland, *Travels in Great Britain,* II (1813), 115–16.

41. Gore and Shaw, *Liverpool's First Directory* (1766), 4, 5; R. Atkinson, *England Described . . .* (1788), 233; Baines, *Lancs* (1824), 164; *The Medical Register 1779,* 96–7.

42. *Gents Mag* (1799), I, 473–4; Anon., *A Short and Candid Account of the Nature and Virtues of the New Iron Pear-Tree Water* (?), Wellcome Institute, Broadsheet No. 457, 19.

43. See Schedule A.

44. A. Pallister, 'The Dinsdale Spa', *Durham County Local Hist Soc,* Bulletin 14, March 1972, 21–2. I thank Dr E. Jenkinson for this reference.

45. J. Hunter, *South Yorkshire* (1831), 475; White, *W. R. Yorks.,* II (1838), 262–3; K. J. Bonser, 'Spas, Wells and Springs of Leeds', *Thoresby Soc,* LIV, I, 29.

46. R. Willan, *Observations on the Sulphur-Water at Croft, near Darlington* (1782), 53–4; R. L. P. and D. M. Jowitt, *Discovering Spas* (1971), 59.

47. *VCH Wilts,* IV, 388; Munk, *Roll of Physicians,* II, 278–9; BJ 3 January 1791; J. Dugdale, *The British Traveller,* IV (1819), 455.

48. Plaque in the Rotunda of the Elisebrunnen, Aachen; GRO D 1833/F1/30 Lord Bath at Spa, 1763; HMC *Rutland* III, 337.

49. S. McIntyre, 'The Mineral Water Trade in the Eighteenth Century', *The Journal of British Transport History,* New Series, II, i, 8, 15; PRO 190/412/9 and

190/243/6; Lafagne, 13.

50. F. Slare, *An Account of the Pyrmont Waters* (1717), Preface, iv–viii 7, 10, 30; McIntyre, 9, 14–15.

51. J. H. P. Pafford, 'The Spas and Mineral Springs of Wiltshire', *WAM,* LV, 13; McIntyre, 3, 8, 12; BL 778.k.15(5), undated advertisement.

52. BJ 4 March 1754, 17, 24 March 1755, 30 June, 8 September 1766; *WAM,* LVI, 388–9.

53. See Schedule D; Pafford, Spas of Wiltshire, *WAM,* LV, 16: BJ 17 March, 20 October 1755.

54. *Candid Account of . . . the New Iron Pear-Tree Water* (?), 4.

55. D. W. Linden, *A Treatise on Chalybeate Waters . . .* (1748), xxi–; Ibid., *Hyde Spa,* 68.

56. GRO D. 1799/A 355; Schedule D.

11   Cheltenham: The Village Spa

1. S. Moreau, *A Tour to Cheltenham Spa* (1783), 36.

2. *The Limner of Bath,* 24; G. Hart, *A History of Cheltenham* (2nd edn, 1981), 115; B & C Gaz 6 August 1838; Little, 'Gloucestershire Spas', 182; J. Goding, *History of Cheltenham* (1863), 256–7.

3. Little, 182; Moreau, 36; mural tablet in Cheltenham parish church.

4. Hart, 88, 113–14, 122–3; Moreau, 26; HMC *13th Report,* App., II, 303; PRO WO 30/48 fo. 67d.

5. *CP;* Little, 'Gloucestershire Spas', 183–4; Moreau, 23, 26; Anon., *Guide to Watering Places* (1806), 155; Goding, 249–50; *Rowe's Illustrated Cheltenham Guide 1850* (S. R. Publishers Ltd, 1969), 39.

6. Goding, 250; Rowe, 37; *Limner of Bath,* 4, 22.

7. Goding, 256; *Limner of Bath,* 23; Hart, 121. *Burke's Peerage & Baronetage* (52nd edn, 1890), 1292.

8. Oliver, 'Diedrick Wessel Linden', 250; mural tablet to Hughes in Cheltenham parish church.

9. *Purefoy Letters 1735–53,* ed. G. Eland (1931), II, 333, 334 fn.

10. Moreau, 23; Goding, 252, 254; Sydenham, *Bath Pleasure Gardens,* 2.

11. L. W. Bayley, *Robert Hughes 1771–1827* (1952), 4; Little, 'Gloucestershire Spas', 187; CC 5 May 1810; Hart, 126, 128.

12. Ibid., 122, 128; Goding, 252; *Purefoy Letters,* II, 331.

13. Hart, 122; B. Smith and E. Ralph, *A History of Bristol and Gloucestershire* (1972), 92; Goding, 292.

14. PRO WO 30/49 fo. 44r; Goding, 259, 261–3; BJ 13 May 1754; Moreau, 29, 33.

15. GRO Batsford Park MS D.1447, Accounts of Mrs (Jane) Edwards of Bristol.

16. Hart, 127; Goding, 268–9; Moreau, 31.

17. Humphris and Willoughby, *At Cheltenham Spa* (1928), 36–9; Villiers, 'Pump and Promenade', 185; Goding, 338; B & C Gaz 21 October 1812.

18. Goding, 262, 286; Moreau, 23; *Limner of Bath,* 24; Pococke, *Travels,* II, 274; *UBD,* II, 549; Anon., *Guide to Watering Places* (1806), 152.

19. B. Little, 'Gloucestershire Spas', 188; B. Little, *Cheltenham* (1952), 35; S. Moreau, *A Tour to the Royal Spa at Cheltenham* (1797), 41; *The Torrington Diaries,* ed. C. B. and F. Andrews (1954); *Guide* (1806), 149.

20. Moreau (1783), 30–2.

21. Mullet, *Public Baths and Health,* 73; Moreau (1783), fn 26; *Torrington Diaries,* 44, 46, 48, 61.

22. GRO D. 1447, Accounts of Mrs Edwards; *Torrington Diaries,* 33–4, 44, 48.

23. Little, *Cheltenham,* 37; *Torrington Diaries,* 44–6.

24. Little, *Cheltenham,* 37–8; Hart, 126–9, 140.

25. Moreau, *Tour* (1797), 41; *UBD,* II, 550; (Symonds), *Companion to the Watering and Bathing Places* (1800), 47; Bayley, *Robert Huges,* 8; Browne, *New Bath Guide* (1811), 159; CC 12 October 1809, 5 April, 25 October 1810; BJ 20 May 1816.

26. Moreau (1797), 41–2; 21 June 1810; *Guide to Watering Places* (1806), 159.

27. A Varley, 'A History of the Libraries of Cheltenham from 1780 to 1900' (unpublished FLA thesis, 1968), 14–15.

28. Hart, 126, 133; Goding, 341; Moreau (1783), 32–3; G. A. Williams, *A New Guide to Cheltenham* (1825), 54.

29. Moreau (1797), 41; Williams, *Guide* (1825), 10; *Commons Journals, 1786,* XLI, 277.

30. Hart, 128–9, 240–1; *Lords Journals, 1786,* XXXVIII, 500, 505.

31. Hart, 241–3; (Symonds) *Companion to Watering Places,* 45; 'An American in Gloucestershire and Bristol: The Diary of Joshua Gilpin, 1796–7', *Trans Bristol and Glos Arch Soc,* XCII, 177.

12   The Challenge of Cheltenham

1. Goding, *Cheltenham,* 305; The London Gazette, no. 13006, 8–12 July 1788, 330; BCM 1 August 1788; *Gents Mag* (1788), ii, 884; Moreau (1793), 4, 5.

2. *Correspondence of George III,* ed. Aspinall, I, 388.

3. Ibid., 380–1; GRO D. 1137, Forthampton MS, File 3, 14 August 1788 (typescript).

4. Hart, 134; Little, 'Gloucestershire Spas', 194; *Gents Mag* (1788), ii, 758, 978; Goding, 343. Hart thinks there were three visits.

5. Little, 'Spas', 191, 197–8; GRO D. 1137, File 3, 9 June 1789; Moreau (1797), 38.

6. Ibid.; La Cave watercolour and etching, Cheltenham Art Gallery; *UBD,* II, 549–50.

7. Ibid.; Moreau (1797), 38.

8. *Bath Herald,* 3 March 1792; M. Barratt, 'An Account of the Journeys undertaken by the Rev Richard and Mrs Boucher 1788–89, *History Studies University Hall Buckland* (1968), I, i, 45; (Symonds), *Companion to Watering Places* (1800), 22, 45; *UBD,* II, 550.

9. Harper, *Directory of Cheltenham* (1844), 121; 'Diary of Joshua Gilpin', 174, 177; Cardiff Reference Library MS 3,127, R. Colt Hoare, Tours in North Wales 1796, fos 1–2, Tour of South Wales 1801, fo. 8r.

10. Colt Hoare, North Wales, 1796, fos 9d, 10r; 'Joshua Gilpin', 178; Moreau (1797), 42.

11. S. T. Blake, *Cheltenham Historical Walks,* No. 3 (1978) (1); Hart, 137; J. Shenton, *Cheltenham Directory* (1800), 15; CC 3 September, 6 October 1814.

12. Hart, 137–8; 25 Geo.III c.cxxv; Moreau (1797), 38, 204–6; Shenton (1800), 23.

13. 32 Geo.III c.lxxxiii; C. Hadfield, *Canals of the West Midlands* (1966), 147–9.

14. Hart, 138; (Symonds), *Watering Places* (1800), 52.

15. Hart, 163; CC 15 March, 5 April 1810; D. E. Bick, *Old Leckhampton* (1971), 5, 7, 10, 15.

16. Symonds, 53; CC 7 December 1809, 15 February, 15 March, 5 April 1810; BL Anon., *Watering Places of England* (SPCK, 1853), 55.

17. R. Howe, 'Joseph Pitt, Landowner', *Gloucestershire Historical Studies*, VII (1976), 20; R. Howe, 'Joseph Pitt and Pittville', *Gloucestershire Historical Studies*, VI (1974–5), 58; *CP;* Hart, 151.

18. Howe, VI, 58; Hart, 146; 11 Geo.IV and 1 Gul.IV c.vi; 45 Gul.IV c.i.

19. S. T. Blake, *Cheltenham Historical Walks*, No. 2 (1977)(4); CC 7 September 1809; R. Howe, 'The Rise and Fall of Joseph Pitt', *Gloucestershire Historical Studies*, VIII (1977), 64.

20. CC 8 February, 15 March, 31 May, 28 June 1810; Goding, 639.

21. E. Lee, *Cheltenham and its Resources* (1851), 12; CC 8 February 1810, 29 September 1814; Williams, *Guide to Cheltenham* (1825), 193.

22. CC 4, 25 May, 8, 29 June, 3 August 1809, 15 March 1810, 19 May 1814; D. Verey, *Gloucestershire: The Vale and the Forest of Dean* (1970), 148–9.

23. Williams, *Guide* (1825) 33, 101; Capper; Humphris and Willoughby, 42–3; H. Ruff, *History of Cheltenham* (1803), 54; CC 21 December 1809; Anon., *Guide to Watering Places* (1806), 160, 161; B & C Gaz 21 October 1812; CC 27 July 1809, 31 May 1810.

24. H. Ruff, *Beauties of Cheltenham* (1806), 16; W. Strange, *The Visitor's Guide to the Watering Places* (1842), 47; CC 27 July 1809, 2 August 1810, 6 Oct. 1814, 11 May 1815, 26 June 1817.

25. War RO Heber-Percy MS, Greatheed's Journal 1812–14, 28 December 1812.

26. Goding, 110; Verey, 123, 143–4; Williams, *Guide* (1825), 24; *Rowe's Guide* (1850), 29; Granville, II, 289.

27. Lewis, I, 507; Anon., *Guide to Watering Places* (1806), 152, 159; Trinder's Map of Cheltenham, 1809; Hart, 245; CC 15 June 1809, 4 April 1816, 20 May 1819; BJ 19 August 1816.

28. *Gents Mag* (1791), i, 513; CC 26 October, 2 November 1809.

29. CC 24 October 1816; Williams, *Guide* (1825), 97. Both Hart, who gives 1806 (p. 152) and Little (1810) in *Gloucestershire Spas* (p. 188), are wrong about the date of Moreau's death. King built a villa in Cheltenham in 1804.

13   The Innkeepers' Rule: Harrogate and Scarborough

1. BL Anon., *The New Brighton Guide; or, Companion . . . to all the Watering-Places in Great Britain* (1796), 20 fn–21.

2. Anon., *Guide to Watering Places* (1806), 238.

3. J. A. Patmore, 'Harrogate and Knaresborough: a study in urban development' (Oxford B.Litt. thesis, 1959), 47–8, 50, 52–3.

4. *A History of Harrogate and Knaresborough*, ed. B. Jennings (1970), 21–2, 231; W. J. Kaye, *Records of Harrogate* (1922), 108, 120–4; W. Grainge, *The History and Topography of Harrogate and the Forest of Knaresborough* (1871), fn 199.

5. HMC *14th Report*, App., IX, 260–1; *The Great Diurnal of Nicholas Blundell*, I, Rec Soc Lancs and Cheshire, CX, 113; *Travels of Richard Pococke*, 57.

6. Anon., *Guide to Watering Places* (1806), 236; Cardiff Central Library, MS 4, 302 R. Colt Hoare, Journal, V, fo. 40r; Rutland, *Travels in Great Britain*, II, 124; Brown, *Essex at Work*, 77–8; HMC *14th Report*, App., IX, 260; Brooke, *George III*, 102.

7. *Richard Pococke*, 58; Kaye, xiii, 79–81, 159.

8. Ibid., xxv, 193; Albert, *Turnpike Road System*, 34, 63 fn, 205, 250; HMC *14th Report*, App., IX, 260–1; HMC *Gorhambury*, 239.

9. Jennings, 287–8.

10. E. Dean, *Spadacrene Anglica* (1736 edn), Preface; Jennings, 236, Plate 15; *Extracts from the 'Leeds Intelligencer' etc.,* Thoresby Soc., XXXVII, 75.

11. Jennings, 258–9; Kaye, 82 fn; Pevsner, *Yorkshire, the West Riding* (1959), 252; Grainge, 118; Colt Hoare, Journal (1800), V, fo. 41r; Patmore, 133; Lafagne, *Spa et les Anglais,* 17.

12. Jennings, 259; Grainge, 89, 117; 29 Geo. III c.lxxvi; Kaye, 86.

13. Grainge, 136 fn, 198; *A Week at Harrogate. A Poem . . . from Benjamin Blunderhead* (2nd edn, 1814), 21; Colt Hoare, Journal, V, 55r; Jennings 236, 295–6; Garnett, *Mineral Waters of Harrogate* (1792), 23–4; Inscription in the Old Pump Room Museum, Harrogate.

14. Jennings, 236–7; Grainge, 119, 120, 188; White, *Yorkshire,* II (1838), 786; (Symonds), *Companion to Watering Places* (1800), 58–9; *Week at Harrogate,* 23, 31, 73; Colt Hoare, Journal, V, 42r; Capper; Anon., *Guide to Watering Places* (1806), 238.

15. Colt Hoare, Journal, V, fos 40r, 41r, 56r, 57r; Jennings, 288; (Symonds), *Watering Places,* 57–9, 70; Mavor, *British Tourists* (1800), VI, 270.

16. Kaye, 92, 96; Jennings, 289.

17. J. A. Patmore, thesis, 113, 120; J. A. Patmore, *An Atlas of Harrogate* (1963), 16; Grainge, 154–5; Capper; White, *W. R. Yorks* (1838), 786; Jennings, 290; *Week at Harrogate,* 23, 31, 73, 77, 80.

18. Patmore, thesis, 121–2; Jennings, 290–1; Grainge, 141.

19. G. C. F. Forster, 'Scarborough 1566–1766', *Scarborough 966–1966,* ed. M. Edwards (1966), 61; J. H. Martin, 'Scarborough 1766–1866', ibid., 67, 68; PRO WO 30/48, fos 208d, 214r.

20. *The History of Scarborough,* ed. A. Rowntree (1931), 256, 347; Forster, 61, 63; BL Anon., *A Dissertation on the Contents, Virtues and Uses of Cold and Hot Mineral Springs Particularly those of Scarborough . . .* (1735), App.; Mullet, 24–5; *Gents Mag* (April 1734), 224; Linden, *Treatise on Chalybeate and Natural Waters* (1748), xxi; McIntyre, 'Mineral Water Trade', 6, 13, 14.

21. Macky, *Journey Through England,* II, 239; Rowntree, 256; *Letters of a Grandmother,* 46.

22. McIntyre, Resorts, 190–9; Macky, *Journey,* II, 239; PRO WO 30/49, fo. 165r; *Letters of a Grandmother,* 46, 57.

23. Gilbert, *Brighton,* 12; Rowntree, 256; Forster, 65; HMC *15th Report,* App., VI, 106, fn 3; *Letters,* 64.

24. T. Whellan, *History of the City of York and the North Riding* (1859), 715, fn 715–16; Kelly, *Dir. N. & E. Ridings of Yorks.* (1905), 299–300; HMC *15th Report,* App., VI, 193; Rowntree, 256; *Gents Mag* (1804), II, 749; Capper.

25. Picture, Scarborough Art Gallery; Rutland, *Travels in Great Britain,* II, 83; *UBD,* IV, 385; McIntyre, 'Mineral Water Trade', 6, 14; Whellan, *North Riding,* 716 fn.

26. Hughes, *North Country Life,* 400–1; Baldwin, *Present State of England,* I, 279; Rowntree, 257.

27. Albert, *Turnpike System,* 42; McIntyre, Resorts, 196; *Extracts from the Leeds Intelligencer 1777–82 . . .,* Thoresby Soc, XL, 7; Rowntree, 266.

28. *The Travel Journal of Philip Yorke, 1744–63,* Beds Hist Rec Soc, XLVII, 131; HMC *Gorhambury,* 237; Rowntree, 258.

29. Rowntree, 263, 266, 279; Forster, plate facing p. 65; Anon., *Guide to Watering Places* (1806), 340–1.

30. Bailey, *British Directory* (1784), III, 678; *UBD,* IV, 384, 386; Rowntree, 261, 266; Mavor, *British Tourists,* VI, 270; BL Anon., *A Guide to the Several Watering*

and Sea-Bathing Places (1813), 53; Anon., *Guide to Watering Places* (1806), 341; Rutland, *Travels,* II, 82.

31. 25 Geo.II c.xxvi; 28 Geo.II c.xix; Rowntree, 267; Mavor, 270; Anon., *Guide* (1813), 53; J. G. Rutter, 'Scarborough 1866–1966: The Holiday Resort', *Scarborough,* ed. Edwards, 81; HMC *Rutland,* III, 415; HMC *14th Report,* App., I, 73; Rutland, *Travels,* II (1831), 85; *UBD,* IV, 383.

32. Rowntree, 263; HMC *Gorhambury,* 237; HMC *14th Report,* App., I, 414, 424; HMC *Rutland,* III, 415.

33. Rowntree, 277, 278, 421; McIntyre, *Resorts,* 201, 203; Anon., *Guide* (1806), 342.

34. Rowntree, 281, 351, 421.

14   The Innkeepers' Spas of Derbyshire: Buxton and Matlock

1. T. Marchington, 'The Development of Buxton and Matlock since 1800' (London University MA thesis, 1961), 20, 31, 33; HMC 13th Report, App., IV, 474; HMC *Gorhambury,* 231; Axon, *Historical Notes on Buxton,* 3rd and 4th Papers (no pagination).

2. Dugdale, *New British Traveller,* II (1819), 15; T. J. Page, *A Month at Buxton* (13th edn, 1828), 12 fn.

3. HMC *Harley,* II, 429, III, 358; *Journal of Mr John Hobson,* Surtees Soc, LXV, 306; *Diary of Richard Kay,* Chetham Soc, XVI, 28, 29, 90, 120.

4. HMC *13th Report,* App., IV, 474; *The Diaries of Thomas Wilson, D.D., 1731–37 and 1750,* ed. C. L. S. Linnell (1964), 248; Axon, 16th Paper; *John Hobson,* 294; Hughes, *North Country Life,* 401; *Correspondence of Mrs Delany,* 2nd Ser. I (1826), 75–6; HMC *Rutland,* III, 429.

5. HMC *Gorhambury,* 232; Axon, 16th Paper; A. Jewitt, *A History of Buxton* (1816), 63–4 (internal evidence shows this to have been written about 1812, see p. 59); R. Grundy Heape, *Buxton under the Dukes of Devonshire* (1948), 26; BL Anon., *Sketch of a Tour into Derbyshire and Yorkshire* (1778), 120.

6. Axon, 16th Paper.

7. Ibid.

8. HMC *14th Report,* App., IV, 508; *UBD,* II, 448; J. A. Goodacre, *Buxton Old and New* (1928), 30; Jewitt, 50; *British Medical Journal,* II (1940), 233; *Medical Register 1779–83,* 71, 124–5; E. G. Cox *A Reference Guide to the Literature of Travel,* III (1949), viii (Spas), 319.

9. S. Glover, *The History and Gazetteer of the County of Derby,* I, ii (1833), 202; *CP;* Grundy Heape, 20; *Torrington Diaries,* 227; F. L. Bickley, *The Cavendish Family* (1911), 222.

10. Albert, *Turnpike Road System,* 203, 209; Axon, 3rd and 12th Papers; *Statutes at Large,* VIII, 31 Geo.II, no. 62, 32 Geo.II, no. 61, XI, II Geo.III, no. 19; Longleat MS, Portland Papers, XIV, fo. 103d; Glover, 202.

11. Lafagne, *Spa et les Anglais,* 16; HMC *10th Report,* App., I, 371; Bickley, *Cavendish Family,* 247, gives 1778 for the Tunbridge Wells visit, but see B. Masters, *Georgiana, Duchess of Devonshire* (1981), 72; also Masters, 52, 77, 84, 99, 106–7, 148, 171, 190, 193, 213; J. Pearson, *Stags and Serpents: the Story of the House of Cavendish . . .* (1983), 95, 100.

12. Grundy Heape, 27–78 ff.; Colvin, *British Architects,* 189–91.

13. Grundy Heape, 28–9, 124.

14. Ibid., 28–9; Burton, *Historic Buxton,* 6–7.

15. Grundy Heape, 29; Axon, 12th and 16th Papers; Jewitt, 34, 54; Glover, 206; Goodacre, 28; Pevsner, *Derbyshire,* revised E. Williamson (2nd edn, 1978), 113–14; W. Bott, *A Description of Buxton and the Adjacent Country* (1795), 5; *UBD,* II, 448; Granville, *Midlands,* 52; Mavor, *British Tourists,* VI, 271.

16. Bott, *Buxton* (1795), 10, 44, (1813 edn), 8; Jewitt, 36.

17. Pevsner, 114; Burton, 8–9; Bott (1795), 56, ibid. (1796), 5; Jewitt, 55–6; Dugdale, British Traveller, II, 28; Page, *Month at Buxton* (13th edn, 1828), 8; *Torrington Diaries,* 241.

18. Bott, *Buxton* (1813), 8; Jewitt, 57, 61, 63, 160–2; Pevsner, 114; Axon, 16th Paper; *UBD,* II, 448; Holden, *Annual Directory* (1811), 111.

19. Axon, 16th Paper; Grundy Heape, 25; Dugdale, *British Traveller,* II, 28 fn; Bott, *Buxton* (1800), 11–12.

20. Marchington, 56; Dugdale, 28; Page, 8; Burton, 9–10.

21. Axon, 12th paper; BL Catalogue; Jewitt, 68–9, 157, 160, 163; *UBD,* II, 448; Page, 19.

22. *UBD,* II, 448; Bott (1795), 54, ibid. (1800), 56; Jewitt, 158.

23. Marchington, 58; Jewitt, 162–4.

24. Axon, 10th Paper; Bott (1813), 48; (Symonds), *Companion to Watering Places* (1800), 36; Jewitt, 60, 156, 164.

25. Jewitt, 25, 140, 141 fn; Bagshaw, *Derbyshire* (1846), 436; Albert, *Turnpike Road Systems,* 219.

26. *Torrington Diaries,* 241, 249; Jewitt, 144; Dugdale, 29; Grundy Heape, 39, 45; Glover, *Hist. of Derby* (1833), I, iii, 208; 51 Geo.III c. lxix.

27. Dugdale, 28; Jewitt, 152–3; Bott (1813), 7; BL Anon., *Guide to Watering Places* (1813), 21; Glover (1833), 202; White, *County of Derby* (1857), 501.

28. HMC *5th Report,* App., 210, *12th Report,* App., IX, 216–17; Jewitt, 151; Page, 113; Hughes, *North Country Life,* 410–12.

29. Grundy Heape, 31–2, 56, 77; Jewitt, 156.

30. Dugdale, 28; Glover (1833), 211; Jewitt, 155–6.

31. Axon, 16th Paper; Grundy Heape, 33.

32. Marchington, 42, 45, 49.

33. Macky, *Journey,* II, 207; Bagshaw, *Derbyshire* (1846), 377; Defoe, *Tour Through England,* II, 160; Dugdale, 69; BL Anon., *Gem of the Peak* (3rd edn, *c.* 1843), 34; *Camden's Britannia,* ed. R. Gough, II (1789), 310–11; Lewis (1849 edn), III, 276–7.

34. Albert, *Turnpike System,* 208; *Diary of Richard Kay,* 120; *Journal of Philip Yorke,* 162.

35. Marchington, 41; Bagshaw, 377; Atkinson, *England Described,* 73; *Tour into Derbyshire and Yorkshire* (1778), 75–7; HMC *Gorhambury,* 233.

36. *Tour* (1778), 76; *Gents Mag* (1774), 353; *Moritz's Travels, 1782* (J. Pinkerton, *Voyages and Travels* [1808], 552).

37. Rutland, *Travels in Great Britain,* II, 280; Bagshaw, 380; Marchington, 56, 91; *Camden's Britannia,* II, 310; *Torrington Diaries,* 251.

38. Bagshaw, 375, 377, 381; Gorton, II, 782; *Gem of the Peak,* 27, 42, 43, 81; *Torrington Diaries,* 179.

39. Mavor, *British Tourists,* VI, 271; Dugdale, 69; *Gem of the Peak,* 28, 35, 38–9; Albert, 220.

40. Colt Hoare, Journals, V, fo. 83; Bott, *Buxton* (1795), 24; (Symonds) *Companion to Watering Places* (1800), 105; *Gem of the Peak,* 63; Dugdale, 69; Capper; *Guide to Watering Places* (1806), 315; *Watering Places* (1813), 46.

15   Georgian Spas of the South: Tunbridge Wells, Epsom and Southampton

1. Chalklin, *Provincial Towns*, 24.

2. St John Colbran, *Guide and Visitor's Handbook to Tunbridge Wells . . .* (1881), 102; Sprange, *Tunbridge Wells* (1780), 40; NRO H(K) 183, John Scattergood's Letters, *c.* 1719/20; Mary Berry, *Extracts from Journals and Correspondence 1783–1852* (1856), II, 332; Onely, *Tunbridge Wells . . .* (1771), 16.

3. 8 Ann. c.xx; Bagshaw, *Kent* (1847), 404; Savidge, *Tunbridge Wells*, 50.

4. HMC *Harley*, II, 118; HMC *15th Report*, App., I, 146; Savidge, 39; *Diary of Dudley Ryder*, 338; Sprange, 43; Bagshaw, 404; HMC *2nd Report*, App., 29.

5. HMC *8th Report*, App., II, 109; HMC *10th Report*, App., I, 269–70; *Letters of a Grandmother*, 92, 95.

6. GRO D. 1833 Rooke MS, Fl/28, F3/7, F4/4.

7. Baldwin, *Present State of England*, I, 137; NRO Scattergood's Letters; Colbran, 107; Macky, *Journey*, I, 118–20.

8. Savidge, 51, gives the date of expiry as 1732; but see Colbran, 42.

9. Savidge, 52–4; P. Amsinck, *Tunbridge Wells and its Neighbourhood* (1810), 7; *Commons Journal 1737–41*, 530.

10. Colbran, 114; Dugdale, *British Traveller*, IV, 260; Savidge, 49.

11. Ibid., 61–2; Amsinck, 13; BJ 30 September, 7 October 1754; Sprange (1780), App., 15; *Dr. Wilson's Diary*, 165.

12. 'A Tour into Kent, 1759', *Arch Cant* LXIX, 174; Amsinck, 14–15; Savidge, 63; *Dr Wilson*, 167; *Verney Letters, Eighteenth Century*, II, 143–4; (Symonds), *Companion to Watering Places* (1800), 135.

13. M. B. and A. D. F. Streeten, 'Another Chalybeate Spring and Cold Bath at Tunbridge Wells', *Arch Cant* LXXXVII, 177–9; Savidge, 63; Sprange, 42; Colbran, 148; *Verney Letters*, II, 144; Mavor, *British Tourists*, VI, 278; Derrick, *Letters from Tunbridge Wells* (1767), 56.

14. Wilson, 160; *Verney Letters*, 232–3; Amsinck, 14.

15. Wilson, 161, 166; Derrick, *Letters*, 57; Savidge, 89.

16. W. A. Shaw, *The Knights of England* (1906), II, 291; Savidge, 65, 66–8, 88; 22 Geo. II c.xxviii, 28 Geo. II c.xxxiv; Pelton, *Illustrated Guide to Tunbridge Wells* (1893), 25.

17. Savidge, 208.

18. BJ 7 October 1816; Berry, *Journals*, II, 332; Savidge, 74–5.

19. Derrick, 48 fn, 56; Albert, *Turnpike Road System*, 202–14; Sprange (1780), App., 7.

20. P. J. Corfield, *The Impact of English Towns 1700–1800* (1982), 10.

21. (Symonds), *Watering Places* (1800), 138, 143; Sprange (1780), Add.1; Savidge, 97.

22. Derrick, 47, 49, 57.

23. HMC *Bath*, I, 254–5, 343; *Dr Wilson's Diary*, 163.

24. Streeten, 'Another Chalybeate Spring', 179–82; Linden, *Treatise on Chalybeate Waters . . .* (1748), 65; Cox, *Guide to the Literature of Travel*, III (1949), 321.

25. Bagshaw (1847), 404; Sprange (1780), 34, 40; Onely, *Tunbridge Wells*, 6; Berry, *Letters*, II, 332.

26. Savidge, 84–5, 103; *Watering Places* (1800), 139; Capper; J. Clifford, *A Descriptive Guide of Tunbridge Wells* (1818), 18; Strange, *Guide to Watering Places* (1842), 84; Savidge, 85, 118.

27. Clifford, 23; Savidge, 81, 84.

28. Ibid., 48–9, 92–4, 96.

29. Ibid., 89; Derrick, *Letters,* 60-1; Addison, *English Spas,* 25.

30. Savidge, 97, 99-100; Mavor, *British Tourists,* vi, 278; Berry, *Journals,* II, 505–6.

31. J. Clifford, *The Directory: or, the Ancient and Present State of Tunbridge Wells* (1816), 64; J. Clifford, *Guide to Tunbridge Wells* (1818), 15; Colvin, *Architects,* 366–7; Amsinck, 34.

32. Anon., *Guide to Watering Places* (1806), 419, 421–4.

33. Dugdale, *British Traveller,* IV, 260.

34. Clark, 'History of Epsom Spa', *Surrey Arch Coll,* LVII, 35–8; Macky, *Journey,* 157; *VCH Surrey,* III, 272.

35. *A Collection of Several Pieces of Mr John Toland* (1726 edn), II, 111.

36. BL Anon., *Some Particulars relating to . . . Epsom* (1825), 85; Clark, *Epsom Spa,* 31; E. W. Brayley, *A Topographical History of Surrey* (1841), IV, 355–6; *Bailey's British Dictionary 1784,* IV, 806.

37. A. Temple Patterson, *Southampton* (1970), 63, 64, 69, 73, facing 85.

38. Ibid., 72–4; T. Baker, *The Southampton Guide* (2nd edn, 1775), 24, 26, 27; K. Denbigh, *A Hundred British Spas* (1981), 127 ff.; Anon., *Guide to Watering Places* (1806), 367.

39. Patterson, 76–8.

40. Ibid., 79–81; Colvin, *Architects,* 514; Robert Newton, Exeter 1770–1780, *Middle Class Housing in Britain,* ed. M. A. Simpson and T. H. Lloyd (1977), 12; Baker, 24–6.

41. Baker, 24; Patterson, 81; Anon., *Guide to Watering Places* (1806), 369.

42. Meyler, *Bath Guide* (1813), 101; Mavor, *British Tourists,* VI (1800), 256; Patterson, 82; Anon., *Guide to Watering Places* (1806), 363–6.

43. Patterson, 96–7.

16   The Severn Spas: The Bristol Hotwells and Malvern

1. V. Waite, 'The Bristol Hotwells', in *Bristol in the Eighteenth Century,* ed. P. McGrath (1972), 113; Atkinson, *England Described,* 377.

2. *Diary of Dudley Ryder,* 242; NRO H(K) 183, Scattergood's Diary, 24 February 1720; BJ 2, 30 March 1772; Chalklin, *Provincial Towns,* 277.

3. S. Rudder, *A New History of Gloucestershire* (1779), 375; Waite, 119–20; W. Ison, *The Georgian Buildings of Bristol* (1978), 124; Little, 'Gloucestershire Spas', 178; BJ 21 July 1755; Atkinson, 378.

4. Rudder, 377, 382; J. Baker, *The New Guide to Bristol and Clifton* (1894), 101–2; Ison, 47, 158–60; Pevsner, *North Somerset and Bristol,* 437; Little, 173.

5. Macky, *Journey,* II, 148; GRO D. 1833 Rooke MS Fl/20; HMC *15th Report,* App., VI, 207; *Passages from the Diaries of Mrs. Philip Lykke Powys . . . 1756–1808,* ed. E. J. Climenson (1899), 49.

6. *Bath and Bristol Guide* (1755), 45; BJ 22 April 1754, 2 June 1755, 29 May 1758, 23 June 1766; Little, 175; Anon., *Guide to Watering Places* (1806), 110.

7. BJ 2 February, 27 May 1754, 12 May 1755, 29 May 1758, 21 April 1766; *Powys Diaries,* 49.

8. Meyler, *Bath Guide* (1813), 97–100; McIntyre, 'Resorts,' 315; Little, 179; Browne, *New Bath Guide* (1811), 152.

9. McIntyre, 'Mineral Water Trade,' 4, 5, 12, 13; Baldwin, *Present State of England,* I, 207; *The Trade of Bristol in the Eighteenth Century,* Bristol Rec Soc, XX, 36, 76, 80.

10. R. Atkyns, *The Ancient and Present State of Gloucestershire* (1768), 188; HMC *Gorhambury,* 251; BL Add. MS 27951 Anon. Travel Diary August–Septem-

ber 1772, fo. 16; BJ 13 April, 11 May 1772; Ison, 198, 202–5; Rudder, *Gloucestershire*, 382–3.

11. Little, 179; Waite, 121; Ison, 213, 224–5; Mavor, *British Tourists*, VI, 256; (Symonds), *Companion to Watering Places* (1800), 29.

12. Ison, 214, 226–8, 231; 'An American in Gloucestershire and Bristol', *Trans. Bristol & Glos Arch Soc*, XCII, 186; E. Clarke, *South of England . . . in 1791* (1793), 151–2, 153.

13. Waite, 113; BJ 8 April 1816; B & C Gaz 5 January 1820; Anon., *Guide to Watering Places* (1806), 118.

14. Waite, 122; GRO D 214 Parsons Letters, Fl/196.

15. 'An American', 186; Ison, 214, 226–7, 228–9, 231–2, 235–6.

16. Ibid., 130–4; B & C Gaz 8 November 1812, 26 May 1813, 15 February 1825; Browne, *New Bath Guide* (1811), 152–3; BJ 15 July 1816; Anon., *Guide to Watering Places* (1806), 112.

17. Waite, 'Bristol Hotwell', 122–3; 56 Geo. III c.vii; Mavor, *British Tourists*, VI, 256.

18. B. S. Smith, *A History of Malvern* (1978 edn), 171–3, 286; HMC *14th Report*, App., II, 416.

19. J. Wall, *Experiments and Observations on the Malvern Waters* (2nd edn, 1757), title page, 5, 17 ff., (3rd edn, 1763), 75, 78 ff.; Mullet, *Public Baths*, 32, 69; Smith, 174–5.

20. J. Chambers, *A General History of Malvern* (1817), 281; Smith, 175.

21. *Torrington Diaries*, 48, 50; Chambers, *Malvern*, 92, 282; Colt Hoare, Journal . . . Tours in North Wales, IV, fos 12r, 15r; Colt Hoare, English Journal, I, fo. 26r; Smith, *Malvern*, 176–7; J. Barrett, *A Description of Malvern* (1796), 52; (Symonds), *Watering Places* (1800), 77.

22. Colt Hoare, N. Wales, fo. 21r; *The Medical Register 1779*, 142, *1783*, 118; Barrett, 42, 51; J. Browne, *The Historic and Local Cheltenham Guide* (1805), 113; Cross, *Historical Handbook to Malvern* (1864?), 136; Smith, 175–6, 185; (Symonds), *Watering Places* (1800), 77.

23. Smith, 160; Barrett, 22.

24. CC 11 May, 10 August 1809; Smith, 184–5; BL Anon., *Letters on Malvern, Descriptive and Historical* (c. 1814), 7.

25. Chambers, 92–3; M. Southall, *Description of Malvern* (1822), 61; Smith, 178; CC 10 August 1809, 3, 24 May 1810, 13 August 1818; Herefordshire Journal 6 September 1815, 26 August 1818.

26. CC 10 May 1810, 19 May 1814, 18 May 1815; *Letters on Malvern* (c. 1814), 12; Chambers, 92; Southall, 60; CJ 15 June 1840; Smith, 180.

27. Smith, 184, 289; Southall, 10, 11, 13–14.

17   Wartime Cheltenham: Problems of Expansion

1. Hart, *Cheltenham,* 138; 49 Geo. III c. xxix; 50 Geo. III c. ii; CC 8 March 1810, 23 June 1814, 30 April, 7 May 1818; B & C Gaz 14 April 1813; Goding, 542; Smith and Ralph, *Bristol and Gloucestershire,* 94.

2. CC 4, 11, 25 May, 9, 16 November 1809, 26 April, 21 June 1810; F. C. Westley, *The New Guide to Cheltenham* (1867), 52.

3. B & C Gaz 3 February 1813; CC 12 May, 16 June 1814.

4. Moreau, *Cheltenham Spa* (1783), 33, (1797), 206; Hart, 273; CC 15 February 1810; Goding, 288.

5. Cheltenham Art Gallery.

6. CC 22 June, 27 July 1809.

7. Williams, *Guide* (1825), 29, 54; Mullet, *Public Baths,* 74; *Gents Mag* (1804), ii, 648–50; CC 10 August 1809.

8. War RO Heber-Percy MS, Greatheed's Journal 1812–14, 28 December 1812; Strange, *Guide to Watering Places* (1842), 57.

9. *Gloucester Journal* 11 September 1815; *Leeds Intelligencer* 6 August 1829; *York Courant* 19 May 1829.

10. *CP;* Goding, 110, 282; Hart, 245; CC 18 May, 30 November 1809.

11. Harper, *The Visitor's Handbook to Cheltenham* (1854), 8; Goding, 103; Hart, 137, 139, 164, 245; Varley, Libraries in Cheltenham, 27; Goding, 287, appears to be wrong in giving Harward's death as 1811; CC 17 August 1817.

12. CC 12 July, 27 September, 11 October 1810, 23 June 1814; Williams, *Guide* (1825), 32.

13. CC 2 November 1809, 26 April 1810, 3 March 1813, 12 May, 23 June 1814, 11 May 1815; Verey, *Gloucestershire,* 144.

14. *UBD,* II, 550–1; Goding, 593; CC 4 May, 2 November 1809, 25 April 1816; Harper, *Directory of Cheltenham* (1844), 121.

15. CC 28 December 1809, 29 March 1810; B & C Gaz 6 January 1813; Hart, 243–4.

16. J. Browne, *The Historic and Local Cheltenham Guide* (1805), 28–9; Shenton, *Cheltenham Directory* (1800), 22.

17. *Gloucester Journal* 2 October, 20 November 1815; CC 27 July, 10 August, 26 October 1809, 23 June, 20 October, 1, 15 December 1814, 4, 11 January, 8 August, 1816; Trinder's Map of Cheltenham, 1809; Cheltenham Library, Williams' Library Subscription Book 1816.

18. Williams, *Guide,* 10, 11; CC 24 August 1809, 26 July, 30 August 1810.

19. CC 7 December 1809, 22 March 1810; B & C Gaz 28 October 1812.

20. Moreau (1793), 106; Hart, 138; CC 4 May, 30 November 1809, 12 April 1810, 4, 23 June, 3 September 1814, 11 May 1815; Blake, *Walks No. 3* (12); D. E. Bick, *The Gloucester and Cheltenham Railway* (1968), 10; B & C Gaz 17 May 1825.

21. Goding, 324, 355; Shenton, *Directory* (1800), 13; Browne, *Cheltenham Guide* (1805), 24; CJ 31 May 1830; BJ 15 December 1800; CC 8, 15 June 1815; B & C Gaz 30 December 1812.

22. CC 22 June 1809, 28 July, 13 October, 17 November 1814; B & C Gaz 27 January 1813; Varley, Libraries, 34, 36.

23. CC 22 June 1809, 8 March 1810.

24. Varley, Libraries, 14–15, 24, 25, 27, 33; Shenton, *Directory* (1800), 8, 16; *Torrington Diaries,* 45; Moreau, *Guide to Cheltenham* (1783), 32, ibid. (1793), 36, ibid. (1797), 43; CC 8 September 1814; (Symonds), *Companion to Watering Places* (1800), 48.

25. *Rowe's Illustrated Cheltenham Guide* (1850), 31; Varley, 34, 36–7; CC 15, 22, 27 June 1809, 12, 19 May, 16, 23 June 1814, 25 May 1815.

26. Varley, 28, 40, 41, 50; CC 26 April, 10 May 1810, 25 May 1815, 28 March 1816.

27. H. Ruff, *History of Cheltenham* (1803), 58; CC 8 February, 14 June 1810, 12 May 1814, 8, 15 June, 3 August 1815, 27 August 1818; 20 May, 3 June 1819; B & C Gaz 21 June 1810, 7 October 1812, 5 May 1813; CJ 8 June 1829.

28. D. A. Bush, 'Bath 1780–1830' (Bath University B.Sc. Dissertation, 1979), 47–8; CC 4 January 1810; B & C Gaz 7 October 1812; *UBD,* II, 549–51; Capper.

29. CC 25 May, 15 June, 27 July, 10 August, 2 November, 21 December 1809, 24 May 1810, 13 October 1814; B & C Gaz 7 October, 4 November 1812.

30. Goding, 273; CC 23 May 1809, 3 May 1810.

31. Moreau (1793), 100–6; Browne, *New Bath Guide* (1811), 155–6; CC 27 October, 24 November 1814, 22 June 1815.

32. Goding, 288; Hart, 108, 162, 241, 246; Browne, *Cheltenham Guide* (1805), 27; CC 5 April 1810.

33. Capper; Hart, 184; B & C Gaz 14 October 1812.

34. *Cheltenham Settlement Examinations 1815–1826,* Records Section, Bristol & Glos Arch Soc, VII, 65, 66, 69, 71; CC 31 August 1809, 28 May 1818.

35. Hart, 251–4; CC 31 August, 14, 21, 28 September 1809, 3 May 1810, 31 March 1813.

36. CC 12 October, 21 December 1809, 4 January 1810.

37. Hart, 252–3; Goding, 283, 418–19.

38. Hart, 247–8; CC 4 August 1814.

39. Goding, 283, 515; CC 15 February, 1, 22 March 1810.

40. CC 2 August 1810; B & C Gaz 31 March 1813.

41. CC 8, 22 June 1809, 8 March, 10 May 1810, 19 May 1814; Williams, *Guide,* 98; B & C Gaz 24 February, 3 March, 5 May 1813; Varley, Libraries at Cheltenham, 34–6.

42. CC 17 August 1809, 19, 26 May, 29 September, 13 October, 10, 17, 24 November 1814; Anon., *Guide to Watering Places* (1806), 149–50; Strange, *Visitor's Guide* (1842), 52.

43. CC 11 January, 15 February, 4 April, 1 August, 24 October 1816, 2 July 1818; BJ 23 October 1816.

18 Bath: The Price of Primacy

1. Diaries of Elizabeth Collett, 1792, 4.

2. Savage, *Bath Guide* (1804), 35–6; Peach, *Bath,* 102, 120, 121; *Letters from Bath,* 81.

3. Peach, 102–3; Browne, *Bath Guide* (1811), 61–2.

4. Walters, *Splendour and Scandal,* 119; Peach, 128–9; Neale, *Bath,* 29.

5. McIntyre, 'Resorts', 53; Warner, 304; Neale, *Bath,* 77, 79; BCA 1709–10.

6. Browne, *Guide* (1811), 74; Walters, 136–7, 140; A. Shaw Mellor, 'Accounts of the Overseers of the Parish of Box, Wilts. . . . 1727–1749', *WAM,* XLV, 344; BJ 19 May 1755; WRO 77/31; Warner, *Bath,* 287, 302.

7. Haddon, *Bath,* 154; BJ 22, 29 September, 6 October, 17 November 1766; Neale, 225.

8. J. A. Williams, *Bath and Rome* (1963), 25, 70–2; BCM 27 June 1780; BRO Chamberlains' Accounts, 1780 fo. 248, 1781 fo. 254; Neale, 310 ff.

9. BCM 2 February 1785; Peach, 158, 167; Browne, *Guide* (1811), 70, 75; Meyler, *Guide* (1813), 66; BJ 15 September 1766, 17 January 1791.

10. Browne (1811), 72, 76; BJ 3 February 1800; Meyler, *Guide* (1813), 63–4; Peach, 157; S. Williams, 'Bath and the New Poor', *Bath in the Age of Reform,* ed. J. Wroughton (1972), 34.

11. Warner, 226; M. Roberts and J. Wroughton, 'Law and Order in Bath', *Bath Reform,* ed. Wroughton, 88, 89, 90, 92, 93; BCM 12 September 1807.

12. BJ 31 January 1791; 26 February, 30 April, 14 May 1810; BCM 19 December, 1792, 24 September 1798; Savage, *Guide* (1804), 46; H. Perkin, *The Origins of Modern English Society 1780–1880* (1969), 30.

13. BJ 20 January, 17 March 1800; R. S. Neale, 'The Standard of Living, 1780–1844', *Ec. H.R.* (December 1966), 591.

14. BCM 16 July 1795; BJ 20, 27 January, 3, 17 February, 3 March, 5, 12 May, 30 June 1800; Neale, *Bath*, 81, 84.

15. BJ 24 March, 21 April 1800.

16. BJ 30 June, 6, 27 October 1800; BCM 2 July 1800, 18 July 1802.

17. D. A. Bush, 'Bath 1780–1830' (Bath University B.Sc. Dissertation, 1979), 47–8; Neale, *Bath*, 86; McIntyre, 'Resorts', 51; Williams, 'Bath and the New Poor Law', ed. Wroughton, 33; B & C Gaz 13 January 1813.

18. Haddon, 157; Meyler, *Guide* (1813), 75; BCM 5 January 1807; B & C Gaz 10 February 1813.

19. CC 25 January 1810; Meyler (1813), 64; BJ 7 February 1791; Haddon, 160; Neale, *Bath*, 324.

20. W. A. S. Hewins, *The Whitefoord Papers* (1898), 244; *Diaries of Mrs Philip Lykke Powys*, ed. Climenson, 332, 358; BCM 13 February 1798.

21. BJ 27 January, 22 September, 6, 20 October, 1 December 1800, 26 January, 9 February 1801, 5 February 1810; B & C Gaz 11, 18 November 1812; W. Lowndes, *They Came to Bath* (1982), 35.

22. *CP;* Neale, *Bath*, 112; Meyler, *Guide* (1813), 123, ibid. (1854), 26; BCM 15, 26 September 1796, 7 February, 10 July 1799.

23. Browne, *Guide* (1811), 132; Meyler, *Guide* (1813), 102, 159; (Symonds), *Guide to Watering Places* (1806), 328.

24. BCM 5 September 1809, 12 January 1810; BJ 1, 22 January, 26 November 1810, 1 January 1816.

25. Meyler (1813), 159; BJ 16 January, 6 August, 29 October, 5, 26 November, 4 December 1810, 15 May, 9 October 1815.

26. B & C Gaz 4, 18 November 1812; BJ 26 November, 4 December 1810.

27. BJ 13 February, 13, 20 March, 17 April, 8, 15, 22 May, 5, 26 June 1815.

28. BJ 25 September, 2, 9, 30 October, 6, 20 November, 11 December 1815; B & C Gaz 5 January 1825.

29. BCM 1 October 1810, 1 January, 12 February 1811, 25 November 1812; 6 Geo. III c.lxx.

30. BJ 2 January, 20 February 1815; BCM 15 May 1815, 6 May 1816.

31. BJ 23 April 1810, 25 November 1812, 6 November 1815, 29 April 1816; Sydenham, *Bath Pleasure Gardens*, 25–6; (Symonds), *Watering Places* (1800), 12.

32. McIntyre, 'Resorts', 50.

33. BCM 4 January 1803, 27 February, 9 July, 30 December 1805, 10 July 1806, 29 March 1808, 4 July 1809; BJ 8 January 1810; Pevsner, *North Somerset* (1958), 119; Meyler, *Guide* (1813), 26.

34. BCM 29 September 1806, 7 May, 9 June 1807, 29 March 1808, 3 January 1809; BJ 15, 22 January, 30 July 1810; Haddon, 172; Ison, Map of City of Bath 1700–1830, ff. 211.

35. Wright, *Historic Guide,* 248, 250, 365; Peach, 114–16, 118, 195, 197; *CP;* BCM 27 October 1807, 19 January, 21 September, 3 October 1808, 4 July 1809, 12 January, 27 June 1810; Haddon, *Bath,* 167; BJ 15 January 1810, 17 June 1816, 26 January 1820; Ison, Map of Bath 1700–1830.

36. Browne, *Guide* (1811), 177–80; *Bath Pleasure Gardens,* 16.

37. Pevsner, 120, 125; Ison, map.

38. Haddon, 160; visitors' list, e.g. B & C Gaz 25 November 1812; BJ 15 October 1810; Neale, *Bath,* 324–8.

39. S. Brooks, 'Bath and the Great Reform Bill', ed. Wrought, 21, 22; B & C Gaz 14, 28 October 1812.

19   Leamington Priors and Wartime Minor Spas

1. Nichols, *Leicester,* II, i, 269; White, *Leicestershire* (1846), 228–9.
2. *Gents Mag* (1799), I, 473–4; Dugdale, *New British Traveller,* IV, 328.
3. T. Garnett, *Experiments and Observations on the Horley-Green Spaw, near Halifax* (1790); Granville, I, 393–6.
4. J. Plymley, *General View of the Agriculture of Shropshire* (1803), 73, 78, 81; J. Piper and J. Betjeman, *A Shell Guide to Shropshire* (1951), 56; I thank Mr G. C. Baugh for information.
5. T. B. Groves, 'Water Analysis a Hundred Years Ago', *Proc. Dorset Nat, Hist. & Antiq. Field Club,* XVII, 143; *UBD,* LV, 730; R. Groves, *An Experimental Inquiry into . . . the Sulphureous Water at Nottington* (1792); McIntyre, 'Resorts', 301–3, 307–8, 315; *Hutchins' History of Dorset,* ed. W. Skipp and J. W. Hodson, II (1863), 487–8; Munk, *Roll,* II, 461.
6. *VCH Glos,* X, 269–70; Gloucester Journal 16 April 1804, 24 April 1815; GRO D 149/M5, Court Leet (1822).
7. *VCH Glos,* VI, 145, 167; GRO D 1375/122 Poem, *The Stow Mineral;* CC 14 July 1814; T. Evans and C. L. Green, *English Cottages* (1982), 126.
8. *UBD,* IV, 768; *Holden's Directory* (1811); *Verney Letters, 18th Century,* III, 273.
9. Pigot, *Nat. Comm. Dir. Somersetshire* (1830), 733–4; BL Anon., *A Few Observations on Mineral Waters particularly Horwood Well, near Wincanton, Somerset,* 9th edn (1807?); Salisbury and Winchester Journal, 5 February 1810, 26 July 1819; Phelps, *Somersetshire,* I (1839), 37, 155; Horwood Well House Sales Catalogue, 7 October 1925; I am indebted to Mr and Mrs Jackson for this last reference, and for allowing me to see the house.
10. BL Anon., *History and Description of Ashby-de-la-Zouch* (pub. W. & J. Hextall, 1852), 52–4; Nichols, *Leicester,* IV, ii, 613; White, *Leicestershire* (1846), 300; Hadfield, *Canals of the West Midlands,* 197.
11. Nichols, *Leicester,* IV, ii, 897; Lewis, IV, 18.
12. Pevsner, *Leicestershire and Rutland* (1960), 263; A. L. Dickens, *Report to the General Board of Health. Wigston Magna* (1855), 20, 46.
13. BL Anon., *A Short Account . . . of the Braceborough Spa Water* (1852), 3–6.
14. *VCH Warwicks,* VI, 156 fn 29; H. G. Clarke, *Royal Leamington Spa* (1947), map, 8–9; LC 18 May 1878.
15. L. Richardson, 'Royal Leamington Spa Medicinal Waters', *Proc. Naturalists' Field Cotteswold Club,* XXII, 14, 177; W. Field, *Historical and Descriptive Account of . . . Warwick and the Neighbouring Spa of Leamington* (1815), 323.
16. C. Loudon, *A Practical Dissertation on the Waters of Leamington Spa* (1831), 61, 87; BL Anon., *The Character of Leamington as a Village . . .* (1847), 32, 35; WA 12, 29 September 1810.
17. War RO Heber Percy MS 1707, Greatheed's Diaries, 21 January, 6 March, 19 May 1812.
18. Albert, *Turnpike Road System,* 31.
19. *VCH Warwicks,* VI, 155; T. H. Lloyd, 'Royal Leamington Spa', *Middle Class Housing in Britain,* ed. M. A. Simpson and T. H. Lloyd (1977).
20. *CP;* Pevsner and Wedgwood, *Warwickshire* (1966), 297–8.
21. R. Chaplin, 'New Light on the Origins of Royal Leamington Spa', *Bir-*

mingham & *Warwickshire Arch Soc Trans,* LXXXVI, 161–2; C. Hadfield, *British Canals* (4th edn, 1969), 121; ibid., *Canals of the West Midlands,* 184; Greatheed's Diaries, 21 September 1810, 19 April 1816.

22. Field, 321; W. T. Moncrieff, *The Visitors' New Guide to the Spa of Leamington Priors* (1824), xi; Greatheed, 28 December 1811, 1 October 1813; WA 3 January 1818.

23. Anon., *Leamington as a Village* (1847), 3, 5–6; Richardson, 165–6; Chaplin, 'New Light on Leamington', 151; Clarke, *Leamington Spa,* 24; Lyndon F. Cave, *Royal Leamington Spa* (1988), 12.

24. Richardson, 166; West (1830), 708; WA 12 September 1810, 25 May 1811, 22 November 1817; CC 3 September 1818; Clarke, 16, 18; J. H. Drew, *The Book of Royal Leamington Spa* (1978), 94; Cave, *Royal Leamington,* 15.

25. Field, 283, 287; Richardson, 167–8; Clarke, 15.

26. Chaplin, 154, fn. 29; Richardson, 168; Greatheed, 18 September 1810, 3 June 1812; Cave 16, 17.

27. WA 4 August 1810, 25 April 1812; J. Bisset, *The Origin, Rise and Progress of Leamington Spa* (1828), 8; West (1830), 712; Clarke, 24.

28. (S. J. Pratt), *A Brief Account of the Rise, Progress and Patronage of the Leamington Spa Charity . . .* (1812), 24; WA 25 July, 15 August 1812; Bisset (1828), 9; Field, 282; *Memoir of James Bisset,* ed. T. B. Dudley (1904), 85.

29. Drew, *Leamington Spa,* 77; Clarke, 25; West, *Warwickshire* (1830), 718, 722; (Pratt), *Leamington Spa Charity* (1812), 7–13; WA 29 August 1812, 22 March 1817; Cave, 66.

30. WA 4 August, 12, 22 September 1810; *Bisset Memoir,* 86; Lloyd, 133.

31. WA 28 September 1811, 1 August 1812; B & C Gaz 7 October 1812; Clarke, 25; Field, 327; J. Bisset, *A Descriptive Guide of Leamington Priors* (1814), 20; Bisset, *Origin of Leamington Spa* (1828), 7.

32. WA 2, 16 June 1810, 4 May 1811; Pratt, 57–8; *Bisset Memoir,* 86.

33. LC 18 May 1878; E. G. Baxter, *Dr. Jephson of Leamington Spa* (1980), 3–4; Lloyd, 119; Chaplin, 155; WA 19 December 1812; Moncrieff, *Guide* (1818), advertisement, August 1818; Field, 326–7.

34. E. G. Baxter, 'The Social Life of Visitors to Leamington Spa in the first half of the nineteenth century', I, *Warwickshire History,* III, i, 29–30; *Bisset Memoir,* 86–8; Chaplin, 153; Drew, 52; Lloyd, 125, 129; WA 30 June 1810, 3 October 1812; Greatheed, 30 April 1813; Clarke, 25; Bisset, *Descriptive Guide* (1814), 29, 32.

35. *CP;* WA 22 February, 19, 26 September, 12 December 1812; Greatheed, 3 November 1812.

36. Pratt, 17, 18 fn.; Moncrieff (1824), vi; ibid. (1833), facing p. 10; West (1830), 707–8; Clarke, 15; Field, 287.

37. Moncrieff (1824), xi; Field, 321, 328; Bisset (1828), 17; WA 23 November 1822; Greatheed, 5 May 1813; Chaplin, 155, fn 35.

38. WA 23 June 1810, 3 October 1812; Clarke, 25, 31; CC 9 June 1814, 2 May 1816.

39. Field, 284, 321; Moncrieff (1824), xi; WA 18 July, 26 September, 3 October 1812, 17 May 1817.

40. Pratt, 28; WA 16 May, 12 December 1812; Baxter, 'Visitors to Leamington Spa', II, *Warwickshire History,* III, ii, 59–60.

41. Bisset, *Descriptive Guide* (1814), 30–1; Field, 333; Moncrieff (1824), x; *VCH Warwicks,* VI, 156 fn 31; Drew, 50.

42. Field, 328; Moncrieff (1824), 59–60; West (1830), 711; Bisset (1814), 20; *Bisset Memoirs,* 88.

43. WA 25 April 1812; Richardson, 169; Anon., *Leamington as a Village* (1847),

8; Clarke, 85; Greatheed, 26 February 1810.

44. Berry, *Extracts from Journals and Correspondence,* II, 352.

45. Lloyd, 128–30; Chaplin, 161, 162; Cave, 96.

46. CC 22 June 1809; Berry, *Journals,* II, 432; Chaplin, 163, quoting D. J. Olsen, *Town Planning in London* (1964), 21–2.

47. Chaplin, 163 fn 85; *CP;* WA 15 September, 17 November 1810; John, Duke of Bedford, *A Silver-Plated Spoon* (1959), 113; Greatheed, 11 January 1810.

48. Chaplin, 165, 166; Greatheed, 15 October 1812, 22 January 1818; Lloyd, 134–5.

49. Chaplin, 156; Field, 336; Lloyd, 129; Greatheed 21 October, 31 December 1810.

50. Ibid., 22, 26, 27 June, 9 October, 2 November 1810, 21 May 1811, 21, 26 September, 29, 30 October, 1, 30 November 1812.

51. Ibid., 9 March, 18, 22, 26, 27 June, 13 September, 21 October 1810, 13 July, 13, 15, 16, 23 September, 25, 27, 28 October, 11 November 1811, 4 November 1812.

52. Ibid., 14 July, 3, 9 September, 23, 28, 29 October, 11 November, 4 December 1811, 26 May, 9 August, 16 October, 30 November 1812, 27 September 1813; WA 23 November, 7 December 1811.

53. WA 9 February 1811; Lloyd, 151; Berry, *Journals,* II, 432.

54. Greatheed, 6, 7, 9 March, 3 August 1811; Colvin, *Architects* (1978), 746; Drew, 51, 56; War RO 1563/140/97 Inventory of the Upper Assembly Rooms (1831); Clarke, 12.

55. Greatheed, 19 May, 24 September, 27 October 1812, 15 March, 21, 30 April, 14 May, 14, 21 June 1813; Clarke, 12; WA 19, 26 September, 10 October 1812.

56. Greatheed, 26 February, 31 May, 2, 4, 9, 17, 21 July, 1, 8 August, 13 September, 4 October, 6 November 1810, 12, 13, 16 September, 27 November 1811, 4, 5 January 1812.

57. Ibid., 15 April, 19 May, 7, 10, 15 June, 10, 11, 13, 22, 29 July, 4, 5, 6, 7 August 1812, 2 April, 7 October 1813.

58. War RO CR 1563/314, Plan; Clarke, 19; Greatheed, 5 September 1812, 26 March 1814.

59. Chaplin, 152, 161; Greatheed, 28 September, 29, 30 October 1812; W. G. Gibbons, *The Royal Baths and Pump Room at Royal Leamington Spa* (1980).

60. Greatheed, 5 November 1811, 19, 20 October, 6 November 1812, 2 April, 26 May, 18, 20, 24, 25 August, 10, 27 September, 1 October 1813; Drew, 21; WA 13 December 1817; Bisset, *Origins* (1828), 13; Clarke, 19.

61. Lloyd, 119–20; Greatheed, 16 March, 4 April 1814.

Conclusion

1. M. Hunter, *John Aubrey and the Realm of Learning* (1975), 96–7, 100–1.

2. Plumb, 'Commercialization of Leisure', *Birth of a Consumer Society.*

3. Barrett, 'Spas and seaside resorts', 48.

4. Schedules A, B, D.

5. Schedule A.

6. *Letters of Lady Mary Coke,* II, 171.

7. *The Journals and Letters of Fanny Burney* (Madame D'Arblay), ed. Warren Derry, X (1982), 746, fn 10.

8. P. Borsay, ' "All the town's a stage": urban ritual and ceremony 1660–1880', *The Transformation of English Provincial Towns 1600–1800,* ed. P. Clark (1984).

9. WRO 77/29 Bradford-on-Avon Settlement Examinations, Hester Bishop; *Letters from Bath,* 84.

10. P. Clark, Introduction, *Provincial Towns,* 46.
11. Ibid., 35.
12. J. Playfair, *A Method of Constructing Vapour Baths* (1783).
13. Schedules A, D.
14. Clark, 13–16.
15. GRO 214 F1/130 Parsons Letters.

Appendix

Schedule A
1

The Chronological Development of the English Spas to 1815

Dating is in many cases approximate, from evidence of use. Some spas are probably earlier than listed here.

Places are given their historic county names.

Elizabethan	Early Stuart & Commonwealth	1660–9
Bath, Somt.	Barnet, Herts.	Astrop, Northants.
Buxton, Derbys.	Castleton, Lancs.	Croft, NR Yorks.
Clifton Hotwell, Bristol	Cuffley, Northaw, Herts.	Gilthwaite, WR Yorks.
Harrogate, WR Yorks.	Epsom, Surrey	Latham, Lancs.
Holy Well (Shoreditch or	Sydenham, Kent	Malton, NR Yorks.
Flints.)	Tunbridge Wells, Kent	Seend, Wilts.
King's Newnham, Warwicks.	Wanstead, Essex	
Newton, St Neots, Hunts.	Wellingborough,	
Utkinton, Cheshire	Northants.	
	Witherslack, Westmorland	
TOTAL 7 (8)	9	6
Improvements or Developments at Existing Spa Centres		Tunbridge Wells, New Well, Kent

2

1670–9	1680–9	1690–9
Alford, Somt.	Bath, Lyncombe, Somt.	Acton, Middx.
Box, Wilts.	Clee Hills, Salop.	Aldfield, WR Yorks.
Leeds, Gipton Spa	Durham, Co. Durham	Aylsham, Norfolk
(Waddington Bath),	Hoxton, London	Bakewell, Derbys.
WR Yorks.	Ilmington, Warwicks.	Canterbury, Kent
Scarborough, NR Yorks.	Islington, London	Chippenham, Wilts.
Shooter's Hill, Kent	London Spa, Spa Fields	Hampstead, Middx.
Streatham, Surrey	Malvern, Worcs.	Horwood, Bucks.
Willowbridge, Staffs.	Sadler's Well, London	Ilkley, WR Yorks.
	Richmond, Surrey	Lambeth, Surrey
	Whitby, NR Yorks.	Leeds, Quarry Hill,
		WR Yorks.
		Matlock, Derbys.
		Pancras Wells, Middx.
		Sissinghurst, Kent
		Witham, Essex
TOTAL		
7	11	15

3

Seventeenth Century
Undated Spas–

Godsall, Staffs.
Kedleston, Derbys.
Leicester (Judd), Leics.
Sutton Park, Routhen
　Well, Warwicks.
Tarleton, Lancs.

TOTAL 5

TOTAL to 1699			
	1558–1603	7	} 16
	1603–60	9	
	1660–9	6	
	1670–9	7	} 39
	1680–9	11	
	1690–9	15	
	Undated	5	
		60	

4

1700–9	1710–19	1720–9
Bath, Widcombe, Somt.	Cheltenham, Glos.	Bungay, Suffolk
Leeds, St Peter's Well, WR Yorks.	Holt, Wilts.	Nevill Holt, Leics.
	Ipswich, Suffolk	Peckforton, Cheshire
Northampton (Vigo), Northants.	Leeds, Eyebright Wells, WR Yorks.	Quarndon, Derbys.
St Chad's, Lichfield, Staffs.		Stainfield, Lincs.
Wigan, Lancs.	Leeds, Woodhouse-Carr, WR Yorks.	Terrington, NR Yorks.
	Somersham, Hunts.	Thirsk, NR Yorks.
	Sunning-Hill, Berks.	
TOTAL 5	7	7

Improvements or Developments at Existing Spa Centres

Bath, Pump Room, Somt.		
Clifton, 2nd Hot Well, Bristol		
Epsom, New Well, Surrey		
Tunbridge, Cold Bath, Kent		
4		

5

1730–9	1740–9	1750–9
Bridlington, ER Yorks.	Bishopton, Warwicks.	Bagnigge Wells, London
Jessop's Well, Claremont, Surrey	Boston, WR Yorks.	Bath, Kingston Pump Room, Somt.
St George's Spa, London	Dulwich, Surrey	East Dereham, Norfolk
Shuttlewood, Derbys.	Gilsland, Cumberland	Glastonbury, Somt.
W. Ashton, Wilts.	Hanly's Spa, Salop.	Godstone, Surrey
W. Tilbury, Essex	Shadwell, Middx.	Kilburn Wells, London
	Southampton, Hants.	Prestbury (Hyde Spa), Glos.
	Spurstow, Cheshire	Reffley, Norfolk
	Thetford, Norfolk	Wivenhoe, Essex
		Welwyn, Herts.
TOTAL		
6	9	10

Improvements or Developments at Existing Spa Centres

Hoxton, bath built, London		Bath, Pump Room, Somt.
Scarborough, Old Spa re-built, NR Yorks.		Malvern, Worcs.
		Somersham, Hunts.

6

1760–9	1770–9	1780–9
Burton Lazars, Leics.	Bermondsey, Surrey	Ashchurch, Tewkesbury, Glos.
Dosthill, Warwicks.	Idle, WR Yorks.	Askern, WR Yorks.
Leeds, Westwood, WR Yorks.	Leamington Priors, Aylesford's Well, Warwicks.	Box (Middlehill), Wilts.
Matlock, New Bath, Derbys.	Liverpool, Lancs.	Flookborough, Lancs.
Newent, Glos.	Marylebone, London	Gloucester, Glos.
St Chad's, London	Mistley, Essex	Gumley, Leics.
Whittington, Derbys.	Stoney Middleton, Derbys.	Leamington, Abbotts' Well, Warwicks.
		Leeds, Peter's Well, WR Yorks.
		Leicester (Nichols), Leics.
		Shap, Westmorland
TOTAL		
7	7	10

Improvements or Developments at Existing Spa Centres

Tunbridge, 2nd Cold Bath, Kent	Bath, Hot Bath, Somt.	Bath, Cross Bath Pump Room, Somt.
Tunbridge, Adam's Well Bath	Hoxton, Bath, London	Buxton, Crescent & Baths, Derbys.
	Malvern, Cold Bath, Worcs.	Clifton, Pump Room in Hotwells Road, Bristol
		Matlock (3rd bath), Derbys.
		Tunbridge, Rusthall Cold Bath, Kent
2	3	5

7

1790–9	1800–9	1810–15
Dinsdale, Co. Durham Horley Green, WR Yorks. Leamington, Wise's Bath, Warwicks. Nottington, Dorset Oldens Spa, Stonehouse, Glos.	Ashby-de-la-Zouch (Moira Spa), Leics. Braceborough, Lincs. Cheltenham, Barrett's Spa, Glos. Cheltenham, Cambray Spa Cheltenham, Montpellier Spa Halifax, WR Yorks. Harrogate, Old Promenade Room, WR Yorks. Horwood, Wincanton, Somt. Leamington, Read's Bath, Warwicks. Leamington, Robbins' Victoria Bath Lower Swell, Stow, Glos. Sandrock, Isle of Wight Sapcote, Leics.	Capland, Somt. Gloucester, New Spa, Glos. Leamington, Royal Pump Room, Warwicks. Melksham, Wilts. Ross-on-Wye, Herefords.
TOTAL 5	13	5

Improvements or Developments at Existing Spa Centres

Bath, Pump Room, Somt. Boston, WR Yorks. Clifton, Sion Spring Pump Room, Bristol Gostone, Surrey	Leamington, Aylesford's Well, Warwicks. Tunbridge Wells Bath House, Kent	Askern, Manor Baths, WR Yorks. Gilsland, Cumberland Newent, Glos.
4	2	3

8

Undated Spa Centres–Eighteenth Century

Axwell, Winlaton, Co. Durham
Birley, Derbys.
Bourne, Lincs.
Brighton, St. Anne's Well, Wick, Sussex
Buglawton, Cheshire

Camberwell, Surrey
Cantley, WR Yorks.
Clitheroe, Lancs.
Cornhill, Northumberland
Cowley, Derbys.
Crickle, WR Yorks.
Gayhurst, Bucks.

Hoveringham, Notts.
Middleton in Wirksworth, Derbys.
Nottingham, St. Anne's Well
Redmire, NR Yorks.

Silbury, Wilts. (McIntyre, 'Mineral Water Trade,' 6).
Sookholme, Notts.
Sutton, Salop.
Welham, Notts.
Wigston Magna, Leics.(?)
Woodford Wells, Essex

Total 22

Spas 1700–1815

Date of Foundation	*No.*	*Further Development or Improvement*	*Total*
1700–9	5	4	9
1710–19	7	—	7
1720–9	7	—	7
1730–9	6	2	8
1740–9	9	—	9
1750–9	10	3	13
1760–9	7	2	10
1770–9	7	3	10
1780–9	10	5	15
1790–9	5	4	9
1800–9	13	2	15
1810–15	(5)	(3)	(8)
	91		
Undated	22		
TOTAL	113		

Periods of Spa Foundation

1558–1659	16
1660–99	39
1770–49	34
1750–99	39
1800–15	18
Undated	27
Total	173

Schedule B

1

Initial Promoters of some Minor Provincial English Spas c. 1660–1815

Date	Place	County	Nobility	Gentry	Medical Men	Ministers	Others
Late C.17	Alford	Somt.				Mr Thomas Earl	
1805	Ashby-de-la-Zouch	Leics.	Marquess of Hastings				
1734	Askern	Yorks. WR		Humphrey Osbaldeston			
1697	Bakewell	Derbys.	Duke of Rutland				
1704	Bath, Widcombe	Somt.					Thomas Greenway (stonemason)
1770	Bermondsey	Surrey					Thomas Keyse (artist)
1742	Bishopton	Warwicks.				Rev Joseph Greene	
1744	Boston	Yorks. WR		Sir Edward Gascoigne			
1783	Box	Wilts.			Dr William Falconer John King (apothecary)		
1728	Bungay	Suffolk					
1760	Burton Lazars	Leics.					Judge Holland
Late C.17	Chippenham	Wilts.		Philip Burton			
By 1739	Claremont (Jessop's Well)	Surrey		James Fox			Mr Vincent

2

Date	Place	County	Nobility	Gentry	Medical Men	Ministers	Others
1789	Dinsdale	Co. Durham	Earl of Durham		Dr John Peacock		Francis Cox
1740	Dulwich	Surrey					
1664	Gilthwaite	Yorks. WR		George Westby			Anne Galloway
1751	Glastonbury	Somt.		Sir Tanfield Lemon			Mr King
mid-C.18	Godstone	Surrey					
1789	Gumley	Leics.		Joseph Cradock	Dr William Morris		
1741	Hanly's Spa	Salop.		Thomas Powys			
1790	Horley Green	Yorks. WR		J. Drake	Dr Thomas Garnett		
c. 1800	Horwood	Somt.		William Gapper			Richard Messiter (attorney)
1772	Idle	Yorks. WR		James Booth			
1684	Ilmington	Warwicks.		Sir Henry Capel	(a) Dr William Cole (b) Dr Samuel Derham		
c. 1702	Kedleston	Derbys.		Sir Nathaniel Curzon			
c. 1670	Latham	Lancs.	Earl of Derby		Dr Edmund Borlase		

3

Date	Place	County	Nobility	Gentry	Medical Men	Ministers	Others
(a) Before 1724	Leicester	Leics.			(a)Mr Judd (apothecary)		(b) J Nichols (grocer)
(b) 1787–90	Leicester						
c. 1702	Lichfield	Staffs.		Sir James Simon	Sir John Floyer		
1773	Liverpool	Lancs.			Dr. Thomas Houlston Dr James Worthington		
By 1673	Lyncombe, Bath	Somt.					Charles Milsom (wine-cooper)
1728	Nevill Holt	Leics.		Cosmos Nevill	Dr Thomas Short		
1751	Prestbury, Hyde Spa	Glos.	Lord Craven				
late C. 18	Reffley	Norfolk		Sir W.J.H.B. Folkes John Frewen Turner			
1806	Sapcote	Leics.			Dr Chessher		
1732	Shuttlewood	Derbys.	Charles Basseldine				
1695 (a) 1717	Sissinghurst	Kent		Mr Baker			
(b) 1758	Somersham	Hunts.	(b)Duke of Manchester		Dr P. Layard		
	"						
c. 1750	Spurstow	Cheshire		Sir Thomas Mostyn			
1720	Stainfield	Lincs.			Dr Edward Greathead		

4

Date	Place	County	Nobility	Gentry	Medical Men	Ministers	Others
c. 1804	Stonehouse	Glos.					Daniel Compton
c. 1807	Stow	Glos.					R. Farmer
c. 1711	Sunning-Hill	Berks.		John Baber	Dr. John Merrick		
c. 1787	Tewkesbury, Ashchurch	Glos.		Richard Smith	Dr James Johnstone		
1746	Thetford	Norfolk			Dr Matthew Manning		
1734	Tilbury, West Welwyn	Essex		John Kellaway	Dr John Andree		
mid-C. 18		Herts.					
(a) c. 1670	Willowbridge	Staffs.	Lady Gerard				
(b) c. 1697	"					Dr Young	
1736	Witham	Essex		Sir Edward Soutcott	Dr James Taverner		
	48		7	24	21	3	12

Although existing spas were sometimes taken over by syndicates for later development, Melksham in Wiltshire was the first spa to be promoted by a company, the Melksham Spa Company (1815), from the outset.

*C. = century

Schedule C

Size of the Long-Rooms or Assembly-Rooms of the Spa Towns

Place	*Rooms*	*Date*	*Measurements*
Bath	Lower Rooms (Thayer)	1730	86 ft long × 30 ft wide × 30 ft high
	Lower Rooms (Harrison)	enlarged 1749	90 ft long × 36 ft wide × 34 ft high
	Upper Rooms	1771	105 ft 8 ins. long × 42 ft 8 in. wide × 42 ft 6 in. high
Bristol Hotwells	Old Room	*c.* 1753	90 ft long × 35 ft wide × 35 ft high
Buxton	Crescent Assembly Room	*c.* 1790	75½ ft long × 30 ft 2 in. wide × 30 ft high
Cheltenham	Old Room, Old Well	1738	35 ft long × 18 ft wide
	Old Room (Mrs Jones's in High Street)	before 1776	60 ft long × 30 ft wide
	Long-room, Old Well (Skillicorne & Miller)	1775–6	66 ft long × 23 ft wide
	Lower Assembly Room (Hughes)	1784	60 ft long × 30 ft wide
	Upper Assembly Room	1791	68 ft long × 28 ft wide
	New Assembly Room	1816	82 ft long × 38 ft wide × 40 ft high
Epsom	Ballroom	*c.* 1707	70 ft long
Hampstead	Ballroom	*c.* 1701	90 ft long × 36 ft wide
Harrogate	Old Promenade Room	1805	75 ft long × 30 ft wide
Leamington	Bowling Green Inn		30 ft long × 15 ft wide
	Upper Assembly Room	1812	82 ft long × 36 ft wide
	Royal Pump Room	1812–14	80 ft long × 36 ft wide
St Pancras Wells	(a) Horn's Room	*c.* 1700	60 ft long × 18 ft wide
	(b) House of Entertainment		135 ft long

Schedule D

The Domestic Trade in Bottled Natural Mineral Waters to 1816

Dates given are those from which there is evidence of trade.

Epsom	{ 1651 { 1664	Harrogate Bourne	1740 { 1748
Alford, Castle Cary	1670		{ 1755
Bath	{ 1673 { 1693/4	Nevill Holt	{ 1748 { 1755
Willowbridge	1676	Shadwell	1748
Sydenham Wells	1678	Hyde Spa, Prestbury	1751
Tunbridge Wells	{ 1679 { 1700–4	Glastonbury Godstone	1751 1752–3
Hampstead	1700	Silbury	1759
Bristol Hotwell	1701	Malvern	1760
Croft	1713	Kilburn	1762
Ipswich	1717	Jessop's Well, Claremont	1767
Streatham	1717	Somersham	1767
Acton	early c. 18	Buxton	1782
Northaw	early c. 18	Horwood Well, Wincanton	1807
Holt, Wilts.	{ 1729 { 1731	Capland, Ashill Gloucester	1815 1815
St George's Spa	1731	Melksham	1816
W. Ashton	1733		
Scarborough	1734		
Cheltenham	1738		
W. Tilbury	1739		

TOTAL 36 places engaged in trade

Schedule E

London Prices of Mineral Waters
(per dozen bottles)

	1730–40[1]	*1762[2]*
Bath	7s. 6d.	9s.
Bristol Hotwells	6s.	8s.
Cheltenham	8s.–10s.	10s.
Holt	10s.	12s.
Scarborough	7s. 6d.	9s.
Acton		6s.
Bourne		18s.
Dulwich		6s.
Epsom		6s.
Harrogate		12s.
Jessop's Well		7s.
Kilburn		6s.
Nevill Holt		12s.
Tilbury		10s.

The waters from Tilbury, which may have come by water transport, and those from a distance were the most expensive.

1. S. McIntyre, 'Mineral Water Trade,' 16
2. GRO D. 1799/A355

Select Bibliography

PRIMARY SOURCES

(a) Manuscript

PUBLIC RECORD OFFICE

E. 190 Port Books.

SP 12/131/2123   Notes of Cures by the new Bath near Coventry.

WO 30/48   Abstract of a Particular Account of all the Inns, Alehouses etc. in England with their Stable-Room and Bedding, 1686.

WO 30/49   Return to Commissioners of Excise, Public Houses and Inns, 1756.

BRITISH LIBRARY

Add. MS 5233.1.3   Dr Edwards Browne's Drawings.

Add. MS 27951   Anon., Travel Journal August–September 1772.

Cotton MS Vitellius, C.I. fos 78–82 (original PRO C.66/1181) Instructions from the Privy Council about St Winifred's Well, 1574.

Egerton MS 3565   Estate book relating to lands and possessions of Rachel, Countess of Kingston.

3647   Manvers Estate leases in Bath.

3648   Rental for the manor of Bath, 1774.

Lansdown MS xcii, No. 114 fo. 203   Michael Hicks about the Earl of Salisbury at Bath, 1612.

Northumberland MS 549/49/5   Letterbook of Col. John Fitzjames 1649–51 (microfilm).

Thomason Tract E. 108.

BRITISH MUSEUM (Prints and Drawings)

Grace Collection

Catalogue of Topographical Drawings.

FOLGER SHAKESPEARE LIBRARY, WASHINGTON

MS v.a. 483   Robert Lesse, A brief view of all baths . . . (microfilm).

ARUNDEL CASTLE ARCHIVES COLLECTION

Autograph Letters 1513–85, Nos 78, 80.

BATH RECORD OFFICE

Weekly list of gentlemen bathing in the King's Bath, 1774–.

Bath Chamberlains' Accounts 1733– and Vouchers 1767, 1768.

BATH REFERENCE LIBRARY

Chamberlains' Accounts of the City of Bath, 1601– vols I, II (typescript).

Bath Council Minutes, Books I, II, III, 1613–1772 (typescript).

Diaries of Elizabeth Collett, 1792, ed. H. Collett (typescript).

Edmund Rack, A Disultory Journal of Events at Bath, 1779.

CARDIFF CENTRAL LIBRARY

MS 4370   J. Verdon, Travel Journal, 1699.

MS 3127   R. Colt Hoare, Tours in North Wales 1796, Tours of South Wales 1801.

MS 4302   R. Colt Hoare, English Journal.

CHELTENHAM PUBLIC LIBRARY (Local History Section)
Williams' Library Subscription Book.

GLOUCESTERSHIRE RECORD OFFICE
D. 123/F4   Winstone Correspondence.

D. 214/F1   Parsons Letters.

D. 1137   Forthampton MS, File 3.

D. 1375/122   Poem, *The Stow Mineral.*

D. 1447   Batsford Park MS, Accounts of Mrs Jane Edwards.

D. 1610/A75   Codrington MS.

D. 1799/A355, C2   Blaithwaite MS.

D. 1833/Rooke MS.

D. 1844/C4, C17   Newton Correspondence.

LONGLEAT HOUSE, WILTS.
Uncatalogued MS, Lord Weymouth's Estate in Bath, 1752.

Portland Papers, XIV.

NORTHAMPTONSHIRE RECORD OFFICE
1C/2093   Isham Correspondence.

H(K) 183   John Scattergood's Letters.

SOMERSET RECORD OFFICE
North Wootton Parish Registers.

STOURHEAD HOUSE, WILTS.
Stourhead MS E.10 J. C. Nattes's Illustrations.

WARWICKSHIRE RECORD OFFICE
Heber Percy MS 1707   Greatheed's Diaries.

CR MS 1707   1563/314   Plan of the Pump-room and baths, Leamington Spa.
             1563/140   Inventory of the Upper Assembly Rooms, Leamington
                        Spa, 1831.

NEWSPAPERS
Bath Herald.

Bath Journal.

Bath and Cheltenham Gazette.

Cheltenham Chronicle.

Cheltenham Journal.

Gloucester Journal.

Norfolk Chronicle and Norwich Gazette.

Warwick Advertiser.

(b) Printed
Acts of the Privy Council of England.

Allen, B. *The Natural History of the Chalybeate and Purging Waters of England*
   (1699).

Allen, B. *The Natural History of the Mineral Waters of Great Britain* (1711).

Amsinck, P. *Tunbridge Wells and its Neighbourhood* (1810).

Anon. *A Guide to Watering and Sea-Bathing Places* (1806, pub. Philipps).

Anon. *A Short and Candid Account of the Nature and Virtues of the New Iron Pear-Tree Water* (?), (Wellcome Institute, Broadsheet No. 457).

Anonymous pamphlets in the British Library:

A brief Account . . . of the Famous Well at Astrop (1668).

A Short Account of the Braceborough Spa Water (1852).

The New Brighton Guide: or, Companion . . . to all the Watering-Places in Great Britain (1796).

A Short Account of the Mineral Waters of Canterbury (1668?).

Sketch of a Tour into Derbyshire and Yorkshire (1778).

Spadacrene Dunelmensis (1675).

Some Particulars Relating to Epsom (1825).

Gem of the Peak (3rd edn, *c.* 1843).

Heliocrene. A Poem in Latin and English on the Chalybeate Well at Sunning-Hill (1744).

A Few Observations on Mineral Waters particularly Horwood Well, near Wincanton (9th edn, 1807?).

Hydro-Sidereon: or a Treatise of Ferruginous Waters, especially Ipswich-Spaw . . . (1717).

Advertisement for the London Spaw.

Letters on Malvern, Descriptive and Historical (*c.* 1814).

Richmond Wells: or, Good Luck at Last (1723).

A Dissertation on . . . Hot Mineral Springs Particularly those of Scarborough (1735).

A Guide to Several Watering and Sea-Bathing Places (1813), (Sissinghurst), Pamphlet Collection BL 778, k, 15(4).

T.G., *A True and Exact Account of Sadler's Well . . . lately found at Islington* (1684).

G. W., *Newes out of Cheshire of the new found Well* (1600).

Atkinson, R. *England Described; or the Traveller's Companion* (1788).

Bailey's British Directory, 1784.

Baily, W. *A Brief Discours of certain Bathes or medicinall Waters in . . . Newham Regis* (1587 edn).

Baker, T. *The Southampton Guide* (2nd edn, 1775).

Baldwin, R. *A New Present State of England* (1750).

Barfoot P. and Wilkes, J. *The Universal British Directory* (1791).

Barrett, J. *A Description of Malvern* (1796).

Bath and Bristol Guide (1755).

Beds Hist Rec Soc XLVII (a) *The Marchioness Grey of West Park*
                                      (b) *The Travel Journal of Philip Yorke 1744–63.*

Berry, Mary *Extracts from Journals and Correspondence 1783–1852* (1856).

Bisset, J. *A Descriptive Guide of Leamington Priors* (1814).

Bisset, J. *The Origin, Rise and Progress of Leamington Spa* (1828).

Memoir of James Bisset, ed. T. B. Dudley (1904).

Blome, R. *Britannia: or a Geographical Description of . . . England* (1673).

Borlase, E. *Latham Spaw in Lancashire* (1670).

Bott, W. *A Description of Buxton and the Adjacent Country* (1795, 1796, 1800, 1813).

Bristol Rec Soc, XX *The Trade of Bristol in the Eighteenth Century.*

Bristol & Glos Arch Soc, Records Section VII *Cheltenham Settlement Examinations 1815–1826.*

Browne, J. *An Account of the Wonderful Cures perform'd by the Cold Baths . . .* (1707, two edns).

Browne, J. *The Historic and Local New Bath Guide* (1811).

Browne, J. *The Historic and Local Cheltenham Guide* (1805).

Calendar of Patent Rolls.

Calendar of State Papers Domestic.

Calendar of State Papers relating to Scotland.

Calendar of Treasury Books.

Camden's Britannia, ed. R. Gough (1789 and 1806 edns).

Cam Soc C.S. 61   *Camden Miscellany,* III.

        O.S. XXI   *Verney Papers. Notes of Proceedings in the Long Parliament.*

        O.S. XCIV   Thomas Dingley, *History in Marble.*

        N.S. XLII   *The Travels of Dr Richard Pococke,* I.

        N.S. L   *The Nicholas Papers 1653–55,* II.

        1st S. XXVI   *Suppression of the Monasteries.*

        1st S. LVI   *Letters and Papers of the Verney Family.*

        3rd S. XXI   *The Nicholas Papers 1657–60,* IV.

        3rd S. XXIV   *Correspondence of Arthur Capel, Earl of Essex 1675–77.*

        3rd S. XCIII   *The Household Papers of the 9th Earl of Northumberland.*

        4th S. XLI   *Wentworth Papers 1597–1628.*

Capper, B. P. *A Topographical Dictionary of the United Kingdom* (1813).

The Chamberlain Letters, ed. E. McClure Thomson (1966).

Chambers, J. *A General History of Malvern* (1817).

Chapman, H. *Thermae Redivivae: the City of Bath Described* (1673).

Chetham Soc 3rd S. XVI *The Diary of Richard Kay, 1716–51.*

Clanny, W. R. *A History and Analysis of the Mineral Waters . . . at Butterby near Durham* (1807).

Clarke, E. *A Tour through the South of England in 1791* (1793).

Clifford, J. *The Directory: or, the Ancient and Present State of Tunbridge Wells* (1816).

Clifford, J. *Descriptive Guide of Tunbridge Wells* (1818).

Journals of the House of Commons.

Crutwell, R. *The Strangers' Assistant and Guide to Bath* (1773).

Davies, J. *A Short Description of the Waters at Glastonbury* (1751).

Deane, E. *Spadacrene Anglica, or, The English Spaw-Fountaine* (1626 and J. Rutherford's edn, 1921).

Defoe, D. *A Tour Through England and Wales,* II (Everyman edn, 1928).

Derbyshire Arch Soc Rec S. I, *Calendar of the Shrewsbury Papers in Lambeth Public Library*.

Derbyshire Arc Soc Rec S. IV, *Calendar of the Talbot Papers*.

Derham, S. *Hydrologia Philosophica, or an Account of Ilmington Waters in Warwickshire* (1685).

Derrick, S. *Letters written from Liverpool . . . Tunbridge Wells, Bath* (1767).

Dugdale, J. *The New British Traveller* (1819).

The Diary of John Evelyn, ed. E. S. de Beer (1955).

Eyre, H. *A Brief Account of the Holt Waters . . .* (1731, 3rd edn 1776).

Eyre, H. *An Account of the Mineral Waters of Spa commonly called the German Spaw* (1733).

Field, W. *An Historical and Descriptive Account of . . . Warwick and the Neighbouring Spa of Leamington* (1815).

Floyer, J. *An Enquiry into the Right Use and Abuses of the Hot, Cold, and Temperate Baths in England* (1697).

Floyer, J. *An Essay to Prove Cold Bathing Both Safe and Useful* (1702).

Garnett, T. *A Treatise on the Mineral Waters of Harrogate* (1792).

Garnett, T. *Experiments and Observations on the Horley-Green Spaw, near Halifax* (1790).

Gentleman's Magazine, 1734–

The Later Correspondence of George III, I (December 1783–January 1793), ed. A. Aspinall (1962).

Gilbert, S. *Fons Sanitatis or the Healing Spring at Willowbridge in Staffordshire* (1676).

Groves, R. *An Experimental Inquiry into . . . the Sulphureous Water at Nottington* (1792).

Gould, W. *An Enquiry into the Origin, Nature and Virtues of the Glastonbury Waters* (1752) (unpublished MS, Stanley Crowe Catalogue, 1973).

Guidott, T. *A Discourse of Bath and the Hot Waters there* (1676).

Guidott, T. *Register of Bath* (1694).

Hales, S. *Philosophical Experiments . . . on Chalybeate or Steel-Waters* (1739).

The Letters and Epigrams of Sir John Harington, ed. N. E. McClure (1930).

Harleian Soc *Miscellany*, VIII, ch. IV, Lodowick Rowzee, *The Queen's Wells . . . a Treatise of the Nature and Virtues of Tunbridge Water* (1632).

Harleian Soc XXVIII *The Registers of the Abbey Church of S.S. Peter and Paul, Bath*, II, ed. A. J. Jewers.

Harrison's Description of England, ed. F. J. Furnivall.

A Week at Harrogate. A Poem . . . from Benjamin Blunderhead (2nd edn, 1814).

Historical Manuscripts Commission *Reports* and *Calendars* of MSS, *Bath, Cranfield, De L'Isle & Dudley, Egmont, Finch, Gorhambury, Harley, Portland, Sackville, Salisbury* and *Rutland*.

Holden, *Annual Directory* (1811).

Hughes, F. L., and Larkin, J. F. *Tudor Royal Proclamations*, II (1969).

The Diary of Thomas Isham of Lamport 1671–73, ed. N. Marlow (1971).

Jeayes, J. H. *Descriptive Catalogue of the Charters and Muniments . . . at Berkeley Castle* (1892).

Jewitt, A. *A History of Buxton* (1816).

Jones, J. *The Bathes of Bathes Ayde* (1572).

Jones, J. *The Benefit of the ancient Baths of Buckstones* (1572).

Jorden, E. *A Discourse of Natural Bathes and Minerall Waters . . . especially of our Bathes at Bathe . . .* (1632 and 1669 edns).

Kaye, W. J. *Records of Harrogate* (1922).

King, J. *An Essay on Hot and Cold Bathing* (1737).

Rec Soc Lancs & Cheshire, CX, CXII *The Great Diurnall of Nicolas Blundell*, I & II.

Diary of William Laud, in *The History of the Trial of William Laud,* ed. H. Wharton (1694).

Layard, D. P. *An Account of the Somersham Water* (1767).

Linden, D. W. *A Treatise on the Origin, Nature and Virtues of Chalybeate Waters . . .* (1748).

Linden, D. W. *An Experimental Dissertation on the Hyde Saline Purging Water* (1751).

Linden, D. W. *Directions for the use of that . . . mineral water commonly called Berry's Shadwell-Spaw, in Sun-Tavern Fields, Shadwell* (1749).

Journals of the House of Lords.

Passages from the Diaries of Mrs. Philip Lykke Powys . . . 1756–1808, ed. E. J. Climenson (1899).

Lysons, D. and S. *Magna Britannia,* II (1810).

Macky, J. *A Journey through England* (1732).

Mavor, W. *The British Tourists* (1800).

Meyler, *Original Bath Guide* (1813).

Letters from Bath 1766–67 by the Rev. John Penrose, ed. B. Mitchell and H. Penrose (1983).

Moncrieff, W. T. *The Visitor's New Guide to the Spa of Leamington Priors* (1818, 1824).

Moreau, S. *A Tour to Cheltenham Spa* (1783).

Moreau, S. *A Tour of the Royal Spa at Cheltenham* (1793, 1797).

Munk, W. *The Roll of the Royal College of Physicians, 1518–1770,* I *1701–1800,* II (1878).

North, Lord Dudley *A Forest of Varieties* (1654).

Onely, R. *A General Account of Tunbridge Wells and its Environs* (1771).

Page, T. J. *A Month at Buxton* (13th edn, 1828).

Pembroke Papers (1780–1794), ed. Lord Herbert (1950).

The Diary of Samuel Pepys (1971), ed. R. Latham and W. Matthews.

Perry, C. *An Account of the Stratford Mineral Water* (1744).

Pierce, R. *Bath Memoirs: or Observations in Three and Forty Years Practice at the Bath* (1697).

Playfair, J. *A Method of Constructing Vapour Baths* (1783).

Pope, *New Bath Guide* (1761).

(Pratt, S. J.) *A Brief Account of the Rise, Progress and Patronage of the Leamington Spa Charity . . .* (1812).

Purefoy Letters 1735–53, ed. G. Eland (1931).

Ruff, H. *History of Cheltenham* (1803).

Ruff, H. *Beauties of Cheltenham* (1806).

Manners, J. H. Duke of Rutland, *Travels in Great Britain* (1813).

The Diary of Dudley Ryder 1715–1716, ed. W. Matthews (1939).

Savidge, J. *The Original New Bath Guide* (1804).

Scott Thomson, G. *Letters of a Grandmother 1732–1735* (1943).

Shardesloe Papers of the 17th and 18th Centuries, ed. G. Eland (1947).

Shenton, J. *Cheltenham Directory* (1800).

Short, T. *A General Treatise on the Various Cold Mineral Waters in England* (1765).

Short, T. *The Natural, Experimental and Medicinal History of the Mineral Waters of Derbyshire, Lincolnshire and Yorkshire* (1736).

Short, T. *Nevill-Holt Spaw-Water* (1749).

Slare, F. *An Account of the Pyrmont Waters* (1717).

Som Rec Soc XXIII *Quarter Sessions Records for Somerset 1607–25.*
    XXXVIII *The Accounts of the Chamberlains of the City of Bath 1568–1602.*
    LXXI *Somerset Assize Orders 1640–59.*

Southall, M. *Description of Malvern* (1822).

Sprange, J. *Tunbridge Wells Guide* (1780).

Stanhope, M. *A Relation of certain particular Cures done by the Mineral Waters near Knaresbrow, . . . (1649, 1654).*

Statutes of the Realm.

Surrey Quarter Sessions Records 1663–66, VIII (Surrey County Council, 1938).

Surrey Quarter Sessions Records 1666–68, IX (Surrey County Council, 1951).

Surrey Rec Soc XVII *Surrey Hearth Tax 1664.*

Surtees Soc XXII *The Injunctions of Richard Barnes, Bishop of Durham, 1575 to 1587.*
    LXVIII *Household Books of the Lord William Howard.*
    LXXVII *The Diary of Sir Walter Calverley of Esholt.*
    CLVII *The Autobiographies and Letters of Thomas Comber,* II.

(Symonds, H. D.) *A Companion to the Watering and Bathing Places of Great Britain* (1800).

Sympson, W. *The History of Scarborough-Spaw* (1679).

Taverner, J. *An Essay upon the Witham Spa* (1737).

Thoresby Soc XXXVIII *Extracts from the 'Leeds Intelligencer' and the 'Leeds Mercury' 1769–1776,* XL *1777–82.*

A Collection of Several Pieces of Mr. John Toland (1726 edn).

The Torrington Diaries, ed. C. B. and F. Andrews (1954).

Turner, W. *A Book of the Natures and Properties as well of the Baths in England as of other baths in Germany and Italy* (1568).

Memoirs of the Verney Family during the Seventeenth Century, ed. F. P. and M. M. Verney, 2 vols (1907).

Verney Letters of the Eighteenth Century, I (1696–1717), ed. M. M. Verney (1930).

Wall, J. *Experiments and Observations on the Malvern Waters* (2nd edn 1757; 3rd edn 1763).

Wiltshire Archaeological & Natural History Magazine XI *Diary of Thomas Smith.*

Warner, R. *The History of Bath* (1801).

Willan, R. *Observations on the Sulphur Water at Croft, near Darlington* (1782).

Williams, J. *Richmond Wells . . .* (1723).

The Diaries of Thomas Wilson, D.D., 1731–37 and 1750, ed. C. L. S. Linnell (1964).

Wilts Rec Soc XXIII *The Earl of Hertford's Lieutenancy Papers 1603–12.*

Wood, J. *A Description of Bath, 1765* (1969 reprint).

SECONDARY SOURCES

References to political biographies and county histories used for background have been omitted here but follow individual chapters. Useful guides to the literature of the subject are:

Cox, E. G. *A Reference Guide to the Literature of Travel,* III (1949), viii (Spas).

Mullet, C. F. *Public Baths and Health in England, 16th–18th Century* (1946).

General

Addison, W. *English Spas* (1951).

Albert, W. *The Turnpike Road System in England 1663–1840* (1972).

Anderson, A. B. & M. D. *Vanishing Spas* (1974).

Anon., *Watering Places of England* (SPCK, 1853).

Chalklin, C. W. *The Provincial Towns of Georgian England* (1974).

The Transformation of English Provincial Towns 1600–1800, ed. P. Clark (1984).

Clark, P. and Slack, P. *English Towns in Transition 1500–1700* (1976).

Cockayne, G. E. *Complete Peerage of England, Scotland, Ireland, etc.,* ed. V. Gibbs *et al.* (1910–49).

Colvin, H. *A Biographical Dictionary of British Architects* (1978).

Copeman, W. S. C. *The Worshipful Society of Apothecaries of London: A History 1617–1967* (1967).

Corfield, P. J. *The Impact of English Towns 1700–1800* (1982), ch. IV, Spas and Resorts.

Denbigh, K. *A Hundred British Spas* (1981).

Dictionary of National Biography.

Granville, A. B. *Spas of England and Principal Sea-Bathing Places* (1841), (1971 edn, introduction by G. Martin).

Hill, C. *Intellectual Origins of the English Revolution* (1965).

Hope, R. C. *The Legendary Lore of the Holy Wells of England* (1893).

Jones, Whitney R. D., *William Turner: Tudor Naturalist, Physician and Divine* (1988).

Jowitt, R. L. P. and D. M. *Discovering Spas* (1971).

Lewis, S. *Topographical Dictionary of England* (1840 and 1849 edns).

McGrath, P. *Papists and Puritans under Elizabeth I* (1967).

McLean, A. *Humanism and the Rise of Science in Tudor England* (1972).

Pevsner, N. *et al., The Buildings of England* (series by counties, 1951–).

Porter, R. *English Society in the Eighteenth Century* (1982).

Raach, J. H. *A Directory of English Country Physicians* (1962).

Simpson, M. A. and Lloyd, T. H. (eds) *Middle Class Housing in Britain* (1977).

Stone, L. *The Crisis of the Aristocracy* (1965 edn).

Strange, W. *The Visitor's Guide to the Watering Places* (1842).

Wernham, R. B. *Before the Armada: The Growth of English Foreign Policy 1485–1588* (1966).

The Victoria Histories of the Counties of England:

County histories, directories and gazetteers by S. Bagshaw and F. and J and W. White.

Local

Abell, H. F. *Kent and the Great Civil War* (1901).

Axon, E. *Historical Notes on Buxton,* 4th Paper (1936), 5th Paper (1937).

Anon., *Leamington as a Village* (1847).

Anon., *History and Description and Ashby-de-la Zouch* (pub. W. & J. Hextall, 1852).

Baker, J. *The New Guide to Bristol and Clifton* (1894).

Barnes, T. G. *Somerset 1625–46: A County's Government During the Personal Rule* (1961).

Barton, M. *Tunbridge Wells* (1937).

Theatre Royal, Bath – A History (Bath Theatre Notes, 1981).

Baxter, E. G. *Dr. Jephson of Leamington Spa* (1980).

Bick, D. E. *The Gloucester and Cheltenham Railway* (1968).

Blake, S. T. *Cheltenham Historical Walks,* No. 2 (1977), No. 3 (1978).

British Association Handbook to Bath, ed. J. W. Morris (1888).

Body, A. *Spa: Histoire et Bibliographie,* III (1902).

Boyce, B. *The Benevolent Man: A Life of Ralph Allen of Bath* (1967).

Burton, I. E. *Historic Buxton and its Spa Era* (1971).

Bush, A. E. and Hatton, J. *Thomas Bellot 1534–1611* (1966).

Cave, Lyndon F. *Royal Leamington Spa* (1988).

Chalklin, C. W. *Seventeenth-Century Kent: a social and economic history* (1965).

Cliffe, J. T. *The Yorkshire Gentry: From the Reformation to the Civil War* (1969).

Colbran, St John *Guide and Visitor's Handbook to Tunbridge Wells . . . (1881).*

Clarke, H. G. *Royal Leamington Spa* (1947).

Collins Baker, C. H. *The Life and Circumstances of James Brydges, First Duke of Chandos* (1949).

Cross, *Historical Handbook to Malvern* (1864?).

D'Arcy Power, *Dr. Walter Bayley and His Works, 1529–1592* (1907).

Drew, J. H. *The Book of Royal Leamington Spa* (1978).

G. Dugardin, *Histoire du commerce des eaux de Spa* (1944).

Scarborough 966–1966, ed. M. Edwards (Scarborough Arch Soc, 1966).

Everitt, A. M. *The Community of Kent and the Great Rebellion 1640–60* (1966).

Fletcher, A. *A County Community in Peace and War: Sussex 1600–1660* (1975).

Foord, A. S. *Springs, Streams and Spas of London* (1910).

Goding, J. *A History of Cheltenham* (1863).

Goodacre, J. *Buxton Old and New* (1928).

Goulding, R. W. *Four Louth Men* (1913).

Grainge, W. *The History and Topography of Harrogate and the Forest of Knaresborough* (1871).

Grundy Heape, R. *Buxton under the Dukes of Devonshire* (1948).

Haddon, J. *Bath* (1973).

Hart, G. *A History of Cheltenham* (2nd edn, 1981).

Hembry, P. M. *The Bishops of Bath and Wells 1540–1640* (1967).

Horton-Smith, L.G.H. *Dr. Walter Baily (or Bayley) c. 1529–92, Physician to Queen Elizabeth* (1952).

Hudson, K. *The Fashionable Stone* (1971).

Humphris and Willoughby, *At Cheltenham Spa* (1928).

Hunter, J. *Hallamshire, The History and Topography of the Parish of Sheffield in the County of York* (1869).

Ison, W. *The Georgian Buildings of Bath* (1948).

Ison, W. *The Georgian Buildings of Bristol* (1978).

Jackson, *Handbook for Tourists in Yorkshire* (1891).

A History of Harrogate and Knaresborough, ed. B. Jennings (1970).

Jewitt, A. *A History of Buxton* (1816).

Lafagne, P. *Spa ancien, figures de Bobelins et pages d'histoire* (1934).

Lafagne, P. *Spa et les Anglais ou l'influence anglaise dans l'histoire de Spa* (1946).

Lee, E. *Cheltenham and its Resources* (1851).

Little, B. *Cheltenham* (1952).

Loudon, C. *A Practical Dissertation on the Waters of Leamington Spa* (1831).

Neale, R. S. *Bath: A Social History 1680–1850* (1981).

Nicholson, N. *Sissinghurst Castle: an Illustrated History* (1964).

Peach, R. E. *Bath, Old and New* (1891).

Pelton, *Illustrated Guide to Tunbridge Wells* (1893).

The Limner of Bath . . . Thomas Robins 1716–1770 (Holburne Museum, Bath, 1978).

Rowe's Illustrated Cheltenham Guide 1850 (S. R. Publishers Ltd, 1969).

Rowland James, P. *The Baths of Bath in the Sixteenth and Early Seventeenth Centuries* (1938).

The History of Scarborough, ed. A. Rowntree (1931).

Savidge, A. *Royal Tunbridge Wells* (1975).

Savidge, A. *The Story of the Church of King Charles the Martyr* (1969).

Scott, B. M. *Boston Spa* (1985).

Smith, B. S. *A History of Malvern* (2nd edn, 1978).

Smith, R. A. L. *Bath* (1945).

Spailier, G. *Histoire de Spa. La plus ancienne ville d'eaux du monde* (2nd edn, 1961).

Sydenham, S. *Bath Pleasure Gardens of the Eighteenth Century* (1907), (2nd edn, 1961).

Temple Patterson, A. *Southampton* (1970).

Thompson, F. M. L. *Hampstead: Building of a Borough 1650–1964* (1974).

Walks Around Tunbridge Wells, No. 1 (Royal Tunbridge Wells Civic Society, 1974).

Turner, A. J. *Science and Music in Eighteenth-Century Bath* (University of Bath, 1977).

Wade, C. *The Streets of Hampstead* (The Camden History Society, 1972).

Walters, J. *Splendour and Scandal, The Reign of Beau Nash* (1968).

Westley, F. C. *The New Guide to Cheltenham* (1867).

Whellan, T. *History of the City of York and the North Riding* (1859).

Williams G. A. *A Guide to Cheltenham* (1825).

Williams, J. Anthony *Bath and Rome* (1963).

Williams, N. *Lady Luxborough Goes to Bath* (1954).

Wright, G. N. *The Historic Guide to Bath* (1864).

Wroughton, J. *The Civil War in Bath and North Somerset* (1973).

Wroughton, J. (ed.) *Bath in the Age of Reason* (1972).

Articles

Barrett, J. 'Spas and seaside resorts, 1660–1780', *English Urban History 1500–1780* (Open University, 1977).

Baxter, E. G. 'The Social Life of Visitors to Leamington Spa in the first half of the nineteenth century', I; 'Visitors to Leamington Spa', II, *Warwickshire History,* III: i, ii.

Bonser, K. J. 'Spas, Wells and Springs of Leeds', *Thoresby Soc, LIV.*

Breeze, G. 'Thomas Hickey's Stay in Bath', *Proc Som Arch NH Soc,* CXXVIII, 83–93.

Bulley, J. A. ' "To Mendip for Coal" ' – a study of the Somerset Coalfields before 1830', *Proc Som Arch Soc,* XCVII, XCVIII.

Chaplin, R. 'New Light on the Origins of Royal Leamington Spa', *Birmingham and Warwickshire Arch Soc Trans,* LXXXVI.

Clark, F. L. 'The History of Epsom Spa', *Surrey Arch Coll,* LVII.

Fessler, A. 'A Spa in 17th Century Lancashire', *Man. Univ. Med. School Gazette,* XXXIII.

Green, E. 'Did Queen Elizabeth visit Bath in the Years 1574 and 1592?', *Proc Bath Field Club,* IV.

Green E. 'The Visits to Bath of two Queens: Anne Consort of James I and Anne Queen Regnant', *Proc Bath Field Club,* VII.

Hammond, E. A. 'Doctor Augustine, Physician to Cardinal Wolsey and King Henry VIII', *Medical History,* 19.

Holland, Elizabeth 'The Earliest Bath Guildhall', *Bath History,* II (1988).

Howe, R. 'Joseph Pitt and Pittville', *Gloucestershire Historical Studies* (1974–5).

Howe, R. 'Joseph Pitt, Landowner', *Gloucestershire Historical Studies* (1976).

Howe, R. 'The Rise and Fall of Joseph Pitt', *Gloucestershire Historical Studies* (1977).

Hull, F. 'A Tour into Kent, 1759', *Arch Cant,* LXIX.

Kite, V. J. 'Circulating Libraries in Eighteenth-century Bath', *A Second North Somerset Miscellany* (Bath and Camerton Arch Soc, 1971).

Lehmann, H. I. 'The History of Epsom Spa', *Surrey Arch Coll,* LXIX.

Little, B. 'The Gloucestershire Spas: an eighteenth-century parallel', in *Essays in Bristol and Gloucestershire History,* ed. P. McGrath and J. Cannon (Bristol and Glos Arch Soc 1976).

Manco, Jean 'The Cross Bath', *Bath History,* II (1988).

McIntyre, S. 'The Mineral Water Trade in the Eighteenth Century', *The Journal of British Transport History, New Series,* II.

Neale, R. S. 'Society, belief, and the building of Bath 1700–1793', in *Rural Change and Urban Growth 1500–1800,* ed. C. W. Chalklin and M. A. Havinden (1974).

Oliver, R. C. B. 'Diedrick Wessel Linden, M.D.', *The National Library of Wales Journal,* XVIII.

Pafford, J. H. P. 'The Spas and Mineral Springs of Wiltshire', *WAM,* LV, LVI, *VCH Wilts,* IV.

Pallister, A. 'The Dinsdale Spa', *Durham County Local Hist. Soc.,* Bulletin 14.

Plumb, J. H. 'England's Travelling Circus', *The Listener,* 5 October 1978.

Plumb, J. H. 'The Commercialisation of Leisure in Eighteenth-century England', in *The Birth of a Consumer Society,* ed. N. McKendrick, J. Brewer and J. H. Plumb (1982).

Richardson, L. 'Royal Leamington Spa Medicinal Waters', *Proc Naturalists' Field Cotteswold Club,* XXII.

Streeten, M. B. and A. D. F. 'Another Chalybeate Spring and Cold Bath at Tunbridge Wells', *Arch Cant,* LXXXVII.

Tongue, C. 'Thomas Thornton at Astrop Spa', *Northants Rec Soc,* IV.

Villiers, M. 'Pump and Promenade', *Quarterly Review* vol. 276 (April 1941).

Waite, V. 'The Bristol Hotwells', in *Bristol in the Eighteenth Century,* ed. P. McGrath (1972).

Wark, K. R. 'Elizabethan Recusancy in Cheshire', *Chetham Soc,* XIX.

Wilcox, R. 'Bath breweries in the Latter Half of the Eighteenth Century', *A Second North Somerset Miscellany* (Bath and Camerton Arch Soc, 1971).

Woolrich, A. P. 'An American in Gloucestershire and Bristol: The Diary of Joshua Gilpin, 1796–7', *Trans Bristol and Glos Arch Soc,* XCII.

Unpublished Theses

Kite, V. J. 'Libraries in Bath 1618–1964' (FLA thesis, 1966).

Marchington, T. 'The Development of Buxton and Matlock since 1800' (London Univ. MA thesis, 1961).

McIntyre, S. 'Towns as Health and Pleasure Resorts, Bath – Scarborough – Weymouth' (Oxford Univ. D.Phil. thesis, 1973).

Patmore, J. 'Harrogate and Knaresborough: a study in urban development (Oxford Univ. B.Litt. thesis, 1959).

Varley, A. 'A History of the Libraries of Cheltenham from 1780 to 1900' (FLA thesis, 1968).

Index

A

Places

Counties are given their historic, not their contemporary, names.

Aachen (Aix-la-Chapelle), Lorraine, 2, 41, 173, 176
Acton, Middx., 102, 168, 177
Aldfield, Yorks., 76
Alford, Castle Cary, Somt., 76–7
Ashby-de-la-Zouch, Leics., 120, 287
Askern, Yorks., 175, 306, 310–11
Astrop, Northants., 70–1, 77, 302, 308
Aylsham, Norfolk, 74

Bagnigge Wells, London, 172
Bakewell, Derbys., 4, 76, 78
Barnet, Herts., 63, 81, 104
Barwick-in-Elmet, Yorks., 18
BATH, Somt.
  as a spa, 52, 66, 113, 119–20, 276, 280, 282, 283, 311; size, 27, 86, 115
  baths, 1–2, 3, 7–8, 12–13, 15, 18, 19, 27, 33–4, 36, 37, 39, 54, 56–7, 62, 88, 123, 129, 134, 145–7; *See also* Bath: Kingston Estate
  Pump Room, 116, 118, 122, 126, 129, 130, 134, 145, 147, 280; Hetling Pump Room, 280
  Abbey House, 25, 26, 34, 88, 92, 93, 116, 123
  accommodation: inns, 27, 57, 87, 141, 142, 154; lodging keepers, 142; lodgings, 27, 54, 87, 93, 121, 125, 126–7, 130–1, 140–3, 280, 281–2; *see also* Bath: New Town, York House Hotel.
  artists, 137, 152–3
  assembly-rooms: Lower, 117–18, 126, 127, 138–9, 144–5, 276–9; Upper, 125–6, 134, 138–9, 144–5, 276, 278, 279

assize town, 89
attorneys, 156
Avon navigation, 118–19, 120, 121, 122
banks, 127, 128
beggars, 31–2, 275
bookshops and libraries, 91, 141, 142, 149–50
bowling greens, 58, 90, 91, 117
bridges: old bridge, 25, 122, 281; Pulteney Bridge, 128
canals, 128, 143
capital investment, 113, 121, 124, 280
chapels, 126, 270–1
charity (*see* philanthropy)
charters, 25, 26, 35, 37, 87, 90, 93, 273
churches, 27, 270–1; Abbey Church, 25–6, 28, 35, 37; others, 26, 28, 121
city debt, 86, 89, 113
Civil War and Commonwealth, 61–3
clubs and societies, 151–2, 277, 278
coal, 142–3, 274
coffee-houses, 91, 115, 117, 121, 123, 147, 273
common fields, 56, 57, 86, 89, 118, 126, 130, 157
corn prices, 272, 274
corporation (common council), 26, 27, 35, 39, 56, 57, 61, 62, 86, 87–9, 90, 93, 118, 119, 120, 122, 123, 124, 126, 129, 130, 136, 137, 139, 140, 143, 145, 146, 147, 212, 273, 274, 276, 277, 279, 281; committees of, 126, 129, 280
developers and architects: Allen, Ralph, 117, 119, 120, 121, 122, 284; Baldwin, Thomas, 126, 128, 129, 130; Cave, Joseph, 281; Chandos, James,

B

People

Only the names of people of national, and some of local, importance or those significant in the argument of the book, e.g. the promoters of spas, are included. Consult Section A for other local people. Members of the Medical Profession are listed (under that heading), but not many of the local residents, transient visitors or individual recusants, e.g. at Bath and Buxton.

C

Subjects

Subjects follow the main themes of the book, and the entries of the major spas, Bath, Buxton, Cheltenham, Clifton Hotwells, Epsom, Harrogate, Leamington Spa, Malvern, Matlock, Scarborough, Southampton and Tunbridge Wells, should also be consulted.

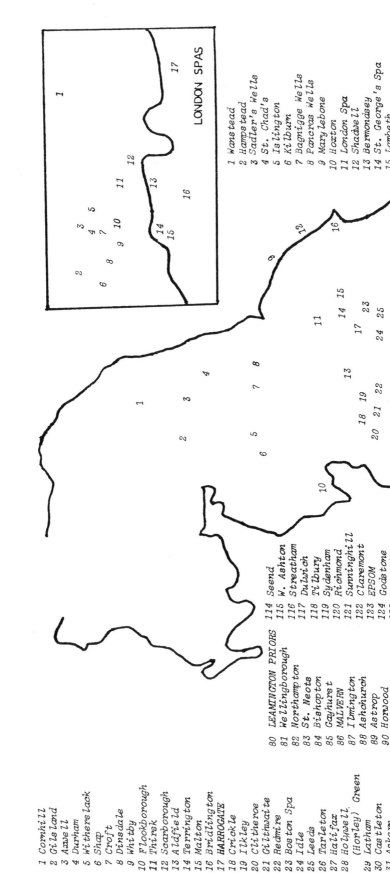

1 Cornhill
2 Gisland
3 Axwell
4 Durham
5 Witherslack
6 Shap
7 Croft
8 Dinsdale
9 Whitby
10 Flookborough
11 Thirsk
12 Scarborough
13 Aldfield
14 Terrington
15 Malton
16 Bridlington
17 **HARROGATE**
18 Crickle
19 Ilkley
20 Clitheroe
21 Gisburn
22 Redmire
23 Boston Spa
24 Idle
25 Leeds
26 Tarleton
27 Halifax
28 Holywell
   (Horley) Green
29 Latham
30 Castleton
31 Askern
32 Wigan
33 Liverpool
34 Birley
35 Cantley
36 Cawley
37 Wetham
38 **BUXTON**
39 Stoney Middleton

80 **LEAMINGTON PRIORS**
81 Wellingborough
82 Northampton
83 St. Neots
84 Bishopton
85 Gayhurst
86 **MALVERN**
87 Ilmington
88 Ashchurch
89 Astrop
90 Horwood
91 Ipswich
92 Newent
93 Ross-on-Wye
94 Prestbury
95 Lower Swell
96 **CHELTENHAM**
97 Gloucester
98 Welwyn
99 Mistley

114 Seend
115 W. Ashton
116 Streatham
117 Dulwich
118 Tilbury
119 Sydenham
120 Richmond
121 Sunninghill
122 Claremont
123 **EPSOM**
124 Godstone
125 Canterbury
126 **Tunbridge Wells**
127 Sissinghurst
128 Glastonbury
129 Alford
130 Wincanton
131 Capland
132 Nottington
133 Southampton

LONDON SPAS

1 Wanstead
2 Hampstead
3 **Sadler's Wells**
4 St. Chad's
5 Islington
6 Kilburn
7 Bagnigge Wells
8 Pancras Wells
9 Marylebone
10 Hoxton
11 London Spa
12 Shadwell
13 Bermondsey
14 St. George's Spa
15 Lambeth
16 Camberwell
17 Shooter's Hill